Treatment of Sexual Problems in Individual and Couples Therapy

←——————→

Treatment of Sexual Problems in Individual and Couples Therapy

$\longleftrightarrow$

Edited By

Robert A. Brown, Ph.D.
University of Maryland
College Park, Maryland
and

Joan Roberts Field Ph.D.
Columbia, Maryland

PMA PUBLISHING CORP.

Library of Congress Cataloging in Publication Data

Treatment of sexual problems in individual and couples therapy /
   edited by Robert A. Brown, Joan Roberts Field
      p.   cm.
      Bibliography: p.
      Includes index.
      ISBN 0-89335-301-9 : $47.50
      1. Sex therapy.   I. Brown, Robert A. (Robert Atkins), 1936-
   II. Field, Joan Roberts.
   RC557.T74   1988
   616.6'906 – dc 19   88-319
                                                              CIP

Printed in the United States of America

Contributors

PETER M. BENTLER, PH.D.
Professor of Psychology
Univ. of California, Los Angeles
Los Angeles, California

ROBERT A. BROWN, PH.D.
Associate Professor of Psychology
University of Maryland
College Park, Maryland

CHRISTINE A. COURTOIS, PH.D.
Washington, D.C.

ANTHONY R. D'AUGELLI, PH.D.
Associate Professor of Human
Development
Department of Individual and
Family Studies
Pennsylvania State University
University Park, Pennsylvania

JUDITH FRANKEL D'AUGELLI, PH.D.
Clinical Psychologist
State College, Pennsylvania

LEONARD R. DEROGATIS, PH.D.
Associate Professor and Director
Division of Medical Psychology
Department of Psychiatry &
Behavioral Sciences
The John Hopkins University
School of Medicine
Baltimore, Maryland

JOEL A. FEINMAN, PH.D.
Amherst Medical Association and
University of Massachusetts at
Amherst
Amherst, Massachusetts

JOAN ROBERTS FIELD, PH.D.
Columbia, Maryland

SHIRLEY P. GLASS, PH.D.
Owings Mills, Maryland

RICHARD P. HALGIN, PH.D.
Associate Professor of Psychology
University of Massachusetts
Amherst, Massachusetts

THERESE R. M. HELBICK, PH.D.
Clinical Associate
Department of Psychology
University of Aukland
Aukland, New Zealand

JAMES E. HENNESSEY, PH.D.
Capital District Psychiatric Center
Albany, New York

JUDITH B. KURIANSKY, PH.D.
Center for Marital and Family
Therapy
New York, New York

GREGORY K. LEHNE, PH.D.
Assistant Professor of Medical
Psychology
Sexual Disorders Clinic
Department of Psychiatry and
Behavioral Sciences
The John Hopkins School of
Medicine
Baltimore, Maryland

MARIA C. LOPEZ, B.A.
Research Associate
The Johns Hopkins University
School of Medicine
Baltimore, Maryland

BARRY W. MCCARTHY, PH.D.
Professor of Psychology
The American University
Washington, D.C.

MICHAEL D. NEWSCOMB, PH.D.
Project Director
Longitudinal Consequences Study
of Adolescent Drug Abuse
Research Faculty, Dept. of
Psychology
Univ. of California, Los Angeles
Los Angeles, California

BARBARA A. PALMERI, M.C.
Fairfield, Connecticut

SUSAN PERKINS
Department of Psychology
Boston University
Boston, Massachusetts

ROGER RUBIN, PH.D.
Associate Professor and Acting
Chairperson
Department of Family and
Community Development
University of Maryland
College Park, Maryland

JUDITH E. SPREI, PH.D.
Co-director, Maryland Institute
for Individual and Family
Therapy, Ltd.
College Park, Maryland

ROBERT N. SOLLOD, PH.D.
Associate Professor of Psychology
Cleveland State University
Cleveland, Ohio

RICHARD C. STUNTZ, M.D.
Instructor in Psychiatry
The Johns Hopkins University
Director, Psychosexual Clinic
Union Memorial Hospital
Baltimore, Maryland

SHEILA STATLENDER, PH.D.
Newton-Wellesley Hospital
Newton, Massachusetts

GREGORY L. WHITE, PH.D.
Associate Professor and Head
Behavioral Science
Psychiatry and Behavioral Science
University of Aukland School of
Medicine
Aukland, New Zealand

THOMAS N. WISE, M.D.
Chairman, Department of
Psychiatry
The Fairfax Hospital
Falls Church, Virginia

THOMAS L. WRIGHT, PH.D.
Associate Professor & Director of
Clinical Training
Department of Psychology
The Catholic University of
America
Washington, D.C.

ELLEN M. ZINZELETRA, B.S.
Research Associate
The Johns Hopkins University
School of Medicine
Baltimore, Maryland

Table of Contents

Preface

Several years ago, one of the editors received a referral from a competent and distinguished colleague for "sex therapy." The patient presented a variety of sexual complaints, from dissatisfaction with the husband's personal hygiene to infrequent intercourse and her usual lack of orgasm. When asked what progress she had made in dealing with her concerns in her two years of therapy, she said "Essentially none. Dr. X seemed sort of uncomfortable talking about it, and that's why he recommended we come to you." Her statement was distressing because it was not unusual.

Why, in the 1980s, would the psychotherapist not have explored her sexual complaints in detail — even if no specific treatment were offered? Her concerns were focused and specific and had bothered her for years. She had read numbers of self-help books, so she could talk clearly about the issues and her past attempts at solutions. The therapist existed in the same social milieu as the patient, where sexual guides were abundant and movies and videos seemed to be desensitizing people to taboos against sexual discussions. Moreover, the therapist had available a wide variety of professional publications and announcements of short courses dealing with sexual dysfunctions.

It was out of concern that patients' sexual problems were not being fully addressed within the context of psychotherapy that the idea for a conference* and later this edited volume was born. We wanted to provide individual, couples and family therapists with an overview of the biological, psychological, interpersonal, and social contexts in which sexual problems arise and to familiarize them with major current trends in assessment and treatment. The emphasis was to be, and is, on demystifying treatment techniques, attempting to maximize the applicability of the therapist's prior training in dealing with sexual complaints, and presenting work with special problems and populations (e.g., sexual trauma, homosexuality) which demonstrates the complex intermingling of sexual and more general personal and interpersonal difficulties.

Perhaps our colleague was not more forceful in dealing with these sexual issues partly *because* of the amount of information available to him; it is clear that there is a great deal to know and that we now have a cadre of professionals who specifically label themselves as sex therapists. In addition to other professional skills and activities, such therapists specialize in dealing with sexual dysfunc-

---

* The conference, *Sexual problems: Advances in understanding and treatment,* was cosponsored by the Maryland Psychological Association and the Health and Education Council and held in Baltimore, Maryland in April, 1981. However, only two of the current chapter authors presented at the conference, and all of the following chapters were written specifically for this volume.

tions such as erectile disorders, orgasmic dysfunction, dyspareunia, disorders of sexual desire and the like.

However, the list of sexual dilemmas is considerably longer than the list of dysfunctions. Therapists are commonly faced with nondysfunctional sexual behaviors such as paraphilias, unusual erotic preferences, or sexual life-styles such as swinging. These may present as a central issue involving guilt or anxiety about the behavior, or as clashes with the law or with partners, or they may be peripheral to the major complaint. Other people will not present a specific problem, but will be dissatisfied with the frequency or quality of their sexual relationships; or they may have social anxiety or interpersonal skill deficits that lead to awkward and strained relations. Others will have concerns related to broader sexual issues such as homosexuality, bisexuality, gender identity or gender roles. Still others will focus on life-stage or circumstance problems, including children's sexuality and sex education, changing sexual capacities and level of interest at different stages of the life cycle, marriage and divorce and their attendant sexual predicaments, or sexual relations involving a partner who is ill or has a chronic disability. Any of these problems may lead to less than satisfactory functioning at any stage of the normal response cycle. So individual, couples, or family therapists are forced to choose among (a) dealing directly with an amazing variety of sexual matters, (b) referring a substantial portion of their cases to someone else, or (c) giving inadequate service by not confronting the problems at all.

A brief digression into the nature and history of sex therapy will be helpful in developing our point of view. The particular phrase "sex therapy" is usually reserved for treatment techniques aimed at remediating a specific set of dysfunctions. Although dysfunctions are defined somewhat differently by different writers, they generally have to do with the inability of an individual or couple to function effectively with respect to one or more phases of the sexual response cycle, in response to socially sanctioned internal or external cues to arousal (e.g., erectile or orgasmic dysfunction, vaginismus, etc.).

In the early 1970s, sex therapy was an emerging specialty. Of course, medical and mental health professionals had been working with sexual complaints for years, but the publication of *Human Sexual Inadequacy* (Masters & Johnson, 1970) provided a seemingly comprehensive diagnostic scheme for sexual problems, a guide for treatment, and a promise of high rates of success. In a familiar sequence of events in developing areas, communications that were targeted to professionals interested in sex therapy quickly expanded, interest groups sprang up overnight, and existing professional associations began claiming the field as their own and setting up standards for training and practice. There were sometimes successful demands that states license or certify sex therapists. Established mental health professionals in turn both accommodated to and assimilated the findings in the area. For example, the behavioral approach was seen to systematize and explain the success of Masters and Johnson's treatment (see McCarthy & Perkins, Chapter 10 in this volume). Kaplan (1981) developed a theory of sexual dysfunction that was compatible with both psychodynamic theory and the empirical successes of Masters and Johnson. She also pointed out that a number of cases that present with sexual complaints may not yield to apparently straightforward sexual therapy exercises, and showed that more traditional treatment approaches could be modified to deal with these cases (see Sollod, Chapter 9 in this volume, for a more detailed analysis of Kaplan's work). These authors at least implicitly suggested that sex therapy could be seen as a mental health subspecialty, not necessarily as a new profession.

Regardless of the issue of specialty versus subspecialty, the popularization of sex therapy has had a great public impact. Paradoxically, developing and publicizing effective procedures for dealing with sexual dysfunctions has made it more difficult to use those same procedures to work with patients who present sexual concerns. The techniques seemed more effective when few people knew about them, probably for several reasons. First, accounts of successful sex therapy have led to the publication of a number of excellent self-help manuals (e.g., Barbach, 1976; Zilbergeld, 1978) in a laudable attempt to give away this information to the public. So some people who could make use of education or specific suggestions may have found the help they needed in the bookstore; these could have been our most dramatically successful cases!

Second, both patients and gatekeepers label problems and make attributions about their causes in order to seek appropriate help. With the amount of lay and professional publicity about sexual issues, in the 1980s it is probably far more likely than before that individuals with a flashback to an assault, with unsatisfactory spousal relations due to marital conflicts, or those with lowered sexual arousal due to depression may self-label their problem as sexual and ask for a sex therapist. Those with low sexual desire or frequency dissatisfaction may now label themselves or their spouses as dysfunctional rather than as incompatible. Thus the referral net for sexual complaints sweeps more broadly than before.

Third, at least partially based on the above, a larger proportion of cases that present now are highly complicated (Kaplan, 1977). They often involve an array of sexual concerns that are determined by a variety of factors. Some of these are individual factors, involving biological functioning or intrapsychic conflicts. Others are related to personality or to interpersonal style, leading to dyadic conflict, which in turn reduces sexual attraction or performance. Still others relate to social or cultural conditions, such as gender-role demands for outstanding sexual performance. And most often these factors intertwine with each other in convoluted ways to produce a sexual dilemma. So, paradoxically, the better we do, the harder it becomes to treat sexual concerns. The more publicity regarding successful, focused sexual treatment, the more likely we are to see patients whose complaints will not yield to the application of these techniques alone.

Finally, dissemination of information on sex therapy has also changed public expectations regarding treatment. Many patients now expect a sophisticated, comfortable therapist who has specific techniques to remediate a wide range of problems, and they may fully expect that dealing with the sexual problem will be possible without tampering with their more general personal or interpersonal functioning. These expectations may be unrealistic, but it does seem reasonable to us that patients should see mental health professionals who are knowledgeable and comfortable regarding sexuality and who are aware of what can and cannot be done to aid them.

We believe, then, that all therapists will be confronted with sexual issues. We noted above that when presented with a sexual concern, a therapist can refer, deal with the problem personally, or give inadequate service by avoiding the topic. From the discussion so far, it is probably clear that we feel that one simply cannot refer all sexual issues to a sexual therapist. Sexual concerns are so ubiquitous that we would refer vast numbers of our patients; those in the private sector could not afford this and those in the public sector would not have enough therapists to whom to refer. Also, information on sexual problems may arise during the course of therapy, after the therapist already has a working relationship with the patient; to reestablish such a relationship with someone else is often difficult or may interfere if the therapist wishes to continue treatment. Some patients, in fact, will refuse such a referral. Moreover, referral may send an ambiguous, possibly destructive message about the patient's sexuality. Also, as noted before, sexual difficulties often involve the intertwining of individual and relationship issues, most of which the therapist understands and can deal with. And since so many factors are involved, often, but not always, sexual therapy will proceed by dealing with sexuality only until these more general individual or dyadic issues impede progress. Only after these conflicts are resolved can one again deal with the sexual issues.

To complicate matters even further, it is now known that the incidence of sexual dysfunctions is very high, not only in distressed couples (Derogatis, Meyer, & King, 1981), but also in nondistressed couples who say that they are quite happy with their relationship. For example, Frank, Anderson, and Rubinstein (1978) reported that 40% of the men and 63% of the women in their sample of "normal" couples reported some type of sexual dysfunction. Moreover, they conclude that "...it is not the quality of sexual performance but the affective tone of the marriage that determines how most couples perceive the quality of their sexual relations" (p. 115). So, regardless of the objective level of sexual functioning, the *perception* of dysfunction is more likely in couples with poorer relationships. Moreover, distressed individuals and couples often have sexual and social concerns that parallel the types of circumstances that are posited to generate sexual dysfunction. For example, sexual dysfunctions are often secondary to depression, anxiety, rage, jealousy, drug and alcohol abuse, or situations such as extramarital involvement or sexual assault (see Masters & Johnson, 1970). Therefore, we expect that distressed individuals and couples, those more likely to seek out a mental health professional, will have a high incidence of sexual complaints and concerns.

Therefore, referral of many of these cases is not feasible. Intentionally giving inadequate service is an option that there is, of course, no need to explore. The important question then is how to help the individual, couples, or family therapist to develop competence in dealing with a wide range of sexual topics and referring when necessary. And that question brings us back to the purpose and organization of this book.

Our suggested solution, certainly neither unique nor a secret to the reader at this point, is to encourage recognition of sex therapy as a subspecialty within the mental health professions, and also to recognize and foster the ability of many competent therapists to deal directly with a wide range of sexual issues. With the amount of information and training available, a psychotherapist should be able to acquire sufficient technical and conceptual skills to be able to deal with many types of sexual problems. Paradoxically, developing competence aids greatly with answering the question of when and when not to refer. The more competent the therapist, the easier it is to recognize one's own limitations. Skilled practitioners know that if their approach does not work, it is the approach that is inappropriate and not that the therapist simply needs to try harder. Greater competence leads to fewer but better referrals to subspecialists.

It would be foolish to suggest that any one book could provide a therapist with the background necessary to work with sexual matters, but we do think that reading can be helpful to therapists in enhancing their competence. We have made several assumptions about necessary information and skills that could be helpful. These assumptions, which led to the selection of chapters and authors for this volume, include (a) the importance of the therapist's comfort with sexual material, (b) understanding of the social/cultural context in which sexual predicaments occur, (c) knowledge of a wide variety of determinants of sexual difficulties, (d) familiarity with theoretical bases and technical skills involved in assessment and intervention, (e) experience with the practical aspects of treatment (enhancing compliance, framing of interventions, etc.), and (f) cognizance of pertinent ethical and professional issues. Finally, we made assumptions about the importance of theoretical and/or technical eclecticism. Many of the chapters address more than one of these concerns.

We do not address the topic of the therapist's comfort with sexual matters directly; we did not believe we could do it justice. Comfort means a freedom from anxiety, sexual arousal, or other affects that may distract the therapist or in some other way interfere with accurate assessment or effective treatment. Achieving comfort involves, at minimum, a general lack of inner conflict over one's own sexuality, insight into transference and countertransference issues involving sexuality, and confidence in one's ability to use sexual language and to deal with whatever sexual content may arise. For most mental health professionals, inner sexual conflicts are probably not due to a simple lack of information, and working through the conflicts is probably best done in one's own therapy (with a therapist comfortable with sexual issues). Insight into transference and countertransference and confidence in language use and dealing with sexual content may come partially from reading. We have addressed these issues here by asking our authors to use case examples liberally; this should give a flavor of the way therapists deal with at least some of the issues that arise. The recent book, *Sexual Dilemmas for the Helping Professional* (Edelwich, with Brodsky,

1982), superbly addresses a wide array of sexual situations that arise between therapist and patient and their implications for treatment; we would recommend this book for all therapists. In addition, formal and peer supervision is exceedingly helpful in sensitizing one to transference/countertransference issues and in learning to speak sexual language publicly. And we would hope that readers would finish this book more confident of their own knowledge and ability to deal effectively with sexual topics. Even if therapists do not do sexual therapy, they may at least ask the kinds of questions that elicit the information about sexual concerns necessary to formulate effective treatment plans.

Another set of assumptions about necessary knowledge has to do with the therapist's understanding a variety of determinants of sexual difficulties and the cultural contexts in which these complaints arise; the first five chapters are devoted to an overview of sexual therapy and to conceptualizing four different descriptive levels of analysis of sexual functioning. First, Richard Halgin and his colleagues give an overview of sexual therapy as it may be practiced in the context of traditional psychotherapy. Judith Kuriansky then discusses the interplay among individual dynamics and conflicts, sexual performance and sexual relationships. Judith and Anthony D'Augelli next bring in literature from a variety of areas, including moral development, exchange theory, and communications to discuss couples factors in sexual functioning. Thomas Wise and Barbara Palmeri then deal with the physical context of sexual functioning from the point of view of problems of physical development, medical illness, and drug and alcohol use. This chapter does not cover the basic anatomy and physiology of sexual function and dysfunction; any number of texts would be useful to the reader in this regard (see Masters & Johnson, 1966, 1970) as will Chapter 8 in this book by Richard Stuntz. Finally, Roger Rubin presents a broad-based, sociocultural view of sexuality in society and its impact on us as social/sexual organisms. Rubin points out the "schizophrenia" of society's demanding chastity while promoting sexual freedom, and he presents a range of sexual conflicts produced by discrepancies between our espoused values and those of our social systems. As we note below, we think it is crucial for therapists to be able to assess the individual and interactional contribution to sexual complaints of each of these levels.

A third set of assumptions regarding sex therapist skills has to do with acquiring theoretical perspectives and technical skills in assessing and treating sexual problems, and gaining knowledge of the practical issues involved in delivering service. The last two sections of the book address these concerns, with the second section dealing with sexual dysfunctions per se and the third section discussing more general sexual issues. In the second section, Michael Newcomb and Peter Bentler give a broad overview of a diagnostic scheme for sexual dysfunctions and a number of specific assessment instruments and techniques. Then Leonard Derogatis, Maria Lopez, and Ellen Zinzeletta discuss the usefulness of one assessment device, the Derogatis Sexual Functioning Inventory, in treatment planning. Richard Stuntz next gives an overview of assessment of organic factors impacting on the sexual response cycle. The remaining chapters in this section, one by Robert Sollod and the other by Barry McCarthy and Susan Perkins, present different but compatible views of treating dysfunctions. The third section presents in-depth treatment approaches for dealing with broader sexual dilemmas. These chapters explore the implications of several sexual predicaments for sexual, personal and interpersonal functioning and present models for treatment. Gregory White and Therese Helbick-White look at jealousy; Judith Sprei and Christine Courtois examine sexual trauma such as incest and rape; Shirley Glass and Thomas Wright discuss their approach to working with couples who are involved in extramarital relationships; and Gregory Lehne presents both a context for understanding and various techniques for working with homosexuality.

We also believe that it is critical for therapists to be familiar with the ethical and professional issues associated with treatment of sexual concerns; some of these issues are simply extensions of those involved in all psychotherapy (e.g. confidentiality) whereas others seem peculiar to work with sexual issues (e.g., use of sexual surrogates). Robert Brown and Robert Sollod address those matters in the final chapter.

Finally, the assumption about technical and theoretical eclecticism, although it is addressed to some extent in the chapters by Halgin et al. and by Sollod, serves more as an orienting framework for the volume than as a particular point of discussion. Technical eclecticism implies that we may maintain a coherent theoretical orientation while selecting from a wide array of existing techniques to deal with specific problems. These techniques are "borrowed" from other theoretical approaches and may or may not be derived from a consistent theory. Theoretical eclecticism would probably almost always involve technical eclecticism, because it consists of choosing the theoretical orientation that seems most applicable to a given situation and then using the appropriate treatment techniques. Even though we agree with Sollod that a systematic or integrated view is useful, our view in pulling together these chapters was that a therapist will intervene most profitably:

1. At an analytical level (i.e. individual, dyadic, social) where the problem is most salient.
2. At a point where the intervention has the best chance for efficient and permanent resolution of the problem.
3. At a level and with a type of intervention that the patient(s) can understand and accept.
4. Where the therapist has adequate conceptual and technical skills.
5. In a format and with a frequency that the environment (e.g. agency, third party carriers, finances) will permit.

We hope that this book will address these points to some extent. For example, intervening at a descriptive level where the problem is most salient demands an understanding of the contributions of individual (biological and psychological), dyadic, and sociocultural factors to sexual distress. Intervening at the point offering the most hope for rapid and permanent change implies accurate assessment and knowledge of the efficiency of various interventions. The third point, intervention at a place and in a way that the patient(s) can understand and accept, is an Ericksonian idea that demands sensitive assessment and flexibility in practice. Intervening where the therapist has knowledge and skills seems self-evident. In fact, intervening by applying specific techniques to remediate sexual dysfunctions sounds at times so straightforward as to lull a therapist into believing that procedures and improvement are automatic and mechanical and that little specific knowledge and skill in sex therapy is needed. This, of course, is not true. However, we do believe that the understanding of the array of determinants of sexual distress and the remedies contained in this volume will be helpful to general therapists in dealing with many of the sexual issues that will arise in their practice. We do not expect that readers of this or any other book will become specialists in sex therapy by reading alone.

This book was conceived in the spirit of following those who have attempted to narrow the gap between sexual therapy and traditional psychodynamic and behavioral approaches to psychotherapy. We hope it will aid in the process of helping therapists make the best use of what they have.

We gratefully acknowledge Carol Fox, who carefully and cheerfully typed and retyped many of the chapters. We also wish to express our great appreciation to all the authors; they were wonderfully responsive to our editorial comments and patient and supportive during the process of birthing this volume.

Robert A. Brown
College Park, Maryland

Joan Roberts Field
Columbia, Maryland

REFERENCES

Barbach, L.(1976). *For yourself: The fulfillment of female sexuality.* New York: Doubleday.

Derogatis, L.R., Meyer, J.K., & King, K.M. (1981). Psychopathology in individuals with sexual dysfunction. *American Journal of Psychiatry, 138,* 757-763.

Edelwich, T., with Brodsky, A.(1982). *Sexual dilemmas for the helping professional.* New York: Brunner/Mazel.

Frank, E., Anderson, E., & Rubinstein, D. (1978). Frequency of sexual dysfunction in "normal" couples. *The New England Journal of Medicine, 299*(3), 111-115.

Kaplan, H.S. (1981). *The new sex therapy: Active treatment of sexual dysfunctions.* New York: Brunner/Mazel.

Kaplan, H.S. (1977). Training of sex therapists. In W.H. Masters, V.E. Johnson, & R.C. Kolodny (Eds.), *Ethical issues in sex therapy and research* (pp.182- 189). Boston: Little, Brown.

Masters, W.H., & Johnson, V.E. (1966). *Human sexual response.* Boston: Little, Brown.

Masters, W.H., & Johnson, V.E. (1970). *Human sexual inadequacy.* Boston: Little, Brown.

Zilbergeld, B. (1978). *Male sexuality: A guide to sexual fulfillment.* New York: Bantam.

Section I

Overview of Sex Therapy and the Determinants of Sexual Functioning

Chapter 1

Treatment of Sexual Dysfunction in the Context of General Psychotherapy

Richard P. Halgin, James E. Hennessey, Sheila Statlender,
Joel A. Feinman, and Robert A. Brown

SEX THERAPY AS A TREATMENT MODALITY

The field of sex therapy has grown and changed remarkably during the past decade. It has become a surprisingly well-accepted treatment modality for many problems that heretofore had been dealt with by traditional insight-oriented therapies. Sex therapy has proven itself to be effective with various sexual dysfunctions with which the traditional therapies often did not succeed. The dramatic outcome statistics reported by sex therapists and the extensive publicity given to this field have generated considerable excitement for mental health professionals as well as a hope for an efficient treatment modality for prospective clients. Sex therapists are receiving an increasing number of referrals for treatment from other professionals as well as from clients themselves.

LoPiccolo (1978) noted that a change in the characteristics of sex therapy applicants occurred during the 1970s. In the early 70s, most couples seeking sex therapy were basically very naive about sex; for these individuals an educational and training approach was often successful. However, with greater societal acceptance of sexuality and the easy availability of good information about sexuality and technique, there are presently fewer such cases. Currently presenting cases more commonly involve deep-seated negative attitudes about sexuality, relational problems, and other problems not fully dealt with by a simple educational program. The hope and promise engenered by the remarkable outcome statistics of the early years of sex therapy research and practice may, therefore, be based on a sample of clients not representative of the clients presenting to sex therapists today (Zilbergeld & Evans, 1980).

3

As this transition has occurred in the type of client presenting for sex therapy, the role of the therapist has become more complicated. For example, criticism has been made that sex therapists have created a new market, and that there are many clients who might tend to look to this new field for simple explanations of much more complex intrapersonal and interpersonal problems. More discriminating assessment procedures must be used to determine the relative contribution of the presenting sexual complaint to the relationship difficulties with which the client is faced. The professional needs to evaluate each applicant in an attempt to understand which factors are playing the primary role in the determination of complaints, and to decide if a therapy excluding sex therapy might not be both more appropriate and more effective. The inclusion of sex therapy in the treatment program of clients presenting with sexual problems must be judged appropriate to the immediate request of the client as well as to the potential relationship bases of these problems. For those cases for which sex therapy techniques seem appropriate, a treatment plan must be formulated so that the clients are given more than just mechanistic directions regarding performance, but rather are given an individualized psychotherapy adapted to their particular needs and problems. This chapter will emphasize the necessity of therapeutic integration and eclecticism in the treatment of sexual problems. To conceive of sex therapy as an independent prescriptive intervention that is automatically applied to sexual complaints is analogous to a pharmacologic treatment of symptoms that ignores emotional, systemic, and historical factors involved in the symptomatology.

In her first text, Helen Singer Kaplan (1974) proposed sexual therapy concepts that were responsive to these complicated presenting problems. She suggested an integrated application of behavioral and psychodynamic approaches in treating sexual dysfunction. She formulated a model of sex therapy, which "when practiced within a psychodynamically oriented multicausal framework, does not rely on sexual tasks alone to resolve conflicts" (p. 153). In Kaplan's second text (1979), she even more emphatically recommended that sex therapy as an isolated behavioral intervention be abandoned. She described a treatment modality that purposefully integrates prescribed sexual experiences with psychotherapeutic exploration of intrapsychic and interactional defenses and resistances. The behavioral prescriptions "are designed to relieve performance anxieties and obsessive self-observations, and desensitize mild sexual tensions. The psychotherapeutic work contains elements of support of sexual pleasure, confrontations with resistance, exploration of unconscious conflicts and marital difficulties, and is aimed at clarifying and resolving those deeper causes which have shaped the sexual problem" (p. 146).

Perhaps Kaplan's greatest contribution in her formulation of a new sex therapy was granting permission for therapists to be pragmatically eclectic. Her model not only permitted, but strongly encouraged behavioral and psychodynamic therapists to incorporate each other's therapeutic strategies into a meaningful and sensible treatment program.

WHAT NEEDS ARE SERVED BY SEX THERAPY

Before discussing the clinical indications and contraindications for the inclusion of sex therapy in a treatment, it is useful to assess both generally and specifically some of the diverse needs that sex therapy or a request for sex therapy may be serving. This should be helpful in understanding sex therapy from the broader perspective of the delivery of mental health services. Moreover, an awareness of such needs may facilitate more informed, responsible, and effective assessment of the clinical indications for sex therapy. With regard to some of the concerns raised in the following sections, the reader is cautioned not to draw simplistic conclusions about the reasons for which sex therapy might be implemented. Various "needs" are spelled out in such a way that each could be perceived as a singular and discrete reason for opting for sex therapy. In actuality, clinical problems are typically multidetermined, and most clients usually present multiple problems. Both the client and the therapist make attributions about the bases of these problems and about which problems are the most important to be addressed in therapy. The following sections enumerate some of the factors that influence decisions as to which problems a client presents, which problems a therapist chooses to treat, and what techniques are deemed most appropriate.

Client Needs

The need of clients to have a more satisfactory sex life is, of course, the need that sex therapy is normally designed to meet. However, a request by a client for sex therapy may be only one of several issues of concern or may even mask other issues or agendas of the client. Just as clients may misattribute tensions arising from sexual conflict to nonsexual aspects of the relationship, they may attribute relational or nonsexual tensions to sexual problems. Or they may present sexual complaints as a strategy to meet nonsexual needs. For some clients, a request for sex therapy may reflect a conscious or unconscious desire for therapeutic help with personal, marital or family problems extending well beyond the sexual sphere.

In some cases, a request for sex therapy may be seen as an attempt to avoid addressing intransigent or potentially explosive relational problems in the hope that the issues are simple and easily resolvable. In cases where the relational discord is secondary to the sexual dysfunction, this strategy may indeed work. Moreover, some people may find it easier to conceptualize an interpersonal problem in sexual terms than to define the problem as one having to do with emotional intimacy or interpersonal anxiety; for example, a woman may be more capable of labeling a problem as orgasmic dysfunction than she would be in recognizing and defining fears of loss of control.

Another factor that may influence some clients to define a problem as sexual in nature is the hope that this new treatment, namely sex therapy, will have a remarkably beneficial impact on solving their problems, just as it has succeeded with so many other individuals and couples whom they have read about or seen on television. Clients may feel that if they present with a circumscribed problem, a quick and easy treatment technique may relieve them of their heavy emotional burden.

It is critical for a therapist to recognize that sexual dysfucntion and relational conflict seldom exist in isolation from one another. Sager (1974) reported that 75% of marital counselees had significant sexual complaints and 70% of sex counselees had marital complaints. These statistics reflect the intertwined nature of sexual and relational concerns; but regardless of the presenting complaint, clients are typically pursuing help in reducing intrapsychic and/or relational conflict. The questions for the therapist are where to start in providing such help, in what proportion should sex therapy techniques be included, and at what point in treatment should they be introduced, if at all.

Therapist Needs

Therapists have needs of their own that can influence a decision to initiate sex therapy. These needs may or may not conflict with the best interests of the clients. Leaving aside unconscious personal, idiosyncratic reactions to clients, there are some broader considerations. Professionals with newly acquired sex therapy skills may be driven to carve out a niche for themselves. Their perception may be quite selective, construing their clients' difficulties in terms of their own particular expertise or interest. Such a perceptual distortion may stem from any of several motivational bases. There is an old folk saying that when one has just acquired a hammer, everything in the world begins to look like a nail. An investment in the acquisition of sex therapy skills may very well tempt a therapist to utilize such skills both to attain a sense of professional validation and to enhance income quickly.

Sex therapy can also function to relieve the therapist's own anxiety about helping clients. It allows for a discrete and specific problem delineation that can be handled by a clearly defined treatment program. In fact, though such an approach may not fully resolve the client's difficulties, it may be indirectly helpful by increasing the confidence of the therapist and the client that the problem is manageable. It is also possible that a therapist may look for structured tasks that promise definitive results when dealing with a client who is demanding and pushing for answers.

There are other therapist needs that are not as easily recognizable, such as the possible unconscious satisfaction of voyeuristic needs of the therapist, or the hoped-for resolution of one's own sexual dysfunction or problem via involvement in the treatment of others' sexual problems. Also there are the more subtle needs, such as the need to enhance one's sense of adequacy as a sexual being, which a therapist may hope (usually futilely) can be accomplished by teaching sexual techniques to others.

Of course there is no easy way to fully understand all the factors that result in a therapist's choice to do work in the area of sexuality. It is presumed that an awareness of these possibilities might sensitize the therapist to some of the needs that could be unconsciously motivating a therapist to do such work. Beyond the level of intrapersonal exploration, there should also be exploration of such issues in the form of solid training, open peer discussions, clinical supervision, and even one's own personal psychotherapy.

Needs of the Profession

In recent years the mental health professions seem to have fostered mental health specialties analogous to the specialties within the field of medicine. Many mental health practitioners have moved from being informed generalists to narrowly defined specialists (e.g., biofeedback, hypnosis, crisis intervention, sex therapy, and so on). Even many graduate programs have urged therapists-in-training to specialize. Professions typically foster such subspecialization in the belief that the results will be greater technical sophistication and ultimately greater prominence and prestige for the profession on the one hand and increased benefit to the public on the other.

There is certainly much to be said for a practitioner who knows a specific field very well and is able to apply special techniques capably. However, a serious problem arises when the practitioner gains special knowledge at the expense of not acquiring a more broad-based familiarity with various theoretical approaches and treatment methods. In some circumstances the narrowly defined technique is acquired in the absence of a solid theoretical base. The result of such a situation can be a therapist who is well trained in a specific technique or other possibly relevant clinical interventions. The profession would be better served if intelligent eclecticism were fostered, so that the good practitioner would be the one familiar with several methods and knowledgeable enough to tailor the treatment to the needs of the client.

Societal Needs

The function of sex therapy as it relates to the larger social structure is an issue that unfortunately receives little attention, even by those therapists most invested in such practice. The presumption underlying society's acceptance of psychotherapy in general is that individual and social mental health can be fostered by the practice of psychotherapy. During this century there has been an increasing awareness that sexual functioning plays a major role in the determination of interpersonal comfort and relational longevity. The presence of a sexual problem often proves to be a threat to the continuance of the relationship, particularly in times such as these when divorce has reached such an unprecedented level in our society. It is possible that society's growing acceptance of sex therapy is directly related to the recognition of a social emergency caused by the growing incidence of relational break-up.

The growth of sex therapy also has been consistent with the increasing level of sexual expression in our society during the past two decades. Not only has society been more permissive in allowing the proliferation of sexual material via the media, but it has allowed and often encouraged public sex education. Concomitant with this end to repression, society has given individuals and couples permission to resolve sexual problems, to achieve healthy sexual functioning somewhat less burdened by the shame that previously accompanied such problems.

On a more practical level, it is possible that sex therapy is increasingly appealing to society because it has a problem- focused technology that usually can be applied in a relatively short period of time. In an age of compulsive technologizing, therapies that can demonstrate functional and cost-effective procedures will be most in demand. And professionals who are able to demonstrate quantifiable competence will be sanctioned. The trend toward narrow publicly recognized specialization is popular in society and is reflected in the myriad of licenses now available in most states. Society needs to know that the purveyors of services are capable of their defined duties, be they automobile mechanics or sex or family therapists.

The professional who chooses to do sex therapy should be sensitive to the social roots and societal implications of such work. First, it would be overly simplistic to presume that sexual problems are the basis for most break-ups. Even in those cases where a sexual problem is defined as a prominent component of the discord, it is necessary for the professional to be able and willing to consider the couple's sexuality within the broad context of their relationship. Second, it is important for the professional to realize that the demise of sexual repression may have been inappropriately perceived by some as a demand or expectation from society that they become "sexual achievers." For example, publicity in the 70s about the female capacity for multiple orgasms left many women feeling incompetent if they experienced a single orgasm during intercourse and a total failure if they experienced no orgasm. Ironically, for some people the increased freedom of sexual expression became a burdensome demand, and for others it led to unrealistically high expectations about achieving characteristically spectacular sexual experiences. In such instances the professional should attempt to foster more realistic expectations and also to educate clients and the public about the wide range of sexual needs and experiences. Third, the professional must be sensitive to the high expectations resulting from the early reports of success and resist being seduced into a potentially lucrative but very narrow provision of services. The professional who chooses to specialize in the delivery of sex therapy should first have the theoretical and technical training to formulate appropriate treatment plans based on comprehensive assessments of clients' needs.

CONSIDERATIONS IN INTRODUCING SEX THERAPY TECHNIQUES

Indications, Contraindications, and Assessment Problems

For the therapist confronted with a client complaining of sexual difficulty, the immediate question is one of determining if and when sex therapy techniques are warranted in the treatment program. The assessment process is necessarily quite complex, and the considerations noted in the previous section should be considered; specifically, what individual or relational needs are being served by the sexual complaint and what therapist needs may be served by offering sex therapy techniques.

Several authors have suggested criteria for determining the appropriateness of offering sex therapy. Clifford Sager (1974) presented a useful model for differentiating couples into three categories, based on the nature of their relational discord and the extent to which the discord is secondary to the sexual dysfunction or vice versa. In the first group, Sager places those clients for whom the sexual dysfunction produces secondary discord within a relationship. For such clients sex therapy is considered the treatment of choice. The second group consists of those clients for whom some degree of relational discord impairs sexual functions. For this most common of circumstances, the incorporation of sex therapy often is indicated when the couple's "desire to improve their sexual functioning outweighs the negative aspects of their relationship" (p. 506); the presumption here is that improved relational functioning can be achieved concomitant with or even as a result of dealing with the sexual problem. In the third group are those with severe relational discord and basic hostility that prevent partners from the expression of loving, intimate feelings on the one hand and from cooperating in the treatment of sexual dysfunction on the other. In such circumstances the undertaking of any kind of treatment is difficult and often impossible, primarily due to the likelihood that such couples are typically unwilling to collaborate regardless of the task. It is conceivable that a therapist might choose to introduce sex therapy into the treatment, and might choose to do so in the hope that structured problem-focused tasks could provide access to more elusive interpersonal problems. However, it is critical that caution be used by the therapist so as not to destroy the relationship or the therapeutic alliance by what might prove to be overwhelmingly threatening issues for the couple.

With regard to couples, Kaplan (1974) specified several pathological factors that should be considered in the assessment process. These factors contribute to sexual dysfunctions and should be considered in light of how they may also seriously interfere with or undermine sex therapy as a viable treatment component. The factors specified by Kaplan that seem most salient to this discussion include lack of trust, power struggles, and communication failure. The therapist should attempt to determine whether such phenomena are general to the relationship or are resulting at least in part from sexual problems. When it is clear that such interpersonal problems derive from areas other than sexual functioning, the implementation of sex therapy will very likely prove frustrating for both the therapist and clients. It is very difficult to teach partners how to make love if they are unable to feel safe and trusting or to talk to each other in nonsexual realms. It is very possible that sex therapy can be incorporated into the treatment if therapeutic progress is made in such areas, but bringing in sex therapy prematurely, or rigidly pursuing it in the face of serious relational issues will likely lead to failure.

Lobitz and Lobitz (1978) specified three important considerations that should enter into the assessment process: (a) the possible presence of organic etiology, (b) motivation for treatment, and (c) the degree of psychopathology in one or both partners. With regard to the first category, it should be a routine practice to rule out any possible organic pathology as an initial step in the assessment process, often by means of a medical consultation. As in any form of psychotherapy, the level and type of motivation bears measurably on the likelihood of treatment success. In this context, it is important to consider the previously discussed client needs that may underlie a request for sex therapy, as well as to consider how serious a commitment clients are willing to make to the treatment process.

The consideration regarding psychopathology is usually quite complex. As Lobitz and Lobitz noted, "Sometimes a person feeling a need for therapy finds it easier to simplify depression or anxiety by labeling it a sexual dysfunction...Patients presenting with a sexual compliant as a target problem are not always accurate in self-diagnosis" (p. 88). If a psychological problem exists in addition to the sexual dysfunction, the therapist must attempt to assess the cause- effect relationship between the two. If the sexual dysfunction is clearly secondary to other psychological problems, then it is generally inappropriate to initiate sex therapy until there is resolution of the psychological problems, if such is possible. For example, sex therapy as an initial treatment is contraindicated for active alcoholics, because alcohol itself has adverse physiological effects on sexual functioning. In addition, there are characteristically many relational problems in the life of an active alcoholic. Immediately focusing on the sexual problems would seem odd, and would even suggest collusion on the part of the therapist in denying the serious implications and role of the patient's alcoholism. Lobitz and Lobitz feel so strongly about this, in fact, that they suggest that sex therapy only be considered following a minimum of six months abstinence from drinking.

Many therapists, including Lobitz and Lobitz, believe that sex therapy can be used with psychotics if the psychosis is not acute and if the client is receiving appropriate medication if needed. Treating an acutely symptomatic psychotic would be obviously inappropriate due to the typically disordered cognitions, perceptions, and behavior during such a state. If psychotropic medication is used, and a decision is made to include sex therapy, the therapist must be especially cognizant of any possible side effects affecting sexual functioning before undertaking treatment of a sexual dysfunction.

Caution must be exercised by a therapist considering the introduction of sex therapy in treating individuals with certain personality disorders. For example, a borderline personality disorder is often characterized by unstable and intense interpersonal relationships, inappropriate and intense anger, identity disturbance, possibly sexual in nature, and affective instability (American Psychiatric Association, 1980). Attempting sex therapy with such people could very well interfere with the possibility of carrying out any of the intense exploratory work typically indicated for such individuals, and exclusive work in the area of sexual problems would likely lead to failure and run the risk of creating increased intrapsychic disturbance and interpersonal turmoil. Similar cautions are recommended for several other personality disorders, namely paranoid, schizotypal, histrionic, narcissistic, and antisocial. Typically the presence of such a disorder reflects a seriously maladaptive interpersonal style. Such individuals often have such disturbed emotional functioning and patterns of relating that the purpose of sex therapy would be defeated. It would make more sense for the therapist to deal first with the personal style; when and if personal change becomes evident, the introduction of sex therapy may be carefully considered. Introducing sex therapy precipitously could very likely result in a tumultuous experience for both the client and the therapist, possibly leaving both parties feeling quite disappointed.

One further factor which requires particular attention in sex therapy assessments is the developmental framework of the client. Sexuality plays a much different role for the seventeen-year-old than it does for the seventy-year-old client. Consequently both the assessment and the treatment of any client should be attentive to particular developmental needs and problems. For example, adolescence is characteristically a period of sexual upheaval in which relationships are quite transient; requests for sex therapy by individuals in this age group can often be best accommodated by an educative approach. For other age groups there are similar age-related factors and life-circumstance issues that impact on sexuality, to which the professional should be sensitive.

Perhaps the clearest indications for sex therapy are in those cases where bad habits have been acquired or good habits have been forgotten or never learned. For example, the man who prematurely ejaculates during sexual intercourse may indeed have never learned ejaculatory control, and instead may have been caught up in the vicious cycle of anxiety related to such a problem. Or the inorgasmic woman who has not adequately learned how to relax and derive pleasure, or whose partner has failed to attend to her needs, may satisfactorily respond to this intervention.

Many other examples of the appropriate or inappropriate use of sex therapy exist, but each case is specific and different in some respects from all others. The major assessment task centers around openness and sensitivity on the part of clients and therapists in their mutual determination of treatment programs that are individually designed to serve client needs; such programs must consider history and current psychological and physical status.

Integrating Different Therapeutic Modalities

Much of the older sex therapy literature seems to presume that sex therapy is being offered independently of any other treatment. From reading some reports, one could easily get the impression that clients have a clear formulation of a sexual problem and therapists have a cookbook treatment ready at the point of intake. Such a perception is naive and such a proposed treatment approach inadequate. Fortunately in the recent past there seems to have been a move away from such simplistic treatment notions. One still finds notices for treatment programs such as five-week therapy groups for inorgasmic women or brief hypnotherapy for sexual problems; for some clients such treatment programs might prove helpful, though there seems the risk that some such approaches might be inclined to ignore the fact that sexual problems are typically quite complex, and thus look for quick and easy solutions for difficult problems. Some therapists assert that the benefit of such programs is that they provide a more comfortable and accessible way for clients to initiate the process of improved sexual functioning. The fact is that many clients who are referred for sex therapy really require other forms of treatment, and many clients who are referred for other forms of treatment might benefit from inclusion of sex therapy into their treatment. It is the ethical responsibility of the professional to attempt a comprehensive and objective appraisal of the client's needs.

A complicated treatment situation involves a client who initiates a course of therapy for a problem not sexual in nature, where it becomes evident to the therapist that sexual problems are prominent and that sex therapy could be helpful. The treatment dilemma becomes one of whether the therapist should refer the client for separate sex therapy or whether the sex therapy can be incorporated into the treatment program by the therapist. A resolution of this dilemma has much to do with both the technical and conceptual styles of the therapist; one who is a rigid adherent to a specific technique would likely find such an integration of methods out of the question, and that therapist might do best to refer the client elsewhere. On the other hand, there are many therapists who strongly identify with particular theoretical conceptualizations, but who are nevertheless willing and able to be flexible with treatment strategy. For example, it is very possible that a rich therapeutic experience can be provided by an interpersonally or psychodynamically oriented therapist who is willing to blend in certain behavioral techniques where they fit appropriately into a therapy.

Several gains can be achieved by integrating sex therapy techniques with other treatment procedures. First, there is the communication of a holistic perspective that regards the client's sexuality as one facet of the person. Secondly, there is the benefit derived from the fact that the therapist has a perspective of the client that goes beyond the sexual sphere, very likely seeing intrapsychic or interpersonal facets that are quite relevant to the client's sexuality.

The pragmatic question arises as to how to integrate the previous therapeutic work (be it interpersonal, psychodynamic, or systems work in nature) with the more behavioral interventions associated with sex therapy. Does one make abrupt transitions from session to session between the "real therapy" and the "sex therapy"? Does the therapist divide the session into two segments? It is hoped that neither of these options would be considered necessary. What could be done involves a process of what these authors refer to as *blending*. Blending is the process wherein the therapist approaches both the whole therapy and each session with an eye toward gauging the ongoing needs of the client and sensitively responding to those needs. Components of sex therapy can be blended into a long-term individual or couples therapy; there may be periods during which attention to sexual functioning seems warranted and primary attention is given to such. There may be other periods during which other issues take precedence, and consideration of nonsexual matters seems warranted. In such a blended treatment where the therapeutic focus must shift as the client's conflicts and anxieties are observed, understood and dealt with, the therapist must attend vigilantly to the client's resistances. In any therapy, unconsciously manufactured crises can effectively divert attention from the more painful tasks at hand. As the sexual focus becomes too anxiety-producing, the therapist can expect the relational context of the couple to become more problematic, perhaps to avoid the anxiety of the sexual focus. Similarly, as the relational issues of the couple become more obvious and anxiety-producing in therapy, one would expect the sexual "problem" to force itself on the therapy and the therapist. By keeping the possibility of such resistances in mind and by confronting the clients with these possibilities as they arise, treatment will be less impeded.

This form of blending was successfully adapted to a group format (Muller & Halgin, 1982) in which the therapists integrated the techniques of a dynamic interpersonal therapy group and a behaviorally directive sex therapy program in the treatment of clients presenting with premature ejaculation. In this group the behavioral intervention served to teach clients ejaculatory control, while the interpersonal intervention facilitated insight and understanding about the intrapersonal and interpersonal significance of the dysfunction, as well as insight regarding the interpersonal issues. Success was achieved through the blending of therapeutic models and strategies; in each group meeting during the 10-week treatment program, neither the sexual dysfunction nor interpersonal issues received consideration to the exclusion of the other. Not only did all the group members achieve improved ejaculatory control, but they also reported an enlightened sense of themselves and the sexual and social roles they played.

Such blending can even more easily be adapted to the individual or couples therapy format. The therapist can start with whatever treatment modality promises to be the most profitable; as it becomes evident that there are problems present for which different therapeutic techniques have been shown to be effective, the therapy is modified so as to integrate such techniques. The major requirement is that the therapist be flexible enough to listen to the needs of the client, both conscious and unconscious, and to choose a treatment path that provides greatest access to therapeutic gain in *both* the sexual and relational contexts. Making interpretations while concomitantly providing behavioral prescriptions need not be considered as contradictory, as some traditionalists might view it. The clinician who perceives such an integration as bizarre would do well to read Paul Wachtel's *Psychoanalysis and Behavior Therapy* (1977), which sensitively and sensibly explains how and why an integration of apparently incompatible perspectives can be achieved.

There are a few problems inherent in the process of blending. There could be a problem with countertransference issues or with the therapist's lack of knowledge in a particular area, so that the therapist moves away from more threatening issues to an area that appears to be safe; the likelihood of this can be diminished with clinical supervision or peer consultation. A second problem is the possible loss of focus with blending; care has to be taken that neither the central issues nor the treatment goals are obscured by the treatment itself.

CASE EXAMPLES

In this section three case examples are provided in order to highlight some of the issues and difficulties involved in sex therapy. The first case describes an unsuccessful treatment that resulted primarily from the therapist's failure to do a thorough assessment upon which a comprehensive treatment could be based. The second case focuses on the process and importance of theoretical and therapeutic integration in psychotherapy. The third case is an example of a situation in which sex therapy considerations helped to focus on and to clarify more pervasive relational problems.

Case Example: An Inappropriate Application of Sex Therapy

John was a 21-year-old college student who requested treatment for premature ejaculation. At the time John initiated therapy he had had four experiences with sexual intercourse, all of which were within the three months preceding his request for treatment. All four experiences were with his girlfriend, whom he had been seeing for one year, and on all four occasions he experienced the frustration of premature ejaculation. John's girlfriend had expressed her willingness to cooperate in any treatment exercises; however, she was not willing to meet with the therapist due to "embarrassment."

In the very first session the client clearly stated his wish that the treatment focus exclusively on the sexual problem. The therapist, a relatively inexperienced graduate student enrolled in a sex therapy practicum at that time, agreed to this request. The therapist asked John to complete a personal history questionnaire prior to the initiation of the sex therapy, and John agreed to do so. In the personal history questionnaire it was evident that John had a lengthy history of interpersonal difficulties and intrapsychic stresses. He characterized himself as "impulsive," prone to "losing control," and "doing things without thinking of the consequences." This picture of impetuosity included an incident in which he had been arrested following an argument in a bar during which he had become assaultive; there were also several incidents with his girlfriend in which he had been physically and emotionally abusive. He also documented his excessive use of alcohol, but vehemently denied that the problem was a serious concern.

Following a review of the personal history data, the therapist suggested that a treatment program should be much broader than sex therapy for John. At that point John threatened to terminate. The impact of that threat on the therapist was considerable and resulted in the therapist's agreement to initiate a circumscribed treatment program for John that would deal solely with his problem of premature ejaculation. Within a few weeks the problematic nature of this choice became apparent to the therapist. The prescription of exercises designed to facilitate sexual sensitivity, awareness and responsiveness appeared inappropriate for a person generally troubled by longstanding maladaptive patterns of relating and specifically troubled by a problem-laden intimate relationship with his girlfriend. Predictably, John became impatient with the treatment, and the therapist grew more anxious and confused. John failed to show for his fifth session and did not contact the clinic thereafter. The therapist expressed relief about John's unilateral choice to terminate, for he had come to recognize the therapeutic fiasco that he had helped to create. What John needed most was a frank assessment of his characterological problems and a treatment program that would address his intrapsychic and relational difficulties. Components of sex therapy could have been blended into such a treatment; the parallels between John's general patterns of behavior and specific patterns of sexuality could have been highlighted in an attempt to bring about change in both areas. Unwillingness on John's part to comply with prescribed exercises could have been used to demonstrate to John his more general problems. However, it is probably evident that John was not a good candidate for therapy in general, and that regardless of the modality, the likelihood for failure would have been considerable.

Case Example: The Appropriate Application of Sex Therapy

Lisa initially requested sex therapy due to her inability to experience orgasm. She was a 25-year-old female undergraduate who was living with her boyfriend Dave at the time she initiated therapy. Dave expressed willingness to cooperate in a therapy program. Lisa and Dave were seen for a total of seventeen 90-

minute sessions over a period of almost 3 months. They were seen twice weekly in one 60-minute conjoint session with the male/female cotherapy team; following this group meeting, each partner was seen for 30 minutes by the same sex therapist.

At the time of intake, Lisa reported that she had never had an orgasm, although she experienced a high degree of sexual arousal, lubricated copiously during lovemaking, and felt strongly attracted to Dave. Although Lisa had never masturbated, Dave had tried on several occasions to bring her to orgasm by clitoral stimulation. Lisa stated that she was extremely frustrated by her failure to climax in the face of a high degree of sexual stimulation and arousal.

Lisa's personal history was relevant in several aspects. She reported that she had sustained severe burns as a young girl and that by the age of 14 had thus undergone a series of medical operations. Lisa stated that as a child and adolescent she had been painfully embarrassed by the scars and chose clothing that would camouflage them. Lisa's first sexual experience occurred when she was 16 with a male friend; her recollection of this experience was somewhat hazy, but she seemed to feel that she had been taken advantage of while she and her partner were both under the influence of drugs. Lisa also described a 3-year relationship with a man who had been both physically and emotionally abusive toward her. She stated that the memory of this relationship still constituted a source of anger, humiliation, and shame. She viewed her current relationship with Dave to be a positive and important development in her life, and stated that she hoped that therapy would also enable her to be freer and more open in her communication with him.

Lisa's strong motivation, high level of erotic arousal and good vasocongestive responding indicated that she was a good candidate for sex therapy. This was reinforced by the fact that she and Dave were engaged in a reasonably harmonious, supportive relationship. According to Kaplan (1974), the prognosis in such cases of primary orgasmic dysfunction is quite good. It was also quite evident that sex therapy alone would not be sufficient.

A treatment program that was composed of both behavioral and psychodynamic components was formulated — a therapy that offered the opportunity for Lisa to recognize and deal with extensive emotional material as well as to acquire sexual competencies. The treatment plan viewed the achievement of Lisa's orgasm as a valid goal, but not the sole criterion of her normal or satisfactory sexual functioning. An emphasis was placed on assertiveness, autonomy and pride in the achievement of a heightened self-image, as well as on a more gratifying sexual relationship. Thus, the treatment strategy involved a dual approach, focused on Lisa's individual functioning as well as on the couple's sexual relationship and interactions. A routine course of individual sex therapy exercises were prescribed for Lisa, including masturbation and the development of a repertoire of erotic fantasies. These were accompanied by couples exercises designed to foster communication and assertiveness.

Throughout treatment Lisa demonstrated a strong commitment to the process, and she was able to develop a strong and positive therapeutic alliance. The treatment evoked a good deal of anxiety and a heightened awareness of her inhibitions, including prohibitions around touching and stimulating herself, dissatisfaction with her body, and a tendency to distract herself from her own pleasure and arousal by worrying about Dave.

Therapy also elicited powerful, emotionally charged memories regarding the past abusive relationship with her previous boyfriend and unpleasant hospital experiences. Extreme dread of anesthesia and of losing consciousness were related to possible fears of losing control during orgasm. It also became apparent that memories of being observed by groups of doctors and medical students led her to adopt an intellectualized attitude toward her own body in order to deal with the embarrassment of exposure. Despite these memories and feelings, Lisa maintained a commitment to the treatment, and she evidenced an increased degree of self- confidence and self-respect. As the treatment progressed, Lisa began experiencing orgasms, initially via self-stimulation and subsequently during intercourse.

Lisa and Dave stated that as a result of therapy there was improved communication between them. Although Dave had not extensively used the therapy sessions to explore the impact the treatment may have had on him, he did express an increased awareness of his own difficulties with assertiveness and ambition. Both Lisa and Dave also stated that therapy had enabled them to feel less, rather than greater, pressure to engage in genital sexuality, and stated that they had a greater appreciation of nonsexual forms of contact and closeness that were pleasurable to them. Lisa stated that she continued to feel better about herself and had a greater sense of satisfaction and pride, not only with regard to her sexual functioning, but in relation to her general sense of self.

With regard to the criteria previously noted, this couple had presented with a high level of maturation, a reasonable level of trust, and evidence of communication and warmth between them. In accordance with the guidelines suggested by Sager (1974), this couple's positive feelings and their desire to improve their sexual functioning were deemed to outweigh any negative aspects of their relationship.

The key to success in this therapy was maintaining a broad perspective and resisting overinvestment in a singular treatment model. At the end of the treatment, Lisa stated that a good deal of emotional material had been dealt with during the treatment, and that she was relieved to have had the opportunity to work through more than just difficulties with inorgasmia.

In this case, there was a marked history of physical trauma, including surgical invasiveness to correct a physical disfigurement. The assessment for sex therapy was necessarily psychologically invasive in an area of extreme vulnerability for this client. The potential for reawakening overwhelming and inhibiting anxiety related to intimacy, body integrity, and body- image was quite high. The therapist's sensitivity to such potential anxiety was crucial in this case. Blending of approaches afforded an understanding of the client's developmental history, some relief for the client around her conflicts about the issues of abnormality in terms of body-image and interpersonal functioning, as well as improved sexual functioning. It was necessary for the therapist to view the significance of the client's complaint both within the client's developmental history and in her current life context. The therapist was able to facilitate improved sexual functioning while addressing the client's past and current conflicts around intimacy as more than just problems secondary to a sexual dysfunction.

Case Example: Using Sex Therapy Considerations as a Means of Assessing Other Problems

Sally and Steven were married and had a 10-year-old son. Sally was 31 years old and was self-employed in a small business. Originally Sally was referred by her physician for individual therapy when no physical etiology could be found for her depression and amenorrhea.

The therapist requested that the entire family attend initially in order to aid in assessment. The pattern of conflict in the family made it clear that Sally's symptoms were, at the least, maintained and supported by the family system. Both spouses were locked into rigid roles vis a vis one another, and their conflict was characterized by a tendency to symmetrical escalation. Sally's role was to be perfectionistic and pessimistic. Steven's role was the easy-going, incompetent optimist. An initial pretense of harmony was shattered in the first session when their son made an analogy between his mother and the dog, noting that they were alike because they both slept on the couch. This was the therapist's first intimation that their conflict was intertwined in their sexual life.

The family therapy rapidly evolved into a couples therapy as Sally and Steven readily acknowledged their interpersonal difficulties and a desire to speak unencumbered by their son's presence. Whereas many conflicts were evident around communication, career choices, and sex roles, there were also frequent statements regarding mutual discontent in their sexual relationship. Steven, who tended to deny problems, acknowledged that it was the one thing that depressed him. In the first couples session they spilled out their relational history, which included their precipitous marriage due to Sally's pregnancy, their sexual inexperience at the time of marriage, and their chronically unsatisfactory sex life. Both seemed relieved by their revelations. Significantly, during the week following the initial couples session, Sally's menstrual cycle resumed after a year's hiatus. Continued reference to their sex life in the first few couples sessions led the therapist to explore with them whether they were interested in a more focused sex therapy. They acknowledged that they had been discussing the issue between themselves and they had decided that they wanted to begin, with the understanding that other aspects of their relationship would not be neglected. The therapist decided to proceed with the incorporation of sex therapy at that point because they both seemed motivated and committed to one another. Their apparent naivete seemed amenable to an educative approach.

Sex histories were taken by the therapist in separate interviews, and it quickly became evident to the therapist that including sex therapy in the treatment would not be a judicious choice at that time. Steven, although admitting his great sexual frustration, was more worried about the quality of the overall relationship. He wanted more warmth and affection and more of a traditional wife. Sally, in her interview, admitted that she was physically repulsed by her husband, felt that they shouldn't have gotten married, had been passive and withholding in the relationship, and had hoped that Steven would have ended it so that she could avoid the guilt and criticism from her parents.

The therapist shared the above impressions with them in the subsequent joint interview and it was agreed that sex therapy was not appropriate at that time. Rather, a continuation of a broader relational treatment was recommended. It had become clear that the criteria suggested by Sager (1974) were not met. Oppressive hostility, lack of commitment and lack of motivation stood as formidable obstacles to improved sexual functioning. The contraindications specified by Kaplan (1974) of lack of trust, power struggles, and communication deficiencies stood out as well.

This was a case in which unsatisfactory sexual relations were present but were inaccessible to direct therapy due to other relational conflicts. Nevertheless the focus on sexuality did facilitate an understanding of systemic difficulties that might not easily have become so apparent. The therapist was able to assess the situation appropriately and make a decision to postpone addressing the sexual problems. Susan and Steven came for couples therapy for several months, during which time they made a mutual decision to separate.

CONCLUSIONS

From the material presented thus far, it should be evident that these authors recommend an approach to treatment in which the therapist adapts the treatment to the needs of the client rather than to a singular theoretical framework. The precise method by which a therapist integrates the treatment of a sexual problem into the psychotherapy is dictated greatly by the therapist's orientation. For example, in the early stage of assessment and treatment, the behaviorally oriented clinician will be particularly attentive to specific behavioral targets and to specific techniques for behavior change. If a sexual problem is initially evident, then a problem-focused treatment that addresses the problem will come easily. Optimally, the recognition and treatment of this problem can be accompanied by consideration also of both intrapsychic and relational issues. The psychodynamically oriented therapist will be most aware of defenses and anxieties about underlying conflicts or impulses; this therapist often faces a theoretically difficult choice when a sexual problem becomes evident, since theoretical biases often pull such a therapist away from problem-focused treatment and toward exploratory work. The acknowledgment that these two strategies can be compatible allows such a therapist to weave together the fibers of a client's developmentally determined issues and current behavioral problem into a fabric that can be comprehensively perceived.

Therapists who permit themselves such flexibility will likely find themselves enjoying a surprising feeling of freedom. Those therapists who have had relatively narrow theoretical and/or therapeutic training may at first feel awkward in their attempt to integrate components of therapies that were previously disregarded or possibly disparaged by them; however, with practice and appropriate supervision, the acquisition of new strategies can add excitement and increased effectiveness to one's work. The acknowledgment that different strategies can be compatible allows a therapist to bring together the factors of a client's history, problematic behaviors, and systemic forces into a meaningful, comprehensive assessment and treatment. Typically clients are not cognizant of the demarcations between different modalities, and thus it would be surprising for the client to be the uncomfortable party in such an amalgamated treatment. It is usually the therapist who must overcome awkwardness determined by theoretical bias.

The goal of this chapter was to convey to the reader a sense of the benefits of therapeutic blending in general, and an appreciation of the value of such blending when treating sexual problems in particular. In sum, these authors wish to convey to the reader the sense that sex therapy *is* psychotherapy; it should not be regarded as an isolated technical process, but rather as one facet of a multimodal therapeutic intervention system. These authors encourage therapists to familiarize themselves with the techniques that sex therapists and sex researchers have demonstrated as effective, and to incorporate such knowledge and techniques into a comprehensive assessment and treatment program that is flexible enough to respond to the particular needs of each client.

REFERENCES

American Psychiatric Association. (1980). *Diagnostic and statistical manual of mental disorders* (3rd ed.). Washington, DC:Author.

Kaplan, H.S. (1974). *The new sex therapy.* New York: Brunner/Mazel.

Kaplan, H.S. (1979). *The new sex therapy (Vol. II): Disorders of sexual desire.* New York: Brunner/Mazel.

Lobitz, W.C., & Lobitz, G.K. (1978). Clinical assessment in the treatment of sexual dysfunctions. In J. LoPiccolo & L. LoPiccolo (Eds.), *Handbook of sex therapy.* New York: Plenum.

LoPiccolo, J. (1978). The professionalization of sex therapy: Issues and problems. In J. LoPiccolo & L. LoPiccolo (Eds.), *Handbook of sex therapy.* New York: Plenum.

Muller, R., & Halgin, R. (1982, March). *A new model for group treatment of sexual dysfunction.* Paper presented at the Annual Meeting of the American Association of Sex Educators, Counselors, and Therapists, New York.

Sager, C.J. (1974). Sexual dysfunctions and marital discord. In H.S. Kaplan, *The new sex therapy.* New York: Brunner/Mazel.

Sederer, L., & Sederer, N. (1979). A family myth: Sex therapy gone awry. *Family Process, 18,* 315-322.

Wachtel, P. (1977). *Psychoanalysis and behavior therapy: Toward an integration.* New York: Basic Books.

Zilbergeld, B., & Evans, M. (1980). The inadequacy of Masters and Johnson. *Psychology Today, 14*(3), 28-43.

Chapter 2

Personality Style and Sexuality

Judith B. Kuriansky

INTRODUCTION

Prior to the last decade, sexologists were prone to think of sexual dysfunctions in psychodynamic terms. For example, a man with erectile dysfunction might have an unconscious unacceptable fear of injuring the female. However, the contributions of Masters and Johnson suggested that sexual dysfunctions are learned behaviors, conditioned by anxiety (Masters & Johnson, 1970). This approach turned the clinician's focus away from internal processes and toward behavior. Later, the "new sex therapy" recognized the value of an integrative view, combining psychodynamic and behavioral approaches to understand and treat sexual dysfunctions (Kaplan, 1974).

With the current trend toward a holistic view of the person, it seems valuable to see sexual dysfunction as one aspect of a person's total adaptation. As such, an understanding of a patient's personality style serves as a context in which to evaluate and treat the particular sexual symptom. Surprisingly little has been written about the relationship between personality style and sexual disorders (Offit, 1977). However, there is clinical as well as research evidence to suggest such an approach would be valuable.

Several researchers have examined the relationship between psychiatric status and sexual dysfunction (Maurice & Guze, 1970; O'Connor & Stern, 1972; Pinderhughes, Grace, & Reyna, 1972). Until recently, these studies have yielded contradictory results. Some studies observed neurosis in a large percentage of patients with sexual problems; others found that only a minority of clients with sexual disorders also suffered from neurotic conditions. However, recent studies by Derogatis (1981) strongly suggest that there is a disproportionate level of psychological distress among individuals suffering from sexual dysfunction.

The Derogatis studies further found evidence that specific sexual dysfunctions manifest characteristic symptom profiles. Men diagnosed as having inhibited sexual excitement also had elevated levels of phobic anxiety and somatization, but low levels of hostility. In contrast, men diagnosed with premature ejaculation demonstrated the opposite pattern, with low levels of phobic anxiety and somatization and high levels of hostility. Women diagnosed as having inhibited orgasm showed elevated levels of depression and interpersonal sensitivity, and very low levels of somatization and phobic anxiety; women with functional dyspareunia or vaginismus had similar but more elevated profiles.

Whereas these results linking psychiatric and sexual status do not prove that high levels of certain psychological distress *cause* a specific sexual dysfunction, they do give support to the view that certain personality characteristics may be consistent with particular symptoms.

In my clinical experience with individuals and couples with sexual dysfunction, it has become useful to me, both in evaluation and treatment, to assess and be continually aware of the patient's personality style. This allows a view of both how the person deals with stress in ways that might lead to specific sexual behavior, and of what underlying needs are motivating and maintaining both the symptoms and the nature of the interpersonal interaction.

This paper explores how the dynamics and defenses of several major personality styles manifest themselves in sexual functioning. The major personality styles explored are the obsessive- compulsive, histrionic, and narcissistic. Paranoid, schizoid, and depressive styles are also discussed briefly. The relationship between personality style and sexual symptoms is highlighted by case examples as well as by descriptions of various aspects of treatment. The treatment style represents an integration of pyschoanalytic, behavioral, interpersonal, and gestalt techniques and theory.

Derogatis's work has shown a connection between sexual functioning and "neurosis" reaching clinical diagnostic levels. However, in this paper I shall discuss personality style as a mode of functioning, which although it is consistent with the symptoms as outlined in the psychiatric criteria of *DSM III* (American Psychiatric Association, 1980), does not necessarily fulfill those criteria to warrant being labeled a clinical diagnostic disorder.

It is important to remember that even though most people function primarily within a particular personality style, they also have characteristics of other styles as well. For example, a predominantly obsessive or histrionic person may also have strong narcissistic characteristics. In addition, these characteristics, rather than being static, may shift over time or in different circumstances. The balance of these styles, as well as their shifts, must be taken into account in order to fully understand someone's functioning and to help them cope with ensuing sexual disorders.

It is also important to point out that sexual problems are not exclusively associated with any one particular personality style. In addition, a person with any one personality style may have a combination of different sexual symptoms. This is partly because many factors may impinge upon the development of the sexual problem within that individual, including sexual history and prior experiences, age, health, life situation, and current life crises. Furthermore, particular personality styles do not by any means lead necessarily to sexual problems. However, when a sexual problem exists, it is consistent with the particular personality style and should be seen in the context of that person's overall character structure and behavior patterns. This is particularly important when determining therapeutic interventions, because these should be applicable not only to the sexual symptom itself, but also to the person's overall psychological functioning.

SEXUAL PROBLEMS IN THE OBSESSIVE-COMPULSIVE PERSONALITY

The typical obsessive-compulsive is marked by control—the need to have it and the fear of losing it. This style is more common in men's sexual functioning than in women's, although it does occur in both sexes.

In *DSM III*, the obsessive is described as someone with a restricted ability to be warm and emotive. People like this are preoccupied with details, insistent on others' submission, overly devoted to work to the exclusion of pleasure, and indecisive for fear of making mistakes.

Following a formulation integrating psychodynamic theory and developmental theory of separation-individuation, the genesis of such behavior can be traced back to early struggles (probably around age two) with the maternal figure over control and independence. In one common interaction, for example, the mother, because of her own needs and dynamics, encourages the child to give full rein to the expression of aggressive impulses. Yet when threatened with her own loss of control, and threat of losing the child, she becomes overly restrictive and controlling. The child consequently becomes fearful of total expression of its dependence on the mother, which could lead to submission of the self. Expressions of aggression then further become a statement of independence and control over the self. Of course, other influences on the expression of control, including identifications with the paternal figure, must also be considered.

In the developmental process of an obsessive, the child becomes flooded with frightening aggressive impulses that become the central theme of character organization. Conflict over the expression of hostility may lead to outbursts (e.g., temper tantrums), and/or withdrawal and emotional constriction. To keep unacceptable feelings in check, the main defenses that become operative are denial and passive aggressiveness, and later on in life, intellectualization. As a result, expression of affectionate as well as aggressive impulses becomes inhibited and behavior appears rigid, over-controlled and routinized.

In adult life, unresolved battles of control with major figures in the person's life can be recapitulated in the sexual arena. This appears to occur in two major ways. The obsessive becomes terrified of allowing expression of dependency, which would signal submission to the "mother" figure. And direct expression of aggression (both a cause and result of the battle over control) is also feared.

Specifically in sexual functioning, the male obsessive can come to perceive the penis as the tool for expression of aggression. Thrusting further stimulates aggressive impulses, ranging from the desire to dominate the partner to the fantasy of overcoming her "hold" on him by symbolically "killing" her. Containment in the vagina may also be perceived as being "controlled" or taken over by the woman.

The unconscious dynamics of the obsessive can manifest themselves in several different sexual behavior patterns and interactions. For example, the obsessive who is defending against feared dependency needs and hostile impulses toward women may develop premature ejaculation, loss of sexual desire, or erection problems, or a combination of these. The sexual problem can be seen itself as a defensive maneuver to protect the person from unacceptable feelings.

Some obsessives develop psychosomatic symptoms, for example, headaches or ulcers. These may be used in turn as excuses to the partner to avoid sex or to control the timing of sexual encounters. Sex would then only occur when he initiates it. The partner of such a man would often complain that he does not respond when *she* wants sex, that he is not considerate of her desire for lovemaking to last longer, and that he criticizes her for being too slow or unresponsive. The woman often blames herself and becomes insecure about her own desirability. Her self-blame often dominates the clinical picture and becomes a chief complaint when she seeks therapy.

The passive-aggressive behavior of the obsessive character may manifest itself in other ways. Instead of directly arguing with the partner about sex, the obsessive might undermine her power by criticizing her for other, nonsexual "inadequacies," such as her housework, cooking, child-rearing, or even personal appearance (e.g., usually of being overweight). This can lead to hostility between the couple such that one or both develop a variety of sexual problems or avoid sex altogether.

Men with sexual problems who use passive aggressiveness as a defense will often ejaculate prematurely. With this symptom, the man deprives the woman of prolonged containment or any intercourse at all, thereby directly protecting himself from the threat of being taken over by her, and indirectly "punishing" her for stimulating his anxiety over uncomfortable feelings.

Because of obsessives' need to stay in control of feelings, and the consequent fear of "letting go" with someone else, they often prefer autoeroticism to sex with a partner. Or when with a partner, obsessives are unadventuresome. Although it is possible that some people compensate for their rigidity in one area of life (for example, in a career in legal or accounting fields where a high degree of rational thinking is required) by expressing more lustful sexuality, it is more common that the sexual and interpersonal behavior remains rigid. Obsessives therefore prefer sticking to "tried and true" positions and partners.

Besides understanding how the individual personality style manifests itself in sexual behavior, it is crucial to observe how the personality styles interact. Couples often pick one another in order to complement their sexual needs and behavior. For example, some obsessives are obsessed with control but harbor desires to loosen up. Thus, they are attracted to partners who are more spontaneous and impulsive. This can be a positive prognostic sign, an attempt to give up some inhibitions. But the obsessive can become frightened by the partner's free expression of sexuality and withdraw from the relationship or attempt to put controls on the partner's behavior.

Such complementary relationships often find the obsessive man pairing with a histrionic woman (to be discussed further in the next section). The following is an example of how this type of relationship presents itself in sex therapy.

Therapy was initiated, as is common, by the wife. The chief complaint was her husband's lack of erection. The wife, Jill, was a 26-year-old teacher who wanted to go back to school to study personnel work. More importantly, she wanted a home and child, both of which her husband was resisting.

The husband, Gordon, was a 30-year-old accountant. In therapy he revealed a classic psychoanalytic dynamic: a fear of vagina dentata (teeth in the vagina). Gordon grew up with a controlling mother and submissive father, and in one therapy session literally stated that he feared a woman would "bite off his penis." Therefore, the vagina was a dangerous place to be and a place his penis should not venture. By losing his erection before intromission, he protected himself from both his aggressive impulses and his anticipation of female hostility, as well as his retaliatory hostility toward his wife (and women in general). Through his impotence, he prevented himself from using his penis as a weapon.

Gordon usually sat in therapy sessions grunting "yes" or "no," his arms tightly crossed, not revealing a glint of emotion. His wife would prod him, complaining he watched too much football on TV, never held her hand in the movies (as she'd like him to), and constantly reviewed his computer printouts after dinner at night. Gordon's withdrawal into routinized work and a rigid approach to both his work and his sexual relationship reflected both his need to control and his fear of aggression and dependency. Under his wife's insistence and criticism (remindful of his mother's domination of his father), he grew more resistant. He lost his erection while making love. It was as if every time they made love he (and his penis) said, "I won't give in to you."

Gordon demonstrates that the obsessive whose need to control is thwarted may withdraw from sexuality. If he cannot be dominant in the relationship or cannot seem effective, he may avoid the situation as a means of self-protection.

Obsessiveness may affect sexual functioning in other ways. For example, he may give to his sexuality and genitalia the same attention to detail he gives to other areas in his life. He may take mental measurements and make constant evaluations of what and how he/it is doing. These judgments lead to extreme anxiety over performance of the sexual act. By constantly checking his erection ("spectatoring"), the man becomes self-conscious, and loses it.

The obsessive often carries over his general rigidity to lovemaking routines. He spends a fixed amount of time and goes through a set pattern of actions. The routine may also include thorough cleansing before or after. Such routines may adversely affect a partner and stimulate her insecurity as she misinterprets his defense as a sign of her own inadequacy. She may object to a "mechanical" touch or feel insulted or rejected by the obsessive getting up to wash immediately after intercourse.

Obsessive-compulsives who are not involved in a committed relationship may apply their rigidity to pursuit of sexual encounters. In addition, although some obsessives protect themselves from sexual urges by redirecting their energies into other activities, others may become overly involved in sexual behavior and consumed with sexual thoughts.

SEX THERAPY APPROACHES FOR THE
OBSESSIVE-COMPULSIVE PERSONALITY

Therapy for sexual problems as they occur in the obsessive character has a unique prognostic factor: The obsessive's main concern is over needing to be in *control,* and behavioral treatment methods for these problems help the patient *develop* control.

For example, the treatment of premature ejaculation in the male and anorgasmia in the female is intended to help the person control the timing of such responses. All behavioral treatments start out with self-exploration and stimulation exercises whereby the person, in the safety of solitude, explores the ways in which to increase or decrease excitement level. This is consistent with the obsessive's comparative comfort with autoerotic behavior, where he or she exclusively exerts control.

An important step in the treatment process of developing control is that during the sessions of experimenting with stimulation, the person is instructed to become aware of the point beyond which full release can no longer be held back. For example, in the man this is the "point of ejaculatory inevitability," that point beyond which physiologically he can no longer hold back ejaculation. Once he becomes aware of this point, he learns to stimulate himself close to this point, yet to stop before reaching it, in order to delay the onset of the orgasmic release and thus continue the sexual experience.

When the obsessive is involved in sensate-focus exercises with the partner, the giving and receiving of feedback needs to be emphasized. In this way the obsessive can constructively exercise control over the sexual experience by giving instructions to the partner about how and where to touch. It may take effort, however, for the obsessive to be comfortable telling others how to please him.

Work to help the obsessive be aware of and express feelings usually has to progress slowly. The therapist can gradually reflect how the patient might feel in a situation. For example, when the patient is recalling a sexual encounter, the therapist might repeat the specifics of the scene (to reassure him by dealing with the *facts*), but then ask questions about how the patient felt, or add comments like "When she said that, you must have been furious." This offers both a model, permission, encouragement for the expression of feelings.

The partner of an obsessive also has to be guided in how to deal with the obsessive's fear of feelings and need to control. For example, Gordon's wife, Jill, was contributing to the problem. When they made love, Jill would say "I can't enjoy it unless you have an erection"; that made it less likely Gordon would. Nagging or prodding by a partner to obsessives, like "Come on, let yourself go," or "Why are you so stuffy?" will just anger them and make them more insecure and rigidly defensive.

Jill and Gordon both had to accept that there were ways other than intercourse (which was difficult since he kept losing his erection) that could satisfy her. Removing the pressure for him to have to perform made it more likely that he would. It is essential that the couple accept that it is not necessary for the man to have an erection (or for the woman to have an orgasm in an analogous situation) for them to enjoy sex and each other.

As mentioned above, when one partner has pressing needs to be emotional or sexual and cannot accept the obsessive partner's slow pace at loosening up, that person will feel cut off, ignored, unsatisfied, and continually frustrated. How these feelings are expressed can be critical for their sexual relationship. For example, each time one couple, Richard and Karen, tried to make love and Richard ejaculated before intromission, Karen would lose her patience and sometimes strike him. "How can you do this to me?" she would scream. Karen had set up a vicious cycle. She saw his premature ejaculation as a message that she was undesirable rather than his being anxious or angry. The more she would press, the more he would withdraw. Clearly, the partner's response to a person's sexual style is crucial in either maintaining or forestalling the symptom.

The obsessive withholds not only feelings and sexual expression, but also communication in general. This causes increased frustration in the couple. The wife of an obsessive will often complain, for example, that her husband refuses to talk to her, refuses to discuss their sexual problem, and furthermore refuses to come to therapy. The therapist can help the wife understand her partner's resistance in terms of his personality style and the underlying issues of anxiety and need for control. Such an understanding will also help the woman plan strategies to cope with her husband's withdrawal.

There are several "homework" assignments in a behavioral treatment program that are helpful for the obsessive. One such exercise is to instruct the obsessive that every time something important happens, stop and think about two aspects: *what* happened (easy for him — he does this all the time) and (a new task) how he *feels* about it (even a tiny feeling).

Another exercise is to locate parts of the body where he feels *something* and to concentrate on the tiniest sensations, particularly during sex. He is to allow himself to be totally relaxed and see where in his body he feels something. If he gets headaches, an upset stomach, or eye twitches, he is to concentrate on that spot and the feeling, since these physical sensations are likely the defensive expression of fear, anger, or even anxiety.

Since obsessives stifle anger, they stifle ability to love, too. When such patients who have dysfunctions finally unload pent-up anger, they may be able to have erections or orgasms. Therefore, the therapist should help the obsessive patient find ways to express anger at home (e.g., by pounding pillows, yelling into a tape recorder). The safe release of unpleasant feelings will eventually free the obsessive to be expressive.

There are several keys to unlocking responsiveness for the obsessive male. First, he has to realize his erection is *his,* not the woman's. If he is able to penetrate her, it is for *his* own pleasure. In making love, he is to concentrate on his own feelings. Second, he must understand he can't *will* an erection. He needs to understand that, ironically, when he worries less about control, he will get better results. Third, he is instructed to think about what he would like to have happen, or to fantasize the sexual experiences he is fearful of expressing. Bringing these out in the open releases guilt and anxiety.

These approaches are effective in overcoming different types of sexual problems in obsessives. In Gordon's case, for example, after many sessions in therapy, he revealed a fantasy of being a macho lover, aggressively seducing a woman. Though he was frightened of expressing this desire, he was given permission to explore the fantasy in his mind and find out what it made him feel. The exploration revealed important clues to his fears and his resistance in his sexual relationship.

Another aspect of the treatment was exploring Gordon's anger toward his wife and women in general. Within the safe context of couples sessions, he was encouraged to let Jill know how he felt in a direct and constructive way. For example, he was able to express his anger toward her for her "nagging." Saying what he did not like, without fear of destroying her or himself, cleared the way for him to say also what he did like about her, about sex, and about their relationship.

SEX PROBLEMS IN THE HISTRIONIC PERSONALITY

More women than men have a histrionic personality style, probably in part because girls are culturally conditioned to be more dependent than boys. In a dynamic framework, the histrionic is locked in an unhealthy dependency bind, called *symbiosis,* with one or both parents. Usually the parent fears separation from the child and inhibits the child's efforts to become a separate person. In comparison with the obsessive character, the histrionic child makes fewer efforts towards independence, and instead maintains attachment to the primary nurturant figure/s. The child is then ruled by the fear of being abandoned. The primary personality dynamic becomes the wish to merge. In childhood, this manifests itself behaviorally in being "the good little girl," either mommy's confidant or daddy's favorite. To keep the union, the child becomes overdramatic and engages in attention-getting behavior. Growing up, she is unable to define her own goals or values separate from those of the parent/s. This wish to merge is then recapitulated in adult relationships, where she often behaves like a devoted and self- sacrificing wife, but lives in the man's shadow, feeding off his identity, and never secure or sure of herself.

The major defense for the histrionic's fear of abandonment is regression. Overdisplays of emotion, flooding of feelings, and creation of "crises" are further defensive maneuvers to protect against the fear of loss. Ironically, although such women appear to "feel" so much, the feelings are shallow; histrionics find it difficult to express real and appropriate emotions.

A diagnosis of histrionic personality disorder, according to *DSM III*, requires display of such exaggerated emotions, incessant drawing attention to oneself, craving excitement, and overreaction. In addition, the person has to show at least two of these disturbances in interpersonal relationships: seen as shallow though acts appear warm; egocentric,; vain; helpless; and possibly threatening suicide.

All these characteristics affect the histrionic's sexual functioning. This type of woman often functions in order to get a response from her partner, rather than taking responsibility (or credit) for *herself*. She can be very sexual yet uses sexuality in order to satisfy her needs to be cared for.

The demands of histrionics on a partner can be great, and their needs are essentially unfillable. An example is an aspect of the relationship between Jill and Gordon, the couple from the previous section. In one session, Jill complained, "I was home and bored. I called Gordon to ask him what I should do for the afternoon, and he said, 'Go to the movies.' How could he?" she cried.

"What did you want him to say?" I asked.

"I wanted him to tell me something that would make me feel better," she answered.

Gordon, in his typically obsessive-compulsive way, had reacted to the *content* of what his wife was saying, but Jill did not want to be taken literally. She was looking for sympathy and fulfillment of her dependency needs — for feelings, not suggestions for action.

Histrionic women run the danger of becoming what is called in the popular literature a "Love Addict." They are Cinderellas waiting for Prince Charming to come to their rescue. Their need for love and attention is like an addiction to drugs and alcohol; life is only tolerable with a fix (a lover saying "I love you") and intolerable when outside affection is withdrawn. Without her love fix, the woman may go into withdrawal-like symptoms, including depression. In serious cases, when she cries "I'll die if you leave me," she means it.

Research psychiatrists Michael Liebowitz and Donald Klein at the New York State Psychiatric Institute have called this type of woman "hysteroid depressive." Oversensitivity to rejection is the primary symptom. Beset with an inadequate sense of self, she endlessly seeks a partner who will "fill her up." But even though they are drawn to merge with the partner, some histrionic women are also fearful of that merging. Or, due to their low self-esteem, they feel unworthy of it. Thus, they become chronically involved with partners who are unavailable to them. This sets up a vicious pattern of inviting the very rejection they fear the most.

Men may be very attracted to the histrionic woman at first. She can be charming, sexy, and coy, and appeal to a man's desire to be strong and protective. But as her needs become more and more demanding and insatiable he may flee, feeling suffocated or "burnt out."

In some situations the histrionic woman herself may flee; ironically this can happen when she gets attached to a man who gives too much to her. What happens in these cases is that once the symbiotic needs are satisfied and the fantasized vision seems complete, the woman may begin to feel suffocated and agitate for differentiation, thereby threatening the stability of the merger.

Usually the histrionic woman likes to merge sexually as well as emotionally with the partner, just as she merged with her parent/s. She thrills at the word "we," and feels threatened in the face of disagreement or separations. Though she prides herself on her ability to have *feelings,* she is often overly sensitive and reacts overly dramatically. If her partner wants to go out with friends one night, she feels rejected or suspects he is having an affair. Because of the tendency to merge her identity in another, she confuses whose behavior is whose. For example, if she misses her alarm clock ring, she could be outraged *he* didn't wake her up. Then, oversensitive to rejection, she interprets her partner's behavior as a sign she is unloved. She may even punish the partner by withholding sex.

Histrionic women have a tendency to overromanticize. As a result, they may make overbearing demands on a partner to act a role consistent with that fantasy. Or they become easily disappointed if an encounter does not live up to the romatic ideal. All men may then seem terrible, all hope lost, and her own self degraded.

Sexually, histrionics often revel in fantasy. They may love to be coquettish one minute, a tigress the next. They may seem to love sex and be ever willing and ready. But they can also be insatiable, because sex is really a means of being taken care of.

Histrionics, in direct contrast to obsessives, will overlook the facts of a situation, and focus instead on their impressions. Asked to describe a lovemaking experience, the response, rather than what happened, is likely "it was great," or

"I felt awful." The elaborations may be colorful, but they focus on feelings and hunches rather than on content. Thus the therapist will have difficulty getting a clear account of any particular experience or encounter.

Often women who are histrionic have an adequate sexual excitement phase, but do not have orgasm. One reason for this is that having orgasm may unconsciously mean she is not a "good girl." Displeasing her parents evokes the fear of being abandoned by them. The woman may also demean her own sexual experience because of a fantasy expectation that it should be earth shattering and, in comparison, her own reactions do not measure up. She may seem to be enjoying sex play, but may "fake it" out of a fear if she did not, her partner would abandon her. Often she may prefer oral sex because of its unconscious connection to being nurtured ("fed" or "devoured"). But, ironically again, she may inhibit pleasure in doing this. Such inhibitions may stem from parental messages that sex is wrong and therefore she cannot risk their disapproval, or from a feeling that she is unworthy of getting what she wants.

The histrionic woman loves to be passionately seduced, but again, because of her need to be a good girl, she may protest this. Her partner may think she wants him to "take her violently," but when he does she may back off.

The histrionic woman's needs become obvious after a while (i.e., her sexy approaches eventually reveal her need to be taken care of). Once the partner realizes this, he can be less manipulated by her demands or less intimidated by her seemingly endless sexual appetite.

The histrionic male may be more difficult to identify and deal with. It is often harder in males to note the urgent dependency needs beneath the pressing sexuality. The difficulty in diagnosis is complicated by cultural stereotypes that affect the reporting of behavior of both members of a couple. For example, partners of such men almost always mistake the man's disappointment at the sexual encounter not having lived up to his romantic ideals for their own inadequacy. They fail to recognize that the disappointment in reality reflects his insatiable, but unstated, dependency needs.

Partners of histrionics run the risk of acting like a parent in response to the histrionic's implicit demand that they set limits. Yet some histrionics will also rebel against their partner, just as a teenager rebels against parents. One result of this dynamic is that the couple stops having sex. For example, the histrionic woman comes to see her partner as a parent figure. This arouses unconscious incestuous desires. In order to avoid these impulses, the couple withdraws from sexual encounters and relates not as lovers, but as "good friends," siblings, or parent and child.

Because of the histrionic's need for attention and volatile nature, she may be excessively demanding on a partner. This can lead to his feeling unable to fulfill her, and therefore "impotent." When this happens, the histrionic may take on affairs, both to fulfill and dramatize her needs and to highlight the partner's inability to fulfill those needs.

SEX THERAPY APPROACHES FOR THE HISTRIONIC
PERSONALITY

The goal of treatment for the histrionic character is maturation: helping the woman to develop a sense of her own body and self, to develop inner supports, and to build independence and self- esteem. Such restructuring of the basic character structure often requires long-term therapy. However, certain techniques in behavioral sex therapy can facilitate the histrionic's becoming more independent in sexual attitudes and behavior. Essentially the woman is encouraged to do things by and for herself, in nonsexual as well as sexual arenas.

In the course of short-term behavioral sex therapy, an important homework exercise requires the woman to take an hour a day for herself to do something pleasurable. I also encourage such a woman to "take herself out on a date." That means getting dressed up exactly as if a favored lover were coming to take her to a nice restaurant or play. That way she gives herself the appreciation and attention she expects from a partner.

Another exercise is to reorder her thinking. Faced with anger or an argument with her mate, she is asked to make a list of all the logical points of her position. In this way histrionics have to do the opposite of obsessive-compulsives; they have to concentrate first on *what* happened and keep their feelings separate from those facts. That is because feelings come all too readily to the histrionic, and cloud her perceptions of reality.

To become more independent, the histrionic is encouraged to stop automatically asking other people for their opinions about what to do. When she feels such impulses coming on, she is instructed to leave the room or hang up the phone, and give herself ten minutes to think the situation through herself. The goal of this exercise is to give her experience in trusting her own judgment.

The steps of such treatment can be seen in the case of Gordon and Jill. Jill showed classic histrionic characteristics of being overly sensitive to rejection, having low self-esteem and being overly attached to her husband, just as she had been to her parents.

"We'll be lying on the bed," her husband described to me in a session with the two of them together, "and Jill will lean over on me as if I'm a chair, just there for her use. If I object, she gets upset, wails, carries on, pestering me."

This experience shows Jill's lack of boundaries; she is seeing Gordon as merged with herself.

Jill herself admitted, "If I ask Gordon a question and he doesn't answer immediately, I feel so angry I don't know what to do with myself. If he ignores me entirely, I feel wiped out." Further, she explained, "If we're driving through the country and I get gleeful over the beauty of the trees, which I love, I start to squeal with delight. If he ignores me, I cry and can't enjoy myself anymore."

The same experience happened in sex, on the few occasions they attempted relations. If she had a sexual feeling, she would rush to him immediately to satisfy it, or at least so he would show as much excitement over her feelings as she did. If he refused, she would get furious and cut off the feeling for herself. This type of response shows histrionic personality features, and also the "mirroring" that occurs in early infant-mother interactions (Winnicott, 1971); if the mother does not respond to the child, the child loses a sense of existing, because there is no solid sense of individual self.

When treating Jill, my first therapeutic task was to help her work through her "symbiosis," that is, to help her "have" her own self and her body. In doing so, she would learn to leave Gordon alone so he too could feel his separate self. This was accomplished in treatment by helping her to give him more space. I gave her the direct message: On those rare occasions when she felt sexual and rushed to him to appreciate her, should he refuse, she was not to badger him, cry or feel devastated. Rather she was to think to herself, "I can have my own sexual feelings. He doesn't have to respond to them for them to be real. They're mine." Then she was to go into another room by herself and fantasize sexual scenes that gave her pleasure, and pleasure herself physically. The message is that you can be sexual without forcing him to acknowledge it or to be sexual as well.

This message was part of the therapy aimed at the most conscious level of her personality functioning. To reinforce the message she was given homework, often part of behavioral sex therapy called sensate-focus exercises (Masters & Johnson, 1970; Barbach, 1976). These involve first looking at her body alone, without criticism, and then touching herself all over (sensing both being touched and doing the touching). Then she was to explore her pleasure through self-stimulation of all parts of her body, including her genitals. These steps are again remindful of the activities in which the infant engages in the primary stages of ego development.

On a deeper intrapsychic level, I worked with Jill to develop a sense that she had a body. We accomplished this primarily by two exercises. The first exercise was to attain solidity. I noted that Jill often came into the office as if floating into the room, that is, hardly touching the floor. So I asked her to purposefully "float" around the room and bump into furniture so she could get the sense of what it was like not to have a body. Then I asked her to imagine what it feels like to be a lamp, that is, to have a base, but a flimsy one, which could be easily pushed over. In the last step of the exercise, she was to imagine being a tree firmly rooted and unable to be swayed; she was to feel her feet that solidly grounded into the floor.

The second exercise involved breathing. Jill's voice was high- pitched and seemed to originate from her throat. Her speech pattern was pressured, all of which also connoted and betrayed her disembodied existence. Consequently I had her focus on where her voice was coming from. This involved breathing exercises, so her voice would originate from lower down in her chest. After much practice at these exercises, she talked in a lower tone of voice and emanated a more solid presence in the room.

Besides working on her body in these ways, the second major therapeutic process, aimed at deeper layers of her personality, was intended to help her separate from her old parental images (or introjects) and to create new supports. Although Jill insisted her real parents had been "totally there for her" and doted on her every whim, she came to realize this was not a true affirmation of her identity or aliveness. Although her mother used to tell her she was beautiful and intelligent and her "diamond," Jill always felt this was an image of a perfect daughter, not her. In therapy, Jill was to replace her old images of her parents with new ones — even a friend or mythical figure — who would be totally attentive and supportive of her every move and feeling, while not getting drowned in her feelings and thereby losing a sense of self. For example, if she returned from school as a little girl crying that the teacher had yelled at her and embarrassed her in class, her real mother would have panicked, feeling exactly the way the little girl did. The "new" mother was to listen to the little girl's upset, and stay inside her own feelings instead of merging with her daughter. To help Jill internalize a new "good-enough mother" (Greenacre, 1957) she was instructed to imagine this person being with her constantly, appreciating her.

Jill put this to work in the following way. When she came home from teaching she was usually anxious to pour out every detail of her day to Gordon, anticipating he would listen to every word. In the past, when he refused to do this, she would get flooded with fear of abandonment and anger and wail in disappointment. Now she would accept his lack of response, go into another room and do something that made her feel good on her own.

As part of a deeper working-through process, once in her room she might have an imaginary interaction, conversation, or comforting from an imagined figure (parent or friend) who would satisfy her every need for as long as she wanted. Eventually, this imaginary nurturance became introjected and she no longer needed to act out the exercise. She became more able to handle her own needs and to consider both herself and Gordon as separate people.

The process had an effect on the relationship with Gordon as well, both immediately and in the long term. Released from fulfilling some symbolic parent role by her expectations that he would respond instantly to her every need, he became more willing to give to her of his own free will. As he became less angry, his sexual feelings gradually returned.

I emphasize that these techniques were geared to stages of development through which Jill moved. I must also stress the point that these exercises and imaging techniques are not applicable for all patients. Imaging techniques, for example, are inappropriate for patients who have primitive personality organizations and are unable to differentiate reality from fantasy. Furthermore, some therapists and/or patients are not comfortable with this approach. Thus, specific exercises should be tailored to suit both the therapist's and the patient's comfort, experience and style.

One important therapeutic task for Jill was to recognize the difference between demands Gordon could fulfill and demands that were romanticized and unrealistic. She also needed to see how she picked a man who was so controlled because of her own fears of her impulsive nature; he, not she, could then be attacked as the dysfunctional one. Deeper in her conscious, however, she revealed she was pleased at first that he was so "tight," not sexually active, and "impotent" because that way he didn't threaten her. It was better to complain about his "impotence" than to be overwhelmed by a "real man." That was *her* way of maintaining control.

The partner of the histrionic woman may facilitate the sexual dysfunction or help in overcoming it. An important task for these partners is to stop reacting to the histrionic's irrational outbursts, and instead to keep her focused on the *facts* of a situation. The partners need to offer support, but need also to set limits on how far they will go before the woman will have to take care of herself. The message that has to be reinforced is that whatever happens is *her* responsibility.

The histrionic is a voracious child, so the partner must resist overindulging her. "I cannot make love now," he might say, "but that doesn't mean I don't love you. I'm doing something now. Let's do it later." The histrionic may protest but in the long run will welcome the controls on her needs and will respect the partner for being his own person. The partner's best approach is to offer *some* support and *lots* of encouragement for them to do *for themselves*.

SEX PROBLEMS IN THE NARCISSISTIC PERSONALITY

In ancient Greek mythology, Narcissus was a beautiful youth who stared in a pool and fell in love with the image he saw reflected there. Of course, the image was himself. Similarly, real life narcissists are filled with all-consuming self-infatuation. The self-love of narcissists seems convincing to an outsider, but underneath the facade, they harbor a deep sense of worthlessness. They are complex, paradoxical personalities given to moodiness and dramatic reactions.

One of the paradoxes of narcissists is that they were either idolized by their parents or not given enough attention at all. Narcissists who were idolized as children never believed they were really loved for themselves, but rather as an image of what others wanted them to be. They were often used as means for the family to gain esteem or status. This burden leaves them with an overinflated sense of self-importance, when really they feel like a nobody. On the other hand, narcissists who were not given enough attention in childhood may compensate by creating an external sense of grandeur to mask their inner emptiness. Or they will choose a partner who is a reflection of the idealized self, and project onto this person inflated characteristics they want for themselves. Merger with this partner is then experienced as a means to incorporate the qualities they desperately need but feel they lack.

Narcissists grow up from childhood with a lack of a solid internal sense of self. They often define themselves by their role or status in life, by saying what they do, where they live or who they know. This usually stems from the parent/s' using the child as their own stabilizing force or status symbol. So, for example, the statement, "I am the mother of this wonderful child," or "I am an actor" becomes a replacement for the more stable personality feature, "I am."

When feeling secure or adored, the narcissist is the glowing light of any social situation. For example, one such woman was often told by her mother, "When you walk into a room, the whole place lights up." Narcissists expect they will achieve great things and indeed they often do. But they expect they can get what they want without having to put up with hardship or tedium. They often feel the whole world owes them a living and they expect to get their due. Feeling inflated like a hero when they are adored, narcissists are in danger of also feeling deflated when ignored or unnoticed. When unappreciated, unadmired, or criticized, they can become self-deprecating, filled with self-loathing and self-doubt, and critical of everyone around them, especially those who care about them. Such people are terrified and incapable of intimacy and emotional and sexual commitment to a partner.

This dynamic discussion of the narcissist fits nicely with the *DSM III* outline of symptoms of the narcissistic personality disorder: grandiose self-importance; preoccupation with fantasies of power, beauty or success; exhibitionism; indifference to others. In relationships, they show lack of empathy, expectations of entitlement, exploitation, and vacillation in commitment.

Sexually narcissists can display extreme lust. They can move around a lot, and display their body in erotic ways. But the narcissist loves love, not the partner. Partners may complain "all he loves is my body." Or they may feel used for their affection. Often there is some validity to these complaints, as the goal of the narcissist in relationships is to inflate his own ego and to incorporate qualities he feels he lacks and perceives the partner as having.

Extreme narcissists often do not give sexual pleasure or attention to their partner in equal measure to what they take. Particularly, male narcissists revere their own genitals. They may insist on being pleasured orally, but not be willing to do this to the partner. Once they have reached their own climax, they may be insensitive to the partner's continuing need. If they do not get the sexual adoration they need, they will either reject the current partner altogether, or supplement that relationship with other affairs.

The narcissist is preoccupied with his or her own body, its functions, and appearance. She or he is often preoccupied with examining and appreciating all parts of the body, including, for example traditionally more taboo parts such as the anus.

The narcissist's ego can be very tied to sexual potency. Being found sexually desirable is essential for the ego and self- esteem. As such, sexual rejection can deal a severe blow to the narcissist. A partner's refusal to make love, or one incidence of an erection problem can make the narcissist overdramatize "failure" and to feel inadequate, and at times even to move on to another partner.

Because the partner becomes a narcissistic projection of oneself, and because of the desperate drive for perfection, the narcissist is very sensitive to a partner's sexual performance. For example, if the female partner does not have orgasm or want to have intercourse at a particular time, the narcissist feels inadequate as a lover and sees the partner as also inadequate. This is why it is essential in therapy to get across the message that each person is responsible for their own sexual response.

The narcissist does not really love the partner, but rather what the partner can do for him. Moreover, he loves being loved. However, once the partner adores the narcissist, the latter demeans the former. It is as if the narcissist is saying, "I don't want to belong to any club that wants me as a member." Acceptance and adoration, once coveted, is eventually worth little to the narcissist, who essentially doesn't feel worth much to begin with. But there is always another challenge who promises to satisfy the narcissist's ego and offer fulfillment.

Narcissists often attract other narcissists. In such a relationship, each is seeking self-gratification. Usually one acts out the role of the adored, and the other of the adoree. The latter then obtains only vicarious need gratification.

The following is an example of this type of relationship. Nicole was a 30-year-old clothing designer who sought therapy for inability to have orgasm during intercourse. The event that precipitated her seeking help was rejection by Stewart, a publicist, who was also 30. Neither had ever been married though they both had long histories of many lovers. They had been seeing each other for two years, the longest relationship for both. Both were attractive and loved a "fast" life. They especially loved going to parties and being seen together. Nicole often pranced around the room hoping everyone would notice her. Stewart often was the only one who did not notice, since he was too busy flirting with other women.

In the middle of one such gala evening out, Stewart, rejected by one woman he was flirting with, searched out Nicole for reassurance. He found her with someone else, giggling gaily. Backing off in anger, he rushed off to talk to another woman. So both of them stood but a few feet apart, pretending not to notice each other. Later that night, they were unable to be sexual with each other (both having suffered a blow to their egos).

Nicole and Stewart both needed to be the center of attention. They used each other both to be in the spotlight and for reflected glory. Two narcissists can enjoy each other's common adoration for a while, but soon at least one ends up either feeling deprived, or seeing the other's imperfections and becoming disillusioned and disinterested.

The partner attracted to a narcissist may temporarily bask in the glory that surrounds their self-centered mate but may be secretly resentful and/or jealous. This is demonstrated in the following case. Roz was in her late 20s and wanted to be an actress. But her parents always discouraged this goal, so instead she worked behind the camera as a production assistant for a movie company. She developed a strong crush on a leading man, Frederick, whom she admired and envied. They eventually began dating. Roz felt she was getting a hold on him, especially since Frederick often had problems getting sexually excited and she was reassuring and flattering. But Frederick started to see another woman who was an actress, and Roz became distraught, could not go to work, and was beside herself with anger. She felt worthless as a person and criticized herself for not being attractive enough sexually. She became desperate for his attention. She would plot how to encounter him, and if he was not responsive, she would go into a severe depression.

One of the biggest traps of partners of narcissistics is expecting the narcissistic mate to be faithful. Narcissists value their own needs too much and undervalue their partner's needs. They may feel guilty if they have an affair but will rationalize their behavior (e.g., it was important for their own growth). Generally, there is always a new man or woman to be conquered, more admirers to collect, more skeptics to be won over to their charms.

Given this situation, the partner of a narcissist has to be prepared to face a possibly rude rejection. For example, one narcissistic man came home one night and announced totally out of the blue to his live-in girlfriend that she should move out because he had met another. "How can you do this to me?" she cried. His reply was "I have to do what's best for me. I only have one life. You want me to be honest, don't you?"

The partner of a narcissistic mate must tread a thin line between giving real substantial support for the narcissist's frail ego and pandering to their grandiose sense of self. Partners need to examine why they are with a person like that to begin with. Most importantly, they must take care of their own needs and find ways to give themselves fulfillment.

It is worthwhile to consider another pairing: the obsessive man attracted to the narcissistic woman. As in the case of the obsessive man attracted to the histrionic woman, this man may be seeking to complement his own personality with characteristics he lacks. An example of this pairing is the following case of Marlene and David.

Marlene thought she was god's gift to this earth, at least on the outside. But inside she felt fat, ugly, and incompetent to do her job as the only woman executive at her magazine publication. She dressed in expensive clothes but was envious of everyone else who she thought was more fashionable.

Marlene picked a boyfriend, Donald, who she thought was totally competent. He was a top government official who seemed perfectly confident. At first she enjoyed sex with him. Though he was somewhat inhibited, she enjoyed feeling expressive and carefree with him. She flaunted her body around him and felt appreciated. But the closer they got, the more she picked on him for his "failings" both in and out of bed. At first she expected merging with him would make up for all her own "imperfections." But after a while, *his* imperfections only made her feel more imperfect. He did not dress high-fashion enough to impress her friends with how fashionable she was. And he did not speak with a classy enough accent to make up for her feeling inadequate that she had not grown up in an upper-class Waspy home. His hesitations about oral sex were no longer an amusing challenge to her, but unnerving. The more she berated his insufficiencies, the more he developed problems having an erection. With that, Marlene could not tolerate his less-than- perfect performance. She began to make constant excuses not to make love, and finally said she wanted to end the relationship.

In therapy, an understanding of Donald and Marlene's personality styles was helpful. Donald was an obsessive man who saw Marlene as fitting into his controlled life-style. He had picked a narcissistic woman to complement his own rigidity. But this match was ultimately destructive to him, because Marlene's criticisms inhibited and threatened him, rather than supporting and encouraging him. His choice of such a domineering woman undermined his own needs to feel in control. His lack of erection was a way to express not only his anxiety but also his anger.

In therapy, Donald learned that his erection problem was partly the result of pressure he put on himself to perform for Marlene. He learned that she would always be dissatisfied, because she was dissatisfied with herself. It was not that he was not good enough (as he feared), but that she would never be pleased.

Donald eventually realized that Marlene was not so perfect herself. There were other women who would appreciate him if he would only give them a chance. He did not need to continue to pursue unrequited love, so he stopped trying to please someone who would never be pleased — and let her go.

SEX THERAPY APPROACHES FOR THE NARCISSISTIC PERSONALITY

Narcissists are highly resistant to change, because it is highly seductive to be overly concerned with self, especially in today's "me" generation. According to Otto Kernberg, narcissists will generally only become motivated to change in middle or late life, when they face frustration in gratifying their needs (Kernberg, 1975).

In dynamic theory, there are two basically conflicting roads to changing self-centeredness, each with an avid professional following. Kernberg, one of the leading authorities on narcissistic personalities, advocates tough treatment. Narcissists should be given strict limits to their behavior. They should not be allowed to indulge self-centeredness.

A conflicting approach as promulgated by Kohut allows the person suffering from narcissism to indulge the need to idealize (Kohut, 1971). Because the narcissist basically feels unworthy, he needs a parent figure to idealize temporarily and to emulate in the process of building self-esteem. Identifying with the idealized figure makes them feel better about themselves until a stronger sense of self can be developed.

Psychiatrist Richard Robertiello (1978), who has treated many narcissists, advocates a method similar to that of Kohut. He insists that the major task of narcissists is not to deprive themselves of searching for "strokes" (or reaffirmation), but to find the people or situations from which those strokes are forthcoming. This view is consistent with the current trend in the self-psychology movement to defend some narcissistic strivings as constructive and healthy, and with the increasing recognition of the difficulty of attempts to totally restructure personality in some patients.

In my treatment of sexual dysfunction in narcissistic patients, I employ an eclectic approach, with a psychodynamic formulation underlying behavioral and gestalt techniques. In the latter, rather than attacking the narcissistic needs in cases where these are being held in check, these needs are first accepted and utilized.

As an example, let's examine different aspects of the therapy for Roz, the woman mentioned above. Therapy proceeded on several levels, each with a set of therapeutic tasks: preserving her dignity in the "here and now" and rebuilding her self-esteem to break the present self-defeating pattern. In dealing with the "here and now," Roz had to exercise self-discipline and restrain herself from approaching Frederick. Whenever she felt desperate to call him she was instructed to call a friend instead who would give her the attention she craved, rather than her giving that attention to Frederick. Should she see him, she was encouraged to resist having sexual encounters with him, because she only felt empty and used afterwards.

Roz was further helped by gaining insight into the nature of the relationship with Frederick. She followed a common dynamic: The person attracted to the narcissist has to be wary of mistaking passion *for* the partner with passion to *be like* their partner. This was clearly true in Roz's case, where she had been unable herself to achieve the narcissistic gratifications she needed. Thus, Roz came to realize that she was not attached to Frederick himself, but rather to how being around him made her feel. She understood that she did not want to "have" him, but rather to be like him. In the long run, she began to see how she would have to develop her own self to have the security or the need satisfaction she imagined he had.

Analyzing the role that Frederick's sexual symptoms played in Roz's attachment to him was also importnat. Though at times she was upset about his not fully responding to her, she felt less threatened to lose him, knowing that he might have trouble with other women. His sexual problem also comforted her:

He was not so "perfect," and she therefore tried to convince herself she did not need him so desperately. Furthermore, his difficulty in performing was a cover for her own lack of full responsiveness, because his problem was more obvious.

Another important aspect of Roz's treatment, geared not only to her sexual symptoms but to her personality characteristics as well, involved identifying the source of her behavior pattern. Roz remembered how, when she was a little girl, she would try to capture her father's attention, but he was often too absorbed in watching television. He may well have been frightened by his own feelings of appreciating his young girl, but the effect on Roz was that of feeling unloved. Frederick represented a repeat of this earlier relationship. Roz now had to face whether she wanted to spend her life trying to reform resistant lovers (as a recapitulation of earlier desires to win her father's approval) or spend her energy on people who would readily respond to her.

Roz's sexual problem, specifically her difficulty achieving orgasm with a partner, was tied to her general personality organization. Part of her sexual withholding reflected her general fear of demonstrating her responsiveness and accepting the attention she so desperately wanted. It was difficult for her to expose her needs for attention to others, and furthermore to let others see her respond. Thus, in a group setting, she was encouraged to go around to each group member and say "Look at me, I want you to see me and how terrific I am." Roz was embarrassed as she did this, but it was important for her to "own" her need to be seen. Then she was to spend lots of time being with people not who were "important" or "showy" in her terms, but who saw *her* as the "star." This was important for her to develop an appreciation of herself as having what she desired. Once her own narcissistic needs were worked through in the safe context of therapy in these ways, she was able to progress to a higher level of personality organization, seeing herself as a worthwhile person separate from her status or what she did.

At the beginning of treatment, Roz, like many types of narcissists, saw sexual functioning as a performance. She, rather than just her partners, saw herself as a sex object, similarly to how she had once been an ego object for her parents' self- esteem. By learning to value her self through some of the above therapy, she no longer needed to score herself or her partners sexually, nor expect that she was the best lover ever. She became able to appreciate her own responsiveness without comparing it to that of others. And she no longer demanded that sexual experiences with desirable partners be a validation of her value.

SEX PROBLEMS IN OTHER PERSONALITY STYLES

The narcissistic, obsessive and histrionic characters are common styles seen in a sex therapy clinical practice. However, other important styles include the paranoid, avoidant (or schizoid), and depressive. The important therapeutic goals in these cases as well as the others covered above in more detail include an accurate diagnosis of the total personality style and its dominant features, an understanding of the operant defenses, and observation of the sexual complaints both as an expression of the personality style and as an attempt to either express important needs or to protect against the expression of unacceptable feelings. Consequent application of behavioral or insight-oriented techniques should then be consistent with the patient's level of emotional development.

Paranoid personalities appear in varying levels of severity, from mild suspiciousness to frankly delusional and psychotic states. In this discussion I will deal with the former. Aside from severity, paranoids may present with two styles: constricted and apprehensive, or aggressive and arrogant.

The paranoid person is characterized by ideas of grandeur and fears of persecution. There is a tendency to see the world and actions of others with predetermined expectations and to continually seek evidence, however small or farfetched, to validate this view. This effort may lead to dismissing contradictory evidence. In contrast to the histrionic person who, under threat, fuzzes details, the paranoid person homes in on details. As a result he is bound to find what he is looking for.

For example, a paranoid person may pick out certain nuances of another person's behavior as rejecting, when in reality he misses the overall picture. For example, one patient, Paul, made overt advances to women and always got turned down. He became hypersensitive to whether they looked at him or avoided his glance, but ignored whether they were simply involved with someone else and could not start up another sexual relationship with him. Being a paranoid personality and starting from his view that he was not a good enough lover, he concluded that passing over him was a sign that indeed he was inadequate.

The well-known defense paranoid people employ is projection. By this mechanism, drives, motives, or feelings that are unacceptable in the self are attributed to another person. In a loose interpretation of this mode, we can include people who ascribe to their lover all the characteristics they themselves either detest or desire, and which may or may not be at all warranted or applicable. Thus, the paranoid person may complain "She thinks I'm inadequate in bed," or "They talk behind my back, saying I'm homosexual."

Paranoid persons are often in such a state of tension underneath that their behavior can unfold like a coil unspringing. As such, they may pounce on partners with comments or attacks on their behavior. They may then hold rigidly to their own position.

An example of this is the case of Don, a 40-year-old man with erectile problems. On each lovemaking occasion, he expected his wife's disapproval. He searched her face and picked on her words, and of course found the evidence he was looking for and jumped to conclusions. When she turned on her side away from him or mentioned she had a hard day, he interpreted that to mean that she did not want sex with him. When once she frowned, he concluded she was wincing at his limp penis. His overall conclusion was that she didn't want sex with him anymore and that she felt he was inadequate.

The treatment of sexual problems within the context of a paranoid personality style can proceed along different directions. With more well-integrated patients who have adequate insight, reality testing is helpful. For example, the man is encouraged to ask his wife for her thoughts rather than putting words into her mouth. This is helpful for people who really hope their deepest fears and expectations of rejection are not true.

In Don's therapy, each interaction with his wife was reviewed, with her giving detailed descriptions of her feelings and actions. This reality testing and feedback was partly helpful. However, adjunctive and deeper therapy work was also necessary.

Another approach involves acknowledgment and confrontation of the feeling evoked by the paranoid person's behavior. The clue to this feeling often lies in the partner's emotional response, because this is a function of the projection defense of the patient. Unsuspecting partners, especially those without strong ego boundaries, may experience the projected feelings as their own. Thus, when I work with a couple in which one partner has paranoid tendencies, I help the partner see that these feelings (anger, fear, guilt) may be their partner's feelings projected onto them. Instead of becoming the object and victim of that feeling, they must separate out their own emotions. And instead of arguing, they are to ask their partner, "What are you feeling now about this?" Getting to the feeling interrupts the immediate cognitive or combative pattern and focuses the interaction on the proper source.

Paranoid people develop fears of sex that can lead to avoidance. They may fear their partner's sexual secretions will infect or harm them. Single people may have extreme fears that partners will give them venereal disease or AIDS. Oral and anal sex pose particular threats, as signs of being humiliated or put down.

Well-adjusted people are generally not self-conscious and are freely expressive with their bodies. However, paranoid characters are rigid and hypervigilant to the point of being uncomfortable when being touched unexpectedly. An accidental poke from a partner may elicit a violent response. Little play or freeform sexuality is allowed. They also may be overly concerned, boastful or ashamed of some body part, such as genitals or breasts. These may be interpreted as either inadequate or superlative examples of manliness or womanliness.

Paranoia is typically evident in cases of complaints of jealousy where the extent of the complaints seem unrealistic or unwarranted. For example, Mr. R was sure his wife was having an affair. True enough, she had once done this and he had found out about it. But that was seven years ago, and she insisted there had not been a recurrence. When she didn't come home exactly on time, when the phone would ring and the person would hang up on hearing his voice, or if a girlfriend would ask her to go out alone, he would insist that this was a plot to meet a lover. An important element in this scenario is that Mr. R himself had fantasies of an affair. He was projecting onto his wife his own desires, and then torturing her as he would himself. In this way, he was also able to stop himself from acting out his impulses.

Schizoid (or avoidant) and depressive styles may also be associated with sexual problems. The most identifiable characteristic of the schizoid person is emotional detachment. These people can manage sexual encounters without affection. They protest that sex and love are separate, not because they feel guilty about having sex without being in love, but because they are incapable of the latter.

Because they do not trust others, schizoid people either avoid sexual encounters altogether, maintain cool distance from any one partner, or have a stream of one-night stands. More likely the schizoid person avoids any real relationships, which would require emotional exchanges and reciprocity, and resorts instead to masturbation or to massage parlors with prostitution.

Schizoid people are unable to establish boundaries between themselves and others. Some men, for example, may avoid intercourse or ejaculation within a partner, because to do so would symbolize giving their penis or their self to the partner. Therapy must include a rebuilding of an intact sense of self.

Depressive personality styles usually involve self-depreciation and withdrawal from pleasure. This can manifest itself in a variety of sexual symptoms, especially low sex drive. In cases where there is no medical or organic basis for low sex drive, the person often gets involved in a vicious cycle. Depression causes a withdrawal from sex, and decreased sexual activity further exacerbates low self-esteem. The depression itself must be identified and treated directly, and the sexual functioning will improve. Effective methods for such treatment of depression as well as low sexual drive has been dealt with extensively elsewhere (Kaplan, 1979) and thus will not be elaborated here.

CONCLUSION

An understanding of underlying personality organization is helpful in both the diagnosis and treatment of sexual problems presented to the general practitioner and/or sex therapist. By seeing the context within which the specific symptoms appear, the therapist can better determine the source of the problem and therefore which of the plethora of therapeutic techniques may be most useful. Furthermore, treatment can then be aimed not only at the chief presenting problem or sexual symptom, but also at the reorganization of the patient's personality to achieve more general adaptive functioning.

REFERENCES

American Psychiatric Association. (1980). *Diagnostic and statistical manual of mental disorders* (3rd ed.). Washington, DC: Author.

Barbach, L. (1976). *For yourself: The fulfillment of female sexuality.* New York: Doubleday.

Derogatis, L.R. (1981). Psychopathology in individuals with sexual dysfunction. *American Journal of Psychiatry, 138,* 757-763.

Greenacre, P. (1957). The childhood of the artist. In A. Freud, H. Hartmann, E. Kris, & R. Eisler (Eds.), *The psychoanalytic study of the child, Vol. 12.* New York: International Universities Press.

Kaplan, H.S. (1974). *The new sex therapy.* New York: Brunner/Mazel.

Kernberg, O. (1975). *Borderline conditions and pathological narcissism.* New York: Jason Aronson.

Kohut, H. (1971). *The analysis of the self.* New York: International Universities Press.

Maurice, W., & Guze, S. (1970). Sexual dysfunction and associated psychiatric disorders. *Comparative Psychiatry, 11,* 539-543.

Masters, W., & Johnson. V. (1970). *Human sexual inadequacy.* Boston: Little, Brown.

O'Connor, J.F., & Stern, L.D. (1972). Developmental factors in functional sexual disorders. *New York State Journal of Medicine, 72,* 1838-1926.

Offit, A. (1977). *The sexual self.* New York: Ballantine Books.

Pinderhughes, C.A., Grace, E.B., & Reyna, L.J. (1972). Psychiatric disorders and sexual functioning. *American Journal of Psychiatry, 128,* 1276-1283.

Robertiello, R. (1978). *Your own true love.* New York: Ballantine.

Winnicott, D.W. (1977). Mirror role of mother and family in child development. *In Playing and Reality.* London: Tavistock.

Chapter 3

Sexual Functioning and Dyadic Relationships: Implications for Therapeutic Practice

Judith Frankel D'Augelli and Anthony R. D'Augelli

Sex is a body-contact sport. It is safe to watch, but more fun to play.

(Szasz, 1980, p. 3)

There is little disagreement that sex is dyadic in nature and that sexual decision making is social in nature. Unfortunately, the fun in playing this dyadic game sometimes gets lost. At those times, couples may seek assistance in understanding how to rekindle or enhance their sexual relationship. How couples think and feel about their overall relationship and how they approach decision making to change it are clearly relevant for the practice of sex therapy. Couples engaged in sex therapy are involved in the process of changing not only specific sexual behaviors, but also the unique norms and guidelines that govern their relationship. In addition, each person's view of a partner's characteristics, dispositions, and attitudes affects the nature of this process of change because it affects, when expressed, how the partner thinks about the relationship. It can therefore be said that couples in sex therapy are immersed in reasoning about their sexual relationships on several levels. They are concerned with their sexual behaviors, their relationship roles, and their personal needs, values, and goals.

The interplay of individual and couple concerns is the subject of considerable discussion in sex therapy. Consider the identification of a sexual dysfunction. Although there exist objective ways of determining sexual performance, clearly the initial diagnosis is highly subjective, based on a conclusion of dissatisfaction with current patterns. As Szasz (1980) has noted, criteria for sexual satisfaction are to a considerable degree culturally conditioned judgments; they depend on the person and the partner comparing subjectively their own situation against these vague cultural standards. Both people bring to this judgment their individual perceptions and standards as well as shared points of view. No

49

doubt many couples live for extended periods of time with an objective dysfunction (absence of orgasm for the woman, for example) but do not define their situation as problematic. Other couples may disagree with each other about whether a certain behavior is indeed a dysfunction and may therefore avoid treatment. And other couples, despite a variety of other disagreements and stresses, at least come to sufficient consensus about a pattern to seek outside help.

As Masters and Johnson (1970) have emphasized, the *relationship* is the focus of sex therapy. Szasz (1980) takes offense at this, decrying its depersonalizing impact and seeming avoidance of each individual's life-style perspective. However, there are important therapeutic considerations that derive from a focus on the relationship. Working with interdependent partners, sex therapists must be attuned to the implicit and explicit dynamic content and dyadic processes of the relationship. From the dynamic interplay of reasoning about and engaging in sexual encounters with one another, the couple develops an idiosyncratic set of norms, attitudes, and behaviors that structure and define their sexual relationship. Because of this, sex therapists should develop knowledge of how to understand and constructively influence the couple *in interaction*.

The purpose of this chapter is to examine some elements of dyadic functioning that relate to aspects of couples' sexual functioning. Three major elements in a multilevel model of interdependence in close relationships will be focused on: (a) social exchange concepts, (b) relationship reasoning, and (c) interpersonal communication. Implications of the theoretical and research observations for actual practice will be drawn.

ELEMENTS OF DYADIC FUNCTIONING

Just as guidelines for behavior change recognize the interaction among the three elements of cognition, emotion, and behavior, those for dyadic sexual behavior change must recognize the interaction and interdependence among *two* sets of cognitive, affective, and behavioral components. Interdependence in a relationship may be defined, following Scanzoni (1979, p. 61), as the reliance of the partners on each other for valued rewards, benefits, and gratifications. Such interdependence evolves over the course of a relationship's development. In Lerner's (1979) dynamic interactional view, relationship development involves a progression from a rather global, perhaps unidimensional, basis of interchange to a highly differentiated, multidimensional basis. The interactionist view (Bolton, 1961; Cottrell, 1942; Foote, 1957; McCall, 1974; Waller & Hill, 1951) asserts that partners mutually influence one another's way of thinking, feeling, and acting. Braiker and Kelley (1979) describe relationship formation as the "mutual influence of two relatively malleable entities in the evolution of preferences and propensities unique to the relationship" (p. 159). They suggest that norms, interpersonal attitudes, and personal goals develop at relationship initiation, at relationship choice points, and at points of conflict as the relationship evolves. And, with the emergence of new relational norms, attitudes, and personal goals, interdependence increases.

From this, one might conjecture that the sexual conflict that brings couples to sex therapy may allow for the growth of the relationship. In Braiker's dissertation study (Braiker-Stambul, 1975) and in subsequent work (Braiker & Kelley, 1979), the amount of interdependence and love in a relationship was found to be independent of the quality of negative feeling and overt conflict. In fact, Braiker and Kelley (1979) assert that conflict of interest in behavioral, normative, and personal goal realms of a relationship and the intra- and interpersonal tensions engendered in dealing with this conflict have central roles in the development of greater interdependence in a relationship. In other words, some challenge, whether individual or dyadic, can solidify a relationship. As the couple struggles with challenge, they make changes on both individual and relational levels. In fact, Braiker and Kelley (1979) theorize that a relationship that successfully copes with conflict episodes will be different than one that is conflict-free. New bases of interdependence evolve, especially on the higher levels of relational norms and personal goals. The degree of closeness will be greater because the conflict or challenge makes possible a *joint* reconceptualization of the relationship. Questions seldom asked in the absence of challenge to the relationship are addressed. Such questions include:

> What are we like as a pair?
> Where do we stand now and where are we headed?
> What kind of relationship should we have or do we want to have?
> To what do we together and separately attach greatest importance?
> How do we really feel about our relationship? (Braiker & Kelley,
> 1979, p. 162)

In confronting such issues, partners influence one another and "incorporate new norms for the relationship, new goals for each other, and a new definition of the relationship" (Braiker & Kelley, 1979, p.162).

As interdependence increases, the partners are likely to progress through the initial exploration stage of relationship development to the expansion stage, in which an increasing number of commonalities are discovered, and finally to the commitment stage of the relationship, in which joint interest predominates (Scanzoni, 1979). Most couples in sex therapy are in the commitment stage of their relationship, usually though not always having formalized their commitment through marriage. However, partners' emotional commitment may have become weakened. Therapists can expect differing degrees of emotional commitment to be manifested in formally committed relationships. Scanzoni (1979) observes the elusive nature of commitment, suggesting that it be understood as the degree to which the partners "feel solidarity with or cohesion in a relationship" (p. 87). Three of the dyadic processes that contribute to the development of solidarity and commitment in a relationship are social exchange, relationship reasoning, and interpersonal communication.

SOCIAL EXCHANGE

George Homans, considered to be the founder of exchange theory, presents its central tenet as follows:

> When I speak of exchange I mean a situation in which the actions of one person provide the rewards or punishments for the actions of another person and vice versa. (Homans, 1961, p. xviii)

Thus social behavior is thought to be shaped by reinforcement patterns, and engaging in certain behaviors is a result of prior history of costs and benefits associated with such behavior. There is considerable debate about the direct applicability of exchange theory to intimate relationships. Fromm (1956) adamantly asserts that "true love" goes beyond exchange. True love is not interested in mechanistic exchange, but rather is altruistic and interested in spontaneous giving. Rubin (1973) argues that the more firmly established the bond in a relationship, the less salient is the notion of exchange for the dyad. On the other hand, Lederer and Jackson (1968) suggest that couples utilize a *quid pro quo* system of responses to one another to assert themselves as equals in the relationship. Foa and his colleagues (Donnenworth & Foa, 1974; Foa, 1971; Foa & Foa, 1974; Turner, Foa, & Foa, 1971) identify classes of resources which are the content for exchange in all relationships, including intimate ones. Hatfield, Utne, and Traupmann (1979) note that exchanges can be made through equity, *quid pro quo,* or power processes. They conclude that intimates do indeed spend time and energy "negotiating the values and exchangeability of various behaviors — the terms, so to speak, of their relationship" (p. 110).

In a partnership, satisfaction with and commitment to the partner are at least partially determined by reciprocity. Gouldner (1960) defines reciprocity as follows: "What one party receives from the other requires some return, so that giving and receiving are mutually contingent" (p. 169). In exchange theory, inputs and outcomes are relevant concepts for understanding reciprocity. According to Hatfield et al., (1979), inputs are each partner's perceptions of the other's contributions to the exchange, both positive and negative. Outcomes are defined as each partner's perceptions of the rewards and punishments the partners have received in the relationship. They make the point that "equity is in the eye of the beholder" (p. 102). For instance, a couple may perceive their relationship to be an equitable one in which reciprocity of inputs and outcomes is satisfactory, with the exception of some aspect of sexual exchange, whereas their sex therapist may view their relationship as inequitable in some other respect. Ultimately, the partners are the only ones who can identify the particular value of each input for them, having developed their own unique definition of reciprocity and its elements. In this way, intimate partners deviate from the direct *quid pro quo* reciprocity that is observable in relationships among strangers (Altman, 1973).

Intimates in interdependent relationships seem to have a wider variety of resources for exchange than do less interdependent partners (Hatfield et al., 1979). It has been suggested, from theory and research (Donnenworth & Foa, 1974; Foa, 1971; Turner et al., 1971), that exchange resources may be classified under six headings: (1) love, (2) status, (3) information, (4) money, (5) goods, and (6) services. The value of a resource from any one of these categories will vary from partner to partner and may vary over the lifespan of the relationship: "One man's (or woman's) nectar is another's poison" (Scanzoni, 1979, p. 67). Partners in a close, interdependent relationship exchange not only specific commodities such as money, goods, and services, but also resources of indeterminate value, such as love, status, and intimate information (Hatfield et al., 1979). This variety of exchange commodities and the likelihood that the rewards that intimate partners give one another are particularly potent and personal (Huesmann & Levinger, 1976) makes the calculation of the equity of exchange a complex task for the partners, much less the therapist.

For the therapist to assist the couple in elucidating aspects of equity in their relationship, a variety of dimensions need to be explored. For example, Blau (1964) observes that rewards (and punishments) are not only differentiated by degrees of tangibility, but also by whether their nature is intrinsic or extrinsic. Extrinsic gratifications, such as having an orgasm, are fairly easy to identify. Intrinsic gratifications, such as *feeling free* to be uninhibited in sexual sounds with that partner, are immeasurably important in interdependent relationships but are difficult to articulate. Perhaps Levinger's (1979) observation that reward resources may also be differentiated by the degree of particularism and concreteness may be helpful in thinking about how to identify and articulate intrinsic and extrinsic rewards. The least particularistic resource is money, which is an extrinsic reward, whereas love is among the most particularistic and it is intrinsic. Those resources of greater concreteness are goods and services. They tend to be extrinsic gratifications. Status and information, especially intimate disclosures, are the least concrete, and they tend to be more intrinsic than extrinsic. The most particularistic and least concrete resources have greatest symbolic content. These tend to be of highest value to partners in a dyad because of their unique intrinsic meaning.

Equity is also germane to the maintenance of a close relationship. Gouldner (1960) suggests that as valued gratifications accrue and continue to be received, each partner develops a strong sense of moral obligation to give benefits to the other. This he terms "gratitude rectitude." He argues that reciprocity is motivated by feelings of both gratification and gratitude rectitude. Further, Scanzoni (1979) asserts that relationships are maintained when reciprocity is ongoing; the partners exchange valued resources and these exchanges "continue to generate ongoing feelings of moral obligation to reciprocate benefits received" (p. 64). This suggests, however, that although a relationship may be perceived as equitable, this equity is always in a state of imbalance. The key to a committed and continuing relationship is for the partners to trust that the other will eventually reciprocate with idiosyncratically valued resources and redeem any imbalance.

The development of partners' mutual trust is closely related to a second relationship process, the emergence of maximum joint profit (Scanzoni, 1979). Maximum joint profit, or MJP, is the perception that each partner seeks the other's best interests (Walster, Walster, & Berscheid, 1978). The more each partner feels that her or his best interests are being met fairly, that distributive justice is occurring, the more the partner is convinced that MJP is operating in the relationship. In addition, the higher the level of perceived MJP, the greater the sense of obligation that is felt to pursue it. A high level of MJP is likely to promote progressive interdependence in close relationships (Scanzoni, 1979) and a sense of solidarity and commitment.

How do partners know *how* to gratify each other or *how* to pursue the other's interests? Blau (1964) argues that unique couple norms emerge when the partners engage in the process of exchanging resources and continue to develop as more and varied resources are exchanged. Ekeh (1974) argues that rules governing exchange exist prior to and apart from the relationship. He asserts that these normative regulations then enter a particular relationship. It seems likely, since neither individuals nor relationships develop in a social vacuum, that both externally derived and relationally developed norms provide some regulatory function in an interdependent relationship. Heath (1976) suggests that partners agree on a "rule which has the function of introducing predictability and regularity into the relationship" (p.68) rather than rely on a process of repeated bargaining. Predictability, of course, is vital for the development of trust. Therefore, expectations begin to develop as a function both of personal needs and relational norms. As the relationship develops a history of sanctions, both rewards and punishments, existing norms are modified or new norms are defined and agreed upon. The relationship grows as a function of the dynamic interplay between expectations and sanctions (Scanzoni, 1979).

RELATIONSHIP REASONING

Coordination of exchange in a relationship involves issues of reciprocity, MJP, and trust. As Carson (1979) observes, partners in a relationship must develop reciprocal patterns of behavior that permit each partner a modicum of outcome profit. Both social and relationship norms regulate this coordination of exchange. These norms lessen power problems and tensions in interdependency (Carson, 1969; Thibaut & Kelley, 1959) by providing the couples with readily available rules for behavior. Relationship norms evolve over time as each partner reacts to the other as a person and as a partner. The norms, in dynamic coordination with personal goals, attitudes, and values concerning dyadic behavior and relationships, provide ways to give meaning to interpersonal events. We have termed the process whereby couples, as individuals and as partners in a dyad, attribute meaning to interpersonal situations *relationship reasoning* (D'Augelli & D'Augelli, 1979).

Relationship reasoning is an individual's unique way of making decisions about the current and future nature and quality of interpersonal life. The process has interrelated intra-individual and inter-individual (interpersonal) consequences. On an individual level, relationship reasoning can explain the actual and idealized direction of someone's interpersonal relationships. On an interpersonal level of analysis, an understanding of a person's relationship-reasoning processes can provide an understanding of the varied relationships within the person's social network — why and how relationships are similar and are different. The relationship-reasoning process underlies the individual's ascription of meaning to her or his own behavior and to the behavior of others with whom she or he is involved. It should be noted that this involvement may be acutal or fantasized. Therefore, from a given individual's perspective, the same behavior observed by self and an uninvolved onlooker will have different meanings depending upon the relationship/s involved. For example, a sexual comment overheard by a partner- in-relationship and an onlooker will be interpreted differently and has distinctly different implications for subsequent action toward the commenter. The partner-in-relationship reasons about the observed behavior, (e.g., the sexual comment) in a specific relational context wherein its meaningfulness has been acquired. The onlooker, unless fantasizing or anticipating a relationship with the commenter, may not even ponder it or may interpret it simply as evidence of an existing relationship between the other two. Future plans for the relationship in response to the observed, interpreted behavior, especially complex plans (e.g., becoming more sexually involved) versus reflective behaviors (e.g., making a casual sexual comment in return) are decided upon using the relationship reasoning process.

The foundation of this social-cognitive developmental view ultimately rests on the individual's cognitive capacities and abilities. Thoughts about behaviors and behaviors-in-relationship are of primary concern. Situational and circumstantial causes of specific interpersonal acts are of secondary interest. Indeed, these behaviors are important *only* to the degree of consistency or inconsistency with the individual's reasoning and the dyad's interactive reasoning. Cognitive processes act as interpreters of behaviors and, as far as the individual is concerned, there are "important" and "trivial" interpersonal, relational behaviors. What is viewed as important or trivial by a partner-in-relationship may be interpreted differently by outsiders to the relationship. Even the partners themselves may not interpret the same interpersonal acts as important from their individual reasoning perspectives, although the intepretations of the partners ought to become more similar as their relationship progresses.

Developmental differences in reasoning processes are critical. Thought processes and interpersonal abilities dependent upon these cognitive abilities develop in a qualitatively advancing manner. Sequential differentiation of cognitive abilities occurs over the developmental lifespan and is contingent upon the processes of accommodation and assimilation. Relationship- reasoning processes are seen as a subset of cognitive-reasoning processes influenced by and influencing the social environment. Thus, there are qualitative changes in one's interpersonal life over the lifespan. Therefore, while the cognitions involved concern self vis-a-vis others, this conceptualization becomes increasingly complex with development. As with cognitive growth conceptualized in Piagetian terms, advancement in relationship reasoning is a complex result of qualitative social interaction experiences as well as a result of psychophysical maturity.

There are likely limits on individual relationship reasoning. Due to differences in basic cognitive processes and to social environments of varying quality, individuals will vary in their abilities to conceptualize their interpersonal lives. Although the association of relationship reasoning to behavior is imperfect, variations in cognitive development can partly explain the inability of certain individuals to engage in intimate, reciprocal relationships. For example, a fairly accurate conception of the partner may be prerequisite for an intimate relationship, because it allows the prediction of the partner's feelings, thoughts, and attitudes. Accurate prediction, in turn, facilitates mutually satisfying interactions. The accurate prediction of a partner's response is fundamentally a role-taking process which is a result of social-cognitive development. Accuracy of role-taking can be enhanced by social interaction: the more one interacts, the more one learns and therefore the more precise one's predictions of the other. The implication of this argument, stressing variation in cognitive and social history, is that individuals differ in level of relationship reasoning achieved. As with the development of formal operations thinking, it cannot be assumed that societal definitions of adulthood imply achievement of the most differentiated level of relationship reasoning.

Complementing interindividual differences in relationship reasoning is intraindividual variability in such reasoning. Although individuals are theoretically capable of reasoning about relationships at a particular high level, it does not follow that *all* of their relationships are subject to processing at that particular level. Like moral reasoning (Kohlberg, 1958, 1969, 1971), an individual's relationship reasoning may be viewed in modal, maximal, or range terms. The modal level is that which most often characterizes the individual's reasoning. The maximal level is the highest level manifested by the individual. The range of reasoning is the span of levels the individual uses among all her or his reasoning about all relationships. An analysis of the individual's relationships will reveal a variety of relationship types, with some conducted using fairly primitive, egoistic notions of immediate costs and benefits, whereas others demonstrate mediation by symbolic reinforcements and formal or informal contractual agreements.

A close relationship is defined both by the reasoning processes of the two partners and the interaction of the partners' unique conceptualizations. The reasoning capabilities of partners may be similar or dissimilar in terms of their current levels of reasoning within that relationship. Indeed, the degree of congruence in relationship reasoning may be a useful dimension to examine in seeking explanation for change within a relationship. Dissimilarity introduces a dynamic quality to relationship development and may produce a tension that leads to enhancement or termination of a relationship. Each partner's conception of the present relationship — its rule, roles, responsibilities, limits and boundaries, in other words, its meaning structure — serves as a framework by which they implicitly and explicitly plan behaviors and evaluate their outcomes. Presumably partners differ in their conceptions of and methods of arriving at the relationship's meaning structure. While homogeneity of reasoning patterns — the processes by which a relationship's meaning structure is articulated — need not exist for relationship development, recognition and articulation of differences could be a preliminary step toward relationship intimacy and growth.

Relationship reasoning is of particular importance at choice points in relationship change and development. In other words, it becomes a mediator of behavior when involvement/disengagement, intimacy increase/decrease, or boundary issues arise. Decision dilemmas evoke the reasoning process of the individual and of the couple. At choice points, decisions can be seen as explicitly following or implicitly adopting one type of relationship reasoning. For example, in explaining to a sex therapist why a couple did not heed the therapist's proscription against intercourse, a partner might say, "We made love even though you told us not to have inercourse, but we thought we should fulfill each others' needs right then." Such a statement involves the use of relationship reasoning to explain the couple's dyadic decision. Similarly, relationship reasoning is being used when one partner acknowledges that, "I didn't want to press my spouse into having sex until I knew we *both* wanted it." Judgments and decisions regarding the relationship are founded in this relationship-reasoning process.

Three levels of relationship reasoning are proposed: Egoistic Reasoning, Dyadic Reasoning, and Interactive Reasoning. Six stages of reasoning development are conceptualized, two within each level. The implicit continuum emphasizes transition from reasoning and relationships based on an individualistic, cost- benefit orientation to a dyadic, role-bound orientation, to a dynamic, consensually interactive orientation. The levels and stages are described below.

Level 1: Egoistic Reasoning

Relationship reasoning within this level is based essentially on a simple cost-reward analysis, in which the individual's cost- benefit ratio is the primary factor. The individual does not view costs and rewards as emergent from the relationship per se, but from the partner: "What I miss in this relationship is your giving me the opportunity to do some things for myself by taking care of the house more than you do." What the individual will give is dependent on the likely returns from the partner. For example, a woman says to her husband, "I pull back from doing what you want when you do so little of what I need from you. When you're more involved with taking care of our son and making the bed and cleaning up the kitchen, then I feel more like giving to you." As is illustrated in the examples, interpersonal interactions are seen as opportunities to give or receive in concrete and reciprocal ways. *Quid pro quo* social exchange is clearly evidenced.

During this stage, there is usually little concern for mutuality and long-term interpersonal reward. The conceptualization of the relationship's normative structures is unilaterally decided. Each partner acts on her or his own view of the relationship's norms with little direct reference to the partner's views: "I thought we always turned off the lights before making love. It's how I'm most comfortable." Relationship change is viewed as a matter of personal rewards and costs, and the locus for change is perceived to lie with the individual, not the dyad. One couple seen in therapy demonstrated this level of reasoning. The husband wanted to maintain the relationship, though the wife had little interest in doing so. She observed, "For years I have kept house for you, worked to put you through school, and postponed doing anything for myself, but I'm fed up! I am going to see people I want to see, go out when I want to go out, spend money on me for a change — not for your schooling! I'm only going to make dinner for me and the baby — you take care of yourself. Do your own laundry. Get your own beer. I'm out for me now." The husband responded, "You've been doing that for months. I can't stand what you're doing to me. You're driving me mad! I take care of the baby, I make her breakfast and change her diaper and get her ready for the sitter. And I give her her bath. I try to be there for you, but you feed the baby and run. You've always gone out with your friends and left me home alone until 3:00 or 4:00 in the morning. I never did that to you. And sex: What's that? You don't do *anything* for me." Obviously, this couple was in severe crisis, with no apparent mutuality in their relationship. Their concerns focused on concrete exchanges, rather than on relational rewards; their comments were very self- oriented, with no mention of their partners. In egoistic reasoning, the optimal relationship is one that provides the most benefits for the individual.

Stage 1: Interpersonal Punishment Avoidance

In this stage, decisions about the relationship are made by minimizing personal loss and avoiding physically, psychologically, or socially punitive consequences of choices or actions. For example, "I'm going to stay with you because I cannot afford to make it on my own" or "If we divorce, I will be humiliated, so I won't consider that" are views reflecting these issues. Consideration of relationship choices at decision points are based upon the probabilities of avoiding punishment or the assessment of being negatively evaluated. For instance: "I've had sex with you only because you threaten to leave when you get frustrated"; or "I enjoy our relationship for the companionship it provides, but marriage? You're too different in background from me—my family disapproves. I can't chance being cut off."

When such reasoning forms the basis for relationship decisions, little value is placed on the other's feedback, needs, or concerns unless they relate to assessing the probabilities of punishment. Seeking out the partner's opinion is infrequent, unless some concern exists about the possibility of the partner's doing emotional or physical harm. For example, "I decided not to have sex with her any more, but I needed to know what she would do to me. When I sounded her out, she got very angry and said she would tell everyone, including my colleagues, about the affair. That unnerved me—I think it would be trouble, given my profession. So I continued." The optimal relationship is barely considered; indeed, the conception of the relationship is superficial and poorly articulated.

Stage 2: Interpersonal Instrumentalism

Decisions are made on the basis of increasing personal gain. Rewards (physical, psychological, and social) in the context of the relationship are of utmost importance. One woman said of her relationship, "I married him because I would gain status and prestige in the community. People would respect me because of his occupation and position. That kind of respect is important to me." A man stated, "I wanted to make love every day. I need it. She was only willing to if I spent a lot of time talking with her before and if I took care of all of my chores. It was worth it to me!"

Interpersonal interactions are viewed as opportunities to receive from the partner: "If I do this for you, what will you do for me?" Giving of self or from self is dependent upon what and how much will be received, thus demonstrating a concrete reciprocity. A client acknowledged that her interest in sex was minimal, but said, "I feel more like meeting your sexual needs when I feel like you are meeting some of my needs. When you don't, I could care less." Decisions are based on what the partner will do or will be influenced to do for the other; the individual will seldom give any more than the maximum amount likely to be attained: "I'm not going to work on changing my sexual activities if you're not willing to change your stance toward household matters. If you're willing to work on that, I'll put some effort into changing sexually." The optimal relationship is one that provides the most essentially immediate benefits for the individual, with little conception of long-term reward.

Level 2: Dyadic Reasoning

At this level, relationship decisions are based on the perceived expectations of the partner or society, as consistent with role stereotypes or standards. Reciprocity and relationship change are based on role responsibilities. One man in therapy with his wife was adamant that "She ought to do that — no question. That's what a wife does. The husband does his things for the family, for the wife, and expects her to take care of a wife's things for him." Choices at decision points support the couple's socially defined conception of their relationship, sometimes to the detriment of personal rewards. The other's view of the relationship is of importance to the individual's decision making. One husband realized, "I did not spend time on my own interests because I wanted to spend time with her. I thought that husbands and wives were supposed to do that. I believe she wanted me there all the time, but now I hear that she felt smothered. It's confusing."

The qualities of a relationship which emerge from dyadic reasoning are more a function of the expectation of a certain kind of mutual relationship consistent with social definitions rather than a function of idiosyncratic dyadic decisions. That is, the dyad makes idiosyncractic decisions regarding the relationship only within the bounds of perceived social expectations, because of perceived obligations to uphold those expectations. For example, "He should be concerned about making sure I have an orgasm because we are husband and wife and should have mutual concerns for each other. *I* want to make sure *he* has one. He should do the same for me because I'm his wife and I'm important to him." Locus of control for change within the relationship is perceived to lie largely with the partner whose role responsibilities are perceived or are socially defined as including dominance and control. In a conjoint interview (D'Augelli, 1972), one unmarried couple stated:

> Male: We decided to pet — light petting I guess — because that's the usual pattern I follow and I enjoy sex. She doesn't, so I try not to do what she doesn't like. Though she didn't like light petting at first, she didn't mind it after we started. She's not afraid of everything as she used to be.

> Female: I would like him to leave me alone more (sexually), but we do stop when I want to. I don't usually engage in sex except necking. Why we decided to pet I can't figure out! I don't mind now.

Due to traditional sex-role expectancies, the male partner was clearly responsible for shifts in their sexual intimacy, although he was concerned about his partner's feelings. There is some sense of tacit agreement. Traditional sex role expectancies are apparent in locus of control and power in this relationship. At this level, the optimal relationship is one that is maintained by promoting fulfillment of most of the other's expectations and enacting one's role/s within the relationship.

Stage 3: Interpersonal Concordance

At this stage, decisions are made on the basis of the perceived expectations of the partner and significant others, such as parents. Perceptions based largely upon role stereotyping of the partner's view of the relationship are of central importance to decision making: "I know he wants to make love more often," said one woman. "Most men do. So, I try to psych up for it."

Unpopular or nonpreferred choices at decision points are justified as well-intentioned and "for the best" in terms of the relationship. "He may not like coming here now, but it's what is best for our relationship and he knows that. We really need help!" Reciprocity as well as relationship change are based on role responsibilities and intentions to fulfill perceived needs or desires. A recognition by a married woman included the following: "I want to meet his sexual needs better than I do because he's such a good husband and is all a wife could want. I know he would like me to be freer than I am with him in bed, and I want to learn how to be so I can be a better wife to him." The optimal relationship is viewed as one that provides the greatest fulfillment of stereotypical role demands as couched in the partner's perceived expectancies.

Stage 4: Social-Convention Orientation

Here, decisions are considered on the basis of the broad social definition of the relationship, with societal givens and normative expectations providing the standard. The partner's expectations are important insofar as they reflect or are consistent with socially established rules and conventions. One man asked, "How many times a week do most couples have sex? Why can't we be like them? We should be – that's what a husband has the right to expect, doesn't he?" His wife replied, "Well, I don't know what other people do, but I suppose husbands have that right. After all, most people believe it. I just have trouble doing what you'd like; that's why we're here."

Unpopular or nonpreferred choices are justified on the basis of perceived standards of external authorities and institutionalized role norms: "Society's views on sex in marriage are more liberal than they used to be. I would place my own views within society's. Even though she doesn't like oral sex, it's socially acceptable nowadays. A lot of couples are doing it. I wouldn't force her to do anything that's not right, but I wish she'd get less uptight about that." Reciprocity and relationship change are based on institutionalized role demands and conventions. One man stated, "I want to meet her needs sexually as best I can. Women these days are supposed to like having a man go down on them. So I thought she'd like it. I know I like her to do that for me." One woman said, "I'd kind of like to experiment in other relationships just to see what it's like. But I know he wouldn't go for it, because it's against the vows of marriage. So I imagine a lot, but I don't say anything." In general, the impetus is toward maintaining the status quo and the given order of the larger society even if this differs from the couple's personal preferences: "Even though both of us would like to get involved with other people, have a kind of open marriage, that's generally not done. So we decided not to rock the boat."

Level 3: Interactive Reasoning

Relationship decisions at this level are based on the couple's consensually developing conception of how the relationship should function. The couple's conception of their relationship is dynamic and fluid. Change is based on agreed-upon responsibilities and norms that are subject to evolving needs and values: "We both agree that we have to approach our relationship openly. We want to work out our own rules so we both feel satisfied." Choices at decision points are made through sharing and discussion, with the *explicit* expectation that both partners contribute to the decision-making process. For instance:

> We approached having intercourse mutually. We are very open with each other, as I believe you have to be, and we communicate well sexually. Earlier, I was preoccupied with the question of virginity, and where the rule to maintain it derived from. I concluded that it was a function of society and particularly the male double standard. No basis for it really, if the two people agree and they are in love.

The locus of control lies with the dyad rather than with one partner. Change results from a process of sharing in which each partner accurately takes the other's point of view and examines the consequences of potential change for self, partner, and dyad. For example, an exchange among partners in one couple went like this:

> Wife: When I want to practice, I feel constrained by your presence. I know you like spending time together, and I do too. But I didn't feel very free to do things for myself.

> Husband: What I hear is that you want more time for yourself. It's not that you are tired of being with me, but that you want to also do other things. I thought you liked me there when you practiced. I didn't realize I was blocking you.

> Wife: You weren't blocking me by *saying* anything. I *felt* like I couldn't go off on my own because it was important to you to be there and to have company. And I like you! But I have felt frustrated lately because *I* don't feel good leaving you to go practice. I'd like to feel freer to do that *as well as* to spend time together.

> Husband: So what we need is to work out a way of handling practice time so we both come to expect it and not plan other things together or feel bound to be together. It sounds important to you. It's important to me too, but I know it'll be harder because I do count on our time together. It means a great deal to me. What do you suggest?

At this level, reciprocity is a function of both individual decisions and relationship norms. The optimal relationship is one that allows for the creation of dyad-specific norms.

Stage 5: Socially Based Contracting

Decisions are reached on the basis of the couple's perspective of socially agreed-upon norms and roles and their fit with personal preferences. This is illustrated in the earlier example regarding mutually agreed-upon premarital intercourse. Another example was provided by a scholarly man who observed, "My wife and I come from vastly different backgrounds. I come from a rural family where roles for men and women were clearly split, not only for chores but also in such things as talking together about politics or personal topics. She's from an urban family where there were less stringent role norms. In fact, her mother worked when her father couldn't. There's a real tug for us — I'm used to having the woman take care of family needs, while the man is the breadwinner. She wants me to be more personally intimate, but I find I'm more comfortable with my men friends and less so with her although I love her. I want her to have her career, but I also want to be taken care of. We've talked a lot about this with each other, and she emphasizes the changes in today's thinking about roles. I am thinking a great deal about it and am changing some of my expectations of myself and her. She seems willing to do the same."

Mutuality and compromise are valued at this stage of relationship reasoning. The optimal relationship is one from which both partners derive mutually satisfying norms founded on social givens.

Stage 6: Interpersonally Based Contracting

At this stage, decisions are arrived at on the basis of the couple's emerging conception of their idiosyncratic relationship roles and norms. Their own concept of interaction is most important to their relationship decision. A reciprocal process of decision making is central. An example is given in Latham and White's (1978) discussion of heterosexual marriages involving a gay partner, where one husband stated: "I think you would have to go into this with a willingness to work out the rules, the expectations" (p. 207). In this instance, no clear or implicit norms exist. Examples of interaction norms worked out by such couples include prohibitions on outside sexual partners being brought into the shared home, introductions of the other partner to gay friends but not to lovers, and directness about involvements with others without specification of sexual details. The couple must be as sharing of their emotional and sexual needs as possible and be focused on working out mutually agreeable guidelines for meeting those needs without hurting or neglecting each other. At this stage of reasoning, socially based and role-derived concepts are relevant only as consistent with the couple's mutually agreed-upon roles.

Some individual autonomy in decision making is provided because it is considered essential to personal development. Take this example: "I am fully supportive of her career and advancement, and we have agreed on ways to handle our time demands to help that come about, but I will not press her about publications as I used to because she sees it as intruding. She had to ascertain the importance to her and make her own choices there. I'd like to see her do that, but I won't interfere anymore." Reciprocity and relationship change are functions of individual decision and relationship norms that have been interpersonally explored and mutually agreed upon. For one couple, agreeing to support one another's friendships involved a process of norm redefinition. They agreed to change their formerly exclusively close relationship to an open one, so long as neither became sexually involved with someone else. Both agreed that for them, as individuals and as a couple, outside sexual involvement would be problematic. Another couple became more at ease sexually when they reconceptualized lines of power in their relationship:

> I was uncomfortable initiating any sex play, although I know that socially it's acceptable for the woman to do that. I worried that it might unconsciously upset him, and that he might take it as a criticism of his masculinity. But as we talked, I see that those things are irrelevant for *our* relationship, and what is important is what it means to us. I have had some emotional blocks initiating and being more assertive, but he has helped me to understand how that fits into our relationship.

The optimal relationship is one that allows for the creation of dyad-specific norms that may or may not fit with social norms.

Relationships in which one or both partners operate at the interactive level of relationship reasoning often resemble what Brickman (1974) has termed "partially structured relationships." In these relationships, "rules constrain certain behaviors, but leave others to the free choice of the parties" (p. 7). In Scanzoni's (1979) view, such relationships are established bargaining relationships since they *regularly* deal with content regarding how to maximize each partner's share of the common resources. Because they are likely to use inducements or reinforcements to influence one another, the couple emphasizes the positive and continuously acts to maximize joint profit. The guidelines and norms by which this is accomlished emerge from each partner and their conjoint process of relationship reasoning.

The relationship-reasoning view has implications for the *process* of relationship development. At any one point in time, two partners may be similar or different in their reasoning orientations. Prior to commitment to an extended relationship, partners may assess differences in relationship matters by verbalizing ideals and observing relationship decision making. This screening process may not be directed by a need to secure a partner with identical views about relationships as much as by an interest in avoiding someone with important incompatibilities. Until relationship decisions are imminent, relationship orientations may not be explored in depth. If and when such discussions occur, each partner may decide that he or she should continue with the relationship, or work to modify it in some way, whether to increase commitment or initiate disengagement. Of course, dissimilarity of relationship orientation between partners does not automatically provoke dissolution, even if it is clearly perceived by both. Just the opposite is possible; differences between partners can spur relationship growth under certain conditions. For example, if a woman operates at the Socially-based Contracting Stage of Interactive Reasoning but her male partner operates at the Social Convention Orientation of Dyadic Reasoning, differences in the meaning of interpersonal behaviors and divergent plans for the relationship may occur. In a nonsexist relationship, the woman's reasoning about the relationship may itself serve to advance her partner's reasoning. In a sexist relationship, the man's reluctance to listen to, much less adapt to, the woman's views might cause conflict and ultimately impede his own interpersonal growth.

On a different level, couples similar in relationship reasoning but operating at Egoistic or Dyadic levels might individually or both develop beyond their current stage or even advance a level with the continuance of the relationship. The ongoing stream of interaction can call for greater role-taking ability over time. However, it is most reasonable to assume stability of the couple's homogeneity in relationship reasoning unless other influences are operative, such as advances in reasoning facilitated by one or both partners' experiences with others who reason in different ways.

Further, it should be stated that relationship satisfaction can occur at any level of relationship reasoning, especially for dyads with homogeneous reasoning. In addition, tolerance of imbalances can occur if the relationship provides additional rewards and if few alternatives exist. Indeed, before the relaxation of divorce laws, partners were strongly committed to a certain type of relationship and "adapted" because few alternatives existed. The current increase in divorce rates may signal the release of heterogeneous couples from previously "unnegotiable" contracts. In sum, couples similar with respect to relationship reasoning might verbally report greater dyadic satisfaction. Nonhomogeneous couples might report more conflict but paradoxically may have greater potential for growth.

INTERPERSONAL COMMUNICATION PROCESSES

How couples discuss the attitudes, goals, and norms of their relationship is a third process of obvious significance in understanding relationships and working with couples. It is widely recognized that promoting effective communication is a vital factor in successful sex therapy (Kaplan, 1974; Lobitz & LoPiccolo, 1972; McCarthy, 1973; Prochaska & Marzilli, 1973; Sadock, Sadock, & Kaplan, 1975; Snyder, LoPiccolo & LoPiccolo, 1975). This section will focus on aspects of the communication process that have direct relevance for therapeutic interventions with couples who wish to modify some aspects of their relationships.

Communication is the process by which couples develop meaning in their relationship. Each message conveys other messages as well, depending on the context of the message, verbal content, nonverbal cues such as vocal and linguistic patterns, body language and meaning ascribed from their history of interaction (D'Augelli & D'Augelli, 1979). Haley's (1963) observations about how relationship development occurs provide an apt link among social exchange, relationship reasoning, and communication processes:

> When any two people meet for the first time and begin to establish a relationship, a wide range of behavior is potentially possible between them. They might exchange compliments or insults or sexual advances or statements that one is superior to the other, and so on. As the two people define their relationship with each other, they work out together what type of communicative behavior is to take place in this relationship. From all the possible messages they select certain kinds and reach agreement that these shall be included. This line they draw which separates what is and what is not to take place in this relationship can be called a mutual definition of the relationship. Every message they interchange by its very existence either reinforces this line or suggests a shift in it to include a new kind of message. (p. 6)

Woody and Woody(1973) note that for partners to make the most of their relationship assets and to minimize their liabilities — one crucial characteristic of a workable marriage according to Lederer and Jackson (1968) — they "must learn to communicate and to continually and consciously negotiate the *quid pro quo*s of the relationship" (p. 23). Further, couples need to learn how to express clearly, verbally and nonverbally, their meaning; how to accurately decode the meaning of messages; and how to give sufficient emphasis to positive meaning so that negative messages are not always the stronger ones. Stuart (1980) asserts:

> Because any inconsistency between the nonverbal message and the spoken word will be resolved in favor of the former and at the expense of the latter, the clarity of communication and the maintenance of a high level of interpersonal regard demands training the couple in two sets of skills: maintaining consistency within the levels of their communication and finding ways to express feelings of interpersonal warmth nonverbally as well as verbally. (p. 213)

Warren and Gilner (1978) have suggested that effective interpersonal communication be viewed as involving three constructs: (a) tenderness expression, (b) rights assertion, and (c) conflict resolution. The expression of tenderness is the ability to convey positive feelings verbally, which makes the person more interpersonally rewarding. The assertion of rights involves the ability to express one's needs without being destructive. Conflict resolution is seen as the ability to resolve interpersonal problems by means of using deescalating actions and listening responses. To be skillful in these three major aspects of interpersonal communication, both the speaker and the listener must be aware of messages sent and capable of both sending and hearing messages accurately.

To decipher dyadic communications it is important to recognize the multiple levels of the communication process. Nierenberg and Calero (1973) suggest that at least three levels of meaning exist: (1) what the speaker is saying, (2) what the speaker believes she or he is saying, and (3) what the listener believes the speaker is saying. We could probably add a fourth level: (4) what the listener believes the speaker believes she or he is saying. Effective communication therefore involves making certain that the spoken and unspoken communication accurately reflects the speaker's intent and that the message sent is the one that is registered and understood by the listener (Stuart, 1980). To foster this understanding, Stuart proposes a five-step communication-change program: listening, measured self- expression, selective request-making, provision of positive and corrective feedback and clarification of intended meanings. From his viewpoint, these are cumulative skills, each one building upon those previously learned. In general, Stuart's model represents thought and practice in relationship communication interventions (e.g., Guerney, 1977; Jacobson & Margolin, 1979; Woody & Woody, 1973). In fact, there is much similarity between opinion of what makes for positive communication and the Rogerian model of client-centered therapy (Rogers, 1951). What receives most emphasis are empathic understanding, concreteness, genuineness, respect, confrontation, and immediacy of communication in descriptions of the process and or skills (cf. Woody & Woody, 1973).

We will draw upon Jacobson and Margolin's (1979) work in order to describe aspects of dyadic communication that can be enhanced by intervention. They conclude that communication includes empathic responding, listening, validating, expressing feelings personally, expressing interpersonally reinforcing positive feelings, and assertion. These skills are explicitly described and modeled by the therapist/s and are practiced by the couple within the therapy session. The therapist/s construct non- emotionally charged practice situations initially, and then when the couple is sufficiently skilled, structure the discussion of sexually related feelings and issues in accord with the communications model. We will also provide a summary of their guidelines for interpersonal problem solving because of their direct relevance for sexual problem solving.

1 *Empathic responding and listening skills.* A variety of communication skills are included under this heading, but the core concept is empathy. Empathy is often defined as the "direct apprehension of the other's experiences, especially the emotional component of the other's experience" (Jacobson & Margolin, 1979, p. 201). This is putting oneself in the partner's shoes and feeling what one senses the partner is feeling. How does one partner demonstrate empathy to the other? Often, several skills are cited as crucial: deep listening (D'Augelli & Weener, 1976); accurate translations of nonverbal cues (D'Augelli & Weener, 1975; Danish, D'Augelli, & Hauer, 1980; D'Augelli, D'Augelli, & Danish, 1980); feeling identification (D'Augelli & Weener, 1975; D'Augelli, D'Augelli, & Danish, 1980); and reflective listening or empathic responding (e.g., D'Augelli & Weener, 1976: D'Augelli, D'Augelli, & Danish, 1980; Gordon, 1970; Guerney, 1977).

Deep listening involves putting aside one's own opinions and feelings for the moment, and focusing intently on what the partner is saying. When the partner completes a thought, the good listener expresses what she or he understood the partner to say, using his or her own words: "You find that just as you reach orgasm, I slow down my tempo—and you lose it." The listener then looks for or specifically asks for feedback regarding the accuracy of her or his understanding, and for clarification of what was missed. The *empathic response* involves the expression of the observed and/or inferred *feeling state* underlying the partner's message and offers the possibility of allowing the partners to check out the accuracy of the perceived and sent message. The empathic response is difficult to learn and incorporate, because it involves complexity of *affect* as well as verbal content. However, it is an interpersonally potent response, indicating a deep interest in and understanding of the partner. For example, "It's been hellish for you over these years because you felt too embarrassed to tell me what you really wanted from me when we make love." Jacobson and Margolin (1979) make the point that listening and empathy skills are more fundamental than problem-solving skills, for they are most likely two of the most powerful social reinforcers a partner provides. Without dyadic skill in listening and empathy, intimacy is unlikely to develop. In addition, listening skills are fundamental to problem solving, since the partners each need to know and understand what the other is talking about before they can work constructively to solve their problems.

2. *Validating responses.* A validating response conveys empathy and understanding, affirming the legitimacy of the feelings expressed by the partner. "Those feelings sound like they come from deep inside you. I hear how important they are. I'm glad you let me know." The responder may be in mild or strong disagreement with specific suggestions regarding dealing with the feelings, but the disagreement does not replace feeling validation.

3. *Feeling talk.* Directed practice at expressing feelings is useful for making feeling talk a more frequent part of the dyad's communication. Again, there are several skills necessary to be able to talk about feelings. Jacobson and Margolin (1979) suggest a four-stage process: (a) tracking feelings and associating them with specific situations, (b) cuing into talking with the partner in feeling terms, (c) being able to recall feelings, and (d) being reinforced (via validating and empathic responding) for such talk. Each stage involves subskills that may require particular attention and practice. An example of feeling talk, or giving a personal message, is, "When we are just cuddling in bed and I feel no pressure to have intercourse, I feel very happy and safe."

4. *Negative feeling expression.* Hostility (Braiker & Kelley, 1979; Gurman & Knudsen, 1978; Levinger, 1979) and other negative emotions inevitably occur in intimate relationships. The question remains how to manage nega-

tive feelings constructively so as to maintain the relationship and promote growth. Jacobson and Margolin (1979) suggest that there is little evidence for the belief that expressing anger diminishes aggressiveness or that unexpressed anger will fester and be released in destructive ways. In other words, expressing anger solely for relief of pent- up feelings is not especially useful, but it is vital to have partners learn to share their discomforts with each other so that change may occur. It is the loss of potentially shared experience that is important to counter, because shared experience is crucial in fostering continued relationship development. In this approach, similar to other models for training effective relationship communication (e.g., D'Augelli & Weener, 1976; Gordon, 1970; Guerney, 1977), certain destructive ways of expressing anger are discouraged (e.g., putdowns, threats, demands, references to the recent or long past as antecedent to their anger). Partners are trained in using "feeling- cause" statements, which include a statement of the feeling and its specific behavioral cause. An example of such a message is, "When you frown and look grumpy when I tell you I'd like to make love, I feel immediately rejected."

5. *Expressing positive feeling.* Personal messages can also be the vehicle for expressing positive feeling (D'Augelli & Weener, 1976): "It makes me feel loved when you give me a hug for no special reason." Expressing appreciation, giving praise and compliments, and conveying affection and caring messages are all important expressions of positive feelings. The assumption that the partner is aware of the positive feelings and/or the self-consciousness which sometimes inhibits expressing loving feelings are two factors in diminished positive reinforcement in a relationship. Discussing these factors and rehearsing various ways to increase verbal reinforcements within the relationship are both important aspects of communication-skills training.

It is Jacobson and Margolin's (1979) belief that these five skill groups not only increase effective tenderness expression, but also increase effective rights assertion. It is useful to frame assertion in terms of saying clearly what one's needs and preferences are in the relationship. In fact, Jacobson and Margolin (1979) caution therapists to avoid assertiveness training *per se* in conjoint relationship therapy. They argue that assertiveness, as typically defined in assertiveness training programs, is rarely an important relationship issue in itself. They propose a set of problem-solving guidelines to help couples improve at conflict resolution. These guidelines are based on the assumption that more basic communication skills have been learned and incorporated. Just as with the five fundamental skill groups, the therapist/s may train the couple by describing, modeling, and structuring the practice of these skills within the therapy session. Thereafter, the therapist/s maintain a mental checklist and intervene to guide the partners to more facilitative and skillful responses.

Problem-solving guidelines include:

1. *In stating a problem, always begin with something positive:* "I enjoy your touching my breasts when we begin to make love. But I am unhappy that you don't spend a lot more time at it."

2. *Be specific:* "You seldom tell me how *you* like to be touched, and I'd like to know."

3. *Express your feelings:* "It's very frustrating to me when you want to come inside me but I want you to continue touching me first."

4. *Admit to your role in the problem:* "I realize that even though I say I would like you to seduce me sometimes, I make it hard for you by not responding to many of your advances. It would be great if we could figure out how to solve this together!"

5. *Be brief when defining problems:* "I am afraid to touch your penis because I always worry that you will get upset."

6. *Discuss only one problem at a time;* avoid sidetracking: "Let's focus on how *you* feel when I'm giving you pleasure; we can talk about how I feel next, okay?"

7. *Paraphrase — summarize each remark before giving your own reaction:* "So you mean that you like it when I touch your chest lightly and kiss your nipples, but you don't like it when I suck them."

8. *Do Not Make Inferences — talk Only About What You Observe:* "I get confused when you tell me to give you space and then tell me you'd like me to be more playful with you" versus "You are trying to confuse me by telling me two different things."

9. *Be neutral rather than "negative," to maintain the collaborative stance:* "When you don't shower before we make love, I feel more inhibited in what we do together" versus "You are smelly when you don't shower before we make love and it turns me off."

10. *Focus on solutions — brainstorm without evaluating the solutions, then discuss the proposals in a careful way.*

11. *Behavior change should include mutuality and compromise;* one rule of thumb is to *begin* the solution phase *with an offer to change some aspect of your own behavior* when beginning a discussion of a problem involving some aspect of your partner's behavior which upsets you. "I would be glad to try that new position you suggested. What I would like is to spend a lot of time beforehand in pleasuring." *Another guideline is to start with a request for change that is possible for the partner, though less than you might ideally want:* "I would like to make love every day. You don't like to. How about if we agree on three times a week, at least one of which you initiate?"

12. *Reaching agreement involves:* (1) Very specific final change agreements, spelled out in clear behavioral terms ("When I want to make love, I will say so clearly. I'd like an affectionate response, like hugging me, whether you want to make love or not. You could tell me, 'I'd love to!'" or "I like the

idea, but I'm too preoccupied right now"); *(2) Cues reminding each partner of the changes agreed upon:* "I'm going to put up a sign on the bathroom mirror to remind me to bathe first!"; and *(3) Record final agreements in writing* (Jacobson & Margolin, 1979, pp. 219-251).

It is clear from these problem-solving guidelines and the prior discussion of communication skills that the emphasis is on the positive and/or the concrete and changeable. Partners are encouraged *and taught* to hear each other and themselves, to express themselves clearly, and to emphasize mutuality. It is the promotion of the "collaborative attitude" (Jacobson & Margolin, 1979) in conjunction with practicing the use of the guidelines that provide the power of this intervention strategy for helping couples to resolve relationship dilemmas.

This collaborative attitude can be understood in terms of maximum joint profit and trust. Encouraging the partners to think in terms of maximum joint profit, how each can be attuned to the best interest of the partner while simultaneously working things out to meet personal needs, is the strategy for fostering trust. Increasing trust will emerge as both partners experience each other's concern and helpfulness. When couples are seen to have differences in relationship reasoning processes, these differences may obstruct the development of the collaborative attitude. As the therapist observes differences, the partners are encouraged to observe and clarify those differences. In doing so, some of the apparent obstacles to collaborative problem solving will become understandable and somewhat less frustrating. Also, those obstacles, such as differing emphases in relationship values, may become open to change through exploration, examination, and behavioral experimentation. Or partners may be able to better meet their partner's needs because each better understands the other's relationship reasoning processes. This is not to suggest that the therapist label the reasoning levels, but rather that the therapist observe to the partners what their reasoning approach or basis seems to be and how that appears to influence their relationship behavior. For example, if a woman has been blocked in sexual expressiveness in part because of her notions of the differences between what a good wife versus mistress does, her husband may be able to show more understanding in both verbal and sexual responses while the couple is working through this in the therapy. Alternatively, if a man has been rigidly locked into an intercourse-only pattern of lovemaking and has difficulty experimenting with nongenital pleasuring, it may be due in part to his relationship reasoning stage with an emphasis on macho image presentation as the good husband or a notion that the way a good husband best satisfies his wife is through intercourse. Therapists attuned to such issues may make observations to the couple and assist them in clarifying and working through such differences.

SEX THERAPY AND DYADIC BEHAVIOR: ADDITIONAL IMPLICATIONS FOR PRACTICE

The structure of sex therapy includes several distinct dimensions well suited to the integration of relationship processes into the general therapeutic procedures. First, the focus on the couple rather than on individual partners provides the framework for working with dyadic processes as they impinge on sexual functioning. This emphasizes the importance of how the couple relates, makes decisions, solves problems, and responds to crises rather than the importance of symptoms *per se*. In this context, individual dispositional variables, such as individual relationship reasoning, and dyadic dispositional variables, such as fighting style and exchange patterns, become important. Second, the use of dual sex teams, when possible, has the potential to provide powerful relationship modeling, implicitly through observation of therapists' interaction and explicitly through deliberate modeling of effective communication and problem-solving skills. Third, certain general and specific aspects of sex therapy offer or actually involve support and training in dyadic processes. Included in the general mechanisms are permission giving and the development of a safe and free atmosphere for exploration. The specific mechanisms include expressed therapeutic support; teaching communication skills; clarification of relationship-reasoning issues, expectations and values; exploration of the couple's attitudes toward sexuality; and therapeutic confrontation. As specific therapeutic strategies are employed, specific and general knowledge of dyadic processes comes into play.

Kaplan (1974) observes that although all sex therapists emphasize improved sexual functioning and relief of the sexual symptomatology, they differ in their degree of focus on broader objectives such as improvement of the couple's communication and general relationship. However, no matter what the point of view, it is probably true that far more than simple behavior therapy occurs in sex therapy (Renshaw, 1975). It is the authors' position that the more explicit and systematic a focus on *both* therapeutic objectives, the more effective will be the outcome for the couple. Both the therapist/s and partners in a couple need to learn how to observe and decipher what is going on in that relationship at the moment:

> To explain and predict the behavior of individuals in a relationship, one must first be able to define the relationship....What is happening in the intimate relationships at the moment of observation.... (Hatfield et al., 1979, p. 111)

To do so, therapists must teach their clients how to draw on listening, expressing, and understanding skills as described earlier. Raising relationship questions, exploring the couple's patterns of exchange, examining the couple's sexual and other norms and goals and observing how those norms are derived and instituted are crucial to successful intervention in sexual relationship functioning.

Promoting effective communication is vital in the reduction of tensions in the relationship and in the subsequent relaxation within the "pleasure bond" (Masters & Johnson, 1975) of the couple's sexual interaction. In discussing sex therapy, Masters and Johnson (1970) develop the notion that effecting satisfying sexual communication is itself an enhancement of couples' overall communication and good feelings about the relationship. To enhance sexual communication most effectively, the couple's intimate communication *skills* must be enhanced. That is, the effects are reciprocal. But general communication must be addressed first in order to provide the means for enhancing sexual bonding.

According to Tullman and colleagues (Tullman, Gilner, Kolodny, Dornbush, & Tullman, 1981), Masters and Johnson emphasize three general concepts in their emerging approach to communication enhancement: (a) self-representation, (b) vulnerability, and (c) problem solving. These three concepts are integral to the notions regarding dyadic processes discussed in this chapter.

Self-representation involves abilities to identify one's own feelings and to express these feelings clearly. Teaching the communication skills discussed earlier, particularly feeling talk, provides the means for enhanced self-representation. However, vitally important to being able to identify feelings and to express them lucidly is developing the understanding of one's own values, expectations, and goals in the relationship and in sexual expression. To this end, the therapist's attention to relationship reasoning and social exchange processes is important in guiding the partners to increased awareness and understanding. Further, in Masters and Johnson's view (1976; Tullman et al., 1981) self-representation includes accepting responsibility for oneself rather than depending on the partner for sexual satisfaction. This focus on sexual self-responsibility is easily misunderstood. The essence of this tenet lies in its emphasis on self-awareness (What is going on in my body now? What sensation am I experiencing? What would I like to feel?) and self- acceptance (It's okay for me to enjoy this feeling; It's all right for me to want that kind of touching). With self-awareness and self-acceptance comes the responsibility to convey to the partner preferences, wishes, and needs, so as to increase the degree of personal satisfaction in sexual interactions. Mutuality is not precluded but rather made possible through clear communication. When the partner is aware of specific preferences and desires, she or he can then act responsively. However, only the individual has the power and knowledge to seek and experience satisfaction.

The essence of *vulnerability* is the willingness to be self- revealing, verbally and physically. Sharing one's feelings, fears, and inadequacies as well as one's pleasures is essential to the ongoing vitality of the relationship. When partners feel close, they are more likely to be willing to be specific about desired changes in their sexual involvement with one another. Being sexually vulnerable means being fully open, verbally and physically, about one's sexual needs and wishes despite one's fears or embarrassment. Vulnerability is possible when the dyad believes that mutual trust and commitment exists, for this belief provides the foundation for mutual emotional support.

Problem solving involves isolating disagreements from other relationship issues and focusing on those disagreements in the *present*. The "rule of neutrality" is essential; references to past feelings or behaviors for predicting present outcomes are taboo. This guideline serves to decrease defensiveness. Teaching couples this rule and working with them to become adept at the twelve problem-solving guidelines summarized earlier will provide the means for sexual problem solving in the therapy. Kaplan (1974) observes:

> It is essential to the couple's future sexual adjustment that they be encouraged to talk to each other in an open, authentic, and non-defensive way. They must continue to listen to and talk to each other, and not feel comfortable until each understands what the other is feeling. Once this pattern of communication has been established, then each can learn to know exactly where the other is in his/her sexual response cycle – what each is feeling – which is essential for a successful sexual relationship. (p. 225-226)

The relationship focus underscores the multidimensionality of relationships and serves as a reminder that the modification of sexual behavior must be approached in terms broader than sexual actions and communication about sexual actions alone.

Understanding the meaning of as well as the feelings about sexual behaviors in the context of the relationship involves not only clarifying the exchange value of various sexual activities but also clarifying their value for the relationship. What is being proposed is that the cognitive process of relationship reasoning holds the interpretive key for understanding what is important and what is trivial to a couple, and how the partners develop expectations and relationship norms about those things. What is viewed as important or trivial by a partner may be interpreted differently by outsiders to the relationship; therefore it is important that the therapist explicitly address valuing issues. Giving meaning to interpersonal behaviors, including sexual ones, stems from the personal and relationship salience of those behaviors based upon one's relationship reasoning. Salience may be associated with the partners' ideals for relationships or with their goals for that relationship. Understanding and influencing behavioral choices requires the understanding of relationship reasoning processes for that couple and the particular social exchange contracts they have made.

Interpretations of each other's behavior by a couple are likely to become more similar as their relationship progresses, if trust and commitment deepen. Sex therapists have the opportunity to facilitate this progression of shared understandings to foster greater commitment, trust, regard, reciprocity and mutuality. The process of facilitation involves therapeutic interventions that clarify relationship reasoning and social exchange issues and teach couples the various communication and relationship skills addressed in this chapter. In Masters and Johnson's view (1975), accommodation and negotiation – that is, mutual problem solving – are the keys to conveying, understanding, and satisfying one's own and one's partner's personal meaning in sexuality. Sex therapy therefore benefits from inclusion of training in these skills. Accommodation and negotiation were essential for Lois and Don White (in Masters & Johnson, 1975) for whom touching became a relationship issue. Lois enjoyed expressing affection and was comfortable doing so in public. However, for Don, touching was a cue for sex and he became embarrassed and frustrated:

> I'd say, "Hey—we're starting to make out in public, and we can't do anything about it. So cut it out until we get home." We'd talk like that, and she'd say, "Well, I'm not making out, I just wanted to touch you." And there was the conflict because I would feel when you touch me it means we *have* to make out. Recently we've had a lot of discussions about that and I think we both understand each other a lot better. (p. 217)

In this example, the implicit social contract is in the process of modification to better fit both partners' sexual values and their views of the relationship. We suggest that relationship reasoning underlies the process of accommodation and negotiation. Lois and Don are reviewing the meaning of public affection in their relationship because of their commitment to each other. Because they are interested in maintaining and enhancing their relationship, their discussions are oriented toward understanding how each one interprets the same behaviors and what meaning they hold for their relationship. Thus they are in the process of renegotiating an unclear norm in the relationship, assisted by their therapists.

The effectiveness of sensate focus or mutual-pleasuring exercises may be understood in part as renegotiation of unclear or unworkable sexual norms. In the atmosphere of permission to explore and specific rules to follow, couples begin to work out new norms by which they interact sexually. The balance of and/or content of sexual exchanges begins to shift. In addition, the content of emotional exchanges shifts as a function of clearer communication, sharing personal feelings, and reinforcing the partner for pleasurable experiences within the mutual pleasuring context. As a function of these factors, there is more impetus toward emphasizing maximum joint profit. Hence, sexual reciprocity is enhanced. Greater trust develops that the partner will be pleasuring and does take an interest in the other's sexual welfare. Although each partner is urged to "be selfish" and concentrate on personally experienced sexual pleasures, each gets a turn in practicing ways to enhance the other's pleasure. The more maximum joint profit and trust are engendered, the greater the interdependence. The greater the interdependence, the greater the feelings of commitment. As increasing trust, commitment, and reciprocity are experienced, the more vulnerable each partner is willing and able to become, and the more risk taking is incurred, sexually and emotionally. Again, the couple continues to develop new relationship norms for their sexual, emotional, and communicational interactions. As sex therapy proceeds, these are further explored, clarified, and developed. Specific sexual goals are delineated and problem solving, in relationship and sexual arenas, is expedited.

GUIDELINES FOR THE PRACTICE OF SEX THERAPY

Some guidelines for sex therapy may be drawn from the multidimensional model of relationships presented in this chapter:

1. Sex therapists may heuristically view the couple relationship as multidimensional, involving cognitive, emotional, and behavioral facets and involving processes important in understanding and intervening in sexuality such as social exchange, communication, and relationship reasoning.
2. Ask relationship questions: Explore the dyad's relationship history — their level of commitment and reciprocity, goals, ideals regarding the relationship, and so on.
3. Explore the couple's explicit norms, expectations, and agreements about sex and the relationship in general.
4. Clarify personal attitudes, values, and goals regarding sex, sexuality, and relationship development.
5. Observe and comment on *implicit* relationship norms, expectations, and agreements.
6. Observe and comment on dyadic processes by which those norms, expectations, and agreements emerge, including relationship reasoning, social exchange, and communication patterns.
7. Elucidate the sexual and relationship exchange patterns.
8. Make observations to the couple about shifts in their exchange patterns and/or equity calculations.
9. Encourage the collaborative attitude and work toward maximum joint profit.
10. Model *and* teach effective communication skills to promote self-assertion, empathic understanding, and mutual regard. Use systematic skills-training strategies to do so.
11. Model *and* teach effective problem solving skills, using systematic skills-training strategies.
12. Be attentive to relationship reasoning in order to better understand power issues and sex-role issues concerning sexual behavior in the relationship.
13. Attend to relationship reasoning stages at both content and process levels as couples discuss their sexual and relationship choices and formulate new ones. Make observations and discuss how they might approach decision making differently or point out the strengths of their current style. Note that a therapist cannot readily change a person's reasoning stage (see D'Augelli & D'Augelli, 1979 for a discussion of limiting factors), but he or she can model, suggest, and reinforce different helpful emphases. By so doing, the therapist increases the possibility of change and enhances mutual understanding.
14. By teaching communication skills, a therapist promotes interactive processes rather than role-based or egoistically oriented interaction. Struc-

turing mutual exploration and analysis and helping couples to avoid acting on assumptions about a partner's preferences or needs is a key element in fostering interactive thought processes, maximum joint profit, and solidarity.

It is important to be aware that it is not only the content of a relationship conflict that is the issue for intervention, but how the couple handles the conflict. So it is not merely the sexual behavior, but how it is talked about and managed, that becomes a potential source of conflict. The tendency for issues to escalate to higher levels of emotional interdependence is seen by Braiker and Kelley (1979) as a dramatic aspect of conflict in close relationships (p. 140). They note that a set of issues at a lower level of relationship issues, such as sexual disagreements, can result in a *general* issue at a higher level, such as worries about commitment in the relationship. However, they believe that resolution of an issue at a higher level (e.g., renewed belief in mutual commitment) may eliminate or reduce conflict regarding lower-level issues (e.g., specific sexual dissatisfactions will become more amenable to problem solving through accommodation, negotiation, and other processes). This suggests that sex therapists should be especially attentive to relationship reasoning and social-exchange processes as the couple proceeds in therapy. We are not suggesting that sex therapy become or is simply one facet of marital therapy, but we are suggesting that sex therapy can be enriched and made even more effective when therapists concern themselves with relationship processes of relevance to sexual interaction. Communication and sexual skills training should be used as a vehicle to elucidate, explore, and resolve higher and lower level relationship issues whether relationship norm, personal goal, or behavioral in nature. As Scanzoni (1979) aptly observes, "Sex has the unique capability of suddenly engendering high degrees of extensive behavioral interdependence quite apart from the kinds of purposive- action processes that ordinarily contribute to solidarity or commitment" (p. 83). Because of this, couples may inadequately clarify and agree on relationship goals, norms, and roles before finding themselves more highly interdependent. Communication concerning these aspects of the relationship is of utmost importance in helping them to enhance pleasure in their sexual interaction, as discussed above. This chapter has been directed towards offering relationship concepts with implications for sex therapists in order to make that challenge more possible.

REFERENCES

Altman, I. (1973). Reciprocity of interpersonal exchange. *Journal for the Theory of Social Behavior, 3,* 249-261.

Altman, I., & Taylor, D.A. (1973). *Social penetration: The development of interpersonal relationships.* New York: Holt, Rinehart & Winston.

Blau, P.M. (1964). *Exchange and power in social life.* New York: Wiley.

Bolton, D.C. (1961). Mate selection as the development of a relationship. *Journal of Marriage and Family Living, 23,* 234-240.

Braiker, H.B., & Kelley, H.H. (1979). Conflict in the development of close relationships. In R.L. Burgess & T.L. Huston (Eds.), *Social exchange in developing relationships* (pp. 135-168). New York: Academic Press.

Braiker-Stambul, H.B. (1975). *Stages of courtship: The development of premarital relationships.* Doctoral dissertation, University of California, Los Angeles.

Brickman, P. (1974). *Social conflict.* Lexington, MA: Heath.

Carson, R.C. (1979). Personality and exchange in developing relationships. In R.L. Burgess & T.L. Huston (Eds.), *Social exchange in developing relationships* (pp. 247-270). New York: Academic Press.

Cottrell, L.S., Jr. (1942). The analysis of situational fields in social psychology. *American Sociological Review, 7,* 370-382.

Danish, S.J., D'Augelli, A.R., & Hauer, A. (1980). *Helping skills: A basic training program.* New York: Human Sciences.

D'Augelli, A.R., D'Augelli-Frankel, J., & Danish, S.J. (1980). *Helping others.* Monterey, California: Brooks-Cole.

D'Augelli-Frankel, J. (1972). *The relationship of moral reasoning, sex guilt, and interpersonal interactions to couples' premarital sexual experience.* Unpublished doctoral dissertation, University of Connecticut.

D'Augelli-Frankel, J., & D'Augelli, A.R. (1979). Sexual involvement and relationship development: A cognitive developmental approach. In R.L. Burgess & T.L. Huston (Eds.), *Social exchange in developing relationships* (pp. 307-349). New York: Academic Press.

D'Augelli-Frankel, J., & Weener, J.B. (1975). *Communication and parenting skills: Research report.* University Park, PA: Addictions Prevention Laboratory.

D'Augelli-Frankel, J., & Weener, J.B. (1976). *Communication and parenting skills.* University Park, Pennsylvania: Addictions Prevention Laboratory.

D'Augelli-Frankel, J., & Weener, J.M. (1978). Training parents as mental health agents. *Community Mental Health Journal, 14,* 14-25.

Donnenworth, G.V., & Foa, U.G. (1974). Effect of resource class on retaliation to injustice in interpersonal exchange. *Journal of Personality and Social Psychology, 29,* 785-793.

Ekeh, P.P. (1974). *Social exchange: The two traditions.* Cambridge: Harvard University Press.

Foa, U.G. (1971). Interpersonal and economic resources. *Science, 171,* 345-351.

Foa, U.G., & Foa, E.B. (1974). *Societal structures of the mind.* Springfield, IL: Charles C. Thomas.

Foote, N.N. (1957). Concept and method in the study of human development. In M. Sherif & M.O. Wilson (Eds.), *Emerging problems in social psychology* (pp. 9-57). Norman, Oklahoma: University Book Exchange.

Fromm, E. (1956). *The art of loving.* New York: Harper & Row.

Gordon, T. (1970). *Parent effectiveness training.* New York: Peter Wyden.

Gouldner, A.W. (1960). The norm of reciprocity: A preliminary statement. *American Sociological Review, 25,* 161-178.

Guerney, L.F. (1977). Description and evaluation of a parenting skills training program for foster parents. *American Journal of Community Psychology, 5,* 361-371.

Gurman, A.S., & Knudson, R.M. (1978). Behavioral marriage therapy: I. A psychodynamic-systems analysis and critique. *Family Process, 17,* 121-138.

Haley, J. (1963). *Strategies of psychotherapy.* New York: Grune & Stratton.

Hatfield, E., Utne, M.K., & Traupmann, J. (1979). Equity theory and intimate relationships. In R.L. Burgess & T.L. Huston (Eds.), *Social exchange in developing relationships* (pp. 99-134). New York: Academic Press.

Heath, A. (1976). *Rational choice and social exchange.* New York: Cambridge University Press.

Homans, G.C. (1961). *Social behavior: Its elementary forms.* New York: Harcourt.

Huesmann, L.R., & Levinger, G. (1976). Incremental exchange theory: A formal model for progression in dyadic social interaction. In L. Berkowitz & E. Walster (Eds.), *Advances in experimental social psychology. Vol. 9.* New York: Academic Press.

Jacobson, N.S., & Margolin, G. (1979). *Marital therapy: Strategies based on social learning and behavior exchange principles.* New York: Brunner/Mazel.

Kaplan, H.S. (1974). *The new sex therapy.* New York: Brunner/Mazel.

Kohlberg, L. (1958). *The development of modes of moral thinking and choice in the years 10 to 16.* Doctoral dissertation, University of Chicago.

Kohlberg, L. (1969). Stage and sequence: The cognitive-developmental approach to socialization. In D. Goslin (Ed.), *Handbook of socialization theory and research* (pp. 347-480). Chicago: Rand McNally.

Kohlberg, L. (1971). From is to ought: How to commit the naturalistic fallacy and get away with it in the study of moral development. In T. Mischel (Ed.), *Cognitive development and epistemology* (pp. 151-235). New York: Academic Press.

Latham, J.D., & White G.D. (1978). Coping with homosexual expression within heterosexual marriage: Five case studies. *Journal of Sex and Marital Therapy, 4,* 198-212.

Lederer, W.J., & Jackson, D.D. (1968). *The mirages of marriage.* New York: W.W. Norton.

Lerner, R.M. (1979). A dynamic interactional concept of individual and social relationship development. In R.L. Burgess & T.L. Huston (Eds.), *Social exchange in developing relationships* (pp. 271-306). New York: Academic Press.

Levinger, G. (1979). A social exchange view on the dissolution of pair relationships. In R.L. Burgess & T.L. Huston (Eds.), *Social exchange in developing relationships* (pp. 169-196). New York: Academic Press.

Lobitz, W.C., & Lopiccolo, J. (1972). New methods in the behavioral treatment of sexual dysfunction. *Journal of Behavioral Therapy and Experimental Psychiatry, 3,* 265-271.

Masters, W.H., & Johnson, V.E. (1970). *Human sexual inadequacy.* Boston: Little, Brown.

Masters, W.H., & Johnson, V.E. (1975). *The pleasure bond.* Boston: Little, Brown.

Masters, W.H., & Johnson, V.E. (1976). Principles of the new sex therapy. *American Journal of Psychiatry, 133,* 548-554.

McCall, G.J. (1974). A symbolic interactionist approach to attraction. In T.L. Huston (Ed.), *Foundations of interpersonal attraction* (pp. 217-231). New York: Academic Press.

McCarthy, B.W. (1973). A modification of Masters and Johnson's sex therapy model in a clinical setting. *Psychotherapy: Theory, Research, and Practice, 10,* 290-293.

Nierenberg, G.I., & Calero, H.H. (1973). *Meta-talk: Guide to hidden meanings in conversations.* New York: Simon & Schuster.

Prochaska, J.O., & Marzilli, R. (1973). Modifications of the Masters and Johnson approach to sexual problems. *Psychotherapy: Theory, Research, and Practice, 10,* 294-296.

Renshaw, D.C. (1975). Sex therapy in the 1970s. *Psychiatric Opinion, 12,* 6-11.

Rogers, C.R. (1951). *Client-centered therapy.* Boston: Houghton-Mifflin.

Rubin, Z. (1973). *Liking and loving: An invitation to social psychology.* New York: Holt Rinehart & Winston.

Sadock, V.A., Sadock, B.J., & Kaplan, H.S. (1975). Comprehensive sex therapy: A new approach. *American Journal of Psychiatry, 132,* 858-860.

Scanzoni, J. (1979). Social exchange and behavioral interdependence. In R.L. Burgess & T.L. Huston (Eds.), *Social exchange in developing relationships* (pp. 61-98). New York: Academic Press.

Snyder, A., Lopiccolo, L., & Lopiccolo, J. (1975). Secondary orgasmic dysfunction: II. Case study. *Archives of Sexual Behavior, 4,* 277-283.

Stuart, R.B. (1980). *Helping couples change.* New York: Guilford Press.

Szasz, T. (1980). *Sex by prescription.* Garden City, NY: Anchor Press.

Thibaut, J.W., & Kelley, H.H. (1959). *The social psychology of groups.* New York: Wiley.

Tullman, G.M., Gilner, F.H., Kolodny, R.C., Dornbush, R.L., & Tullman, G.D. (1981). The pre- and post-therapy measurement of communication skills of couples undergoing sex therapy at the Masters & Johnson Institute. *Archives of Sexual Behavior, 10,* 95-109.

Turner, J.L., Foa, E.B., & Foa, U.G. (1971). Interpersonal reinforcers: Classification in a relationship and some differential properties. *Journal of Personality and Social Psychology, 19,* 168-180.

Waller, W., & Hill. R. (1951). *The family: A dynamic interpretation.* New York: Dryden.

Walster, E., Walster, G.W., & Berscheid, E. (1978). *Equity: Theory and Research.* Boston: Allyn & Bacon.

Warren, N.J., & Gilner, F.H. (1978). Measurement of positive assertive behaviors: The behavioral test of tenderness expression. *Behavior Therapy, 9,* 178-184.

Woody, R.H., & Woody, J.D. (1973). *Sexual, marital, and familial relations.* Springfield, IL: Charles C. Thomas.

Chapter 4
Sexual Dysfunction In The Medically Ill

Barbara A. Palmeri and Thomas N. Wise

Physical illness, acute or chronic, forces an individual to modify a preexisting self image, adopt new behaviors and alter roles and relationships. Sexual function may be altered by a medical condition.

The past decade has witnessed a remarkable growth of information regarding the role of sexuality in individuals with medical illnesses (Sha'ked, 1978). Since Masters and Johnson described the normal sexual response cycle, this area of study has gained much attention. The recent addition of behavioral treatment techniques and specific medical and surgical procedures to the clinician's armamentarium demands ever-increasing familiarity with sexual dysfunction in the medically ill.

This chapter will focus on medical illness that may compromise sexual functioning in each of Kaplan's (1979) three phases of the normal sexual response. Following a review of the clinical assessment of sexuality in the medically ill, the impact of specific medical conditions upon each phase of Kaplan's cycle will be discussed. The reader will develop an increased familiarity and ease with evaluation of sexual function in the medically ill.

NORMAL SEXUAL RESPONSE

The sexual response cycle is a complex repertoire of affective, cognitive, behavioral and physiological phenomena. Kaplan has modified Masters and Johnson's initial description of the normal sexual response into a three part cycle (Figure 4-1). The initial component is the *desire phase,* an appetitive drive stage that consists of fantasies and subjective desire for sexual activity. The second phase, *arousal or excitement,* is characterized by penile tumescence in the male and vaginal lubrication in the female. The final phase of the sexual response is the *release phase,* denoted by an orgasm followed by a resolution and, in males,

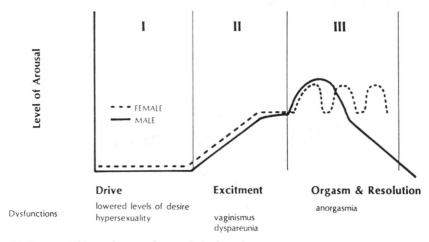

Figure 4.1 Three phases of sexual dysfunction

a refractory period. Due in part to the peripheral visibility of the male sexual response, much more is known about sexual difficulties in males.

In order to fully assess and understand sexual dysfunction in the medically ill, the clinician should be conversant with the normal sexual response. The physiology of normal sexuality is elaborated on in a variety of texts. However, a brief summary follows.

The Desire Phase

The biological basis of sexual desire is complex and poorly defined. Animal studies indicate that outflow tracts from the limbic system to the hypothalamus result in the release of gonadotropic releasing hormone (Levine, 1982). The pituitary gonadoaxis further modulates androgenic release. In males, plasma testosterone levels may transiently increase during sexual arousal (Laferta, Anderson, & Schalach, 1978). Androgenic deficiency may lower sexual arousal. Congenital hypogonadism that causes low testosterone levels has been reported to be associated with lowered levels of sexual desire or drive. The relationship is complex, however, because lower testosterone levels due to surgical castration or medical antiandrogenic substances vary in their effect upon sexual drive (Davidson, Camargo, & Smith, 1979).

In premenopausal women, normal cyclical variations of estrogen and progesterone do not necessarily modify sexual drive. Persky et al. (1982) were unable to document a relationship between sexual drive and estrogen and progesterone levels. Abplanalp, et al. (1979) have also questioned the cyclical nature of sexual drive in women and report only minimal psychological changes throughout the menstrual cycle (Abplanalp, Rose, & Donnelly, 1979).

Schreiner-Engle, Schiavi, & Smith (1981) suggest a tentative relationship between androgens from the adrenal cortex and sexual arousability in women.

The central nervous system is also important in promoting sexual desire. The cortex, as well as hypothalamic and preoptic areas within the brain, process visual, sensory, olfactory, and gustatory sensations, in addition to fantasy production, to foster sexual drive (Robinson, 1983). Blumer (1971) has demonstrated that individuals with temporal lobe epilepsy are often hyposexual yet improve in sexual drive following drug treatment for the seizure disorder. In summary, cortical, subcortical, and endocrinological factors clearly modify sexual desire, although clear delineation of such physiologic phenomena is not yet available.

The Arousal Phase

The arousal or excitement phase is the next element of normal psychosexual response and is characterized by penile tumescence in the male and vaginal lubrication in the female. Concurrent physiological changes include increasing heart rate, development of a sex flush over the upper thoracic area, and a quickening respiratory rate. In addition to psychological factors, the basic biology of the arousal phase includes endocrinologic, vascular and neurologic contributions. Hormonal contribution to male tumescence involves interaction between pituitary gonadotropin follicle stimulating hormone and luteinizing hormone, which stimulates testosterone production. Hemodynamic changes promote male tumescence with the arterial blood-flow shift into the penile corpus cavernosa. Recent data suggest that arteriodilatation is under the control of the adrenergic nervous system to initiate this fluid transfer. Both arterial and venous disease may ablate male arousal. Finally, the neurologic input of both the parasympathetic and sympathetic systems promotes tumescence. Adrenergic nerve fibers supply the trabeculae of the penile musculature as well as moderate penile blood pressure. Vaginal and clitoral tumescence also is under control of both sympathetic and parasympathetic input, so peripheral vascular disease in women can significantly diminish arousal.

The Release Phase

The final phase of the sexual response cycle is that of orgasm or the release phase. The orgasmic phase is under both sympathetic and parasympathetic control. For males, sympathetic nerve response stimulates introduction of seminal fluid into the posterior urethra, which in turn closes the bladder duct. The presence of fluid stimulates parasympathetic fibers, which force contraction of the perineal muscles resulting in ejaculation. The hypogastric, pelvic and pudendal nerves all carry fibers contributing to emission. The neurologic contribution to the release phase is poorly understood in women.

CLINICAL ASSESSMENT OF SEXUAL DYSFUNCTION

A careful clinical history and psychosocial evaluation is essential to assess an individual's level of functioning and to formulate a treatment plan. The best method of initiating such a history is by the open-ended interview technique of asking broad questions to prompt the patient's response. In the initial history gathering session, too many direct questions may discourage more subjective, informative replies.

The clinician must make an orderly, systematic assessment of the emotional impact of the disease state and then assess the role of sexuality in the lives of the individual and the sex partner. As patients recount their symptoms, ideas about etiology, reactions to discomfort and inconvenience, and previous experiences with disease, the clinician may learn of idiosyncratic behavior patterns. To best manage individuals, assessment of sterotypic personalities, such as the obsessional personality or the histrionic character type, is helpful. The orderly, obsessive individual will require more information about the illness. It is helpful to utilize this need for order and structure by having the individual chart out various parameters of the treatment regimen such as weight, medicines and activities. The histrionic individual, on the other hand, will often not be able to tolerate a rigid regimen but will need support, direction and continued encouragement. An individual who is more dependent will also need more aid from the medical care givers as well as from family members.

In the male, the presence or absence of nocturnal emissions, early-morning erections and tumescence with masturbation is important to help differentiate psychogenic from physically based sexual dysfunctions. The absence of tumescence in any situation strongly suggests an organic factor, although depression may also ablate the erective response. The clinician should inquire about the onset of the difficulty and the time course from full- functioning to present status. The female patient should be asked about the presence of vaginal lubrication and orgastic response in addition to other difficulties such as dyspareunia, urinary dribbling or uterine cramping during sexual activity, whether it be intercourse or masturbation. A careful medical history, with specific emphasis upon the presence of symptoms or history of illnesses such as cardiovascular disease or diabetes or any pharmacological treatment, is mandatory to reveal the source of the individual's difficulties. Ingestion of tranquilizers, neuroleptic medication and previous surgical procedures, including urological or gynecological surgery must be delineated. In the absence of specific diagnostic information, careful attention should be directed to the presence of shortness of breath, weakness, sensory difficulties, mobility problems, polydipsia and polyuria. Family history for chronic diseases is also important.

Physicians who will perform the physical examination must assess both vascular and neurologic symptoms. Presence of chest pain or problems in the healing of minor scrapes and abrasions in the lower extremities may denote cardiovascular disease. The presence of calf pain upon exertion may suggest a peripheral vascular disease. Direct examination should be made of the extremities to determine hair distribution, skin texture, and color. Assessment of skin temperature and detection of peripheral pulses by palpation is necessary to determine blood flow.

Neurological assessment includes review of an individual's motor system, sensory discrimination, autonomic nervous system and higher cortical functions. Physical examination includes assessment of peripheral sensory discrimination and motor strength. The presence and symmetry of deep tendon reflexes and long tract signs, such as Babinski, elucidate input of higher nervous centers. The integrity of the lumbosacral spinal pathways that are essential to sexual functioning may be determined by the following tests. S1-S2 may be evaluated by intact mobility of the small muscles of the foot. S2-S4 may be evaluated by the ability to contract and relax both the internal and external anal sphincters. This may be ascertained by digital examination of the anus to test the initial contraction and the relaxation of the external sphincter. The finger should then be advanced to test the internal sphincter tone. S2-S4 may be further tested by the bulbocavernous reflex. The absence of anal sphincter contraction is common even in normal subjects, thereby requiring electromyographic studies to further investigate the potency of the sacral segments (Hollander & Meker, 1976). S2-S5 is documented by the presence of perianal sensations.

Evaluation of endocrine status is important. Physical inspection of the distribution of body hair may indicate endocrinological pathology. Distribution of body fat, including presence of gynecomastia in the male, is also important. Thyroid status must be assessed by noting the individual's ability to tolerate temperature changes, as well as appetitive and energy levels. Direct examination of the thyroid gland is necessary in addition to appropriate laboratory screening.

The patient will often need appropriate laboratory testing for various endocrinologic problems including assays of follicle stimulating hormone (FSH), luteinizing hormone (LH) and testosterone in the male. In the female, measurement of FSH and LH should be accompanied by that of prolactin and growth hormone levels. Vaginal cytologies may also be helpful. Measurement of the thyroid axis is also necessary (Leiber et al., 1976). Doppler techniques to measure blood flow as well as pelvic angiography may be necessary to elucidate areas of pathology in male sexual functioning.

Finally, the patient should undergo a complete mental status exam and be asked about emotional status. It is important to ascertain how the illness affects personal relationships and occupational and recreational functioning.

In summary, careful history taking with appropriate physical examination and laboratory testing is imperative. Attention to endocrinologic and neurologic systems may uncover physiological causes for sexual dysfunction. In both men and women with diagnosed systemic illness, the role of organic factors in compromising sexual functioning cannot be ignored.

THE ROLE OF SPECIFIC MEDICAL ILLNESSES IN SEXUAL DYSFUNCTION

In order to aid the clinician in assessing and treating sexual dysfunction in the medically ill, we will review several specific illnesses. Our review will focus on how each phase of the sexual response cycle is compromised. Treatment considerations will follow.

Cardiovascular Disease: Coronary Artery Disease

Cardiovascular disease covers a wide range of pathologic entities that affect both the heart and peripheral vasculature.

Disorders of desire. The role changes that result from chronic illness may seriously hamper sexual satisfaction by affecting the desire phase. Such interpersonal difficulties are often demonstrated in patients who survive a myocardial infarction. Fears regarding resumption of sexual activity are common, but the cardiovascular requirements for sexual intercourse are equivalent to a brisk walk around a city block. Most patients with uncomplicated myocardial infarctions are capable of almost twice the physiological energy necessary for intercourse. The actual heart rate maximally achieved during an orgasm averages 117 beats per minute with a wide range of variation in systolic blood pressure (Hellerstein & Friedman, 1970). Convalescence at home may promote tension between the heart patient and the spouse; convalescence is often the first time in years that the couple has been together without interruption. Subsequent marital conflict may seriously impede sexual desire.

Disorders of arousal and release. As noted above, sexual functioning is generally preserved in patients with coronary artery disease who do not have widespread peripheral vascular disease. Specific problems in the postcoronary patient, such as anginal pain, may require further medical treatment. Patients with congestive heart failure may be treated with cardiac glycosides; this may lower testosterone and increase estrogen, causing lower sexual drive and erectile problems in men.

Treatment considerations. Sexual activity may be safely resumed approximately twelve weeks following hospital discharge. Nevertheless, many studies indicate a marked reduction in intercourse following an infarct. McLane demonstrated that few subjects recovering from myocardial infarction were counseled regarding sexuality despite the fact that most individuals feared the effects of the cardiac insult upon their sexual ability (McLane, Krop, & Mehta, 1986). Papadopoulos et al. (1980) found similar results in studying the spouses of recent myocardial infarction victims. Direct information does not always allay anxieties regarding sexual activity in these spouses, so ongoing support and sexual counseling by medical personnel is often necessary to prevent sexual difficulties in such situations.

Understanding the individual's fears about sexual activity following a myocardial infarction is mandatory. Both patient and spouse should be included in such a discussion. If a patient does not bring up the role of sexuality, the clinician must inquire tactfully if this has been a worry. Resumption of sexual activities has been recommended 8 to 12 weeks following acute infarct. The patient should be warned that during this time the couple may have disagreements over various minor or trivial issues, which may be displacements from the psychological effects of the infarct. Gradual resumption of sexual activity is advisable using sexual behavior such as touching exercises prior to actual intercourse. Utilization of the male-superior position may increase isometric tension, which increases cardiovascular demand, thus alternative positioning such as side-by-side may be advisable. Sexual problems that occur must be dealt with actively by the physician, with appropriate referral if necessary.

Cardiovascular Disease: Peripheral Vascular Disease

Disorders of the desire phase. Pain due to deficient peripheral vascular circulation may make sexuality less enjoyable and distract the individual. The presence of wounds and abrasions that fail to heal due to compromised circulation further create shame and embarrassment as well as difficulties in mobility.

Disorders of arousal and release. Peripheral vascular occlusion may limit blood supply to the pelvic area. This may cause microvascular and neuropathic changes that create erectile dysfunction within the male. Leriche's syndrome, occlusion of the bifurcation of the abdominal aorta, will create erectile dysfunction due to insufficient genital blood supply. Although the sexual effects of peripheral vascular disease in women are not fully known, peripheral changes do significantly reduce the capacity for vaginal lubrication and engorgement.

Treatment considerations. Certain individuals with peripheral vascular disease, such as Buerger's disease, have been shown to be difficult patients who do not comply with treatment (Farberow & Nehemkis, 1979). These individuals tend to be dependent and dissatisfied, and they often continue to use cigarettes and tobacco products, which advance the progression of their disease. They also tend to be complaining, demanding, aggressive and negativistic. Supportive individuals are thus distanced. Patients with intermittent claudication may become depressed and dissatisfied because of the advance of their illness, so depression must be evaluated and treated.

Chronic Pulmonary Disease

Chronic obstructive pulmonary disease ranks second only to coronary artery disease in its prevalence in adult males of middle age. A heterogeneous group of conditions, including chronic obstructive pathology as well as the asthmatic diseases, are noted when referring to chronic obstructive pulmonary disease.

Disorders of desire. The fatigue and dyspnea upon exertion that is common in individuals with chronic pulmonary disease may severely limit sexual enjoyment. In advanced pulmonary disease, the use of auxiliary oxygen as well as muscular wasting may create actual mechanical difficulties for sexual activity. The physical requirements during intercourse have been cited as catalysts for asthmatic attacks in a selected population of individuals. Depression that results from the chronic incapacitation of pulmonary disease may limit libidinal drive.

Disorders of Arousal and Release. Recent studies (d'A Semple et al., 1979) have demonstrated that chronic obstruction to the airways may be associated with low testosterone values. Thus arterial hypoxia is directly related to testosterone depression. Symptomatically this may result in penile impotence in the male with chronic obstructive airway disease. One study demonstrated 17% of a sample of men with chronic lung disease were impotent on an organic basis. (Koss, Updegroff, & Muffly, 1972). Erectile dysfunction in individuals with chronic obstructive lung disease may be due to psychological factors as well. No data is available regarding orgasmic response in women with similar pulmonary pathology.

Treatment considerations. Premedication for individuals with exercise-induced asthma will modify any pulmonary symptoms induced during sexual activity. For those individuals with chronic obstructive disease, utilization of various positions to minimize exertion will often be necessary to maximize sexual enjoyment.

Adult-Onset Diabetes Mellitus

Diabetes mellitus affects over 2 million adults and adolescents. The disease forces the individuals to regulate diet carefully and to medicate themselves with parenteral insulin.

Disorders of desire. Complications from diabetes may result in renal failure, blindness, skin changes due to diabetic lipodystrophy, and pain from peripheral neuropathies. Sensory deficits may limit sexual enjoyment due to discomfort and general malaise. Shame about leg ulcers and poorly healing abrasions may further modify sexual enjoyment. The adolescent who suffers from uncomplicated diabetes may feel ostracized and different because of the necessary dietary limitations and fears of peer group rejection. This may result in social withdrawal or promiscuity to prevent abandonment.

The diabetic patient may be depressed from a variety of factors. The adult with sequelae may be depressed due to actual limitations of the disease, such as the visual diminution due to retinopathy, the implications of diabetic neuropathy and resultant hemodialysis, or the pain and suffering of peripheral vascular disease. These may all limit libidinal drive and make sexual activity more difficult. As noted, the young diabetic may feel ashamed and different.

Disorders of arousal and release. Diabetes, although an endocrine disorder, has serious effects on the small vessels, nervous system, and kidneys. The progressive neuropathy found in many diabetics will eventually render almost one half of diabetic men impotent. The erectile dysfunction appears to be unrelated to the severity or duration of diabetes. There is no evidence that plasma testosterone is involved in the dysfunction. Recently, Ellenberg (1980) has replicated an early study by Kolodny (1971) and found no diminution of libido or orgastic potential in the female diabetic with peripheral neurologic changes. Autonomic neuropathies found commonly in diabetics may cause retrograde ejaculation in the diabetic male. This can produce a serious problem in individuals who wish to procreate, but specific urologic techniques have been developed to allow extraction of semen for full reproductive capacity. Psychological reactions to diabetes may also potentiate arousal-phase disorders. The differential diagnosis of diabetic impotence is difficult because of the poor reliability of clinical symptoms that differentiate organic versus psychogenic causes of erectile difficulties in such patients.

Treatment considerations. In males with diabetic neuropathy and impotence, the use of a mechanical penile implant is often indicated. The use of either a siliastic rod or a fluid-pump prosthesis has been very successful in restoring potency. In individuals who have managed their diabetic status poorly, nutritional malnourishment and fatigue may inhibit sexual functioning. Restoration of diabetic control is needed to restore full sexual functioning. In those individuals who are depressed, psychotherapy is clearly indicated to restore full sexual expression in the absence of organic limitation (Abel et al., 1982).

Renal Disease with Hemodialysis or Transplantation

Chronic renal disease often requires maintenance hemodialysis. The individual is thus dependent upon routine hemodialysis via a "kidney machine." In addition, severe limitations of fluid and food are necessary to maintain life. Other individuals may be treated by transplantation by a donor or cadaveric kidney. This requires major surgery as well as ongoing follow-up utilizing multiple ongoing medications.

Disorders of Desire. Women on chronic hemodialysis report sexual dysfunction, which appears to be primarily related to psychological and social difficulties. In men, the neurologic and vascular effects of chronic renal disease are not reversed by hemodialysis. Therefore, men may have problems with tumescence, ejaculation and emission. Additionally, fatigue and chronic malaise compromise sexuality in men and women. Orgastic potential through masturbation often appears to be intact, although orgasm during intercourse is less commonly achieved.

Maintenance hemodialysis augments dependence and fosters depression. These factors may limit sexual interest. Commonly, however, the individual with such a chronic disease wishes to be considered a loved and attractive individual and may crave sexuality. However, the partner may be fearful of hurting the individual and thus sexual distancing may result.

Disorders of arousal and release. Individuals undergoing chronic renal dialysis commonly have sexual dysfunctions. In one series, 45% of men undergoing hemodialysis reported diminished potency following onset of chronic renal diseases and subsequent hemodialysis (Levy & Wynbraut, 1975; Stickler et al., 1974). The source of this diminished potency appears to be related to dysfunction between the pituitary and Leydig axis (Chen et al., 1970). Exogenous testosterone, although it may restore sexual functioning, augments atherosclerosis and therefore cannot be utilized. Following renal transplantation, many dysfunctional males report restoration of sexual potency, indicating that uremia and hemodialysis treatment are the etiological agents (Milne, Golden & Fibus, 1978; Procci, Hoffman & Chatterjee, 1978). Dysfunction in transplantation patients can be due to the medications used such as corticosteroids and immunosuppressant agents.

Treatment considerations. Attention to sexual functioning is necessary in individuals undergoing hemodialysis. Discussion with the patient and the sexual partner is needed to clarify sexual potential and desire. The posttransplant patient may also experience sexual difficulty. Although this may have an organic basis, the psychological meaning of having another individual's organ inside oneself also may provoke distress which can be translated into sexual difficulties. Exploration of the meaning of surgery is often necessary to define the parameters leading to the sexual dysfunction in a posttransplant individual.

The stress of a serious and chronic illness may upset a marriage, but the added insult of erectile dysfunction and sexual inability can further wreak havoc in an already-troubled relationship. Conjoint counseling can be directed toward alternative forms of lovemaking including mutual masturbation and oral genital activity, if this is acceptable to each individual. Recognition of realistic limitations by the therapist is essential to prevent pushing the patient and spouse to more than they are capable of achieving.

Breast Cancer

Cancer is the disease process most feared by both laymen and health professionals. As advances in medical chemotherapy, radiation therapy, and surgical techniques have allowed the cancer victim to live longer, quality of life and sexual functioning have become increasingly important concerns of the individual with neoplastic disease. Rehabilitation rather than palliation is often a major goal. This has shifted the focus of psychosocial treatment from acute care to a longitudinal approach that will allow patients to reenter their social system and perform occupational tasks that maximize their potential abilities. Each neoplasm has its own idiosyncratic features.

Disorders of desire. The anger and discouragement that result from the narcissistic blow of breast neoplasia may modify sexual functioning (Jamison, Wellison & Pasnau, 1978). Pain and discomfort from the incisional scar of a mastectomy as well as swelling edema, and discomfort of an arm due to blocked lymphatic drainage may augment this discomfort and prevent maximal sexual enjoyment. Shame at disfigurement of a mastectomy may limit sexual interest.

Only a small percentage of women with breast cancer develop sufficient psychological distress for it to be defined as a clinical syndrome. Nevertheless, certain women become discouraged and depressed because of their disease and resultant mastectomy. This may develop into a collusive relationship with their sexual partner, where the withdrawal of the spouse of the sexual partner may enhance the individual's sense of shame. In those couples where there was not a discussion of the meaning of a mastectomy prior to surgery and/or where there was infrequent visiting within the hospital, postsurgical sexual problems frequently develop and present as marital discord.

Disorders of arousal and release. Mastectomy following carcinoma of the breast obviously limits tactile pleasure from breast caressing. Nipple stimulation is thus ablated unless there is preservation of areolar tissue in breast reconstruction. Decreased libidinal drive and orgastic inability may also result from chemotherapy. Dyspareunia also may result from vaginal epithelial atrophy when estrogens are withheld in postmenopausal women.

Treatment considerations. Witkin (1978) recommends that immediately following a mastectomy, the spouse be present as the mastectomy wound is unbandaged and inspected. This provides a professional setting in which the husband may view the site of the absent breast and help allay the woman's fears and anxieties. Rapid resumption of sexual activity has also been recommended to avoid sexual difficulties that foster lack of self-esteem. Reconstructive breast surgery following mastectomy is becoming increasingly utilized to repair the absent breast.

Noting the individual's psychosocial history allows the health professional to assess the extent to which an individual's self-esteem has been assaulted. The clinician can give the patient permission to discuss various dysphoric feelings or thoughts, provide specific information and, if need be, recommend intensive psychotherapy.

Prostatic cancer

Disorders of desire. The discouragement and depression from the neoplastic disease itself as well as severe pain, if present, may modify libido and inhibit sexual activity. Despite the fact that prostatic cancer often occurs in older individuals, many of these patients will still have libidinal wishes and drives; understanding of their psychological and sexual needs is mandatory. Gynecomastia from estrogenic therapy may also create shame and inhibit sexual expression.

Disorders of arousal and release. The various treatments for prostatic cancer differ in their effects on sexual functioning (Maruto & Osborne, 1978). Potency is lost in only 10% of individuals who undergo transurethral resection for well-differentiated and localized adenocarcinoma of the prostate. If radiotherapy is utilized, organic impotence increases to 50% of patients. Concurrent use of estrogenic hormonal therapy may lower libido, but potency is preserved in most individuals undergoing hormonal treatment. Adjunctive use of orchiectomy in metastatic and prostatic lesions may also create erectile dysfunction.

Arthritis

Arthritis, either inflammatory or degenerative disease of the joint, covers a wide spectrum of specific disorders that occur throughout the life cycle. Juvenile forms of arthritis may severely disfigure a young adolescent, whereas degenerative joint disease can incapacitate and immobilize the older individual.

Disorders of desire. The depression that accompanies the constant pain of arthritis, as well as the shame of physical disfigurement, changes and diminishes one's self-esteem and can lower libidinal drive. The psychological changes due to steroid medication, such as depression or severe cognitive deficits, can also compromise sexual function.

Disorders of arousal and release. Functional limitations from arthritis most commonly occur due to lack of mobility of the hips, knees, or the back; this may make intercourse difficult because of mechanical impediments. Bilateral hip contractions may make intercourse impossible, as well as interfere with perianal hygiene. Medications used for treatment for arthritis may further compromise sexual functioning. Steroid medication may render males impotent.

The pain from musculoskeletal joint disease can inhibit orgasmic enjoyment. The stiffness common to many forms of arthritis may further make the physical activity in sexuality problematic. Sjogren's syndrome, which accompanies rheumatoid arthritis, inhibits mucosal secretions and can cause atrophic vaginitis or male urethritis, making intercourse painful. Fatigue from systemic disease as well as exhaustion from the prolonged pain of the degenerative joint disease further diminish sexual activity.

Treatment considerations. In order to enhance sexual functioning, attention must be paid to alleviation of arthritic pain (Richards, 1980). Salicylates and other antiinflammatory aids may diminish discomfort and increase mobility. Many individuals with rheumatoid arthritis note that certain periods of the day correlate with greatest mobility and comfort, so it is during this time that individuals may best use their preferred sexual positions. Good communication patterns between the arthritic patient and the sexual partner are necessary. In juvenile arthritic patients, it is necessary to be aware of the fears pertaining to peer-group relationships and self-worth.

Obesity

Obesity severely compromises an individual's health status and may be considered a pathologic entity.

Disorders of desire. Obesity has been suggested by psychoanalytic theorists to be a defense against sexuality. This may occur in a selected group of individuals and may prevent their engaging in sexual activities. Frequently, however, depression from isolation and the stigmatization of an unattractive body results in withdrawal and limited social and sexual opportunities.

The obese adolescent male may be ashamed of gynecomastia and refrain from heterosexual activities and sexual experiences. The hyperobese woman appears to have more frequent sexual opportunities than her male counterparts. This may be due to the obese woman's utilization of sexual activity as the only attractive facet of her femininity. Another factor that diminishes enjoyment of sexuality is the difficulty in finding an adequate position for intercourse because of the large body mass of the obese individual.

Disorders of arousal and release. The few studies of morbidly obese individuals suggest that there are few if any sexual dysfunctions in the obese and hyperobese that are directly a result of weight problems (Wise, 1977a). Nevertheless, individuals who are severely overweight do experience difficulties such as shortness of breath during intercourse. Potency problems in obese men and orgastic difficulties in women appear to be no more common than in the general population.

Treatment considerations. In the obese individual, the major focus must be on achieving a more realistic body weight. This is usually a difficult and chronic task, which results in repeated dieting via various methods that range from modified protein fasts to more drastic surgical techniques such as ileal bypass or gastric stapling in the morbidly obese. The vast majority of overweight individuals, however, engage in chronic dieting. As the obese individual loses weight, sexual opportunities become more available. This may become a problem if the individual has no previous sexual experience and is confused by new intimate relationships.

Genitourinary Surgery

Urologic conditions that affect the male genitalia have emotional significance as well as a clear mechanical impact upon adequate sexual functioning. The treatment for certain congenital and acquired defects of the penis may further complicate effective sexual functioning. Similarly, surgical procedures that affect female genitalia and reproductive organs will have a distinct emotional as well as frequent physical effects upon sexual activity.

Disorders of desire. The mechanical inability to successfully penetrate the vaginal canal in severe hypospadias produces shame and distress. Urinary spray due to the abnormal urethral opening further embarrasses the individual. Individuals with Peyronie's disease are also embarrassed. Those individuals with priapism are agitated and distressed by the pain and persistence of the erection. Patients with prostatic cancer who are on estrogen therapy may be threatened by the gynecomastia. Severe depression and inhibition may result from any of these urologic situations. The limitation on enjoyment and actual functional limitations augment distress.

Disorders of arousal and release. Mechanical derangements, such as in hypospadias, where the urethral meatus is abnormally located, may make vaginal penetration difficult. Procedures to correct this difficulty may create erectile dysfunction. Peyronie's disease is a painful deformity of the penis due to fibrous tissue within the tunica albuginea. Surgical treatment involves dermal grafting, which may result in impotence. Priapism is the painful prolongation of an erection. It is caused by blood dyscrasia such as sickle-cell disease or leukemia, neoplastic disease and drugs such as phenothiazines, antihypertensives, and anticoagulants. This condition may lead to tissue destruction and erectile dysfunction. Surgical treatment to detumesce the penis via saphenous vein shunt will often cause impotence. The effects of both surgical and radiological treatment for carcinomas of the prostate have been discussed previously.

Treatment considerations. Impotence from any of these causes may be treated by surgical prosthesis. Some patients will not be candidates for such a procedure because of their debilitated medical state or their need for various treatments such as anticoagulation. Careful psychological assessment and follow- up is recommended if urological procedures cause impotence.

Gynecological Surgery

Disorders of desire. The depression resulting from major and minor gynecologic procedures originates not only in reaction to the actual illness and surgery, but also in the fantasies of the cause of surgery. Individuals may blame former sexual activities or other factors in their life as the cause of their disease. This can augment depression and shame and limit libidinal drive.

The disfigurement from genital surgery may shame the patient or disgust the sexual partner. The presence of the radiation implant for uterine carcinoma may create fears and fantasies for the sexual partner that he will be radiated through sexual activity.

Disorders of arousal and release. The specific gynecologic procedure will determine the actual organic limitations upon sexual functioning. Massive surgical procedures, such as pelvic exenteration, ablate the vaginal canal (Brown et al., 1972). Surgery may permit reconstruction of the vaginal canal and allow intercourse. However, clitoral tissue is frequently not present, resulting in anorgasmia. Hysterectomy for cervical carcinoma involves removal of the cervix with subsequent vaginal shortening and stenosis (Decker & Schwartzman, 1962; Donahue & Knapp, 1977; Seibel, Freeman, & Graves, 1980). This may result in dyspareunia. Following oophorectomy, the removal of the ovaries, the relative steroid deprivation may create vaginal epithelial thinning, which may result in atrophic vaginitis and dyspareunia.

Treatment considerations. In individuals with vaginal shortening due to total hysterectomy for cervical carcinoma, frequent intercourse will elongate the vaginal canal for functional utilization. Fantasies about the impact of radiation implants must be elicited and discussed with both the patient and the sexual partner if normal sexual activity is to be resumed. Finally, a full discussion of the fantasies and fears regarding the etiology and course of any gynecological carcinoma is necessary to prevent needless psychological side effects. The sexual partner should be included whenever possible.

Pregnancy

Although not a disease, pregnancy, delivery and the post partum period are significant medical experiences for mother, father, and neonate. The effects upon sexuality are important.

Disorders of desire. Sexual activity may be limited during the first trimester due to nausea and breast swelling, which make breast caressing painful. Fear of injury to the baby may also diminish enjoyment of sexual activity. During the later stages of pregnancy, the abdominal girth may demand use of new positions such as side-by-side placement for comfortable intercourse. Postpartum fatigue from infant care as well as from nursing may diminish libidinal drive.

Postpartum depression will diminish libidinal drive and preclude effective sexual response. It has been suggested that unexpected cesarean delivery will make the mother feel less of a "complete women." This appears to be true only in a selected group of individuals postcesarean. A variety of reactions toward the birth of a child, however, should be investigated and treated. In these situations sexuality is only one part of a complex reaction to the birth of a child. The nursing mother may feel less sexually responsive because of the investment in the nursing process. The role of prolactin in limiting libidinal drive is not clear. An essential variable in the role of sexuality during pregnancy and during the postpartum period is the perception of the husband. Psychologically vulnerable men may feel abandoned or threatened by the emergence of a new individual in their family, which can provoke withdrawal. The clinician must be aware of this possible development.

Disorders of arousal and release. Fears of fetal harm are common in expectant mothers. In fact, prepartum coitus is well tolerated until the last trimester. However, prostaglandins in semen may stimulate uterine contractions and thus make intercourse without a condom inadvisable in the later part of pregnancy (Miles, Harlop, & Harley, 1981). Immediately postpartum, the tissue trauma in the perianal and vaginal areas due to delivery precludes intercourse until 4 to 6 weeks postpartum.

Alcohol

Excessive ingestion of alcoholic beverages becomes a serious medical problem. Psychological factors are significant in the etiology of alcoholism, which may be looked at from a disease, social-learning or cultural-variant model. The effects of alcohol on sexual functioning are significant (Gad-Luther, 1980).

Disorders of desire. Chronic alcoholism has been associated with numerous psychological characteristics. Passivity, dependence and depression common in individuals addicted to alcohol can modify sexual functioning and the ability to relate to a partner. Chronic alcoholics, both men and women, report problems finding suitable sexual partners. This is often due to diminished capacity for interpersonal relationships.

The chronic alcoholic may be decidedly offensive to the sexual partner, with a presence of alcohol on the breath and a disheveled demeanor. The physical consequences of alcoholism, such as gynecomastia, have been reported to be a source of shame to men who have retained or regained their potency. Likewise, a woman suffering from chronic alcoholism may find her own physical deterioration a source of shame to herself as well as to her partner.

Disorders of arousal and release. Alcohol has a biphasic effect upon sexual functioning. Low blood levels of alcohol (25 mg/100 ml) actually accelerate sexual arousal in males who are not chronic alcoholics. Moderate blood levels of alcohol (less than 50 mg/100 ml) affect an individual's belief system and modify psychological defenses against sexuality and aggression. At this level, alcohol may diminish an individual's sexual control and lessen guilt and negative attitudes toward sexuality. Increased blood levels of alcohol (greater than 75 ml/100 ml) depress and impair erection and ejaculation.

In addition to the acute effects of alcohol, chronic alcoholism is a disease that affects the peripheral nervous system, the central nervous system, and the liver. Impotence is a frequent finding in chronic alcoholics. The significant prevalence of impotence in chronic alcoholics is not fully understood. The role of peripheral neurologic changes is a major factor. In addition, many chronic alcoholics with cirrhosis have gynecomastia and testicular atrophy. Despite these signs, there is usually a normal plasma estradiol. The initial alcohol-induced hypoandrogenicity may continue until chronic irreversible liver damage produces irreversible testicular germ-cell injury. Chronic alcohol ingestion in women has been noted to result in lowered sexual desire and anorgasmia. Acute alcohol ingestion lowers blood flow to the vaginal area, which may be analogous to the finding that high alcohol blood levels diminish erectile response in males.

Treatment considerations. Sexual rehabilitation of individuals suffering from chronic alcoholism demands direct confrontation of the problem and the promotion of sobriety. Drugs utilized for alcoholism may produce difficulties.

Antabuse has been reported to produce impotence. Certain neuroleptic medications occasionally used in the treatment of anxiety states from alcoholism, such as Mellaril, may further foster sexual dysfunction. Ongoing support and managment as well as utilization of sexual marital counseling are useful adjuncts in the treatment of the primary disease of alcoholism (Murphy et al., 1980).

SUMMARY

Sexuality in the medically ill is an important issue, even though some patients may minimize its significance (Wise, 1980). This may be appropriate in the face of other concerns, as well as due to their own history, but it may also indicate a denial and a sense of hopelessness associated with feelings that they are unattractive and rejected. The clinician should listen patiently and allow the individual to reveal fears and concerns. While sexuality is only one area of psychosocial concern to the individual with a chronic medical illness, failure to investigate and, if necessary, to treat this issue may promote despair, fear, and isolation. For these reasons, comprehensive care mandates evaluation and, if possible, treatment of sexual dysfunction in the medically ill (Wise, 1977b).

REFERENCES

Abel, G.G., Becker, J.V., & Cunningham-Rathner, J. (1982). Differential diagnosis of impotence in diabetes. *Neurology and Urodynamics, 1,* 57-69.

Abplanalp, J.M., Rose, R.M., Donnelly, A.F., & Livingston-Vaughn, L. (1979). Psychoendocrinology of the menstrual cycle: II. The relationship between enjoyment of activities, moods, and reproductive hormones. *Psychosomatic Medicine, 43,* 199-214.

Blumer, D. (1971). The sexual behavior of patients with temporal lobe epilepsy before and after surgical treatment. *Journal of Neuro-visceral Relations, 10,* p. 469-476.

Brown, R.S., Haddox, V., Posada, A., & Robio, A. (1972). Social and psychological adjustment following pelvic exenteration. *American Journal of Obstetrics and Gynecology, 114,* 162-171.

Chen, J.C., Vidt, D.G., Zorn, E.M., Hallberg, M.C., & Wieland, R.G. (1970). Pituitary-Leydig cell function in uremic males. *Journal of Clinical Endocrinology, 31,* 14-17.

d'A Semple, P., Watson, W.S., Beastall, G.H., Bethel, M.I., Grant, M.K., & Hoone, R. (1979). Diet, absorption and hormone studies in relation to body weight in obstructive airways disease. *Thorax, 34,* 783-788.

Davidson, J.M., Camargo, C.A., & Smith, E.R. (1979). Effects of androgen on sexual behavior in hypogonadal men. *Journal of Endocrinology and Metabolism, 48,* 955-958.

Decker, W.H., & Schwartzman, L. (1962). Sexual function following treatment for carcinoma of the cervix. *Obstetrics and Gynecology, 83,* 401-411.

Donahue, V.C., & Knapp, R.C. (1977). Sexual rehabilitation of gynecologic cancer patients. *American Journal of Obstetrics and Gynecology, 49,* 118-121.

Ellenberg, M. (1980). Sexual dysfunction in diabetic patients. *Annals of Internal Medicine, 92*(part 2), 331-333.

Farberow, N.L., & Nehemkis, A.M. (1979). Indirect self-destructive behavior in patients with Buerger's disease. *Journal of Personality Assessment, 43,* 86-96.

Gad-Luther, I. (1980). Sexual dysfunctions of the alcoholic. *Sexuality and Disability, 3,* 273-290.

Hellerstein, H.D., & Friedman, E.G. (1970). Sexual activity and the postcoronary patient. *Scandanavian Journal of Rehabilitation Medicine, 2*(2), 109.

Hollander, M.H., & Meker, A.J. (1976). The wish to be held and the wish to hold in men and women. *Archives of General Psychiatry, 33,* 49-51.

Jamison, K.R., Wellison, D.K., & Pasnau, R.O. (1978). Psychosocial aspects of mastectomy: The woman's perspective. *American Journal of Psychiatry, 135,* 432-436.

Kaplan, H.S. (1979). *Disorders of sexual desire.* New York: Brunner/Mazel.

Kolodny, R.C. (1971). Sexual dysfunction in diabetic females. *Diabetes, 20,* 557-559.

Koss, I., Updegroff, & Muffly, R.B. (1972). Sex in chronic obstructive pulmonary disease. *Medical Aspects of Human Sexuality, 7,* 33-38.

Laferla, J.J., Anderson, D.L., & Schalch. (1978). Psychoendocrine response to sexual arousal in human males. *Psychosomatic Medicine,40,* 166-172.

Leiber, L., Plumb, M., Gerstenzag, M.L., & Holland, J. (1976). The communication of affection between cancer patients and their spouses. *Psychosomatic Medicine, 38(6),* 379-389.

Levine, S. (1982). The biology of sex. In I.M. Zales (Ed.), *Eating, sleeping and sexuality* (pp. 203-225). New York: Brunner/Mazel.

Levy, N.B., & Wynbrandt, G.D. (1975). The quality of life on maintenance hemodialysis. *Lancet,* June 14, *1* (7920), 1328-30.

Maruto, T., & Osborne, D. (1978). Sexual dysfunction following therapy for cancer of the prostate, testis and penis. *Frontiers of Radiation Therapy and Oncology, 11,* 42-57.

McLane, M., Krop, H., & Mehta, J. (1986). Psychosexual adjustment and counseling after myocardial infarction. *Annals of Internal Medicine, 92,* 514-519.

Mills, J.L., Harlap, S., & Harley, E.E. (1981). Should coitus late in pregnancy be discouraged. *Lancet,* July 18, *2* (8238), 136-138.

Milne, J.G., Golden, J.S., & Fibus, L. (1978). Sexual dysfunction of renal transplant recipients. *Journal of Nervous & Mental Disease, 166,* 402-407.

Murphy, W.D., Coleman, E., Hoon, E., & Scott, C. (1980). Sexual dysfunction and treatment in alcoholic women. *Sexuality and Disability, 3,* 240-255.

Papadopoulos, C., Larrimore, P., Cardin, S., & Shelley, S.I. (1980). Sexual concerns and needs of the postcoronary patient's wife. *Archives of Internal Medicine, 140,* 38-41.

Persky, H., Dreisbach, L., Miller, W.R., O'Brien, C.P., Khan, M.A., Lief, H.A., Charneo, N., & Strauss, D. (1982). The relation of plasma androgen levels to sexual behaviors and attitudes of women. *Psychosomatic Medicine, 44,* 305-319.

Procci, W., Hoffman, K., & Chatterjee, S.A. (1978). Sexual functioning of renal transplant recipients. *Journal of Nervous and Mental Disease, 166,* 402-407.

Richards, J.S. (1980). Sex and arthritis. *Sex and Disability, 3,* 97-99.

Robinson, R.G. (1983). Sexual differentiation of the brain and human sexual behavior. In J.K. Meyers, C.W. Schmidt, & T.N. Wise (Eds.), *Clinical Management of Sexual Disorders.* Baltimore, MD: Williams and Wilkins.

Schreiner-Engel, P., Schiavi, R.C., & Smith, I.I. (1981). Sexual arousability and the menstrual cycle. *Psychosomatic Medicine, 43,* 199-214.

Seibel, M.M., Freeman, M.G., & Graves, W.L. (1980). Carcinoma of the cervix and sexual function. *Obstetrics & Gynecology, 55,* 484-487.

Sha'ked, A. (1978). *Human sexuality in physical and mental illness and disabilities.* Bloomington, IN: Indiana University Press.

Strickler, R.C., Woolever, C.A., Johnson, M., Goldstein, M., & Deveber. G. (1974). Serum gonadotropin patterns in patients with chronic renal failure on hemodialysis. *Gynecological Investigations, 5,(4),* 185-198.

Wise, T.N. (1977a). Sexual functioning in the hyperobese. *Obesity and Bariatrics Medicine, 6,* 84-85.

Wise, T.N. (1977b). Sexuality in chronic illness. *Primary Care, 4,* 199-208.

Wise, T.N. (1980). Sexuality in the aging and incapacitated. *Psychiatric Clinics of North America, 3,* 173-189.

Witkin, M.H.(1978). Psychosexual counseling of the mastectomy patient. *Journal of Sex and Marital Therapy, 4,* 20-28.

Chapter 5

The Social Context of Sexual Functioning: Lifestyles, Values, Behavior and Gender Roles

Roger H. Rubin

INTRODUCTION

Social and behavioral scientists are attempting to understand the powerful force called sexuality that sustains the survival of the species yet evokes intense emotional and intellectual debate. Murstein (1970) notes that mammalian human beings are subject to biology, but not bound by it. They can suppress their sexual urge by will. "The attempt to successfully take into account the pushes of biological inheritance, his own wishes, and those stemming from his social environment constitute the warp and woof of the continuously changing sexual image of man" (Murstein, 1970, p. 121). The eminent sociologist Pitirim A. Sorokin, writing in 1956, even predicted sexual anarchy and eventual collapse of the nation if the "sexualization" of American society continued. He claimed Americans were becoming obsessed, sexual addicts. Sexual freedom was pushing the limits of safety and perhaps the time had arrived to fight back. The new sex freedom was one factor "in the drift toward social revolution and political disorder, toward international conflict, toward a general decline of creativity and irremediable decay of our culture" (Sorokin, 1956, p. 134).

Kinsey, Pomeroy and Martin (1948) maintained that the tension between highly restrictive sexual standards and the values of personal freedom and individuality created the primary characteristic of American sexuality. According to Money and Ehrhardt (1972) this public restrictiveness was important in shaping popular and private morality, yet it is in sharp contrast to the mass media's message of sexual pleasure. The sexuality portrayed in the "ideal culture" of norms and values and the actual experiences in the "real culture" reflect this discrepancy and represent the gap between "ought" and "actual" behavior of Americans.

Brown and Lynn (1966) and Gagnon and Simon (1973) contend that sexual attitudes are the products of social learning and therefore represent a great range of opinion. For example, Gaylin (1982) described adultery as "the most dramatic breach of confidence or trust in a marriage...which strikes at the very heart of the union" (Gaylin, 1982, p. 51). Clark (1977) pointed out that, "We do not become jealous or panic if a spouse shares himself or herself in other ways, but we have been trained to respond with alarm if sex is shared elsewhere. Love is expressed by the quality of hundreds of daily interactions, not just in sexual intercourse. But programming does not yield to mere factual truth. We are apt to cling to the belief that love and sex are synonymous, and that if one's lover or spouse is sharing sex with someone else, presumably they are sharing love" (Clark, 1977, p. 143-144).

Sex, then, appears to be special, mysterious, private, and unique. It can both enrich and destroy our lives. Sex exposes the most intimate side of who we are. Perhaps it is the momentary loss of physical and mental control during orgasm that frightens us. After all, can a woman be a good mother and succumb to the animalistic yearnings of her sexual drive? We think of pure thoughts as being nonsexual, and forbidden words are sex words both smutty and dirty. Some are concerned that knowledge about sex may corrupt the young.

This fear of the power of uncontrolled sexuality eroding the social system and individual personalities stands in contrast to those who perceive contemporary sex standards, rooted in the past, as already an array of irrational and contradictory ideologies, often repressive and ultimately confusing and destructive. The inconsistencies between what is publicly prescribed and actual behavior creates a sexually schizophrenic society, which produces a clinically needy population.

THE CONTEMPORARY SOCIAL CONTEXT OF SEX

Technological Change

Sexual change cannot be examined in isolation from the situations in which it occurs. The social context within which the individual determines her or his sexual participation has been profoundly altered by an array of technological events. For example, medical advances allow more Americans to live longer than ever before. Such longevity has changed the expectations for length of marriage and put a strain on traditional values of fidelity. The number of golden wedding anniversaries being celebrated today exceeds that of previous generations. Yet, how realistic is it to expect most couples to live together in an exclusive monogamous relationship for 50 or more years? Toward the end of World War Two, medical advances provided penicillin with its social and health impact on venereal disease. The current herpes and AIDS epidemics are also beginning to have significant impact. Contraceptive technology has advanced and become more readily available than at any previous time.

Contraception coupled with legalized abortion has allowed women to control their fecundity. This leads to greater equality in sexual bargaining between males and females. Increasing recognition is being given to the need for negotiation and dialogue between the sexes rather than an assignation of fixed and permanent sexual roles. Masculine and feminine gender-role scripts for sexual expression may become more similar as such discussion persists and may already be evidenced by increasing female sexual activity. Likewise, there is increasing similarity in gender-role scripts for men and women in the world of work. Along with the advances in technology which have provided economic self-sufficiency for individuals, this has led to a weakening of the economic basis of the familial bond. This is true especially for women.

Nutritional advances also are contributing to change. The earlier beginnings of menarche for American females is one example, falling from approximately age 15 in 1900 to age 12 today. This frequently ignored factor in the debate on adolescent pregnancy cannot be overlooked, considering the increased sexual activity of teenagers and the delaying of their entrance into marriage.

Benign-appearing inventions have had a profound effect on sexuality. The mass-produced automobile provided Americans with a vehicle to release them from their immediate surroundings and provided them simultaneously with a place to express their sexual longing. The motel was its by-product. Likewise, Melville (1983) observed that telephones contributed to a decline in parental control over the dating system.

Radio, television, movies, and magazines brought a mass communications information explosion, helping to create new images of love, sex, and romance, and they made available sexually explicit materials such as guides to masturbatory and lovemaking techniques. Video recorders, tapes, and cable television are the latest providers of mass-marketed sexually oriented merchandise. Even computers can be utilized to establish a format for the day's sexual activities or to play games that assist in communicating sexual desires between verbally reticent partners.

Urbanization has also had a pervasive influence on modern sexuality. It provided anonymity to individuals and freed them from the social controls of the rural, small-town setting. The social invention of dating and its acceptance by the 1920s was a result of the need to institutionalize a method of mate selection among increasing numbers of strangers with no closely shared social roots. Today, singles communities with their implicit suggestion of permissive sexual conduct are the latest manifestation of the free life-styles of the urban center.

New work modalities, such as the flextime practices of the federal government and the increasing feasibility of working at home via the computer provide further options for physical and emotional intimacy. More leisure time, shorter work weeks, and earlier retirements also expand our opportunities beyond the restrictions of work roles.

Technology has given many people the affluence that provides them with opportunities to indulge themselves and explore new paths to personal fulfillment.
How wisely we utilize these new options is a fundamental challenge of our time.

Social Trends

The extraordinary acceleration of change during the twentieth century has
produced several trends that have changed sexual opportunities and behaviors.
The increasing divorce rate has catapulted a large number of obviously non-
virginal participants into the dating market. Unfortuantely, virtually no scientific research has been done on postmarital dating patterns and the social dilemmas involved in the sexual lives of the divorced. However, it is probably not too
farfetched to speculate that the sexual participation of the previously married
includes dynamics that are considerably different from their premarital court-
ships. For example, those with children find themselves contending with everything from acceptable sleeping arrangements with partners to seeking advice
from older children as to the appropriateness of a weekend tryst with a lover.

The delaying of first marriages by both males and females has extended the
premarital period. This extension reflects in part the desire for more education,
travel, independent living, and the pursuit of economic opportunity. Among
members of this group we might also find a less reticent attitude about sex. A
frequent goal is to combine personal autonomy with a fulfilling sexual life, even
though they do not always achieve this. The slowed pace of remarriage after
divorce also implies increasing numbers of nonmarital sexual activities.

The continuing influx of women into the work force strengthens the bargaining power of women regarding sex. The traditional exchange of male economic
resources in return for female sexual favors is altered when economic opportunity becomes more equally balanced between genders. Sexual intimacy as a
more mutually agreed-upon component of the dating relationship may emerge
as the necessity for sex as a token of exchange begins to diminish. Moreover,
the work trend assumes increasing social contact between men and women in
the workplace. The separation of work roles and private- life roles is a complicated issue, predicated partially on personal standards of self-discipline, values,
character, life circumstances, and so forth. However, it is possible that the workplace will not undermine marriage, but rather that it will serve as the forum to
bring out one's marital discontents and then will determine one's social and
sexual opportunities.

Approximately one fifth of American households today consist of one person. This figure includes never-married singles, divorced persons, widows and
widowers. The sexual opportunities of these individuals have been enlarged as
they maintain control over an unshared environment and invite into their lives
and homes those people they desire. This form of autonomy enhances the concept of personal privacy well beyond that of the more shared quarters of previous generations.

These various trends produce a dramatic pluralism in contemporary American life-styles. Although it remains true that the vast majority of Americans will get legally married and become parents, their lifelong profile will show an array of life-style experiences. People may choose different sexual life-styles at different stages of their lives to meet their relational and sexual needs adequately. With this in mind, then, perhaps a suggestion by Kassel (1970) to legalize polygyny over the age of 60 might not seem so outrageous.

Interpersonal Life-styles

Although much attention has been paid to the belief that the 1980s began as a more conservative political period than the past two decades, reality dictates otherwise in regard to interpersonal life-styles. What Toffler (1981) referred to as the de-massification of the society and the family has led to increasing diversification and choice. The needs of the individual have become primary. Compared to a decade ago, three times as many people are heterosexually cohabitating, twice as many are heading single parent households, stepfamily formation continues to increase, the singles population proliferates daily, dual work/career families multiply as women leave the home for the paid employment market, homosexuals increase their visibility, child-free and child-delayed marriages are popularized and romanticized, large numbers of post-child-rearing couples plan their futures, and social scientists speculate on the size of populations of communards, mate-swappers, and group-marriage participants.

The previous discussion, on the sweeping changes in American society, described the foundation from which today's multitude of life-style choices arose. Admittedly many find themselves in life-style situations not of their choosing; that has always been true and will remain so. What has changed are the possibilities for people to select consciously from a variety of increasingly socially acceptable options to traditional marriage.

Sexually, the traditional nuclear family was predicated on exclusivity and male dominance. This has been somewhat tempered by the paid "working wife" of the contemporary nuclear family. The increased emphasis on female sexuality, coupled with women's new economic and social supports, has induced more sexual equality, or at least expectations of such. However, the concept of exclusivity remains a mutually shared understanding. Moreover, several interesting subtypes of the contemporary nuclear family have arisen, including commuter, long-distance, or weekend marriages where sexual congress becomes more restricted and less spontaneous. The rules of exclusivity remain the same in these subtypes, and recent research (Gerstel & Fross, 1983) indicates no greater chance of having an affair in these than in more conventional marriages. Some couples who report themselves to be happily married have established separate housing for themselves in the same general locale, even though the bond of sexual exclusivity is assumed to remain intact. Such couples are referred to as "apartners."

The sexual dynamics of stepfamilies have usually focussed on incidences of incest between stepparent and child. The growing number of "unrelated" males living in households and families that include teenage females has claimed the greatest attention. The sexual tensions between unrelated stepsiblings has been virtually ignored. Of course, the presumption of spousal sexual exclusivity in the stepfamily remains the same as that of first marriages.

Singles represent a heterogeneous variety of sexual life-styles. Included are the "swinging singles" and their ideological openness to new sexual partners. However, there are many celibate singles, ranging from members of the clergy to those simply reticent about sexual activities. Although steeped in popular myth, little is known about the sexual patterns of the divorced, and less about the in-limbo circumstances of those who are separated or have been deserted. Singlehood resulting from the death of a spouse is a common situation, especially for older females. For some the loss of their partner may mean the termination of their sexual interests, whereas others may discreetly turn to autoerotic behavior or to a new sex partner. The chances of the latter occurring are limited by the scarcity of single older men and societal prejudices regarding the appropriateness of sexual activity among the nation's elders.

Unmarried heterosexuals living together without benefit of marriage have been relabeled from living-in-sin to cohabiting. This semantic change partially captures the significant change of societal attitude over the past two decades. As an area of emerging research, the cohabitation of unmarried heterosexuals has suffered from the usual vagueness of definition and from population parameters that often plague and challenge the social and behavioral scientist. However, there is general agreement that such dyadic formations have increased dramatically, and recent census figures indicate that 3% of the American adult populace is currently cohabiting (Macklin, 1983). This is roughly three times the rate of cohabitation a decade ago. Macklin (1978) earlier reported that one fourth of college undergraduates in the United States will have experienced heterosexual cohabitation by graduation time. Ignored in all these figures is homosexual cohabitation, a category of which we remain ignorant. Moreover, speculation reigns about the sex lives of cohabitators. A recent comprehensive review by Macklin (1983) of research on nonmarital heterosexual cohabitation barely mentions the quality of sexual relationships.

Census experts have described the increase in single-parent households as the most dramatic social development of the 1970s. The rapid rise is due primarily to increased divorce and out-of-wedlock births, including a threefold increase in births among unmarried American teenagers from 1960 to 1980. Trying to explain the pregnancy trend among single teenagers in sociopsychological terms underscores the complexity of deciphering the sexual and childbearing decision-making process. The work of Zelnik and Kantner (1972, 1977, 1978, 1979, 1980) and their associates has provided some of the most helpful insights. Ignorance about contraception, human sexuality, and physiology is apparent among the females in their samples. But the far more intractable issues lie in the self-concept of these females and in the social environment within which they dwell. Often lacking a vision of future opportunities, many place themselves on a path of limited economic, educational, and interpersonal growth. Some teenagers even report a conscious desire to become pregnant, perhaps out of a desire to have a child to love or to love them, something to do, or as a symbol of womanhood. The social environment may also promote sexual activity as a commodity in bargaining for material goods and emotional needs, especially when financial resources are scarce. These factors are deeply rooted and the circumstances are difficult to alter.

Child-free marriages have thus far not been established as a distinct variable in examining sexual relationships. For example, we have often drawn on circumstantial evidence regarding sex among postchildrearing couples. For some middle-aged women the cessation of menses may increase sexual interest as fear of pregnancy declines. For others the ending of the childbearing years justifies the termination of sexual activity. This may also include men. Others may seek new and more youthful sexual partners, contributing to the estimated one fourth of all divorces now being filed by middle-aged couples. The lack of developmental, lifespan longitudinal data on the evolution of the sex lives of couples stifles any more data-based discussion.

Another form of child-free marriage is that in which children have been either voluntarily or involuntarily not conceived. Studies of the marital success of such couples compared with that of those couples who have children appear contradictory (Veevers, 1983). The methodology is often weak, the samples not clearly distinguishable, and little is written that specifically focuses on the sexual interactions of voluntarily and involuntarily childless marriages versus marriages with children.

The term *open marriage* received much public attention during the 1970s. It was popularized by the best-selling book *Open Marriage* (1972) by George and Nena O'Neill. Interestingly, they assiduously avoided the topic of sex, leaving it primarily to the imagination of the reader. However, by advocating the loosening of the stranglehold of traditional husband-wife roles, their ideas were easily distorted by many, as a license for extramarital sexual indulgences. This, coupled with the reports of mate swapping during the 1970s, gave new dimension and meaning to the word *affair.* This was consensual extramarital sex, a clear violation of traditional marital expectations and values. Estimates of mate swapping run from 0.5% to 4% of the adult population. The "institutionalizing" of this behavior can be seen in the clubs, magazines, and formal rituals and rules adopted by the "swinging" population. However, for most couples, "cheating" will remain a clandestine adventure. See Weis (1983) and Glass and Wright (Chapter 13 of this volume) for extensive reviews of this topic.

On the more exotic end of the life-style continuum, and perhaps the next step from mate-swapping, is group marriage. The most definitive book on this topic is *Group Marriage* (1973) by Larry and Joan Constantine. Although this practice is rare in the United States, the study of group marriage may still provide valuable insights into the state of American family life. Most groups are composed of triads and quads, often with legally married couples involved. Although shared economic and childbearing responsibilities are stated as among the practical reasons for forming such alliances, the emotional and sexual components often receive the most attention. Sexual arrangements may include group sex, dyadic relationships, and heterosexual and/or homosexual couplings. The consequences of all this on the participant are not well known, but the long-term stability of group marriage is quite tenuous.

The term *commune* has been applied to a plethora of group-living arrangements where those involved often share an ideological, economic, social, political, religious, and/or sexual reason for living together. Some are sexually pair-bonded and others are sexually open. Whether the extent of sexual gratification is any more or less than in more conventional relationships is not known.

Finally, over the last two decades, there has been a dramatic increase in the visibility of the homosexual in America. This has led to a heightened interest in clinical and descriptive material on male homosexuals and on lesbians. The assortment of interpersonal relationships found in these populations challenges the stereotypic images of butch-femme lesbian couples and male partners who model themselves after traditional male-female roles. Yet, once recognizing this great variability, the next step is to determine any qualitative emotional differences between homosexual and heterosexual couples, including sexual satisfaction. Other questions abound. What should we know about the evolution of the sex lives of long-term committed lesbians and gay males? What are the consequences of sexual nonexclusivity among lesbians and gays? How do heterosexually married gays and lesbians deal with their sexual desires?

Clearly this proliferation of life-styles raises many new issues for the sex therapist and other clinicians. A recognition of the increased presence and social tolerance of these life-styles may impact on who presents for treatment as well as on the selection of treatment modalities and approaches. These changes also represent a challenge to many psychotherapists' beliefs and values regarding sexuality and bonding.

IDEOLOGY AND SEX IN A CHANGING SOCIETY

The United States has undergone enormous technological and life-style changes, particularly during the 20th century; many of these changes have affected sexual behavior and relationships. How successful the society has been in absorbing these changes may be reflected upon by comparing American sexual ideologies with actual practices.

American Sexual Ideologies and Behavior

American sexual beliefs are rooted in the Judeo-Christian heritage. Jesus Christ, a Palestinian Jew, was born at a time when his people believed everything that came from God was good, including sex. It is not surprising, then, that Christ said little about sex. Restrictions on sexual expression were established later by disciples and theologians. According to Whitehurst (1972), sexual self-denial was a way to sacrifice for the second coming of Christ. Sex represented desires of the flesh and became equated with sin, and virginity was associated with purity and spiritual salvation. Judaic and Christian theology eventually placed sex solely within marriage, and in Christianity "sexual relations were condemned except for procreation" (Murstein, 1974, p. 86). Even sex in marriage was considered shameful. Celibacy was elevated above marriage, and Bardis says that "sex was condemned with boundless fanaticism" (Bardis, 1969, p. 185). He maintained that Christianity's disapproval of sex led to demonic beliefs regarding carnal love. Murstein (1974) described one bizarre Church edict that male and female corpses could not be buried next to one another until she decomposed!

Such attitudes also reflected a contempt for women. She was thought to be the root of all evil, since it was Eve who had lured Adam to sin in the Garden of Eden. "In sum, most Church leaders saw women as weak, frail, slow-witted, simple, unstable, deceptive..." (Murstein, 1974, p. 94). However, much of this negativism preceded Christianity, and in its favor Murstein (1974) argued that Christianity improved the position of women by criticizing the double standard and making marriage a sacrament.

North America was to be settled by a variety of ethnic, racial, and religious groups carrying with them often conflicting views of sexuality. Columbus's encounters with nude Indian women illustrates a clash of cultures. Later, black slaves, as well as American Indians, Oriental and South American laborers, and many European nationalities experienced blatant sexual exploitation by mainstream American societal groups (Francoeur, 1982). A more popular image in America is that of the conservative Puritans. The Puritans believed sex was only for reproduction within the context of marriage. How shocking, then, to discover that a scarcity of women led to illicit sexual intercourse (Morgan, 1978) and to the not-uncommon practice of bestiality (Francoeur, 1982). However, reality for most Puritans probably fell between these extremes. Morgan (1978) maintained that realistically, sex was accepted as long as it did not interfere with religion. Within this religious framework, even sexual pleasure was not denied and violations of the strictest sexual codes were treated leniently. The Puritans recognized human fallibility and were not as rigid and cold as commonly depicted.

Conflicting sexual customs developed in America due to a lack of privacy in the small homes of the early pioneers. Strict societal and religious views regarding nonmarital and nonreproductive sex coexisted with the reality of chamber pots and bundling boards. A bundling poem captures the spirit of the time:

Since in a bed a man and a maid
May bundle and be chaste,
It does no good to burn out wood
It is a needless waste.

(From Bardis, 1969, p. 1K).

Francoeur (1982) describes sexual mores in the 18th century as paradoxical. In the 1770s and 1780s, 30% of brides were pregnant at marriage (Rothman, 1983). Francoeur (1982) reported that of 200 people joining a Groton, Connecticut church, between 1761 and 1775, one third admitted fornicating. Skolnick (1980) estimated premarital pregnancies at 10% of all first births in America during the 18th century.

Finally, the extramarital escapades of such founding fathers as Benjamin Franklin and Thomas Jefferson belie the idea that even among the most prominent citizens there was always a strict following of the ideological dictates of the time. Indeed, according to Francoeur (1981) these men may have been following the English and French aristocracy's idea of marital flexibility rather than the more rigid American beliefs.

Francoeur (1982) linked economic conditions and sexual values in American history. To illustrate, in the 19th century, the financial panic of 1837 led to "The Second Great Awakening of Protestantism" wherein revivalist ministers proclaimed the panic to be a punishment from God, who demanded more conservative sexual behavior. Simultaneously, another trend emerged from religious belief justifying sexual experimentation. With the "Second Coming of Christ" everyone should fully love everyone else, including sexual loving. These dichotomous religious interpretations were reflected in some of the communal movements of the 19th century. For example, John Humphrey Noyes' Oneida Community (1831-1881) abolished sexual exclusivity in marriage.

The Victorian period (reign of Queen Victoria, 1837-1901) is thought of as a time of sexual repression involving innocent childhood and female nonsexuality. "Most of our negative sex attitudes came...from the Victorians" (Francoeur, 1981, p. 7). The era was rooted in a rising middle class whose affluence promoted the industrialization that increasingly took men out of the home and placed women in a non-income-producing domestic environment. Industrialization stimulated sex-role segregation. Barker-Benfield (1978) believed men saw the world as a competitive battlefield, whereas women were idealized as the protectors of morality.

What was considered appropriate sexual behavior for males and females became increasingly restrictive. In retrospect, the antisexual ideology at times reached hysterical proportions. Masturbation was seen as destructive to men's energies, and the number of orgasms and ejaculations was considered finite for each individual. Victorian sex expert Dr. William Acton said unchecked masturbation could lead to "...frequently flaccid penis, a permanently sunken visage, epilepsy, insanity, heart disorders, and tuberculosis" (Murstein, 1974, p. 252). A masturbator would pass on such maladies to his innocent offspring as well (Nass, Libby, & Fisher, 1981). Crude and cruel antimasturbation devices were marketed. Part of the context of these concerns was that until the end of the 1800s it was not known how conception occurred (Family Life Educator, 1982). For those who believed sperm contained all the ingredients to make a human, masturbation was the equivalent of murder (Nass, Libby, & Fisher, 1981).

An obsessive desire to control women and a sexually paranoid atmosphere is vividly reflected by the gynecological surgery of the Victorian period. Barker-Benfield (1978) points out that a paradox gripped the sexes. Men feared that women, although supposedly sexless, were potentially quite sexual and had to be controlled. Thus, female masturbation was to be abhorred because it represented sexual desire. Men's anxieties were most brutally manifested by the doctrine that the emotional state of females could be controlled by altering their physiology. According to Barker-Benfield (1978), clitoridectomy was performed in the United States from around 1867 to perhaps 1925. Circumcision of females was also practiced in the 1890s and continued as late as 1937. Female castration, invented in 1872 by Robert Battey of Georgia, was widespread. "Castrated women became 'tractable, orderly, industrious and cleanly.' A wife should be a faithful servant, as tractable and undemanding as a castrated animal" (Barker-Benfield, 1978, p. 390). Although castration ended a woman's chances for pregnancy, the ideology of the period paradoxically promoted impregnation as another way of controlling women.

Finally, Shorter (1981) contends that many women had aversions to sexuality, but that these aversions were a product not only of such excessive procedures, but also of the genital disorders they suffered due to medical ignorance. It was less ideological subjugation than it was the real bodily pain they suffered that generated sexual anxiety and discomfort.

On the other hand, some Victorian beliefs did encompass the idea that females were sexual; this is often ignored in examining this period. Following the Civil War, Degler (1983) implies that sexual ideology and medical opinion regarding female sexuality fell into two camps: "...the 'idealists' who defined women as sexually pure, morally superior creatures, and the 'realists' who concluded — as much from observation as theory — that women as well as men experience and act on sexual feelings" (Degler, 1978, p. 406). Indeed, Degler (1978) doubts that there was a 19th century consensus on female sexuality. He cites medical literature directed at urban, middle-class women that encouraged sexual activity at the risk of losing one's health! Much 19th century writing, Degler (1978) maintains, assumes the existence of strong female sexual feelings and that in practice women were sexually expressive. He notes the work of Dr. Clelia Duel Mosher, whose rare questionnaire data from Victorian women indicate considerable acceptance of sexuality. Therefore, he argues that the negative ideas concerning women's sexuality were not a consensual ideology and did not represent the prevalent view or practice.

In spite of the current confusion over prevalent beliefs in the 19th century, the Victorian period did bring greater sexual restraint to the United States. The range of sexual activities decreased over the course of the century. By the end of the century more women embraced "the central tenet of Victorian sexual ideology—female passionlessness" (Cott, in Rothman, 1983, p. 399). Premarital intercourse was increasingly replaced by "the invention of petting" (Rothman, 1983, p. 400). The decline of bridal pregnancies during the latter part of the Victorian period was partial evidence of the increasing restrictiveness.

Thus, the Victorian era was full of contradictions. The prevailing antisexual ideology should not be interpreted as having been pervasive; actual behavior often did not follow ideology.

At the turn of the 20th century the works of Sigmund Freud, Havelock Ellis, Margaret Sanger and other pioneer researchers, educators, and social activists promoted acceptance of the idea that sexual interest is normal for both sexes. This was also a period of advancement in the medical sciences, sociology, psychology, and anthropology, further eroding the myths and ignorance surrounding human sexuality. Feminists began attacking the image of Victorian womanhood at the beginning of the century. However, it was World War I that served as a catalyst for sexual change, as soldiers were exposed to different cultures, as well as venereal diseases, and women increasingly went into the paid work force. Francoeur (1982) reports that divorce and premarital and extramarital sex increased from 1915 to 1920. In response to these changes, state legislatures passed laws limiting contraception and nonprocreative sex. Prohibitionist Anthony Comstock attempted to repress sex legally by outlawing the mailing of "obscene" material and contraceptive information; these laws were not overturned until 1957. These events may be interpreted as a panicked stampede to institutionalize antisexual ideology.

The "roarin' 20s" brought new freedoms and opportunities. Clothing and dance styles changed, secularization increased, women were more emancipated, disposable sanitary pads were made available, radios and automobiles became commonplace, and urbanization and industrialization advanced. Certainly the overt image projected during this period was one of less repressed emotional and physical expression.

With the Great Depression of the 1930s a reversal occurred. Unemployment, poverty, and the unpredictability of the social and economic order were not conducive to a liberal sexual ideology. Once again, some claimed the economic depression was God's punishment for the excesses of the previous decade. Sexual repression, at least with respect to the public ideology, prevailed again.

Francoeur (1982) describes the 1940s as a period of continued sexual hypocrisy. This was again a decade of war, and again soldiers were in contact with different cultures and women were required in the labor force. But now penicillin was available to combat venereal disease, and the relationshp between the sexes began to shift once more. The publication of Alfred Kinsey's *Sexual Behavior in the Human Male* (Kinsey, Pomeroy, & Martin) in 1948 exposed the myth of "puritan" America. The discovery that males were very sexually active prior to, during, and beyond their marriages illustrated, as before, the contradictions between public ideology and private behavior.

Kinsey had "shocked" the nation in 1948; he shocked it more so in 1953 with the publication of *Sexual Behavior in the Human Female*. This is often seen as a key event in the changing American sexual climate. Statistics indicating the loss of virginity by 30% of unmarried American women before age 23 was only one of the dramatic findings. It was further evidence that the behavior of many Americans did not conform to public moral ideology.

By the 1960s the scene had been set for more profound changes in how Americans viewed sex. The birth control pill became available and the perception that sex was recreational as well as procreational became more evident and more practical. The number of individuals who were involved in premarital and extramarital sexual activities increased. By the late 1960s images of free love, hippies and flower children abounded. Masters and Johnson became household names, as middle-class Americans gobbled up copies of the esoteric medical text *Human Sexual Response* (1966) and later the more readable *Human Sexual Inadequacy* (1970). A multitide of social-sexual taboos collapsed, ranging from nudity on the stage to the availability and mass consumption of sexually explicit material.

The 1970s was also an era of continued change. For example, the Supreme Court overturned abortion statutes in 1973. The power of the gay rights movement asserted itself, as male homosexual and lesbian groups formed and individual gays stepped "out of the closet." It was also a decade of mate-swapping, swingers, ever-increasing divorce rates, and rising opposition to many of the sexual changes of the previous decades.

The 1980s may prove to be a decade of political conflict over sexual issues. However, once more there may be many discrepancies between ideological struggles and personal behaviors.

The Sexually Schizophrenic Society

We have seen in the preceding discussion that ideology and actual behavior often differ. Francoeur (1982) says that we have formal values (what we think is right or wrong) and informal values (what people actually do). Both sets of values are valid sources for social analysis and can be viewed as distinct phenomena. But because we say one thing and do another, it is a potential source of guilt, anxiety, personal conflict and confusion. Using the word *schizophrenic* as an adjective and in a pejorative manner, we may speak of a sexually schizophrenic society. The concept may assist in explaining why so many people are sexually disturbed and in need of therapy.

References to a sexually schizophrenic society are not new. Gordon (1978) uses the term in discussing the sexual ambiguity and contradictions of 19th-century America. A decade ago, Whitehurst (1972) described Americans as living in a sexually polarized society. "On the one hand it seems sexually obsessed, tending by indirect and subtle means to give sexual messages, while on the other it is often sex-denying in terms of formal socialization procedures" (Whitehurst, 1972, p. 2). Recently Derek Freeman criticized Margaret Mead's contention, drawn from her Samoan studies, that free sex and a desire for virginity can coexist. "Surely no human population could be so cognitively disoriented as to conduct their lives in such a schizophrenic way" (Freeman, 1983, p. 69). In his book *Sexual Bargaining,* Scanzoni (1982) underscored the frustration of social scientists in studying the lack of correspondence between stated preferences and actual behavior.

Examples abound to document the existence of the sexually schizophrenic society. The following discussion describes some.

The increasing nonmarital cohabitation rate in the United States was noted earlier. Yet, much of this behavior, especially among the young and elderly, tends to be kept secret from family members. College students who fear discovery often keep two residences, one serving as an "empty" address to ward off suspicious parents. In the true spirit of the double-standard, women are much more likely to deceive their parents than are males, who probably anticipate greater social tolerance of their behavior. Sadly, one of the major complaints that students have about the cohabitation experience is that they could not share this significant occurrence with their parents. The charade of parents denying the sexuality of their children and children denying the sexuality of their parents is common in spite of the frequency of sexual activity before marriage, in marriage, between marriages, after marriage, and without marriage.

Senior-citizen cohabitators also use various ploys when their children or grandchildren come to visit the retirement community. Ageism in our society may deprive the young from recognizing the need for physical intimacy among the elderly, further promoting discomfort and embarrassment among older Americans that such needs exist, and leading them to mask actual sexual behavior.

Highly sexually active unmarried people who are not cohabitating may be called *swinging singles;* their free life-style has been popularized by the mass media. In the United States, one can be raised with a celibate ideology, become a sexual swinger, and find praise for both! However, the sexual problems and anxieties of singles are often ignored by researchers and the public. The most common noncoital sexual activity is masturbation and, although frequently practiced, especially by singles, it is still rarely discussed. The recent herpes and AIDS epidemics may have at least contributed to more realistic concerns regarding the sexuality of single people.

The term *premarital sex* refers to a wide variety of people and situations. What peculiar messages are derived from an ideology that does not distinguish between the sexual relations of two 14-year-olds and the sexual activities of two unmarried 25- year-olds? Although there may be more tolerance for the latter relationship, the abstinence standard is the same. In addition, the divorced, widowed, and separated are publicly denied their sexuality, but privately they must contend with personal feelings and leering societal stereotypes that mock the celibate ideology.

Today the majority of states still have archaic sex laws that would punish consenting adults, and even married couples, for indulging in their favorite sexual acts. If these laws were enforced, the majority of Americans would be in jail by age 25, serving long sentences. Next to treason, rape, murder, and kidnapping, violation of these laws has historically carried the heaviest maximum sentences, although they are rarely enforced or judgments made to the full extent allowed (Myricks & Rubin, 1977). Male homosexuals have suffered disproportionately from such laws. The homophobic fears of Americans characterize schizophrenic thinking. In spite of estimates that 5% to 10% of the general population is exclusively homosexual, sexual orientation remains one of the few categories that the nation has not seen fit to protect as a civil right.

The secretive sexual affair involving at least one married participant is a classic illustration of a schizophrenic situation. Decades ago, Kinsey et al. (1953) reported that by age 40 approximately one fourth of American women and almost half of American men had "cheated" on their spouses at least once. By breaking the vows of marital sexual exclusivity some people have had to lead "two lives" to conceal their infidelity.

Sexual silence in American families is common and indicates the strain and tension induced by an ideology that promotes the idea that sex belongs only in marriage. When the topic of sex is broached, often this ideology is stated and discussion is discouraged. With so little family discussion regarding sex, it is not surprising that we do not celebrate healthy sexual development as a positive life event. Greeting cards do not congratulate us on our first ejaculation or the start of menses! Instead these events are often hidden or dismissed with the presentation of a book and a curt "If you have any questions, ask." Sexual information may belong in the home, but that is not where it is to be found. Rather, most people learn from peers, books, and personal experiences.

Is it any wonder that Masters and Johnson observed that at any one time perhaps half the couples in the United States suffer from some form of sexual dysfunction? Sexual problems in marriage may be the clearest indicator of the confused state of American sexuality, for within the marital bond persons should feel relatively free to express themselves sexually. Yet impotence, lack of orgasm, premature ejaculation and sexual dissatisfactions are not unusual. Many of these sexual problems are psychosocial in origin rather than biophysical.

Sexual assaults in marriage reflect a more brutal side of the schizophrenic society. Once the marital boundary is crossed, acts that are prosecutable when they occur between unmarried individuals become legally and socially acceptable within the institution of marriage. This schizophrenic scenario is often defended in terms of marital rights, but the acts and victims remain the same. Fortunately, some legal changes are occurring today to ease this situation.

We are a nation reputedly concerned about teenage pregnancy, out- of-wedlock births, unplanned and unwanted conceptions, abortion, and sexually transmitted diseases — but we have only recently permitted the marketing of birth control devices on television. Americans spend an average of six hours a day in front of a television set, yet they will infrequently see a condom advertised.

Societal denial of sexuality operates elsewhere. The reproductive practice of artificial insemination by donor, conducted throughout this century, remains legally confused. It is often performed clandestinely. Yet the issues surrounding artificial insemination are simple in comparison to the complexities of the issues brought up by advancing reproductive technologies. Another example is the abortion controversy, in which males have been socially and psychologically ignored and legally dismissed. Perhaps this is consistent with the lack of attention paid to unwed fathers.

A related topic and consequence of our sexual behavior is childbearing. We live in a pronatalist society in which 90% of American women will bear a child during their lives. Parenthood remains a major rite-of-passage into adulthood. Yet, there is virtually no parenting education provided in the formal educational system. What little is available barely reaches males at all. This remains another paradox in a society that has prided itself on being child centered.

The ongoing debate over sex education and what it should encompass further illustrates sexual schizophrenia. Some fear that sexual information will lead to experimentation. Others contend that sexual behavior occurs regardless and education leads to responsibility. Resolving the debate is not the issue here. Rather, it is important to recognize that an educational solution to sexual social problems has faced tremendous opposition in a society that values education as an instrument in solving social problems.

Americans, however, may be getting an education of another sort. This comes from the booming video cassette and cable television market. Interest and sales in sexually oriented material have spurred discussions about how to control access to such products and, in reaction, outcries of invasion of personal privacy. This is only the latest twist in the schizophrenic scenario. Sex in the mass media titillates us in advertising, commerical programming, and now in sexually explicit visuals. Educators, politicians, and clerics will publicly denounce it and private consumption will continue.

A number of authors have suggested explanations for the existence of the sexually schizophrenic society. Francoeur (1983) postulates a dichotomy existing in the world view of humans. An absolutist view is that "...everything was created perfect and complete in the beginning of time, after which the human race fell from grace and began a painful, guilt-ridden, penitential return to Eden" (Francoeur, 1983, pp. 380-381). In this view, values are absolute and do not change over time. The counterpoint to the absolutist view is one which is process- oriented and sees the human race as constantly evolving and changing, hopefully improving as it moves toward a more perfect world. Values may also evolve and change. Due to social changes, tension between these two perspectives is increasingly manifesting itself. The clash between the absolutist fixed philosophy and the process-oriented world view can be seen in the debate on sexual morality. Religious, political, medical, educational, and economic institutions are all involved in this controversy. Some common issues include abortion, sex education, contraception, homosexuality, nonmarital sex, and pornography. On these issues, advocates of each of the two world views appear to be polarized under various labels. The absolutists are often perceived as members of or sympathetic to the former Moral Majority organization, as being against a federal Equal Rights Amendment, as Protestant fundamentalists, strict Catholics (including both the Roman and the Eastern Orthodox churches), or ultra-Orthodox Jews, and as political "New Rightists" and extreme conservatives. The process-oriented are characterized as very liberal, secular humanists. They may be viewed as feminists, gay activists, prochoice on abortion, and supporters of such organizations as People for the American Way and the National Organization for Women.

Whatever the actual meaning of these labels, they have tended to politicize the competing camps. Francoeur maintains that the absolutist position may have been historically functional in restricting sexually transmitted diseases, maintaining family stability, protecting inheritance rights and so forth. But new technology and medical advances have shifted society away from a need to control sexual behavior and have thus moved more people in the direction of the process-oriented end of the sexual morality spectrum. Self-determination in sex and reproduction become increasingly attractive, and resistance to societally imposed standards rises. The present confrontation between the two philosophical world views regarding sexuality may serve as a basis for understanding the schizophrenic appearance of the American sexual scene. Yankelovich's (1981) extensive study of changing American attitudes indicates the vast majority of people shifting their values, to some degree, to adapt to a changing social environment. The absolutists, although vocal and visible, appear to be a distinct minority.

MALE-FEMALE RELATIONS

Sexuality and Gender Roles

For most males and females, socially acceptable sexual expression is limited by the definitions of masculinity and femininity in society. As young children, the passivity and conformity that characterizes female socialization versus the more aggressive and forceful stance adopted by males (see Scanzoni, 1982) carries over into the sexual interaction of adulthood. Males continue to have more sexual partners than do women, and they remain the primary sexual aggressor. Perhaps this reflects the common finding that females, more so than males, are taught to seek some emotional commitment prior to sexual intercourse.

The sexual and gender role relationships between American males and females have changed dramatically during the 20th century. Catalyzed by technological innovations and social upheavals, women today have moved into the paying economy. Toffler (1981) states that the increasingly shared and similar experiences of men and women is the result of the latter's growing paid-work role and in some respects is more similar to the shared experiences of preindustrial villages, which were altered by the segregating of gender roles during industrialization. Scanzoni (1982) argues that the desire for equity by women is the central force in the changing of family patterns and the quest for an equal-partner marriage. Less subordination to males is the goal, and conflict, bargaining, and exchange is the process that leads to change. As gender roles change, interpersonal conflict increases, and one of the areas of struggle is in men's sexual coercion of women.

Tavris and Offir (in Nass, Libby, & Fisher, 1981) maintain that men and women live in dissimilar symbolic worlds based upon different sexual scripts. Mistrust was built into the courtship process, and the classic exchange was male economic status and security for female sex appeal and domestic services. "Sex making was socially structured as a battlefield" (Nass, Libby, & Fisher, 1981, p. 107). Moreover, Whitehurst (1972) believes that men fear that women will gain power over them and that the society is really femiphobic rather than sexophobic. If this is correct, then a by-product of increasing equity between men and women may be the demise of the sexually schizophrenic society, at least to the extent it is rooted in antifemale passions.

The women's movement, both in political terms as well as in social subtleties, has altered the instrumental, expressive and physical relationships beween males and females. Within this changed gender role context comes a shift in intimate sexual relationships. The sexual bargaining positions of men and women have become more similar as has the congruence of their sexual requests.

Dating and Marriage Patterns

With the emergence of contemporary dating in the 20th century, sex became an increasingly important commodity in the social exchange between the sexes. Waller's (1937) pioneering studies on college campus dating in the 1930s suggested a system of mutual exploitation in which males sought sex and females pursued material goods and services, with neither party openly communicating their goals to one another. By this time in history, McCall (cited in Murstein, 1974) maintains that premarital sex no longer necessarily disqualified a person from marriage. Later, Farber (cited in Murstein, 1974) would suggest his "permanent availability" model, implying that one is never totally off the marital and sexual market if the price is right.

Bargaining with one's sexuality is a major component in a variety of contemporary dating theories. Murstein's (1974) Stimulus, Value, Role (SVR) theory holds that individuals try to maximize the profits of social interaction. Sex may be a profit or cost depending upon one's bargaining position vis-a-vis a particular partner. Broderick's (1967) double-funnel theory of courtship contends that there are two gender-role-related dating goals. Females pursue commitment in a relationship, but males control the extent of such commitment. Males on the other hand seek sexual intimacy, but women have power to control the situation by denying sexual access. It is these two distinct agendas that form the basis of a trade-off of sex for commitment and vice versa. The daters entangle themselves in this exchange while slipping and sliding down the funnels of commitment and sexual intimacy, moving toward possible marriage. Although many factors may end the relationship, individuals are likely to repeat the process, although at an accelerated pace, with the next partner.

Such exchanges can operate only within a social environment of unshared, gender-specific expectations and goals. The sexually schizophrenic society promotes double standards, avoidance of communication, and mutual exploitation. If males and females shared the same goals, Broderick's double-funnel theory would be inoperable. The mixed and confused sexual messages of modern America promote interpersonal adversity.

If the present courtship and dating system can be characterized as schizophrenic, then it is potentially destructive in a society that expects success and stability in marriage to emerge from such a system.

The broad applicability of contemporary dating and marriage theories is tempered by social-class and racial/ethnic differences. Although these differences are eroding, gaps still do exist. People of less privileged classes are more likely to experience premarital sexual involvement than others, but this does not imply a high degree of sexual satisfaction. One possible reason for this lessened satisfaction is that their sexual repertoire is more limited than that of higher social classes. Also, Murstein (1970) states that the rigidity of and gratification from sex roles that characterize the lower classes lead to husband-wife difficulties. Feelings and emotional communication are focused on same-sex friends and the family of orientation, not on the spouse. Work fatigue and economic instability also may be partial explanations for strained spousal relationships. "However, whatever the source, their lack of solid psychological interacting is highly correlated with poor sexual adjustment" (Murstein, 1970, p. 130). Less sexual satisfaction among lower income couples was also reported by Rainwater (1964) and Gagnon and Simon (1973).

Generally, less gender-role segregation is found among higher social classes, with more equality and sharing between the sexes. Middle-class people are more successful in contending with sexual issues through a greater use of romance, erotic discussion and sexual fantasizing. In addition, the middle class indulges in a greater variety of sexual acts, often initially in order to avoid intercourse.

Racially, much discussion has focused on the greater frequency and perhaps tolerance of nonmarital sexual behavior among Blacks when compared with whites. The explanation is partly rooted in the prominence of sex as a bargaining commodity, especially among poor Blacks, who have few other resources. Middle-class Blacks are much more similar in their sexual values and behavior to middle- class whites. There is, of course, no evidence to support the popular myth that Blacks are more sexually potent than are whites.

THEORETICAL PERSPECTIVES

Today, social and behavioral scientists recognize the value of studying sexuality as a specific variable. From the macro-level theories of the structural-functionalist comes the perspective that individual sexuality cannot be isolated from the larger social scene. By analyzing societal events, writers such as Francoeur (1982) theorized about a new ecosystem consisting of virtually irreversible social changes impacting upon human sexuality. Many factors sparked this 20th-century sexual revolution. The changing status of women was one. There were also wars, new knowledge in the human sciences, advances in communication and transportation, and the realization that sexual responsiveness is a product of social events and interpersonal relationships as well as of biological urges. Researchers began linking marital happiness with sexual adjustment and also discovered the extent to which people violated society's sexual codes. The sexually schizophrenic society had become exposed.

The structural-functional framework of analysis provides a method of viewing personal decision making through the examination of external pressures placed upon the individual. Reiss's (1967, 1971) four competing premarital sexual standards have become widely acclaimed examples of the choices contemporary society furnishes. Although his work focused on college students, Reiss (1967, 1971) discovered that even at different social levels there is little consensus regarding any one sexual standard. Rather, he found support for the existence of four standards: (1) abstinence — premarital sex is wrong for males and females under all circumstances; (2) orthodox double standard — intercourse is more acceptable for males than females; traditional double standard — intercourse is still preferred for males, but if a woman is engaged or in love it may be all right; (3) permissiveness with affection — intercourse is okay for both sexes when a stable, caring relationship exists; and (4) permissiveness without affection — this is recreational sex.

Reiss's four standards illustrate the potential for friction and confusion, which seems to occur often between parents and children. These standards are rooted in religious as well as in secular world views and they pose for individuals the decision as to which one is most appropriate for them at any one time. Conflict and guilt manifested as sexual problems may result for those individuals unsure of the justification for their choice.

The opportunity that individuals have to select from different standards makes choice and exchange theory at the micro-level of analysis particularly attractive. Indeed, that which has been described as societal sexual schizophrenia may be partly a consequence of the many choices available to individuals today. From a theoretical perspective, it is reasonable to recognize that rapid social change has altered and increased the items human beings could barter in their interpersonal relationships. The flooding of the marketplace with viable and numerous life- style choices further widened the gap between past sexual ideology and current behavior.

According to classic choice and exchange theory, one ideally offers the least and seeks the most in relationships. In this manner, people attempt to maximize their "profits." Rooted in the works of Thibaut and Kelley (1959), Homans (1961), Blau (1964), Levi-Strauss (1969) and Heath (1976), it was Nye (1978) who suggested that individual behaviors via exchange can explain broader social behavior, even to the macro-level.

Robert Winch's theory of complementary needs (Winch, 1958; Winch, Ktsanes, & Ktsanes, 1954) is often cited in the mate-selection literature as a pioneering contribution in recognizing personal needs and attributes as the basis for a trade-off or exchange with a potential partner. Others have followed (see Hendrick & Hendrick, 1983, for a detailed discussion), but all remain in an exchange-theory format.

The direct application of choice and exchange theory to sexual attitudes and behavior has been attempted. According to Nye (1979) men and women report differences in their attitudes and values regarding sexual intercourse, thus creating an opportunity for bargaining. An early example of this was Waller's (1937) rating-dating system and the emphasis on the female's exchange of sex for the male's material goods and services. Other previously discussed dating theories by Murstein, Broderick, and Farber also recognize sex as a commodity for exchange. It is often external influences that establish the exchange criteria. For example, Reiss and Miller are cited by Nye (1979) as noting that youth culture rewards sexuality. The more institutional support there is for sexual permissiveness, the more sexual activity occurs. If marriage is less valued as an immediate goal, more people, especially women, will lose their virginity premaritally. With contraceptive availability and legalized abortion, choice and exchange theory might predict reductions in the personal cost of nonmarital intercourse, with a consequent increase in such behavior. D'Augelli and D'Augelli (Chapter 3 in this volume) also addresses exchange theory as it applies to dyadic sexual relationships.

CLINICAL IMPLICATIONS

During the time when abortion was illegal in the United States, Schur wrote that "Perhaps some illusory satisfaction is felt by maintaining formal standards to which few attempt to conform" (Schur, 1964, p. 328). He quotes Radcliffe-Brown "...the application of any sanction is a direct affirmation of social sentiments by the community and thereby constitutes an important, possibly essential, mechanism for maintaining these sentiments" (Schur, 1964, p. 379). Today the price of preserving "some illusory satisfaction" with the "social sentiments" of the community is prohibitive as we come to recognize the existence of the sexually schizophrenic society and seek a reduction of its costs.

Although the Protestant ethic apparently has made America rich and affluent beyond the dreams of other nations, it seems to have left us with a sexual legacy very much out of touch with the reality of the contemporary social situation. Throughout history, man seems to have polarized sexual expression. Either it is suppressed and denied, with those activities which come to attention severely punished, or it is sanctified to the point where it cannot be discussed or dealt with realistically. In either case, heavily repressed or distorted variable expressions of sexuality often manifest themselves in obsessive concern with the subject. Obviously, healthy integration of sex into normal life becomes almost impossible. That some people manage to achieve a workable solution to this problem is a tribute to the resilience and flexibility of the human being. (Whitehurst, 1972, pp. 13- 14)

Therefore, clinicians should recognize that the source of much of the anxiety and confusion regarding sex comes from the society. Sexual problems and dysfunctions may be the residue of societal madness. Acknowledgment of this might serve in establishing treatment goals in which one can maintain personal integrity while accepting the imperfections of the world in which one lives.

McCary and McCary (1984) believe that socially induced guilt is used to control sexual behavior among the young even when no moral rationale exists to justify prohibiting the behavior. Rigid rules are incorporated into the youngsters' value system, and stress occurs when the rules are broken. Especially criticized is "guilt-instilling" religion as a menace to psychosexual health. For some, a religiously grounded belief that sex is sinful cannot be dispelled by a marital ceremony, and the consequences may include "...guilt, pain, frigidity, impotence, and premature ejaculation" (McCary & McCary, 1984, p. 8). It is a positive move that increasingly some religious groups are trying to counter this via church-sponsored sex education (Smith, 1975). However, what happens when the society not only condemns all premarital sexual behaviors "...but also depicts them as desirable and exciting" (McCary & McCary, 1984, p. 5)? This describes the present state of the situation.

Rapid changes in contemporary society require that young people be prepared for the world they will live in rather than the one their parents were raised to live in. The crisis of adaptation that Toffler (1971) calls "future shock" consists of transience, novelty, and diversity, and clinicians' need to understand the convergence of these factors if they are to appreciate fully the clientele they serve. That is only the beginning of the multitude of challenging issues facing the clinical professions. A new generation of ideas, models, and prescriptions to guide clinical judgments is needed. The proliferation of life-styles and shifting gender relationships offer challenges and questions with no prior solutions. This is to be expected, according to Murstein (1974), who points out that "...in an affluent society in which men and women are becoming more equal...sex is commanding greater interest than ever before" (Murstein, 1974, p. 442).

Phillips (1983) notes that the therapy literature is lacking in its reporting on alternative life-styles. Practitioners may be poorly prepared to deal with nontraditional relationships. Already we are challenged by many questions. How do we assess the intricacies of sexual rules in stepfamilies? How do single parents successfully fulfill their sexual needs and their parenting responsibilities? How do dual career/work marriages manage their sexual time? How does the single person relate to the several sex partners he/she is dating simultaneously? How does one deal with jealousy when communicating the existence of other partners? Is silence golden? How are sexual boundaries established between cohabitators? How well do we understand gay and lesbian relationships? How do we feel about celibacy?

What is the essence of marriage, asks Murstein (1974)? For some, he says, it may be sexual fidelity, for others shared values, emotions, or intellectual pursuits. The therapist must explore the meaning of marital sex during a time when normative sexual behavior often defies the prevailing values. Toffler (1971) predicts marital partners will increasingly be selected by stage, not age, therefore producing more relationships between older men and younger women, who may share more values and interests than those of the opposite sex in their own age group. What consequences might this have for sexual compatibility?

Some clinicians may have to deal with unusual sexual issues such as questions related to embryo transplants and surrogate mothers. What is the impact of these procedures on the spousal, parental, and sexual roles and feelings of couples? Other practitioners are already employed in sifting out the traumas of sexual assault and abuse.

More mundane and common controversies center on issues related to social class, ethnic and racial distinctions in sex therapy, as well as on an increasing sensitivity to the sexual needs of older people.

CONCLUSION

We are at the early stages of our understanding of human sexuality. As stated earlier, it was only about 100 years ago that Western science recognized that human conception occurs when sperm and egg unite (*Family Life Educator*, 1982). The power of sexuality is still seen as a frightening and uncontrolled force.

The sexual schizophrenia of the society will begin to fade as expectations and reality become more consistent with one another. This will occur when personal behavior, life-styles, family life and the social environment become more mutually supportive. Until then a substantial number of people will find personal unhappiness and confusion requiring clinical assistance.

REFERENCES

Bardis, P.D. (1969). Early Christianity and the family. In P.D. Bardis (Ed.), *The family in changing civilizations* (2nd ed.). New York: Selected Academic Readings.

Barker-Benfield, G.J. (1978). The spermatic economy: A nineteenth century view of sexuality. In M. Gordon (Ed.), *The American family in social-historical perspective* (2nd ed.). New York: St. Martin's.

Blau, P. (1964). *Exchange and power in social life.* New York: Wiley.

Broderick, C.B. (1967). Going steady: The beginning of the end. In S.M. Farber & H.L. Wilson (Eds.), *Teenage marriage and divorce.* Ann Arbor, MI: Diablo Press.

Brown, D., & Lynn, D. (1966). Human sexual development: An outline of components and concepts. *Journal of Marriage and the Family, 28,* 155-162.

Clark, D. (1977). *Loving someone gay.* New York: Signet.

Constantine, L., & Constantine, J. (1973). *Group marriage.* New York: Macmillan.

Degler, C.N. (1978). What ought to be and what was: Women's sexuality in the nineteenth century. In M. Gordon (Ed.), *The American family in social-historical perspective* (2nd ed.). New York: St. Martin's.

Degler, C.N. (1983). The emergence of the modern American family. In M. Gordon (Ed.), *The American family in social-historical perspective* (3rd ed.). New York: St. Martin's.

Family Life Educator. (1982).Where do babies come from? *Family Life Educator, 1,* 5-7.

Francoeur, R.T. (1981). Sex in America. *Sexology Today, 47,* 1-36.

Francoeur, R.T. (1982). *Becoming a sexual person.* New York: Wiley.

Francoeur, R.T. (1983). Religious reactions to alternative lifestyles. In E.D. Macklin & R.H. Rubin (Eds.), *Contemporary families and alternative lifestyles: Handbook on research and theory.* Beverly Hills, CA: Sage.

Freeman, D. (1983). Bursting the South Sea bubble. *Time Magazine, 124,* 68-69.

Gagnon, J., & Simon, W. (1973). *Sexual conduct.* Chicago: Aldine.

Gaylin, N. (1982). Trust: The overlooked essential of marriage. *Medical Aspects of Human Sexuality, 16,* 50-57.

Gerstel, N., & Gross, H. (1983). Commuter marriage: Couples who live apart. In E.D. Macklin and R.H. Rubin (Eds.), *Contemporary families and alternative lifestyles: Handbook on research and theory.* Beverly Hills, CA: Sage.

Gordon, M. (Ed.). (1978). *The American family in social- historical perspective* (2nd ed.). New York: St. Martin's.

Heath, A. (1976). *Rational choice and social exchange.* London: Cambridge University Press.

Hendrick, C., & Hendrick, S. (1983). *Liking, loving, and relating.* Monterey, CA: Brooks/Cole.

Homans, G. (1961). *Social behavior: Its elementary forms.* New York: Harcourt, Brace & World.

Kassel, V. (1970). Polygyny after sixty. In H. Otto (Ed.), *The family in search of a future.* New York: Appleton-Century-Crofts.

Kinsey, A.C., Pomeroy, W.B., & Martin, C.E. (1948). *Sexual behavior in the human male.* Philadelphia: Saunders.

Kinsey, A.C., Pomeroy, W.B., Martin, C.E., & Gebhard, P.H. (1953). *Sexual behavior in the human female.* Philadephia: Saunders.

Levi-Strauss, C. (1969). *The elementary structures of kinship.* Boston: Beacon Press.

Macklin, E.D. (1978). Non-marital heterosexual cohabitation: A review of research. *Marriage and Family Review, 1,* 1-12.

Macklin, E.D. (1983). Nonmarital heterosexual cohabitation: An overview. In E.D. Macklin and R.H. Rubin (Eds.), *Contemporary families and alternative lifestyles: Handbook on research and theory*. Beverly Hills, CA: Sage.

Masters, W.H., & Johnson, V.E. (1966). *Human sexual response*. Boston: Little, Brown.

Masters, W.H., & Johnson, V.E. (1970). *Human sexual inadequacy*. Boston: Little, Brown.

McCary, S., & McCary, J. (1984). *Human sexuality* (3rd brief edition). Belmont, CA: Wadsworth.

Melville, K. (1983). *Marriage and family today* (3rd ed.). New York: Random House.

Money, J., & Ehrhardt, A.A.(1972). *Man and woman, boy and girl*. Baltimore: Johns Hopkins University.

Morgan, E.S. (1978). The puritans and sex. In M. Gordon (Ed.), *The American family in social-historical perspective* (2nd ed.). New York: St. Martin's.

Murstein, B. (1970). The sexual image in marriage throughout history. In C. Presvelou & P. de Bie (Eds.), *Images and counter images of young families*. Louvain, Belgium: Catholic University of Louvain.

Murstein, B. (1974).*Love, sex, and marriage through the ages*. New York: Springer.

Myricks, N., & Rubin, R.H. (1977). Sex laws and alternative life styles. *The Family Coordinator, 26*, 357-360.

Nass, G.D., Libby, R.W., & Fisher, M.P. (1981). *Sexual choices*. Monterey, CA: Wadsworth.

Nye, F.I. (1978). Is choice and exchange theory the key? *Journal of Marriage and the Family, 40*, 219-233.

Nye, F.I. (1979). Choice, exchange, and the family. In W.R. Burr, R. Hill, F.I. Nye, & I.L. Reiss (Eds.), *Contemporary theories about the family* (Vol. 2). New York: The Free Press.

O'Neill, G. and O'Neill, N. (1972).*Open marriage*. New York: Evans.

Phillips, R., Jr. (1983). Clinical issues in alternative lifestyles. In E.D. Macklin & R.H. Rubin (Eds.), *Contemporary families and alternative lifestyles: Handbook on research and theory*. Beverly Hills, CA: Sage.

Rainwater, L. (1964). Marital sexuality in four cultures of poverty. *Journal of Marriage and the Family, 26*, 457-466.

Reiss, I. (1967). *The social context of premarital sexual permissiveness*. New York: Holt, Rinehart & Winston.

Reiss, I. (1971). Premarital sexual codes: The old and the new. In D.L. Grummon & A.M. Barclay (Eds.), *Sexuality: A search for perspective*. New York: Van Nostrand Reinhold.

Rothman, E.K. (1983). Sex and self-control: Middle-class courtship in America, 1770-1870. In M. Gordon (Ed.), *The American family in social-historical perspective* (3rd ed.). New York: St. Martin's.

Scanzoni, J. (1982). *Sexual bargaining* (2nd ed.). Chicago, University of Chicago.

Schur, E. (Ed.). (1964). *The family and the sexual revolution*. Bloomington, IN: Indiana University.

Shorter, E. (1981). Women's diseases before 1900. In M. Albin & D. Cavallo (Eds.), *Family life in America 1620-2000*. St. James, NY: Revisionary Press.

Skolnick, A. (1980). The American family: The paradox of perfection. *American Educator, 4*, 8-23.

Smith, L. (1975). Religion's response to the new sexuality. *SIECUS Report, 1*, 14-15.

Sorokin, P.A. (1956). *The American sex revolution*. Boston: Porter Sargent.

Thibaut, J., & Kelley, H. (1959). *The social psychology of groups*. New York: Wiley.

Toffler, A. (1971). *Future shock*. New York: Bantam.

Toffler, A. (1981). *The third wave*. New York: Bantam.

Veevers, J. (1983). Voluntary childlessness: A critical assessment of the research. In E.D. Macklin & R.H. Rubin (Eds.), *Contemporary families and alternative lifestyles: Handbook on research and theory*. Beverly Hills, CA: Sage.

Waller, W. (1937). The rating and dating complex. *American Sociological Review, 2*, 727-734.

Weis, D. (1983). "Open" marriage and multilateral relationships: The emergence of nonexclusive models of the marital relationship. In E.D. Macklin & R.H. Rubin (Eds.), *Contemporary families and alternative lifestyles: Handbook on reserach and theory*. Beverly Hills, CA: Sage.

Whitehurst, R. (1972). American sexophobia. In L.A. Kirkendall & R.N. Whitehurst (Eds.), *The new sexual revolution.* New York: D.W. Brown.

Winch, R. (1958). *Mate-selection: A study of complementary needs.* New York: Harper.

Winch, R., Ktsanes, T., & Ktsanes, V. (1954). The theory of complementary needs in mate selection: An analytic and descriptive study. *American Sociological Review, 19,* 241-249.

Yankelovich, D. (1981). *New rules: Searching for self-fulfillment in a world turned upside down.* New York: Random House.

Zelnik, M., & Kantner, J.F. (1972). Sexuality, contraception and pregnancy among unwed females in the United States. In Commission on Population Growth and the American Future, *Demographic and social aspects of population growth.* Washington, DC: U.S. Government Printing Office.

Zelnik, M., & Kantner, J.F. (1977). Sexual and contraceptive experiences of young unmarried women in the United States, 1976 and 1971. *Family Planning Perspectives, 9,* 55-71.

Zelnik, M., & Kantner, J.F. (1978). Contraceptive patterns and premarital pregnancy among women aged 15-19 in 1976. *Family Planning Perspectives, 10,* 135.

Zelnik, M., & Kantner, J.F. (1979). Reasons for nonuse of contraception by sexually active women aged 15-19. *Family Planning Perspectives, 11,* 289.

Zelnik, M., & Kantner, J.F. (1980). Sexual activity, contraceptive use and pregnancy among metropolitan-area teenagers. *Family Planning Perspectives, 12,* 230.

Section II

Assessment and Treatment of Sexual Problems

Chapter 6

Behavioral and Psychological Assessment of Sexual Dysfunction: An Overview*

Michael D. Newcomb and Peter M. Bentler

Only a few years ago, outcome studies examining the effectiveness of short-term behavioral sex therapies boasted of success rates of 80% to 100%. This phenomenal record of positive outcomes in treating sexual disorders was due primarily to the seminal work on direct short-term behavioral interventions of Semans (1956) and Wolpe (1958). This earlier work gained focus, refinement, and expansion through Masters and Johnson (1970) and Kaplan (1974). Unfortunately, these initial, almost miraculous success rates have declined more recently (Hogan, 1978). Reasons for this apparent decrease have focused on three essential aspects of sex therapy.

One important component of sex therapy is education and information. Ignorance, naivete, and misunderstanding have fueled, if not generated, many sexual difficulties. For instance, Masters and Johnson (1970) have asserted that "...ignorance of sexual physiology, rather than psychiatric or medical illness, constitute the etiological background for most sexual dysfunction." However, because of the current upsurge in self-help and education material available to an eager general public, this facet of sex therapy has diminished in central importance. In other words, people presenting now with sexual problems typically have more basic knowledge of sexual functioning and behavior than previously, and thus arrive with more complex and severe sexual disturbances resistant to treatment with education and information (Chapman, 1982). In fact, Derogatis and Meyer (1979) have noted that even though individuals with sexual dysfunctions have significantly lower levels of accurate sexual information than do control subjects, this difference only accounted for 4% of the variance between the groups.

---

* Preparation of this chapter was supported in part by USPHS grant DA01070. Appreciation is given to J. Speckart for production assistance.

127

A second reason offered to explain the decrease in success rates for sex therapy concerns the theoretical model utilized by noted practitioners. In particular the Masters and Johnson (1970) model, as well as that implicit in *DSM-III* (American Psychiatric Association, 1980), have received extensive criticism for not accounting for the numerous facets or multiple causes of sexual disorders. Specifically, satisfaction and subjective components have not been adequately incorporated in the assessment and treatment of sexual dysfunctions (Zilbergeld & Ellison, 1980). Therefore, treatment models that narrowly address only the physiological response cycle have been facing increasing difficulty with patients who present with satisfaction problems (e.g., lack of sexual interest or arousal).

Finally, Chapman (1982) has argued convincingly that many diagnostic and treatment methods for sexual dysfunction do not adequately assess or acknowledge complex interactions of relationship problems with sexual disorders. This has resulted in many couples with major relationship and/or individual pathology being treated in a brief sex therapy format, which has little power to deal with these serious, nonsexual issues.

Each of these three speculative reasons for the decrement in success rates for sex therapy can be dealt with by more careful and thorough assessment prior to treatment. Thus, a meticulous evaluation allows more effective screening for the appropriateness of sex therapy and the information with which to design a more individualized and detailed treatment plan. This chapter provides an overview and conceptual model to help address these deficiencies in typical assessment procedures. Numerous methods, in addition to the clinical interview, are presented and discussed to allow a more detailed, useful, and multifaceted evaluation of sexually dysfunctional patients.

COMPONENTS OF SEX THERAPY ASSESSMENT

Lobitz and Lobitz (1978) have delineated three important steps or stages in the assessment component of treating sexual dysfunctions. They suggest first gauging the patients' appropriateness for sex therapy via an initial evaluation. Then, if the patients are found to be suitable for treatment in a sex therapy format, detailed sexual interviews are conducted to diagnose the dysfunction, delineate sexual histories, and specify goals for treatment. The final stage of sex therapy assessment is the ongoing evaluation of progress during treatment and follow-up evaluation subsequent to termination.

Since the goal of this chapter is to familiarize general- psychotherapy practitioners with assessment procedures in sex therapy, we have expanded the general three-part assessment formulation of Lobitz and Lobitz (1978) into a general model for assessing and effectively discriminating relationship-therapy prospects from sex-therapy prospects. This conceptual model is depicted graphically in Figure 6.1.

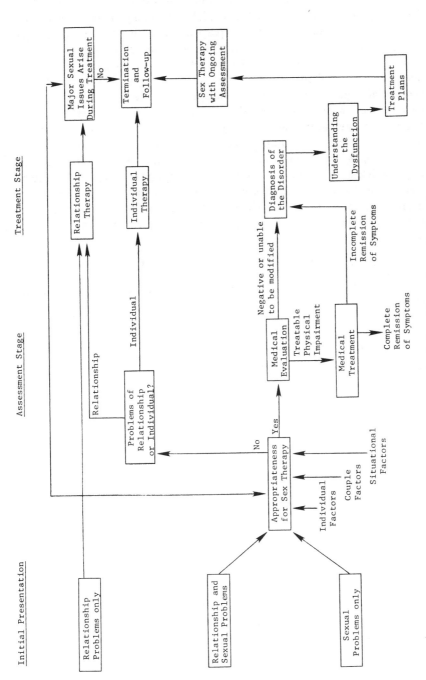

Figure 6.1 Model for the assessment and treatment of relationship and sexual disorders.

This model divides the treatment process into several components, including initial presentation, assessment, treatment, termination, and follow-up stages. The components and focus of this model clearly emphasize the assessment aspects of the treatment process with particular attention given to screening for the appropriateness of using sex therapy, even if sexual problems are the only major presenting complaints of the patients. The greater part of this chapter addresses in detail five important assessment stages in this model. These sequential stages include evaluating the appropriateness for sex therapy, medical consultation, diagnosis of the disorder, understanding the dysfunction, and ongoing assessment during treatment. In addition, research instruments used in studying sexual dysfunctions and disorders, which may in the future be useful tools for the practitioner, are presented briefly. However, prior to embarking on a discussion of these specific areas, it is useful to review and appreciate some of the basic antecedent or etiological factors implicated in the development of sexual dysfunctions. Then, the various modes or techniques practitioners should or do employ to measure these factors are presented.

ETIOLOGICAL FACTORS OF SEXUAL DISORDERS

Sexual functioning is a complex interaction of biological (physiological), psychological, relational, and cultural factors, requiring a great deal of harmonious interplay among these components. Dysfunctions can occur because of problems in any one of these areas. Thus, assessment and treatment procedures need to confront problems arising in any of these essential aspects of sexual functioning. Even though extensive, but not exhaustive, research has been devoted to understanding the sexual dysfunctions, typically no single consistent etiological factor has been identified for any one of them. Consequently, a multicausal perspective has gained favor when attempting to understand and treat sexual dysfunction.

In this section, we examine several factors that contribute to sexual dysfunction. Consideration and appreciation of these influences help construct a complete picture of sexual disorders and are essential for a thorough assessment. In other words, these are not facets or perspectives that should only be considered idly or academically; they are, rather, essential features that should underlie a comprehensive appraisal of the patient. These areas include biology, psychology, the dyad, culture, and a general appreciation of remote and immediate causes.

Biological Factors

Biological processes form the potential for engaging in sexual activity, and as such constitute a primary level or area where dysfunction can occur. Age, drugs, and illness are three important factors that can impair sexual functioning from a physiological perspective.

Age. The aging process, through its inexorable impact on the physiology of the body, profoundly affects sexual functioning. Kaplan (1974) emphasizes that aging represents a prime example of how biology and psychology interact in creating sexual behavior.

Loss of interest in and avoidance of sex are frequent behaviors that emerge in response to the physiological changes associated with growing older (Kaplan, 1974). In fact, researchers have noted consistent age-related decrements in sexual interest and activity for men and women (e.g., Kinsey, Pomeroy, & Martin, 1948; Kinsey, Pomeroy, Martin, & Gebhard, 1953). One study, however, suggests that this inverse relationship between age and sexual activity is moderated by sexual guilt, which was higher in older men (DiVasto, Pathak, & Fishburn, 1981). Yet, sex guilt cannot account for the many biological differences that have been noted (e.g., Masters & Johnson, 1966, 1970). Masters and Johnson (1966) have documented some of the physiological changes that occur with increasing age. Older men need a greater degree and duration of erotic stimulation to attain and maintain erection (Solnick & Birren, 1977), the force of ejaculation is decreased, and the refractory period is lengthened. The surgical trauma of prostatectomy (a not-infrequent procedure in older men) should not interfere with erotic ability, although ejaculation might be retrograde into the bladder rather than through the penis. In older women, vaginal lubrication occurs after longer foreplay and the amount of lubrication is diminished. Hormone-replacement treatment is sometimes used for postmenopausal and posthysterectomy women patients.

Men and women differ greatly in their patterns of aging in regard to sex (Kinsey et al. 1948; Kinsey et al. 1953; Masters & Johnson, 1966, 1970). Men reach their peak of sexual interest and activity in their late teens, which then diminishes gradually during the rest of their life. Women, on the other hand, attain their sexual peak in their late thirties and then decline more slowly than men.

These changes, however, do not in and of themselves create sexual dysfunction. It is the psychological reaction to such changes, the ignorance or unwillingness to adapt, that produces a disorder. Many older men and women remain sexually interested and active, including those who are institutionalized (White, 1982). In addition, older patients are also responsive to treatment (Sviland, 1975), although perhaps not in group formats (Schneidman & McGuire, 1976). Martin (1981) has noted that among 60- to 79-year-old males, previous level of sexual functioning was an excellent predictor of present sexual activity. Thus, sexual activity in the aged is not so much a product of the aging process per se, but of the general, lifelong interest and behavior patterns.

Growing older does not need to signal the "beginning of the end" of sexual pleasure, and Kaplan (1974) suggests that clinicians help older patients "…recognize that normal age-related sexual changes exist, that they are not identical for husband and wife, that these changes are a product of biological rhythms and not of the quality of their love or attractiveness" (p. 114). Kaplan further asserts that therapists can assist in this adaptation process, because "it is the manner in which the general differences in sexual aging are resolved, the degree of openness, love and acceptance...which determine how they will function sexually as they grow older."

During the assessment process it is important to determine what physical changes may be present as a result of growing older, and the psychological reaction in response to these. These may prove to be central issues to be addressed in treatment.

Drugs. Various chemical substances, either medicinal, illicit, or recreational, may enhance or more likely hinder sexual functioning. Drugs can affect sexual functioning both centrally in the brain, resulting in alteration of sexual desire and pleasure, and more peripherally, by changes in nerve receptors and blood flow in the genital area (Kaplan, 1974). Unfortunately, most drugs interfere with and diminish sexual functioning and enjoyment rather than enhance it.

As with age, drugs may not affect sexual functioning in a consistent manner for all people (Kaplan, 1974). The pharmacological action of a chemical substance is only one factor in the complex interaction of context and expectations that surround sexual behavior. However, certain substances can usually be expected to alter sexual behavior to some extent. Alcohol has been implicated repeatedly in sexual dysfunctions of men and women (e.g., Briddell & Wilson, 1976; Wagner & Jensen, 1981; Wilson & Lawson, 1976, 1978). Any drug that has anticholinergic effects (e.g., atropine, propantheline) will dampen mechanisms that allow the excitement and arousal stages of the sexual process (e.g., erection of the penis and lubrication of the vagina), while any drug that has antiadrenergic qualities (e.g., methyldopa, phentolamine) will impair orgasm (Kaplan, 1974). Types of medications that contribute to decreased sexual potential and enjoyment include sedatives, narcotics, antiandrogens, hypertension regulators, and many psychotropic preparations (e.g., Blair & Simpson, 1966; Cohen, 1981; Neri, Aygen, Zuckerman, & Bahary, 1980; Kotin, Wilbert, Verburg, & Soldinger, 1976).

Since use of many of these drugs is essential for physical and/or emotional well-being, it may not be feasible to discontinue the medication solely on the basis that it has potentiated sexual dysfunction. In such cases, sex therapy may be quite appropriate, in fact very important, to help the patient adjust and adapt to the limitations in sexual functioning the drugs create. For other substances, which do not serve a clearly medicinal purpose, such as alcohol and narcotics, it may be necessary to require discontinuation of their use prior to commencing sex therapy, depending upon the quantity and frequency of their use. Recent evidence also suggests that tobacco may cause erectile failure in some men (Wagner & Green, 1981), even in small quantities (Forsberg, Gustavii, Hajerbac, & Olsson, 1979).

Various street drugs may also affect sexual behavior and interest, although their effects have not been well documented. For instance, narcotics generally decrease sexual interest and impair sexual responses due to their analgesic and central nervous system depressant effects. On the other hand, amphetamines and cocaine may enhance sexual interest and functioning at low dosage levels due to their stimulant effects, whereas at higher levels they become systemically toxic and inhibit sexual responses. Marijuana has also been reported by some to enhance sexual responses, although this effect seems to have wide variation among people.

A thorough assessment should determine any and all drugs (including cigarettes, alcohol, and caffeine) used by individuals seeking sex therapy. This information is vital for evaluating appropriateness for sex treatment, diagnosing the disorder, specifying its etiology, and developing a treatment plan.

Illness. Physical sickness, emotional disturbance, and natural physiological processes can impair sexual functioning. The presence of such conditions is not sufficient to preclude sex therapy. In fact, sex therapy with patients who have chronic illnesses may be essential for them to adapt and find ways to enjoy sexual encounters despite difficulties or impairments resulting from the disease process.

Various illnesses and/or injuries have been found to affect sexual functioning in men and women, including cardiovascular disease (e.g., Stein, 1980), myocardial infarction (e.g., Derogatis & King, 1981; Wabrek & Burchell, 1980), diabetes (e.g., Jensen, 1981; Wagner, Hilsted, & Jensen, 1981), spinal cord injury (e.g., Flitting, Salisbury, Davies, & Mayclin, 1978; Higgins, 1979), cerebral palsy (e.g., Steinboch & Zeiss, 1977) and pelvic surgery in women (e.g., Levine & Yost, 1976). Natural physical processes such as pregnancy (e.g., Grudzinskas & Atkinson, 1984; Toler & DiGrazia, 1976) and menopause (e.g., Green, 1977) frequently result in declines in sexual interest, activity, and satisfaction.

Emotional conditions such as depression, anxiety, stress, and fatigue (Kaplan, 1974), as well as most psychoses (e.g., Nestoros, Lehman, & Ban, 1981; Rozan, Tuchin, & Kurland, 1971), typically interfere with sexual functioning. Raboch (1984) found that schizophrenic women had retarded sexual development resulting in lowered sexual activity and arousability in adult life, exacerbated by social isolation. Similarly, Friedman and Harrison (1984) found greater problems with sexual functioning (e.g., disinterest, orgasm difficulties) for schizophrenic women than for controls.

Of course, it is expected that experiencing a sexual dysfunction will be accompanied by anxiety and depression. However, when the emotional condition is severe and most likely the cause of the sexual dysfunction, sex therapy may be contraindicated until the emotional disturbance is treated or at least stabilized.

Clearly, all physical and emotional conditions must be carefully assessed and evaluated, including consultation with a physician, prior to engaging in sex therapy. Patients with chronic illnesses and/or permanent physical impairments will be in special need of sex counseling and should not be turned away because of their condition. Careful collaboration with their physician to determine specific limitations and to aid in coordinating a well- planned sex therapy program may foster the return of sexual interest and pleasure to the patient's life.

Psychological Factors

Despite the obvious contribution of physiological mechanisms, the vast majority of sexual dysfunctions are considered to be psychogenic in origin (Masters & Johnson, 1966, 1970). However, there is no agreement regarding the specific nature of the psychological processes involved (Kaplan, 1974).

An early perspective is offered by Freud (1953), who considers sexual problems to be the result of conflict, repression, and other defenses against anxiety relating to unresolved infantile sexuality. He places particular emphasis on the oedipal stage of psychosexual development and the unconscious conflicts typical of that period. Assessment within this model is extremely difficult because it necessitates accessing processes that are remote, both in time and in abstraction level, and largely unconscious in nature.

A more recent conceptual model offered by Helen Singer Kaplan in *The New Sex Therapy* (1974) weds dynamic and behavioral therapies in a way that is compatible with a variety of treatment approaches. This model is more amenable to direct assessment and posits that certain obstacles intrude in the natural sexual process, creating dysfunction, frustration, and dissatisfaction (Kaplan, 1974). Kaplan (1974) has identified several of these obstacles. One problem may be the failure to engage in adequate and effective stimulation, due to a lack of knowledge and/or ambivalence toward enjoying sexual activity. Sexual anxiety emanating from a fear of failure, pressure to perform, or an excessive need to satisfy one's partner, can also intrude on pleasurable sexual functioning. Observing, cognitively removing oneself from the sexual encounter, or "spectatoring," resulting from a lack of trust, insecurity, or fear of losing control can frequently adversely affect sexual encounters and create dysfunction.

Finally, behaviorists have emphasized the role of conditioning and reinforcement in the development of sexual disorders. Learning theory does not specify particular etiological factors, but rather argues that certain mechanisms and events underlie sexual problems (e.g., Annon, 1977; Lobitz & LoPiccolo, 1977; Wolpe, 1969, 1977). Frequently, early traumatic, negative or humiliating experiences associated with sexuality or the sexual organs are central in acquiring or learning sexual dysfunctions. These events range from extreme trauma resulting from rape or incest, to insidious messages from partners, religion, or society that sex is dirty, unhealthy, or sinful and that only "bad" or "fallen" people derive pleasure from masturbation or intercourse. In addition, fear and anxiety about being caught engaging in sexual activities (including masturbation), and perhaps having actually been discovered, may initiate a cycle of fear, failure, humiliation, anxiety, and then more fear, that is difficult to break.

Each of these factors or mechanisms can play a major role in disturbing the sexual process from a psychological perspective. It is essential to assess carefully and accurately the psychological features and components that may have created or at least help maintain a sexual dysfunction.

Dyadic Factors

Transactions within the relationship may also be at the root of sexual disorders (Sager, 1974). This may take the form of partner rejection based on physical or psychological incompatibility. On the other hand, conflict and discord within the dyad, frequently arising from unexpressed rage or hostility and fear of abandonment, may prevent a pleasurable and satisfying sharing of sexual experience. These difficulties may involve problems of trust and openness, power struggles, disappointed expectations, inadequate or destructive communication, and alternative attractions outside of the relationship. Kaplan (1974) has delineated several ways these more general relationship problems are translated or carried over into the sexual arena and wind up sabotaging the possibility of pleasurable sexual activity. These techniques of sexual sabotage include creating a pressured and tense environment for the partner, using improper timing, and making oneself unattractive. In addition, unresolved transferences brought into the relationship may disturb interpersonal functioning, not based on current transactions, but by triggering earlier fears of abandonment, humiliation, and failure.

It is expected that sexual problems will lead to a certain degree of relationship disturbance. However, if the sexual dysfunction is only one facet of a generally troubled relationship, sex therapy may be contraindicated, because it will not treat the basic disturbance. This is a critical distinction to make during assessment, when, as is frequently the case, patients present with both relationship and sexual problems. This must be determined on a case-by-case basis because some couples are able to work on sexual problems in spite of other difficulties in their relationship; that is, providing that these other issues do not undermine or sabotage treatment of the sexual dysfunction. In addition, it is essential to be aware that no assessment is perfect and that a more general or pervasive relationship problem may emerge or unfold during the treatment process. This highlights the importance of ongoing assessment during therapy.

Cultural and Situational Factors

Attitudes, mores, and values in our environment and society affect how sexuality is developed and expressed. In particular, restrictiveness, severe religious proscriptions, and equating sex with sin can engender conflict and frustration when attempting to find a manner in which to express this both intensely pleasurable and powerful need.

This potential constrictiveness is manifested in many ways, including child-rearing practices, discomfort with physical contact and intimacy, and guilt, and is occasionally institutionalized in prohibitive laws. A sense of security and trust in one's partner and immediate surroundings are important for full and uninhibited expression of sexual pleasure. Where apprehension and vulnerability are paramount, sexual functioning is impaired, if not impossible. This is true regardless of whether the concern involves fear that lovemaking will be interrupted by children entering the bedroom or fear that one is doing something wrong and sinful that will deserve punishment (e.g., from the conscience, if internalized).

During the assessment phase of sex treatment, it is important to review and examine these remote and immediate environmental conditions that can impede and disrupt sexual functioning. For example, it is useful to explore how the parents felt about sex and nudity, and prevailing subcultural attitudes toward sex. In addition, the immediate circumstances under which lovemaking is attempted need to be discussed. For example, is it safe, secure, and private, or vulnerable to disruption and intrusion?

Each of these etiological factors points to essential components and areas vital to assess. In the next section, we present various methods of assessment that can be used during the evaluation process to gather appropriate information.

METHODS OF ASSESSMENT

The clinical interview has been the most frequently used mode of assessment in sex therapy. However, many other very informative and useful methods are available that are accessible to most clinicians. These do not necessarily include specialized methods such as biochemical assay of blood or urine (e.g., Schwartz, Kolodny, & Masters, 1980), genital response indicators such as the penile strain gauge (e.g., Barlow, Becker, Leitenberg, & Agras, 1970), or the vaginal photoplethysmography transducer (e.g., Geer, Morokoff, & Greenwood, 1974). These assessment methods may be quite informative and useful, particularly in research, but they are not typically meaningful or practical for most sex therapists. Various methods of assessment are examined that can be used by a general psychotherapist, with specific examples given within each mode.

Interview

As mentioned above, the clinical interview is the common method therapists use to assess patients for sex therapy. A wealth of information can be gathered in this manner if the right questions are asked, the therapist is a good observer, and a comfortable, nonthreatening environment is provided. Interviews are often, but not necessarily, conducted by a male-and-female sex therapy team. It is frequently useful to interview a couple together, and then separately, in order to get a more complete appraisal of the individual and the relationship. More secretive material may not emerge when both are seen at once (e.g., extramarital affairs), while important interactions are not observable if patients are interviewed separately.

Green (1977) presents an outline for conducting a clinical interview with a focus on assembling a complete sexual history. In particular, he offers brief comments and questions that may help facilitate the process of collecting information within several main areas. These areas include discussion of the sexual dysfunction, teenage sexuality, current situation, sexual myths, masturbation, homosexual feelings, "unusual" sex interests, concerns with aging, sexual diseases, and contraception.

An alternate interview protocol is offered by LoPiccolo and Heiman (1978). They divide important content to be assessed into two general areas relating to historical data and current situation. Under *historical information* they suggest examining background and early childhood circumstances, including family background, religious influences, attitudes toward sex in the home. They also explore emerging sexuality in the period of puberty and adolescence, including sexual education, dating and petting behavior, coital and other sexual experiences, and premarital attitudes and behavior. In the area of *current information,* various concerns are examined, including sexual attitudes and beliefs, nonintercourse sexual activity, extra-relationship sex, homosexuality, communication, quality of the relationship, life-style, and a detailed questioning about the sexual difficulty of dysfunction.

Lobitz and Lobitz (1978) offer a slightly different interview format, although they do not provide the specificity and, in some cases, precise wording as the two mentioned above. They suggest that the assessment interview should cover parent sex attitudes and behavior, sources and content of early sexual information, early sex play, self-discovery of one's own sexuality, social-sexual experiences during adolescence, social-sexual values, first intercourse, involvement with present partner, other major sexual relationships, onset and course of specific sexual dysfunction, and previous attempts to change the dysfunction.

Each of these various protocols are suggestions of appropriate interview schedules. They are offered to sensitize clinicians to the broad areas that are important to assess in a systematic and thorough manner. The specific format can be individually tailored to suit the therapist's style.

Although content of the information is crucial for understanding the patient and formulating a treatment plan, the style of presentation is equally as important. Nonverbal behavior, discomfort, avoidance, and numerous other styles of interaction and engagement provide further information regarding how sexual material is handled and dealt with by the individual and couple.

The inclusion of topics of intimate sexual behavior, attitudes, and feelings in sex therapy assessment increases the need for sensitivity and self-awareness in the therapist. This potential "blind spot" must not be taken lightly. The therapist's comfort and openness with discussing intimate and sexual issues with the patient provides a model for the patient and facilitates disclosure and exploration. Thus, the clinician's comfort guides the assessment and interventions in therapeutically useful ways and can profoundly influence the outcome of treatment.

In a recent analogue study of therapist's responses to sexual material and seductiveness in the patient, Schover (1982) noted some disturbing patterns and potential problems. Using professionally trained psychologists, psychiatrists, and social workers, she found that men responded more inappropriately to sexual themes than women, by both overemphasizing and underemphasizing sexual materials. Female therapists tended to be more comfortable and make fewer therapeutic errors than male clinicians. Attitude and awareness problems were also noted. For example, male clinicians rated a female patient who was not achieving "vaginal" orgasms as highly disturbed, and several clinicians seemed unware of the availability of effective short-term treatment for cases of mild premature ejaculation and secondary orgasmic dysfunction, and tended to overpathologize the problems.

It is important that therapists be aware and open to their own discomfort when assessing through a clinical interview. A great deal of information is available when the therapist provides a safe and supportive environment.

Questionnaires

Various types of objective questionnaires are the second most frequently used assessment method in sex therapy (for review see Conte, 1983). There are three classes of instruments typically employed: Single-item measures to determine frequency, desire, and satisfaction with specific sexual behaviors; psychometrically developed multi-item instruments designed to assess particular sexual attitudes, qualities, or behavior; and tools that measure nonsexual but relevant aspects of the individual and/or couple.

Sexual history and background information can be obtained easily from a general attitude and behavior frequency questionnaire. Data from this source can be an excellent springboard for issues to examine more closely in the clinical interview. For example, in studying male dysfunctions, Price et al. (1981) used a background-information questionnaire that assessed "...current and desired frequency of masturbation, intercourse, and other sexual behavior; frequency of problems getting and maintaining an erection; problems with rapid and delayed ejaculation; self-reported satisfaction with sexual self-image and sexual relationship." A variation of this format suitable for women would include questions regarding pain, discomfort, or difficulty having intercourse, and problems with orgasm, both during intercourse and by other means (e.g., oral, masturbation, vibrator).

A 28-item sexual history form that is particularly useful has been developed by Schover, Friedman, Weiler, Heiman, and LoPiccolo (1980). Through multiple-choice questions, various qualities are assessed, including actual and desired frequency of intercourse, initiations for sex, satisfaction, specific problems, and duration of important activities. The unique feature of this form is that it has been incorporated into a diagnostic system (Schover, Friedman, Weiler, Heiman, & LoPicolo, 1982), with norms for each sex. This will be described more fully in the section of this chapter headed Diagnosis of the Disorder.

Background information and sexual history questionnaires should be coordinated with a specific interview protocol. For instance, subjective orgasmic responsiveness for women has been related to the number of sexual partners (Newcomb, 1985) and to the type of relationship, for example, cohabitation (Newcomb, 1986). Thus, the paper-and-pencil test should include enough general and specific information to sensitize the clinician to areas that need to be explored in depth during the assessment interviews. They should also give an initial diagnostic impression.

A vast number of instruments have been designed to assess particular sexual qualities, including attitudes, responsiveness, knowledge, and actual behavior.

Types of attitude measures that have been used include flexibility assessment (Sewell & Abramowitz, 1979; Sperlich, 1975), Love Scale (Rubin, 1975), Behavioral Test of Tenderness (Warren & Gilner, 1978), Sexual Anxiety Scale (e.g., Kockott, Feil, Revenstorf, Aldenhoff, & Besinger, 1980), Sex Guilt (Mosher, 1968), Sexual Fear (Annon, 1975), Negative Attitudes Toward Masturbation (Abramson & Mosher, 1975), and attitudes toward masturbation, premarital sex, extramarital sex, menstruation, guilt, simultaneous orgasm, nudity, and homosexuality (e.g., Schneidman & McGuire, 1976), to name but a few. In terms of utility, because masturbation is a frequent assignment during treatment (LoPiccolo & Lobitz, 1972), the Negative Attitudes Toward Masturbation may be particularly illuminating to assess, as well as is flexibility, which is an essential ingredient for optimistic prognosis (Sewell & Abramowitz, 1979).

Types of responsiveness measures include Subjective Orgasmic Responsiveness during coitus, masturbation, and with a partner (Bentler & Peeler, 1979; Newcomb & Bentler, 1983), Sexual Responsiveness Survey (Pion, Anderson, & Wagner, 1970), Sexual Arousability Inventory (Hoon, Hoon, & Wincze, 1976), and the Physiological Arousal Scale (Griffitt, 1975), as examples. Although these may be important research tools, their present usefulness in clinical treatment may be limited due to inadequate norms in some cases. Of these various measures, the Sexual Arousability Inventory has demonstrated adequate discriminant validity, high internal consistency, and percentile norms (Hoon et al., 1976). In addition, five subscales have been identified (Hoon & Hoon, 1978), relating to breast stimulation, genital stimulation, gentle seduction (foreplay), intercourse, and media arousability.

Since knowledge of sexual processes is an important aspect of adequate and effective sexual functioning, several measures have been developed to assess this knowledge base. Such measures include the information scale of the Derogatis Sexual Functioning Inventory (DSFI: Derogatis, 1976), which includes percentile norms, the Sexual Knowledge and Attitude Test (Lief & Reed, 1972), the Sex Knowledge Inventory (McHugh, 1967), and the Sex Questionnaire (Zuckerman, Tushup, & Finner, 1976). The patient's level of sexual knowledge and sophistication is useful to be aware of in testing sexual dysfunctions, and these types of self- administered tests are practical for determining this information.

Measures have also been developed to assess actual behavior of the individual or couple. For example, Bentler (1968a, 1968b) has developed heterosexual Sexual Behavior Inventories for men and women, which include Guttman-type ordering of specific behaviors. This has been used frequently to study both sexuality (e.g., DiVasto et al., 1981) and relationships (e.g., Newcomb & Bentler, 1980). Other similar instruments include the Sexual Experience Scale (Zuckerman, 1973), and the Experience scale of the DSFI (Derogatis, Melisaratos, & Clark, 1976).

Finally, more specific scales have been developed, such as the Goals for Sex Therapy Scale (Lobitz & Baker, 1979), and the Erectile Difficulty Questionnaire (Reynolds, 1978). At a more general level, extensive inventories have been created that assess a wide variety of important factors. These include the Sexual Interaction Inventory (LoPiccolo & Steger, 1974) and the DSFI (Derogatis, 1976; Derogatis & Meyer, 1979). These more complex inventories are discussed in greater depth in the section of this chapter headed Understanding the Dysfunction, and in chapter 7 of this volume.

Several other questionnaire-type instruments have been used to assess nonsexual aspects of the patient. Most important and useful of these have been the Minnesota Multiphasic Personality Inventory (Hathaway & McKinley, 1967) and the Short Marital Adjustment Scale (Locke & Wallace, 1959). Use of these instruments is discussed in the chapter section headed Appropriateness for Sex Therapy.

Observation

Direct observation of sexual and semisexual behavior has occasionally been used to assess dysfunction. This can range from noticing how a couple gives each other hand massages in the clinician's office (e.g., Lobitz & Lobitz, 1978), to actually observing overt sexual behavior including intercourse (e.g., Hartman & Fithian, 1972, 1974; Serber, 1974). Some therapists even go one step further by physically engaging the patient in sexual activity (e.g., Hoch, 1980).

Clearly, many of these techniques may not be appropriate for most clinicians or for most patients. In fact, the observation of and participation in overt sexual activity raises serious questions around professional ethics, patient privacy, and perhaps result in deleterious effects on the doctor/patient relationship. In particular, sexual activity between patient and clinician is considered unethical within most professional organizations and such conduct may be quite destructive to the patient's welfare and psychological well-being.

However, observing less explicit sexual behavior of a couple may yield important information regarding how they interact in a nonverbal and tactile manner. Having the couple give each other hand, foot, or face massages in the therapist's office may not be overly intrusive for some patients and does not seem to raise major ethical concerns. However, the decision to use this method must be made on a case-by-case basis.

Behavioral Experiments

Assigning specific behavioral activities for the individual and/or couple can be useful for a variety of reasons from an assessment, as well as from a treatment perspective. These activities are designed to be carried out in the privacy of the patient's home. Feedback from these assignments gives the therapist a practical sense of how the couple will respond to the demands of sex therapy, which typically involve assignment of many diverse tasks to be done together and individually. It allows the therapist to gauge how well the patient follows instructions. Also, it may pinpoint problems or circumstances preventing the execution of the assignment. It will evaluate the patient's motivation and willingness to set aside time for sexuality. Finally, it will help assess how well the couple works together in structuring time and situations alone and together, and the general quality of their interactions.

Assuming that the assessment process involves more than one interview, an assignment can be given during the first session and evaluated during the second. It is useful to assign an activity for both to do together, and one that they must do separately. Types of couple activities might include a ban on intercourse, or massages, or assigned discussions. Individual activities might include body exploration, tactile experiments, or writing down sexual or sensual feelings and associations.

Fantasy

The use of sexual fantasy plays an important role in masturbation and intercourse for many men and women (e.g., Hariton & Singer, 1974; Stock & Geer, 1982). Although fantasy, particularly when sexual in nature, is a very sensitive topic, assessing the role of fantasy in sexual behavior can shed light and perspective on how sex is dynamically integrated into a patient's life, the character of erotic and sexual needs, and the ease and comfort with which fantasy is used. This information can be used to develop treatment plans that involve imagery and fantasy, which have proven useful in modifying sexual activity (e.g., Echeandia, 1981).

Several methods have been utilized to assess the range and content of sexual fantasy. The projective Thematic Aperception Test (Stein, 1948) has been employed as a measure of sexual modeling effects (e.g., Sach & Duffy, 1976) and as an outcome indicator when treating male erectile dysfunction (Lobitz & Baker, 1979). Objective measures have also been developed to assess fantasy, such as the Imaginal Processes Inventory (Singer & Antrobus, 1972), which has been used to assess sexual fantasy behavior in women (Stock & Geer, 1982) and found to be correlated with sexual behavior in men (Giambra & Martin, 1977). A short form of the Imaginal Process Inventory is available, which is easily administered and scored (Huba, Singer, Aneshensel, & Antrobus, 1982). Important second-order factors of positive- constructive daydreaming, guilt-fear of failure daydreaming, and poor attentional control have been identified in this short form (Huba, Aneshensel, & Singer, 1981). Coen (1978) suggests an interview method to elicit sexual fantasy material, which is discussed in a psychoanalytic framework.

Physiological Indicators

Physiological reactions are excellent indicators of various components and stages of sexual behavior (e.g., Masters & Johnson, 1966). Although currently unavailable to the general psychotherapist, several physiological measures may prove to be quite useful in the assessment, diagnosis, and treatment of sexual dysfunctions (e.g., Geer, 1975, 1976; Heiman, 1976).

Nocturnal penile tumescence has been found to be a good discriminator between psychogenic and organic impotence in men (e.g., Karacan, 1978; Marshall, Surridge, & Delva, 1981). Penile circumference and number of penile tumescence episodes during REM sleep have been found to significantly differentiate types of erectile dysfunction in males (Marshall et al., 1981). Other physiological reactions have also been related to sexual response, such as those measured by the EEG, ECG, plethysmography, and vaginal pulse amplitude (e.g., Heiman, 1976, 1977, 1978; Rogers, Van de Castle, Evans, & Critelli, 1985). For example, Wincze, Hoon, and Hoon (1976) found that sexually dysfunctional women showed significantly less vaginal vasocongestion and lower diastolic blood pressure than nondysfunctional women, when viewing an erotic film.

A major drawback to these methods is that they typically require a specialized laboratory and obtrusive devices that have not been feasible to be used in the privacy of the patient's home. However, recent advances in recording capabilities have allowed these various physiological measures to be gathered by a small cassette recorder, which can be taken home when the patient has been properly trained (e.g., Sarrel, Foddy, & McKinnon, 1977). A radiotelemetric device have been developed that can monitor vaginal temperatures in the woman's home (Fugl-Meyer, Sjogren, & Johansson, 1984). For the male, portable nocturnal penile tumescence monitors have been developed, which will permit physiological assessments in the privacy of home (e.g., Procci & Martin, 1984). In addition, physiological measures have been used in an analogue treatment study using biofeedback (Hoon, Wincze, & Hoon, 1977).

Verbal and Written Reporting

A final essential assessment method is feedback from the patient during treatment in response to assignments and interventions. This can be either verbal or written, but a combination of both may be most useful.

A typical type of report or feedback sheet includes several components. First, the actual activity engaged in should be described in detail. The duration of activity is indicated in minutes. Subjective ratings may also be gathered in this manner. For example, the perceived amount of pleasure or arousal elicited by the activity can be indicated on a 1- to 10-point rating scale. Finally, positive and negative comments and reactions to the activity may be written in a narrative or short-phase format. All of this written information should be read by the therapist and addressed and discussed during the treatment sessions as a part of therapy.

APPROPRIATENESS FOR SEX THERAPY

The initial task in sex therapy assessment is determining whether the patient is suitable for treatment in a brief behavioral format focused only on sexual issues. This is essential, because sex therapy is a powerful but specific treatment that is designed to address sexual dysfunction and not other complicating problems. These other interfering issues generally reside in the individual, dyad, and/or situation.

Chapman (1982) examined sex therapy failures and successes and found several aspects of treatment and the patients that differentiated these outcomes. She noted that treatment failures spent considerable therapeutic time struggling with what material was appropriate for the treatment session; nonsexual issues and problems frequently intruded upon and often became the focus of treatment; and they often had trouble beginning or completing homework assignments. In particular, Chapman (1982) noted that "...failure to initially conduct a thorough diagnosis was associated with treatment failure." In other words, many nonsexual issues and faulty processes in the relationship were either ignored or simply not noted during assessment, which then interfered with the sex therapy procedures and resulted in treatment failure. Individual, dyadic, and situational components all need to be carefully evaluated, with particular attention devoted to whether sex therapy is contraindicated for these patients at this particular time.

Individual Factors

Lobitz and Lobitz (1978) suggest three individual factors necessary to assess when considering appropriateness for sex therapy: (1) organic pathology, (2) psychopathology, and (3) motivation. Several of these components have already been discussed, and thus are reviewed here only briefly.

Involvement of organic pathology with sexual dysfunction has been found to vary between 3% and 30% (Kaplan, 1974; Lobitz & Lobitz, 1978; Shrom, Lief, & Wein, 1979). It is important to have all patients evaluated by a competent physician aware of problems of sexual functioning. In addition, possible infections or drug side effects need to be evaluated (Chapman, 1982), as well as do age, natural physical events, and other physiological processes previously mentioned.

Presence of major psychopathology also needs to be carefully assessed. An MMPI (Dahlstrom, Welsh, & Dahlstrom, 1972) can be quite valuable in ruling out gross emotional disturbance and is highly recommended for regular use in patient screening. In general, severe psychiatric impairment is a poor prognostic indication for sex therapy (e.g., Meyer, Schmidt, Lucas, & Smith, 1975). Depression and alcohol abuse can severely disrupt the treatment regime, since depression decreases energy and motivation (e.g., Lobitz & Lobitz, 1978) and alcohol interferes with natural sexual functioning (e.g., Briddel & Wilson, 1976). However, not all patients with apparent psychopathology need to be excluded from sex therapy. Lobitz and Lobitz (1978) suggest that if the psychological disorder does not interfere with the patient's everyday functioning and the treatment process, sex therapy can be considered.

A final individual factor to consider when assessing for the appropriateness for sex therapy is attitude and personal characteristics. Sewell and Abramowitz (1979) found that flexibility was the best predictor of persistence in sex therapy. Flexibility was measured using the sum of eight items rated on a 7-point rating scale (Sperlich, 1975). This flexibility assessment accounted for almost 50% of the variance between couples who dropped out and those who completed the sex therapy program. Motivation is another personal quality essential for successful treatment of sexual dysfunction (Lobitz & Lobitz, 1978). The patients must be willing and hopefully eager to participate in the treatment process, and possess a genuine desire to improve their relationship.

Although patients of all ages benefit from sex therapy, some evidence suggests that older patients of both sexes tend to respond best to individual rather than group treatment (e.g., Price et al., 1981; Schneidman & McGuire, 1976). Younger patients seem to respond equally well to either individual or group therapy formats. Some difficulty in treatment has also been noted in lower class patients (e.g., Lansky & Davenport, 1975), perhaps because behavioral sex therapy requires relative sophistication regarding values confrontation and an interest in self-awareness (e.g., Sewell & Abramowitz, 1979). In addition, it is important that the patient have some degree of "therapy positive" attitude and a belief that therapy can be effective (e.g., Chapman, 1982).

Dyadic Factors

Quality of the relationship is another component to weigh when evaluating the suitability for sex therapy. It is common for couples presenting with sex problems to have other relationship difficulties as well (e.g., Frank, Anderson, & Kupfer, 1976; Sager, 1976). Although at times difficult to assess, it is important to determine whether the relationship problems are a result of the sexual dysfunction, or whether the dysfunction in only one aspect of a troubled relationship. Sex therapy is usually contraindicated when the sexual problems are only one facet of a general relationship disturbance.

Lobitz and Lobitz (1978) suggest that the level of hostility and amount of intimacy are important indicators of whether sex therapy is advisable. A high degree of intimacy and minimal hostility are positive prognostic indications for effective sex therapy treatment. In addition to being able to identify and determine that a particular sexual dysfunction is present, Chapman (1982) has established basic relationship requirements or criteria for patients to be suitable for sex therapy. These criteria include (1) an established and clear commitment agreement, (2) adequate communication skills, (3) that relationship material is not withheld, and (4) mutually compatible life and relationship goals. These requirements may be overly strict in specific instances; however, they represent important areas of strength upon which successful sex therapy must build. If sex therapy is attempted when these criteria are not met, the clinician must be sensitive to where these deficits may be impeding therapeutic progress.

These qualities can be evaluated by a combination of verbal interview material, clinical observation, behavioral experiments, and written tests or questionnaires. One of the most commonly used relationship assessment devices is the Short Marital Adjustment Scale (Locke & Wallace, 1959), which should be completed by both partners of the couple independently. This measure attempts to assess one general factor of relationship adjustment using 15 items. The single large factor has been confirmed factor-analytically (Bentler & Newcomb, 1978; Newcomb, 1983; Kimmel & van der Veen, 1974). The items tap various areas of relationship functioning, including sexual relations, and are formed into a single composite score, which has a mean of 100 by a weighted summation formula (Locke & Wallace, 1959). Recent attempts to delineate various aspects of relationship satisfaction and adjustment have located one large general second-order factor and several first-order factors, one of which is a problem with sex and affection (Newcomb, 1983).

Thus, two methods are suggested for decision making using the Locke-Wallace Scale. First, total scores of 80 or less have been shown to be poor sex therapy prospects (e.g., Leiblum, Rosen, & Pierce, 1976), and would best be treated for their general relationship troubles before undertaking therapy for their sexual dysfunction. A second method involves examining specific responses to particular items. It is often useful to compare ratings given to the sexual relations item to those given for other areas of the relationship (e.g., recreation, in-laws, finances), by examining the scatter of responses to these items. It is also important to notice if either patient endorsed the statements regarding whether they would have preferred to have married another person or wished they had never married their present spouse. Agreement with either of these statements is a very poor prognostic indication.

Situational Factors

Various situational or circumstantial components may also preclude sex therapy as an optimal treatment choice. For example, an active extrarelationship sexual involvement, whether or not it is known and/or condoned by both members of the couple, can be very disruptive and detrimental to the treatment process. Typically, sex therapy is denied to those couples wherein one or both partners are actively involved in an outside sexual affair.

Other situational factors that may preclude or postpone sex therapy include crises in the family, death of a relative or close friend, and the stress involved in moving, divorcing, or changing jobs. These outside impinging factors clearly limit the time, attention, energy, and emotional involvement that are necessary for sex therapy to be successful.

MEDICAL EVALUATION

If the couple has been found to be appropriate for sex therapy, a medical evaluation and consultation should be conducted before proceeding with treatment.

Not all physicians are sensitive to or aware of the complex interaction of emotional and physiological processes that occur in sexual functioning. As a result, some less-enlightened physicians convey disturbing suggestions and advice to their female patients, such as, "Don't worry about it, just pretend you enjoy sex," and "Your childhood masturbation is what made you frigid," (LoPiccolo & Lobitz, 1973); and to their male patients in the form of "So join the club. It happens to all of us sooner or later." (Lobitz & Lobitz, 1978). Until recently, medical schools have not included curriculum on sexual behavior (Vincent, 1968), and preliminary evidence indicates that its inclusion is effective in changing attitudes and increasing sexual knowledge of medical students (e.g., Garrard, Vaitkus, Held, & Chilgren, 1976; Marcotte & Logan, 1977).

Thus it is imperative to select carefully a physician to do the medical consultation. If no organic impairment is evident, sex therapy assessment and treatment can continue. If an organic problem is discovered that is not amenable to medical treatment, sex therapy may still continue in many cases, with close coordination with the physician to clarify the extent and nature of the organic deficit. If the organic impairment is treatable, appropriate referrals should be expedited. If medical treatment cannot completely remediate the condition, sex therapy may be needed to help the couple adjust to the limitations in sexual functioning brought on by the impairment. In this case, the physician should be actively consulted regarding specifics of the organic or physiological problem.

Important areas of which to be particularly sensitive are discussed by Wagner and Green (1981) and Hatch (1981).

DIAGNOSIS OF THE DISORDER

DSM III (1980) defines a sexual dysfunction as an "...inhibition in the appetitive or psychophysiological changes that characterize the complete sexual response cycle" (p. 275). Chapman (1982) and Zilbergeld and Ellison (1980), however, emphasize the role of "subjective satisfaction and personal meaningfulness of sexual encounter," rather than simply completing the sexual response cycle. Schover et al. (1980, 1982), on the other hand, attempted to minimize the etiological implications of previous diagnostic systems, with careful and explicit descriptions of the various disorders using a multiaxial perspective. In other words, they wanted to provide clear and useful behavioral descriptions of the sexual disorders without relying upon unobservable constructs and dynamics that may have contributed to the development of the dysfunction, but that cannot be readily assessed and evaluated.

Males and females seem to present different types of disorders. In general, men tend to suffer from dysfunctions of performance (e.g., erectile failure), while women typically suffer from dysfunctions of satisfaction (e.g., orgasm) (Derogatis & Meyer, 1979). Following the multiaxial approach of Schover et al. (1980, 1982), various disorders of men and women are presented within six areas, including desire, arousal, orgasm, coital pain, frequency dissatisfaction, and qualifying information. Overall, the Schover et al. (1980, 1982) delineation is an expansion and important refinement of the relatively minimal typology offered by *DSM III* (1980). The first three areas or axes—desire, arousal, and orgasm—follow the conceptualization of Kaplan (1979), while the last three axes—coital pain, frequency dissatisfaction, and qualifying information—have been added by Schover et al. The Schover et al. (1980, 1982) diagnostic system also requires disorders to be refined along two dimensions. One dimension specifies the problem as lifelong or not lifelong, while the other dimension categorizes the dysfunction as either global, occuring in all sexual activity, or situational, present in only certain activities.

Desire

DSM III (1980) provides one classification for a desire dysfunction called "inhibited sexual desire" (302.71), and suggests that this diagnosis will rarely be given. However, there is an apparent increase in observed cases of low sexual desire (e.g., LoPiccolo, 1980), although this may be an artifact of more careful assessment and outcome evaluation (Kaplan, 1977). Problems of low desire and desire discrepancies have received increased research attention, thus providing a more accurate appraisal of the disorder.

Kaplan (1979) offers a more differentiated typology of cases of low sexual desire. She suggests that the classification of "inhibited sexual desire" be used when the dysfunction is clearly psychogenic and "hypoactive sexual desire" be used when etiological factors are unclear. This distinction is reflected in *DSM III* (1980) where the diagnosis of "inhibited sexual desire" may be given only if "the disturbance is not caused exclusively by organic factors (e.g., physical disease or medication) and is not due to another Axis I disorder" (p. 279). Where these conditions are not met, according to *DSM III*, one must diagnose the nonsexual Axis I disorder, and/or specify the physical impairment on Axis III, and not give a sexual dysfunction diagnosis. Kaplan (1979), however, suggests that the diagnosis of "hypoactive sexual desire" be given in these instances. Kaplan further categorizes disorders of desire on a primary (lifelong) or secondary (not lifelong) dimension, and a global (all sexual activity) or situational (certain activities) dimension.

Schover et al. (1980, 1982) provide two basic classifications on their Desire Axis: low sexual desire and aversion to sex. Each should be modified by stipulating whether it is lifelong or not and whether it is global or situational. Low sexual desire is characterized by a subjective component (a lack of desire for sex) and by a behavioral component (a low frequency of sexual activity). Although absolute numbers are extremely difficult to state for frequency (e.g., Zilbergeld & Ellison, 1980), a rule of thumb suggests that a total sexual outlet less than once every two weeks is considered a sign of low desire (Schover et al., 1982). Aversion to sex is characterized by low sexual desire and obvious negative emotional reaction to sexual activity, including fear, disgust, guilt, shame, or anxiety.

LoPiccolo (1980) has noted several predisposing factors associated with various problems of low sexual interest and desire. These include depression, restrictive religions (e.g., rigid Catholicism), other sexual dysfunctions, aversion to oral sex activity, aversion to female genitals, total absence of or conflict about masturbation, and relationship disturbance not acknowledged by the patients. However, she does not indicate whether these factors differentially help generate low sexual desire versus an aversion to sex. Frank, Anderson, and Rubinstein (1978) noted that problems of low sexual desire and interest occur in both men and women, yet over twice as many women than men reported "disinterest" and being "turned off" by sex. Others have noted differences between men and women regarding various aspects of sexual encounters (Denney, Field, & Quadagno, 1984). Women desired more time for foreplay and afterplay than men, who desired longer intercourse than women. If these differences are pronounced in a couple, a lack of desire may result due to frustration from unmet needs and preferences.

Arousal

Arousal disorders are typically ones of performance and thus appear most frequently in men. *DSM III* (1980) categorizes arousal problems in one diagnosis called "inhibited sexual excitement" (302.72), which has been characterized in men as "...partial or complete failure to attain or maintain erection until completion of the sexual act..." and in women as "...partial or complete failure to attain or maintain the lubrication-swelling response of sexual excitement until completion of the sex act" (p. 279).

Schover et al. (1980, 1982) offer nine specific, mutually exclusive diagnoses on the Arousal Axis: six of these are specific to men. These involve combinations of decreased subjective or physiological arousal and difficulty achieving and/or maintaining an erection. In other words, erectile dysfunction (trouble attaining and/or maintaining erection) may or may not be accompanied by decreased subjective arousal. Again, these diagnoses must be refined by determining whether they are lifelong or not (primary versus secondary impotence as defined by Masters & Johnson, 1970), and whether they are global or situational. It is important to ascertain that adequate sexual stimulation is provided and continued, and that arousal difficulties occur in spite of sexual activity.

An important distinction to make is between organic and psychogenic causes of arousal dysfunction (Wagner, 1981; Wagner & Green, 1981). Previously, virtually all erectile failure dysfunctions had been considered psychological in nature (e.g., Ellis, 1980; Masters & Johnson, 1970). Recently, however, as many as one third of erectile dysfunctions have been found to have an organic involvement (e.g., Shrom et al., 1979). Ellis (1980) suggests that careful and direct questioning can make the distinction between organic and psychogenic erectile failure. He argues that if "...the client sometimes achieves erection in intercourse, usually does so during masturbation, has little trouble during petting, and often has good erections while asleep, it is fairly certain that his problems are of psychological origin" (p. 236). Although these are essential facts to determine, we do not believe that they replace a careful and thorough medical evaluation. Other researchers have been able to distinguish psychogenic from organic impotence on the basis of standard personality inventories such as the MMPI and California Personality Inventory, although differences were evident on only a few items or scales (Martin, Rodgers, & Montague, 1983).

Orgasm

DSM III (1980) provides one diagnostic category for orgasm dysfunction in women (inhibited female orgasm — 302.73) and two possible diagnoses for men (inhibited male orgasm — 302.74; and premature ejaculation — 302.75). Clearly, these limited classifications offer little utility in assessment and treatment. Fortuantely, other systems offer more detailed understanding of orgasmic dysfunctions.

In men. Typically men can have either retarded ejaculation or premature ejaculation as orgasmic disorders.

Retarded ejaculation is defined as the inability of the man to achieve orgasm during coitus, or "recurrent and persistent inhibition of the male orgasm as manifested by a delay in or absence of ejaculation following an adequate phase of sexual excitement" (*DSM III*, 1980, p. 280). It is a relatively rare phenomenon (Apfelbaum, 1980; Kaplan, 1974; Masters & Johnson, 1970), though perhaps more common than previously assumed (Munjack & Kanno, 1979), that is often resistant to treatment. Apfelbaum (1980) takes issue with the intercourse-specific nature of the diagnosis and emphasizes that ability to ejaculate in other contexts (particularly masturbation) needs to be more carefully evaluated. He contends that most patients labeled as retarded ejaculators can have orgasms in other manners than coitus, and thus considers the problem a coitus-specific desire disorder. The Schover et al. (1980, 1982) diagnostic system allows this specification for "inhibited ejaculation" by determining whether the problem is lifelong or not, and whether it is situational (during coitus only) or global (during all activities and forms of stimulation). Munjack and Kanno (1979) suggest that fear, guilt, resentment, and passivity may be important psychological factors in the etiology of retarded ejaculation.

The second, more common male orgasmic dysfunction is premature ejaculation. *DSM III* (1980) defines premature ejaculation as when "ejaculation occurs before the individual wishes it, because of recurrent and persistent absence of reasonable voluntary control of ejaculation and orgasm during sexual activity" (p. 280). If a man ejaculates before or immediately upon entering the vagina there is little doubt that this is premature. However, beyond this, the definition of "reasonable control" becomes difficult. Early researchers attempted to define the duration of coitus or number of thrusts prior to orgasm as premature ejaculation (reviewed by Perelman, 1980). Masters and Johnson (1970) redefined premature ejaculation in terms of the partner's satisfaction and the inability of a responsive partner to achieve orgasm during 50% of their intercourse experiences. However, individual variations limit the usefulness of this definition (Kilmann & Auerbach, 1979). Perelman(1980) emphasizes the "lack of a learned ability to delay orgasm, once sexually aroused, regardless of time" (p. 201) as a defining characteristic of a premature ejaculator. These men have not been able to discriminate effectively their own internal cues to sexual arousal.

Schover et al. (1980, 1982) describe six categories of premature ejaculation: before entry; less than 1 minute; 1 to 3 minutes; 4 to 7 minutes; with flaccid penis; and with anhedonic orgasm. The use of specific durations is somewhat arbitrary but based on some normative research. For example, 4 to 7 minutes has been noted as the median duration of intercourse in one sample (Jemail, 1977), while Hunt (1974), in his national survey, estimated that the median duration of coitus was 10 minutes. Again, the diagnosis should be refined in terms of whether it is lifelong or not and whether it is global (during all activities, including masturbation, as well as partner manual or oral stimulation) or situational (e.g., only during coitus).

Schover et al. (1980, 1982) also include diagnoses for male orgasm with anhedonia and/or flaccid penis. Anhedonic orgasm is defined as one with no pleasurable sensations or wherein the ejaculatory phase is inhibited and only the emission phase occurs (seepage of ejaculate from urethra), again with no pleasurable sensations. Ejaculation with flaccid penis indicates an orgasm without the presence of a firm erection.

In women. Inability to achieve orgasm is the only orgasmic dysfunction in women. Primary inorgasmia (Masters & Johnson, 1970) and anorgasmia (Barbach, 1980) are categories for women who have never been able to reach orgasm all their lives by any means (see review by Anderson, 1983). *DSM III* (1980) provides one diagnosis for orgasmic dysfunction in women that is called "inhibited female orgasm." This may be used in the case of anorgasmia or if the dysfunction is situational (i.e., the woman is orgasmic in some circumstances but not in others). Situational orgasmic dysfunction, or secondary inorgasmia (Masters & Johnson, 1970), frequently involves the inability to reach orgasm during intercourse, although other variations also occur.

Inability to achieve orgasm during intercourse is so common that it is not generally considered a dysfunction unless the patient is concerned with it (e.g., Schover et al., 1980, 1982). However, secondary orgasmic dysfunction should not be considered a catch- all category, because the range and nature of activities in which a woman is orgasmic helps determine treatment strategies and sexual satisfaction subsequent to therapy (e.g., McGovern, McCullen, & LoPiccolo, 1975). Toward this end, Schover et al. (1980, 1982) have specified six types of orgasmic difficulty in women. These diagnoses are all situationally specific except for totally inorgasmic, which is typically a global diagnosis unless the woman's sexual behavior (orgasmic ability) differs between partners. The remaining five diagnoses are restricted types of inorgasmia, such as the one of inorgasmic except during specific situations (or combinations of situations). Other circumstances include masturbation, partner manipulation, mechanical stimulation (e.g., vibrator), and infrequent coital orgasms. These diagnoses must be refined by determining whether or not they are lifelong.

Barbach (1980) has reviewed the various etiological factors contributing to orgasmic dysfunction in women. She noted that a lack of information or misinformation, role scripting that teaches women to be passive and relinquish control of their lives, and fear of losing control may predispose a woman to develop orgasm difficulties. Newcomb (1984) has noted that increased female orgasmic responsiveness (both coital and masturbatory) is significantly associated with high levels of sexual behavior, dating competence, social assertiveness, and early sexual involvement. Positive parental attitudes toward sex indirectly influence high orgasmic responsiveness via the women's social and dating competence. Attempts have also been made to link orgasm difficulties in women to insufficient foreplay and duration of coitus. In general, however, such an association has not been found (e.g., Fisher, 1973; Huey, Kline-Graber, & Graber, 1981). Kline-Graber and Graber (1978) have emphasized the role of pubococcygeal muscle deficiencies in women with orgasmic dysfunctions, although research linking muscle tone to orgasmic capacity is generally inconclusive (e.g., Freese & Levitt, 1984; Graber & Kline-Graber, 1979; Messe & Geer, 1985; Chambless,

Sultan, Stern, O'Neill, Garrison, & Jackson, 1984; Trudel & Saint-Laurent, 1983).

Coital Pain

Problems can arise that make intercourse impossible, such as vaginismus, or uncomfortable, such as pain or dyspareunia.

DSM III (1980) defines "functional vaginismus" (306.51) as a "...recurrent and persistent spasm of the musculature of the outer third of the vagina that interferes with coitus" (p. 280). In addition, a good deal of pain is often experienced if intercourse is attempted (e.g., Schover et al., 1980, 1982). Fuchs, Hoch, Paldi, Abramovici, Brandes, Timor-Tritsch, and Kleinhaus (1973) suggest that vaginismus is comparable to primary impotence in men because they both can preclude the physical possibility of sexual intercourse. They further assert that it is essential to treat vaginismus immediately, before the symptoms become fixated, the partner becomes conditioned to faulty intercourse, major disruptions in the relationship occur, and pathological reactions such as guilt, shame, depression, and hostility emerge.

Leiblum, Pervin, and Campbell (1980) reviewed some of the etiological factors associated with vaginismus. They noted that vaginismus is a conditioned involuntary phobic response, that, as Masters and Johnson (1970) have noted, may be "...due to imagined, anticipated, or real attempt at vaginal penetration" (p. 250). This may result from specific trauma (e.g., rape), fear of pregnancy, sexual conflict, fear of punishment, religious orthodoxy, and secondary response to dyspareunia, or partner sexual dysfunctions. Fertel (1977) has noted that husbands of sexually inexperienced women (virgins prior to marriage) are frequently passive-dependent, weak, overly protective and considerate, exhibiting little persistence and assertion. In fact, Masters and Johnson (1970) have observed that "...the syndrome has a high percentage of association with primary impotence in the male partner." Ellison (1972) has noticed that husbands of wives with vaginismus typically are "...timid, gentle, over permissive men who have either overt or hidden anxieties about their own sexual role and potency" (p. 45). Both partners seem to fear the aggressiveness of sexual activity and they apparently create symptoms to prevent it. In other words, if a diagnosis of vaginismus is established, it is essential to assess carefully for sexual dysfunction in the male partner as well.

DSM III (1980) defines "functional dyspareunia" (302.76) as when "coitus is associated with recurrent and persistent genital pain, in either the male or female," (p. 280) with rule-outs for a physical disorder, arousal difficulty (e.g., insufficient vaginal lubrication), and vaginismus. Many physical diseases, infections, and abnormalities can precipitate coital pain and need to be carefully evaluated (e.g., Abarbanel, 1978). If organic involvement has been ruled out, a detailed description is obtained of the "...frequency, intensity, and duration of pain and discomfort in order to appreciate the level of sexual and relational disruption" (Lazarus, 1980: p. 150). It is important to consider contributing factors to coital pain. These may be developmental (such as sexual misinformation, associating sex with guilt and shame, and a strict religious upbringing, traumatic events associated with intercourse, relationship with the partner), or situational, such as inadequate foreplay, fear of being interrupted by children, or problems with contraception (Lazarus, 1980).

Schover et al. (1980, 1982) provide four diagnoses for painful sexual activity. "Dyspareunia" is defined as pain located in the genital area that occurs during sexual activity. This diagnosis must be modified by either being situational (e.g., only during coitus) or global (all forms of sexual activity), as well as by whether it is lifelong or not. In addition, they provide categories for "pain on ejaculation," "pain after ejaculation," and "other pain exacerbated by sexual activity," such as arthritis or low-back pain.

Frequency Dissatisfaction

Schover et al. (1980, 1982) provide two diagnoses for frequency dissatisfaction, one higher and one lower than desired. The categories clearly incorporate a subjective component in the form of desire (Zilbergeld & Ellison, 1980). It is important to assess actual frequencies of various sexual behaviors and desired frequencies of the same behaviors. If large differences emerge, this diagnosis should be considered. It is also relevant to determine that the desire frequencies are approximately in a normal range. As with the other diagnoses, these must be evaluated as either situational (only with particular activities or partners) or global (all sexual outlets), and whether the discrepancy has been lifelong or not.

Qualifying Information

Schover et al. (1980, 1982) provide a sixth axis, where additional information can be recorded that does not specify a sexual dysfunction, but specifies behaviors or conditions that definitely can impact on sexual activity. These include homosexuality, fetishism, voyeurism, exhibitionism, transvestism, masochism, sadism, psychopathology, marital distress, substance abuse, spouse abuse, extramarital affairs, medical conditions, and medication.

For insurance purposes and various government and agency requirements, *DSM III* (1980) diagnoses may be mandatory. However, they are rather deficient in providing a clear and usable diagnosis for the sexual dysfunctions. For clinical use, the multiaxial system developed by Schover et al. (1980, 1982) seems the most comprehensive and provides the greatest utility currently available. Specific diagnoses can be made on each of the six axes, providing a relatively clear picture of the various sexual dysfunctions and potential complicating factors present.

UNDERSTANDING THE DYSFUNCTION

Once a specific diagnosis has been established and the nature of the sexual disorder determined, it is necessary to evaluate how the dysfunction is maintained in the relationship and the strengths available to overcome it. A sexual dysfunction does not occur in isolation, but rather is manifested by the interplay between two people. It is the quality of this ecology that must be determined in this next step of sex therapy assessment.

Results of the various instruments discussed in the section on the Appropriateness of Sex Therapy (e.g., MMPI, Marital Adjustment Scale) are important input to this phase of assessment. Discussion of these will not be repeated here. However, two other assessment instruments and an assessment model are discussed in relation to fleshing-out the diagnosis, defining the dysfunction more accurately, and characterizing the partners and their interaction in a more detailed manner.

Derogatis Sexual Functioning Inventory

One of these assessment tools or instruments is the Derogatis Sexual Functioning Inventory (DSFI: Derogatis, 1975, 1976, 1977). This is a complex, evolving inventory that assesses 10 primary content areas relevant to sexual functioning. These dimensions include information, experience, desire, attitudes, emotions, symptoms, gender-role definition, fantasy, body image, and sexual satisfaction. In addition, an overall measure of Global Sexual Satisfaction is included. This inventory is designed to be completed and scored for an individual — not a couple — with appropriate norms provided to evaluate the responses. Results are plotted on a psychological profile sheet with each scale having a mean of 50 and a standard deviation of 10.

Since the following chapter is solely devoted to presenting clinical uses of the DSFI (Derogatis et al., 1988), it is only touched on briefly here in order to highlight its use in defining sexual dysfunction. Derogatis and Meyer (1979) compared males and females diagnosed with a variety of sexual disorders with a group of male and female nonpatient controls on the scales of the DSFI. They found that dysfunctional men had less accurate sexual information, less sexual experience, less sexual drive, more depression, more anxiety and more interpersonal sensitivity (symptoms), less positive and more negative affect, less androgyny (more inflexible gender role), and were less sexually satisfied than the control males. Dysfunctional women, on the other hand, had less accurate sexual information, more psychological distress, more negative and less positive affect, less androgyny, and less sexual satisfaction compared with nonpatient control women. This clearly indicates that possessing a sexual dysfunction is accompanied by other psychological changes, often regardless of the specific diagnosis.

Sexual Interaction Inventory

Similarly, informative data can be obtained from the Sexual Interaction Inventory, a very useful instrument for both assessment and outcome evaluation (SII; LoPiccolo & Steger, 1974). The SII was developed to assess dissatisfaction with the frequency and range of sexual activity, self-acceptance, pleasure, accurate knowledge of the partner, and acceptance of the partner. Data about these areas does not permit making a specific diagnosis, but rather helps to evaluate qualities of the individual and couple that surround and perhaps maintain or initiate a particular sexual dysfunction.

The administration format of the SII involves responding to six standard questions regarding each of 17 specific sexual behaviors. The 17 behaviors or activities were derived from the Guttman-type Heterosexual Behavior Inventories of Bentler (1968a, 1968b). Items ranged from "the male seeing the female when she is nude" (1), through "the female caressing the male genitals with her hand" (10), to "the male and female having intercourse with both of them having an orgasm (climax)") (17). For each of the 17 activities, six questions are asked that assess (a) current frequency, (b) desired frequency, (c) pleasure derived, (d) perceived partner's pleasure, (e) desired pleasure, and (f) desired partner's pleasure. It is essential that each partner independently complete these 102 items, since certain derived scales require comparison of the couple's responses.

Eleven scales are derived from the SII by summing individual items or differences between items across all 17 sexual behaviors. These 11 scales include male and female frequency dissatisfaction (the differences between current frequency and desired frequency), male and female self-acceptance (the differences between derived pleasure and desired pleasure), male and female pleasure (simple sums of pleasure responses), male and female spouse's perceived accuracy (differences between perceived partner's pleasure and the other partner's actual derived pleasure), male and female mate acceptance (differences between perceived partner's pleasure and desired partner's pleasure), and total disagreement (a sum of the eight difference scores). These scores are plotted on a profile sheet that is standardized to a mean of 50 and a standard deviation of 10.

LoPiccolo and Steger (1974) have evaluated the SII in regard to reliability (test-retest and internal consistency) and validity (convergent and discriminant), and they found all scales to be adequate and acceptable. In addition, the measure has been standardized in a sample of 124 volunteer couples with satisfactory sexual relationships. In terms of discriminant validity, sexually functional control couples were found to be significantly different on 9 of the 11 scales when compared with pretreatment sex therapy couples. The only scales that did not differ between the samples were male pleasure and female acceptance of the male (LoPiccolo & Steger, 1974).

The SII has been used in clinical assessment, research, and as an outcome measure for sex therapy, and through all of these trials it has proven to be useful (e.g., Golden, Price, Heinrich, & Lobitz, 1978; Kilmann, Mills, Caid, Bella, Davidson, & Wanlass, 1984; LoPiccolo & Miller, 1975; McGovern, Kirkpatrick, & LoPiccolo, 1976; McGovern, McMullen, & LoPiccolo, 1975; Zeiss, Rosen, & Zeiss, 1977). However, McCoy and D'Agostino (1977) have criticized the SII on several issues, based on factor-analytic results attesting to the multidimensionality of the 17 sexual behavior activities. Many problems are evident in this critical article, which precludes it from being taken too seriously in condemnation of the SII. For example, items rather than scales were examined, only rotated solutions of the factor analyses were considered, eigenvalues were not reported to determine the number of useful factors (only a greater-than-1 criterion, which often captures many meaningless factors), and finally the sample size was simply too small for any stable loadings to emerge with multivariate analyses.

In general, the SII represents a very clinically useful instrument that should fill in much of the individual and couple ecology that surrounds a sexual dysfunction. It can also be important in treatment planning and outcome evaluation. It is somewhat unique in the use of difference (or relative) scores and intracouple comparisons, which, although perhaps a little complex at first glance, make the information rich and informative.

A Multimodal Model

A final method to be discussed for defining and refining the sexual dysfunction and the ecology surrounding it, is the multimodal model offered by Lazarus (1976, 1980). This model emphasizes the assessment of seven important aspects of the individual and couple that can be conveniently remembered in the mnemonic BASIC ID: *B*ehavior, *A*ffect, *S*ensation, *I*mages, *C*ognitions, *I*nterpersonal, and *D*rugs (or biology). Although designed as a basic psychotherapeutic assessment model (Lazarus, 1976), it has been specialized to deal with assessment in sex therapy (Lazarus, 1980, Lobitz & Lobitz, 1978).

Behavior. The actual behavior in which a couple engages is paramount to determine and to examine in detail. A step-by- step appraisal of what each person does, and when, allows an evaluation of the activities with regard to appropriate timing, duration, intensity, range, focus, and responsivity.

Affect. Anxiety is a frequent affect associated with sexual dysfunction. This may take the form of performance anxiety, an overemphasis on such goals as reaching orgasm or delaying ejaculation, rather than on enjoying the sensual pleasure and involvement of making love. Anxiety of most any form can contribute to maintaining a dysfunction, as well as perhaps being an important etiological factor in itself. Depression is another affect that frequently accompanies sexual dysfunction, and it must be assessed for severity and etiology.

Many other feelings and emotions are associated with sexual activity and particularly dysfunction, which also must be brought into the open and discussed.

Sensation. Effective and fulfilling sexual behavior requires an ability to experience and enjoy bodily sensations and sensuality. Many people cut themselves off from feelings and sensations because of a disruptive focus on goals and performance. Principal sensations include those that are positive and desired, such as pleasure, warmth, and arousal, as well as those that are more noxious or neutral, such as pain, discomfort, or anaesthesia.

Images. The capacity to use imagery is an important element in pleasurable sexual activity. Men with erectile dysfunctions and women suffering from inorgasmia are frequently unable to fantasize sexually arousing images. A thorough assessment must determine the comfort and ease with which patients use fantasy and images during sexual activity and involvement. In general, men tend to fantasize more than women. If a deficit or avoidance of fantasy is noted, this may be an area to address in treatment.

Cognitions. Many people with sexual dysfunctions have destructive or inappropriate thoughts or cognitions around their sexual behavior. Lobitz and Lobitz (1978) have identified three categories of problematic cognitions. Patients may be ignorant of accurate sexual knowledge, and this misinformation may interfere with effective sexual functioning. Destructive attitudes regarding sexual behavior and involvement—such as "sex is dirty or wrong"—may inhibit responses and/or generate guilt, fear, or shame. Finally patients may have self-defeating thoughts or "self-statements" (Meichenbaum, 1974, 1977). These various inappropriate cognitions need to be elicited during assessment and confronted as a part of treatment.

Interpersonal. The nature and quality of the interpersonal relationship is obviously an essential area to assess meticulously in patients with sexual dysfunctions. Important areas to evaluate include communication, life-style, commitment, degree of mutual responsibility for resolving the dysfunction, and general mutuality of the relationship (Lobitz & Lobitz, 1978).

Drugs. Medical, physical, and drug-related concerns and contributions to sexual dysfunctions also need to be taken into consideration. These areas, however, should have been evaluated much earlier in assessment than this point.

Personality. In addition to the aspects related to the BASIC ID, personality is another component to be aware of during assessment (Lobitz & Lobitz, 1978). For example, Lassen (1976) has identified several personality traits in men with erectile dysfunction, such as achievement-oriented, aggressive, and driven, that help maintain the dysfunction. An understanding of individual and couple personality dynamics aids in formulating treatment goals and strategies (Lobitz, LoPiccolo, Lobitz, & Brockway, 1974).

Based on all of the information gathered in the assessment process, treatment goals, plans, and strategies need to be developed. These should be determined cooperatively with the patients, giving them an active role in the treatment formulation. This promotes greater commitment and motivation to the therapy process (Lobitz & Lobitz, 1978). Obviously, the particular treatment strategies and interventions will be based on and derived from the therapist's own theoretical and practical model of sex therapy, as well as the disorders and specific ecology of symptoms and qualities presented by the patients.

ONGOING ASSESSMENT DURING TREATMENT

Two other areas of assessment are essential for a thorough sex therapy treatment program: ongoing evaluation during therapy and follow-up. It is beyond the scope of this chapter to address these areas, since the first is integrally involved with treatment and the latter is both a quality-control and clinical therapy issue. In brief, ongoing assessment during treatment typically involves written and/or verbal feedback after completing various specific assignments. Methods of possible and appropriate assessment of these areas have been discussed earlier. Follow-up assessment will often involve an interview and/or questionnaires assessing change in relevant areas of sexual and nonsexual behavior, attitudes, and relationship quality.

CONCLUSIONS

Adequate and thorough diagnosis and assessment are essential for treating any disorders or dysfunctions. Responsible treatment cannot occur without competent appraisal of the problems and circumstances surrounding them. This is no less true in the area of sex therapy than for medical treatment or psychotherapy. Poor assessment assures poor prognosis.

A battery of tests to be used in general sex therapy assessment can be suggested from the preceding discussion. These would include a thorough sexual history and behavior questionnaire (e.g., that provided by Schover et al., 1980), an MMPI, and the Locke-Wallace Marital Adjustment Scales. These are all very easy to administer and quickly scored. If both partners are seeking treatment, each should complete the preceding tests and the SII. The DSFI is also quite useful, and its specific usefulness is discussed at length in Chapter 7. Depending upon the clinician's therapeutic perspective, other methods of assessment may include fantasy, observation, or physiology; these should be chosen to match the intervention techniques. In all cases, a careful and thorough clinical interview is essential and indispensable for proper assessment and to prepare the patients for treatment.

This chapter was intended to sensitize the general psychotherapist to the areas of importance and methods of evaluation in sex therapy assessment. Depending upon the qualifications of the clinician, it may not be appropriate to perform the entire assessment procedure—nor the therapeutic interventions.

Expertise with psychological tests is an important qualification for a complete evaluation of therapeutic appropriateness. Doctoral level clinical psychologists have typically been trained in this area. The medical evaluation obviously needs to be conducted by a licensed physician with specialty in sexual disorders. Often, urologists or gynecologists are consulted. Diagnosis and definition of the disorder and dysfunction also require familiarity with psychological tests, sexual physiology, as well as interview and clinical skills. Comfort with discussing and probing for intimate sexual material is vital. In general, if not always, therapists who treat patients with sexual dysfunctions should have specialized training in sex therapy and assessment. Reading this chapter, or this book alone will not ethically qualify anyone to engage in sex therapy. Schover (1982) has clearly documented that clinicians are not typically or naturally equipped to handle sexual problems in their patients without specific supervised training. As an integral part of this training, clinicians should be given a careful and thorough understanding of why assessment is needed and how to go about it.

REFERENCES

Abarbanel, A.R. (1978). Diagnosis and treatment of coital discomfort. In J. LoPiccolo & L. LoPiccolo (Eds.), *Handbook of sex therapy* (pp. 241-259). New York: Plenum.

Abramson, P.R., & Mosher, D.L. (1975). Development of a measure of negative attitudes toward masturbation. *Journal of Consulting and Clinical Psychology, 43,* 485-490.

American Psychiatric Association. (1980). *Diagnostic and statistical manual of mental disorders* (3rd ed.). Washington, DC: Author.

Anderson, B.L. (1983). Primary orgasmic dysfunction: Diagnostic considerations and review of treatment. *Psychological Bulletin, 93,* 105-136.

Annon, J.S. (1975). *The sexual fear inventory—female and male forms.* Honolulu: Enabling Systems.

Annon, J.S. (1977). The PLISSIT model: A proposed conceptual scheme for the behavioral treatment of sexual problems. In J. Fischer & H.L. Gochros (Eds.), *Handbook of behavior therapy with sexual problems. Vol. 1* (pp. 70-83). New York: Pergamon.

Apfelbaum, B. (1980). The diagnosis and treatment of retarded ejaculation. In S.R. Leiblum & L.A. Pervin (Eds.), *Principles and practice of sex therapy* (pp. 263-296). New York: Guilford.

Barbach, L. (1980). Group treatment of anorgasmic women. In S.R. Leiblum & L.A. Pervin (Eds.), *Principles and practice of sex therapy* (pp. 263-296). New York: Guilford.

Barlow, E.H., Becker, R., Leitenberg, H., & Agrass, W.S. (1970). A mechanical strain gauge for recording penile circumference change. *Journal of Applied Behavior Analysis, 3,* 73-76.

Bentler, P.M. (1968a). Heterosexual behavioral assessment. I. Males. *Behavior Research and Therapy, 6,* 21-25.

Bentler, P.M. (1968b). Heterosexual behavioral assessment. II. Females. *Behavioral Research and Therapy, 6,* 26-30.

Bentler, P.M., & Newcomb, M.D. (1978). Longitudinal study of marital success and failure. *Journal of Consulting and Clinical Psychology, 46,* 1053-1070.

Bentler, P.M., & Peeler, W.H. (1979). Models of female orgasm. *Archives of Sexual Behavior, 8,* 405-423.

Blair, J.H., & Simpson, G.H. (1966). Effect of antipsychotic drugs on reproductive functioning. *Diseases of the Nervous System, 27,* 645-647.

Briddle, D.W., & Wilson, G.J. (1976). Effects of alcohol and expectancy set on male sexual arousal. *Journal of Abnormal Psychology, 85,* 225-234.

Bridges, C.F., Critelli, J.W., & Loos, V.E. (1985). Hypnotic susceptibility, inhibitory control, and orgasmic consistency. *Archives of Sexual Behavior, 14,* 373-376.

Chambless, D.L, Sultan, F.E., Stern, T.E., O'Neill, C., Garrison, S., & Jackson, A. (1984). Effect of pubococcygeal exercise on coital orgasm in women. *Journal of Consulting and Clinical Psychology, 52,* 114-118.

Chapman, R. (1982). Criteria for diagnosing when to do sex therapy in the primary relationship. *Psychotherapy: Theory, Research and Practice, 19,* 359-367.

Coen, S.J. (1978). Sexual interviewing, evaluation, and therapy: Psychoanalytic emphasis on the use of sexual fantasy. *Archives of Sexual Behavior, 7,* 229-241.

Cohen, S. (1981). *The substance abuse problems.* New York: Haworth Press.

Conte, H.R. (1983). Development and use of self-report techniques for assessing sexual functioning: A review and critique. *Archives of Sexual Behavior, 12,* 555-576.

Dahlstrom, W.G., Welsh, G.J., & Dahlstrom, L.E. (1972). *An MMPI handbook. Vol. 1. Clinical interpretation.* Minneapolis: University of Minnesota Press.

Denney, N.W., Field, J.K., & Quadagno, D. (1984). Sex differences in sexual needs and desires. *Archives of Sexual Behavior, 13,* 233-246.

Derogatis, L.R. (1975). *The brief symptom inventory.* Baltimore: Clinical Psychometrics.

Derogatis, L.R. (1976). Psychological assessment of the sexual disabilities. In J.K. Meyer (Ed.), *Clinical management of sexual disorders.* Baltimore: Williams & Wilkins.

Derogatis, L.R. (1977). *SCL-90-R: Administration, scoring, and procedures manual I.* Baltimore: Clinical Psychometrics.

Derogatis, L.R., & King, K.M. (1981). The coital coronary: A reassessment of the concept. *Archives of Sexual Behavior, 10,* 325-335.

Derogatis, L.R., Melisaratos, N., & Clark, M.M. (1976). Gender and sexual experience as determinants in a sexual behavior hierarchy. *Journal of Sex and Marital Therapy, 2,* 85-105.

Derogatis, L.R., & Meyer, J.K. (1979). A psychological profile of the sexual dysfunctions. *Archives of Sexual Behavior, 8,* 201-223.

Derogatis, L., Zinzeleta, E., & Lopez, M. (1988). Behavioral and psychological assessment of sexual dysfunction: Clinical use of the DSFI. In R.A. Brown & J.R. Field (Eds.), *Treating sexual problems in individual and marital therapy.* Great Neck, NY: PMA Publishing Corp. Spectrum.

DiVasto, P.V., Pathak, D., & Fishburn, W.R. (1981). The interrelationship of sex guilt, sex behavior, and age. *Archives of Sexual Behavior, 10,* 119-122.

Echeandia, D. (1981). *The drive-facilitation role of sexual fantasy: Effects of female-active sexual fantasy rehearsal upon female-active sexual arousal and response.* Doctoral dissertation, University of California, Los Angeles.

Ellis, A. (1980). Treatment of erectile dysfunction. In S.R. Leiblum & L.A. Pervin (Eds.), *Principles and practice of sex therapy* (pp. 235-261). New York: Guilford.

Ellison, C. (1972). Vaginismus. *Medical Aspects of Human Sexuality, 8,* 34-54.

Fertel, N. (1977). Vaginismus: A review. *Journal of Sex and Marital Therapy, 3,* 113-121.

Fisher, S. (1973). *The female orgasm.* New York: Basic Books.

Flitting, M.D., Salisbury, S., Davies, N.H., & Mayclin, D.K. (1978). Self-concept and sexuality of spinal cord injured women. *Archives of Sexual Behavior, 7,* 143-156.

Forsberg, L., Gustavii, B., Höjerback, T., & Olsson, A.M. (1979). Impotence, smoking, and beta-blocking drugs. *Fertility and Sterility, 31,* 589-591.

Frank, E., Anderson, C., & Kupfer, D.J. (1976). Profiles of couples seeking sex therapy and marital therapy. *American Journal of Psychiatry, 133,* 559-562.

Frank, E., Anderson, C., & Rubinstein, D. (1978). Frequency of sexual dysfunction in "normal" couples. *New England Journal of Medicine, 299,* 111-115.

Freese, M.P., & Levitt, E. (1984). Relationships among intravaginal pressure, orgasmic function, parity factors, and urinary leakage. *Archives of Sexual Beahvior, 13,* 261-268.

Freud, S. (1953). Three essays on the theory of sexuality. In the *Complete psychological works of Sigmund Freud. Vol. 7.* London: Hogarth Press.

Friedman, S., & Harrison, G. (1984). Sexual histories, attitudes, and behavior of schizophrenic and "normal" women. *Archives of Sexual Behavior, 13,* 558-568.

Fuchs, K., Hock, Z., Paldi, E., Abramovici, H., Brandes, J.M., Timor-Tritsch,I., & Kleinhaus, M. (1973). Hypnodesensitization of vaginismus. *International Journal of Clinical and Experimental Hypnosis, 21,* 144-156.

Fugl-Meyer, A.R., Sjogren, K., & Johansson, K. (1984). A vaginal temperature registration system. *Archives of Sexual Behavior, 13,* 247-260.

Garrard, J., Vaitkus, A., Held, J., & Chilgren, R.A. (1976). Follow-up effects of a medical school course in human sexuality. *Archives of Sexual Behavior, 5,* 331-340.

Geer, J.H. (1975). Direct measurements of genital responding. *American Psychologist, 30,* 415-418.

Geer, J.H. (1976). Genital measures: Comments on their role in understanding human sexuality. *Journal of Sex and Marital Therapy, 2,* 165-172.

Geer, J.H., Morokoff, P., & Greenwood, P. (1974). Sexual arousal in women: The development of a measurement device for vaginal blood volume. *Archives of Sexual Behavior, 3,* 559-564.

Giambra, L.M., & Martin, C.E. (1977). Sexual daydreams and quantitative aspects of sexual activity: Some relations for males across adulthood. *Archives of Sexual Behavior, 6,* 497-505.

Golden, J.S., Price, S., Heinrich, A.G., & Lobitz, W.C. (1978). Group vs. couple treatment of sexual dysfunctions. *Archives of Sexual Behavior, 7,* 593-602.

Graber, B., & Kline-Graber, G. (1979). Female orgasm: Role of the pubococcygeus muscle. *Journal of Clinical Psychiatry, 40,* 348-351.

Green, R. (1977). Taking a sexual history. In J. Fischer & H.K. Gochros (Eds.), *Handbook of behavior therapy with sexual problems. Vol. 1* (pp. 15-21). New York: Pergamon.

Griffitt, W. (1975). Sexual experience and sexual responsiveness: Sex differences. *Archives of Sexual Behavior, 4,* 529-540.

Grudzinskas, J.G., & Atkinson, L. (1984). Sexual functioning during the puerperium. *Archives of Sexual Behavior, 13,* 85-92.

Hariton, E., & Singer, J. (1974). Women's fantasies during sexual intercourse. *Journal of Consulting and Clinical Psychology, 42,* 313-322.

Hartman, W.E., & Fithian, M.A. (1972). *Treatment of sexual dysfunction.* Long Beach, CA: Center for Marital and Sexual Studies.

Harman, W.E., & Fithian, M.A. (1974). *Treatment of sexual dysfunction: A bio-psycho-social approach.* New York: Aronson.

Hatch, J.P. (1981). Psychophysiological aspects of sexual dysfunction. *Archives of Sexual Behavior, 10,* 49-64.

Hathaway, S.R., & McKinley, J.C. (1967). *The Minnesota Multiphasic Personality Inventory.* New York: Psychological Corporation.

Heiman, J.R. (1976). Issues in the use of psychophysiology to assess female sexual dysfunction. *Journal of Sex and Marital Therapy, 2,* 197-204.

Heiman, J.R. (1977). A psychophysiological exploration of sexual arousal patterns in females and males. *Psychophysiology, 14,* 266-274.

Heiman, J.R. (1978). Uses of psychophysiology in the assessment and treatment of sexual dysfunction. In J. LoPiccolo & L. LoPiccolo (Eds.), *Handbook of sex therapy* (pp. 123-135). New York: Plenum.

Higgins, G.E. (1979). Sexual response in spinal cord injured adults: A review of the literature. *Archives of Sexual Behavior, 8,* 173-196.

Hoch, Z. (1980). The sensory arm of the female orgasmic reflex. *Journal of Sex Education and Therapy, 6,* 4-7.

Hogan, D.R. (1978). The effectiveness of sex therapy: A review of the literature. In J. LoPiccolo & L. LoPiccolo (Eds.), *Handbook of sex therapy* (pp. 57-84). New York: Plenum.

Hoon, E.F., & Hoon, P.W. (1978). Styles of sexual expression in women: Clinical implication of multivariate analyses. *Archives of Sexual Behavior, 7,* 105-116.

Hoon, E.F., Hoon, P.W., & Wincze, J.P. (1976). An inventory for the measurement of female sexual arousability: The SAI. *Archives of Sexual Behavior, 5,* 291-300.

Hoon, P.W., Wincze, J.P., & Hoon, E.F. (1977). The effects of biofeedback and cognitive mediation upon vaginal blood volume. *Behavior Therapy, 8,* 694-702.

Huba, G.J., Aneshensel, C.S., & Singer, J.L. (1981). Development of scales for three second-order factors of inner experience. *Multivariate Behavioral Research, 16,* 181-206.

Huba, G.J., Singer, J.L., Aneshensel, C.S., & Antrobus, J.L. (1982). *Short imaginal process inventory.* Port Huron, MI: Research Psychologists Press.

Huey, C.J., Kline-Graber, G., & Graber, B. (1981). Time factors and orgasmic response. *Archives of Sexual Behavior, 10,* 111-118.

Hunt, M. (1974). *Sexual behavior in the 1970's.* Chicago: Playboy Press.

Jemail, J.A. (1977). *Response bias in the assessment of marital and sexual adjustment.* Doctoral Dissertation, State University of New York, Stony Brook.

Jensen, S.B. (1981). Diabetic sexual dysfunction: A comparative study of 160 insulin treated diabetic men and women and an age-matched control group. *Archives of Sexual Behavior, 10,* 493-504.

Kaplan, H.S. (1974). *The new sex therapy.* New York: Brunner/Mazel.

Kaplan, H.S. (1977). Hypoactive sexual desire. *Journal of Sex and Marital Therapy, 3,* 3-9.

Kaplan, H.S. (1979). *Disorders of sexual desire.* New York: Brunner/Mazel.

Karacan, I. (1978). Advances in the psychophysiological evaluation of male erectile impotence. In J. LoPiccolo, & L. LoPiccolo, (Eds.), *Handbook of sex therapy* (pp. 137-145). New York: Plenum.

Kilmann, P.R., & Auerbach, R. (1979). Treatments of premature ejaculation and psychogenic impotence: A critical review of the literature. *Archives of Sexual Behavior, 8,* 81-100.

Kilmann, P.R., Mills, K.H., Caid, C., Bella, B., Davidson, E., & Wanlass, R. (1984). The sexual interaction of women with secondary orgasmic dysfunction and their partners. *Archives of Sexual Behavior, 13,* 41-50.

Kimmel, D., & van der Veen, F. (1974). Factors of marital adjustment in Locke's Marital Adjustment Test. *Journal of Marriage and the Family, 2,* 57-63.

Kinsey, A.C., Pomeroy, W.B., & Martin, C.E. (1948). *Sexual behavior in the human male.* Philadelphia: Saunders.

Kinsey, A.C., Pomeroy, W.B., Martin, C.E., & Gebhard, P.H. (1953). *Sexual behavior in the human female.* Philadelphia: Saunders.

Kline-Graber, G., & Graber, B. (1978). Diagnosis and treatment procedures of pubococcygeal deficiencies in women. In J. LoPiccolo & L. LoPiccolo (Eds.), *Handbook of sex therapy* (pp. 227-239). New York: Plenum.

Kockott, G., Feil, W., Revenstorf, D., Aldenhoff, J., & Besinger, U. (1980). Symptomatology and psychological aspects of male sexual inadequacy: Results of an experimental study. *Archives of Sexual Behavior, 9,* 457-475.

Kotin, J., Wilfert, D.C., Verburg, D., & Soldinger, S.M. (1976). Thioridazine and sexual dysfunction. *American Journal of Psychiatry, 133,* 82-85.

Lansky, M.R., & Davenport, A.E. (1975). Difficulties in brief conjoint treatment of sexual dysfunction. *American Journal of Psychiatry, 132,* 177-179.

Lassen, C.L. (1976). Issues and dilemmas in the treatment of sexual dysfunction. *Journal of Sex and Marital Therapy, 2,* 32-39.

Lazarus, A.A. (1976). *Multimodal behavior therapy.* New York: Springer.

Lazarus, A.A. (1980). Psychological treatment of dyspareunia. In S.R. Leiblum & L.A. Pervin (Eds.), *Principles and practice of sex therapy* (pp. 147-166). New York: Guilford.

Leiblum, S.R., Pervin, L.A., & Campbell, E.H. (1980). The treatment of vaginismus: Success and failure. In S.R. Leiblum & L.A. Pervin (Eds.), *Principles and practice of sex therapy* (pp. 1-24). New York: Guilford.

Leiblum, S.R., Rosen, R., & Pierce, D. (1976). Group treatment format: Mixed sexual dysfunctions. *Archives of Sexual Behavior, 5,* 313-322.

Levine, S.B., & Yost, M.A. (1976). Frequency of sexual dysfunction in a general gynecological clinic: An epidemiological approach. *Archives of Sexual Behavior, 5,* 229-238.

Lief, H.I., & Reed, D.M. (1972). *Sex knowledge and attitude test* (2nd ed.). Philadelphia: Center for the Study of Sex Education in Medicine.

Lobitz, W.C., & Baker, E.L. (1979). Group treatment of males with erectile dysfunction. *Archives of Sexual Behavior, 8,* 127-138.

Lobitz, W.C., & Lobitz, G.K. (1978). Clinical assessment in the treatment of sexual dysfunctions. In J. LoPiccolo & L. LoPiccolo (Eds.), *Handbook of sex therapy* (pp. 85-102). New York: Plenum.

Lobitz, W.C., & LoPiccolo, J. (1977). New methods in the behavioral treatment of sexual dysfunction. In J. Fischer & H.L. Gochros (Eds.), *Handbook of behavior therapy with sexual problems. Vol. 1* (pp. 7-14). New York: Pergamon.

Lobitz, W.C., LoPiccolo, J., Lobitz, G., & Brockway, J. (1974). A closer look at "simplistic" behavior therapy for sexual dysfunction: Two case studies. In H.J. Eysenck (Ed.), *Case studies in behavior therapy.* London: Routledge & Kegan Paul.

Locke, H.J., & Wallace, K.M. (1959). Short marital adjustment and prediction tests: Their reliability and prediction. *Marriage and Family Living, 21,* 251-255.

LoPiccolo. L.(1980). Low sexual desire. In S.R. Leiblum & L.A. Pervin (Eds.), *Principles and practice of sex therapy* (pp. 29-64). New York: Guilford.

LoPiccolo, L., & Heiman, J.R. (1978). Sexual assessment and history interview. In J. LoPiccolo & L. LoPiccolo (Eds.), *Handbook of sex therapy* (pp. 103-112). New York: Plenum.

LoPiccolo, J., & Lobitz, W.C. (1972). The role of masturbation in the treatment of orgasmic dysfunction. *Archives of Sexual Behavior, 2,* 163-177.

LoPiccolo, J., & Lobitz, W.C. (1973). Behavior therapy of sexual dysfunction. In L.A. Hammerlynk, L.C. Handy, & E.J. Mash (Eds.), *Behavior change: Methodology, concepts, and practice.* Champaign, IL: Research Press.

LoPiccolo. J., & Miller, V.H. (1975). A program for enhancing the sexual relationship of normal couples. *The Counseling Psychologist, 5,* 41-45.

LoPiccolo. J., & Steger, J.C. (1974). The Sexual Interaction Inventory: A new instrument for assessment of sexual dysfunction. *Archives of Sexual Behavior, 3,* 585-595.

Marcotte, D.B., & Logan, C. (1977). Medical sex education: Allowing attitude alteration. *Archives of Sexual Behavior, 6,* 155-162.

Marshall, P., Surridge, D., & Delva, N. (1981). The role of nocturnal penile tumescence in differentiating between organic and psychogenic impotence: The first stage of validation. *Archives of Sexual Behavior, 10,* 1-10.

Martin, C.E. (1981). Factors affecting sexual functioning in 60-70 year old married males. *Archives of Sexual Behavior, 10,* 399-420.

Martin, L.M., Rodgers, D.A., & Montague, D.K. (1983). Psychometric differentiation of biogenic and psychogenic impotence. *Archives of Sexual Behavior, 12,* 475-486.

Masters, W.H., & Johnson, V.E. (1966). *Human sexual response.* Boston: Little, Brown.

Masters, W.H., & Johnson, V.E. (1970). *Human sexual inadequacy.* Boston: Little, Brown.

McCoy, N., & D'Agnostino, P. (1977). Factor analysis of the sexual interaction inventory. *Archives of Sexual Behavior, 6,* 25-35.

McGovern, K.B., Kirkpatrick, C.C., & LoPiccolo, J.(1976). A behavioral group treatment program for sexually dysfunctional couples. *Journal of Marriage and Family Counseling, 2,* 397-404.

McGovern, K.B., McMullen, R.S., & LoPiccolo, J. (1975). Secondary orgasmic dysfunction I: Analysis and strategies for treatment. *Archives of Sexual Behavior, 4,* 265-275.

McHugh, G. (1967). *Sex knowledge inventory.* Durham, NC: Family Life Publications.

Meichenbaum, D. (1977). *Cognitive-behavior modification.* New York: Plenum.

Meichenbaum, D. (1974). Self-instructional methods. In F.H. Kanfer & A.P. Goldstein (Eds.), *Helping people change.* New York: Pergamon.

Messé, M.E., & Geer, J.H. (1985). Voluntary vaginal musculature contractions as an enhancer of sexual arousal. *Archives of Sexual Behavior, 14,* 13-28.

Meyer, J.K., Schmidt, C.W., Lucas, M.J., & Smith, E. (1975). Short-term treatment of sexual problems: Interim report. *American Journal of Psychiatry, 132,* 172-176.

Mosher, D. (1968). Measurement of sex guilt in females by self-report inventories. *Journal of Consulting and Clinical Psychology, 32,* 690-695.

Munjack, D.J., & Kanno, P.H. (1979). Retarded ejaculation: A review. *Archives of Sexual Behavior, 8,* 139-150.

Neri, A., Aygen, M., Zuckerman, Z., & Bahary, C. (1980). Subjective assessment of sexual dysfunction of patients on long-term administration of digoxin. *Archives of Sexual Behavior, 9,* 343-349.

Nestoros, J.N., Lehmann, H.E., & Ban, T.A. (1981). Sexual behavior of the male schizophrenic: The impact of illness and medications. *Archives of Sexual Behavior, 10,* 421-442.

Newcomb, M.D. (1983, April). *First and second order factors of marital distress: A confirmatory factor analysis model.* Paper presented at the Western Psychological Association Meetings, San Francisco.

Newcomb, M. (1984). Sexual behavior, responsiveness, and attitudes among women: A test of two theories. *Journal of Sex and Marital Therapy, 10,* 272-286.

Newcomb, M. (1985). Sexual experience among men and women: Associations within three independent samples. *Psychological Reports, 56,* 603-614.

Newcomb, M. (1986). Sexual behavior of cohabitors: A comparison of three independent samples. *Journal of Sex Research, 4,* 492-513.

Newcomb, M.D., & Bentler, P.M. (1980). Cohabitation before marriage: A comparison of married couples who did and did not cohabit. *Alternative Lifestyles, 3,* 65-85.

Newcomb, M.D., & Bentler, P.M. (1983). The dimensions of subjective feamle orgasmic responsiveness. *Journal of Personality and Social Psychology, 44,* 862-873.

Perelman, M.A. (1980). Treatment of premature ejaculation. In. S.R. Leiblum & L.A. Pervin (Eds.), *Principles and practice of sex therapy* (pp.199-233). New York: Guilford.

Pion, R.N., Anderson, S.N., & Wagner, N.N. (1970). *Sexual responsiveness survey.* Seattle: Northwest Counseling Associates.

Price, S., Reynolds, B.S., Cohen, B.D., Anderson, A.J., & Schochet, B.V.(1981). Group treatment of erectile dysfunction for men without partners: A controlled evaluation.*Archives of Sexual Behavior, 10,* 253-268.

Procci, W.R., & Martin, D.J. (1984). Preliminary observations of the utility of portable NPT. *Archives of Sexual Behavior, 13,* 569-580.

Raboch, J. (1984). The sexual development and life of female schizophrenic patients. *Archives of Sexual Behavior, 13,* 341-350.

Reynolds, B.S. (1978). *Voluntary facilitation of erection in men with erectile dysfunction: Effects of continuous tumescence feedback and contingent erotic film.* Doctoral dissertation, University of California, Los Angeles.

Rogers, G.S., van de Castle, R.L., Evans, W.S., & Critelli, J.W. (1985). Vaginal pulse amplitude response patterns during erotic conditions and sleep. *Archives of Sexual Behavior, 14,* 327-342.

Rozan, G.H., Tuchin, T., & Kurland, M.L. (1971). Some implications of sexual activity for mental illness. *Mental Hygiene, 55,* 318-323.

Rubin, Z. (1975). *Liking and loving: An invitation to social psychology.* New York: Holt, Rinehart & Winston.

Sach, D.H., & Duffy, K.G. (1976). Effects of modeling on sexual imagery. *Archives of Sexual Behavior, 5,* 301-311.

Sager, C.J. (1974). Sexual dysfunctions and marital discord. In H.S. Kaplan (Ed.), *The new sex therapy* (pp. 501-516). New York: Brunner/Mazel.

Sager, C.J. (1976). The role of sex therapy in marital therapy. *American Journal of Psychiatry, 133,* 555-559.

Sarrel, P.M., Foddy, J., & McKinnon, J.B. (1977). Investigation of human sexual response using a cassette recorder. *Archives of Sexual Behavior, 6,* 341-348.

Schneidman, B., & McGuire, L. (1976). Group treatment for nonorgasmic women: Two age levels. *Archives of Sexual Behavior, 5,* 239-247.

Schover, L.R. (1982). Male and female therapists' responses to male and female client sexual material: An analogue study. *Archives of Sexual Behavior, 10,* 477-492.

Schover, L.R., Friedman, J.M., Weiler, S.J., Heiman, J.R., & LoPiccolo, J. (1980). *A multi-axial descriptive system for the sexual dysfunctions: Categories and manual.* Stony Brook, N.Y.: Sex Therapy Center.

Schover, L.R., Friedman, J.M., Weiler, S.J., Heiman, J.R., & LoPiccolo, J. (1982). Multiaxial problem-oriented system for sexual dysfunctions. *Archives of General Psychiatry, 39,* 614-619.

Schwartz, M.F., Kolodny, R.C., & Masters, W.H. (1980). Plasma testosterone levels of sexually functional and dysfunctional men. *Archives of Sexual Behavior, 9,* 355-366.

Semans, J.H. (1956). Premature ejaculation: A new approach. *Southern Medical Journal, 49,* 252-257.

Serber, M. (1974). Videotape feedback in the treatment of couples with sexual dysfunction. *Archives of Sexual Behavior, 3,* 377-380.

Sewell, H.H., & Abramowitz, S.I. (1979). Flexibility, persistence, and success in sex therapy. *Archives of Sexual Behavior, 8,* 497-506.

Shrom, S.H., Lief, H.I., & Wein, A.J.(1979). Clinical profile of experience of 130 consecutive cases of impotent men. *Urology, 13,* 511-515.

Singer, J., & Antrobus, J. (1972). Daydreaming, imaginal process, and personality: A normative study. In D. Sheehan (Ed.), *The function and nature of imagery.* New York: Academic Press.

Solnick, R.L., & Birren, J. (1977). Age and male erectile responsiveness. *Archives of Sexual Behavior, 6,* 1-9.

Sperlich, P.W. (1975). *Crimes without victims, but laws with victims.* Paper presented at the Annual Meeting of the Western Political Science Association, Seattle, WA.

Stein, M. (1948). *The TAT.* Cambridge, MA: Addison-Wesley.

Stein, R.A. (1980). Sexual counseling and coronary heart disease. In S.R. Leiblum & L.A. Pervin (Eds.), *Principles and practice of sex therapy* (pp. 301-319). New York: Guilford.

Steinboch, E.A., & Zeiss, A.M.(1977). Sexual counseling for cerebral palsied adults: Case report and further suggestions. *Archives of Sexual Behavior, 6,* 77-83.

Stock, W.E., & Geer, J.H. (1982). A study of fantasy-based sexual arousal in women. *Archives of Sexual Behavior, 11,* 33-47.

Sviland, M.A.P. (1975). Helping elderly couples become sexually liberated: Psychosocial issues. *The Counseling Psychologist, 5,* 67-72.

Toler, A., & DiGrazia, P.V. (1976). Sexual attitudes and behavior patterns during and following pregnancy. *Archives of Sexual Behavior, 5,* 539-551.

Trudel, G., & Saint-Laurent, S. (1983). A comparison between the effects of Kegel's exercises and a combination of sexual awareness, relaxation and breathing on situational orgasmic dysfunction in women. *Journal of Sex and Marital Therapy, 9,* 204-209.

Vincent, C.E. (1968). *Human sexuality in medical education and practice.* Springfield, IL: Charles C. Thomas.

Wabrek, A.J., & Burchell, R.C. (1980). Male sexual dysfunction associated with coronary heart disease. *Archives of Sexual Behavior, 9,* 69-75.

Wagner, G. (1981). Methods for differential diagnosis of psychogenic and organic erectile failure. In G. Wagner, & R. Green (Eds.), *Impotence: Physiologial, psychological, surgical diagnosis and treatment* (pp. 89-130). New York: Plenum.

Wagner, G., & Green, R. (1981). General medical disorders and erectile failure. In G. Wagner & R. Green (Eds.), *Impotence: Physiological, psychological, surgical diagnosis and treatment* (pp. 37-50). New York: Plenum.

Wagner, G., Hilsted, J., & Jensen, S.B. (1981). Diabetes mellitus and erectile failure. In G. Wagner & R. Green (Eds.), *Impotence: Physiological, psychological, surgical diagnosis and treatment* (pp. 51-62). New York: Plenum.

Wagner, G., & Jensen, S.B. (1981). Alcohol and erectile failure. In G. Wagner & R. Green (Eds.), *Impotence: Physiological, psychological, surgical diagnosis and treatment* (pp. 81-88). New York: Plenum.

Warren, N.J., & Gilner, F.H. (1978). Measurement of positive assertive behaviors: The behavioral test of tenderness expression. *Behavior Therapy, 9,* 178-184.

White, C.B. (1982). Sexual interest, attitudes, knowledge, and sexual history in relation to sexual behavior in the institutionalized age. *Archives of Sexual Behavior, 11,* 11-21.

Wilson, G.T., & Lawson, D.M. (1976). Effects of alcohol on sexual arousal in women. *Journal of Abnormal Psychology, 85,* 489-497.

Wilson, G.T., & Lawson, D.M. (1978). Expectancies, alcohol, and sexual arousal in women. *Journal of Abnormal Psychology, 87,* 358-367.

Wincze, J.P., Hoon, E.F., & Hoon, P.W. (1976). A comparison of the physiological responsivity of normal and sexually dysfunctional women during exposure to erotic stimulus. *Journal of Psychosomatic Research, 20,* 44-50.

Wolpe, J. (1958). *Psychotherapy by reciprocal inhibition.* Palo Alto: Stanford University Press.

Wolpe, J. (1969). *The practice of behavior therapy.* New York: Pergamon.

Wolpe, J. (1977). The treatment of inhibited sexual responses. In J. Fischer & H.L. Gochros (Eds.), *Handbook of behavior therapy with sexual problems, Vol. 1* (pp.46-58). New York: Pergamon.

Zeiss, A.M., Rosen, G.M., & Zeiss, R.A. (1977). Orgasm during intercourse: A treatment strategy for women. *Journal of Consulting and Clinical Psychology, 45,* 891-895.

Zilbergeld, B., & Ellison, C.R. (1980). Desire discrepancies and arousal problems in sex therapy. In S.R. Leiblum & L.A. Pervin (Eds.), *Principles and practice of sex therapy* (pp.65-101). New York: Guilford.

Zuckerman, M. (1973). Scales for sexual experience for males and females. *Journal of Consulting and Clinical Psychology, 41,* 27-29.

Zuckerman, R., Tushup, R., & Finner, S. (1976). Sexual attitudes and experience: Attitude and personality correlates and changes produced by a course in sexuality. *Journal of Consulting and Clinical Psychology, 44,* 7-19.

Chapter 7

Clinical Applications of the DSFI in the Assessement of Sexual Dysfunctions

Leonard R. Derogatis, Maria C. Lopez, and Ellen M. Zinzeletta

INTRODUCTION

Although modern psychometrics was a turn-of-the-century innovation, techniques for the formal psychological assessment of sexual behavior did not emerge until much later. Terman (1936) and other pioneers in the area accomplished some work on measuring masculinity and femininity, but social prohibitions concerning the explicit discussion of sexual activities precluded any systematic attempts at psychological measurement in this area. With the increasing liberalization of sexual attitudes in the 1960s, sexual behavior became a legitimate topic of scientific inquiry. It was not until the 1970s, however, that psychological tests specifically dedicated to the measurement of sexual behavior were systematically published, and it was during this era that the Derogatis Sexual Functioning Inventory (DSFI) was developed (Derogatis, 1975c).

THE DEROGATIS SEXUAL FUNCTIONING INVENTORY

The DSFI is a multidimensional test designed to measure the *current* level of sexual functioning of the *individual.* The test is multidimensional, consistent with the view that sexual functioning inherently involves components from multiple domains and cannot be adequately assessed unidimensionally (Derogatis, 1980; Derogatis & Melisaratos, 1979). The individual was chosen as the unit of measurement because it is the simplest and most straightforward to work with and because, ultimately, quality of sexual functioning must be experienced by an individual. In our clinic, the most frequent general question posed during an evaluation of a sexual complaint is, "What is the patient's current level of sexual functioning?" This is essentially the question the DSFI is designed to answer, with questions concerning diagnosis, prognosis and treatment left as questions to be answered empirically.

The DSFI is composed of 10 subtests developed from a like number of substantive domains of sexual functioning. These specific domains were selected on the basis of clinical experience, empirical findings and psychological theory. In its original formulation the DSFI contained only 8 subtests (Derogatis, 1976). However, more recently, subscales for the important domains of *Body Image* and *Satisfaction* were added (Derogatis & Melisaratos, 1979). The DSFI was designed as an "omnibus" test of sexual functioning, reflecting features inherent in effective and satisfying sexual activities. A brief exposition of the 10 subscales follows below.

SUBTESTS OF THE DSFI

I. Information

The Information subtest is designed to measure the patient's general fund of knowledge regarding sexual functioning. It consists of 26 items in a true/false format. By selecting the majority of items with moderate difficulty, and a lesser number with minimal and maximal difficulty, we anticipated providing effective clinical discrimination along the information dimension.

II. Experience

The Experience subtest assesses the variety of sexual behavior that the patient has experienced. It is composed of 24 distinct sexual behaviors that cover the typical spectrum of sexual experiences from simple to relatively complex. This particular series of sexual experiences has been developed into a scaled hierarchy using direct-magnitude-estimation techniques, and it shows very high levels of agreement between males and females regarding hierarchical position (Derogatis, Melisaratos, & Clark, 1976). The subtest also indicates recency of sexual experiences by specifying which activities have occurred during the past 60 days, although recency is independent of the experience score.

III. Drive

The Drive subtest measures the level of interest or investment in sexual matters as estimated by the frequency of intercourse, masturbation, kissing and petting, and sexual intercourse.

Although low or high sex drive is not, per se, an indication of sexual dysfunction, disproportionate levels of drive between sexual partners may contribute to the development of sexual disorders. Also, many disorders of a sexual nature, regardless of etiology, will influence the level of interest or investment the individual manifests in sexual activities. Another important aspect of sexual functioning is sexual precociousness. Two drive items, D6 and D7 ("age of first sexual interest" and "age of first intercourse") do not contribute formally to Drive score, but they may be used clinically.

IV. Attitude

The Attitude subtest is designed to measure liberalness or conservativeness of attitudes toward sexual activities or relationships. The 30 statements comprising the subtest represent varying degrees of liberalism and conservatism regarding sexual behavior. Fifteen of the items are liberal in nature; the other 15 are judged to be conservative. These assignments were made as a result of psychophysical scaling procedures with a panel of judges representative of the general population. Participants were asked to respond to each item via a 5-point Likert-type scale in which there were 2 degrees of agreement, a neutral point, and 2 degrees of disagreement.

In general, conclusions from a variety of studies suggest that people espousing a more liberal, accepting posture regarding sexuality tend to have richer and more satisfying personal sexual experiences. Although there is no one-to-one relationship between conservative sexual attitudes and the experience of sexual dysfunction, there is consistent evidence to suggest that constriction of sexual behavior, inhibitions and negative emotions (e.g. guilt) concerning the experience of pleasure, and a tendency toward reduced communication about sexual performance and satisfaction are often associated with conservative sexual views.

V. Symptoms

The Symptom subtest of the DSFI is designed to assess the distress arising from psychological symptoms that the patient is currently experiencing. There is strong evidence (Derogatis, Meyer, & King, 1981) that psychological disorders are more likely in individuals with sexual dysfunctions, and such disorders are an important discriminating characteristic of the clinical picture.

The DSFI subtest that measures psychological symptoms is in fact a distinct psychological test instrument termed the Brief Symptom Inventory (Derogatis & Melisaratos, 1983; Derogatis & Spencer, 1982). The Brief Symptom Inventory is a self-report symptom inventory that measures psychopathology in terms of nine major symptom dimensions and three global indices of distress. It takes approximately 10 minutes to complete, and is the brief form of the 90-item SCL-90-R, which uses the same symptom dimensions and global distress indicators (Derogatis, 1975b, 1977).

The primary symptom dimensions of the Brief Symptom Inventory are Somatization, Obsessive-Compulsive, Interpersonal Sensitivity, Depression, Anxiety, Hostility, Phobic Anxiety, Paranoid Ideation, and Psychoticism. There are three global indices of distress, including the General Severity Index, the Positive Symptom Distress Index, and the Positive Symptom Total. Of the global indices, the General Severity Index measures a combination of numbers of symptoms and intensity of distress, while the Positive Symptom Distress Index is a pure intensity measure. The Positive Symptom Total reflects only numbers of symptoms. The symptom configuration of the Brief Symptom Inventory may be scored and plotted separately on profile forms; however, the General Severity Index is the only measure contributing to the DSFI total score.

VI. Affects

Because negative affects are frequently involved in the development and expression of sexual disorders, we have incorporated a subtest to measure specifically the patient's mood status. The Affects subtest defines the balance between the patient's positive and negative emotional experiences, and in addition represents the spectrum of the patient's affective experience across a multidimensional mood profile.

The Affects measure is the Affects Balance Scale, the second of the DSFI subtests that is, in itself, a distinct psychological measuring instrument. The Affects Balance Scale represents 8 affect dimensions (4 positive and 4 negative) and 3 global affect indices drawn from a series of 40 selected adjectives. The respondents indicate the degree to which each adjective descriptor is typical of their emotional experiences during the previous two weeks (Derogatis, 1975a).

VII. Gender Role Definition

The Gender Role Definition scale provides a measure of the balance between the patient's conscious self-attribution of masculine and feminine characteristics. A series of 30 adjectives is presented, reflecting primarily "masculine" or "feminine" character traits as defined by traditional societal standards. The respondent indicates the degree to which each trait is characteristic of him or her. The series of adjectives was selected from a much larger set on the basis of consistency and extremity ratings of a panel of male and female judges.

A number of formal studies have indicated that, particularly in females, more integrated role definition (i.e., the balanced adoption of characteristics considered both masculine and feminine) tends to be associated with a superior capacity to develop and sustain interpersonal relationships and achieve life goals. It has also been frequently noted in clinical observations that gender-role polarization (either hypermasculine or hyperfeminine) is often associated with the development and maintenance of sexual dysfunction.

VIII. Fantasy

The Fantasy subtest measures the number of different sexual fantasies experienced by the patient. Sexual fantasy is almost universal, even though fantasy experience varies widely from one person to another. Some individuals experience detailed sexual fantasies several times a day, but others rarely have conscious sexual fantasies and are limited to sexual ideation in dreams.

It has been observed clinically that within a certain range, individuals with sexual dysfunction tend to be constricted in the variety of sexual themes they entertain. In other instances, the quality or nature of the dysfunctional individual's sexual ideation may be found to be incompatible with healthy sexual functioning. The 20 themes that comprise the Fantasy subtest were selected from clinical interview material.

IX. Body Image

The Body Image subtest assesses patients' appreciation of and satisfaction with their own bodies. It is composed of 15 items, the first 10 of which are to be completed by respondents of both sexes. An additional 5 items are specifically gender-keyed for males and females. Items on the Body Image subtest relate to general physical appearance as well as to the respondents' perception of specific genital body parts. We have observed a strong, consistent relationship between body image and quality of sexual functioning, so this subtest has become an important clinical indicator in dysfunctions.

X. Satisfaction

The Satisfaction subtest measures the degree to which patients are gratified by their sexual activities. It is constructed to reflect the fact that sexual satisfaction is a multifaceted phenomenon, and the 10 items deal with varied aspects of sexual fulfillment. This subtest is constructed on a true/false basis with items balanced as to positive and negative orientation.

XI. The GSSI

The Global Sexual Satisfaction Index is a unidimensional 9-point scale on which the patient makes a simple evaluation of his or her present sexual relationship. The ratings vary from "could not be worse," which receives a value of 0 to "could not be better," for a value of 8.

SCORING THE DSFI

In determining scores for the 10 subtests of the DSFI, each of the 10 distinct raw score distributions is converted to a standardized score distribution with a mean of 50 and a standard deviation of 10. Such a standardized score distribution is referred to as a *T-score* distribution (Nunnally, 1970). In the case of the DSFI, we have developed *area* T-scores in making the raw score transformations, which have the important advantage of normalizing the distribution. This means that DSFI T-scores may be interpreted in the standard fashion as areas under the normal curve. A T-score of 60 (i.e., +1 standard deviation) on any of the DSFI subtests places the client in the 84th centile. Similarly, a T-score of 40 (i.e., -1 standard deviation) would establish the individual in the 16th centile of the distribution. The use of area T-scores, although more complex than simple linear transformations, allows us to establish the proportion of individuals in the normative standardization group that scored above or below the individual under evaluation.

In addition to the 10 subtest scores, two global scores were developed for the DSFI. The first of these is the Global Sexual Satisfaction Index (GSSI), which essentially represents the patients' subjective evaluation of the quality of their sexual functioning on a nine-point Likert-type scale. The GSSI is transformed to standardized scores in the same fashion as the 10 DSFI subtests. The Sexual Functioning Index is a more comprehensive, global score. This measure is the quantitative summary statement of the patient's overall level of sexual functioning. It is derived by summing the standardized scores from the 10 subtests and representing this linear combination of scores as though it were a basic raw score distribution. Because the subtest components are represented in the SFI in terms of the same area T distribution (i.e., mean = 50, standard deviation = 10), they each have approximately equal weight in determining the global score.

Once the DSFI is scored, the subtest profile and global scores are represented graphically on DSFI Score/Profile Forms (see Figure 7- 1 to Figure 7-7). These forms essentially provide the norms for the subtest and global scores and give a visual presentation of areas of effective and impaired functioning. Separate norms have been developed for males and females, because on 8 of the 10 subtests and on the GSSI there are significant differences by sex in the score distributions.

RELIABILITY AND VALIDITY

In self-report measures, there are essentially two forms of reliability that concern us: *internal consistency* and *test-retest*. Internal consistency is involved with the issue of the consistency with which items of a test or subtest sample the construct domain, that is, the homogeneity of the items. Test- retest reliability addresses the issue of consistency of measurement from a temporal perspective, that is to say, the stability across time of observed test scores. We have developed estimates of both forms of reliability for the DSFI, and coefficients of both types are given in Table 7-1.

These coefficients demonstrate acceptable levels of reliability for the DSFI subtests, although there are variations in the level from scale to scale. Because raw score distributions for the Attitude, Affect and Gender Role subtests are essentially difference scores, internal consistency coefficients are more meaningfully developed for their respective components (i.e., Liberalism-Conservatism, Masculinity-Femininity) than for the subtest scores themselves. Test-retest coefficients for the DSFI are also quite good on the whole, although there are some exceptions. For the 8 subtests on which test-retest studies have been done, 4 show coefficients above .90, and 3 more reveal coefficients in the .80 range. Only the Information subtest demonstrates a coefficient below .70. A

Table 7.1 Internal Consistency and Test-Retest Reliability
Coefficients for the Subtests of the DSFI

Subtest	Internal Consistency* (N = 325)	Test-Retest** (N = 60)
I. Information	.56	.61
II. Experience	.97	.92
III. Drive	.60	.77
IV. Attitude	—	.96
A. Liberalism	.81	.92
B. Conservatism	.86	.72
V. Symptoms	—	.90
VI. Affect	—	.81
A. Positive Total	.93	.75
B. Negative Total	.94	.42
VII. Gender Role	—	.84
A. Masculinity	.84	.60
B. Femininity	.76	.58
VIII. Fantasy	.82	.93
IX. Body Image	.58	—
X. Satisfaction	.71	—

*Internal consistency coefficients for the 9 primary symptom dimensions of the BSI are as follows: Som = .80, OC = .83, Int = .74, Dep = .85, Anx = .81, Hos = .78, Phob = .77, Par = .77, Psy = .69.
**Test-Retest coefficients are based on a 14-day retest interval.

more detailed discussion of DSFI reliability may be found in Derogatis and Melisaratos (1979).

Although establishing the reliability of a psychological test requires a substantial number of "school figure" psychometric exercises, it usually may be accomplished in a relatively brief period of time. Validation of a test, on the other hand, is an inherently programmatic endeavor that requires multiple studies and years to accomplish. It can even be argued that the validation of a test is a perpetual exercise in that, strictly speaking, the test must be validated anew for each new predictive context in which it is used. In actual practice, the tendency is to generalize from previous validation studies to the study of current interest. Even this approach, which assumes that new measurement contexts are sufficiently like the old to allow generalization, still requires much effort and many studies before evidence is compelling that the fundamentals of validation have been accomplished.

Although the current report is not an appropriate place for an in-depth discussion of DSFI validation studies, it is important that the keystones of the instrument's validation be reviewed briefly. To begin with, the instrument possesses both face and content validity: the former by virtue of the fact that the items of the test are clearly about sexual behavior, and the latter by a very careful review of the domains critical to adequate sexual functioning; within each domain, there is representative sampling of domain items. Derogatis and

Melisaratos (1979) discuss these aspects of validation and in addition report on a structure-confirming factor analysis based on a sample of 380 subjects. The analysis identified seven major factors that conformed in large measure to the primary subtests of the DSFI and provided strong support for the construct validity of the test.

Another important aspect of validation has to do with criterion- oriented or predictive validity. Often this type of validity is demonstrated through clinical discrimination studies. To date, the DSFI has been used to discriminate males and females with sexual dysfunctions from heterosexual normals (Derogatis & Meyer, 1979b), male transsexuals from heterosexual males (Derogatis, Meyer, & Vazquez, 1978), female transsexuals from heterosexual females (Derogatis, Meyer, & Boland, 1981), males with psychogenic versus biogenic impotence (Derogatis, Meyer, & Dupkin, 1976), and male and female partners of patients with sexual dysfunctions (Derogatis & Meyer, 1979a). In addition, we have been able to distinguish distinct psychological subtypes of anorgasmia on the basis of DSFI profiles (Derogatis, Fagan, Schmidt, Wise, & Gilden, 1986). These and continuing studies like them cumulatively contribute to the validation of the scale.

In evaluating the validity of a psychometric instrument, the evaluations of the performance of the instrument that are accomplished by other investigators are clearly as important as the validation studies done by the test's author. Conte (1983, 1986) has completed two comprehensive reviews of psychometric measures of sexual functioning. Concerning the DSFI, she states in her first review (1983), "Derogatis's DSFI appears to be the most comprehensive [of the inventories reviewed]...it also provides the most complete psychometric data" (p. 574). In her second comparative evaluation (1986) she states, "For general clinical use Derogatis's DSFI appears to be the most comprehensive and potentially useful inventory" (p. 151). Although certainly not the last word, positive peer review for the DSFI tends to confirm its validity and utility.

CLINICAL INTERPRETATION

In any discussion concerning the clinical assessment of sexual disorders, it is important to recognize that most sexually dysfunctional individuals who become involved with the health care system are often self-referred and consciously aware that they have a sexual dysfunction. This means that psychological assessment with these patients rarely serves the screening and detection function that is so often associated with psychological assessment in regard to psychopathology. In addition, although we have made important strides in our attempts to develop a useful contemporary nosology of psychosexual disorders, our current system essentially assigns individuals to diagnostic categories on the basis of where in the sexual-response cycle (i.e., excitement, plateau, orgasm, resolution) dysfunction occurs (American Psychiatric Association, 1980). Often the presenting complaint is in and of itself sufficient information to make an accurate psychosexual diagnosis (e.g., premature ejaculation). This observation should help us to realize that comprehensive psychological assessment may not be a cost-efficient service if our major goal is to make a precise nosologic assignment, because the information required for these operations usually can be obtained through an initial evaluation interview. Until such time as our nosology encompasses more carefully delineated, naturally occurring, or functionally determined subtypes of sexual disorders, it is unlikely that psychological assessment will make a major contribution to such diagnostic assessment.

If psychological assessment does not perform a significant screening function, and if it is not essential to diagnostic operations, then in what fashion does it make a contribution to the evaluation of the patient with a sexual disorder? We believe that the answer to this question is that *psychological assessment dimensionalizes the psychosexual disorder* — it goes beyond simple taxonomic categorization and provides data on the nature and breadth of the problem. Comprehensive psychological assessment of the sexually dysfunctional patient should tell us about the patient's strengths and weaknesses with regard to sexual functioning, about the patient's current level of sexual functioning, and should also describe the patient's current emotional status. This information helps the clinician make more effective and meaningful treatment and disposition plans.

The DSFI has been developed to be interpreted at three distinct levels: *global scores, primary domain scores,* and *individual items* (Derogatis, 1976, 1980). The globals, the Sexual Functioning Index and the Global Sexual Satisfaction Index, are designed to provide an estimate of the patient's current level of sexual functioning in a single quantitative statement. The Sexual Functioning Index is a more complex, psychometrically developed indicator, whereas the Global Sexual Satisfaction Index represents the patient's current overall subjective appraisal. Discrepancies between the levels represented by the two global scores will often signal unappreciated strengths or liabilities associated with the patient's sexual behavior.

Each of the 10 primary domains represented in the DSFI was selected because it was felt to be highly relevant and important to effective and satisfying sexual behavior. Quality of sexual information, breadth of sexual experiences, the nature of an individual's attitudes about sex, and sexual fantasies have all been shown to have a marked influence on quality of sexual functioning. Lowered sex drive, although it may appear suppressed in response to chronic dysfunctional status, more often than not is seen in a causal rather than a resultant role in sexual disorders. Less intuitively obvious, gender role behaviors can also play a major part in initiating and sustaining dysfunctional sexual status, and recent evidence has shown us that body image is an extremely potent determinant of quality of sexual functioning. Each of these components represents an important determinant of quality of sexual functioning, and for this reason each has become the basis for a DSFI subtest.

Since current evidence strongly suggests that sexual dysfunction and psychological disorder are related (Derogatis, Meyer, & King, 1981), we thought it imperative to provide a comprehensive measure of psychological disorder. Two such areas, symptoms and affect, have been judged to have particular relevance for the assessment of sexual functioning. Symptoms and affect are both measured via independent multidimensional psychological tests that function as subtests within the DSFI. Measurement of symptoms is accomplished through the Brief Symptom Inventory (BSI) (Derogatis, 1975b; Derogatis & Melisaratos, 1983); affect is assessed through the Affect Balance Scale (ABS) (Derogatis, 1975a). In both cases, only a single global score contributes to the DSFI index; however, each test may itself be scored for its primary-dimension scores and additional global measures.

DSFI CLINICAL CASES

In this section, we will provide a series of clinical cases with a brief descriptive history of each case, and a discussion and interpretation of the patient's DSFI profile. Obviously, a comprehensive review of the clinical interpretation of a complex test such as the DSFI would require a substantial monograph and a great deal more case material than we can provide here. As a practical alternative, we have chosen to review a small series of cases that are both exemplary of the kinds of patients the clinician will confront in this area and that will enable us to demonstrate the utility of the DSFI in psychosexual evaluation. Moreover, it will be helpful for the clinician to bear in mind that these cases were selected from those presenting to a medical school clinic with a multidisciplinary staff who deal with a wide variety of sexual problems. The DSFI was one of a number of sources of information available to them. The following discussion will focus on the contributions of the DSFI, even though the case dispositions were also influenced by interviews and other diagnostic procedures.

Case 1: Impotence. Mr. D is an attractive 20-year-old Black male who is currently a college freshman. He has presented with a complaint of impotence. Neither the patient nor his family have a previous history of impotence, diabetes or psychiatric illness. The patient appears to be in excellent physical condition.

Mr. D attributes his impotence to "working roots," a "black magic" spell cast upon him by a former girlfriend. Mr. D had terminated the relationship with this woman in his senior year of high school in order to become sexually active with another female. Although he was not impotent in the first relationship, Mr. D reports that in subsequent sexual encounters over the last two years he has been partially or completely impotent with five other women. He has noticed a decrease in early morning erections, and he is not certain that the erections that he does experience are full. Mr. D reports, however, that he is able to ejaculate with masturbation.

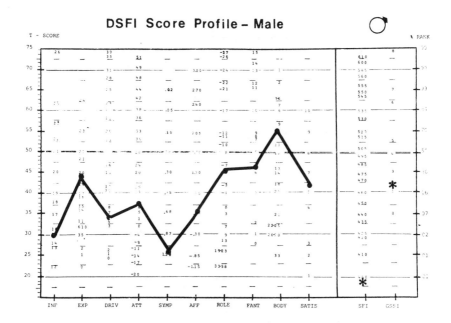

Figure 7.1 DSFI Profile of Mr. D, a 20-year-old male with impotence.

Although the idea of "working roots" is an accepted part of the patient's cultural surroundings, Mr. D is fairly convinced that his current dysfunction has a psychological base.

In evaluating Mr. D's profile, the very low scores on the globals tell us that he appears to have significant decrements in his overall sexual functioning. His subjective estimate of quality of functioning (Global Sexual Satisfaction Index) is substantially in agreement with the Sexual Functioning Index. One of the most striking aspects of the patient's profile is the marked lack of accurate sexual information available to him. Also, although indicating sexual relationships with multiple partners, the patient reveals a somewhat constricted sexual repertoire. Drive appears lowered, but item-by-item evaluation reveals that this score is a result of current difficulties, and that Mr. D's ideal frequency of sexual contact would be two or three times per week. Mr. D is quite conservative in his sexual attitudes, which, although somewhat unusual for a man of his age, is consistent with a constriction in the variety of his sexual experiences. Gender Role and Fantasy are essentially unremarkable, and Mr. D's Body Image score is actually above the mean. This latter finding is a somewhat atypical source of strength in this man's profile, since very often body image problems are a salient source of difficulty, particularly for younger patients. As anticipated, the patient indicates a certain degree of sexual dissatisfaction. More importantly, the patient indi-

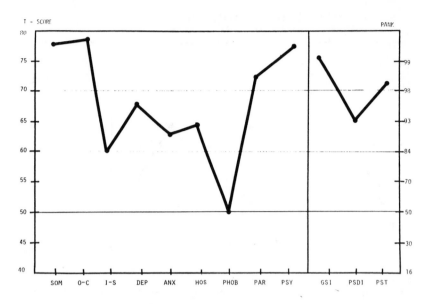

Figure 7.2 BSI Symptom profile of Mr. D, a 20-year-old male with impotence.

cates he is extremely distressed emotionally; both the symptom score and the affect score are quite low. Because dramatic psychological distress is a significant aspect of this patient's presentation, we have also reproduced his Brief Symptom Inventory (BSI) symptom profile below in Figure 7-2.

On the Brief Symptom Inventory, Mr. D's overall GSI score (the score that is calculated into the overall DSFI index) places him in the 99th centile of the normative distribution. On the primary symptom dimensions he reveals particular elevations on Somatization, Obsessive-Compulsive, Psychoticism and Paranoid Ideation, with a secondary peak on Depression. Review of the specific symptoms endorsed indicates that Mr. D has for the most part somaticized his anxiety, and the very high obsessive- compulsive score results from cognitive-performance difficulties (e.g., trouble concentrating, difficulty with memory) that could be associated with either clinical anxiety or depression. He appears to have a substantial paranoid coloring to his mode of thinking, and although some of his elevation on Psychoticism is due to social alienation, his particular superstitious orientation accounts for the remainder of the elevation.

Mr. D is a patient who presents as a particularly symptomatic and unhappy young man whose style of thinking and cultural experiences have combined with a marked lack of reliable information concerning sexual functioning to render him highly susceptible to sexual dysfunction. He shows strong conscious denial of anxious affect, and tends to experience conflict in somatic terms. His superstitious beliefs, coupled with a clear lack of knowledge about sexual matters, have contributed significantly to his problem.

In the disposition of Mr. D's case, it was recommended that the patient undergo short-term psychotherapy oriented toward providing a better understanding of the personal meaning sexuality held for him, and receive supplemental education concerning sexual anatomy and physiology as well as relaxation techniques.

Case 2: Premature Ejaculation. Mr. and Mrs. B are both white, 28 years old and have been married for four years. They have no children, and both members of the couple work in real estate. They were referred with a presenting complaint of premature ejaculation, which Mr. B indicates has been a difficulty for him since his first attempt at intercourse during adolescence. Although he has had experiences with many different women, he has never been free of the problem and is now quite preoccupied with it. Mr. and Mrs. B report having had premarital intercourse late in their courtship, which lasted on and off through high school and his college years. They were aware of his sexual problem, but they felt that it would correct itself over time. Although they have successfully completed intercourse on several occasions, most of their sexual experiences have been disappointing due to premature ejaculation prior to penetration. Their attempts at sexual play occur every couple of weeks, during which Mr. B is quickly brought to a state of arousal and ejaculates. Mrs. B frequently achieves orgasm through his manual stimulation. Mr. and Mrs. B present as being concerned about the possibility of having children unless their problem can be corrected. In spite of the difficulties, both partners feel that the marriage has been fairly successful. They have, however, noticed a growing distance between themselves over the past several years.

Although Mr. B is not currently being treated for psychological problems, Mrs. B is under treatment for depressive reaction to the current situation.

The DSFI profiles of Mr. and Mrs. B are provided in Figures 7-3 and 7-4 respectively.

Taking Mr. B first, we observe a Sexual Functioning Index that is 418 (two standard deviations below the mean), and a Global Sexual Satisfaction Index that is in essential agreement with this indicator. Mr. B shows striking dissatisfaction with all aspects of his sexual relationship, which lends poignancy to this couple's request for help. Again with this patient, we see an individual with a somewhat constricted library of sexual experiences, coupled with a much less than adequate fund of information about sexual functioning. Mr. B's drive level is relatively unimpaired, however, which is much more typical of premature ejaculation than of impotence among males. The patient reveals a symptom T-score of approximately 32 with an affect score of 36. He shows elevated levels of depressive and anxious symptoms on the Brief Symptom Inventory (not shown), with a particular peak on Interpersonal Sensitivity. The latter reveals

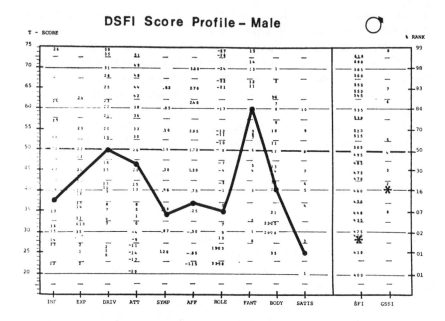

Figure 7.3 DSFI profile of Mr. B, a 28-year-old male with premature ejaculation.

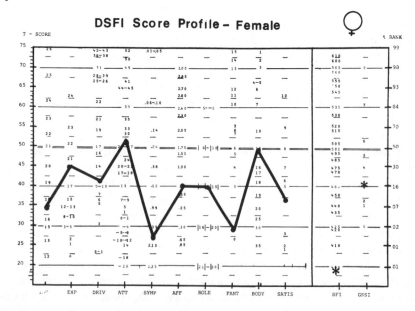

Figure 7.4 DSFI profile of Mrs. B, the 28-year-old wife of a premature ejaculator.

high levels of self-doubt and self-deprecation, and the GSAI score suggests clinical levels of psychological distress. The patient also reveals an androgynous gender role definition, which is not optimal for sexual functioning among males, and a moderately negative body image. His elevated sexual-fantasy score is consistent with his unimpaired drive levels and did not reveal any perverse content.

Mrs. B is currently under treatment for a depressive condition described by the couple as reactive to their sexual difficulties, but which is more accurately depicted as being reactive to the broader marital difficulties they appear to be having. Although less dissatisfied with the sexual relationship than was her husband (Figure 7-4), Mrs. B's Brief Symptom Inventory profile revealed a marked sense of alienation and loneliness, with clinical levels of depression. Mrs. B is also uninformed regarding sexual matters, with mild limitations in sexual experiences. Drive levels are notably reduced and she indicates little or no sexual fantasy. Mrs. B evidences a gender role definition that, although somewhat more feminine than optimal for females, is not really remarkable, and a normal body image score. Her Sexual Functioning Index of 399 is primarily a result of her dramatic symptom posture and reduction in Fantasy and other drive measures.

Treatment disposition of this case involved starting Mr. and Mrs. B in a dual-sex-therapist treatment program for their problem with premature ejaculation while maintaining Mrs. B in her individual psychotherapy for depression.

Case 3: Primary Anorgasmia. Mrs. Q is an attractive 30-year-old white school teacher who presents with a complaint of never experiencing an orgasm. The patient has had an extensive psychiatric history, which began at age 14 with a suicide attempt. Subsequently, she has been assigned a psychiatric diagnosis of hysterical personality.

The patient's history involves an unhappy childhood, a first marriage that ended in divorce, and her present marriage, which she describes as happy but sexually unfulfilling. Although she reports being well adjusted to the changes involved in puberty, she describes her reaction to learning about the mechanics of sex as one of disgust and repulsion.

Mrs. Q reports that she did not masturbate in adolescence, and that although she tried masturbation several times recently, she had never experienced orgasm. This is so, although she engaged in ritual intercourse at least 10 times a week with her first husband. She did not lubricate and reports finding the experience distasteful. In her present marriage, sexual foreplay between Mr. and Mrs. Q lasts from 10 to 30 minutes and consists of kissing, hugging, petting, and manual and oral vaginal stimulation. Although the patient does not lubricate, intercourse follows foreplay. Mr. Q states that he is dissatisfied with his wife's lack of responsiveness, and Mrs. Q claims she does not know what to do.

Mrs. Q's Sexual Functioning Index of 468 is less than one standard deviation below the mean and contradicts her poor subjective evaluation of her sexual relationship via the Global Sexual Satisfaction Index. In large measure this dis-

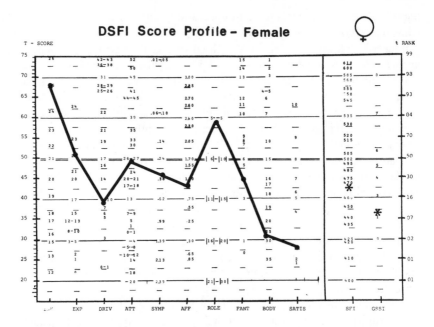

Figure 7.5 DSFI profile of Mrs. Q, a 30-year-old woman with primary anorgasmia.

crepancy is due to the high score on information achieved by the patient and her optimal gender role definition. Attitude and symptom scores are essentially unremarkable, and although the patient complains of dysphoric affect, it is mild. Of particular note in her profile is the very low body image score of 30 and the similar satisfaction score of 28. The former occurs in spite of the fact that Mrs. Q is an obviously attractive woman, and the latter suggests dissatisfaction with most aspects (e.g., variety, interest, communication, foreplay) of her sexual relationship. Reductions in drive and fantasy scores are also consistent with her lack of interest and inability to gain satisfaction from sexual behavior.

In the disposition of this case the couple was referred for dual-sex team therapy oriented toward treatment of the anorgasmia, and it was strongly recommended that the patient enter into individual psychotherapy with another therapist.

Case 4: Functional Vaginismus. Mrs. J is an attractive 24-year-old Black female who enjoys good physical health and is employed as a part-time food-service worker in a school. The patient's presenting complaint is of vaginismus.

Mrs. J reports an unusual family situation during her childhood and adolescence, in which her father was physically abusive and used alcohol excessively. Due to a fear of her father, Mrs. J lived with her maternal grandmother for ex-

DSFI Score Profile - Female

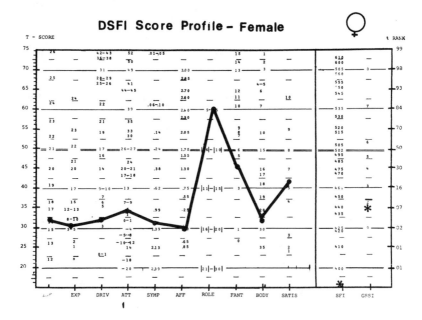

Figure 7.6 DSFI proflie of Mrs. J, a 24-year-old woman with vaginismus.

tended periods of time. She describes her upbringing as restricted. She dated no one before her husband and has had no sexual contact outside of the marriage. Mrs. J was married shortly after graduating from high school. Although Mr. and Mrs. J engage in sexual contact they have not consummated the marriage to date. Mr. J is able to stimulate the patient vaginally with his fingers, but she becomes rigid and tense throughout her entire body if he attempts penile penetration. The patient performs fellatio on her husband to satisfy him sexually. Mrs. J reports that she has never been orgasmic, although on occasion her vagina does lubricate. The patient states that she and her husband have never tried lubricants or artificial aids to facilitate vaginal penetration.

Mrs. J's Sexual Functioning Index score of 370 is more than three standard deviations below the normative mean, revealing a broad range of sexual deficits. This evaluation is consistent with her subjective assessment represented by the GSSI score of one. The patient reveals significant constrictions in sexual experiences, and her attitude toward sex is extremely conservative. Drive is suppressed, although her fantasy score and quality suggest this suppression is far from complete. Interestingly, she shows an optimal gender role definition score, and although satisfaction is somewhat low, it is clear that the patient receives pleasure and satisfaction from her sexual activities.

It is interesting to note that as a result of our evaluation, in addition to receiving a sexual diagnosis of functional vaginismus, the patient also received a psy-

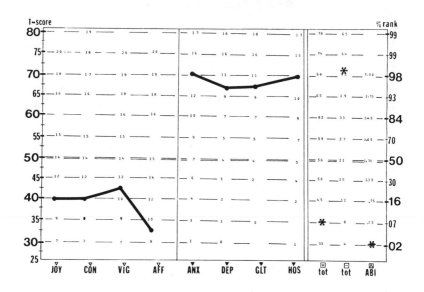

Figure 7.7 ABS profile of Mrs. J, a 24-year-old woman with vaginismus.

chiatric diagnosis of generalized anxiety disorder. Although we do not show it here, the patient's Brief Symptom Inventory profile supports such a diagnosis. The global score was elevated, with pronounced peaks on Anxiety, Phobic Anxiety, and Hostility. Although her particular pattern of symptoms is somewhat unique, the high symptomatic elevation is typical of our series of patients presenting with vaginismus (Derogatis, Meyer, & King, 1981).

Mrs. J's affect profile also supports such a judgment, and is reproduced from the Affect Balance Scale in Figure 7-7. This profile shows a marked negative affect balance, with decrements in all positive affect states and particular elevations on the anxiety and hostility dimensions.

In making a disposition, it was decided to treat the vaginismus first, with a recommendation that the patient should subsequently become involved in treatment for her anxiety disorder. Mrs. J was referred for systematic desensitization therapy through progressive vaginal dilation and was observed to respond well to this treatment.

These few brief vignettes and profiles only begin to communicate the potential richness inherent in the DSFI as a clinical assessment measure. The current format does not lend itself to communicating great detail concerning interpretation of the DSFI, and our goal here is to provide an initial clinical exposition. A more comprehensive document on clinical applications of the DSFI is currently being developed and will become available at a future time. The multiple dimensions of the DSFI profile, plus the detailed multidimensional presentation of symptoms and affects afforded by the Brief Symptom Index and the Affect Balance Scale, deliver high levels of relevant information concerning the current status of the sexually dysfunctional patient. Appropriate applications of the instrument can be extremely useful in initial patient evaluations, and can provide an excellent benchmark to evaluate the relative efficacy of therapeutic interventions.

REFERENCES

American Psychiatric Association. (1980). *Diagnostic and statistical manual of mental disorders* (3rd ed.). Washington, DC: Author.

Conte, C.R. (1983). Development and use of self-report techniques for assessing sexual functioning: A review and critique. *Archives of Sexual Behavior, 12*(6), 555-576.

Conte, C.R. (1986). Multivariate assessment of sexual dysfunction. *Journal of Consulting and Clinical Psychology, 54*(2), 149-157.

Derogatis, L.R. (1975a). *The Affect Balance Scale.* Baltimore: Clinical Psychometrics Research.

Derogatis, L.R. (1975b). *The Brief Symptom Inventory.* Baltimore: Clinical Psychometrics Research.

Derogatis, L.R. (1975c). *Derogatis Sexual Functioning Inventory.* Baltimore: Clinical Psychometrics Research.

Derogatis, L.R. (1976). Psychological assessment of sexual disabilities. In J.K. Meyer (ed.), *Clinical management of sexual disorders.* Baltimore: Williams & Wilkins.

Derogatis, L.R. (1977). *The SCL-90-R Manual I: Scoring, administration and procedures for the SCL-90-R.* Baltimore: Clinical Psychometrics Research.

Derogatis, L.R. (1980). Psychological assessment of psychosexual functioning. *Psychiatric Clinics of North America, 3,* 113-131.

Derogatis, L.R., Fagan, P.J., Schmidt, C.W., Wise, T.N., & Gilden, K.S. (1986). Psychological subtypes of anorgasmia: A marker variable approach. *Journal of Sex and Marital Therapy, 12(3),* 197-210.

Derogatis, L.R., & Melisaratos, N. (1979). The DSFI: A multidimensional measure of sexual functioning. *Journal of Sex and Marital Therapy, 5,* 244-281.

Derogatis, L.R., & Melisaratos, N. (1983). The Brief Symptom Inventory: An introductory report. *Psychological Medicine, 13,* 595-605.

Derogatis, L.R., Melisaratos, N., & Clark, M.M. (1976). A sexual behavior hierarchy via direct magnitude estimation. *Proceedings of the 46th Annual Meeting of the Eastern Psychological Association.* New York.

Derogatis, L.R., & Meyer, J.K. (1979a). The invested partner in sexual disorders: A profile. *American Journal of Psychiatry, 136*(12), 1545-1549.

Derogatis, L.R., & Meyer, J.K. (1979b). A psychological profile of the sexual dysfunctions. *Archives of Sexual Behavior, 8,* 201-223.

Derogatis, L.R., Meyer, J.K., & Boland, P. (1981). A psychological profile of the transsexual. II. The female. *Journal of Nervous and Mental Disease, 169,* 157-168.

Derogatis, L.R., Meyer, J.K., & Dupkin, C.N. (1976). Discrimination of organic versus psychogenic impotence with the DSFI. *Journal of Sex and Marital Therapy, 2,* 229-239.

Derogatis, L.R., Meyer, J.K., & King, K.M. (1981). Psychopathology in individuals with sexual dysfunction. *American Journal of Psychiatry, 138,* 757-763.

Derogatis, L.R., Meyer, J.K., & Vazquez, F. (1978). A psychological profile of the transsexual. I. The male. *Journal of Nervous and Mental Disease, 166,* 234-254.

Derogatis, L.R., & Spencer, P.M. (1982). *The Brief Symptom Inventory Manual I: Administration, scoring, and procedures for the BSI.* Baltimore: Clinical Psychometrics Research.

Nunnally, J. (1970). *Introduction to psychological measurement.* New York: McGraw-Hill.

Terman, L.M., & Miles, C.C. (1936). *Sex and personality: Studies in masculinity and femininity.* New York: McGraw-Hill.

Chapter 8

Assessment of Organic Factors in Sexual Dysfunctions

Richard C. Stuntz

INTRODUCTION

Sexuality refers to a relational process between persons of the same or opposite sex who mutually share physical and psychic intimacy, and thus vulnerability, with the aim of relieving emotional tension in a manner perceived as pleasurable. Sexual *function* describes the use of genital and nongenital organs in the pursuit of the release of these erotic psychic tensions. Such pursuit may be both separately and simultaneously goal-oriented, as in the striving for orgasm, or non-goal- oriented, as in the development of a sense of fusion with the partner.

We may define sexual *dysfunction* as an impairment or inhibition of one or several aspects of sexuality, which impedes the discharge of erotic tensions. Sexual dysfunction may be of organic (impaired) or psychogenic (inhibited) etiology, though it is impossible for me to conceive of organically produced sexual dysfunction which is not also concurrently compounded by psychogenic factors.

Pauly and Goldstein (1970) indicated that a conservative estimate of the prevalence of sexual dysfunction would be 10% of the general population. In a report of sexual problems encountered in a general medical practice in the United States, 15% of all contacts were related to sexual problems (Burnap & Golden, 1967). Others have estimated that from 30% to 50% of all people in the United States have sexual difficulties even though they may not seek assistance for them. Though I have no figures to sustain the belief, my 25 years of experience as a gynecologist convinces me that nearly half of the patient population that I encountered had sexual difficulties that merited attention. The lower reported figures may reflect the still-powerful societally imposed restrictions on, and the resulting embarrassment in, discussing sexuality on the part of *both* the patient and the physician or therapist.

Whatever the true incidence, only a minority of sexual dysfunctions arise solely from organic pathology; the majority originate in reaction to psychologic processes or are compounded by psychologic reaction to organic pathology (Masters & Johnson, 1970; Kaplan, 1974, 1979). Having said this, we are still left with the question of which problems fall into the minority group of sexual dysfunctions due to organic causes, and the even more perplexing problem of *how much* of the individual's sexual dysfunction is attributable to organic factors. For example, not every diabetic, nor every alcoholic, nor even every person with a transection of the spinal cord is impotent, anorgasmic, sexually unarousable, or sexually disinterested. And yet, estimation of this distinction is imperative if we are to establish a valid diagnosis, initiate proper therapy, and project an appropriate prognosis (Stuntz, 1983a).

THE DEPORD MODEL OF THE NORMAL HUMAN SEXUAL RESPONSE CYCLE

An understanding of the normal physiologic changes that accompany the human sexual response cycle is basic to the assessment of sexual function. We are in debt to Masters and Johnson, who gave us most of the data concerning the human sexual response cycle (Masters & Johnson, 1966). They divided the sexual response cycle, arbitrarily but of necessity, into four phases: Excitement, Plateau, Orgasm, and Resolution. Kaplan has added the concept of the Desire phase which both precedes the Excitement phase, and resumes following completion of the Resolution phase (Kaplan, 1979). Combining these concepts produces the DEPORD model to describe the normal human sexual response cycle.

The DEPORD Model: General

If we plot level of sexual tension against time we develop a graph similar to Figure 8-1. The actual dimensions of sexual tension, the elapsed time of each phase, and the total elapsed time are variables of each sexual encounter and vary with each individual in each sexual encounter. However, every individual normal response cycle will pass consecutively through each of the phases.

In general, the model is descriptive of the normal sexual response cycle for both men and women, though it is probable that the rise of sexual tension from baseline levels to plateau levels is normally more rapid for males, and the resolution phase is probably slower for females.

In the following sections I shall make general comments concerning each phase and describe the major physiologic changes that occur during each phase. I shall emphasize those physiologic changes that may be self-evident to the individual, and therefore recognizable and reportable to the interviewer.

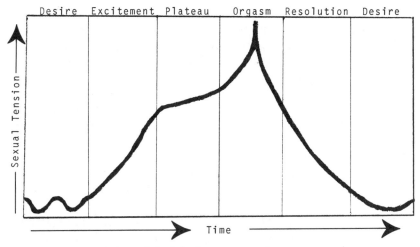

Figure 8.1 DEPORD model of the human sexual response cycle.

Desire Phase: General

Forty percent of the patients applying to the Marriage Council of Philadelphia for help with sexual problems were suffering from what was described by psychiatrists as Inhibited Sexual Desire, or ISD (Lief, 1977). Sexual desire consists of thoughts and fantasies including dreams about sexuality, and includes interest or longing to participate in sexual activity. Sexual desire can be thought of as an appetite for sexual activity. The judgment of the presence of persistent or pervasive inhibition of sexual desire should be made only when one takes into account those factors that may affect sexual desire, such as age, health, intensity and frequency of available sexual partners, and the context of that individual's life. In fact, the diagnosis of ISD should not be made unless this lack of desire is a source of distress to the individual or to that individual's sexual partner (American Psychiatric Association, 1980).

Desire phase: males and females. The presence of the hormone testosterone at a certain not-too-well-defined baseline level appears to be a prerequisite for the presence of sexual appetite in both men and women. This may be the most important androgenic effect of testosterone (Bancroft, 1980). Bancroft quotes the typical response of hypogonadal men during periods of testosterone deficiency, "I have the basic incliniation [for sex] but I don't seem to have the energy to put it into effect; I can easily put myself off" (Bancroft, 1980, p. 258). And further, in relation to intellectual tasks, he quotes, "I lose concentration and tend to leave things half finished. I get distracted by other things" (Bancroft, 1980, p. 258).

Hormone-behavior relationships, particularly in the area of sexual desire, are more difficult to assess in women than in men. Testosterone is believed to have a positive effect in women. It has frequently been used to increase sexual desire in postmenopausal women, but there have been no well-designed treatment-outcome studies. There is also a risk of the masculinizing effect of testosterone, such as the development of hirsutism and of voice changes. There does not appear to be a direct estrogen effect on sexual desire in women parallel to that of testosterone in men; the role of estrogen in the maintenance of sexual appetite and sexual arousability remains uncertain. A secondary effect, however, is present in the requirement of estrogen for the maintenance of normal vaginal mucosal functions. If such functions (i.e., distensibility and lubrication) are lost through lack of estrogen, as may occur naturally in some postmenopausal women, the result will be painful coitus. The anticipation of coital discomfort, or dyspareunia, may be difficult to separate from the perceived lack of sexual desire.

A separate problem has to do with the social mores concerning sexual activity. In our present society, though this appears to be changing, most men would still feel in some way abnormal if they did not *usually* indicate the level of their sexual appetite by initiating sexual activity with their partners. Many (and until recently, most) women would agree and would themselves feel in some way abnormal if they were required *regularly* to take the initiative in sexual encounters. Thus the woman with normal or even strong sexual desire might exhibit the same level of sexual activity as the woman with low or poor drives toward sexual activity. In each case the male partner would be setting the frequency rate. Appropriate questions in the sexual interview would not be limited to the frequency of sexual activity but rather would explore areas concerning the satisfaction with that usual frequency.

Table 8.1   Physiologic Changes: Desire Phase

Male	
Normal	No known changes
ISD	Possible low serum testosterone
Female	
Normal	No known changes
ISD	Possible low serum testosterone

Excitement Phase: General

The excitement phase of the sexual response cycle is defined as that period of time during which sexual tension rises from the relatively low level of the usual or, for that individual, normal desire level to the relatively high level of sexual tension that then merges into the plateau level.

We are not here interested in the mental activity or the physical sensations that produce sexual excitement, but rather the physiologic changes produced by whatever it is that causes this increase in sexual tension. Traditionally, penile erection and vaginal lubrication have been used as indicators of the presence of sexual excitement. By that definition, if erection or vaginal lubrication does not occur or is not maintained in what is for that individual a sexually appropriate and sexually stimulating situation, then in that situation there has been inhibition of sexual excitement (ISE), regardless of the causative factors. We do not have available at present any other valid markers of sexual excitement; we cannot determine whether the individual who cannot develop a penile erection or become lubricated due to the presence of organic pathology is nevertheless sexually excited, other than by self-report. We can, however, in some cases to be discussed later, determine whether ISE is partially or primarily related to organic pathology.

The term *Inhibited sexual excitement* (ISE) is, I believe, preferable to *impotence* or *frigidity,* both of which have belittling implications. Also, neither impotence nor frigidity has been defined and accepted universally to include the same constellation of signs and symptoms. ISE indicates a recurrent or persistent absence or decrease in sexual excitement during sexual activity. In males this is manifested by partial or complete failure to attain or maintain penile erection sufficient for vaginal intromission and completion of the sexual act. In females there is partial or complete failure to attain or maintain the swelling-lubrication response until completion of the sexual act. Both of these must be judged in the context of sexual activity that is adequate in focus, intensity, and duration (American Psychiatric Association, 1980).

Excitement phase: males. The physiology of the changes occurring during the excitement phase in males has been thoroughly detailed and updated in several recent papers (deGroot & Booth, 1980; Finkle, 1980; Newman & Northrup, 1981) and is a major part of the February 1981 issue of the *Urologic Clinics of North America* on male sexual dysfunction.

Very briefly summarized, penile erection is produced by a combination of penile arterial dilatation and decreased venous outflow from the penis. With increased blood inflow and decreased outflow, there is a resulting engorgement of the corpora cavernosa, the spongelike erectile tissue lying on the posterior and lateral aspects of the penis, which are closely surrounded by a dense fibrous covering. It can be thought of as similar to pumping up a rodlike football. The degree of rigidity is of more functional concern sexually than is the degree of penile enlargement, but both are dependent on the amount of blood compressed into the corpora cavernosa.

These vascular changes are the result of nerve-reflex responses of two separate origins. One is the genital organ stimulation that activates spinal reflex centers; this is the nerve reflex that produces penile erections in the newborn male infant. The second reflex response is produced by stimuli from all the senses: visual, tactile, auditory, olfactory and perhaps gustatory, plus the stimuli produced by the cognitive functions of thoughts, fantasies, and dreams, all of which impinge on the supraspinal centers. Both the higher and lower nervous system stimuli are responsible for erections in the normal adult male. Sacral parasympathetic and thoracolumbar sympathetic nerves provide the efferent vasodilatory input to the penis. As with the desire phase, all of the above neurocirculatory changes will occur only in the milieu of an "adequate" supply of testosterone. What consitutes the critical lower limit of this adequate amount of testosterone cannot at present be determined for the individual, though most laboratories have established their own maximum and minimum norms. The critical minimum probably varies for each individual, it may vary diurnally for each individual, and it does vary with increasing age for all males. Therefore, for penile erection to occur, the cardiovascular, neurologic, and hormonal systems must be functioning. Major insults or combinations of minor insults to any of these systems may be reflected in impaired erections. For example, castration, which may be required in the treatment of cancer of the prostate, usually results in loss of erectile capability due to the almost complete loss of testosterone. On the other hand, minor degrees of decreased peripheral circulation combined with minor degrees of peripheral nerve conduction loss, as is frequently seen with diabetes mellitus, will in many cases produce the same degree of erectile disability.

Presumably the same general body systems must be functioning for nipple erection to occur, as it does in most males during the sexual excitement phase (Masters & Johnson, 1966), and for contraction of the cremasteric muscle, which elevates the scrotum toward the base of the penis at the perineum late in the excitement phase.

Excitement phase: females. As stated above, the most commonly described physiologic change in women during the excitement phase is the development of increased vaginal fluid, or lubrication (Hoon, 1976, Levin, 1980). This fluid is a transudate (a fluid that passes through the vaginal wall lining rather than being produced by glands in the vagina), which is the direct result of increased perivaginal circulatory congestion. Female sexual excitement was portrayed in early Greek drama by a male (playing the female part) who wore sacks of water attached to a belt so as to hang down in the groin area. It is believed that the increased circulation in the perivaginal tissues is produced by similar if not identical stimuli and responses as were described for the males, and which in the male produces penile erections. At present we do not know whether this transudate is quantitatively or qualitatively related to the kinds or degree of stimulation. It is believed that changes in the production of this fluid are related to the same pathophysiologic changes that in the male result in erectile dysfunctions.

It must be remembered that, pleasure aside, the female vagina can function purely as a physical receptacle for the erect penis, regardless of whether there is sexual desire or excitement. Female prostitution is made possible by this fact. The male must be able to demonstrate his sexual excitement with a penile erec-

Table 8.2. Physiologic Changes: Excitement Phase

Male
1. Penile erection
    (a) Result of filling and engorgement of the corpora cavernosa.
2. Scrotum
    (a) Flattening of the skin, beginning elevation of the testes
3. Nipple erection in 2/3 of men.

Female
1. Vagina
    (a) Lubrication by transudate due to vasocongestion of perivaginal tissues
    (b) Beginning dilatation of upper 2/3 of vagina and constriction of lower 1/3
2. Clitoris
    (a) Enlarged in diameter, but not in length
3. Vulva
    (a) Color changes: from pink through red to purple
    (b) Labia majora thinned and flattened in primipara, enlarged 2/3 in multipara
4. Uterus
    (a) Beginning elevation out of the deep pelvis
5. Breasts
    (a) Nipple erection in 2/3 of women
    (b) Beginning areolar enlargement and deepening color

tion for him to be able to participate in coital activity. This is an absurdly simple but amazingly important difference in sexual functioning that is frequently overlooked or not appreciated. For example, it is rare for a man to complain to a woman, "You are not lubricated, therefore you are not excited, and that must mean that you don't love me." On the other hand, I frequently hear the litany, "You don't get an erection because I don't excite you anymore. You must not love me!"

The other factors listed in Table 8-2 are also related to neurovascular changes that are under the influence of higher and lower neural centers. Dilatation of the upper third of the vagina and elevation of the uterus may be due to contraction of the smooth muscle of the suspensory ligaments of the uterus.

Plateau Phase: General

The Plateau phase emerges from the Excitement phase at very high levels of sexual tension (Masters & Johnson, 1966). During the Plateau phase, sexual tension increases more gradually until a level of orgasmic inevitability is reached, which marks the border of the following Orgasmic phase. The more readily recognized physiologic changes are listed in Table 8-3.

Plateau phase: males. The same vasocongestive changes and autonomic stimulation that were present during the Excitement phase continue during the Plateau phase. The penis, including the glans, continues to enlarge and deepen in color. There is a 50% to 100% increase in the size of the testes. Parasympathetic stimulation of Cowper's glands produces a drop or two of mucoid secretion at the external urethral meatus, which acts as an additional lubricant. Viable sperm are often found in this secretion, which may in part explain the frequent failure of pre- ejaculatory withdrawal from the vagina (coitus interruptus) as a birth-control measure. Similar autonomic stimulation is also responsible for continued elevation of the scrotum. In the late Plateau phase the testes lie snugly against the base of the penis at the perineum.

As the Plateau phase continues toward orgasm, there is increased generalized muscle tension, increased heart and respiratory rate, and elevation of the blood pressure. It is difficult to separate how much these changes are due to autonomic stimulation and how much to increased physical activity.

Absence of the Plateau phase, that is, progression of the Excitement phase directly and rapidly into the Orgasmic phase is diagnostic of premature ejaculation. Following ejaculation, there is at all ages a refractory period for another ejaculation and with this an almost inevitable loss of penile rigidity, because of which the terms *premature ejaculation* and *impotence* are frequently confused. The diagnostic criteria for premature ejaculation as listed in the *Diagnostic and Statistical Manual of Mental Disorders (DSM III)* is that ejaculation has occurred before the individuual wishes it, because of recurrent or persistent absence of reasonable voluntary control of ejaculation and orgasm during sexual activity (American Psychiatric Association, 1980). However, ejaculation occurring after 10 or 15 mintues of coital activity could not reasonably be called premature ejaculation even if that individual were unable to control his ejaculation at that point. Therefore the period of time from vaginal intromission to ejaculation is critical diagnostically but, retrospectively, difficult to measure. The Sexual Behaviors Consultation Unit at Johns Hopkins has empirically adopted the standard of 15 thrusts. Ejaculation occuring before 15 thrusts is defined as premature ejaculation.

Premature female orgasm is infrequently if ever a presenting complaint. Given a woman's capacity for multiple orgasms without loss of the vasocongestion of sexual excitement, the first rapid orgasm may be perceived as a valuable adjunct to the total sexual experience.

There are no known pathophysiologic causes for premature ejaculation. As far as is known today, it is always etiologically related to emotional distress, usually to anxiety.

Plateau phase: female. Increasing vasocongestion under the influence of autonomic stimulation is responsible for the physiologic changes that continue to develop as the Plateau phase emerges out of the Excitement phase and mounts slowly toward the Orgasmic phase. The perivaginal tissues of the outer third of the vagina, that is, the outer 2 or 3 inches, become increasingly engorged. This area has been named the "orgasmic platform" by Masters and Johnson (1966), and is composed of the mucosal and perivaginal tissues directly overlying the pubococcygeus muscle, which has both voluntary and involuntary functions during the entire coital act from intromission through or-

Table 8.3. Physiologic Changes: Plateau Phase

Male
1. Penis.
    (a) Increase in diameter and color of glans
    (b) Drop of secretion from Cowpers gland appears at urethral meatus; may
         contain viable sperm
2. Testes
    (a) 50% to 100% increase in size over baseline
    (b) Elevation to perineum at base of penis
3. General
    (a) Appearance of sex flush, rash resembling measles spreading over upper half of
         body including face
    (b) Generalized muscular tension, tachycardia, hyperventilation and elevated
         blood pressure

Female
1. Vagina
    (a) Vasocongestion increases, producing orgasmic platform
    (b) Ballooning of upper 2/3 of vagina
2. Clitoris
    (a) Shaft and glans retract against pubic symphysis
    (b) Engorgement of labia "hides" glans
3. Breasts
    (a) Increase in breast size up to 50%, more marked in women who have not
         breast-fed
4. General
    (a) Appearance of sex flush, rash resembling measles spreading over upper half of
         body including face
    (b) Increased muscular tone, heart rate, respiratory rate, and blood pressure

gasm. With contraction of the pubococcygeus muscle, or simply by its increased muscle tension plus engorgement of the orgasmic platform, the penis is more snugly encompassed by the vaginal canal. This in turn produces more friction on both the penis and the walls of the outer third of the vagina, all of which increases the sensory stimulation leading to heightened sexual tension.

During the plateau phase, and particularly just prior to the Orgasmic phase, the vault of the vagina (the inner two thirds) is expanding to produce a ballooning cavity that acts as a holding pool for the ejaculation produced by the male orgasm. Because of this ballooning effect, the male may complain that he cannot feel anything with the tip of his penis, which may lead to the further observation/complaint that his partner's vagina is too large.

Breast engorgement during the Plateau phase, or for that matter at any time during the normal sexual response cycle, is usually not described as painful even though there may be as much as a 25% increase in size, particularly in women who have not breast- fed (Kolodny, 1980).

A sex flush closely resembling the rash of measles is reported by three out of four women, spreading over the trunk, chest, face, and arms. This is the same distribution found in the postmenopausal woman who complains of "hot flashes."

As in the male, during the Plateau phase there is increased generalized muscle tone, increased heart rate and respiratory rate due both to the autonomic stimulation and to increased physical activity.

Orgasmic Phase: General

The orgasmic phase in both women and men is predicated on the attainment of high levels of sexual tension. As mentioned above, sexual tension is produced by both mental activity and by stimulation of erogenous areas, which may be more or less specific for each individual. Most men will require penile stimulation and most women clitoral stimulation directly or indirectly to produce the orgastic or ejaculatory response. In essence, orgasm can be described as a neurophysiologic release, considered by most people who have experienced the event to be the acme of pleasure. If one compares descriptions of orgasm written by both men and women, and if specific references to the gender of the author or to the genitals being stimulated are deleted, it is impossible to identify whether the description was written by a man or by a woman. This suggests that orgasm is either not a gender-specific reaction or that the sensation of orgasm cannot properly be described (Levin, 1980).

There is one gender difference, however, and that is the association of ejaculation with orgasm in the male. The production and expulsion of a bolus of ejaculate through the length of the penile urethra is considered a pleasurable part of male orgasm. When this does not occur, as in the case of retrograde ejaculation, men will describe the sensation as being less enjoyable. Part of this decreased enjoyment may be related psychologically to the infertility that accompanies the loss of the ejaculate.

A secondary but nevertheless important distinction between male and female orgasm relates to the time and frequency of orgasm. Most men can achieve orgasm, if they wish, within a few minutes of coital activity. Usually, women require considerably longer. Perhaps as many as 30% to 50% of women never achieve orgasm through coital activity alone, many requiring additional clitoral stimulation. And there is a residue of some 10% of women who never experience orgasm regardless of the mode of stimulation (Levin, 1980). Inhibited male orgasm—the recurrent or persistent absence of ejaculation or prolonged delay in ejaculation in the presence of an adequate level of sexual excitement (American Psychiatric Association, 1980)—is uncommon. Usually, inability to ejaculate due to organic causes is accompanied by loss of erectile capability. When the individual describes good functional erections but complains of grossly inhibited or absent ejaculation, I would suspect psychogenic causes.

Because orgasm is dependent on increasing sexual tensions, anything that interferes with or represses sexual excitement, be it organic or psychologic, will interfere with or inhibit orgasm as well. We do not at present have available clinical tools with which to measure levels of sexual excitement and can only infer such levels from self-reports of women and from penile tumescence studies in men.

Evidence suggests that the functional status of the pubococcygeus muscle is important for orgasm in women. This is the muscle that surrounds the vaginal outlet, which has both voluntary and involuntary sexual functions. Women may contract this muscle at will; it is the muscle that in part controls the escape of urine during micturition. During high levels of sexual tension there is some involuntary contraction of this muscle, and during orgasm there are repeated involuntary spasmodic contractions. A statistically significant difference has been found between orgasmic and anorgasmic women in the physiologic status of their pubococcygeus muscles (Graber, 1981; Kegel, 1952). Loss of the normal contractive function of this muscle is frequently associated with the vaginal delivery of many and/or large infants, and may usually be remedied by exercises designed to increase pubococcygeus muscle strength.

Multiple orgasms, a series of repeated identifiable orgasmic responses, may occur in the woman who is normally orgasmic and who desires further orgasms if the level of sexual tension is maintained at high plateau levels by continued vaginal and/or clitoral stimulation. Males do not have this potential. Immediately following ejaculation the male enters a period during which he is refractory to ejaculation. During his teen years the male may be able to maintain an erection during this refractory period but he usually loses this ability by his middle 20s. The length of this refractory period is directly related to age, from a few minutes in the teens to several hours in the older population (Kolodny, Masters, & Johnson, 1979).

Orgasmic phase: males. Most men will describe a feeling of increased pressure and heat in the perineal area as the orgasmic phase beings. This is due to contraction of the capsule of the prostate gland as it propels the prostatic secretion into the proximal portion of the urethra. This constitutes the major portion of the seminal fluid bolus. If the man has an infection of the prostate gland, this capsular contraction may be quite painful. The seminal vesicle and the vas deferens also eject their fluids into the proximal urethra, and it is this portion of the ejaculate that will contain the sperm in fertile men (deGroot & Booth, 1980).

As the seminal fluid accumulates in the proximal urethra, a sensation of ejaculatory inevitability develops, that is, the feeling that ejaculation is impending and will occur regardless of further penile stimulation. This is followed within 2 or 3 seconds by simultaneous rhythmic contractions of the prostate, of the perineal muscles, and of the shaft of the penis, all of which, acting simultaneously, cause rapid propulsion of the seminal bolus down and out of the urethra. These contractions occur at a rate of one per 0.7 to 1.2 seconds for a total of 3 to 10 contractions. Both the quantity of the ejaculate and the force of the ejaculation normally decrease with age. During the ejaculation period the sphincter muscle at the urethrovesicle (bladder) junction is tightly closed. If this sphincter does not close due to previous urologic surgery or due to damage, or because of lack of parasympathetic stimulation, the seminal bolus is ejaculated in a retrograde manner into the bladder.

Orgasmic phase: females. Orgasm, and particularly female orgasm, has been described and both specific and generalized importance attached to it in psychiatric, philosophic, sociologic, anthropologic, poetic, and fictional literature. But orgasm per se remains a neurovascular physiologic event. It may in some ways be compared to a reflex arc, with an efferent or motor reaction to an afferent or sensory stimulus. We can describe the efferent response as a series of contractions of the perivaginal musculature, primarily the pubococcygeus muscles, but also involving the ileococcygeus, the ischiocavernosus, and the bulbocavernosus muscles. This is, however, a description of the efferent response, and not of orgasm itself. We do not at this time know all of the neuroanatomic pathways for either stimulus or response.

The afferent loop has been studied primarily in relation to stimulation of the clitoris and vagina, though orgasm has been induced from other afferent receptor sites, such as the breast (Masters & Johnson, 1966). Krantz, in a study of the histology of the vagina, found few receptors of any kind in the vaginal wall and reported that the most common receptors in the clitoris were pressor receptors (Krantz, 1959). An intact and functioning pubococcygeus muscle, which when contracted produces circumvaginal pressure on the coital penis and thus reciprocal friction, is essential in many women to the attainment of orgasm (Graber, 1981). The most common cause for the loss or decreased function of this muscle in women is the trauma and vaginal lacerations incurred during childbirth. Appropriate stimulation of the clitoris manually, orally, or by penile friction and pressure will augment the frequency of orgasm in most women, and is essential for orgasm in from 30% to 50% of women (Levin, 1980).

The uterine contractions that occur during orgasm resemble the contractions of labor in kind, though not in degree. They begin in the upper body of the uterus and proceed downward in waves toward the cervix. The number and frequency of these contractions as well as the perivaginal muscle contractions are almost identical to the male orgasmic contractions. Because of the similarity to labor contractions and the possibility of inducing in this manner the premature termination of a pregnancy, physicians recommend to some of their pregnant patients that sexual activity not be carried on to orgasm particularly during the latter months of the pregnancy.

There will be an occasional woman who is unable to recognize within her own sexual response whether orgasm has occurred. This may be due to genital anesthesia, lack of sufficient sexual stimulation, or to psychologic defenses. If, ac-

Table 8.4. Physiologic Changes: Orgasmic Phase

Male
1. Contractions of prostate, seminal vesicles and vas deferens, producing pooling of seminal fluid in the proximal urethra
2. Sensation of ejaculatory inevitability
3. Simultaneous contractions of the prostate, of the perineal muscles, and of the shaft of the penis propels the seminal bolus down the urethra
3. 5 to 12 contractions at 0.7- to 1.0-second intervals

Female
1. Sudden surge of sexual tension
2. Followed very rapidly by equally sudden release of sexual tension
3. Simultaneous rhythmic contractions of the uterus, orgasmic platform, and rectal sphincter
4. 5 to 12 contractions at 0.7- to 1.0-second intervals

cording to a woman's description of her own sexual response cycle, there is, following several minutes of appropriate sexual stimulation during which lubrication has developed, an episode of rather sudden increase in sexual tension followed by an equally sudden release of that tension (usually described as more intensely pleasurable than other sexual activities) then orgasm has almost certainly occurred. On the other hand, the anorgasmic sexual response cycle is characterized by a slow increase of sexual excitement and tension, but not usually to very high levels, followed by a slow decrease in sexual tension—almost as if the tension was dribbling away faster than it could be accumulated in spite of whatever sexual stimulation was being employed. The separating dimension in the two descriptions is the rapid rise and rapid release of sexual tension associated with orgasm. At present we do not have any simple clinical means of determining whether orgasm has occurred, and therefore must depend on self report.

Resolution Phase: General

This is the phase during which sexual tension subsides to baseline desire levels—if we presume that sexual stimulation ceases. As stated previously, if the female is continuously stimulated and if sexual tension levels remain at high plateau levels, the orgasmic response may be repeated for as long as the woman considers this to be desirable. Not all women are multiorgasmic, but presumably this potential exists for all orgasmic women.

The anatomic and physiologic changes that developed during the earlier phase of the sexual response cycle now dissipate. This is a period of psychologic vulnerability, which has variously been described to me as being "a pleasurable afterglow" or as "being uncomfortably exposed," and which may prompt such behaviors as continuing the warm embraces, or slipping off into sleep, or as expressing the need to "wash off."

Table 8.5.   Physiologic Changes: Resolution Phase

Male
1. Immediately following ejaculation, refractory period for repeated ejaculation, though partial or full erection may be maintained.
    (a) Length of the refractory period is a function of age and of the frequency of ejaculation.
2. Increased generalized perspiration
3. Anatomic and physiologic changes previously developed are now slowly reversed
4. Period of afterglow, which my be experienced as a sense of psychologic vulnerability

Female
1. The potential for multiple orgasms is related to the maintenance of high plateau levels of sexual tension
2. Increased generalized perspiration
3. Previous physiologic and anatomic changes are slowly reversed
4. The relaxation following orgasm, the "afterglow," may be experienced as joyful or as psychologically threatening

Resolution phase: males. Once ejaculation has occurred, there is a refractory period for ejaculation though not necessarily for erection, the period of time being a function of age.

As resolution occurs, there usually is increased perspiration and decreased blood pressure. Heart rate and respiratory rate return toward normal and general muscle tone relaxes. These changes appear to occur more rapidly in men than in women.

Resolution phase: females. If there is no continuous sexual stimulation, the previously described anatomic and physiologic changes gradually return to normal desire baseline levels. As with men, there is a generalized perspiration; this may be another indication that orgasm has occurred. In the absence of orgasm, the decrease in sexual tension dissipates much more slowly. This is a frequently indicted cause of chronic pelvic pain.

The period of relaxation at the end of the normally completed sexual response cycle has been described by many women as being a goal in and of itself. They report that the pleasure of this time is longer lasting, and that the openness, the sharing, and the emotional closeness of this period is for them of equal value to the evanescent peak experience of orgasm.

The DEPORD Model: Summary

The DEPORD Model of the human sexual response cycle allows us somewhat better understanding of the physiology of sexual activity. The basic physiologic response to sexual stimulation is widespread vasocongestion and increase in muscle tension. Associated with each stage, with the possible exception of the Desire phase, are specific organ responses. Because of their visibility and the sensations produced by these responses, some of them may serve as diagnostic markers for that particular stage of sexual arousal.

SEXUAL HISTORY

The single most important diagnostic instrument the therapist has available in attempting to separate organic from functional sexual dysfunctions is the clinical interview. The purposes of this interview are not simply limited to "history taking." It is the beginning dialogue with the patient, which fills in the informational gaps, and it is the initial evaluation of both the patient's dysfunction and of the patient who has the dysfunction. It may be the initial introduction of the patient to an interviewer/therapist, and it is frequently the first step in therapy.

Very little sexual disclosure will be made by most patients when the interviewer has a distaste for such discussion. Disclosure will increase when questions are asked about sexual matters that are indicated by the patient's condition or complaints; disclosure will increase even more when sexual questions are included routinely in the interview by a therapist who is undisturbed by their inclusion (Group for the Advancement of Psychiatry, 1973).

The full sexual interview is usually accomplished on three levels: (a) elaboration of the chief complaint, (b) review of the sexual response cycle, and (c) the longitudinal developmental history. The experienced interviewer may be able to assess the organicity of the sexual dysfunction without obtaining the full psychological developmental history. However, when the etiology and the diagnosis are obscure, the full history will be required.

Elaboration of the Chief Complaint

The patient is asked to give a "journalistic" report on the problem which has brought the individual to the interview. This should include the what, when, where, and why of the problem from the patient's perspective.

What: The patient's description of the problem completely and specifically as possible.

When: Time of onset, characteristics of the problem since onset, life situation at the time of onset.

Where: Only at home, only in bed, on vacation, at certain times, with certain partners only, or pervasive.

Why: The patient's perception (belief, guess, thoughts, fantasy) of the cause; this question is asked too infrequently.

In addition to the above questions, I usually inquire as to the timing of the search for help, that is, why the patient is seeking help at this time rather than previously. This gives me some indication of the pressure being applied to the

Table 8.6.   Organic versus Psychologic Sexual Dysfunction: Clues from the History

Psychologic Dysfunction
1.   Frequently abrupt in onset, not related to specific trauma
2.   Fluctuating functional ability
3.   Responsive to situational factors
     (a)   Time, place, partner
4.   In males, unimpaired nonsexual erections

Organic dysfunction
1.   Frequently insidious in onset with steady decline in function unless related to
     trauma
2.   Consistently decreased function or completely nonfunctional
3.   Unresponsive to situational changes
4.   In males, decreased or absent nonsexual erections

individual by the sexual partner. If I am interviewing a couple with a sexual dysfunction, I usually interview them together initially and then separately. In the conjoint session I ask them both to specify the reasons for coming in to see me, and then I go over the elaboration of the chief complaint again when in individual sessions. Not infrequently I find that there is considerable disagreement concerning the primary problem.

The distinction between organic and functional sexual problems frequently hinges on the chronicity and unrelenting nature of the organic problem, and the fluctuating or situational nature of the functional ones (Meyer, 1983).

Review of the Sexual Response Cycle (DEPORD)

The next step in obtaining the sexual history is to review the sexual response cycle. This is probably the most effective means of assessing organic factors in the sexual dysfunction, and involves reviewing the practices and problems the patient encounters in each phase of the DEPORD model as described previously.

In practice this can best be accomplished by asking the patient to describe in as much detail as possible a recent typical sexual encounter during which the problem was in evidence. For example, I usually request that the patient start from the moment he or she believed a sexual encounter would take place (i.e., who initiated the encounter), how this request for sexual activity was made known, and how it was received and the request acknowledged. From that point on I ask the patient to describe the perceived physical responses as well as psychologic and sensory changes. I then attempt to relate these changes to those usual changes in the normal response cycle. For example, if a woman states that her chief complaint is that she cannot have an orgasm with coitus, and on reviewing the sexual response cycle she describes entirely normal desire, excitement and plateau phases, I would certainly be concerned by the presence or absence of the physiologic changes of the orgasm phase. On the other hand, if that same woman stated that in a sexual encounter "Nothing at all happens" (a not too unusual complaint), then I would be more interested in desire-phase and excitement-phase anomalies.

At the conclusion of the review of the sexual response cycle it should be possible to state at what phase difficulties arise and to specify the accompanying physical and emotional events. As the sexual response cycle is reviewed, it is also important to inquire about related genitourinary and bowel function. For example, loss of urinary control during coitus may indicate loss of perivaginal muscle tone or, less frequently, neurologic damage, both of which might interfere with the development of sexual excitement. Another example would be the rectal pain of hemorrhoids or rectal fissures, which may be exacerbated by vaginal-penile penetration and containment, and which might readily lead to a loss of interest in coitus. Also, associated difficulties in these anatomically and neurologically related areas may signal some organic pathology (Meyer, 1983).

The Psychologic Developmental History

When the intention is simply to take a sufficient history to distinguish between organic and psychologic problems in the interest of appropriate referral, it is probably not essential to obtain the full developmental history. When the intent is to select among appropriate psychologic treatment modalities, the development history is essential. For the reader interested in exploring the process of obtaining the developmental history, I suggest the following references: Meyer, 1977, 1980a, and 1980b.

THE PHYSICAL EXAMINATION

Sexual activity is the physical expression of erotic feelings, pursued with the goal of discharging sexual tensions. The presence of physical pathology may interfere grossly with sexual activity, as in the case of organic impotence. Or it may interfere more subtly, as might be the case with vaginitis, which produces dyspareunia (painful intercourse), and thus interferes with sexual satisfaction and possibly, secondarily, with sexual desire. Therefore, a careful, complete physical examination is necessary for the proper evaluation of the individual with a sexual dysfunction.

The primary purpose of the physical examination, of course, is to determine the presence or absence of organic factors that cause or contribute to the sexual dysfunction. An important secondary purpose is to reassure the individual who in fact does not have organic factors involved; this may allow that person to focus on the psychologic aspects of the problem. And finally, the physical examination can also serve a sex-education function for those individuals or couples who have little or no understanding of the anatomy, physiology, or sexual functioning of their genital organs (Stuntz & Stuntz, 1983).

The methodology of pelvic and genital examinations has been well covered in recent medical literature and need not be repeated here (Smolev, 1983; Stuntz, 1983b). However, in the examination of patients who complain of sexual difficulties, a special note of caution is in order. All physical examinations occur in an ambience of anxiety, the more so with the genitals, for this area is so highly invested with emotional content, and in these patients so frequently with conflict. Fears associated with the genital examination may be related to anticipation of pain, perhaps the remembrance of previous examinations. There also may be fears about the possibility of discovering a dread disease, of simply exposing the genitals, which they were "taught" to believe were "nasty," or that their genitals may not be "large enough," or "tight enough," or "rounded enough." A frequent fear is related to the concerns about "having someone touch me down there." And finally, the examiner may also be subject to sexual anxieties, and therefore needs to address those concerns in order to be of help to these patients. The physical examination should not become a psychologically alienating experience.

LABORATORY STUDIES

Laboratory studies should be used in conjunction with the sexual history and physical examination to assess the health of the individual with sexual complaints. Though laboratory tests are important, that is a relative term. Physicians tend to rely on "facts" in making diagnoses and in projecting prognoses; we tend to rely heavily on "numbers" and "lab reports." I personally have seen *normal* Pap smears from women with advanced cancer of the cervix, *normal* fasting blood sugars from known diabetics, and very *low* testosterone levels in young, sexually active, adult males. The laboratory can only report on the findings of the specimen sample submitted. Randomly submitted specimens may, randomly, be either in the normal or abnormal range. And finally, laboratories as well as individuals can make mistakes. Laboratory reports may substantiate your clinical impression, they may lead you to the correct diagnosis, but they should rarely if ever be the sole basis for that diagnosis (Stuntz, 1983a).

There are no laboratory screening tests that will universally and unerringly indicate an organic cause for a sexual dysfunction. However, because of the frequency of association of sexual dysfunction with certain illnesses, it has proven fruitful to search for these. For example, in a recent unpublished survey of 72 impotent males seen in the Sexual Behaviors Clinic at Johns Hopkins Hospital, 10 were known to have diabetes mellitus. Of the remaining 62, as the result of screening all impotent patients by means of blood glucose determinations, an additional 2 were found to have unsuspected diabetes. In addition, Spark reported that in his clinic a study of 105 impotent males revealed that 36 had abnormally low serum testosterone levels, and he strongly recommended that testosterone levels be obtained on all impotent males (Spark, 1980). Although no screening studies indicating abnormal testosterone levels in women with sexual dysfunctions have as yet been reported, it is appropriate to test for this in women with serious desire-level abnormalities when no other causative factors can be identified.

Nocturnal penile tumescence studies are based on the observation that from early infancy to extreme old age the physiologically normal male will undergo several episodes of involuntary penile erection while asleep. The number, duration, and to some extent the rigidity of these "normal" erections is a function of age — with maximum frequency, duration, and rigidity normally occurring in late adolescence and decreasing linearly over the ensuing years. Psychologically impotent males will continue to experience these nocturnal erections during their sleep and in proportion to their age, whereas organically impotent males will have no or markedly impaired erections. The critical factor in all erections is the rigidity, which usually though not always is related directly to the degree of engorgement. Therefore, the rigidity must be tested for in addition to the enlargement. It seem obvious that there may be both organic and psychologic factors impeding the erection, and interpreting the result requires considerable experience and clinical acumen (Karacan, 1975).

Vaginal photoplethysmography is an indirect method of studying sexual excitement in the female. Increasing sexual excitement produces, in the physiologically normal female, increased perivaginal circulation, which in turn causes a color change in the vaginal wall from pink through deep red to purple. These color changes are measured by the photoplethysmography equipment. Similar tests are being developed that use heat changes in the vaginal wall, which presumably also relate to changes in the perivaginal circulation. However, both of these tests are intrusive and as yet have not been refined suitably for clinical use in determining the presence or absence of organic sexual dysfunction (Hoon, 1976).

SUMMARY

Appropriately assessing the organic factors in sexual dysfunction requires detailed knowledge of the physiologic changes of normal sexual functioning. Using the DEPORD model, the normal physical changes experienced during the sexual response cycle have been detailed. Based on this understanding, a sexual history is then accompanied by a general physical examination, and by both appropriate screening and specific laboratory studies, the organic factors in the sexual disturbance can most often be identified.

There are, however, situations that can be described as gray areas, when both organic and psychologic factors are thought to be affecting the sexual functioning. One such example would be depression in an impotent diabetic male who shows decreased but not absent penile erections during the nocturnal penile tumescence studies. I personally believe it is best in such circumstances to attempt to obtain the maximum psychologic benefit possible with psychotherapy

Table 8.7. Laboratory Examinations

DEPORD Phase	Male	Female
Desire-phase disorders	Testosterone CBC*	Testosterone CBC* Vaginal smear for estrogen effect Culture of vaginal discharge
Excitement-phase disorders	Testosterone CBC SMA 12, SMA 18** T3 and T4[†] NPT Studies[††]	CBC SMA 12, SMA 18** T3 and T4[†] Vaginal smear for estrogen effect Vaginal photoplethys- mography studies
Plateau-phase disorders	No known tests	No known tests
Orgasm-phase disorders	CBC SMA 12, SMA 18 T3 and T4	CBC SMA 12, SMA 18 T3 and T4
Resolution-phase disorders	No known tests	No known tests

*CBC = Complete blood count.

**SMA 12 and SMA 18 = Packages of screening blood studies usually included in general work-up. Will include basic liver enzyme studies for liver function.

[†]T3 and T4 = Thyroid function tests.

[††]NPT Studies = Nocturnal Penile Tumescence studies to help separate psychogenic from organic erectile problems.

first, rather than to turn immediately to surgical implantation of a penile prosthesis or to the newer penile injection therapies. If psychologic treatment is effective, surgery has been avoided; if psychologic treatment has not proven beneficial, surgery has only been postponed.

REFERENCES

American Psychiatric Association. (1980). *Diagnostic and Statistical Manual of Mental Disorders* (3rd ed.). Washington, DC: Author.

Bancroft, J. (1980). The endocrinology of sexual function. *Clinics in Obstetrics and Gynecology, 7,* 253-281.

Burnap, D.W., & Golden, J.S. (1967). Sexual problems in medical practice. *Journal of Medical Education, 42,* 673-680.

deGroot, W.C., & Booth, A.M. (1980). Physiology of male sexual function. *Annals of Internal Medicine, 92,* 329-331.

Finkle, A.L. (1980). Sexual impotence — current knowledge and treatment. *Urology, 16,* 449-452.

Group for the Advancement of Psychiatry. (1973). *Assessment of sexual function: A guide to interviewing.* (Report No. 88). New York: Author.

Graber, B. (1981). Circumvaginal musculature and female sexual function. *Journal of Sex and Marital Therapy, 7,* 37-48.

Hoon, P.W. (1976). Physiologic assessment of sexual arousal in women. *Psychophysiology, 13,* 196-204.

Kaplan, H.S. (1974). *The new sex therapy.* New York: Brunner/Mazel.

Kaplan, H.S. (1979). *Disorders of sexual desire.* New York: Brunner/Mazel.

Karacan, I. (1975). Sleep related penile tumescence as a function of age. *American Journal of Psychiatry, 132,* 932-937.

Kegel, A.H. (1952). Sexual function of the pubococcygeus muscle. *Western Journal of Surgery, Obstetrics, and Gynecology, 60,* 521-524.

Kolodny, R.C., Masters, W.H., & Johnson, V.E. (1979). *Textbook of sexual medicine.* Boston: Little, Brown.

Krantz, K.E. (1959). The gross and microscopic anatomy of the human vagina. *Annals of the New York Academy of Sciences, 83,* 89-104.

Levin, R.J. (1980). The physiology of sexual function in women. *Clinics in Obstetrics and Gynecology, 7,* 213-249.

Lief, H. (1977). What's new in sex research? Inhibited sexual desire. *Medical Aspects of Human Sexuality, 7,* 94-95.

Masters, W.H., & Johnson, V.E. (1966). *Human sexual response.* Boston: Little, Brown.

Masters, W.H., & Johnson, V.E. (1970). *Human sexual inadequacy.* Boston: Little, Brown.

Meyer, J.H. (1977). The treatment of sexual disorders. *Medical Clinics of North America, 61,* 811-823.

Meyer, J.H. (1980a). Paraphilia. In: H. Kaplan, A. Friedman, & B. Saddock (Eds.), *Comprehensive textbook of psychiatry* (3rd ed.). Baltimore: Williams & Wilkins.

Meyer, J.H. (1980b). Psychotherapy in sexual disorders. In: T. Karasu & L. Bellak (Eds.), *Specialized techniques in individual psychotherapy.* New York: Brunner/Mazel.

Meyer, J.H. (1983). Consultative interview. In J.H. Meyer, C.W. Schmidt, & T.N. Wise (Eds.), *Clinical management of sexual disorders* (2nd ed.). Baltimore: Williams & Wilkins.

Newman, H.F., & Northrup, J.D. (1981). Mechanisms of human penile erection: An overview. *Urology, 17,* 399-408.

Pauly, I.H., & Goldstein, S.G. (1970). Prevalence of sexual dysfunction. *Medical Aspects of Human Sexuality, 4,* 48-52.

Spark, R.E., et al. (1980). Impotence is not always psychogenic. *Journal of the American Medical Association, 245,* 750-755.

Smolev, J. (1983). Physical examination of the male. In J.H. Meyer, C.W. Schmidt, and T.N. Wise (Eds.), *Clinical management of sexual disorders* (2nd ed.). Baltimore: Williams & Wilkins.

Stuntz, R.C. (1983a). Laboratory evaluation. In J.H. Meyer, C.W. Schmidt, & T.N. Wise (Eds.), *Clinical management of sexual disorders* (2nd ed.). Baltimore: Williams & Wilkins.

Stuntz, R.C. (1983b). Physical examination of the female. In J.H. Meyer, C.W. Schmidt, and T.N. Wise (Eds.), *Clinical management of sexual disorders* (2nd ed.). Baltimore: Williams and Wilkins.

Stuntz, R.C., & Stuntz, S.S. (1983). The sexological examination. In J.H. Meyer, C.W. Schmidt, & T.N. Wise (Eds.), *Clinical management of sexual disorders* (2nd ed.). Baltimore: Williams & Wilkins.

Chapter 9

An Integrated Eclectic Approach to Psychosexual Therapy

Robert N. Sollod

Sexual dysfunctions, often consisting of specific behavioral complaints that are presented by individuals in the context of an interpersonal relationship, are well suited to an eclectic psychotherapeutic approach. Generally, such eclecticism consists of the application of concepts and/or of methods from a variety of schools or traditions of psychotherapy. These traditions, such as the various psychoanalytic or behavioral approaches, usually consist of sets of clinical procedures explicitly connected to underlying concepts of personality, psychopathology and the therapeutic process. Practitioners have often used concepts or methods from more than one of these systems in the service of the pragmatic goal of facilitating therapeutic progress.

There is a current trend toward integrated approaches (Feather & Rhoads, 1972; Garfield, 1980; Goldfried, 1982a, 1982b; Greenspan, 1975; Marks & Gelder, 1966; Silverman, 1974; Wachtel, 1975, 1977; Woody, 1968). This integration can range from suggesting that two different schools of therapy are simply using two terms to describe the same concept, to recognizing that fundamentally different assumptions about human behavior can still lead to similar interventions, through developing new theories incorporating elements of a variety of schools. This chapter will focus on systematic or integrated eclecticism, which consists of the delineation and specification of the particular therapeutic methods to be used as well as the underlying theoretical rationale for the selection of approaches derived from various psychotherapeutic traditions. Such systematic eclecticism usually justifies itself not purely on the basis of pragmatic results, but more fundamentally on the basis of a model of psychopathology and therapeutic change that necessitates the utilization of elements from more than one therapeutic approach. Systems theory is helpful in explaining the potential usefulness of eclectic integration; the combination of approaches ideally should have an impact greater than the sum of each approach taken alone. There should be a synergistic effect of the combination, such that the resulting therapeutic approach will, in many ways, have qualities different from its component parts.

The primary integrated eclectic approach to psychosexual therapy is the new sex therapy, as developed by Dr. Helen Kaplan at the Cornell University College of Medicine and the Payne-Whitney Psychiatric Clinic (Kaplan, 1974, 1979). Her approach, specifically designed to facilitate the remediation of a variety of sexual disorders in brief outpatient psychotherapy, in many ways epitomizes the general characteristics of an integrated or systematic eclectic approach to psychotherapy (Sollod, 1975; Sollod & Kaplan, 1976).

A short historical review is helpful in order to understand the nature of Dr. Kaplan's eclectic integration. Prior to the pioneering work of Masters and Johnson, the major psychotherapeutic approach to sexual dysfunction was psychoanalytic. In this approach, the sexual dysfunctions were seen within the framework of Freudian or other psychodynamic theories as being caused by deepseated developmental problems or by unconscious conflicts. In either event, the sexual dysfunction was viewed not as the problem to be addressed per se, but rather as a symptom of a more pervasive disorder. Symptomatic improvement, without indication of more fundamental changes in personality make-up or in individual psychodynamics, was viewed suspiciously within this conceptual framework. Patients with sexual dysfunction often underwent intensive psychoanalytic treatment for many years. Unfortunately, although psychoanalytic treatment was successful in some cases, the available evidence indicates that only a modest percent of men with the most common psychogenic sexual dysfunctions experienced significant improvement. In addition, psychoanalytic theorizing was not congenial to the treatment of female sexual dysfunction, because there was a devaluation of orgasms that were attained, in whole or in part, through clitoral stimulation. Finally, the psychoanalytic view of sexual dysfunction as indicative of a more profound problem contributed to the intense concern and sense of helplessness that an individual with a sexual dysfunction might experience.

Masters and Johnson's approach to the treatment of sexual dysfunctions represented a significant departure from the psychoanalytic tradition and a major advance in treatment technique (Masters & Johnson, 1970). They, for the first time, described the physiology of the normal sexual response, developed a theory of the processes underlying normal sexual functioning, devised a taxonomy of the variety of sexual dysfunctions, and designed innovative treatment approaches for the sexual disorders. The treatment approach they developed, now familiar to all sex therapists, was a residential program involving an educational component, highly structured couple-therapy sessions, and a set of specified exercises for each dysfunction. Although Masters and Johnson did not appear to use explicit behavioral or psychodynamic theories in the development of these therapeutic exercises, such concepts can be used to understand the efficacy of many of their procedures. The sensate-focus exercise, which involves relaxation and mutual pleasuring without demand for intercourse, may be viewed as efficacious because it involves in vivo desensitization, reciprocal inhibition, shaping of desired responses, and assertiveness training, as participants learn to express their needs or likes and dislikes. A paradoxical approach may also be operative, because the couple is instructed to "avoid intercourse." Some psychodynamic components may also be helpful in explaining the utility of sensate focus, because the strength of superego taboos may be attenuated by the cotherapists who, acting as parental figures, give the dysfunctional couple permission to experience pleasure. The Masters and Johnson approach is, thus, implicitly eclectic in that the structured exercises contain a variety of elements, and that their effectiveness can be explained by a variety of psychological theories. It is interesting to note that these innovations were not apparently derived from formal psychological theories. In regard to this point, it can be noted that many fields — such as education, athletics, the performing arts, or animal training — have also developed effective techniques implicitly incorporating major psychological principles without being formally derived from psychological theories.

Masters and Johnson's approach was markedly more effective in the treatment of sexual dysfunctions than psychoanalytic methods had been (Masters & Johnson, 1970). Cure rates for many dysfunctions far exceeded 50% and in some instances were reported to be 90%. In addition, methods were developed to facilitate female orgasmic responsiveness. In spite of revolutionary successes in dealing with sexual dysfunctions, the Masters and Johnson approach had a number of limitations that gradually became more evident. The structured exercises were relatively inflexible in dealing with idiosyncratic differences. Intrapsychic issues or conflicts, which might have interfered with therapeutic progress, were not specifically addressed. In addition, the residential nature of treatment limited it to those couples who were able and willing to make a major commitment of time and financial resources to improvement of their sexual functioning.

These limitations became more apparent as there was a progressive change in the composition of the patient population. Originally, Masters and Johnson's client consisted of a disproportionate percentage of highly motivated, psychologically healthy couples who had strong commitments to one another. Gradually, with increased publicity about the treatment of sexual dysfunctions, more clients with moderate to severe psychopathology or significant interpersonal problems began to seek treatment for their sexual dysfunctions. In addition, many of the new potential clients had more limited economic resources and could not afford an extended period of residential treatment.

The new sex therapy, as developed by Helen Kaplan (1974), was designed to overcome many of the limitations of the Masters and Johnson approach. Couples are usually seen for between 5 and 20 weekly 1-hour sessions in an outpatient clinic or private office, and they carry out various behavioral exercises in their homes. The new sex therapy is a systematic integration of behavioral and psychodynamic elements, including informational and educational components and a specific focus on dyadic or interpersonal aspects of behavior. Disorders treated include lack of sexual desire, general sexual dysfunction, vaginismus, orgasmic dysfunctions, primary and secondary erectile dysfunctions, premature ejaculation, and retarded ejaculation.

Kaplan's theoretical rationale for her systematic eclecticism rests on her understanding of the origins of sexual dysfunction. Normal sexual responsiveness consists of an autonomic component, which is highly susceptible to anxiety. The causes of such anxiety may be relatively superficial, in which case behavioral approaches such as relaxation and in-vivo desensitization alone could be effective. In other cases, the anxiety can be traced to unconscious intrapsychic conflicts, deep-seated personality traits, or to interpersonal dynamics. In such instances, even though behavioral approaches alone might be helpful, Kaplan believes that a therapeutic approach that acknowledges the deeper roots of the dysfunction is preferable to a purely behavioral approach. Moreover, sexual responsiveness may be viewed as a learned sequence of behaviors. Learning can proceed normally through behavioral processes such as imitation learning, reinforcment, and shaping. Personality factors or intrapersonal dynamics may, however, prevent or impede the individual from acquiring a repertoire of sexual responses.

Sexual dysfunctions may be viewed as part of a multilevel interlocking cycle involving both partners (Sollod & Kaplan, 1976). In such a pattern — regardless of the etiology of the dysfunction — behavioral, interpersonal, psychodynamic and cognitive factors may all eventually become involved. Effective intervention would necessarily require change at more than one level. The cases presented later are illustrations of the manner in which intervention at many levels may be required in psychosexual therapy.

Another major aspect of Kaplan's argument for an integrated therapeutic approach to sexual dysfunctions is that marked improvement in sexual functioning may have a major impact on the overall personality. Considerable therapeutic skill and understanding of the dynamics involved is necessary to enable the client to adjust or accommodate to a real or anticipated improvement in sexual functioning. The possibility of change, even of potential change, may provoke major resistance to the therapeutic process.

In addition to the behavioral, psychodynamic, and interpersonal aspects of Kaplan's eclectic approach, there is an awareness of the importance of the physical or biological causes of dysfunction and the necessity of adequate information or education about sexual functioning. Many cases of sexual dysfunction have an organic rather than psychogenic cause, so appropriate medical examination is necessary. In addition, an inventory of all medications should be made because a wide variety of drugs may have a deleterious impact on sexual functioning. The biological level of this approach is largely for assessment purposes and, although hormonal treatments and penile prostheses have been used for the treatment of some dysfunctions, such treatment is not part of the current discussion of eclectic psychotherapeutic intervention. In each case, the therapist should also assess the areas of misinformation or lack of information about sexuality. In many cases, it is necessary for the therapist to assume the role of providing necessary information about sexual anatomy, physiology, and behavior.

Each of the approaches or levels indicated above plays a role in Kaplan's "new sex therapy." How and when each approach is used and the considerations underlying therapeutic tactics and strategy comprise the essence of the eclecticism embodied in Kaplan's approach. In general, the new sex therapy can be classified as a behavioral form of treatment (Krasner, 1971). The therapist is active, behavioral principles are used, and there are definite intervention procedures for specified problems. There is even the use of environmental reinforcement that is unknown in more psychodynamic approaches, which view sexual symptoms as indicative of intrapsychic processes. Treatment may proceed on a primarily behavioral course. This is true particularly when there is little interpersonal or individual psychopathology. When there is resistance or great difficulty in the successful completion of the behavioral exercises, then the therapeutic focus is shifted toward the intrapsychic or interpersonal causes of such resistance or difficulty (Hartman, 1983; Weissberg & Levay, 1981). Unlike the effects of such an intervention in individual psychodynamically oriented therapy or in couples therapy, the goal is not personality reorganization or change in the nature of a couple's relationship per se (although such "deeper" changes may occur as a result of even brief exploration). Instead, the focus consists of intrapsychic or intrapersonal processes inasmuch as they prevent the successful completion of the behavioral tasks.

In addition to the use of explicit psychodynamic or interpersonal methods, the sex therapist uses knowledge of intrapsychic or interpersonal processes in the choice and design of behavioral exercises, the manner in which they are presented to the couple, and/or in various decisions regarding resistance to the exercises or to aspects of the therapeutic process itself. For example, in the treatment for premature ejaculation, the male is requested to engage in the stop-start exercise with his partner. In this exercise, the partner stimulates his penis while he lies on his back. For men with conscious or unconscious conflicts concerning passivity, this exercise is often not effective, as a result of the interference of anxiety or other emotions. The therapist who adopts Kaplan's eclectic method will explore the client's feelings and may restructure the exercise, for example, by asking the client to be more active in initiating the exercise, perhaps by suggesting that the exercise could be preceded or followed by another one in which the client was more active and giving to his partner.

An alternative approach of a more cognitive nature would be to reframe the two exercises as one exercise, which after a temporary period of passivity would enable the client to be more active and masculine as he attains significant ejaculatory control. Or perhaps there could be an assertion or interpretation by the therapist, in particular if it became apparent that conflicts over homosexual tendencies were involved, that it is not unmasculine for a person, at times, to relax and enjoy the attentions or caresses of a caring partner. In other cases, exploration of the client's thoughts and feelings about the exercise, even without some type of interpretation, might be effective. Various interpretations might be effective. For example, the therapist could indicate, "You seem to feel anxious about the passivity involved in this exercise," or "You seem to feel that being so passive is not masculine," or "Being passive seems uncomfortable to you for some reason." Deeper levels of interpreting or "uncovering" interpretations, which in such a case would refer to homosexual motivations, are not appropriate because they would lead in the direction of individual psychotherapy rather than toward the successful completion of the behavioral exercises.

Interpersonal dynamics could also be involved in resistance to the stop/start exercises. For example, the client might feel that his partner would reject him for being so dependent upon her. Or he might feel a lack of trust in her interest or ability to help him. Another common dynamic in these situations is that the client would feel, possibly justifiably, that his partner would be angry for giving him pleasure without receiving any in return. These types of interpersonal issues can be dealt with by the eclectic sex therapist in a manner analogous to that of dealing with intrapsychic conflict; the exercise itself could be modified to meet relational concerns. For example, if the issue of lack of reciprocity of pleasure giving is paramount, then the exercise can be coupled with one in which the client caresses or stimulates his partner. In other cases, exploration of the issues involved and the resolution of them to the extent that the stop/start exercise can proceed successfully is possible. For example, if the client feels he cannot trust his partner, some exploration of the issues might lead to reassurance by the partner or to the partner's own expression of concern that she might not perform the exercise in a helpful manner. Expression of thoughts and feelings by the couple, combined with therapeutic support, reflection of feelings or limited interpretation on the therapist's part, can lead to a resolution of the issues involved.

General dyadic issues may also be involved when there is difficulty completing a behavioral exercise. A couple who cannot cooperate in any other area of their life, for example, cannot reasonably be expected to cooperate in sex therapy without considerable therapeutic support and intervention.

Finally, intrapsychic issues having to do with the partner herself may be involved in problems the couple is having with the stop/start exercise. The partner may experience emotions having to do with childhood feelings associated with parental indifference or sibling rivalry. After all, she is the one who has suffered years of frustration from her partner's ejaculatory difficulties; and now, in therapy, she is expected to provide pleasure for him. Another possible dynamic could be her ambivalent feelings about the male sexual organ, or about having to take an active role in providing pleasure. Again, in these situations, the therapist has the options of modifying the exercises in light of the apparent dynamics, of merely exploring the thoughts and feelings of the partner, of cognitively reframing or restructuring the way the client views the exercises in order to reduce the negative impact of the presumed dynamics, or of providing interpretations in order to facilitate insight or exploration of the issues involved.

It is as a result of the eclecticism inherent in Kaplan's approach that the sex therapy techniques developed by Masters and Johnson have been made more flexibly suited to an outpatient format serving clients of diverse levels of motivation and varying degrees of pathology. In addition, by avoiding the structured format of the Masters and Johnson approach, more rapid and economical treatment is possible in many cases. It is possible that some patients with more severe pathology might never be able to seek treatment within the Masters and Johnson format or would be unable to obtain the desired outcome.

To understand more fully the flexibility inherent in Kaplan's eclectic approach, it is helpful to note the explanations and responses to therapeutic failure given by behaviorists and psychodynamic therapists. As far as behavioral approaches are concerned, therapeutic failure is not seen as being based on client characteristics but rather on a problem with the therapeutic technique or lack of practice with the technique. Thus, there is often a reliance on repetition and more repetition if therapeutic goals are not reached. Psychodynamically oriented therapists assume that if specified symptomatic goals are not reached, it is a result of lack of sufficiently deep exploration of the underlying hidden dynamics. So the therapeutic watchword is "Dig deeper." Both of these forms of "nothing-but-isms" have as dangers the possibilities of therapeutic culs-de-sac, in which a therapeutic strategy is pursued more ardently—in spite of, or perhaps as a result of, negative results. In Kaplan's eclecticism, even though there is a behavioral structure that guides therapeutic progress, any major intrapsychic or interpersonal processes that might impede such progress are acknowledged by the therapist and are often the focus of therapeutic exploration. In cases of significant resistance, the therapist assumes a flexible approach and may often engage in exploration of intrapsychic conflicts, interpersonal factors or other material.

One feature of the therapeutic eclecticism in the new sex therapy is the use of sexual exercises on many levels. These exercises, such as sensate focus (mutual pleasuring) and stop/start, may be viewed as behavioral approaches in which new learning occurs. Behavioral principles such as desensitization, shaping, or reinforcement, are relevant. The exercises may be seen as including elements of assertiveness training or as a means of encouraging couple communication (Fensterheim, 1972). Another viewpoint is that the exercises are a problem the couple must learn to solve together. Additionally, the exercises should be used as a means of continual assessment. The sensate-focus exercise provides a basic structure that is handled in different ways by different participants. In this way, the exercise can serve as a type of in-vivo conjoint projective test.

Therapists should note the thoughts, feelings, and behaviors reported by each participant as well as the couple's interaction. Was there any distortion of the instructions of the therapist? What were the areas of cooperation, of disagreement? In particular, any sources of anxiety should be carefully explored. It is precisely the exploration of the dynamics underlying difficulties with the exercises that will enable the eclectic therapist to develop therapeutic approaches that will be effective with a particular couple. Regardless of the positive or negative results of a particular exercise, information that can be of assistance in the treatment process will be provided.

Another feature of the eclectic integration characteristic of the new sex therapy is the consideration of the psychodynamics of rapid symptomatic improvement — particularly when therapeutic resistance or a major impasse occurs. It is a psychoanalytic cliché that rapid symptomatic improvement (e.g., transference cure, flight to health, etc.) is to be mistrusted. The new sex therapy, as a form of brief, focused therapy, encourages symptomatic improvement, but it acknowledges that such rapid progress may occasionally be difficult for the individual to assimilate and maintain.

Even anticipated improvement in sexual functioning may arouse deep resistance. A woman with primary orgasmic dysfunction may be afraid that the orgasmic experience will be accompanied by an irreversible loss of impulse control, by personality dissolution, or by the destruction of current relationships. Even positive changes in the person's life, which might in fantasy be anticipated, could be threatening.

These and other fears and concerns should be explored. Patients should be asked how their personalities, relationships, and lives would change as a result of significant amelioration of their sexual difficulties. Often, what is needed is mere reassurance that many, if not all, of the threatening changes will not occur automatically as a result of the hoped-for (and feared) improvement in sexual functioning. In other instances, the fears are more complex and pervasive, and require more extensive exploration and possible interpretation. In certain cases, resistance occurs in order to maintain a system in which the sexual dysfunction is a stabilizing element. For example, a woman who is insecure about her attractiveness may be married to a man with erectile dysfunction. This dysfunction, which on one level causes him much distress, also enables her to trust the faithfulness of her husband. On his side, her commitment might be seen as especially valuable in light of his dysfunction, and he may feel dependent upon her. To the extent that the dysfunction is maintaining the relationship, the couple will evidence a variety of resistances. The eclectic therapist should not aim for symptomatic improvement in such a case without first exploring the couple's interpersonal dynamics and without helping them to explore the nature of their concerns and to strengthen their commitment. A question such as, "Can you think of any negative consequences of improvement in his sexual dysfunction?" or, more pointedly, "Do you think he will remain with you if he learns to function better?" could lead to a helpful exploration of issues interfering with symptomatic improvement.

The interpersonal aspects of sexual dysfunction and treatment are most apparent when both partners have sexual dysfunctions. Improvement of either client may dramatically affect the relationship and create significant anxiety and/or increased motivation to change for the other partner. Treatment of a woman with vaginismus who is married to a man with secondary erectile dysfunction is illustrative. As the woman develops the capacity to enjoy intercourse, her partner's inability to obtain or maintain an erection may become increasingly frustrating for her. At the same time, the prospect of meeting his wife's newly expressed sexual desires may cause even more dysfunctional anxiety on the part of the male (Dickes & Strauss, 1980). As a result, without sufficient therapeutic support, such a male may interfere with or sabotage the treatment of his wife's dysfunction. In addition to exploring the issues involved and supporting the relationship, the therapist may also decide to begin the treatment of erectile dysfunction prior to the completion of the exercises designed to alleviate vaginismus.

The particular pattern of intrapsychic and interpersonal problems involved in a given case depends on many factors and may vary considerably depending on the disorder/s involved, the specific personality make-up of the individuals, as well as their relationship. For a woman with vaginismus or primary orgasmic dysfunction, the issues involved are often concerned with her lack of accurate information about sexuality or with her guilt and conflict about meeting her needs or obtaining sexual pleasure. This is not always true, however. In some cases none of these factors may be relevant, and in other cases there may be a combination of causes. Although the therapist may have an informed opinion about the contributory causes, it is only by carefully assessing the results of the behavioral exercises that the therapist can gain accurate knowledge about the factors involved, and their relative importance.

For example, one female client may proceed through the various stages of treatment for vaginismus without any resistance or difficulty. Such treatment may be conceptualized in behavioral terms as a combination of in-vivo desensitization, reciprocal inhibition of anxiety and shaping. In the treatment for vaginismus, the woman learns to relax and to place, at first, a finger in her vaginal entrance until a painful spasm occurs. Then she stops, relaxes again, and continues very slowly to move her finger around the inside of the vaginal entrance. Gradually she learns to tolerate the presence of two or three fingers inside her vagina without painful spasm. Then the exercises proceed to the insertion of her partner's finger/s and finally to the insertion of his erect penis. In such an uncomplicated case, vaginismus may be conceptualized as a learned response to painful stimuli.

Other reactions to treatment may also occur. The woman may find the exercises difficult to perform because of lack of information about sexuality, guilt or shame. She may have had childhood experiences in which she was severely punished or humiliated by her parents for masturbatory behavior. In certain more psychopathological cases, she may have concerns about her own wholeness or integrity occasioned by penetration. In other cases, phobic ideation and imagery may occur. Occasionally, a woman will have painful spasms or anxiety when her partner's fingers or penis are inserted, even though they provide no more vaginal stimulation than her own fingers. In such cases, alternative explanations must be sought — including deep-seated fears about male sexuality, guilt that is related to incest fantasies, fear of loss of control, anxiety that is related to actual rape or incest, and lack of trust of her partner. Such issues may lead not only to symptoms and overt anxiety but also to resistance to the treatment process. The new sex therapy relies on the therapist's receiving feedback from the clients about the sexual exercises. Through such feedback, the therapist will modify the standard behavioral approaches in unique ways to meet the requirements of therapeutic progress in a specific case and will also focus on those particular issues that impede progress for a particular client or couple.

In Kaplan's new sex therapy, transferential feelings are supported by the therapist and are not interpreted unless they interfere with the treatment process. When such interference occurs, the therapist may either modify the approach in light of presumed dynamics or interpret the patient's transferential feelings. For example, homework assignments in sex therapy are commonly prescribed in a directive manner. This approach is helpful to most clients, who benefit from the structure provided. Some clients, however, may resent the assignment of behavioral exercises. These clients may complain about the lack of spontaneity, misconstrue the directions, or even refuse to participate (Munjack & Oziel, 1978). The therapist has the option to become less directive by encouraging the patient to choose exercises from among a variety presented by the therapist. Or the therapist could present the basic structure of the recommended exercise in a more collaborative way and discuss possible modifications of the suggested procedures. In some cases, it might be necessary to point out the nature of the patient's view of the therapeutic relationship and interpret the transferential pattern.

Knowledge of personality style and the couple's relational pattern is also important if the therapist is to facilitate the impact of the behavioral exercises. Hysterical, obsessive- compulsive, depressive, schizoid, and other personality types have characteristic ways of relating to the treatment program. They also have different patterns of emotional needs (Shapiro, 1965). Whereas the hysterical personality may require approval and attention from the therapist, for example, the obsessive- compulsive may find such approval cloying and uncomfortable. The therapist should try to accommodate to a great extent to the varying needs of the clients, as their personality pattern is not in itself the focus of therapeutic intervention.

The new sex therapy, as developed by Kaplan, is thus a very sophisticated and well-articulated example of eclectic integration. This therapeutic approach makes many demands upon the therapist's judgment, skill, and creativity, and requires a broad base of knowledge and therapeutic experience. The therapist who is to be trained in this approach should have a good background in behavioral, psychodynamic, and interpersonal or couples-therapy principles and techniques; a thorough understanding of personality theory and psychopathology; and a knowledge of the causes of sexual dysfunctions and their treatments. The benefits gained from the therapeutic flexibility in Kaplan's approach will result only with a well-trained and skilled therapist.

A good sense of timing of interventions, as well as both a tactical and strategic grasp of the course of intervention, is also necessary. Therapists who are engaged in this type of eclectic approach should find the appropriate balance between too much adherence to a strict behavioral regimen and too much exploration of intrapsychic or interpersonal material. If there is too much of a focus on interpersonal or intrapsychic issues, the therapeutic momentum of improvement derived from the sexual exercises may be interrupted, and the clients will find themselves preoccupied with a variety of emotions and conflicts that could interfere with the course of sex therapy. Such activity may satisfy the therapist's professional needs for thoroughness and completion, particularly for someone who is psychodynamically oriented, even though it may not be in the best interests of the couple. On the other hand, too little attention to such issues may result in either an ineffective approach or in an approach that results in the desired behavioral outcome – but one not well integrated into the couple's relationship or into the personalities of the clients. There must also be a balance between focus on the individual clients and support of the couple's relationship.

Another consideration that should occur to the sex therapist is that improvement of sexual functioning may be accomplished even with the presence of major underlying problems. In such cases, the achievement of adequate sexual functioning often represents a major personal victory for the client. The sex therapist, however, should occasionally refer some clients for individual or marital therapy when significant resistance occurs, even though there are techniques to bypass such resistance. Such judgments require careful professional evaluation and include ethical considerations.

One example that is not uncommon is that of a couple with problems in the area of trust and commitment who present as sex therapy clients. Sexual functioning may be enhanced by treatment, and after therapy the couple will continue in an unsatisfactory relationship. In such a case the therapist will have collaborated with the couple in agreeing with their notion that their problem was primarily sexual. The therapist may decide, when lack of trust, love, or commitment exists, to focus on these issues even at the cost of progress in sexual functioning. Or, in other cases, individual psychopathology might be so marked that improvement in sexual functioning is deeply distressing to the individual. A borderline personality, for example, in a stable but unsatisfying relationship, may feel that her relational problems stem from her husband's erectile dysfunction. Upon normal penetration and experience of orgasm as a result of the course of sex therapy, she may become severely depressed or suicidal as she realizes that adequate sexual functioning did not help her feel more connected with her partner. Such an experience can be deeply destructive to her partner, to the stability of the relationship, and to the quality of her own life. The therapist should try to develop a balanced and caring approach to these types of problems. Many types of people in a wide variety of relational patterns can benefit from improvement in their sexual lives. On the other hand, if the therapist keeps the overall happiness of the client in mind, the therapist will be sensitive to unhappiness or suffering which will not be ameliorated by sex therapy.

The integrated eclecticism of the new sex therapy, although developed specifically for the treatment of sexual dysfunctions, can be viewed as a model for a more general psychotherapeutic eclecticism. In a more general approach based on structural features of the new sex therapy, there would be an emphasis on rapid amelioration of a behaviorally defined symptom or set of symptoms. Psychodynamic and interpersonal considerations would be included in planning the course of treatment. If there were difficulties in the course of behavioral treatment, the therapist would focus on relevant intrapsychic or interpersonal difficulties. In fact, some therapists use such a model in working with phobias. A marital therapist might facilitate a couple's reaching certain goals using a similar therapeutic strategy.

In a more general way, the new sex therapy suggests that the insights and methods of conceptually divergent therapeutic approaches may be complementary, or even synergistic, in clinical practice. The complex model of pathology presented by Kaplan involves many contributory dimensions, including unconscious dynamics, relational factors, as well as learned behaviors. As a result, more than one approach is therapeutically relevant. The therapeutic approach of the new sex therapy is a demonstration of one way that various psychotherapeutic stances can be systematically integrated. As such, it is a model for the type of therapeutic sophistication and conceptualization required for the careful integration of complex theoretical and therapeutic traditions.

REFERENCES

Dickes, R., & Strauss, D. (1980). Adverse reaction of the apparently healthy partner in response to improvement in the overtly dysfunctional partner. *Journal of Sex and Marital Therapy, 6,* 109-115.

Feather, B.W., & Rhoads, J.M. (1972). Psychodynamic behavior therapy: I. Theory and rationale. II. Clinical aspects. *Archives of General Psychiatry, 26,* 496-511.

Fensterheim, H.(1972). Assertive methods and marital problems. *Advances in behavior therapy.* New York: Academic Press.

Garfield, S.L. (1980). *Psychotherapy: An eclectic approach.* New York: John Wiley.

Goldfried, M.R. (Ed.). (1982a). *Converging themes in psychotherapy: Trends in psychodynamic, humanistic, and behavioral practice.* New York: Springer.

Goldfried, M.R. (1982b). A behavior therapist looks at rapprochement. *Journal of Humanistic Psychology, 23,* 97-107.

Greenspan, S.I. (1975). A consideration of some learning variables in the context of psychoanalytic theory: Toward a psychoanalytic learning perspective. [Special issue, No. 33]. *Psychological Issues, 9*(1).

Hartman, L.M. (1983). Resistance in directive sex therapy: Recognition and management. *Journal of Sex and Marital Therapy, 9,* 283-293.

Kaplan, H.S. (1974). *The new sex therapy.* New York: Brunner/Mazel.

Kaplan, H.S. (1979). *Disorders of sexual desire.* New York: Brunner/Mazel.

Krasner, L. (1971). The operant approach in behavior therapy. In A. Bergin & S. Garfield (Eds.), *Handbook of psychotherapy and behavior change.* New York: Academic Press.

Marks, I.M., & Gelder, M.G. (1966). Common ground between behavior therapy and psychodynamic methods. *British Journal of Medical Psychology, 39,* 11-23.

Masters, W.H., & Johnson, V.E. (1970). *Human sexual inadequacy.* Boston: Little, Brown.

Munjack, D.J., & Oziel, L.J. (1978). Resistance in the behavioral treatment of sexual dysfunction. *Journal of Sex and Marital Therapy, 4,* 122-138.

Shapiro, D. (1965). *Neurotic Styles.* New York: Basic Books.

Silverman, L.H. (1974). Some psychoanalytic considerations of nonpsychoanalytic therapies: On the possibility of integrating treatment approaches and related issues. *Psychotherapy: Theory, Research, and Practice, 11,* 298-305.

Sollod, R. (1975). Behavioral and psychodynamic dimensions of the new sex therapy. *Journal of Sex and Marital Therapy, 1,* 335-340.

Sollod, R., & Kaplan, H. (1976). The new sex therapy: An integration of behavioral, psychodynamic and interpersonal approaches. In J. Claghorn (Ed.), *Successful psychotherapy.* (pp. 140-152). New York: Brunner/Mazel.

Wachtel, P.L. (1975). Behavior therapy and the facilitation of psychoanalytic exploration. *Psychotherapy: Theory, Research and Practice, 12,* 68-72.

Wachtel, P.L. (1977). *Psychoanalysis and behavior therapy: Toward an integration.* New York: Basic Books.

Weissberg, J.H., & Levay, A.N. (1981). The role of resistance in sex therapy. *Journal of Sex and Marital Therapy, 7,* 125-130.

Woody, R.H. (1968). Toward a rationale for psychobehavioral therapy. *Archives of General Psychiatry, 19,* 197-204.

Chapter 10

Behavioral Strategies and Techniques in Sex Therapy

Barry McCarthy and Susan Perkins

The three major components of the behaviorally oriented approach to sex therapy are (a) techniques to reduce sexual anxiety, (b) sexual skills training, and (c) a program of individually designed sexual exercises to be done between therapy sessions. The goal of this therapy is for people to develop a comfortable, functional, and satisfying sexual style. Therapists usually work with established couples, but behavioral sex therapy can be implemented with individuals who do not have regular sexual partners. The concepts of this approach to sex therapy are based largely on the pioneer work of Masters and Johnson (1970), behavioral research done outside the sexual area (Bandura, 1977; Lazarus, 1976; Wolpe, 1973), and specific behavioral work in the sexual area (Annon, 1974; Leiblum & Pervin, 1980; LoPiccolo & LoPiccolo, 1978; McCarthy & McCarthy, 1984). The approach utilizes a broad range of behaviorally oriented strategies and techniques tailored to the specific sexual problem.

Behavioral sex therapy is best conceptualized as a form of behaviorally oriented couples psychotherapy. There are three major aspects of this therapeutic approach that differentiate it from traditional marital psychotherapy: (a) the focus is on the sexual relationship; (b) the therapy contract is time-limited, usually 12 to 20 sessions; and (c) it emphasizes the practice of sexual exercises between sessions. The most common therapy format consists of one session a week with a single therapist, beginning with assessment and proceeding to a treatment program tailored to the particular presenting problem.

ASSESSMENT

Assessment of sexual functioning and complaints is a critical first step in behavior therapy, with a major tool for assessment being the detailed sex history. Standardized tests, such as the Sexual Adjustment Inventory (Stuart, Stuart, Maurice, & Szasz, 1975), have been used also. Referral to a physician is important whenever there is a possibility that organic factors may be causing or contributing to the sexual impairment. Such medical assessment can be as straightforward as a single office visit, or as complex as two days of testing for hormonal, neurological, and vascular functioning combined with three nights of monitoring penile tumescence during sleep cycles.

A clinician taking a behaviorally oriented sex history uses the following guidelines to obtain information most useful for treatment planning: (a) beginning with non-anxiety-provoking material and progressing to material that is more emotional and intimate; (b) being nonjudgmental in order to allow the client to reveal socially undesirable or traumatic sexual experiences; (c) discussing strengths in the client's sexual development as well as problems; and (d) assessing the client's level of comfort and skill in a variety of sexual situations. The sex history is a semistructured individual interview that typically follows a chronological framework. In addition to gathering information, it is equally important for the clinician to establish rapport, increase comfort with sexual language, and counter sexual myths with accurate information. Unlike some traditional psychotherapies wherein the clinician acts as a neutral observer, the behaviorally oriented sex therapist attempts to model a comfortable, tension-free attitude toward sexuality. The clinician can reduce guilt and provide a positive model by discussing behaviors such as masturbation, oral-genital stimulation, and fantasy. It is important that the client feel *permission* to talk about and to experience these activities, rather than *pressure* to engage in them.

The client is told at the beginning of the assessment interview that if there is information the client does not want shared with the partner, this information will be held in confidence. For example, if the difficulty brought to therapy is an inability to maintain an erection with his wife, and the clinician learns that the male has erections with an extramarital partner, then an anxiety-reduction strategy to deal with the erection problem would not be the appropriate intervention. This information would not be revealed to the partner without the client's permission, even though it would be used to plan the treatment strategy.

In comparison with other approaches, the unique element in a behaviorally oriented sex history is the detailed focus on assessment of sexual anxieties and sexual skills. Typical areas of sexual anxiety include nudity, touching of partner's genitals, specific parts of one's own body being looked at or touched, guilt over sexual fantasies, avoidance of specific sexual behaviors, fear of loss of control, fear of physical harm, and fear of pregnancy. The assessment of sexual skills is, of course, more difficult than assessing such behaviors as public speaking or assertiveness, because the clinician does not observe the target behavior. Although there are some sex therapy programs in which couples' sexual interactions are directly observed (Hartmann & Fithian, 1972), this is rarely the case and is not advocated.

Because the clinician must rely on self-report, comfortable, clear, and detailed communication is essential. One of the most important areas to understand is use of sexual language. Clients might use proper terms such as *penis* and *intercourse,* colloquial terms such as *prick* and *make love* or have their own language, such as *junior* and *afternoon delight.* It is important to clarify the meanings of terms so that the therapist and clients fully understand one another and can thus make the details of sexual activities (affectionate touching, manual and oral stimulation, and intercourse techniques) clear. Many clients believe the myth that "good lovers just naturally know what to do," so it is helpful for the clinician to preface discussion of skills by noting that sexual functioning is complex, learned behavior.

There are several important considerations in predicting the couple's response to sex therapy. The ideal couple for behaviorally oriented sex therapy has a specific sexual dysfunction, is committed to the marriage, does not have severe nonsexual relationship problems, and is willing as a couple to relearn a sexual interaction style. Conversely, a difficult couple for behaviorally oriented therapy has more diffuse sexual and relationship problems, is angry and blaming, and has a tenuous commitment to the relationship.

BEHAVIORAL TECHNIQUES FOR TREATMENT OF SPECIFIC DYSFUNCTIONS

There are specific behavioral interventions for each problem, but each person, each couple, and each sexual dysfunction is complex and unique. Far from being a mechanically oriented cookbook approach, successful sex therapy requires implementation of treatment principles by clinicians who use clinical judgment in timing, sequencing, and processing sexual exercises with clients.

For males the most common sexual dysfunctions are involuntary ejaculation (also called rapid or premature ejaculation), erectile difficulty (also called impotence), inhibited sexual desire (also called hypoactive sexual desire or low libido), and ejaculatory inhibition (also called ejaculatory incompetence or retarded ejaculation).

For females the most common sexual dysfunctions are nonorgasmic response with partner, inhibited sexual desire, preorgasmic dysfunction (also called anorgasmic dysfunction), sexual aversion, and vaginismus.

The key elements in all successful behavioral sex therapy are the anxiety reduction and skill building that occur during the sexual exercises. This is different from many forms of psychotherapy that focus on change occurring within the therapy session itself. In behavioral therapy, detailed sexual exercises done by the couple in the privacy of their home serve as in-vivo desensitization experiences. The exercises provide the couple with the opportunity to build an increasingly complex, flexible, and problem-free sexual repertoire. The first set of exercises focuses on initiation, touching, and developing feedback and guiding skills. The premise is that nondemand, nongenital touching exercises will increase comfort with nudity and touching as well as reduce performance anxiety.

As the couple's sexual comfort increases, exploratory nondemanding genital pleasuring exercises are introduced. The couple is instructed to add to their sexual repertoire gradually and comfortably. The task focus is shared pleasure, exploration, and increased comfort, rather than performance demands for sexual expertise and orgasm. Stress is placed on increasing sexual awareness without falling into the trap of becoming self-conscious and clinical about sexuality.

Each individual of the couple is encouraged to assume responsibility for his/her own comfort and arousal. This includes giving feedback to the partner and making clear, direct sexual requests. This emphasis on self-responsibility is followed by a focus on mutual couple responsibility for sexual satisfaction. You cannot "give" your partner an erection or orgasm; however, you can facilitate your partner's sexual functioning by being active and emotionally involved and by being receptive to guidance and sexual requests. Individual responsibility for comfort and arousal and mutual responsibility for couple satisfaction are consistently reinforced throughout the exercises and therapy sessions.

Typically, the first two weeks of the sex therapy exercises, regardless of the particular problem, focus on learning basic sexual communication and touching skills. The process of the couple is carefully monitored, especially regarding anxiety reduction. Most behaviorally oriented sex therapists do not believe anxiety must be at a zero level, but it is important with continued sexual exercises that anxiety continues to decrease. Exercises can be repeated, with modifications to maximize comfort as well as to minimize boredom. In cases where there is a specific anxiety factor or where overall anxiety remains high, the client is taught deep-muscle relaxation procedures (Rosen, 1976). If necessary, subsequent sessions may then be conducted using imagery desensitization or guided imagery (Lazarus, 1981). This consists of constructing imagined scenes within the therapy session, and then instructing the couple to practice the imagined exercises in-vivo at home.

The couple is usually requested to refrain from intercourse or from attempting orgasm during the initial phase of sex therapy in order to reduce performance orientation and to increase comfort with the pleasuring process. A crucial clinical judgment is when to lift those prohibitions. Some clinicians lift them simultaneously, although the recommended strategy is to lift the prohibition on orgasm after the first or second week and to keep the prohibition on intercourse for at least a week longer. The rationale is that nonfunctional habits revolving around intercourse are overlearned behaviors. Focusing on nondemanding pleasuring exercises can improve comfort and sexual skills (especially stroking, manual stimulation, and oral stimulation) without the performance pressure and rigid sexual behaviors often associated with intercourse.

Another crucial clinical judgment involves the degree to which the therapist focuses specifically on the sexually dysfunctional behavior. Zilbergeld and Ellison (1980), for example, have argued persuasively that rather than focusing on erections (which tends to increase self-consciousness and performance demands), the client should instead be encouraged to focus on comfort, arousal, and erotic stimulation. The exercises prescribed for treatment of the specific dysfunction build on the nondemand and pleasuring experiences. Intercourse can be integrated into exercises as another pleasuring experience, rather than thought of as a totally separate sexual behavior. This allows intercourse to be relearned in the context of a comfortable, mutually satisfying couple activity and helps prevent regression to old dysfunctional intercourse patterns.

MALE SEXUAL DYSFUNCTIONS

In considering specific strategies for treating each dysfunction, it is important to remember the *central principles* of the behavioral sex therapy approach: (a) reduction of sexual anxiety, (b) building functional sexual skills, and (c) utilizing specific sexual exercises.

The best illustration of these principles can be seen in the treatment of involuntary ejaculation. From a learning point of view, the key element in involuntary ejaculation is the association of high sexual excitement and high performance anxiety. This association leads to a decrease in the male's awareness of his arousal pattern, especially the point of ejaculatory inevitability, and to a lack of appreciation of the sensations that accompany building arousal gradually. In helping the male to increase voluntary ejaculatory control, the first step is discrimination learning. The "do-it-yourself" techniques have emphasized trying to ignore or downplay arousal by such tricks as wearing two condoms or thinking of unpleasant things such as how much money you owe. In contrast, the sex therapist instructs the male to focus on increasing his awareness of sensations and identifying the point of ejaculatory inevitability. This can be accomplished by means of masturbation training (Zilbergeld, 1978), use of the "squeeze" technique by his partner (Masters & Johnson, 1970), or use of the "stop-start" technique (Perelman, 1980).

Initially, the couple is instructed to focus on learning control by means of extravaginal stimulation and then in female-on-top, "quiet vagina" intercourse exercise. After control has been achieved in these exercises, the couple moves to slow thrusting controlled by the female, then to slow thrusting controlled by the male, and finally to rapid thrusting. This process is repeated using other intercourse positions. Voluntary control is achieved by a gradual learning process, with the most difficult learning involving rapid thrusting in the male-on-top position. Sex therapy sessions need not continue until the top of this hierarchy is reached, but it is crucial that the male develop a sense of mastery and experience voluntary control before termination of therapy.

At present, the most commonly used technique for promoting ejaculatory control is the stop-start technique, in which, as the man approaches the point of ejaculatory inevitability, he signals his partner to stop movement and stimu-

lation. When his urge to ejaculate subsides, he signals his partner to start stimulation. As he repeats this procedure, the male gains confidence in his ability to
monitor and to control his ejaculation voluntarily. Eventually, rather than stopping completely, he maintains control by making subtle shifts in the speed and
type of intercourse thrusting. In comparison to other procedures, this technique
is viewed as less mechanical and more easily transferable to the couple's sexual
relationship. Instead of being a "mechanical squeezer" or a "wooden doll," the
woman plays an integral role in the treatment program. This also helps prevent
a regression after termination of therapy, because it lays a firm foundation for
a cooperative, mutually responsible approach to sexual satisfaction.

The second most frequent male sexual problem is secondary erectile dysfunction. This has traditionally been called *impotence,* but this term has fallen out
of favor in the professional community because of its negative connotations.
Erectile dysfunction means that the man is having trouble getting and maintaining an erection, not that he is less powerful or masculine.

One common sequence in the development of erectile difficulties starts with
the male trying to control ejaculation by reducing arousal, which can result in
the loss of erection during intercourse. This may progress to the point at which
the male loses erections at intromission, loses erections during foreplay, has difficulty gaining erections, and eventually avoids sex. By the time the man comes
for therapy, he is enmeshed in this failure- negative anticipation cycle.

Performance anxiety and the taking of a spectator role on the male's part,
and to a lesser extent by his partner, are key factors in erection problems. The
behavioral strategy to reduce performance anxiety and to break the failure-
negative anticipation cycle is to start with a prohibition on intercourse and orgasm. This allows the male to learn about and to experience the normal physiological process involved in the waxing and waning of erections. Most males immediately push toward intercourse as soon as they have obtained an erection.
The series of nondemand exercises prescribed at the beginning of a treatment
allows the man and his partner to become aware of a wider range of sensations
and arousal patterns. It is important for the man to realize that if the arousal
does not result in orgasm, his erection will naturally wane, and that he can become erect again with continued sexual stimulation.

The nondemanding pleasuring exercises may help the male to (a) reduce his
performance anxiety, (b) reassert his role as an active and involved sexual participant, (c) identify the types of sexual stimulation that he finds most sensual
and arousing, (d) improve his sexual communication skills, and (e) learn to approach intercourse not as a separate performance task, but as a continuation of
the pleasuring sequence. One additional sexual exercise is for the woman to insert the man's flaccid penis into her vagina. In addition to helping the woman
develop skills in initiating and guiding intercourse, this serves to make clear to
the couple that a strong, firm erection is not a prerequisite for intercourse.

Zilbergeld (1978) has suggested that even when anxiety is low, the conditions for good sex have been met, and the stimulation is effective, there still may be times when the male has erectile difficulty. Thus, it is important for the therapist to teach the client cognitive and behavioral strategies that will enable him to deal with an occasional erectile difficulty without overreacting. One such strategy is to teach him that the male penis is not a perfectly functioning machine, and that when he has erectile difficulties he can satisfy his partner and himself by using manual and/or oral stimulation techniques.

Ejaculatory inhibition, also referred to as retarded or incompetent ejaculation, is a more commonly experienced sexual difficulty, especially of middle-years males, than previously thought (McCarthy, 1977; Schull & Sprenkle, 1980). Although traditionally described as the total inability of the male to ejaculate within the vagina, there are many varieties of this dysfunction. Perhaps the most common is an intermittent pattern where the male has previously ejaculated intravaginally but now is unable to do so at least 25% of the time. One variant pattern is the male who is only able to ejaculate while using a very narrow range of sexual stimulation similar to a fetish. A common inhibition involves blocking oneself off emotionally from the partner and her sexual stimulation. This may be the result of anger or feeling uncomfortable in requesting additional stimulation.

The behavioral strategy used in treating ejaculatory inhibition is to identify and reduce blocks and inhibitions, to increase arousal by using multiple stimulation techniques, such as testicle stimulation and/or fantasy during intercourse, and to increase the sexual expressiveness of the couple by increasing verbalization and movement during sex (McCarthy, 1981).

FEMALE SEXUAL DYSFUNCTIONS

The emphasis in defining female dysfunctions has been on the presence or absence of orgasm. Orgasm is one natural response to sexual arousal, a positive and integral aspect of female sexuality. However, the requirement of orgasmic response at each sexual opportunity is an unrealistic performance demand for many women. This demand is one major cause of secondary nonorgasmic response, the most frequent female sexual dysfunction. A woman with this dysfunction had at one time been orgasmic with a partner, but now is either totally nonorgasmic or reaches orgasm on an infrequent or irregular basis. The causes of this dysfunction include performance anxiety, poor sexual communications, relationship problems, anger, and depression. Treatment strategy places a major emphasis on the woman's awareness and responsibility for her own sexual response.

Through nondemand pleasuring exercises the woman has an opportunity to reexperience sensual and erotic stimulation without pressure for arousal, intercourse, or orgasm. The couple is requested not to have or to attempt orgasm, which allows the woman to experience a range of sensations and arousal without being self-conscious about orgasm. In some cases, the woman quickly regains her ability to respond orgasmically to nonintercourse stimulation.

Barbach (1980) states that each woman has a unique orgasmic pattern; this view is communicated to the couple and is strongly reinforced. At a given sexual opportunity, the woman might be nonorgasmic, singly orgasmic, or multiply orgasmic. Orgasmic response might occur during the pleasuring/foreplay period, during intercourse, or during the afterglow/afterplay period. There is no "right" pattern of orgasmic response. The woman and her partner are encouraged to develop a sexual style with which they are comfortable and that is satisfactory for them.

There is less consensus in the literature about how to approach a complaint from either partner about the woman's not reaching orgasm during intercourse. In our view, if the woman is orgasmic during sexual activity with her partner and enjoys the intercourse experience, there is no need for therapeutic intervention. The woman's having an orgasm during intercourse is not the definition of "normal female sexual functioning." If the woman desires to increase her sensations and responses during intercourse, several techniques can be utilized, such as intercourse with simultaneous clitoral stimulation, intercourse positions involving greater pelvic contact, the woman controlling the timing and rhythm of coital thrusting, and the use of pubococcygeal muscle exercises during intercourse. The couple is also told that there is wide professional acceptance that the distinction between "vaginal" and "clitoral" orgasms is not scientifically meaningful. Physiologically, an orgasm is an orgasm, whether obtained through vibrator stimulation, masturbation, manual stimulation by partner, cunnilingus, or intercourse. Moreover, the experience of orgasm will differ from one time to another, as will the subjective feelings of satisfaction.

The woman's learning to be more sexually assertive, to make requests, to guide her partner, and generally to assume responsibility for her own sexual response is crucial to the development of a mutually satisfying sexual relationship. Many people feel it is the male's responsibility to ensure his partner an orgasm each time, so that the woman's orgasm has become a measure of the man's sexual prowess. This male-oriented performance pressure has proven immensely destructive to female sexuality and to couple satisfaction. The appropriate association is between sexuality and pleasure, not between sexuality and performance. The woman is advised not to fall into the trap of trying to "force" an orgasm, but rather to take a more active, involved, expressive role in the sexual interaction. With the woman assuming responsibility for her sexuality, the male's role is to be an involved and caring partner who is open and responsive to the guidance and requests of his partner.

Exercises to improve sexual skills are introduced once the couple has established a comfortable, sensuous touching relationship. These techniques focus on multiple stimulation to build arousal. Depending on the woman's desires, breast and vulva stimulation, manual and oral stimulation, fantasy and/or vibrators can be helpful. The woman is encouraged to take a more active and guiding role during intercourse and to continue multiple stimulation, such as kissing, breast stroking, clitoral stimulation, the woman setting rhythm, and fantasies. Orgasm is seen not as a performance goal, but rather as one natural response to the giving and receiving of sexual pleasure.

A second common dysfunction is one in which the woman has never been orgasmic with her partner, but does reach orgasm through masturbation. This often involves a power/control issue, when the woman either fears "letting go" in front of the partner or feels angry or distrustful of him. A valuable technique in the former instance is for the woman to masturbate to orgasm in front of the partner (Heiman, LoPiccolo, & LoPiccolo, 1976).

Anxiety and anger are the two emotional states most likely to inhibit sexual response. The nondemand pleasuring exercises followed by the multiple-stimulation exercises are the treatment of choice with anxiety-based problems, but such treatment will be less successful with anger-based problems. Sexual expression will be inhibited until the angry feelings have been expressed and/or resolved. Where the inhibiting factor is anger, the treatment of choice involves communication and problem-solving techniques.

Preorgasmic (also called primary nonorgasmic) is a term referring to women who have never been orgasmic by any means. Two intervention strategies are available for treating this dysfunction. Short-term preorgasmic women's groups (Barbach, 1974) appear to be of particular value for women without partners; this will be discussed in the section on treating individuals. If the woman is married or has an involved partner, an alternative strategy is to view the problem as a relationship one and to treat the couple. In addition to couple-pleasuring exercises, the woman engages in a personal program of self- exploration and masturbation. The rationale is that if she is aware of her arousal pattern and can experience orgasm herself, then she can share that learning with her partner. Heiman, LoPiccolo, and LoPiccolo (1976) have an excellent program of behavioral pleasuring exercises that allows the woman to explore her arousal and orgasmic patterns and to integrate her partner into this experience. Initial orgasmic response will occur typically in either masturbatory activity or in manual or oral stimulation; it is relatively rare during intercourse. Rather than viewing the initial orgasmic response as the end of therapy, it is seen as a beginning step in the couple's sexual growth.

Recently, attention has been focused on the problem of sexual aversion (Kaplan, Fyer, & Novick, 1982; Kolodny, Masters & Johnson, 1979), which is often misdiagnosed as inhibited sexual desire or as nonorgasmic response. Sexual aversion involves the process of a specific element (or stimulus) in the sexual interaction becoming so negative that it reaches phobic proportions. Although sexual aversion occurs in males, it is predominantly a female syndrome. Common aversive stimuli include semen, buttocks, vaginal secretions, breast stimulation, smells, and tongue kissing. Some women are sexually functional if they can avoid the aversive stimuli, whereas others are still dysfunctional.

An effective behavioral strategy in treating sexual aversion is an in-vivo desensitization program, similar to treatment of a phobia. The woman gradually and comfortably approaches the aversive stimulus. Couples are instructed neither to avoid sex nor to end a sexual interaction when the woman becomes anxious, because this would reinforce the discomfort and avoidance. They are advised to move to a more comfortable and secure pleasuring position and can either end the exercise at that point or again approach the anxiety-arousing sexual interaction. Sexual aversion is replaced by feelings of increased comfort and mastery.

A rarer sexual problem, but one especially amenable to behavioral techniques, is vaginismus. The definitive diagnosis of vaginismus requires a gynecologist to perform a physical examination and observe the spasming of the vaginal introitus. The strategy for overcoming vaginismus is use of in-vivo desensitization. The manner of desensitization can be dilators, the woman's finger, or innovative materials of increasing sizes such as candles. When initial comfort is established, additional stimuli, including the male's finger/s and eventually his penis, are introduced. Use of additional modalities such as relaxation training, couple communication, and assertiveness training is not only helpful in this process but may also be helpful in other aspects of the couple's sexual relationship.

TREATMENT OF MORE COMPLEX SEXUAL PROBLEMS

In this section we will discuss three particularly complex sexual issues: inhibited sexual desire, couple sexual dissatisfactions, and patterns of fetish arousal.

Inhibited sexual desire (ISD), also referred to as low libido or as hypoactive sexual desire, has recently received a good deal of attention (Kaplan, 1979; Kolodny, Masters, & Johnson, 1979). Lief (1977) estimates that approximately 30% of sex therapy referrals involve ISD. Although there has not been a definitive behavioral paper on ISD, it has been discussed by LaPointe (1979), LoPiccolo (1980), McCarthy (1984), and Schover and LoPiccolo (1982).

Behavioral approaches to ISD emphasize not only behavioral but also cognitive, attitudinal, and expectational factors, particularly the importance that one take responsibility for one's own sexuality. In the assessment phase, it is crucial to identify anxieties, inhibitions, anger, and guilt that may be responsible for blocking sexual feelings. Moreover, careful assessment must be undertaken of the variety of thoughts, images, sensations, fantasies, and interpersonal feelings the person labels "sexual." Some people have a very limited repertoire of activities they consider sexual. If the woman labels only intercourse and orgasm as being sexual and if she enjoys neither, she adopts a self-label as "frigid" or is so labeled by her partner. She then views sexual expression as not being "her" and develops a negative view of sexual interactions and of herself as a sexual being. This turns into a self-fulfilling prophecy leading to continued unsatisfactory sexual experiences.

Therapeutic intervention in this self-defeating cycle involves a strategy for expanding the boundaries of what is thought of as sexual, and increasing awareness of these cues. The individual's taking responsibility for her or his own sexuality is a cornerstone of this approach. Clients are encouraged to keep a daily diary of broadly defined sexual thoughts, feelings, and images. Therapists give permission and encourage clients to develop a range of sexual fantasies, perhaps by reading sexual books and magazines or attending sexually explicit movies. The individual may be encouraged to develop an ideal sexual scenario, including as many contextual, sensual, and interpersonal cues as possible. Labeling oneself as "frigid" or "nonsexual" is directly confronted. A variety of cognitive restructuring techniques, including self-instructional training, rational disputation, and identification of cognitive distortions (Lazarus, 1981), are used to refocus the individual on comfort, receptivity, and responsivity, and away from the judgmental performance criteria of intercourse and orgasm. In working with couples who have a discrepancy in sexual desire, the concepts of Zilbergeld and Ellison (1980) are used to assess the motivations and patterns of both partners, not just the one with ISD. The concepts of naturally occuring discrepancies in sexual desires and preferences, as well as the range of alternatives to meet sexual and emotional needs, allows viewing the issue from a couple problem-solving perspective. It is particularly important to discuss the quality of the sexual experience rather than to stay stuck on the frequency problem.

In sexual exercises, special attention is focused on initiation patterns, level of involvement of the individual, and increasing assertiveness so that the expression of feelings and needs becomes part of the sexual experience. The person with ISD is encouraged to increase activity and involvement rather than to view sex as a passive "servicing" of the partner.

An important behavioral exercise involves establishing a "safe" position. This means if the person becomes anxious or uninvolved she or he can request switching away from explicit sexual behavior to a focus on a warm, close, comfortable interaction. This could include a position in which they just lie together and hold each other, where one person puts their head on the other's lap and has their hair stroked, or where they lie back to chest in a "spoon" position and breathe together in a slow, rhythmic manner.

Couple interaction is an area requiring special attention in assessing and treating ISD. In some couples, sexuality is used as the arena in which to play out control struggles or to act out anger that is not directly expressed and dealt with in nonsexual areas. Sexual interaction is a cooperative venture in giving and receiving pleasure. At its best, it is an intimate, open sharing of feelings and sensations. Unfortunately, sex can also be an angry, coercive, and manipulative experience. In these cases, a marital intervention focused on learning direct expression and problem-solving approaches to anger is necessary, either as prerequisite to or as concomitant with sexually focused therapy. The sexual exercises will often elicit these issues so they can be dealt with therapeutically.

A second complex sexual problem involves couple sexual dissatisfactions. This refers to couples who do not have a specific sexual dysfunction, but who report chronic dissatisfaction with their sexual relationship. Sources of dissatisfaction include initiation patterns, frequency issues, variety issues, interfering aspects of anger, and dissatisfaction with the afterplay/afterglow experience. These couples usually report that the arousal and orgasm phases are mechanically satisfactory, although emotional satisfaction is often low. In some couples, a sexual dissatisfaction can be a sign of dissatisfaction with the marital relationship. In these cases, marital therapy would be the treatment of choice.

When applying behaviorally oriented strategies and techniques to the treatment of dissatisfied couples, it is important to clarify expectations about the role they want sexuality to play in their marital relationship (McCarthy & McCarthy, 1981). Clarifying expectations and suggesting guidelines to make marital sex more satisfying is a new concept for most couples and helps them break out of their self-defeating cycle. The therapeutic focus is on shared responsibility for developing a mutually satisfying and flexible sexual style. They are told that each couple is unique, and that there is no "right" way to initiate, nor is there a "normal" number of times to have intercourse per week. Some suggested sexual guidelines include setting aside couple time, accepting occasional unsatisfactory sexual experiences, and increasing intimate communication. The therapist may stress that the primary functions of marital sex are shared pleasure, greater emotional intimacy, and tension reduction, and that an unsatisfying sexual life can serve to devitalize a marital relationship.

The therapeutic strategy for dealing with sexual dissatisfactions is to take the sexual interaction from the realm of a nonverbal power struggle cloaked in romantic mystique, and to present it as a positive, cooperative experience open to discussion, negotiation, and problem solving. Emphasis is put on use of "I" communications combined with clear and assertive requests.

One of the most effective techniques is to structure a ping-pong pattern of initiation, in which each person has a day when he or she is responsible for sexual initiation. Assertiveness training and behavioral rehearsal can facilitate setting up the time, milieu, and the form of the sexual interaction. Ideally, both partners would learn to initiate, be able to say "no" in nonhostile ways, and to offer a wide variety of sensual or sexual alternatives. Such an exercise can be an especially powerful learning experience for the woman who is not comfortable with sexual initiation.

The therapist confronts the myth that each sexual experience has to be equally involving and satisfying for both partners. Frank, Anderson, and Rubinstein (1978) found that among couples who did not complain of sexual problems, fewer than half of their sexual experiences are rated as equally satisfying. Moreover, cognitive restructuring can be used to attack the "every sexual encounter should be dynamite" myth. Couples are encouraged to be affectionate in and out of the bedroom, and to be aware that touching has its own rewards, rather than each touch being a prelude to intercourse.

The importance of the afterplay/afterglow experience is not recognized by many couples. This period can be a time of quiet emotional sharing, intimacy, or playfulness, but men particularly tend to fall into the trap of going to sleep or going back to a chore or to watching television after sex. Not only does this behavior ignore the potential to reinforce intimate feelings, it can lead to a partner who feels frustrated or uncared for. The therapist can clarify the couple's expectations and desires and design exercises to allow the couple to experiment with different afterplay/afterglow experiences.

Another complex sexual problem involves patterns of fetish arousal. Behavioral interventions have been effective with a range of paraphilias, including exhibitionism, voyeurism, and fetishes (Brownell & Barlow, 1980). Most of the literature consists of reports on individual treatment of the male. Even if the man is married, the traditional approach is not to do couple work, or to limit such work to supportive marital counseling. Although this treatment regimen might be all that is necessary in some cases, a systems viewpoint that emphasizes multiple determinants of the behavior and mutual couple responsibility for change is usually beneficial and often necessary. In this treatment regimen, the male is seen individually on a weekly basis, focusing on decreasing the paraphiliac arousal, and the couple is seen conjointly once a week to improve their sexual relationship.

Arousal to paraphiliac stimuli has little transferability to couple sex. The combination of high sexual excitement and guilt/obsessiveness attached to the sexual behavior has a multiplicative effect that makes this a very powerful sexual experience. In individual sessions, the male is encouraged to take responsibility for not acting out his patterns of paraphiliac sexual behavior. At the same time, he is encouraged to reduce his guilt about this "deviant" arousal by understanding more objectively the maladaptive learning process and by focusing his energy into the present and future rather than obsessing about past sexual transgressions. Guilt is not a motivator to promote positive change, it rather lowers self-esteem and contributes to the continuation of the maladaptive pattern. A number of therapeutic techniques, including aversive conditioning, are used to stop the client from acting out the paraphiliac pattern. One strategy is to eliminate paraphiliac fantasies using techniques of masturbation monitoring, where he gradually and systematically alters the fantasies he uses as he approaches orgasm until the fetish fantasy is extinguished (Marquis, 1970). An alternative approach is for the male to learn, utilizing cognitive restructuring, to view fantasies as "old friends." Rather than controlling sexual arousal, they are combined with other fantasies and stimulation to serve a bridging function for greater sexual interaction with his partner.

The woman is relieved of the pressure to keep track of or to worry about the man's paraphiliac behavior. Rather, during couple sessions she is encouraged to assume mutual responsibility for making their sexual relationship more satisfying by increasing her sexual and emotional involvement. These couples have often had a passive, uninvolved, nonsatisfactory sexual relationship in which the entire experience revolved around the male's paraphiliac activity. They are informed that when the male is dysfunctional or dissatisfied in his partner relationship, the probability becomes greater of returning to traditional paraphiliac arousal.

TREATMENT OF PEOPLE WITHOUT PARTNERS

The behavioral sex therapy model is primarily couple oriented, but there are many individuals with sexual problems who do not have regular partners. Typically, singles are seen by a therapist of the same sex. At one time, sexual surrogates were utilized, but use of surrogate partners proved extremely problematic both in terms of legal issues and the "burn-out" effect on the surrogate.

Preorgasmic women's groups have received widespread attention in the literature (Barbach, 1974). These groups are the treatment of choice for females without partners who have not experienced orgasm. Treatment most commonly involves 10 sessions on a twice- weekly basis. The group design includes education, permission giving, behavioral homework assignments, and modeling by group leaders (especially on taking responsibility for one's own sexuality and being sexually assertive). The group process also provides support, confrontation, and problem-solving opportunities.

Through self-exploration and masturbation the woman learns her individual arousal pattern. This program has achieved considerable success in reducing anxiety and increasing awareness of orgasmic response, but the results of transferring these responses to partner sex are more ambiguous (Payn & Wakefield, 1982).

Group approaches to male sexuality have also been explored, though they have been less popular due to the reluctance of males to admit sexual problems to others of their gender. Erectile difficulties are the sexual problem most frequently treated in a group setting (Lobitz & Baker, 1979; Reynolds, Cohen, Schochet, Price, & Anderson, 1981). The male groups focus on information, permission-giving, behavioral exercises concentrating on masturbation, fantasy training, as well as a special segment on role playing (behavioral rehearsal of talking to women about sexuality, using female cotherapists or paraprofessionals). Results have generally been positive, although the utility of the group model for men remains questionable.

Individual sex therapy for men without partners has focused on education, masturbation retraining, relaxation and guided imagery techniques, cognitive restructuring, and improvement of heterosocial skills (McCarthy, 1980). The most common problem presented is erectile dysfunction, although single males are also seen for involuntary ejaculation, ejaculatory inhibition, and inhibited sexual desire. The male is encouraged to break self- defeating patterns of interaction with women, such as drinking to reduce anxiety, playing the macho role, and attempting intercourse on first dates. The client is encouraged to choose partners with whom he is comfortable, is attracted to and trusts. For males with specific sexual phobias, desensitization is the treatment of choice.

Sex therapy with the individual female client usually involves a female therapist and follows the same basic format. As a result of culturally scripted sexual patterns, the single woman is often placed in the position of fending off unwanted sexual advances and being labeled "frigid" if she does so. The female therapist models the concept that the woman should be comfortable with her own sexuality and that she has the option of choosing how and with whom she can most enjoy sexual expression. Cognitive restructuring and assertiveness training are used to allow the woman to feel more in control of her sexuality.

INTEGRATING BEHAVIORAL SEX THERAPY TECHNIQUES

Strategies and techniques of behaviorally oriented sex therapy can be integrated into more traditional individual and couple psychotherapy if needed, as addressed in more detail in Chapter 1 of this volume. A useful framework for such integration was also developed by Annon (1974), called the PLISSIT model. Four levels of intervention are conceptualized:

P: Permission-giving

LI: Limited information

SS: Specific suggestions

IT: Intensive sex therapy (similar to the model of behaviorally oriented sex therapy presented in this chapter).

When sexual issues are brought out during psychotherapy, the clinician can employ a range of interventions. Using permission giving, the therapist indicates that sex is a proper issue to be dealt with therapeutically. The therapist's positive conceptualization is "Sex is a good part of life; your sexuality is an integral part of your personality, and you can choose to express your sexuality in ways that enhance your life rather than cause problems for you." The therapist also gives permission for sexual expression to be planful and choiceful. The therapist promotes acceptance of certain behaviors such as masturbation, arousal by socially nonacceptable fantasies, use of oral-genital stimulation, and the occasional sexual difficulty that is within the normal scope of human sexuality.

The limited information level of intervention builds on permission- giving and helps the client/s establish alternatives to deal with particular issues. Bibliotherapy can be particularly helpful in this process. Unlike many of the self-help sexuality books that overemphasize sexual variations and sexual performance, the most useful sex literature attempts to (a) provide information; (b) set reasonable expectations; (c) reduce the negative emotional states of anxiety, guilt, and anger; and (d) establish guidelines for functional communication and stimulation techniques. Some of the books that are useful adjuncts for ongoing therapy for females include *For Yourself* (Barbach, 1976), *Becoming Orgasmic* (Heiman, LoPiccolo, & LoPiccolo, 1976), and *The New Our Bodies, Ourselves* (Boston Women's Health Collective, 1984). Books recommended for males are *What You Still Don't Know About Male Sexuality* (McCarthy, 1977), *Male Sexuality* (Zilbergeld, 1978), and *Prime Time* (Schover, 1984). For couples, *Sex and Satisfaction After 30* (McCarthy & McCarthy, 1981) can be useful.

Limited information may include reassuring the couple that alternate intercourse positions are appropriate and showing diagrams depicting different positions. Myths about "vaginal" and "clitoral" orgasms are refuted. Possible reasons for erectile problems are described, as are ways to avoid making performance anxiety a chronic problem. For example, if one partner feels guilty or humiliated about a sexual incident (i.e., having been molested as a child, having had an abortion), the therapist provides information that identifies the situation as a negative, but not uncommon, human sexual experience. The clinician discusses ways to accept and to cope with the incident, and ways not to feel guilty or to lower one's sexual self-esteem.

Specific suggestions or tasks may also be integrated into the ongoing therapy experience. These directed tasks could take part of a single session or be incorporated into therapy for an extended number of sessions. Assignments may include giving instructions for self-exploration, or prohibiting intercourse and focusing the couple on pleasuring exercises. A committed couple with a cooperative, communicative relationship could be instructed on how to use the stop/start process for gaining ejaculatory control.

COMMON THERAPEUTIC DILEMMAS

There are several difficulties that nonbehavioral clinicians have in applying behavioral sex therapy techniques. These include (a) not giving clear, direct instructions; (b) abandoning exercises at the first sign of resistance or avoidance; (c) not processing the exercises in detail; (d) emphasizing performance goals rather than increasing comfort and skills; (e) appearing aloof and uninterested in therapy; and (f) not ensuring generalization and maintenance of change.

A crucial skill in the practice of sex therapy is the ability to give clear, direct instructions for sexual exercises. In clinical training, the proper use of empathic response and interpretations are highly valued skills, whereas giving instructions is seen more as counseling or education than as "real therapy." However, in behavioral sex therapy the clinician must become competent and comfortable with prescribing sexual tasks.

Abandoning a sexual exercise when it is resisted can often be a mistake. Exercises have two major functions: (a) to increase comfort and skills and (b) to elicit discussion of anxieties, inhibitions, and skill deficits, often referred to as resistances in psychodynamic therapy. Stopping the exercises in order to explore feelings, to do in-depth interpretation, or to point out secondary gains from the sexual problems has the effect of reinforcing avoidance of sexual interaction. The couple can be encouraged to continue a sexual experience until they reach a sense of comfort or move to a more comfortable sexual interaction and end the sexual exercise in a positive manner. The problems elicited by the exercises can be dealt with in the therapy session and/or by redesigning the exercise.

Clinicians are often comfortable exploring orgasms, feelings, and past psychological functioning in detail, but many have a reluctance to do a detailed processing of sexual exercises. Therapists report a feeling of being a "voyeur" by being invasive in an area that is private and sensitive, or they may fear appearing to be sexually seductive or feeling sexual arousal. However, since the therapist does not observe the sexual behavior, there *is* a need for clear, detailed feedback, both to assess progress and to help design the next steps of the behavioral program. For example, sometimes the difference between a neutral and a highly arousing stimulus involves only a slight modification in the pressure, rhythm, or area of stroking. These details need to be explicated in processing the sexual experience.

A typical performance-pressure mistake made by clinicians doing sex therapy is to say something like, "Now you should have intercourse" or "Get an erection and insert halfway in the vagina" or "Experience orgasm during clitoral stimulation." This puts pressure on the client to perform and to strive to reach this goal immediately. The most useful strategy in sex therapy is not to tell the clients they "should" experience anything, but rather to give them permission to do so by removing a prohibition and telling them that they "can." Arousal, erection, and orgasm are the natural responses to involving, effective stimulation. The clinician focuses the couple on increasing comfort, improving sexual involvement, and utilizing multiple stimulation.

One of the major reasons that behavioral therapy is not more popular among experienced clinicians is that they find the structure, information giving, and task assignments less personally involving and emotionally rewarding than other forms of therapy. Sometimes when doing a standard behavioral intervention, the clinician appears minimally attentive, and only becomes more involved when problems or crises occur. Since an involved therapist is reinforcing to a client, couples may present problems with the structured program in an attempt to get the therapist's attention. Such problems can be avoided if the therapist reinforces success with the program throughout the course of treatment.

Generalization and maintenance of sexual changes are often not fully addressed in the literature. There are assumptions in traditional psychotherapy that, once a person gains insight or gets in touch with feelings, these breakthroughs (a) result in behavioral changes, which (b) generalize to a large number of areas and (c) are easily maintained. In any particular case, these assumptions may be erroneous (Lazarus, 1976), particularly so in the sexual area.

Clients often regress after termination of therapy, so the therapist may wish to deal directly with maintaining changes. Strategies to help the clients maintain gains emphasize that the sex therapy has given them a basic sexually functional repertoire. They can now develop their own unique style as a sexual couple. Couples are encouraged to engage in do-it-yourself exercises, to set aside at least two times a month to share emotional and sexual feelings, and to schedule a six-month follow-up therapy session that will focus on maintenance and generalization of their marital and sexual gains.

SUMMARY

The purpose of this chapter was to highlight the strategies and techniques used in behavioral sex therapy. A focused, time-limited approach that emphasizes well-designed, sequential exercises done at home is a core factor in sex therapy. Central to the behavioral approach is the strategy of first increasing comfort and awareness and then learning more functional and flexible sexual skills. In reviewing the dysfunctions and dissatisfactions, it is clear that the more specific the sexual problem is and the more it involves anxiety and/or poor skills, the more appropriate is the behavioral approach. Moreover, behavioral techniques can be integrated with other therapeutic interventions in the treatment of more complex sexual problems. The behavioral sex therapy approach provides a good conceptual framework for understanding and treating sexual dysfunction.

REFERENCES

Annon, J. (1974). *The behavioral treatment of sexual problems.* Honolulu: Enabling Press.

Bandura, A. (1977). Self-efficacy: Toward a unifying theory of behavioral change. *Psychological Review, 84,* 191- 215.

Barbach, L. (1974). Group treatment of preorgasmic women. *Journal of Sex and Marital Therapy, 1,* 139-145.

Barbach, L. (1976). *For yourself.* New York: Doubleday.

Barbach, L. (1980). *Women discover orgasm.* New York: Free Press.

Boston Women's Health Collective. (1984). *The new our bodies, ourselves.* New York: Simon & Schuster.

Brownell, K., & Barlow, D. (1980). The behavioral treatment of sexual deviation. In A. Goldstein & E. Foa (Eds.), *Handbook of behavioral interventions.* New York: Wiley.

Frank, E., Anderson, C., & Rubinstein, D. (1978). Frequency of sexual dysfunction in "normal" couples. *New England Journal of Medicine, 299,* 111-115.

Hartmann, W., & Fithian, M. (1972). *Treatment of sexual dysfunction.* Long Beach, CA: Center for Marital and Sexual Studies.

Heiman, J., LoPiccolo, L., & LoPiccolo, J. (1976). *Becoming orgasmic.* Englewood Cliffs, NJ: Prentice-Hall.

Kaplan, H.S. (1979). *Disorders of sexual desire.* New York: Brunner/Mazel.

Kaplan, H., Fyer, A., & Novick, A. (1982). The treatment of sexual phobias. *Journal of Sex and Marital Therapy, 8,* 3-28.

Kolodny, R., Masters, W., & Johnson, V. (1979). *Textbook of sexual medicine.* Boston: Little, Brown.

LaPointe, C. (1979). A short term cognitive and behavioral treatment approach to sexual desire phase dysfunctions. *Journal of Sex Education and Therapy, 1,* 35-38.

Lazarus, A. (1976). *Multi-modal behavior therapy.* New York: Springer.

Lazarus, A. (1981). *The practice of multimodal therapy.* New York: McGraw-Hill.

Leiblum, S., & Pervin, L. (Eds.). (1980). *Principles and practice of sex therapy.* New York: Guilford.

Lief, H. (1977). Inhibited sexual desire. *Medical Aspects of Human Sexuality, 11,* 94-95.

Lobitz, W., & Baker, E. (1979). Group treatment of single males with erectile dysfunction. *Archives of Sexual Behavior, 8,* 127-138.

LoPiccolo, J., & LoPiccolo, L. (Eds.). (1978). *Handbook of sex therapy.* New York: Plenum.

LoPiccolo, L. (1980). Inhibited sexual desire. In S. Leiblum & L. Pervin, *Principles and practice of sex therapy.* New York: Guilford.

Marquis, J. (1970). Orgasmic reconditioning: Changing sexual object choice through controlling masturbatory fantasies. *Journal of Behavior Therapy and Experimental Psychiatry, 1,* 263-271.

Masters, W.H., & Johnson, V.E. (1970). *Human sexual inadequacy.* Boston: Little, Brown.

McCarthy, B. (1977). *What you still don't know about male sexuality.* New York: Crowell.

McCarthy, B. (1980). Treatment of secondary erectile dysfunction in males without partners. *Journal of Sex Education and Therapy, 6,* 29-34.

McCarthy, B. (1981). Strategies and techniques for the treatment of ejaculatory inhibition. *Journal of Sex Education and Therapy, 7,* 20-23.

McCarthy, B. (1984). Strategies and techniques for the treatment of inhibited sexual desire. *Journal of Sex and Marital Therapy, 10,* 97-104.

McCarthy, B., & McCarthy, E. (1981). *Sex and satisfaction after 30.* Englewood Cliffs: Prentice-Hall.

McCarthy, B., & McCarthy, E. (1984). *Sexual awareness: Sharing sexual pleasure.* New York: Carroll & Graf.

Payn, H., & Wakefield, J. (1982). The effect of group treatment of primary orgasmic dysfunction on the marital relationship. *Journal of Sex and Marital Therapy, 8,* 133- 150.

Perelman, M. (1980). Treatment of premature ejaculation. In S. Leiblum & L. Pervin (Eds.), *Principles and practice of sex therapy.* New York: Guilford.

Reynolds, B., Cohen, B., Schochet, B., Price, S., & Anderson, A. (1981). Dating skills training in the group treatment of erectile dysfunction for men without partners. *Journal of Sex and Marital Therapy, 7,* 184-194.

Rosen, G. (1976). *Don't be afraid.* Englewood Cliffs: Spectrum.

Schover, L. (1984). *Prime time: Sexual health for men over 50.* New York: Holt, Rinehart & Winston.

Schover, L., & LoPiccolo, J. (1982). Treatment effectiveness for dysfunctions of sexual desire. *Journal of Sex and Marital Therapy, 8,* 179-197.

Schull, G., & Sprenkle, D. (1980). Retarded ejaculation: Reconceptualization and implications for treatment. *Journal of Sex and Marital Therapy, 6,* 234-246.

Stuart, F., Stuart, R., Maurice, W., & Szasz, G. (1975). *Sexual adjustment inventory.* Champaign, IL: Research Press.

Wolpe, J. (1973). *The practice of behavior therapy.* New York: Pergamon.

Zilbergeld, B. (1978). *Male sexuality.* Boston: Little, Brown.

Zilbergeld, B., & Ellison, D. (1980). Desire discrepancies and arousal problems in sex therapy. In S. Leiblum & L. Pervin (Eds.), *Principles and practice of sex therapy.* New York: Guilford.

Section III

Special Problems and Special Populations

Chapter 11

Understanding and Treating Jealousy

Gregory L. White and Therese R.M. Helbick

> *But through the heart*
> *Should Jealousy its venom once diffuse,*
> *'Tis then delightful misery no more,*
> *But agony unmixed, incessant gall,*
> *Corroding every thought and blasting all*
> *Love's paradise*
>
> Othello, III, iii

Romantic jealousy is one of the most common sources of distress in couples, and it is perhaps one of the most complex and difficult relationship problems to resolve. It is also a problem for society in that roughly 15% to 25% of all murders and a great deal of spouse abuse are committed in a jealous rage (Daly, Wilson, & Weghorst, 1982; Whitehurst, 1971). Unfortunately, therapists have little in the way of empirical research to guide their search for either an understanding of the causes and consequences of jealousy or for successful treatment methods (Clanton & Smith, 1977; White, 1981d; White & Mullen, in press).

In this chapter we make some distinctions that we have found useful in understanding jealousy. We then review theoretical and empirical work from four traditions, including psychoanalyic- psychodynamic, anthropological-sociological, biological, and social-psychological perspectives. Implications for short-term therapy are especially noted. We also review short-term treatment methods for the normal romantic jealousy most likely to be encountered by therapists (White & Devine, in press).

Though this chapter focuses on the more problematic aspects of normal jealousy, we think that coping with jealousy can help the couple to redefine their relationship in more mutually satisfying ways. We like to think that one's feeling jealous can be a useful cue to the person and couple that choices need to be

245

made about the relationship and about the manner in which the person's needs are met. As we hope to make clear, we think jealousy is a normal part of romantic relationships that cannot be avoided realistically but that can affect the relationship for better as well as for worse.

Definition of Jealousy

We have found it clinically useful to conceptualize romantic jealousy as *a complex of thoughts, feelings, and actions that follow threats to self-esteem and/or threats to the existence or quality of the relationship, when those threats are generated by the perception of a real or potential romantic/sexual attraction between one's partner and a (perhaps imaginary) rival.* We use the term *complex* to capture the interrelatedness of the behaviors, thoughts, and feelings people have when they are jealous. The pattern of thoughts, feelings, and actions are assumed to be relatively stable — individuals, couples, and cultures reveal repeating patterns of reaction to the twin threats posed by rivals to relationships.

Threats to the self and to the relationship are conceptually distinct yet empirically difficult to untangle, as Freud (1922/1955) suggested. A number of theorists have also suggested that either or both threats are at the psychological root of jealousy (Bohm, 1961; Fenichel, 1955; Jones, 1937; Mead, 1931, Simmel, 1950, pp. 406-407; Spielman, 1971). These threats may be rather specific and situationally defined, as, for example, when one partner flirts at a party at a time when the other is feeling unattractive. Or the threats may be general and chronic to the relationship, as when one partner repeatedly talks about attractions to potential rivals or frequently complains of unhappiness with the relationship.

This definition implies that it may be useful to think of jealousy as a label given to particular configurations of thoughts, feelings, and behaviors. From this point of view, jealousy is not a primary or even a complex emotion. It is apparent that the emotional states involved in jealousy differ from person to person, situation to situation, and relationship to relationship. A variety of emotions are experienced by the jealous person, including rage, anger, fear, suspicion, envy, sadness, sexual passion, vengefulness, and curiosity. We assume that the particular mix of emotions is dictated partly by personality, partly by situation (including culture), and partly from the interaction of individual and situational characteristics. If so, trying to specify the particular blend of emotions that characterizes jealousy in all cases is a futile task.

Likewise, we think that the behavior of the jealous person is not automatically programmed but reflects idiosyncrasies of person and situation. Jealous behavior thus should vary qualitatively over different romantic relationships, although the same type of event may generate the sense of threat. Jealous people may compete with the rival, may develop hobbies, may kill their lovers, or may propose marriage (Hupka, 1981; White, 1981c; White & Mullen, in press). Part of the planning and execution of these behaviors also includes a number of cognitive activities such as comparison of self with the rival ("What's he got that I don't?"), motive attribution to the partner ("What's in it for her?"), and assessment of alternatives to the relationship ("So what if they get together?"). How people behave, what they think about the situation, and how they feel are interrelated processes and we have chosen the term *complex* to denote this fact.

Clinically, thinking of jealousy as an interrelated complex of thoughts, feelings, and actions that develop within an interpersonal context has given us some freedom to move among a variety of perspectives when developing interventions. We may elect to focus on the personality and needs of the individual, on the personality and needs of the nonjealous partner or the rival, on the couple's dynamics, on the dynamics of the romantic triangle, or on cultural factors such as sex roles, norms regarding treatment of romantic rivals, and prescriptions about which situations should "naturally" produce jealousy. Shifting among these perspectives often suggests interventions that we could otherwise overlook.

It may be useful here to distinguish between jealousy and envy, an emotion often felt by the jealous. Envy is usually considered a primary emotion like anger or fear, whereas jealousy has no primary quality; people do not *feel* jealous (Bohm, 1961; Spielman, 1971; Sullivan, 1953, p. 347). Envy involves the desire for something *like* that possessed by another, jealousy involves the desire for what *is* (believed to be) possessed by another, such as the affection seen going to a rival. Jealousy is also profoundly interpersonal in a way that envy is not, because the desired object in jealousy is always a person (or process involving a person) with feelings, motives, and independent behavior. We may be envious of another's good romantic relationship, but when we start wanting that same relationship for ourselves the interpersonal situation is transformed.

Jealousy and Sexuality

Jealousy and sexual feelings and behavior have been linked in a variety of ways, including operation of instinct (Kinsey, Pomeroy, Martin, & Gebhard, 1953); projection of homosexual impulses (Freud, 1922/1955; Lagache, 1949); increases in libido from the excitement and intrigue of the triangle (Seeman, 1979); and the change through reaction formation of hostility toward the nonjealous partner into sexual feelings (Schmideberg, 1953). Inducing jealousy in a partner has been described as a sadistic act that may reflect confusion of sexuality and so-called pregenital aggression or hostility (Jones, 1937; Riviere, 1932). To date, there is no systematic research on the relationship between jealousy and sexuality, though it appears that the dynamics of jealousy can affect sexuality and vice versa.

We have not found it useful to assume an innate link between sexual drives and jealousy. We do think that there is a biological imperative to protect the self. However, we assume that the ways in which self-concept and sexual behavior are linked are prescribed through culture and social learning history. The

biological imperative to protect the self may or may not be engaged in a particular situation, depending on the perceived situation's implied (and learned)
linkages of sex, self, and threat.

Our definition of jealousy implies that the self is most vulnerable to threat in
intimate relationships in which sexual intimacy is often experienced as a powerful self-disclosure. Sex is not always so construed by individuals. In certain situations or relationships sex may be a form of play, manipulation, or religious
duty (Turner, 1970, pp. 320-325) with a much less direct implication of the self.
In this point of view there is nothing inherently threatening to the self about a
partner's sexual attraction to others except insofar as the jealous person's perceptions of the relationship between sex and self dictates the threat.

Pathological Versus Normal Jealousy

Pathological jealousy is characterized by obsessional concern with a mate's
real or potential infidelity when evidence available for reality testing would dis-
confirm the seriousness of the threat. Such jealousy is associated with extreme
behaviors such as constant surveillance, locking up one's spouse, spouse abuse,
and even murder (Bernard, 1971; Cobb & Marks, 1979, Ellis, 1977; Hafner,
1979; Mooney, 1965; Seeman, 1979; Sokoloff, 1947; Whitehurst, 1971). This type
of jealousy can be relatively independent of other dysfunction, cuts across
various diagnostic categories of hospitalized patients, and is three times as common in men as in women (Mooney, 1965).

Though the clinical research is sparse, it appears that pathological jealousy
may in some cases be symptomatic of a severe underlying disorder, typically
paranoid schizophrenia, paranoid psychosis, paranoid personality disorder, or
some alcoholic dementias (Langfeldt, 1961; Mowat, 1966; Seeman, 1979). The
person may have had a history of delusions about themes other than sexual infidelity, and the jealous delusions and accompanying rage can emerge suddenly.

This chapter is concerned with the treatment of less extreme jealousy, which
we will call normal jealousy. Although there may be a continuum between normal and morbid jealousy, we focus on those persons whose reality testing is relatively intact and who would also be considered good candidates for verbal therapy. In fact, the great majority of people who seek counseling for their jealousy
are not at pathological extremes (White & Devine, in press).

Romantic Versus Other Jealousies

Very little work has been done with other jealousies such as sibling rivalry
(Ausubel, Sullivan, & Ives, 1980, pp. 296-297), professional jealousy, or jealousy
among same-sexed friends. There is some conjecture that sibling rivalry may be
related to adult romantic jealousy (Clanton & Smith, 1977; Erikson, 1963; Levy,
1940; Sokoloff, 1947, p. 241), but there is no research evidence linking romantic jealousy with other jealousy. The exception is Bringle's work on "dispositional" jealousy (Bringle, Roach, Andler, & Evenbeck, 1979; Bringle & Willi-

ams, 1979). Bringle's Self-Report Jealousy Scale consists of four 5-item subscales assessing sibling, work, social (among friends), and romantic jealousy. The mean correlation among these four subscales is in the low .40s. Part of this mean intercorrelation is probably due to using the same paper-and-pencil technique of measurement, but it does suggest that some weak underlying trait may account for some consistency among different types of jealousy (White, 1984).

JEALOUSY RESEARCH AND THEORY

Psychodynamic-Psychoanalytic Perspectives

Freud (1922/1955) distinguished between normal jealousy (about which he had little to say except that it was common), projection jealousy, and delusional or paranoid jealousy. Projection jealousy is a mildly pathological state normally susceptible to treatment that occurs when heteroerotic impulses are projected onto one's romantic partner. Delusional jealousy was held to be more resistant to analysis, because it results from the projection of more anxiety-laden homoerotic impulses. Fenichel (1955, p. 433) thought that "a bit of such projection of homosexuality is to be found in every case of jealousy."

Psychoanalytic theory also suggests that those who repeat patterns of jealousy with no satisfactory resolution may have failed to work through the oedipal conflict satisfactorily (Freud, 1959/1914; Klein & Riviere, 1964). The rage and depression consequent to losing the beloved parent to the other of the same sex is still active in the unconscious and reemerges when adult reality approximates the same triangular set of relations as in the oedipal conflict. Such individuals may also repeatedly seek out triangular romantic relationships.

The oedipal explanation generates a number of largely untested hypotheses. For example, male castration anxiety should dispose adult males to compare themselves to rivals more so than do adult females, as Francis (1977) reported in a sample of 15 couples. Docherty and Ellis (1976) reported on three pathologically jealous men who as adolescents had seen their mothers engaged in extramarital sex. The interpretation was that the latent oedipal conflict became reactivated by this event, and the subsequent romantic relationships of these men were infiltrated by rage projected onto rivals and by feelings of worthlessness as partners.

Psychoanalytic treatment of jealousy has stressed examination of narcissistic pathology. The real or potential loss of narcissistic supplies leads normally to (conscious or unconscious) feelings of helplessness and depression over being unlovable. The resulting rage is defended against by projection onto a rival (or sometimes the partner) who is seen as evil and destructive. The external enemy can then be attacked in a way that allows for the expression of rage compatible with superego constraints (Klein & Riviere, 1964).

Others have stressed narcissistic pathology that predisposes a person to jealousy. Jones (1937) emphasized that narcissistic gratifications of romantic relationships may be needed by some to combat unconscious feelings of self-hate rooted in preoedipal dynamics. The defensive use that is made of partner's love is endangered by any sign of transfer of love to a rival. The resulting anger and depression would be greater than normally experienced by those who do not need partner's love as a defense against self-hate. Recent work in object-relations theory (Kernberg, 1975; Kohut, 1971) on narcissistic pathology suggests that projection of a grandiose view of self onto a romantic partner underlies rigidly idealized views of the partner. This idealization serves as a defense against fears that the partner will attack the self, an unconscious fear that itself is the result of projection of so-called oral rage. An attraction between rival and partner would threaten this idealization, leading to fearful withdrawal from or attack upon the partner.

Several psychoanalytically oriented observers have suggested that jealous feelings themselves might serve a defensive purpose. Fenichel (1955, p.512) noted that the jealous person becomes obsessional and clinging, seeming to embrace anxiety rather than to ward it off. To Fenichel this made sense only if there was a greater underlying anxiety deflected by the anxiety of jealousy. Riviere (1932) and Docherty & Ellis (1976) suggest that unconscious sadistic desires, perhaps acted out by becoming a rival for others' partners, could be defended against by projection onto one's own partner. The resulting jealousy could be seen as a defense against the primitive envy and rage thought to generate the unconscious sadism.

Anthropological-Sociological Perspectives

Surveys of different cultures have shown jealousy to be universal but incredibly varied in precipitating events, intensity, quality of emotional experience, and behavioral manifestations (Daly, Wilson, & Weghorst, 1981; Hupka, 1981; Mead, 1931; Seidenberg, 1967; Tellenbach, 1974). One common observation is that culture specifies the situations in which sexual attraction or behavior between spouse and another person threatens the self. Many cultures allow and encourage sexual practices such as wife-lending and ceremonial license that would make the average Westerner jealous. Instances and practices in which sexual possession is not related to self- or communal esteem are relatively free of jealousy.

Davis (1936) suggested that jealousy is a reaction to violation of sexual property norms. Ownership rather than self-esteem maintenance is the principle at work. Those who violate culturally defined sexual property rights can be punished in ways prescribed by the culture. Daly et al. (1982) extend this to argue that the "rights" are usually those of males trying to protect paternity confidence. Because females are always certain that the children they bear are their own and males cannot usually be confident of their paternity through observation, sanctions against female infidelity should tend to be stronger cross- culturally in order to protect the "right" of the male to raise his own children, not those of another male.

Hupka (1981) reviewed and summarized the available cross-cultural evidence by citing four conditions that appear to be independently associated with the frequency and intensity of jealousy typical of the culture. Jealousy seems more common if (1) there are strong norms favoring personal (vs. communal) property, (2) sex is restricted to marriage, (3) there are strong economic or moral values of having progeny, making it important to establish paternity, and (4) marriage is the required vehicle for achieving economic or social status.

A number of sex differences in jealousy have been found (White, 1981d). One major difference is that jealous males are more focused on the sexual aspects of the rival relationship, whereas jealous females are more fearful of losing the relationship. Research on swinging reveals that husbands, who typically initiate swinging, do not anticipate jealousy. However, once partner swapping begins, the male's jealousy is a major problem and is primarily centered on anxieties over his sexual performance relative to other men. Wives are more likely to be jealous prior to the start of swinging. Their jealousy centers on fears of relationship disruption and is much less concerned with sexual rivalry either before or after swinging begins (Denfeld, 1974; Varni, 1974).

Other research supports this sex difference. Francis's (1977) survey of 15 couples found men more concerned with sexual aspects of the rival relationship, whereas females were more concerned with loss of contact, affection, and support. Teismann & Mosher (1978) had 80 couples role play jealousy situations. Eighty percent of the men spontaneously chose sexual themes to enact as the jealous partner compared to only 18% of the women. Women were much more likely to choose themes around loss of time, attention, and companionship posed by the rival. Shettel-Neuber, Bryson, and Young (1978) showed jealousy-inducing videotape scenes of flirtation to subjects who indicated what their response might be in a similar situation. Females were less likely to think they would use relationship-threatening actions such as aggression and withdrawal, perhaps because of their greater concern (when jealous) with maintaining the relationship. White (1981c) reported that women were more likely than men to report trying consciously to improve their relationships in order to reduce their jealousy. Finally, Gottschalk (1936) interviewed Northern Europeans and found a strong sexual threat component in the jealousy of 80% of the men but in only 22% of the women. Women were more concerned about qualities of the rival relationship, such as communication and emotional intimacy. These sex differences are compatible with traditional sex roles that emphasize female dependency on men and that for males define romantic relationships as arenas for sexual display and competitiveness (Gross, 1978; Peplau, 1978).

Biological Perspectives

Darwin (1888) traced jealousy to an instinctual defense of the pair bond. The feelings and behavior of jealousy served to increase the likelihood that the pair would stay together and hence replicate their genes. Men came to be the aggressively jealous sex because such tendencies were reinforced by selection operating through the hunting role. Because to Kinsey, human jealousy appeared similar to "jealousy" in lower species (Kinsey et al., 1953, p. 411), he also concluded that male jealousy is inherited. Jealousy acts to maintain monogamy, and many human and primate societies are monogamous. This is the reverse of Davis's (1936) assertion that monogamy (a property distinction) maintains jealousy (a reaction to violation of property rights).

Daly, Wilson, & Weghorst (1982) present a more modern version of this evolutionary theory. Males who jealously guard against sexual rivals would be more likely to raise their own children, not their rivals' children. Even if this did not confer a survival advantage to the children per se, it would still insure that the jealous male's genotype would become more established than the genotypes of males who diverted their energies into raising children with other men's genotypes. A different process is hypothesized to apply to females who would always be raising their own progeny. If a stable pair bond conferred survival value, then those females better able to maintain the pair bond would be more likely to have their genotypes established. Eventually these two parallel evolutionary processes would lead to a male jealousy focused on sexual threat, whereas female jealousy would center on relationship maintenance and enhancement. Daly et al. present a good deal of animal and cross- cultural evidence in support of their argument.

Social-Psychological Perspectives

Since the mid 1970s there has been an upswing in empirical work on romantic jealousy, almost all of it conducted by social psychologists and personality theorists (Bringle & Williams, 1979; Buunk, 1980; Shettel-Neuber, Bryson, & Young, 1978; White, 1980a, 1980b, 1981a, 1981b, 1981d). Much of this work has been reviewed by White (1981d). The following variables have been found to be rather consistently correlated with self-report measures of jealousy: (1) sexual exclusivity, (2) low self-esteem, (3) feelings of inadequacy as a partner for the current mate, (4) overdependence on one's partner for one's own self-esteem, (5) dependence on the relationship, (6) sensitizing (vs. repressing) defensive style, (7) external locus of control, (8) sex role traditionalism, especially for men, and (9) greater relative involvement or greater effort put into the relationship compared to partner.

White (1981d) presents a coping paradigm to understand how the jealous person perceives and reacts to threats to self and relationship. The *primary appraisal* of such threats (cf. Lazarus & Launier, 1978) involves estimation of the presence and strength of threat and is likely to be affected by the nine variables listed above. The *secondary appraisal* of jealous threats involves recalling or gathering information that could help the person cope. Discerning partner's motives, comparing oneself to the rival, and surveying alternatives to the threatened relationship are examples of this process (White, 1981a, 1981c).

Such information may be gathered consciously or unconsciously and is probably rarely systematically sought out. Also, it is likely that information gleaned in the process of coping may affect the estimation of the degree of threat ("My rival is no match for me.") and that information that originally generated the perception of threat may also be used in developing coping responses ("My partner has always wanted a better sex life so maybe I should try to be more attractive.").

The information yielded by primary and secondary appraisal should affect the jealous person's emotional response. This initially resembles the flight/fight stress response and then may resolve predominantly into emotions associated with anger, depression, or both. These emotions and the information gleaned via secondary appraisal are assumed to interact in complex ways with the person's actual coping behavior. For example, those who think that their partner is attracted to another because the rival relationship is high in quality and who are angry seem more likely to try to interfere with that relationship (White, 1981c). However, such interference may backfire by making the jealous person seem even less attractive than the rival, which in turn could increase the anger of the jealous person.

White (1981c) identified seven major strategies of coping with jealousy. These were classes of specific behaviors that clustered together empirically. The effect of the strategies is seen to be either to reduce the threat to self-esteem, to reduce the threat to the relationship, or sometimes to reduce both threats simultaneously. The strategies include (1) improving the relationship, (2) interfering with the rival relationship, (3) denying the threat implications of partner's or rival's feelings and behavior, (4) developing romantic or nonromantic alternatives to the relationship, (5) derogating the rival or partner, (6) introspectively examining one's own role in the drama, and (7) demanding greater commitment. Females were more likely to try to improve the relationship and to demand commitment whereas males reported greater use of denial. Conceptually, all possible coping behaviors can be seen as combinations of these different strategies. For example, late-night phone calls to the home of a lover to "check up" can have elements of (a) trying to make partner and rival feel guilty and thus diminish the quality of their interaction (interference), of (b) derogating the partner as untrustworthy and hence less valuable as a partner, and of (c) a thinly disguised demand for greater commitment. These strategies may or may not be consciously developed and enacted by the jealous person.

Implications for Short-Term Therapy

In this section we sketch some suggestions for short-term treatment of normal jealousy that are based on the theory and research reviewed above. Since there is no outcome research on treatments for jealousy, these suggestions are meant to guide clinical intervention, not to constrain development of other methods.

Screening and initial assessment. Short-term therapy appears to be inappropriate for cases of pathological jealousy characterized by delusions associated with alcoholism, paranoid disorders, or prominent elements of narcissistic character disorder. Because jealousy develops within relationships (Sullivan, 1953) conjoint sessions with the partner are to be preferred when possible. Potential clients should be queried as to the possibility of bringing in the rival as well. Cultural background should be noted so that the therapist can start assessing the role of culture in shaping the perception of threat and the choice of coping behaviors. Two relationship histories should be taken, one of the current relationship and one of the course of previous romantic relationships. The role of jealousy in relationship history and recurrent patterns of unsuccessful attempts to cope with jealousy should be explored.

Build self-esteem. The jealous person may be low in self-esteem, in part due to the threats implied by the rival relationship and in part due to self- and others' judgments that the jealousy is somehow a mark of an insecure personality or other personality flaw. If the jealous person does have low self-esteem, in order to design interventions it would be important to know if this were caused by recent experiences (including the jealousy situation) or if it were an enduring aspect of the person's self-image. Building self-worth may reduce depression and anger, increase a sense of resourcefulness to cope with the situation, and help the person negotiate more as an equal with the partner about resolving the dilemma. The focus of building esteem might be on either the aspects of self outside the relationship (job, friendships, etc.) or on the ways in which the jealous person does satisfy the partner.

Look for repetitive patterns. Either the jealous person or the partner may have a history of acting the jealous role and/or acting the role of the target of jealousy. Several reasons for such patterns are plausible, including problems with resolution of oedipal conflicts, the use of jealousy as a solution to relationship problems, the use of jealousy as a defense against more threatening internal states, the use of jealousy as a way of avoiding intimate relationships, or an implicit definition by either partner or jealous person that jealousy is an affirmation of love.

Assess subjective meaning of events and their implications for self-esteem. The task here is to assess and address the subjective meaning of the events triggering jealousy, with a focus on how such meanings affect and are affected by self-esteem. This should be done with both partners. Self- judgments could be focused on by questions oriented to specific behaviors of the rival, partner, and jealous person, such as "When partner does X, what kind of person do you think you are?" and "What do you think other people would think about you if they knew that your rival and partner did X?" or "What is the right thing to do when your partner does X?" Clients should be asked about what they think are "natural" reasons to be jealous and to explain their cultural models defining how to react to jealousy-provoking situations.

Try to develop hope and reassurance about the relationship. Fears about losing the relationship may disable the person from effective use of therapy. The person may be unable to assess self-needs because of an overwhelming desire to please the other at all costs. The therapist could obtain a time-limited commitment from the nonjealous partner not to leave the relationship or not to see the rival. How this commitment is negotiated and communicated is in itself an important process of reassurance; if the partner appears forced into commitment, reassurance is probably minimal.

If jealousy is one of several problems affecting the couple, attention could first be given to the more tractable issues to provide increased satisfaction with the relationship. If present, the strong attractions of the relationship to the non-jealous partner could be given emphasis.

Expose both cultural and relationship-specific norms and roles that are operating. Both partners should be asked to describe how self and other should behave according to general cultural norms and according to more idiosyncratic norms and roles that have developed over the course of their relationship. Norms would include dating norms, norms about extramarital friendships and extramarital sexual involvement, norms about disclosing relationship problems to others, expectations about how the partners should acknowledge their sexual feelings about others, and ideas about the importance and place of loyalty to each other that are focused on specific behaviors that imply loyalty or disloyalty. Important roles to consider include sex roles and marital roles with respect to tasks (e.g., the man does the heavy work) and emotions (e.g., the woman discusses the man's feelings). The purpose is to make expectations explicit, to shift attribution of conflict away from unchangeable personality characteristics to more malleable role and norm definitions, and to increase the range of alternative solutions to the jealousy problem by making the acceptance of norms and roles a more conscious act.

Explore relationship-related dependencies. Overdependence on one's partner's evaluation of oneself and overdependence on the emotional and material rewards of the relationship are both associated with jealousy. Because these dependencies are normal in romantic relationships, the jealous person and partner may fear examination and reduction of overdependencies because to do so might imply that no romantic bond would be left. The less dependent person might also fear the reduction in power that could ensue if the overdependent jealous partner became less dependent. Exploration of what love means and of fears about losing love in order to reduce jealousy should be useful.

Address issues of power and equity. Jealousy may be symptomatic of an asymmetric distribution of power in which one partner is less able to get desired outcomes and hence is in a position of greater vulnerability to external threats to the relationship. We assume that the person low in power has relatively fewer and less attractive alternatives to the relationship than the partner (cf. Thibaut & Kelley, 1959). In addition, inducing jealousy can be in itself a power tactic to force partner to behave in a desired way or to punish the partner for past inequities (White, 1980a). Equity considerations are also important because the partner who has put more effort into developing or maintaining the relationship may be more likely to screen for threats to this investment. Such screening could easily be interpreted as jealousy by the other partner.

There are many reasons for an imbalance of power, some endemic to the re-lationship and some culturally dictated (e.g., women having less access to job markets). Structural changes in the relationship may need consideration, such as reaching new agreements about how to distribute spouses' incomes. Helping the couple develop more open and effective decision-making norms, changing roles so that both partners think that the other's contribution is equitable, and addressing feelings of impotence and depression over low power status could all be useful in preparing for such changes.

Identify previous solutions and their effects. The couple should be asked about the specific behaviors each has used in order to cope with the jealousy problem. The usefulness of these behaviors in reducing the twin threats to self and relationship can be assessed by each partner. Solutions that have led to more problems should be identified and the reasons for the failure of the solu-tions should be explored. Problem solutions should be differentiated from the intended consequences, for there is likely to be more agreement on goals than on methods.

THERAPY FOR JEALOUSY

There are no published outcome studies of jealousy therapies. However, White and Devine (in press) have recently surveyed 159 relationship counselors concerning their experience in treating normal jealousy. Their results are sum-marized below, followed by an overview of published reports of different ther-apeutic strategies.

Clinical Dimensions of Jealousy: Therapists' Reports

Sixty relationship counselors responded to a nationwide mailing sent to a ran-domly selected sample of members of the American Association of Marriage and Family Therapy. Respondents averaged 12.4 years of clinical experience and were heterogeneous with respect to degree (27% MSW, 13% PhD Clinical Psychology, etc.) and to theoretical background (e.g., systems, behavioral, psy-chodynamic). There was no effect of therapist degree status, gender, theoreti-cal background, or length of experience, on any of the measures discussed below.

Prevalence of jealousy. The therapists reported that jealousy was *the major* problem in about 10% of those who sought counseling for relationship problems. Jealousy was a *major* problem for another 22% and a *minor* problem for about 30%. These percentages held across client gender and race. Apparently jealousy is a major factor for about one third of all clients seeking relationship therapy.

The incidence of problem jealousy seemed to diminish with age. Fifty-nine percent of clients under 30 were judged to have a major problem with jealousy compared with 39% for those in the 30-45 age group, 21% for those 46-60, and only 13% for those over 60.

Contributory factors. Therapists rated the importance of 15 possible contributing factors to jealousy. For both men and women, chronic feelings of low self-esteem and being overly dependent on partner for self-esteem were the most potent causes. This was followed by feeling inadequate as a partner and by being overly demanding of attention and sexual exclusivity. These four factors were on the average estimated to be contributory factors in well over half the therapists' cases. For women, the next most potent causes were feeling more involved in the relationship than is partner, feeling the inequity of effort put into the relationship, being in a position of low power in the relationship, and transient feelings of low self-esteem. This list was the same for men except that the position of low power was not rated as important. These factors were on the average estimated to be contributing to the jealousy of 30% to 50% of the cases. Contrary to psychodynamic formulations, oedipal complications were not seen as important even among therapists with a psychodynamic orientation. Surprisingly, therapists indicated that the length of the marriage (more or less than 5 years) and presence of children were not related to the frequency of jealousy among their clients. Finally, couples were more likely to present with an actual rival relationship rather than one that was imaginary to the jealous person.

Sex differences in jealous feelings and behavior. Therapists indicated the relative frequency of different feelings and behaviors separately for male and female clients. Men were reportedly more likely to have long-term desires for revenge and to have long-term anger. Females were reportedly more likely to have short- and long-term depression, to blame themselves, and to be envious of the quality of the rival relationship. Jealous men were supposedly more likely to respond by developing alternative relationships, whereas women were reportedly more likely to try to improve their relationship, to attempt to interfere with the rival relationship, and to examine introspectively their role in the situation. Overall, the therapists indicated that women seemed better able to cope with their jealousy.

Treatment Reports and Therapeutic Strategies

There are many case reports of standard psychoanalytic- psychodynamic therapy that have happened to involve jealousy (Docherty & Ellis, 1976; Fenichel, 1955; Jones, 1937; Lagache, 1949; Langfeldt, 1961; Mooney, 1965; Riviere,

1932; Seeman, 1979; Sokoloff, 1947; Todd & Dewhurst, 1955). With the exception of Seeman (1979), these authors did not formulate guidelines that might be useful for the therapy of normal jealousy. There are also reports of the use of behavioral techniques to reduce agoraphobia of women married to abnormally jealous men (Hafner, 1979) and to reduce obsessive-compulsive behaviors of jealous clients (Cobb & Marks, 1979). Neither of these reported strategies is appropriate to jealousy as a problem focus.

Ard (1977) drew from his decades of experience as a marriage counselor to suggest that unchallenged assumptions that jealousy implies love need to be addressed in therapy. He also suggests a careful review and negotiation of expectations and boundaries regarding affectionate behavior with others. Ellis (1977) and Hibbard (1975) suggest use of rational-emotive therapy to challenge *irrational* beliefs of the jealous person, such as "it's awful" that my mate is attracted to another, "I can't stand" my mate's being involved with another, beliefs that the self is incompetent compared with a rival, that the mate is ungrateful, that the jealous person would be embarrassed if the partner left, or that the partner "makes" the person angry. Realistic deprivations and fears should be addressed in couples therapy through communication and negotiations. Hawkins (1976) also stressed the challenging of unspoken assumptions about the meaning of the rival relationship and exploring feelings of low self-worth related to psychological and economic dependency. In particular, love and jealousy should be separated.

Clanton and Smith (1977) suggest three levels of therapeutic intervention that may proceed simultaneously. At the personal level, the jealous person should . focus on feelings, behaviors, and assumptions. At the relationship level, the couple should discuss rules of their relationship, share positive feelings, and develop their communication and negotiation skills. Reassurance of the primacy of the bond is critical. At the situational level, both the nonjealous partner and the rival are responsible for minimizing the threat to the jealous person. Clanton and Smith suggest that these interventions can be geared toward the goals of marriage enrichment, remodeling of roles and rules of the marriage, or revolutionizing the marriage into an alternative to the monogamous standard.

Morgan (1975) notes that the jealous partner often tries to impose rules arbitrarily on the partner in order to lessen the chances that partner will get involved with another. Such rules include prohibitions against wearing appealing clothes or using makeup, enforced avoidance of potential rivals, and daily reports on activities. Partner may accept such prohibitions out of concern, fear, or frustration. Morgan thinks that acceptance of these rules can lead to a less satisfying relationship for the nonjealous partner and hence may increase the level of felt anger and frustration. Morgan first addresses therapy to whatever serious potential there may be for violence and then tries to build the low self-esteem of the jealous partner. Explicit attention is given to renegotiating the rules that have developed to contain the jealousy of one partner.

Seeman (1979) reports the results of psychodynamically oriented therapy of 5 jealous women. She focused on increased libido as a secondary gain of the expression of jealousy as evidenced by increased sexual desire, greater frequency of orgasm, and greater pleasure in orgasm. Mooney (1965) also reported increased libido in about a fifth of his pathologically jealous clinical sample. Seeman suggested that increased libido could be due to reaction formation, evolutionary mechanisms that prevent separation, homoerotic fascination with the rival, pleasure at being the center of attention, and a reawakening of childhood sadomasochistic fantasies. It is also possible that the arousal due to jealous anxiety may be relabeled as passion (Walster & Walster, 1977; White, Fishbein, & Rutstein, 1981). Seeman's findings suggest that the secondary gain of increased sexual pleasure may be a source of resistance to change. Her treatment included reducing stress by support and medication, allowing for separate ventilation by each partner, getting the jealous person involved in esteem-raising activities, helping the nonjealous partner understand and support the mate, and exploring the reality of the threatening situation in order to clear up distortions and facilitate negotiations.

Baute (1978) gives a somewhat flippant transactional analysis account of jealousy, emphasizing the hypnotic power of the principal drama between partner and rival to place the jealous partner in a powerless, reactive role. Baute's objectives are to diminish the infatuation of partner and rival, build ego strength and role awareness in the jealous person, and to bring some comic relief into a depressed situation. In a so-called love-is- war-anything-goes strategy, Baute suggests that the jealous person be encouraged to engage playfully in unpredictable behavior that out-dramatizes the other two actors. In particular, the victim and rescuer roles inherent in the jealous triangle should be played up. Examples of such playful enactment that emphasize the victim role would include leaving home suddenly, deliberately creating an uproar, shopping binges, and seeming to alternate between divorce counseling and loving approaches to the mate. By making the melodrama more overt, Baute thinks power to influence behavior would be weakened.

Teismann (1979, 1982) has used short-term strategic therapy in work with couples and triangles. Individual insight is played down in favor of symptom-oriented direct interventions by the therapist who is attempting to alter the dyadic/triadic system with behavioral prescriptions. For example, the therapist must use the therapeutic triangle to overcome the influence of the rival in the romantic triangle. Teisman suggests that one way to do this is for the therapist to phone the rival in the presence of the couple and urge the rival to come into therapy. Upon refusal (the expected response), the therapist requests the rival to continue to see the nonjealous partner so that the therapist will know how to treat the couple. Whether the rival refuses or not, this interaction begins to establish the therapeutic control of the triangle's dynamics. Teisman also reinterprets the jealous person's behavior in more benign ways than perceived by either partner in an attempt to show that the jealous behavior may be directed toward admirable goals accepted by both partners. For example, a jealous partner's suspicious prying could be reinterpreted as wanting to save the nonjealous partner the potential embarrassment of being found out. Feelings — such as anxiety over the relationship, anger, and sadness — that the nonjealous partner is having that are similar to those of the jealous partner are discussed in an attempt to build empathy.

There are two published accounts of short-term jealousy workshops. Blood & Blood (1977) conduct a 2-day workshop for couples, individuals, and triads. Most participants are in couples, about half of which are married. The purpose of the workshop is to get beyond the impasse of constricted alternatives as typically perceived by participants. Each partner starts by describing her or his feelings about the mate. Triangles are then assembled, usually involving the couple and a stand-in for the rival (or for the missing partner). Each member of the triangle then forms a static sculpture of the three actors, which is then put into movement and discussed for relevance to the actual situation. Actors then draw a picture of the jealousy of the jealous person in the triangle and take turns describing how parts of the picture represent parts of themselves.

After a break, each couple identifies a specific problem that is threatening the relationship and contributing to the jealousy. Behavioral resolutions of this problem are negotiated with the aid of the group and facilitators. Next each triangle performs a freeform dance in front of the group, followed by a triangle massage where two members rotate massage of the third. Finally the workshop is reviewed.

Blood and Blood report a variety of outcomes of this diverse program, though no structured assessment is used and no follow-up is reported. Reported outcomes include discovery that the relationship is too weak to withstand external involvements, more realistic norms concerning the handling of alternative attractions and relationships, the development of jealousy by the partner who originally presented as nonjealous, and the decision to seek further counseling. However, it seems to us that the use of the triangle and some of the nonverbal exercises has the potential to create fairly intense and explosive confrontations that may be inappropriate to a short-term workshop setting. Blood and Blood provide little information about the ways in which they monitor and incorporate emotional crises that conceivably develop in their format.

Constantine (1977) conducts 1- and 2-day workshops for couples and triangles. The avowed purpose is to promote resolutional behaviors such as joint problem-solving, exploration of feelings, negotiation around the jealousy situation, and discouragement of isolational, antagonistic, or intellectualizing coping behaviors. Constantine stresses the usefulness of jealousy in limiting the complexity of relationships by setting boundaries and in suggesting the need to look at self- and relationship dissatisfaction.

The workshop focuses first on specifying the actual behaviors, feelings, and interpersonal events of the jealousy situation. The real relationship between the nonjealous partner and the rival is examined with the aim of reducing unwarranted and threatening fantasies and to diagnose the possibility that the nonjealous partner may be playing rival and mate off against each other. The nonjealous person also discusses ways in which the rival relationship is beneficial (as well as harmful) to himself or herself. Individual and couple's boundaries are then explored and negotiated with a strong focus on the unique needs of each partner that would be most threatened if a rival relationship were to progress in specific ways. Nonverbal "boundary sculptures" supplement discussion, and other semistructured exercises are given in order to increase positive feelings about the relationship. Constantine routinely gives training in communication and negotiation skills as well. Unfortunately, Constantine has not reported on outcomes of this workshop format.

We have developed a 2-day workshop for couples only. We have five goals for this workshop: (1) education about the causes and consequences of jealousy, (2) training in communication and negotiation skills so the couple has a structure with which to communicate during and after the workshop, (3) helping the couple assess the utility of current coping strategies, (4) designing new coping strategies, and (5) promoting discussion of the possibility of seeking relationship counseling. Each person is interviewed separately to screen for pathological jealousy or psychological disorder that would contraindicate a workshop approach.

We first present evidence for the universality of jealousy and stress its usefulness in helping the couple develop a more satisfying relationship. We also stress the self-protective and relationship-protective intent of coping behaviors. This leads to exploring negative self-evaluations about being jealous in the first place, which we think is important because we and others have found a strong social desirability bias against being jealous (Lobsenz, 1977).

After this introduction, *each* partner is asked to list specific situations that would or do trigger their own or their partner's jealousy. This list is then presented to the partner. The partners then each describe how they feel or would feel in that situation listed. The partners are advised merely to listen to their mates and then to paraphrase back to them the eliciting situation and attendant feelings. These lists are then shared with the group and their commonalities discussed.

At this point in the workshop some of the common correlates of jealousy outlined earlier in this chapter are presented (White, 1981d) and illustrated by the specific situations listed by participants. Sex role and cultural influences are also presented, in part to take some of the focus off of the "flaws" of the jealous partner. We also point out some of the power implications that may be present in jealousy. We then introduce some basic communication-skills training (cf. Stuart, 1980), focusing on differentiating thoughts from feelings, making "I" statements, and negotiating behavioral contracts. Participants are then given structured individual homework to list their and their partner's most common behaviors when jealous and what effect these behaviors seem to have.

On the second day of the workshop, participants share their behavior-consequences lists and engage in a guided fantasy reenacting two or three of the least successful and most successful of their own coping behaviors. Couples then discuss with each other how they are affected by the coping behavior of the other, with an assessment made as to whether the coping behavior is useful for reducing the threat to self-esteem of the jealous person, reducing the threat to the relationship, or both. The group is then reassembled and new coping behaviors are designed with the help of the group and facilitators. These new solutions focus largely on (1) more explicit communication and negotiation around jealousy-provoking behaviors and coping behaviors, (2) examination of the positive benefits of the jealousy situation to help uncover how each partner may have played a (perhaps unwitting) role in maintaining jealousy, and (3) helping the couple identify how they could reduce the threat posed by real or potential rivals by improving the primary relationship or developing nonthreatening sources of satisfaction for needs that are not being met in the relationship.

The last step of the workshop is for couples to role play situations they had previously identified as actually or potentially threatening. New coping strategies are explicitly practiced with the aid of group participation and feedback. Finally, the workshop is evaluated and couples are asked to discuss how they might go about continuing to reduce the unwanted aspects of jealousy. We give a structured evaluation of the workshop and self-report scales assessing jealousy. Though our sample size is small, our early experience with this format is favorable enough to continue.

Summary. There are a number of themes common to treatments developed specifically for jealousy. These include (1) challenging irrational beliefs and assumptions, (2) training in communication skills, (3) explicitly negotiating over behaviors acceptable to both partners relevant to one partner's jealousy, (4) addressing the low self-esteem of the jealous partner, including negative self-evaluation about being jealous, (5) working at the personal, relationship, and contextual (e.g., triangle) levels, (6) developing new ways for the person/couple to interpret the meaning of the jealous feelings and behaviors, and (7) developing new coping behaviors to reduce the threats to self and relationship while potentially strengthening the relationship. No outcome research is available to judge the relative merits of the reported interventions.

THE FUTURE OF JEALOUSY

We see contemporary interest in jealousy as a reflection of changing sex roles, loosening norms regarding premarital and extramarital sexual and nonsexual relationships, the demise of the extended family, and geographical and job mobility that can place the couple in new interpersonal contexts. The tendency to perceive threat to self and relationship would be realistically greater given relative normlessness concerning relationship boundaries, greater availability of alternative relationships, greater ease in leaving relationships, and contemporary fascination with sex and physical attractiveness. Since Western and particularly American culture has placed a high premium on the ability of romantic love and romantic relationships to help the individual through the stresses of modern life, we think it especially true today that people will be sensitive to threats to their primary source of love, support, and economic stability. Our prediction is that jealousy will continue to be a major issue for premarital couples and will increase in importance for married people. We obviously think it is important for the relationship counselor or to understand the variety of causes and consequences of jealousy and for the field to continue to develop short-term treatments for normal jealousy.

REFERENCES

Ard, B. (1977). Avoiding destructive jealousy. In G. Clanton & L.G. Smith (Eds.), *Jealousy* (pp. 166-169). Englewood Cliffs, NJ: Prentice-Hall.

Ausubel, D.P., Sullivan, E.V., & Ives, S.W. (1980). *Theory and problems of child development.* New York: Grune & Stratton.

Baute, P. (1978). The love is war—anything goes ploy in triangles. *Psychotherapy Bulletin, 13,* 13-24.

Bernhard, J. (1971). Jealousy in marriage. *Medical Aspects of Human Sexuality, 5,* 200-215.

Blood, R., & Blood, M. (1977). Jealousy workshops. In G. Clanton & L.G. Smith (Eds.), *Jealousy* (pp. 199-208). Englewood Cliffs, NJ: Prentice-Hall.

Bohm, E. (1961). Jealousy. In A. Ellis & A. Abarbanel (Eds.), *The encyclopedia of sexual behavior* (Vol. 1). New York: Hawthorn.

Bringle, R.G., Roach, S., Andler, C., & Evenbeck, S. (1979). Measuring the intensity of jealous reactions. *Journal Supplement Abstract Service.* (Ms. No. 1832).

Bringle, R.G., & Williams, L.J. (1979). Parental-offspring similarity on jealousy and related personality dimensions. *Motivation and Emotion, 3,* 265-286.

Buunk, B. (1980, July). *Attributions and jealousy.* Paper presented at the meeting of the 22nd International Congress of Psychology, Leipzig.

Clanton, G., & Smith, L.G. (Eds.). (1977). *Jealousy.* Englewood Cliffs, NJ: Prentice-Hall.

Cobb, J.P., & Marks, I.M. (1979). Morbid jealousy featuring as obsessive-compulsive neurosis: Treatment by behavioral psychotherapy. *British Journal of Psychiatry, 134,* 301- 305.

Constantine, L.L. (1976). Jealousy: From theory to intervention. In D.H. Olson (Ed.), *Treating relationships.* Lake Mills, IA: Graphic.

Daly, M., Wilson, M., & Weghorst, S.J. (1982). Male sexual jealousy. *Ethology and Sociobiology, 3,* 11-27.

Darwin, C.R. (1888). *The descent of man and selection in relation to sex.* New York: Hurst.

Davis, K. (1936). Jealousy and sexual property. *Social Forces, 14,* 395-405.

Denfeld, D. (1974). Dropouts from swinging: The marriage counselor as informant. In J.R. Smith & L.G. Smith (Eds.), *Beyond monogamy.* Baltimore: Johns Hopkins University Press.

Docherty, J.P., & Ellis, J. (1976). A new concept and finding in morbid jealousy. *American Journal of Psychiatry, 133,* 679-683.

Ellis, A. (1977). Rational and irrational jealousy. In G. Constantine & L.G. Smith (Eds.), *Jealousy* (pp. 170-180). Englewood Cliffs, NJ: Prentice-Hall.

Erikson, E.H. (1963). *Childhood and society.* New York: Norton.

Fenichel, O. (1955). *The psychoanalytic theory of neurosis.* London: Routledge & Kegan Paul.

Francis, J.L. (1977). Toward the management of heterosexual jealousy. *Journal of Marriage and Family Counseling, 10,* 61-69.

Freud, S. (1955). Some neurotic mechanisms in jealousy, paranoia, and homosexuality. *Standard edition* (Vol. 18). London: Hogarth Press. (Original work published 1922).

Freud, S. (1959). On narcissism: An introduction. In E. Jones (Ed.), *Collected papers.* (Vol. IV, pp. 30-59). New York: Basic Books. (Original work published 1914).

Gross, A.E. (1978). The male role and heterosexual behavior. *Journal of Social Issues, 34,* 362-367.

Gottschalk, H. (1936). *Skinsygens problemer* [Problems of jealousy]. Copenhagen: Fremad.

Hafner, R.J. (1979). Agoraphobic women married to abnormally jealous men. *British Journal of Medical Psychology, 52,* 99- 104.

Hawkins, R.O. (1976). Jealousy: A solvable problem. *Journal of Sex Education and Research, Spring-Summer,* 39- 42.

Hibbard, R.W. (1975). A rational approach to treating jealousy. *Rational Living, 10,* 25-27.

Hupka, R.B. (1981). Cultural determinants of jealousy. *Alternative Lifestyles, 4,* 310-356.

Jones, E. (1937). Jealousy. In E. Jones (Ed.), *Papers on psychoanalysis.* London: Balliere, Tindall & Cox.

Kernberg, O.F. (1975). *Borderline conditions and pathological narcissism.* New York: Jason Aronson.

Kinsey, A.C., Pomeroy, W.B., Martin, C.E., & Gebhard, P.H. (1953). *Sexual behavior in the human female.* Philadelphia: Saunders.

Klein, M., & Riviere, J. (1964). *Love, hate, and reparation.* New York: Norton.

Kohut, H. (1971). *The analysis of the self.* New York: International Universities Press.

Lagache, D. (1949). From homosexuality to jealousy. *Psychoanalysis, 13,* 351-366.

Langfeldt, G. (1961). The erotic jealousy syndrome: A clinical study. *Acta Psychologica Neurologica Scandinavica, 36*(Suppl. 151). 7-68.

Lazarus, R.S., & Launier, R. (1978). Stress-related transactions between person and environment. In L.A. Pervin & M. Lewis (Eds.), *Perspectives in interactional psychology.* New York: Plenum.

Levy, D.M. (1940). Jealousy. *Journal of Pediatrics, 16,* 515-518.

Lobsenz, N.M. (1977). Taming the green-eyed monster. In G. Clanton & L.G. Smith (Eds.), *Jealousy* (pp. 26-35). Englewood Cliffs, NJ: Prentice-Hall.

Mead, M. (1931). Jealousy: Primitive and civilized. In S.D. Schmalhausen & V.F. Calverton (Eds.), *Woman's coming of age.* New York: Liveright.

Mooney, H.B. (1965). Pathological jealousy and psychochemotherapy. *British Journal of Psychiatry, 111,* 1023-1141.

Morgan, D.H. (1975). The psychotherapy of jealousy. *Psychotherapy and Psychosomatics, 25,* 43-47.

Mowat, R.R. (1966). *Morbid jealousy and murder.* London: Tavistock.

Peplau, L.A. (1978). Power in dating relationships. In J. Freedman (Ed.), *Woman: A feminist perspective.* Palo Alto: Mayfield.

Riviere, J. (1932). Jealousy as a mechanism of defense. *International Journal of Psychoanalysis, 13,* 414-424.

Schmideberg, M. (1953). Some aspects of jealousy and of feeling hurt. *Psychoanalytic Review, 40,* 1-16.

Seeman, M.V. (1979). Pathological jealousy. *Psychiatry, 42,* 351-361.

Seidenberg, R. (1967). Fidelity and jealousy: Socio-cultural considerations. *Psychoanalytic Review, 54,* 27-52.

Shettel-Neuber, J., Bryson, J.B., & Young, L.E. (1978). Physical attractiveness of the "other" person and jealousy. *Personality and Social Psychology Bulletin, 4,* 612-615.

Simmel, G. (1950). *The sociology of Georg Simmel* (Kurt Wolff, Ed.). New York: Free Press.

Sokoloff, B. (1947). *Jealousy: A psychiatric study.* New York: Howell, Soskin.

Spielman, P.M. (1971). Envy and jealousy. *Psychoanalytic Quarterly, 40,* 59-82.

Stuart, R.B. (1980). *Helping couples change: A social- learning approach to marital therapy.* New York: Guilford.

Sullivan, H.S. (1953). *The interpersonal theory of psychiatry.* New York: Norton.

Teismann, M.W. (1979). Jealousy: Systematic, problem-solving therapy with couples. *Family Process, 18,* 151-160.

Teismann, M.W. (1982). Persistent jealousy following the termination of an affair: A strategic approach. In A.S. Gurman (Ed.), *Questions and answers in the practice of family therapy* (Vol. 2). New York: Brunner/Mazel.

Teismann, M.W., & Mosher, D.L. (1978). Jealous conflict in dating couples. *Psychological Reports, 42,* 1211-1216.

Tellensbach, H. (1974). On the nature of jealousy. *Journal of Phenomenological Psychology, 4,* 461-468.

Thibaut, J.W., & Kelley, H.H. (1959). *The social psychology of groups.* New York: Wiley.

Todd, J., & Dewhurst, K. (1955). The Othello syndrome — A study in the psychopathology of sexual jealousy. *Journal of Nervous and Mental Disease, 122,* 367-374.

Turner, R.H. (1970). *Family interactions.* New York: Wiley.

Varni, C.A. (1974). An exploratory study of spouse swapping. In J.R. Smith & L.G. Smith (Eds.), *Beyond monogamy.* Baltimore: Johns Hopkins University Press.

Walster, E., & Walster, G. (1977). Sexual jealousy. In G. Clanton & L.G. Smith (Eds.), *Jealousy* (pp. 91-100). Englewood Cliffs, NJ: Prentice-Hall.

White, G.L. (1980a). Inducing jealousy: A power perspective. *Personality and Social Psychology Bulletin, 6,* 222-227.

White, G.L. (1980b). Some correlates of romantic jealousy. *Journal of Personality, 49,* 129-147.

White, G.L. (1981a). Jealousy and partner's perceived motives for attraction to rival. *Social Psychology Quarterly, 44,* 24-30.

White, G.L. (1981b). Relative involvement, inadequacy, and jealousy: A test of a causal model. *Alternative Lifestyles.*

White, G.L. (1981c). *Social comparison, motive attribution, alternatives assessment, and coping with jealousy.* Paper presented at the annual convention of the American Psychological Association, Los Angeles.

White, G.L. (1981d). A model of romantic jealousy. *Motivation and Emotion, 5,* 295-310.

White, G.L., Fishbein, S., & Rutstein, J. (1981). Passionate love and the misattribution of arousal. *Journal of Personality and Social Psychology, 41,* 56-62.

White, G.L. (1984). Comparison of four jealousy scales. *Journal of Research in Personality, 18,* 115-130.

White, G.L., & Devine, K. (in press). Romantic jealousy: Therapist's perceptions of causes, consequences, and treatments. *Family Relations.*

White, G.L., & Mullen, P.E. (in press). *Jealousy: A multidisciplinary and clinical approach.* New York: Guilford.

Whitehurst, R.N. (1971). Violence potential in extramarital sexual responses. *Journal of Marriage and the Family, 33,* 683-691.

Chapter 12

The Treatment of Women's Sexual Dysfunctions Arising from Sexual Assault

Judith E. Sprei and Christine A. Courtois

The sexual distress and dysfunction that results from sexual assault received repeated mention in the descriptive studies of rape that were conducted during the early 1970s (Burgess & Holmstrom, 1974; Hilberman, 1976; Notman & Nadelson, 1976) and in a few of the early studies of childhood sexual molestation and incest (Barry, 1965; Halleck, 1962, 1965; Kaufman, Peck, & Tagiuri, 1954; and Lukianowicz, 1972). More recent empirical and controlled investigations are offering substantiation that sexual maladjustment can result from various types of sexual assault, while treatment for assault-precipitated sexual dysfunction is only now beginning to be addressed (Baisden & Baisden, 1979; Becker, Abel, & Skinner, 1979; Burgess & Holmstrom, 1979b; Courtois, 1979; Feldman-Summers, Gordon, & Meagher, 1979; Meiselman, 1978; and Westerlund, 1983).

Becker et al. (1979) list reasons they believe that the impact of sexual assault on sexual functioning has not been investigated adequately in the past. These same reasons would also seem to account for the scarcity of treatment information.

> The majority of literature and information regarding the impact of sexual assault on a woman's sexual life is anecdotal rather than empirical. There are several reasons such as (a) rape treatment and research are new and minimal research has been conducted, (b) individuals providing needed services to assault victims have been busy providing these services and often do not have the time or means to investigate victims' sexual lives in detail, (c) in general, there is a timidity by people in our society to discuss sexuality, especially with victims traumatized by rape, and (d) rape counselors and clinicians are generally at a loss as to how to treat sexual problems they may uncover during an interview and usually avoid such inquiries. (p. 230)

To this list we would add that many assault victims/survivors are too ashamed and embarrassed to discuss the assault itself, much less its sexual aftereffects. Victims of incest and of other types of childhood molestation often repress the experience altogether and/or do not relate the past assault to their current level of functioning. Finally, much of the literature written during the 1970s described rape as an act of power with sexual behavior constituting the modus operandi; more recent writing cautions that the sexual aspects and aftereffects of rape cannot be overlooked (Becker et al., 1979; Burgess & Holmstrom, 1979b).

In this chapter, several topics will be covered in some detail. The different types of assault and the full range of consequences, including the sexual, will be discussed, because the therapist who treats sexual dysfunction needs a general understanding of the dynamics and consequences of assaults in order to develop a treatment plan. The focus will then shift to a consideration of the sexual sequelae of assault, particularly as they relate to specific types of sexual dysfunction. Special issues for therapists to consider in treating these dysfunctions will also be addressed.

The needs of victims of assault will receive primary attention, even though it is clear that others involved in the trauma, including the perpetrators and family members, may have treatment needs also. For example, investigators of offenders have found that many males who molest and abuse children were themselves sexually abused as children (Groth, 1982); therefore, some sexual offenses are the dysfunctional consequence of prior assault. The spouses and significant others of assault victims/survivors may find their own sex lives disrupted or made dysfunctional. They too become sexual casualties of the assault.

Although the term *dysfunction* will be used in this chapter, the functional value of certain sexual problems must be recognized and addressed in treatment. As will be discussed, certain sexual activities reminiscent of the abuse may result in flashbacks, hyperventilation, or panic attacks disrupting further sexual activity. Avoiding these activities allows the client to engage in other sexual behaviors and may thus be considered functional. The clients must be allowed to decide for themselves what is and what is not dysfunctional. A client may, for example, choose to be celibate and be satisfied with this life-style. Although celibacy is not considered the norm in our society except in certain occupations (e.g., priests, nuns), it is not dysfunctional if the client is comfortable with this choice.

Some sexual dysfunctions were functional during the abuse. The incest survivor's ability to dissociate and disconnect her body from her mind may have been her means of tolerating the abuse. In later sexual relationships, the use of this defense becomes maladaptive resulting in inorgasmia. Understanding the original functional value of the defense helps explain its resistance to traditional sex therapy treatment methods. This and similar defenses and/or survival mechanisms need to be approached gently with appreciation for the value they served in the past, and may in some cases continue to serve in the present.

DEFINITIONS, CHARACTERISTICS AND GENERAL EFFECTS

Three types of sexual assault, including rape, incest and childhood sexual molestation, will be defined with an emphasis on psychiatric/psychological definitions and criteria rather than legal ones. Legal definitions vary by jurisdiction and are much more restrictive than their psychological counterparts. The psychological definitions recognize that circumstances do not always meet legal or prosecutable criteria even though the victim is psychologically affected by the assault.

Rape

Rape has been defined as carnal knowledge of a person, other than one's spouse, by force and against that person's will. Recent reforms in the rape laws in many states have expanded the definition to include oral sex, anal or digital intercourse, and the placing of foreign objects in the vagina or anus. Some reforms have eliminated physical injury or an eyewitness as necessary evidence for lack of consent. Statutes now recognize both males and females as possible victims or perpetrators. In some jurisdictions, marital rape is defined as illegal.

The incidence of rape is increasing more quickly than that of any other violent crime in the United States, according to the Uniform Crime Reports, which are gathered from local police jurisdictions, FBI statistics, and the statistics compiled by rape-crisis centers around the country. Although the treatment accorded the rape victim has improved greatly during the last decade in most jurisdictions across the country, with increased reporting as a result, it is believed that rape remains a very underreported crime.

The demographics of rape show that women of all races, classes and age groups are victimized. The assailant may be a complete stranger, although approximately 50% of all victims know their assailant to some degree and half of all assaults occur in either the victim's or the assailant's home. Some victims are brutally injured, marred or killed, but the majority do not sustain severe physical injury. Coercion — including threats of violence to the victim or to other persons — is usually enough to force submission.

In order to work effectively with rape victims, it is crucial to understand that rape is primarily an act of violence acted out sexually. A popular misconception about rapists is that they are motivated only by sexual desires.

> Quite to the contrary, careful clinical study of offenders reveals that, in fact, rape serves primarily nonsexual needs. It is the sexual expression of power and anger. Forcible sexual assault is motivated more by retaliatory and compensatory motives then by sexual ones. Rape is a pseudosexual act, complex and multidetermined, but addressing issues of hostility (anger) and control (power) more than passion (sexuality). (Groth & Birnbaum, 1980,p. 18)

For the victim,

> Rape represents an act of violence and humiliation in which the victim experiences not only overwhelming fear for her very existence, but an equally overwhelming sense of powerlessness and helplessness which few other events in one's life can parallel...Rape becomes the ultimate violation of the self, short of homicide, with invasion of one's inner and most private space, as well as the loss of autonomy and control. (Hilberman, 1976, pp. ix-x)

Rape is often nonsexually motivated, but it is an assault upon the victim's sexuality and thus may affect profoundly this aspect of her life. The general effects of the assault will be covered next. The sexual effects will be discussed in detail later in this chapter.

Rape-response syndrome. Several authors have described response syndromes specific to rape (Burgess & Holmstrom, 1974; Frieberg & Bridwell, 1976; Sutherland & Scherl, 1970). Although these authors use different terms to define stages of the response syndrome, general agreement exists regarding symptoms and their development over time. Immediately after the assault, the first stage, that of acute disorganization, is experienced. The victim is often in shock and totally overwhelmed. She may have no emotional reactions other than feeling numb. During this stage, some victims are able to express themselves and to show their distress through words, tears and trembling, whereas others exhibit a controlled style with little outward evidence of distress.

After the initial shock reaction, victims often demonstrate reactions common to the second stage, outward adjustment or pseudoadjustment, in which denial and suppression of feelings are predominant coping mechanisms. The woman will attempt to get her life back to normal and may discount or deny reactions associated with the assault. It is typical however for the woman to make some changes in her life vis a vis her personal safety, such as not going out alone or at night, while outwardly continuing to deny reactions.

In the third stage, reorganization, the initial feelings are usually less overwhelming due to the passage of time. The loosening of denial and suppression will give way to feelings of depression, anxiety, fear, guilt, isolation, confusion, and shame. Changes in life-style such as social withdrawal, less effective functioning at work and at home, and changes in residence are common expressions of these emotions. Anger and fear often predominate. Anger may be difficult for the victim to express due to her fear or due to female socialization that conditions women to hide rather than to express directly their angry feelings. Such feelings may be displaced onto the self or onto others, or on unrelated events or be expressed in a passive-aggressive manner rather than directly. Extreme irritability is also a common emotion during this stage. The fear aroused by the assault may generalize beyond the rapist to other men and to sexual activity. Sexual impairment may range from minimal to total.

Long-term reorganization/recovery may show wide variations between individuals, from those who regain full functional capacity to those who remain totally impaired. Many victims fall somewhere in between, having some areas of functioning that are impaired while others are not. How well the individual resolves the aftereffects of the assault depends on many factors, such as: the nature of the assault itself (e.g., its degree of violence, the physical damage the victim may have incurred); the individual's prior mental health and the absence or presence of other unresolved crises in her life; the postassault response from families and friends and from the personnel of any involved agencies (e.g., police, medical, legal, judicial); whether the rapist is free, apprehended and on bail or incarcerated; whether the assault is brought to trial. Both the short- and long-term effects of a rape experience are currently under study by a number of researchers. The predominant findings are presented next.

Short- and long-term effects of rape. Most studies on the reactions of rape victims have followed the subjects for less than one year and have involved victims who reported to the police and received some crisis intervention services. These studies appear to indicate a decrease in symptoms after 1 month with substantial adjustment in 3 to 4 months. For example, Burgess and Holmstrom (1974) found that in a few weeks to months following the assault, half of the victims claimed to be almost recovered from the event. Kilpatrick, Veronen and Resick (1979) found that 46 victims rated themselves as highly distressed 6 to 10 days after the assault and again at 1 month assessment. By 3 and 6 months, this distress was diminished, leaving a residual of fear and anxiety that remained as a relatively long-term problem. Similarly, Atkeson, Calhoun, Resick and Ellis (1982) found that although victims of rape experienced significantly more depressive symptoms immediately following the assault, most of them returned to normal levels by 4 months postrape.

These studies of early adjustment of victims must be viewed with caution due to the now-recognized widespread use of denial and suppression to cope with the reaction to rape. Even studies employing interviewer-observers, rather than self-report, have at times overlooked the importance of denial and suppression as early coping mechanisms. This was demonstrated in a 6-year follow-up study by Burgess and Holmstrom (1979b) of 81 rape victims studied in their earlier counseling-research project. Although originally half of the victims claimed to be almost recovered or completely recovered in a few weeks to months, 6 years later only 37% of these same subjects felt they had recovered within months of the assault. Thirty-seven percent stated it took them years to recover and 26% still did not feel recovered 4 to 6 years postrape.

Many clinical observers (DeFrancis, 1969; Hilberman, 1976; Medea & Thompson, 1974; and Notman & Nadelson, 1976) report permanent psychological damage as a result of rape, and many victims feel they have chronic psychological scars (Katz & Mazur, 1979). In fact, it is not uncommon for rape victims to seek therapy many years after the assault in order to explore the impact the rape had on their lives. Recognizing that rape victims often do not return to a precrisis level of functioning, Williams and Holmes (1981) suggest that rape be viewed as a prolonged crisis. They write:

> Although victims do manage to cope and function, the impact of the rape experience persists in the form of residual crisis effects. By and large, victims do not simply reestablish their pre-crisis state of equilibrium. Rather, they experience fundamental changes, affectively and behaviorally. In general, they seem to experience both fear and anxiety to the extent that they become more defensive and self-protective. As a result, their behavior is changed in substantial and specific ways; they restrict their mobility, their interaction with men is hampered by distrust and generalized discomfort; they are comparatively apathetic and withdrawn from a variety of routine activities; and they suffer from some assault-related health concerns. One victim may have unknowingly articulated the essence of the residual impact for us when she said, very matter of factly, "I will never be the same because the worst thing about rape is that you learn how vulnerable you are." (p. 109)

Still other rape victims feel the assault precipitated a crisis that in turn led to self-exploration which resulted in growth and higher self-esteem. The experience of having one's life disrupted may lead to a process of life evaluation, leading to new plans for the future and a clearer picture of life goals. The statement, "If I can survive this, I can survive anything" is not uncommon and typifies the new strength and confidence eventually experienced by some rape victims.

Incest

Densen-Gerber and Benward (1975) provide a most comprehensive definition of incest:

> It [incest] refers to sexual contact with a person who would be considered an ineligible partner because of his blood and/or social ties (i.e., kin) to the subject and her family. The term encompasses, then, several categories of partners, including father, step-father, grandfather, uncles, siblings, cousins, in- laws, and what we call "quasi-family." This last category includes parental and family friends (e.g., mother's sexual partner). Our feeling is that the incest taboo applies in weakened form to all these categories in that the "partner" represents someone from whom the female child should rightfully expect warmth or protection and sexual distance. Sexual behavior recorded as ...incest ranged from intercourse or seduction; molestation; primarily fondling of breasts and genitals; and exposure. We included other sexual behaviors as intercourse; namely, all penetration, anal, oral, and vaginal, both passive and active. Cunnilingus and fellatio were not uncommon activities, nor was sodomy. (p. 326)

Even though the causes and development of incest are too complex and varied to discuss in detail in this paper, it will be useful to highlight the most salient characteristics of incest, including prevalence, onset, context, duration, frequency and progression of sexual activity. Incest was formerly believed to be rare (Weinberg in 1955 estimated 1 case per million population) but is now estimated to occur frequently. In the most recent survey (Russell, 1983), consisting of a random sample of 930 adult women, 14% had experienced intrafamilial sexual abuse before the age of 18, 12% before the age of 14. Even this estimate may be conservative. As Russell states: "[Even] these figures err on the side of underestimation, even presuming that all respondents were willing to disclose their experiences of intrafamilial sexual abuse; this is undoubtedly a poor presumption" (p. 137).

Unlike rape, the onset of incest is gradual, usually beginning when the child is prepubertal. The most common sexual pattern begins with hugging, exhibitionism, fondling, masturbation, and possibly oral contact, progressing to intercourse as the child matures (although intercourse with a young child is not unusual). The activity may occur within a loving although misdirected relationship, such as a father who turns toward his favorite child for love, affection and ego enhancement, or it may be part of a generally cold or abusive relationship. For many children, it may fall somewhere between these two extremes, occurring with someone they are not particularly close to or with whom they are not frequently in contact (e.g., relatives who visit only occasionally). For still others, it signifies an abrupt change in a relationship that may have been close or distant. With respect to duration, the average case of incest occurs over a time period ranging from several months to several years. The frequency of the contact varies by case, ranging from a one-time contact to several times daily. Often, the contact will cease only when the child breaks the secrecy surrounding it or takes steps to end the behavior (e.g., saying no, disclosing to someone, leaving home, running away, fighting back, or getting married). Male perpetrators and female victims constitute, by far, the most prevalent pattern.

Incest is a form of sexual assault with effects compounded by its occurrence within the family, with related or quasi-related individuals. This compounded effect is seen most directly when the behavior occurs with a parent in the nuclear family, where a pattern of secrecy, rivalry, power and intense guilt is often established. Incestuous relationships with siblings and with relatives outside the nuclear family, such as grandparents, aunts, uncles, or cousins, are also compounded by kinship ties. The taboo does not extend as directly to these individuals, but intense emotions of guilt, shame and fear may be stirred up by these relationships. Even though the family atmosphere in such cases is sometimes distant and hostile, the effects of incest are frequently complicated by its occurrence in the context of or under the guise of love and affection. Thus, the betrayal by sexual misuse is often embedded within the broader context of a caring relationship. The victim may be left with both tender and negative feelings toward the perpetrator, and almost always with guilt and self-doubt.

When incest is disclosed within the family, its members may experience divided loyalty and attempt to suppress the information. The perpetrator may be protected or shielded as the victim is left to fend for herself, a common occurrence in father-daughter or sibling incest, and in grandfather-daughter cases as well. The uninvolved family members, because of divided loyalties, may be unwilling or unable to confront the perpetrator effectively and defend the child. A second-level betrayal occurs when the child is not believed and is made to feel as though she caused the situation. Butler (1979) has noted that the child also may come to disbelieve or suppress her own experience and feelings, thereby creating a third level of betrayal, that of the self.

Sexual Molestation/Victimization of Children

This type of sexual abuse includes incest and rape activities but is broader in context, encompassing all forms of pedophilic activity by related and nonrelated individuals. The National Center on Child Abuse and Neglect (1978) defines sexual abuse of children as:

> ...a wide range of behavior from fondling and exhibitionism to forcible rape and commercial exploitation for purposes of prostitution or the production of pornographic material. It takes many forms and involves varying degrees of violence and emotional traumatization. (p. 1)

Several other types of molestation, notably child-sex rings, child prostitution, and child pornography, are only now being investigated to determine their etiology, circumstances and effects.

The popular image of child sexual abuse is that the perpetrator is a "pervert," a "dirty old man," or a stranger who materializes to molest the child and then disappears. Research studies have exploded this view. In a 1968 study conducted by the American Humane Association of 9,000 cases of sex crimes against children, 75% were found to be perpetrated by members of the victim's household, relatives, neighbors, or acquaintances of the victim (DeFrancis, 1969). Finklehor (1979) found strangers involved in only 24% of the cases of victimized females and in 30% of the victimized males. Similar to rape and incest, the majority of perpetrators are male. Molestation patterns are often similar to those found in incest: the development of a relationship with the child and use of the child's trust or of the power of the adult over the child to engage the child; progressive sexual activity over an extended time period, beginning with less-threatening behavior that may be perceived by the child as affection; and an injunction to secrecy, which the perpetrator may use to coerce the child as the behavior progresses (e.g., the child is told that he or she will not be believed, or will be blamed for the behavior or for not reporting it sooner). Force or violence may be used when the child is older or in cases of child rape.

General effect of incest and childhood molestation. Two opposing traditions exist in the literature concerning the effect of incest and, to a lesser degree, molestation. Childhood incest and molestation tend to be viewed as non-traumatic on the one hand (Henderson, 1975; Weiner, 1962) or as highly traumatic on the other. Several reasons may account for these disparate conclusions, including:

1. The many varieties of childhood assault and molestation, ranging from enmeshed nuclear-family involvement to a happenstance involvement with strangers. Duration, frequency, sexual behavior and relationship may vary dramatically from case to case.

2. The very nature of childhood sexual assault is surrounded with taboo, and results in reactions of disgust, horror, or outrage (particularly father-daughter incest and child rape). A child who seeks help is often faced with either disbelief, denial, and no response, or with extreme overreaction; each of these may greatly intensify the child's response.

3. For many children, the sexual involvement may have had pleasurable aspects, especially if the child was young at onset, the adult was gentle, and/or the behavior fulfilled the child's need for affection. In such cases, some children may have a stronger reaction to the secrecy and to the adults' reactions to disclosure than they have to the behavior itself.

4. The reactions of children may be masked or may not appear to be negative. Children often exhibit their response in behavior related to their age/stage of development. They may regress to younger behavior during a crisis to exhibit their distress. Examples are bed-wetting that is post-toilet-training in young children or refusal to engage with peers by formerly well- adjusted individuals of all ages. Adults (including professionals) have often ignored or misinterpreted these signs or used them to prove the child's complicity (e.g., the child who, because of adult stimulation, exhibits sexually provocative behavior that is beyond what the child would be expected to know at that age and then is said to cause sexual molestation).

5. Children who receive no response or assistance often internalize their feelings and cope as best they can. Adults seen in therapy with unacknowledged, untreated history of childhood molestation, whether intra- or extrafamilial, present many and varied symptoms. These may be the direct result of the childhood experience or may be indirect in that they contributed to the development of problems that later become presenting concerns (e.g., the woman who presents with a marital crisis that in part developed from her distrust of men). The remainder of this section will be devoted to aftereffects noted in adults. The reader is referred to Burgess, Groth, Holmstrom and Sgroi (1978) for a comprehensive discussion of child and adolescent victims.

The short- and long-term effects of incest/molestation are manifest in many ways. Courtois (1979) clustered these effects into eight life-sphere categories:

(1) social (including vocational); (2) psychological/emotional; (3) physical; (4) sexual; (5) family; (6) sense of self; (7) relation to men; (8) relation to women, each short- and long-term. These categories also organize the presenting concerns brought to therapy, described by Courtois and Watts (1982) as concerns about self and relations to others. They write:

Concerns pertaining to self seemed to fit into four main areas: identity, self-esteem, physical functioning, and sexual functioning. Concerning identity and self-esteem, many of these women have a very negative self-image, have a sense of being different and distant from "ordinary" people, have a sense of being powerful in a malignant way, express self-hatred, and are depressed and anxious. They may also be self-destructive and suicidal. Physical complaints include feelings of dissociation, migraine headaches, severe backaches, gastrointestinal and genitorurinary problems, inability to concentrate, lethargy, anxiety, phobic behavior and substance abuse. Sexual identity conflicts and impairment in sexual functioning are also presenting complaints.

Concerns pertaining to relationships also have four main areas of manifestation; relationships in general, marital relations, and parental relations with both their own parents or their in-laws and their children. Relationships, in general, are often described as empty, superficial, conflictual, or sexualized. The inability to trust is pronounced. Good or pleasurable relationships often increase guilt and shame because they are viewed as undeserved or impossible.

Conflict is most apparent in marriage or other intimate relationships with men. Many of these women have very negative feelings toward men but at the same time overvalue men and search for a protector. Paradoxically yet predictably, these women very often end up with men who, like themselves, have been abused. These men are often abusive to or neglectful of them so this type of relationship serves to recapitulate early experience and reinforce a negative sense of self-worth.

Conflicted relations often exist with parents and in-laws. Many of these women (most especially those who had been involved with fathers or stepfathers) have severely strained relations with parents marked by feelings of mistrust, fear, ambivalence, hatred, betrayal, and an inability to relate in a positive way or to receive much nurturance or support from the parents.

Individuals who experienced poor relationships with their own parents or within their own families often adapt this mode of relating to in-laws and to their own children. Many express fear of their male children and fear for their female children and feel they cannot be good mothers. (p. 276)

Based on available literature, it is safe to conclude that the most frequent response to being abused in childhood is negative, although effects vary by individual and circumstance, and intrafamily abuse may intensify and confound reactions to being victimized. Some victims do indeed suffer long-term devastation and trauma affecting many areas of their lives, whereas others have few, if any, negative aftereffects. It appears that severity of aftereffects cannot be ascribed definitively to certain aspects of the experience, as has been hypothesized by researchers. For example, in the past, longer duration, use of force, and closer degree of relationship were believed to determine more severe aftereffects, but at this time research evidence remains inconclusive.

The long- and short-term reactions associated with rape and childhood sexual molestation/incest may be classified as traumatic neurosis (Gelinas, 1983) or as post-traumatic stress disorder (American Psychiatric Association, 1980) with the sexual assault or its memory being the stressor. The disorder is defined as acute when the onset of symptoms occurs within 6 months of the trauma and lasts no longer than 6 months; as chronic if the duration of symptoms is of 6 months or more; and as delayed if the onset of symptoms occurs at least 6 months after the trauma. Common reactions to any type of sexual assault, such as intrusive thoughts and nightmares, recurrent dreams of the event, numbing of responsiveness or reduced involvement with the external world, startle responses, guilt, and impaired concentration, all conform to the diagnostic criteria of post-traumatic stress disorder.

Sexual Effects

Given that some of the predominant feelings resulting from rape and incest/molestation (i.e., anxiety, guilt, fear, depression, mistrust, helplessness, ambivalence and anger) are the same emotions frequently related to sexual dysfunctions in general, and that the locus of the assault is sexual, it follows that sexual dysfunction may be a consequence of sexual victimization. Many recent investigations have documented sexual disruptions and dysfunctions postassault. The postassault problems have been found for both lesbians and heterosexual women although the literature focuses almost exclusively on heterosexual women.

The percentage of rape victims reporting some type of sexual difficulty ranged from a low of 14% reported by Becker et al. (1979) to a high of 89.5% reported by Williams and Miller (1979). Across studies the average is about 50%. Because longitudinal studies of rape victims are scarce, the crisis or short-term nature of sexual problems has been emphasized. In the studies in which follow-up was conducted several years after initial data collection (Burgess & Holmstrom, 1979a, 1979b; Nadelson, Notman, Zackson & Gornick, no date), long-term effects have been found. Symptoms may continue over time or recur, or new symptoms may emerge (Nadelson, 1982).

Sexual problems as a long-term consequence of intra- and extra- family molestation were mentioned in several of the studies published from the 1930s to the 1960s. More often, these sexual aftereffects received no mention because child and adolescent subjects were not followed into adulthood, the time at which sexual symptoms are most likely to develop. Two main types of sexual problems received repeated mention as possible consequences: promiscuous sexual behavior at one extreme or the total avoidance of sex at the other. More recent empirical studies are documenting these as well as a host of other problems. These findings may be accounted for because more investigations of long-term effects (including sexual ones) have been undertaken and more is now known about female sexual functioning in general and sexual dysfunction in particular. In recent studies, the percentage of sexual problems arising from incest/molestation ranged from 24% when the sexual activity was with a friend of the family (Baisden & Baisden, 1979) to 87% in intrafamily activity (Meiselman, 1978).

The specific type, severity, and duration of the dysfunction will vary depending upon the individual's life history, personality, mental health and coping style, characteristics of the assault, the presence or absence of a usual sexual partner, and the reactions of the partner, significant others and societal caregivers such as social service, police, hospital and legal personnel. It is important to note that sexual problems are not a consequence for all individuals who are raped or molested. Sexual consequences, like psychological effects, vary a great deal. Sexual functioning may not be a client's first treatment priority nor may it be a greater issue than other postassault problems (Westerlund, 1983). The findings of several research studies suggest that childhood molestation experience, particularly incest, is more indicative of later sexual dysfunction than is rape in adulthood (Herman, 1981; Meiselman, 1978). Becker, Abel, Skinner and Treacy (1982) found no statistical difference in the mean number of sexual problems between rape and incest victims but did find differences in the types of problems experienced by each. These will be discussed in more detail in the next section.

SEXUAL PROBLEMS AND TREATMENT CONSIDERATIONS

Victims of sexual assault bring special issues and problems into counseling due to the victimization and its sexual focus. These issues will be discussed in the first part of this section as they relate to major aspects of therapy in general and to sex therapy in particular. The second part of the section will address assessment issues, a detailed examination of the sexual problems most common to sexual assault victims, their likely etiology or relation to the assault/abuse situation, and recommendations for treatment.

Therapist's Attitudes, Values, and Therapeutic Stance

The attitudes, values and therapeutic stance of the therapist are of course of vital importance in successful treatment. The therapist needs to be aware of the negative societal attitudes, especially victim-blaming, associated with sexual assault. Even contemporary therapists may be influenced by the Freudian tradition, which viewed sexual molestation as for the most part either fantasy or wish fulfillment. It is helpful for the therapist to focus on the nonconsensual aspects of the behavior and to view the client as a victim. Because of societal stereotypes, many assaulted or abused individuals do not see themselves as victims (i.e., as acted upon against their will or without informed consent) but believe rather that they somehow caused the situation. Maintaining the assault and victimization in focus may be difficult, because many clients are all too ready to "forget" or shelve the experience due to its painfulness, and thus may resist the therapist's best efforts to address it. The therapist may need to return to the topic and to explain as concretely as possible how the assault experience may be related to current functioning.

The therapist also must guard against overprotecting or overidentifying with the victim. This may lead to: treating the client as overly "special" or particularly fragile; encouraging a helpless or "victimly" style on the part of the client; treating the sexual assault/abuse as the client's only issue or to the exclusion of other concerns; and treating the client as *so* special or difficult that the therapist is inadequate to assist or is overly quick to refer. Therapists may also find themselves enraged at the client's experience. It is often helpful for a client to experience that someone is angry about what happened; however, therapists must be cautious about overexpressing these feelings and should vent or work them through away from the client. The client can feel validated and reassured by some expression of anger by the therapist, but it is not appropriate for therapists to use the session to work through their own unresolved feelings.

The therapist's gender may be a significant factor for both the therapist and the client. Female therapists may overidentify with the client, males may not be able to identify enough to understand the client fully or may even, in some cases, identify with the perpetrator. Clients may be very fearful of males or be enraged at the powerlessness of females and transfer these and other gender-related feelings to the therapist. Clients may also attempt to sexualize the therapy relationship. Incest victims in particular may confuse sex and affection, or they may attempt to engage in sexual contact due to feelings of inadequacy and as a means of self-abuse. Whereas sexual contact between client and therapist is detrimental and unethical in any case, it is particularly harmful to sexual-molestation victims for whom it recreates aspects of the original betrayal.

Dynamics of Abuse as Related to the Therapy Relationship and Process

Many of the dynamics of abuse/assault may be brought into the therapy relationship. Most victims have had their trust in others violated. The victim of rape may have concluded that men are untrustworthy, and the incest victim may have decided that no one can be trustworthy because even family members were not. The feelings associated with being betrayed may be transferred to the therapist, who will then find the establishment of a therapeutic alliance to be slow and difficult work. Of course, this process is particularly important work in furthering recovery from a victimization experience, and it is often crucial to the success of therapy. At times, the therapist may be sorely tried by a client who engages in behavior designed to prove the therapist's untrustworthiness, or one who is slow to open up. It may be difficult for the therapist to maintain the necessary firmness, consistency, patience, and nonpunitive attitude.

A second, related issue is that of low self-esteem resulting from abuse. Some clients test their therapists in order to prove their own unlovability and thus confirm their sense of "badness," "guilt," or "nothingness." Self-hatred and disgust may result in many forms of self-abusive behavior, such as self-mutilation, drug and alcohol abuse, suicide attempts, or prostitution. These are best viewed as symptoms of the underlying pain. It often takes a considerable amount of time and much discussion and testing before the client shows improvement in self-esteem. The therapist can reflect back to the client the self-denying, self-defeating or self- destructive aspects of the behavior and can help her consider how and why she is hurting herself. Many of these clients do not realize the intensity of their feelings of self-blame or self- hatred — or the degree to which they have made themselves the only guilty party. Therapist statements explaining the client's behavior, and therapist behavior such as concern, respect and consistency despite the client's behavior, will often assist a client in examining feelings about herself. She may be surprised at how cruel she is to herself or by how hard it is to accept regard and warmth from others. These insights are often a first step in the change process.

The issue of shame is also important. Most victims feel disgraced sexually and incorporate feelings of guilt or badness about themselves, their sexuality, and sexual behavior. These feelings may be compounded by cultural and societal taboos and attitudes. Many women have hidden the assault for years for fear of the reactions of others. The secret is usually kept at the cost of great personal anguish.

Concerns about responsibility for or complicity in the assault are involved in these self-esteem and shame issues and must be addressed directly. The victim needs to place major responsibility where it belongs, on the offender, and to explore what role, if any, she played in the victimization or in its maintenance. Rape victims often believe the societal notion that they caused or deserved the assault. Incest victims frequently exhibit a great deal of confusion about their role. They wonder *what about themselves* made the perpetrator do what he did and/or why no one believed them when they tried to tell or to stop the behavior. Incest victims may also be caught by their ambivalent feelings when they consider the issue of responsibility; they often have love as well as hate feelings for the perpetrator and other family members. The habit of protecting or taking care of the family members may be hard to break. The ambivalent feelings may make it difficult for the victim to place responsibility on the perpetrator. She may suppress her feelings of anger and hatred, fearing that if she experiences or expresses them she will be ostracized by the family or will herself want to reject them. Additionally, the victim may fear that expression of her anger will lead her to behave like the perpetrator and to abuse others. It may seem safer to internalize the anger or to take it out on herself.

Assault and abuse, by definition, imply lack of consent (at a minimum, a lack of informed consent on the part of a minor child). As a result, the issues of control and personal power are very important and may be manifested in a variety of ways. For example, both rape and incest victims may have concluded they had no control over the situation, with resultant feelings of powerlessness and passivity. On the other hand, the incest victim may have learned enormous self-control in order to survive her ordeal and her lack of control of it. She may have gone so far as to train herself not to feel (i.e., deny, dissociate) physical sensations or emotions during the molestation. One of our clients described her dissociation as divorcing her head from her body. This self-control and lack of emotional or physical response, coupled with lack of trust in others, may later extend to many life arenas, producing an individual who is detached and numb. This "survival skill" may remain long after it is needed, interfering in many pleasurable activities including sex. Because rape is usually a one-time occurrence, its victim does not develop this same control mechanism to lessen the impact; rather rape victims acutely feel the sudden nature of its occurrence, the violation, and the lack of consent. Postassault contact with police, medical, and judicial authorities, and such factors as whether the rapist is caught, whether he is out on bail, or whether he knows her identity and address, may accentuate feelings of being out of control. As mentioned earlier, many rape victims make major changes in their lives, such as moving, changing jobs, or changing schedules, in an attempt to regain stability and control. Because of the sexual nature of the assault, they also may have major changes in their attitude toward sexual activity. Therapy can assist the woman to develop self-control that is not overly rigid or dissociative on one hand or overly passive or helpless on the other.

One natural consequence of victimization is anger, yet many female victims appear devoid of this emotion. Women are taught from childhood that positive, caretaking emotions are feminine, but that negative, hostile emotions are not. Women may imagine their anger as uncontrollable and violent if it is acknowledged. Moreover, many victimized females feel they have no right to anger. Anger is often repressed, and is expressed in disguised, alternative forms, such as passive-aggressive behavior, self-blame, depression, self-contempt, anxiety, or somatic complaints. It may subvert sexual activity and thus may be implicated in many forms of sexual dysfunction. Therapy often involves expression of the repressed anger and rage as well as the development of techniques to manage emotions.

Feelings of loss and grief may also ensue from a victimization experience. The rape victim may have lost her sense of innocence, her trust in others, and her sense of invulnerability. In fact, she may think of her life in terms of prerape and postrape. Incest/molestation victims may have similar feelings, often expressed as "I never had a chance to know the real me" or "The incest experience made me different from what I might have been." This self-loss may be accompanied by feelings of loss involving other family members (e.g., "I never knew what it was like to have a real father" or "My mother never took steps to protect me", or "I've completely cut off my family to get away from their crazy system. It protects me but I no longer have a family. It hurts"). Therapy can assist the grieving process by freeing the emotions engendered by the loss. Defenses, including denial, repression, intellectualization, rationalization, minimization, projection, splitting, and dissociation, also influence the therapy process. Often these defenses were used by the woman to cope with the pain or get through the experience. Myers (no date/1980) has the following to say about the utility of detachment or splitting defenses to cope with a paternal incest experience:

> Victims of incest learn this detachment early in their lives. Some have learned to detach their minds from their bodies, pretend that all fathers are sexual with their daughters, pretend that it is a dream, pretend that it really isn't abuse, pretend that it is happening to someone else...Other victims have learned to pinch themselves during the abuse and put all their energy into concentrating on self-abuse, rather than sexual abuse. Then there are those who pretend they are sleeping so they can block out what is happening. It is important to understand that this detachment was probably what helped them to survive the experience. (p. 5)

The therapist will hear victims say "I just want to forget the whole thing" or "It was no big deal" or "It's too painful/shameful/scary to talk about." We have a number of clients who openly tell us "the wall just went up," "I just blanked out" or "I know I'm here but I'm not experiencing anything" when attempts are made to explore the assault and its attendant emotions. An exploration of the defense and what it is defending against is useful. Most victims fear not only the pain of reexperiencing the situation and its emotions but also the judgment of the therapist as well. It can be helpful to explain to the client that her defensive style is how she took care of herself and got herself through a bad situation. We encourage clients to give themselves credit for their self- sustaining behavior, and to explore the possibility that such strong defenses are no longer needed and may, in fact, be maladaptive when used extensively. Because of the degree of anxiety involved, these defenses need to be dismantled slowly. The client may need a great deal of support and reassurance when attempting to examine her defenses and will need to have established a trusting relationship with the therapist before doing so.

Obviously, all of these defenses, in conjunction with the dynamics of abuse/assault, can play a part in the development and maintenance of sexual dysfunction. Therapy involves uncovering and analyzing these dynamics and defenses and aiding the client to modify or dismantle the latter as appropriate. Through therapy, many incest clients learn skills that were not taught in the family. The appropriate expression of emotion (rather than its denial), relationship skills, parenting skills, and sexuality skills, may all be involved in the therapy. Simply uncovering and analyzing, although crucial functions, may not be enough to fully assist the client in recovery. Similar to conditions found in alcoholic or battering families, real skill deficits or faulty skill development may have occurred in the family. The growth and development in these areas incorporate learning from the uncovering aspects of the therapy but may also require direct instruction and behavioral training from the therapist.

Assessment and Therapy Approaches

Assessment. Newcomb and Bentler, in Chapter 6 of this volume, provide comprehensive overview of the assessment of sexual dysfunction. They emphasize a thorough appraisal of several life areas in order to determine the etiology of sexual dysfunction. Some aspects of these areas are especially problematic for sexually abused women and should be examined in detail. Under *biologic aspects,* particular attention should be paid to physical damage, chronic pain or dysfunction, drug and alcohol use and the possiblity of a biologic base for emotional disturbance. *Psychological factors* have been discussed in detail. Of particular importance is the assessment of the use of denial or repression as a means of defending against the trauma of the early or current assault/abuse experience. *Dyadic factors,* although not focused on in this chapter, may be very important because the dynamics of the abuse may be reflected in the dyad. Working with a partner or spouse may be helpful in identifying and overcoming problems in the treatment. *Remote and immediate environmental conditions and circumstances,* such as past and present sexual attitudes, behavior and education within the family, the larger cultural group, and society at large, may be important influences as we have sought to explain above. These also should be part of a comprehensive assessment.

The therapist should ensure that assessment methods employed include questions about intra- and extra-family contact and sexual assault. The more recent interview and questionnaire forms usually include such items. Older ones typically do not. Many victims of sexual abuse/assault will not disclose their experience spontaneously, but may do so if asked directly. It is important to note, however, that even with explicit questioning, the individual may not disclose the experience either because it has been repressed and is not consciously available to her or because it is too emotionally laden to disclose. Nadelson (1982) writes that the therapist must be vigilant and open to the possiblity that current dysfunction/s are related to antecedent events of which even the client is unaware. Even after the formal history taking, the therapist must continue to sift data and be open to the possibility of unacknowledged or repressed assault as etiological. Nadelson further notes that a request for sex therapy may be a way for a client to avoid painful discussion or confrontation about sexual assault.

She writes: "Sex therapy alone is unsuccessful unless underlying concerns about sexual trauma are confronted" (p. 64).

Newcomb and Bentler mention the special importance of therapist style of presentation and comfort in discussing intimate and sexual issues. As discussed, therapist attitudes and communication styles are crucial when working with sexual assault victims. The therapist must ask about sexual assault issues in a calm, straightforward and matter-of-fact way and must be prepared to return to the topic in those cases where it is suspected but not disclosed. Gelinas (1983) states that: "Inquiry by the therapist implies permission to talk of such things and signals the therapist's ability to tolerate the anxiety such discussion might generate" (p. 326). We have noted that an overly aloof, analytic or uninvolved stance on the part of the therapist can serve to reinforce feelings of fear, shame and embarrassment. Far preferable is a therapeutic stance that communicates empathy along with a willingness to speculate about and verbalize that which the client cannot.

Once a client has been found suitable for sex therapy, a medical evaluation and consultation is needed prior to treatment. This may prove particularly difficult for women who have had a sexual assault experience. A sensitive physician is important for individuals suffering from any sexual dysfunction, and especially important for those who have been sexually traumatized. Gynecologists in particular need to be sensitive to the fact that they are examining the locus of an assault, and they should exhibit patience and tact. The therapist would do well to anticipate reactions ranging from mild fear to a mistrust of doctors that borders on paranoia. Acute fear and mistrust often arise from past negative experience with medical personnel. One example is the rape victim whose doctor questioned her complicity during the examination and whose physical examination was insensitive and painful. Another is the incest victim whose family doctor ignored obvious physical signs and symptoms of the abuse or who never correlated them with abuse.

The therapist and physician will usually need to prepare and educate the client and may need to be active in working with her. For example, it may be important for the client to learn how the examination will occur, what instruments will be used, what she will likely feel. One or two preliminary meetings with the physician to gain familiarity and to ask questions may be helpful. Therapist support may be crucial; at times, it may be useful for the therapist to be present physically during the examination. The client should be given as much control as possible and should be encouraged to ask questions and to be an active participant rather than a passive, acted-upon spectator. Successful completion of a medical/gynecological examination may offer relief and, in itself, be a therapeutic experience.

Therapy approaches. A modified version of Annon's PLISSIT model (1977) is a useful conceptualization for the treatment of sexual dysfunction in sexually victimized individuals. Annon arranges sexual disorders in a hierarchy ranging from simple to complex. Treatment is geared to the nature and etiology of the dysfunction, with each level of therapy building upon the level that precedes it.

Annon's first treatment step (P) is to give the client *permission* to do or not to do something as a means of alleviating distress. For example, for sexual assault victims, permission to refuse certain forms of sexual activity which are aversive may be therapeutic. On the other hand, permission to try a certain activity may also be helpful.

Annon's second treatment step (LI) is a to give *limited information* to the client. Lack of information about sexual physiology and about normal sexuality and functioning may contribute to sexual disorders. For victims of any type of sexual assault, education about previously discussed issues such as victimization, and locus of responsibility for (and societal myths about) assault may serve to relieve anxiety or conflicted feelings that contribute to disorders. Incest victims in particular may have distorted information and misinformation regarding sexual issues. For example, a victim's father may have explained or rationalized the abuse by calling it sex education. The secrecy surrounding the activity and resultant feelings about the self may prevent a woman from gaining information. In many incest families (as in many nonincest families) sex education and discussions of sexuality are nonexistent. The children often receive conflicted messages about sex as being bad and something not to be discussed or involved in—even though they are being sexually abused within the family. Sex education, including specific information about sexual assault, may provide relief and reassurance as well as knowledge.

The third step of the PLISSIT model (SS) is *specific suggestions* for behavioral exercises or strategies. With permission, information and participation in suggested exercises, sexual dysfunction may abate rapidly. The assignment of exercises such as masturbation training or giving or receiving sexual pleasuring may enable the sexual assault victim to attempt new behavior or to achieve pleasure in ways that were previously unavailable or unsatisfying.

Annon's fourth step (IT) is *intensive therapy* for individuals who need to go beyond the sexual disorder to explore etiological factors that contributed to its development. Many sexual assault victims do not connect current disorders with the past assault or have repressed the assault entirely. Often, the past will surface during the specific suggestion or behavioral exercise stage. Nadelson (1982) describes such a circumstance involving couple counseling. The woman could not comply with the prescribed sexual exercises because she experienced them as coercive. She reluctantly disclosed having been raped 15 years earlier, prior to knowing her husband. She had told no one of the rape, including her husband, for fear of being blamed and rejected. She pretended to have sexual feelings although she had not had any postrape. Therapy then focused on the past event and on communication between the couple.

Nadelson emphasizes that no one treatment modality or approach will be effective in every case. Victims of incest, rape or molestation are affected in different ways and to different degrees by the experience. Treatment must be flexible, offering a combination of information and exploration, along with the opportunity to develop trust and alliance. The treatment of some victims will be long term and will require patience on the part of both therapist and client. It may take years for conflicts to lessen, for trust to develop, and for repressed feelings and sensations to emerge or reemerge. Some clients may be successful in achieving only partial recovery.

SPECIFIC SEXUAL AFTEREFFECTS AND THEIR TREATMENT

In this section, we will outline specific sexual problems resulting from sexual trauma and will then discuss treatment issues. Schover, Friedman, Weiler, Heiman and LoPiccolo's (1980, 1982) multiaxial diagnostic system for sexual dysfunctions will be employed in categorizing sexual aftereffects. This system delineates six axes for diagnosing sexual disorders, each with a number of specific disorders subsumed under it, including the areas of desire, arousal, orgasm, coital pain, frequency dissatisfaction, and qualifying information. Within each area, dysfunctions are modified by two additional axes: lifelong versus not-lifelong and global versus situational. The reader is referred to Chapter 6 (on assessment) for a more complete discussion of this classification system.

Desire Disorder

Disorders of desire are classified into two areas: low sexual desire wherein desire is inhibited and results in a lack of desire and low frequency of sexual activity; and aversion to sex, characterized by low sexual desire and negative emotions such as fear, shame, disgust that are associated with sex. Both of these disorders are common for rape and sexual molestation victims and may represent an attempt to cope with unresolved assault conflicts through denial of sexuality or dampening of sexual desire, or they may be due to ambivalence about the body.

Many women report a global fear of sex with resulting low sexual desire or sexual aversion for a period of time postrape; nevertheless, their desire for nonsexual affection and reassurance may actually increase during the same time period. The woman may have difficulty communicating her fear and distinguishing between affection and sexuality with her partner; she may end up forsaking affection due to her perception that any physical contact will be interpreted as a desire for sex. The partner (whether male or female) is often affected by the assault. According to Holmstrom and Burgess (1979), the typical response of the male partner is to want to have sex quite soon postassault, possibly as reassurance for himself or his partner that the rape will not interfere with their sexual relationship and/or that his partner will continue to be sexually interested in and involved with him. On the other hand, some men and women are reluctant to touch their partner or to initiate a discussion of sexual matters for fear of triggering memories and upsetting the partner. Men in particular may shun their partner because they consciously or unconsciously view her as "damaged goods" or as having done something to precipitate the assault. The woman will most likely interpret any lack of contact as rejection or repulsion. Lack of understanding of the possible impact of rape on sexual functioning, coupled with lack of communication, may result in termination of relationships, adding a further tragic dimension to the impact of the assault.

Williams and Miller (1979) found that the average time for avoidance of sex is 6 weeks to 2 months postrape. Although avoidance is common, some women initiate sex almost immediately postrape in a desire to return to normal, to regain control, and to prove that they can still be sexual.

Fear of sex and intimacy is a common issue for a number of molestation victims as well, especially incest victims (Becker et al., 1982; Courtois, 1979; Herman, 1981; and Meiselman, 1978), due to many physical and/or psychological aspects of the past experience. For example, assaulted children may experience intense pain because of body immaturity and size. Some victims never resolve feelings of guilt or ambivalence about the molestation/incest. On one hand, they fear or avoid sex because they fear being coerced, being out of control of their bodily reactions, being in physical pain, or doing things that were once so repulsive to them and that awake negative memories. On the other hand, they may have experienced pleasure during the childhood activity, which they are ashamed of or are afraid of reactivating and, as a result, avoid being sexual. These assault-related issues must be addressed before more specific sex therapy techniques can be effectively employed. As Kaplan (1979) comments, in comparison with conventional sex therapy, the treatment of disorders of sexual desire is lengthier and has to be more flexible and individualistic. The underlying difficulties are usually deeper and require exploration of defenses and resistances as well as an emphasis on fostering insight.

Victims of all types of sexual assault may have aversions to specific sexual acts that occurred during the assault, with oral sex most frequently cited as problematic. Certain smells, positions and words may also become aversive. One treatment of aversion to specific sexual acts, developed by the first author, combines an awareness of assault-related issues and traditional sex therapy techniques. The approach is similar for both rape and incest victims although the course of treatment may be extended and more complex with the latter. The treatment involves a three-phase approach: recognition and understanding; temporary acceptance of the aversion; sensate-focus and desensitization.

The first goal in treating aversions is to help the client to recognize and understand them. While individuals assaulted as adults usually attribute their specific aversions to the assault, those assaulted as children may not be aware of a connection between their present behavior and their earlier experience.

Making the connection helps the client gain awareness and control. This under-standing does not automatically produce a cure, but it often relieves guilt and anxiety, making it possible eventually to treat the aversion.

The second treatment phase is the temporary, or in some cases permanent, acceptance of the aversion. The client's anxiety in sexual relationships is further relieved and the sense of control enhanced when the client can accept that she has a right not to enjoy particular activities, and has a right to tell her partner not to touch her in ways she does not enjoy. Couple therapy and assertiveness training are often helpful, in that it is crucial that the client learn to articulate her needs and that her partner respect her right and understand her need to limit their sexual repertoire. Once the woman is confident that the partner will not force behavior against her wishes, treatment can proceed to the third phase, sensate focus and desensitization. Depending on how severely the aversion dis-rupts the couple's sexual pleasure, the couple may either decide to work to over-come the aversion or to accept the limitation. The following example demon-strates how this technique was used with a woman for whom breast fondling was aversive.

> Ms. A desired a sexual relationship but believed that no man would ac-cept her unless she allowed him to fondle her breasts. When her breasts were fondled, she felt anxious, "turned off," and unable to enjoy other aspects of the sexual relationship. Furthermore, she felt helpless to do anything about the fondling since she believed that all men would ignore her desire not to have her breasts fondled and would ultimately desert her.

> Through exploration in therapy, the client was able to connect her aversion with the sexual abuse she experienced by her father as a child and adolescent. Among other forms of sexual abuse, her father would come up behind her at various times throughout the day and grab her breasts. She felt anxious, never knowing when he would grab her, and helpless to do anything about this behavior. In therapy she was able to first accept that she had a right not to have her breasts fondled and then to articulate her desire to her sexual partner. Her partner did not comply with her request at first. Assertiveness training helped her to state her desire directly and clearly to her partner. After an extended period of testing her partner and finding out that he would not touch her breasts against her wishes, she was able to relax and on occasion ask him to fondle her breasts. Once she felt in control of her body and assured that she would not be touched against her will, the aversion to the fon-dling diminished.

Arousal Disorders

Arousal disorders involve performance and the ability to become sexually aroused. Schover et al. (1980, 1982) delineate nine areas of arousal disorders consisting of various combinations of subjective and physiological arousal and erectile difficulties, most of which apply solely to men.

Lubrication difficulties, which include partial or complete failure to attain or maintain lubrication-swelling response throughout the sex act, constitute the most common arousal disorder for women. Lubrication difficulties are frequently not assessed and, in fact, are not mentioned in the rape/molestation literature except by Masters and Johnson (1976b), who mention it as a postrape problem. Although clients may not specify lack of lubrication as a problem, they may report a lack of sensation or feeling in the vaginal or pelvic area that results in an inability to become sexually aroused. The therapist must ascertain whether the arousal problem is organic or psychogenic; using the suggestion by Ellis (1980), quoted in Chapter 6 and applying it to women, careful and direct questioning can make the distinction between organic and psychogenic lubrication swelling failure.

If a client sometimes lubricates in intercourse or does so during masturbation or petting, the problems are more likely to be of psychological origin. We echo the recommendation for a careful and thorough medical evaluation in order to rule out organic causes. Hartman and Fithian (1972) describe many physical causes of diminished vaginal perception, including scarring, fibrosity, pain, slack musculature, and the separation of muscle from the vagina. Psychological factors may include sexual anxiety, body ambivalence, ignorance and misperception about sexual feelings and responses, and resistance to pleasurable or sexual feelings.

These and other physical and psychological concerns may be due to or interact with the effects of forced sexual experiences. The PLISSIT hierarchical approach may be used with this class of dysfunction. For some sexual assault clients, lack of arousal constitutes a conversion symptom and should be treated as such with intensive therapy as the treatment of choice. The therapist would work toward allowing unconscious memories to emerge within the safety of the therapeutic environment while monitoring ego strength and ensuring that the client is not overwhelmed by the new learning. Conversion symptoms often diminish or disappear once the client becomes conscious of and works through the anxiety- producing materials. We have found that conversion reactions may occur in other body areas besides the vagina. For example, one of our clients experienced soreness in her finger for a period of weeks, during which time she was discussing her incest experience. She was able to recall that her father had forced her to put her finger in his anus, an activity that repulsed her.

Interestingly, Masters and Johnson (1976a) also note the development of impotence in male partners of rape victims as another postrape arousal disorder. This impotence is a reflection of the male partner's own emotional reaction to the assault. He may be anxious about how his partner will react to renewed sexual activity and/or be afraid that sexual activity will cause her physical pain. He may feel guilty that he was not able or available to protect her from being raped, or he may feel angry at the rapist, his partner, and/or himself. In the midst of crisis and the trauma of assault, the victim is the center of attention and concern. The male partner may feel left out and helpless. Like the victim, he too needs to express and to work through his emotional reactions.

Individual therapy with the partner, whether male or female, and support groups for significant others of rape victims, can be extremely useful in helping the partners explore their feelings about the rape. Couples therapy to facilitate communication between the partners may also prove beneficial.

Sarrel and Masters (1982) report loss of erectile capacity as the most frequent sexual dysfunction in men who have been raped by women. As with female victims, treatment must address the underlying feelings and issues (i.e., loss of personal dignity, loss of confidence in one's masculinity) in addition to the specific sexual dysfunction.

Orgasmic Disorders

Schover et al. (1980, 1982) specify several types of situationally specific orgasmic difficulties in women (i.e., inorgasmic except during masturbation, partner manipulation, mechanical stimulation, infrequent coital orgasm) in addition to the global diagnosis of inorgasmia.

Orgasmic disorders are common for both rape and sexual molestation victims, constituting a response to the fear of being out of control or a manifestation of guilt and anxiety associated with sexual pleasure. Orgasmic disorders may also result from the defenses employed to cope with the anxiety or from fixation on a particular activity. Goodwin, McCarthy, and DiVasto (1981) report impairment of ability to orgasm as the most commonly reported sequela of incest, occurring in 20% to 75% of victims. Orgasmic difficulties are reported in 23% (Becker et al., 1979) to 41% (Burgess & Holmstrom, 1979b) of rape victims. Anorgasmia except during masturbation appears to be the most common orgasmic dysfunction for this population, perhaps because masturbation does not involve trusting another person or relinquishing control.

Although our emphasis here is on the sexually assaulted woman, it should be noted that similar issues emerge and may lead to anorgasmia in women who have not been sexually victimized. Barbach (1980) writes that fear of losing control is a common concern. This fear is often heightened by socialization that teaches females to be passive and thus may predispose a woman to orgasmic difficulties. Sexual victimization further highlights these concerns. These issues may be explored prior to focusing on orgasmic difficulties or may only emerge as the specific treatment of the sexual dysfunction is underway. The therapist needs to be aware that themes of control, trust, and passivity as amplified by sexual victimization are possible sources of orgasmic inhibition. With this awareness, treatment of orgasmic disorder can proceed using traditional sex therapy techniques for the treatment of this disorder (e.g., Barbach, 1976).

Two members of an incest therapy group illustrate the relationship among orgasm, guilt and control. Both women disclosed that they could only orgasm if, while masturbating, they pictured their fathers. They suffered great guilt over the behavior which, coupled with shame, self-hatred, and fear that the association of orgasm with memories of father meant that they were insane, made disclosure extremely difficult.

The relief at finally admitting this secret and finding out that they were not alone was apparent. While there are obviously a multitude of issues related to this behavior, an issue of particular interest arose as we explored their masturbatory fantasies. In their fantasies, both women were at an age when the incest behavior was just beginning and when the fondling behavior and attention had been pleasurable. As the sexual activity progressed and became painful (for example, one woman was anally assaulted at age 5), the women employed a dissociative defense (previously described) to block themselves from experiencing physical sensations. One hypothesis is that the masturbation fantasies allowed each woman to regress to a time before their mind-body sensations were dissociated, thus allowing them to experience sexual feelings and achieve orgasm.

Coital Pain

Schover et al. (1980, 1982) offer four diagnoses for painful sexual activity, two of which apply to women: dyspareunia, defined as pain located in the genital area that occurs during the sexual act, and other pain, such as lower back pain, exacerbated by sexual activity. Vaginismus, the conditioned involuntary phobic response that causes musculature spasms and interferes with coitus, is included in this category by other diagnostic systems.

In discussing factors contributing to coital pain, Lazarus (1980) includes sexual misinformation, associating sexual feelings with guilt and shame, and traumatic events associated with intercourse. It is not surprising, therefore, that vaginismus and dyspareunia have been documented as resulting from sexual assault (Burgess & Holmstrom, 1979b; Kaplan, 1979; Masters & Johnson, 1976b). Individuals whose first sexual encounter was assault or abuse may be at a particularly high risk for developing these disorders. Crisis intervention, particularly with individuals with no prior sexual activity, needs to include sexual education and a clear differentiation between assaultive and consensual sexual activity. It may even be helpful to explain positive sexual feeling and response and that not all sex is abusive or painful.

Gynecological examination and consultation is essential to determine whether any physiological damage resulting from the assault may be causing the pain. Once physiological damage is ruled out or treated, traditional sex therapy techniques for these disorders (Kaplan, 1979; Masters & Johnson, 1976b) may be employed.

Frequency Dissatisfaction

Frequency-dissatisfaction disorders are classified by Schover et al. (1980, 1982) into two categories: higher or lower frequency than desired. Although general sexual dissatisfaction is not included in their diagnostic system, we will include it at this point in our discussion.

Once rape victims begin to resume sexual activity, they do not immediately return to their prerape level of frequency or satisfaction. Burgess and Holmstrom (1979b) found that 71% of previously sexually active women reported decreased sexual activity following rape, with 38% of them being abstinent for at least 6 months and some having no sexual activity for a number of years. Of the 19% who reported no change in frequency, half reported problems such as flashbacks, lack of orgasmic response, and aversion to specific sexual acts. Ten percent reported increased sexual activity, including self-defined promiscuity, prostitution and general confusion concerning their sexual activity.

Feldman-Summers et al. (1979) conducted a retrospective evaluation of the impact of rape on sexual satisfaction. The time lapse between the assault and the survey varied from 2 months to 7 years with a median of 1 year. Following the assault, satisfaction on a wide variety of sex-related behaviors, including kissing, stroking, and intercourse, decreased substantially. Autoerotic (masturbation) and affectional (holding hands, hugging) experiences were unaffected by the rape. In terms of sexual behavior at the time of the survey, frequency of such behaviors as oral sex, vaginal intercourse and orgasm did not differ between victims and nonvictims, but level of satisfaction did, with victims receiving significantly less satisfaction from these activities. The authors conclude that some long-term residual associations of sexuality with pain and fear appeared to be present still, which put a damper on the extent of sexual satisfaction.

The rape literature often mentions the importance of prior level of sexual activity, suggesting that a virgin suffers greater distress from rape due to her prior lack of experience. However, the 4- to 6-year follow-up study conducted by Burgess and Holmstrom (1979b) indicates that prior level of sexual activity does not affect the length of recovery from rape. This finding supports Medea and Thompson's (1974) statement that "...it seems likely that the effect depends much more on the woman's personality than on the existence or nonexistence of her hymen" (p. 105). However, this does not lessen the possible impact of loss of virginity or its significance as a therapeutic issue for any individual client.

Satisfaction difficulties may also result from childhood molestation (Becker et al., 1982; Courtois, 1979; Meiselman, 1978; and Tsai, Feldman-Summers, & Edgar, 1979). According to Tsai et al.:

> It is worth noting that at least in terms of current sexual satisfaction, the impacts of molestation on women...appear to be similar to the impacts of rape on the victim several months after the assault. (p. 414).

Frequency and satisfaction problems can be worked on by exploring the assault experience and its effect on sexual functioning. In particular, the client may need assistance addressing issues of control and intimacy, and working through feelings of fear and anger. She may or may not return to preassault levels of sexual satisfaction, a fact that should be discussed along with resulting feelings such as loss and anger. The therapist can also provide encouragement and support for the client who is becoming sexually active after an inactive period or who is attempting new sexual behavior.

Ms. B, an incest victim, has been celibate by choice for a number of years because she feels she handles sexual encounters so poorly. In the past, she has had periods of promiscuity characterized by her "servicing" her partner but deriving no pleasure for herself. She is now able to masturbate and understands her body responses. What she does not know is how to be with someone else in a normal sexual encounter.

She shows many obsessive defenses, illustrated by her determination to function perfectly and normally while she berates herself for not being able to do so. Consequently, she is never satisfied. Therapy has involved behavioral approaches, but is now focused on the psychological and psychogenetic aspects of her functioning.

Qualifying Information

Schover et al. (1980, 1982) use this category to discuss factors that impact on sexual functioning. They include such issues as homosexuality, fetishism, masochism, sadism, marital distress, substance abuse, and extramarital affairs. Many of these factors are involved in cases of rape and childhood molestation. We will discuss flashbacks and other problems, including promiscuity, prostitution, spouse abuse, masochism, confused sexual identity, and substance abuse. In discussing treatment, we will limit ourselves to the treatment of flashbacks, because the treatment of such issues as spouse abuse and substance abuse is beyond the scope of this chapter.

Flashbacks. Similar to other post-traumatic stress disorders, flashbacks to the actual incident is one of the most frequently mentioned problems following sexual assault. Flashbacks are especially likely to occur in situations that bear some resemblance to the original, so that any sexual activity may cue the flashbacks. Burgess and Holmstrom (1979b) report that half of the sexually active rape victims in their sample had flashbacks during sexual activity.

Molestation/incest victims often report being unable to separate the present from the past. The memories and images are intrusive and often paralyzing. In fact, some victims have described a sudden onset of flashbacks or of incomplete memory fragments during their adult sexual activities as the way in which they "remembered" the childhood experience.

Flashbacks may result in cessation of the present activity and hesitation to reinitiate or resume sexual activity in the future. Indeed, the fear of experiencing the images can lead to a phobic reaction to all sexual activities. Flashbacks are treated in a manner similar to the treatment of phobias (Dupont, 1982). The client is helped to control the panic rather than avoid the object or activity that cues the fear. It is imperative that the victim change her goal from one of eliminating all flashbacks (a goal over which she has little control and is bound to fail) to one of reducing her anxiety and improving her manner of coping with the flashback.

The following procedure, developed by the first author, has been effective in helping clients deal with flashbacks. In therapy, the client is first taught that flashbacks are normal and will reduce in frequency and intensity over time but may occur periodically throughout her life. She is then taught, with the aid of her partner, to control the anxiety when the flashbacks do occur. For example, the client is taught to inform her partner when she is having a flashback. For some clients, a nonverbal signal may be used. She is told to open her eyes, look around and, with her partner's assistance, test reality by focusing on her present surroundings. Her partner can reassure her that she is safe and that he or she will not do anything she does not desire.

The issue of control is again of crucial importance. As in the treatment of other phobias, the client needs to know that she has a way out of the situation at all times. With this knowledge, and her partner's assurance, she can leave the bedroom or the house or create space between herself and her partner if that is what she needs. Alternatively, she can be encouraged to remain in the situation for long enough for her anxiety to lessen. It may take a number of attempts before she is able to return to sexual activity once the anxiety is alleviated or under control.

Another example of how the restoration of control is employed in the treatment of flashbacks involves changing the ending of the event to one of mastery and control. The client might envision herself becoming Superwoman and fighting off her assailant, or she might see the United States Cavalry riding to her rescue. With the understanding that she may not have been able to act any differently during the actual assault, she is taught to recognize that the flashback is in her mind and no longer in reality. Thus, she has complete control over it. This same method is used in treating assault-related nightmares (Sprei & Goodwin, 1983).

Other factors impacting on sexual functioning. Promiscuity and indiscriminate sexual behavior appear to be less common aftereffects for victims of rape than for victims of incest/molestation, according to reports in the literature. It has been increasingly recognized, however, that many rape victims were abused as children, a circumstance that may have increased their vulnerability to sexual assault as adults. Compulsive sexuality may alternate with periods of sexual inhibition. As has been underscored in this chapter, sexual assault/molestation may have devastating effects on self-esteem and may confuse the victim in her interpersonal functioning. Promiscuity, as well as masochistic behavior and spouse abuse, may become means of acting out a negative self-concept, proving worthlessness and, often, reenacting the abuse. These are means of further self-punishment and degradation. These behaviors may also reflect an overvaluation of men, a craving for attention, and a reenactment of giving or receiving affection through sexual means.

In discussing masochism, Shainess (1979) describes the acting out of a hypnotic-type suggestion.

> The masochistic person is in fact, carrying out a long- range post-hypnotic suggestion from childhood. The effect of a particularly cruel parent...(p. 180)

> The all-pervasive feeling of badness, and of guilt, is so easily triggered in masochistic persons, that they are magnetized into self-abusing behavior, into victimization. (p. 182)

> [The masochist thus] unwittingly chooses a dangerous figure to relate to because it is the only kind of figure appearing real to her, and then acts out her defensive style. (p. 179)

This analysis of masochistic behavior correlates with the cross- generational pattern that has been discussed in the battered child and battered spouse syndromes. Without intervention, many of these problems will be repeated from generation to generation.

Prostitution may be another consequence of childhood sexual molestation, according to the research of James and Myerding (1977) and Silbert and Pines (1981). Similar to the dynamics of promiscuity, the woman may be seeking to abuse herself and men. As one incest victim states:

> Prostitution was a way for me to capitalize on what I thought was the only thing I had to offer. I didn't know how to get pleasure, but I knew how to give it, and, anyway, that was what I was used to.

> I felt marked. I knew that, wherever I went, men would find me and abuse me. So, my attitude toward prostitution was, "Why not?" If I had to have sex, I thought, why not get something for it? I felt I deserved the money: other men were going to have to pay for every time my father had me. Nothing they did could repulse me. I had lived with too much of it while I was growing up.

> Since I thought that the only thing men wanted was sex, the only way I could see to get power in a relationship was by them paying for it. It was my only control, and I could keep it as long as the men didn't mean anything to me; once I cared about them, I felt they had all the control. Prostitution was another way of expressing my rage, of getting back at all of them for what had been done to me. (Myers, no date/1980, p. 13)

Confusion about sexual identity and preference may be another consequence of childhood rape and molestation. Westerlund (1983) states: "Confusion about sexual orientation is not uncommonly a complaint although the majority of women with incest histories maintain heterosexual relationships. Causal connections between incest and lesbianism have not been established or supported by study" (p. 7). In helping a client assess her sexual orientation or preferences, the therapist must be careful not to devalue same-sex orientation or to imply that it was caused by the abuse. On the other hand, the client may need assistance in clarifying and/or working through her fear and hatred of men, which may prevent her from any sexual involvement with them.

Substance abuse may be a means of escaping the thoughts, feelings and reality of sexual abuse, as explained by Myers (no date/1980):

> Drugs became my great escape; there was nothing I wouldn't try in order to get high. I never knew how I'd feel dealing with different people, but on drugs, I could be anything I wanted to be. I could make up my own reality; I could be pretty, have a good family, a nice father, a strong mother, and be happy. When I was on drugs, I felt high, happy, and in control of my life. When I was high, I had peers; I finally belonged somewhere — in a group with other kids who took drugs.

> For me, drinking had the opposite effect of drugs, which is probably why I did so much of it. Drinking got me back into my pain; it allowed me to express my anger (which, of course, I couldn't do on drugs because I couldn't feel any pain).

> Neither of them gave me what I needed, but, in a negative way, they gave me ways of coping with what I had. (pp. 11-12)

The reactions described in this section are less prevalent in individuals assaulted as adults than in those molested as children. Treatment of such reactions must look beyond the acting-out behavior to focus on the molestation experience and its aftereffects, including issues of self-esteem, identity, shame and guilt. As discussed previously, building the alliance may be difficult, particularly with the acting-out, hostile client. Firmness, consistency, and support on the part of the therapist are essential, as is an expectation of being tested over and over again.

SUMMARY

In this chapter, we have presented an overview of the dynamics of sexual assault and molestation as they relate to the development of sexual distress and dysfunction. The effects of these same dynamics on the therapy relationship and its development were discussed in detail to offer specific guidelines to the therapist. Finally, assessment and treatment approaches, particularly where modifications were needed from standard sex therapy approaches, were discussed for six categories of dysfunction.

The changes in sexual functioning resulting from sexual assault and abuse must not be overlooked in treatment. An appreciation of the functional value these current dysfunctions served previously in helping the victim to survive the abuse is essential. Certain dysfunctions may still serve to inhibit flashbacks, intrusive memories and feelings associated with the abuse. Therefore, traditional sex therapy treatment methods alone may not suffice. Therapists need to be aware of the dynamics of abuse as they affect sexual functioning and the therapy process.

REFERENCES

American Psychiatric Association (1980). *Diagnostic and statistical manual of mental disorders* (3rd ed.). Washington, DC: Author.

Annon, J.S. (1977). The PLISSIT model: A proposed conceptual scheme for the behavioral treatment of sexual problems. In J. Fischer & H.L. Gochros (Eds.), *Handbook of behavior therapy with sexual problems* (Vol. 1). New York: Pergamon.

Atkeson, B.M., Calhoun, K.S., Resick, P.A., & Ellis, E.M. (1982). Victims of rape: Repeated assessment of depressive symptoms. *Journal of Consulting and Clinical Psychology, 50,* 96-102.

Baisden, M.J., & Baisden, J.R. (1979). A profile of women who seek counseling for sexual dysfunction. *American Journal of Family Therapy 7,* 68-76.

Barbach, L. (1976). *For yourself: The fulfillment of female sexuality.* New York: Anchor Books.

Barbach, L. (1980). Group treatment of anorgasmic women. In S.R. Leiblum & L.A. Pervin (Eds.), *Principles and practice of sex therapy.* New York: Guilford.

Barry, J., Jr. (1965). Incest. In R. Slovenko (Ed.), *Sexual behavior and the law.* Springfield, IL: Charles C. Thomas.

Becker, J.V., Abel, G.G., & Skinner, J. (1979). The impact of sexual assault on the victim's sex life. *Victimology: An International Journal, 4,* 229-235.

Becker, J.F., Abel, G.G., Skinner, L.J., & Treacy, E.C. (1982). Incidence and types of sexual dysfunctions in rape and incest victims. *Journal of Sex and Marital Therapy, 8,* 65- 74.

Burgess, A.W., Groth, A.N., Holmstrom, L.L., & Sgroi, S.M. (1978). *Sexual assault of children and adolescents.* Lexington, MA: Heath.

Burgess, A.W., & Holmstrom, L.L. (1974). Rape trauma syndrome. *American Journal of Psychiatry, 131,* 981-986.

Burgess, A.W., & Holmstrom, L.L. (1979a). Adaptive strategies and recovery from rape. *American Journal of Psychiatry, 136,* 1278-1282.

Burgess, A.W., & Holmstrom, L.L. (1979b).Rape: Sexual disruption and recovery. *American Journal of Orthopsychiatry, 49,* 648-657.

Butler, S. (1979). *Conspiracy of silence: The trauma of incest.* New York: Bantam.

Courtois, C.A. (1979). Characteristics of a volunteer sample of adult women who experienced incest in childhood or adolescence. *Dissertation Abstracts International, 40,* 3194-3195.

Courtois, C.A., & Watts, D. (1982). Counseling women who experienced incest in childhood or adolescence. *The Personnel and Guidance Journal,* January, 275-279.

DeFrancis, V. (1969). *Protecting the child victims of sex crimes committed by adults.* Denver: The American Humane Association.

Densen-Gerber, J., & Benward, J. (1975). Incest as a causative factor in antisocial behavior: An exploratory study. *Contemporary Drug Problems,* Fall, 323-340.

DuPont, R.L. (Ed.). (1982). *Phobia: A comprehensive summary of modern treatments.* New York: Brunner/Mazel.

Ellis, A. (1980). Treatment of erectile dysfunction. In S.R. Leiblum & L.A. Pervin (Eds.), *Principles and practice of sex therapy.* New York: Guilford.

Feldman-Summers, S., Gordon, P.E., & Meagher, J.R. (1979). The impact of rape and sexual satisfaction. *Journal of Abnormal Psychology, 88,* 101-105.

Finklehor, D. (1979). *Sexually victimized children.* New York: The Free Press.

Frieberg, P., & Bridwell, M. (1976). An intervention model for rape and unwanted pregnancy.*The Counseling Psychologist, 6,* 52-53.

Gelinas, D.J. (1983). The persisting negative effects of incest. *Psychiatry, 46,* 313-332.

Goodwin, J., McCarthy, T., & DiVasto, P. (1981). Prior incest in mothers of abused children. *Child Abuse and Neglect, 5,* 87-95.

Groth, A.N. (1982, May). *The child molester: Treatment issues.* Paper presented at the Second National Conference on Sexual Victimization of Children, Children's Hospital National Medical Center, Arlington, Virginia.

Groth, A.N., & Birnbaum, H.J. (1980). The rapist: Motivations for sexual violence. In S.L. McCombie (Ed.), *The rape crisis intervention handbook.* New York: Plenum Press.

Halleck, S.L. (1962). The physician's role in management of victims of sex offenders. *Journal of the American Medical Association, 180,* 273-278.

Halleck, S.L. (1965). Emotional effects of victimization. In R. Slovenko (Ed.), *Sexual behavior and the law.* Springfield, IL: Charles C. Thomas.

Hartman, W.E., & Fithian, M.A. (1972). *Treatment of sexual dysfunction.* Long Beach, CA: Center for Marital and Sexual Studies.

Henderson, D.J. (1975). Incest. In A.M. Freedman, H.I. Kaplan, & B.J. Sadock (Eds.), *Comprehensive textbook of psychiatry.* Baltimore: Williams & Wilkins.

Herman, J.L. (1981). *Father-daughter incest.* Cambridge, MA: Harvard University Press.

Hilberman, E. (1976). *The rape victim.* Washington, DC: American Psychiatric Association.

Holmstrom, L.L., & Burgess, A.W. (1979). Rape: The husband's and boyfriend's initial reactions. *The Family Coordinator, 21,* 321-330.

James, J., & Myerdling, J. (1977). Early sexual experience as a factor in prostitution. *Archives of Sexual Behavior, 7,* 31-42.

Kaplan, H.S. (1979). *Disorders of sexual desire: The new sex therapy, Vol. II.* New York: Brunner/Mazel.

Katz, S., & Mazur, M. (1979). *Understanding the rape victim: A synthesis of research findings.* New York: Wiley.

Kaufman, I., Peck, L., & Tagiuri, K. (1954). The family constellation and overt incestuous relations between father and daughter. *American Journal of Orthopsychiatry, 34,* 267-279.

Kilpatrick, D.G., Veronen, L.J., & Resick, P.A. (1979). The aftermath of rape: Recent empirical findings. *American Journal of Orthopsychiatry, 49,* 658-669.

Lazarus, A.A. (1980). Psychological treatment of dyspareunia. In S.R. Leiblum & L.A. Pervin (Eds.), *Principles and practice of sex therapy.* New York: Guilford.

Lukianowicz, N. (1972). Incest. *British Journal of Psychiatry, 120,* 301-313.

Masters, W.H. and Johnson, V.E. (1976a, April). Incest: The ultimate sexual taboo. *Redbook, 54,* 57-58.

Masters, W.H. and Johnson, V.E. (1976b, June). The aftermath of rape. *Redbook, 74,* 161.

Medea, A., & Thompson, K. (1974). *Against rape.* New York: Farrar, Straus and Giroux.

Meiselman, K.C. (1978). *Incest: A psychological study of causes and effects with treatment recommendations.* San Francisco: Jossey-Bass.

Myers, B. (no date). *Incest: If you think the word is ugly, take a look at its effects.* Minneapolis, MN: Christopher Street. Also in National Center on Child Abuse and Neglect, Children's Bureau. (1980). *Sexual abuse of children: Selected readings* (DHHS Publication No. 78-30161). Washington, DC: U.S. Government Printing Office.

Nadelson, C.C. (1982). Incest and rape: Repercussions in sexual behavior (pp 56-66). In L. Greenspoon (Ed.), *The Annual Review of Psychiatry.* Washington, DC: American Psychiatric Press.

Nadelson, C., Notman, M., Zackson, H., & Gornick, J. (no date). *The long-term impact of rape: A follow-up study.* Unpublished manuscript.

National Center on Child Abuse and Neglect. (1978). *Child sexual abuse: Incest, assault, and sexual exploitations.* (DHEW Publication No. 78-30166). Washington, DC: U.S. Government Printing Office.

Notman, M.T., & Nadelson, C. (1976). The rape victim: Psychodynamic considerations. *American Journal of Psychiatry, 133,* 408-412.

Russell, D.E.H. (1983). The incidence and prevalence of intrafamilial and extrafamilial sexual abuse of female children. *Child Abuse and Neglect, 7,* 133-148.

Sarrel, P.M., & Masters, W.H. (1982). Sexual molestation of men by women. *Archives of Sexual Behavior, 11,* 117-131.

Schover, L.R., Friedman, J.M., Weiler, S.J., Heiman, J.R., & LoPiccolo, J. (1980). *A multi-axial descriptive system for the sexual dysfunctions: Categories and manual.* Stony Brook, NY: Sex Therapy Center.

Schover, L.R., Friedman, J.M., Weiler, S.J., Heiman, J.R., & LoPiccolo, J. (1982). Multi-axial problem-oriented system for sexual dysfunctions. *Archives of General Psychiatry, 39,* 614-619.

Shainess, N. (1979). Vulnerability to violence: Masochism as process. *American Journal of Psychiatry,* 174-189.

Silbert, M., & Pines, A. (1981). Sexual child abuse as an antecedent to prostitution. *Child Abuse and Neglect, 5,* 407-411.

Sprei, J.E., & Goodwin, R.A. (1983). The group treatment of sexual assault survivors. *Journal of Specialist in Group Work, 8,* 39-46.

Sutherland, S., & Scherl, D.J. (1970). Patterns of response among victims of rape. *American Journal of Orthopsychiatry, 40,* 503-511.

Tsai, M., Feldman-Summers, S., & Edgar, M. (1979). Childhood molestation: Variables related to differential impacts on psychosexual functioning in adult women. *Journal of Abnormal Psychology, 4,* 407-417.

Weinberg, S. (1955). *Incest behavior.* New York: Citadel Press.

Weiner, I.B. (1962). Father-daughter incest: A clinical report. *Psychiatric Quarterly, 36,* 607-631.

Westerlund, E. (1983). Counseling women with histories of incest. *Women and Therapy, 2,*(4) 17-30.

Williams, A.M., & Miller, W.R. (1979). *Sexual assault victims and their husbands, boyfriends: Presenting complaints and therapy goals.* Paper presented at Eastern Association of Sex Therapists.

Williams, J. and Holmes, H. (1981). *The second assault: Rape and public attitudes.* Connecticut: Greenwood Press.

Chapter 13

Clinical Implications of Research on Extramarital Involvement

Shirley P. Glass and Thomas L. Wright

Extramarital involvement (EMI) is one of the most frequent problems encountered by marital therapists, but it is infrequently addressed in the marital literature. Surveys indicate that approximately 25% of couples seen in marital therapy present extramarital sex (EMS) as a problem at the outset, and as therapy proceeds an additional 30% may disclose EMS (Greene, 1981; Humphrey, 1983a, 1983b; Sprenkle & Weiss, 1978). The incidence of EMS in surveys of nonclinical populations ranges from 25% to 50% (Athanasiou, Shaver & Tauris, 1970; Bell, Turner & Rosen, 1975; Glass & Wright, 1985; Hunt, 1974; Kinsey, Pomeroy & Martin, 1953; Levin, 1975; Petersen, 1983). Divorced and separated men and women have reported a higher incidence of EMS than those who have remained married (Glass & Wright, 1977; Hunt, 1974; Petersen, 1983).

It is perplexing that the research and clinical literature seldom addresses EMS among the proliferation of topics related to marital, sexual and family issues despite the prevalence of EMS among both clinical and nonclinical populations of married couples and the even higher incidence among divorced individuals. Humphrey (1983a) surveyed the content of quarterly journals dealing with marriage and family issues for the year 1982. He found only one article dealing with EMS out of 428 marital and family articles. We searched 60 marital and family therapy manuals, handbooks, and texts in preparation for this chapter and were amazed that "extramarital" (behavior, involvement, relations, sex) was most often not cited at all in the subject index. It was infrequently cited or referred to in conjunction with other topics (Ables, 1982; Dicks, 1967; Greene, 1981; Jacobson, 1981; Jacobson & Margolin, 1979; Liberman, et al., 1980; Whitaker, Greenberg & Greenberg, 1981) and EMI was addressed in a separate chapter only by Humphrey (1983b) and Mace (1965). There have been few books on EM relationships addressed to professionals in the field (Neubeck, 1969; Smith & Smith, 1974; Strean, 1980), although there has been a proliferation of books written for the general public (Berger, 1972; Block, 1978; Ellis, 1969; Hunt, 1969; Leigh, 1985; McGinnis, 1981; Wolfe, 1976). Because extramarital relationships are so prevalent in the general population and are such a common problem for couples in marital distress, it is important for clinicians and researchers to pay more attention to extramarital relationships and to address EMI directly.

Our use of the terms extramarital involvement (EMI) and extramarital sex (EMS) should *not* be taken as interchangeable nomenclature. The use of *EMS* by therapists, researchers, and the public reflects the prevailing assumption that *extramarital sexual* intercourse defines an extramarital involvement; this common usage of EMS ignores other extramarital sexual behaviors and overlooks extramarital emotional involvement. We consider extramarital emotional involvement and noncoital extramarital sexual intimacies important enough to be included in a comprehensive exposition of EMI. Therefore, we use *EMI* as a comprehensive term that can represent either sexual and/or emotional extramarital involvement.

The clinical and empirical literatures are separate, and each is biased according to the specific population under observation. Research evidence that consistently cites the high incidence of extramarital sex (EMS) among the general population suggests that EMS can and does occur among "normal" men and women and in stable marriages. On the other hand, therapists often conclude from their clinical populations that extramarital involvement should be attributed to pathological processes in either the individual or the marital relationship. Partly because of this lack of consensus, clinicians who conscientiously base their interpretation of client's behavior on theoretical writings and empirical findings may abandon an objective stance and project their personal biases when their clients discuss extramarital behavior. Knapp (1975) reported that therapists' attitudes toward EMS are directly associated with their own extramarital experience. Nearly one third of marriage counselors surveyed who engaged in secret EMS had more accepting attitudes than those with no EMS experience. Therapists without EMS experience tended to judge EMS clients as neurotic, antisocial, or characterized by a personality disorder.

Our goal in this chapter is to integrate the clinical, theoretical, and empirical research on EMI in order to broaden clinicians' perspectives on EMI and to provide a basis for their therapeutic interventions regarding EMI. We approach the area of EMI as both therapists and empirical researchers. Each of these perspectives has enriched the other and strengthens our belief in the value of such integration.

OVERVIEW

This chapter will synthesize empirical and clinical literature pertaining to extramarital involvements and propose clinical implications of this literature. We differentiate sexual, emotional, and "combined-type" extramarital involvement and link these three types of EMI to gender differences and sex roles. We propose a double code of EMI for men and women that describes different paths toward and sanctions against combined- type involvement. We address whether there is a connection between the state of the marriage and the occurrence of different types of extramarital involvement. We consider a range of individualistic explanations for EMI including social-demographic characteristics, attitudinal variables, and psychodynamic formulations.

Treatment issues that will be considered include: individual versus conjoint sessions, problems of confidentiality and therapeutic alliances, whether conjoint therapy can proceed if the EMI continues, the effects of disclosure on the marriage, and signs of resistance in involved and noninvolved spouses. We distinguish between secret EMI and EMI that is known prior to therapy, and we propose a model for marital therapy after an EMI disclosure or discovery. We present our approach for assessing marital and extramarital relationships and for establishing a therapeutic contract. We review specific marital therapy techniques that strengthen the marriage through caring behaviors and that improve communication patterns. We discuss ways of using information about the EMI to improve aspects of the marriage and suggest a structure for spouse disclosure that considers motivations, trust, jealousy, forgiving, alliances, and long-range effects.

TYPES OF EMI: HOW DO EM RELATIONSHIPS DIFFER?

It is a mistaken notion to consider EMI as a single entity: there are as many variations of EMI as there are different types of marital relationships and individual differences in personality. Two important EMI variables are: (1) sexual versus emotional involvement, and (2) gender of the participant.

Sexual versus Emotional Involvement

Knowledge and attitudes about extramarital relationships have been limited in scope by the traditional sexual criteria for defining EMI. The prevailing criterion for extramarital involvement in the culture and the literature includes only those interactions where extramarital sexual intercourse (EMS) has occurred. This narrow definition excludes extramarital relationships where sexual and/or emotional intimacies have taken place without coitus. However, it is important to distinguish between sexual and emotional EMI (Buunk, 1980; Glass, 1981; Neubeck & Schletzer, 1962; Spanier & Margolis, 1983; Sprey, 1972; Thompson, 1983, 1984). Bernard (1974) described different forms of "infidelity that include flirtations, sex as play, and noncoital nonfantasy relationships that involve a profound sharing of the self with another" (p. 146). Sprey (1972) proposed that "sex per se may be as great a threat to the marriage as emotional extramarital intimacy" (p. 36). Zetterberg (1966) emphasized that it is not sexual as much as

emotional involvement that violates the privacy taboo. We have studied empirically and observed in our practice that a wide range of extramarital experiences
that may or may not include intercourse can be associated with marital distress.
We broadened the criteria for EMI to include a range of sexual intimacies
(kissing...petting, sexually intimate without intercourse, intercourse) and
added a separate continuum of extramarital emotional involvement (slight...ex-
tremely deep) (Glass & Wright, 1985). A one-night stand or a series of casual
sexual encounters may not have the same implication for the marital relationship as a deep emotional involvement that does or does not include sexual intercourse. Humphrey (1983b) has observed in his clinical practice that some extramarital affairs are virtually exclusively sexual, with little love, but that at the
other extreme an affair may be totally devoid of sexual intercourse and involve
deep levels of loving. Therapists will be more adequately prepared to help
couples if they acknowledge that extramarital involvements can be characterized by this broad range of emotional and sexual experiences.

Extramarital emotional involvement is distinguishable from platonic friendships by the presence of secrecy, intimacy, and sexual chemistry. The "extra" in
extramarital often connotes a relationship that is "outside" of the common
knowledge within the marriage. Spouses may be informed about the relationship in question, but they are usually not aware of or informed about the extent
of the involvement. In fact, when opposite-sex "friendships" become a source
of marital conflict, therapists cannot assume from the absence of sexual involvement that the spouses are fighting about autonomy issues. Before lending support to the right of marital partners to have close friendships outside the
marriage, therapists need to assess the degree of emotional intimacy, secrecy,
and sexual attraction in such a friendship in order to determine the potential or
actual threat to the marriage.

Gender Differences in Type of EMI

The prevailing literature in the field reflects the traditional masculine bias
toward *sexual* EMI; most of the EMI gender differences reported pertain to
differences in *sexual* attitudes and behaviors and generally ignore emotional involvement. The most widely reported gender difference in the EMS literature
is the greater male incidence of extramarital intercourse (Athanasiou et al.,
1970; Buunk, 1980; Glass & Wright, 1985; Hunt, 1974; Johnson, 1970; Kinsey et
al., 1953). Men experience EMS earlier in marriage than women and have more
extramarital partners (Athanasiou et al., 1970). Men report more actual opportunities for EMS, and more men than women who have never experienced EMS
would welcome the opportunity (Glass, 1981; Johnson, 1970b). Men have a
more approving attitude than women toward EMS (Johnson, 1970b; Kinsey et
al., 1953; Singh, Walton, & Williams, 1976; Thompson, 1984).

Men and women differ in type of extramarital involvement in ways that reflect traditional sex roles. Men characterize their EMI as more sexual, whereas

women characterize their EMI as more emotional (Glass & Wright, 1985; Gurgul, Bowers, & Furstenberg, 1969). The degree of emotional involvement in extramarital relationships is greater for women than men (Glass & Wright, 1985; Gurgul, Bowers, & Furstenberg, 1969; Spanier & Margolis, 1983). Roebuck and Spray (1967) observed a group of married men who were sexually involved with single women whom they met in cocktail lounges. These men were happily married, were loving at home, and were particularly careful not to become emotionally involved with their extramarital partner. Thompson (1984) found that both men and women predicted that a greater proportion of married men than women would engage in extramarital intercourse without an emotional involvement. Mace (1965) has observed clinically that extramarital sexual experience generally means a deeper level of emotional involvement for women than for men. Blumstein and Schwartz (1983) reported that "...when a woman has sex outside her marriage, it is more likely to be a 'meaningful love affair'" (p. 583). We also found that women are more likely than men to combine emotional and sexual involvement in their extramarital relationships and that women are seldom involved sexually without also having some type of emotional involvement (combined-type involvement) (Glass & Wright, 1985).

We have proposed that sex roles in extramarital involvement may be reflected in differential codes for women and men that inhibit or delay movement toward combined-type extramarital involvement. When an EMI consists primarily of one aspect (sexual or emotional), men are more likely than women to engage in extramarital intercourse without emotional involvement, whereas women tend to be more inclined than men to be emotionally involved without sexual intercourse (Glass & Wright, 1985). A double code of EMI may allow for the prevailing type of involvement for each sex while inhibiting the secondary type. The male "code" appears to reflect a sanction against adding emotional to sexual EMI whereas the female "code" appears to reflect a sanction against adding sexual intercourse to emotional EMI. Francis (1977) found that husbands' jealous reactions are related to sexual involvement of their wives with another man, and wives' jealous reactions are associated with their husbands' spending time talking or sharing common interests with another woman. It appears that men begin with *sexual* EMI and may or may not add *emotional* EMI, whereas women begin with *emotional* EMI and may or may not add *sexual* EMI (Glass & Wright, 1985). Women are more likely to be involved in a combined-type EMI. Both men and women perceive combined-type involvements as having the most serious implications for the marriage because of the implicit codes for EMI that will have been broken.

Reiss, Anderson, and Sponaugle (1980) proposed that most male extramarital relationships would be "pleasure-centered" and that most female extramarital relationships would be "love-oriented." They noted that traditionally males have been socialized to take a more pleasure-oriented approach to sexuality and females have been socialized to take a more affection-oriented approach.

Hunt (1969) has described two types of EMI but has not linked them to a particular gender. The "pagan-courtly" person views EMS as perfectly normal and is primarily seeking fun and excitement. The "puritan- romantic" person believes that sex and affection are bound together and views EMS as a momentous event that often may be linked with feelings of guilt. Among our EMI subjects, the puritan-romantic label describes the majority of women and some men whose extramarital relationships are strongly emotional, whereas the pagan-courtly label appears to describe the majority of men whose extramarital relationships are mainly or entirely sexual (Glass & Wright, 1985).

These gender differences in type of EMI are parallel to consistent gender differences in expressions of sexuality and emotionality in premarital and marital relationships (Glass & Wright, 1985). Studies of premarital sex have consistently found that females more frequently associate sex with feelings of love whereas males often separate sex and affection (Ehrmann, 1959; Kanin & Davidson, 1972; Reiss, 1960, 1967; Simon & Gagnon, 1970). Marital research studies report that men place greater importance than do their wives on the sexual aspects of marriage whereas women are more concerned than their husbands with the affectional and emotional aspects of the marital relationship (DeBurgher, 1972; Levinger, 1964). These gender differences may stem from different biological processes in the development of sexual behavior (Simon & Gagnon, 1970), that are further embedded by far-reaching sexual learning histories and sex roles perpetuated by the culture (Gross, 1978).

Clinical Implications

Extramarital sexual intercourse isn't everything you need to know about EMI. It is important to discover the depth of emotional involvement as well as the extent of sexual involvement in relationships outside the marriage. EMI can be characterized as primarily emotional, primarily sexual, or as a combination of sexual and emotional involvements. Combined-type involvement can have more serious implications for the marriage than primarily sexual or primarily emotional EMI.

Husbands and wives appear to observe a double code when they discuss their EMI. Wives are generally more willing to admit emotional involvement and are often reluctant for their husbands to know they have had sexual intercourse with their extramarital partner. Husbands are generally inclined to discount the seriousness of their own extramarital sexual involvement, but they may withhold the extent of emotional extramarital involvement from their wives. These apparent sanctions against telling about a specific aspect of extramarital involvement reflect gender differences in EMI characterized by strong reactions of men to their wives' extramarital intercourse and strong reactions of women to their husbands' extramarital emotional involvement.

We suggest that therapists approach men and women differently when exploring the ramifications of their extramarital involvement because of this apparent double code. Namely, ask women about emotional involvement first; ask men about sexual involvement first. Clients may find it easier to share initially the dimension of EMI that is consistent with traditional sex roles. Then they may be more comfortable disclosing the extent of their involvement on the dimension of EMI that has greater sanctions for that gender.

MARITAL STATE AND EMI

Does EMI Reflect an Unhappy Marriage?

Extramarital sex is commonly assumed to be associated with an unhappy marriage. However, analyses based on clinical observations (Ellis, 1969; Johnson, 1972; Myers & Leggitt, 1972) and interview data or surveys (Cuber & Haroff, 1963; Hunt, 1969; Kinsey et al., 1953; Sprey, 1972) have concluded that some marriages are enriched, some are harmed, and others appear to be relatively unaffected by extramarital involvement. Another source of confusion when a negative association is found between EMI and the state of the marriage is that marital dissatisfaction can be a cause or an effect of EMI. Spanier and Margolis (1983) found that divorced and separated men and women regarded spouse EMS as the *cause* of marital problems but viewed their own EMS as the *result* of marital problems.

Empirical research on the relationship between marital dissatisfaction and extramarital involvement is inconsistent. Mixed findings may be attributed partly to lack of differentiation by gender and/or by type of extramarital involvement, because most of these studies only addressed extramarital *sex*. In studies with single-sex populations, Whitehurst (1969) found that EMS was associated with negative marital adjustment for men, and Bell et al. (1975) found EMS associated with low marital happiness and sexual dissatisfaction for women. Neubeck and Schletzer (1962) combined the sexes and found no relationship between marital satisfaction and extramarital sexual or emotional involvement, but they studied a small sample with a low incidence of EMS.

In studies where the data have been analyzed separately for men and women, the findings between studies also have been mixed (Buunk, 1980; Glass & Wright, 1977, 1985; Johnson, 1970b). Johnson found that EMS husbands had lower marital and sexual satisfaction than non-EMS husbands, wives showed the same general pattern, but the differences were not significant. Buunk (1980), in a Dutch study, found that dissatisfaction with the affective aspects of marriage was associated with potential extramarital involvement for both sexes but was associated with actual involvement for men only. For both men and women, sexual and/or emotional extramarital involvement were associated with general marital dissatisfaction (Glass & Wright, 1985) and with dissatisfaction over specific sexual or emotional aspects of marriage (Glass, 1981); these associations were consistently stronger for women than men. Among those who experienced extramarital sexual intercourse, the proportion of women who were happily married was significantly lower than the proportion of men who were happily married (34% vs. 56%) (Glass & Wright, 1985). Hunt's (1969) findings are remarkably similar; 33% of EMS women versus 50% of EMS men reported high marital satisfaction. In a magazine survey with 100,000 respondents, Petersen (1983) found that women who are sexually satisfied in their marriages are less likely to engage in EMS, but men "cheat" despite the quality of marital sex. Petersen suggests that it may be inappropriate for wives to blame themselves for their husbands' affairs; we would like to add the same cautionary note for marital therapists. Even in those studies where marital and sexual satisfaction is significantly lower for those who have engaged in extramarital relationships, there are still a substantial number of EMS participants who report happy marriages and enjoyable marital sex.

Research suggests that the relationship between marital dissatisfaction and EMI is moderated by gender and by type of involvement. Extramarital involvement that is mainly sexual is less likely to be associated with marital dissatisfaction than EMI that combines sexual intercourse and deep emotional involvement (Glass & Wright, 1985; Kinsey et al., 1953). Since women are more likely than men to participate in a combined-type involvement, there is often a greater association between the state of the marriage and EMI for women than for men. It may be that deficits in their marriages lead women to look outside their marriages to satisfy unmet emotional needs, or it may be that the greater depth of emotional involvement of women in their extramarital relationships has a stronger adverse impact on their marriages. In contrast, men's extramarital involvements are related more to their attitudes, beliefs, values, and opportunities for EMS than to an unhappy marriage (Glass, 1981). Kinsey et al. (1953) reported that sexual variety appears a reasonable desire to men, but most women could not understand how a "happily married" man would want sexual intercourse with another woman.

When men become emotionally involved in their extramarital sexual relationship, their EMI is similar to women's EMI and they too are likely to report an unhappy marriage (Glass & Wright, 1985; Gurgul et al., 1969). These empirical findings of greater marital dissatisfaction in emotionally involved EMS are consistent with treatment implications stated by family therapist Elbaum (1981), that "The type of extramarital sex that is most destructive to a marital relationship is the ongoing affair where there is an emotional commitment...") (p. 490).

Clinicians make different conclusions about whether extramarital relationships are "good" or "bad" depending on their own observations; their value-laden vocabulary often reflects their individual perspectives. Johnson (1972) characterizes "adulterous" marriages as "replete with untrustworthiness, paranoia, disappointment, and utter frustration" (p. 190). Salzman (1974) asserts that "infidelity" represents dissatisfaction, discontent, and a questionable commitment to the individual's marital partner. Humphrey and Strong (1976) consider EMS affairs a severe threat to marital happiness and stability. Ables (1982) believes that extramarital affairs are detrimental to marriage because they decrease involvement in the marriage, reduce motivation to negotiate, and stimulate unrealistic expectations; marriage cannot compete with an affair in terms of romantic intensity. Boylan (1971) categorically states that "sexual infidelity is the best known symptom of an unhealthy marriage" (p. 16).

Myers and Legitt (1972) strongly advocate that clinicians consider that there are positive aspects of EMI, and they have made a deliberate effort to offset the more widely reported destructive effects. They report that a marriage may benefit from EMI by reducing resentment or feelings of deprivation caused by lacks in the marital relationship. The involved spouse can increase self-esteem, improve personal attractiveness, develop new dimensions of sexuality, and enhance his or her own capacity for warmth; the implication is that these personal enrichments can then be a resource for an improved marriage. They assert that there is no scientific evidence that sexually monogamous couples have more (or less) fun in bed, or have better (or worse) overall relationships than couples in which one or both spouses have engaged in EMS. Weil (1975) suggests that "marriages may have more permanence because many individuals find an answer to unmet needs in such (EMS) relationships" (p. 725). She contends that not all EMS is the result of a problem marriage and that not all EMS creates problems for the marriage.

Low marital satisfaction is commonly associated with low need satisfaction in the marriage. A common assumption has been that the involved spouse is looking elsewhere because of deficits in the marriage. A supplementary need hypothesis of EMI has been proposed but only inconsistently supported by empirical evidence (Glass, 1981; Neubeck & Schletzer, 1962).

We have found that marital dissatisfaction may be experienced by both spouses in an inequitable relationship; that is, the spouse who does less for his partner may be as unhappy or in some cases more unhappy than the spouse who does more in the marriage. The underbenefitted spouse may be dissatisfied by lack of reciprocity in the relationship, but a strong personal investment in the marriage often creates an unwavering commitment. On the other hand, the overbenefitted spouse, who may have never put much energy into the marriage, can be more vulnerable to opportunities for EMI because one foot is already out the door.

How is EMI Associated with Length of Marriage?

Length of marriage and stage in the family life cycle are aspects of the marital relationship that can be associated with EMI. Research on length of marriage consistently reports that marital satisfaction decreases and unfavorable perceptions of one's spouse increase the longer a couple is married. Glass and Wright (1977) found that the relationship between EMS and marital satisfaction varied according to length of marriage in different patterns for men and women. For men, EMS was associated with low marital satisfaction in young but not old marriages. The earlier in the marriage a man had extramarital intercourse the lower was his subsequently reported marital satisfaction. EMS men in older marriages reported high marital satisfaction, whereas EMS women in older marriages reported the lowest marital satisfaction of any other group in the study. Spanier and Margolis (1983) found that more than half of their subjects began EMS within 4 years after their marriage but did not divorce or separate until many years later. Hunt (1974) found that divorced people had experienced EMS earlier than those in stable marriages. Bell et al. (1975) found that modern women with high marital happiness and liberal sexual values were more likely to engage in EMS when they had been married more than 5 years. In general, EMS early in a marriage can be indicative of marital dissatisfaction or potential instability.

Elbaum (1981) has asserted that stages of marriage can provide insight into conflicts in the relationship that may contribute to EMI. In the initial stages of marriage, extramarital relationships often revolve around dependence-independence issues. In the next stage of marriage, when pregnancy and childbirth occur, it is not unusual for the husband to seek another relationship if the wife's attention to the baby causes the husband to feel excluded. We would further note that young mothers are unlikely to engage in EMI because of lack of opportunity, time, and energy. In the middle stages of marriage, the male sexual responsiveness slows down and female sexuality increases (Elbaum, 1981). The peak incidence of EMI for women is mid to late 30s (Kinsey et al., 1953; Levin, 1975); we suggest that this seems to coincide not only with increased responsiveness but also with children going to school and mothers going to work. Whitehurst (1969) suggested that EMS among males married 10 to 20 years is associated with loss of youthful idealism and decreased interdependency in the marriage. Mace (1965) observed that middle-aged men were impelled by curiosity or were susceptible to feelings of inadequacy. In polygamous societies, old men use their old first wife for understanding and companionship and their young second wife to renew their sex lives (Blood & Wolfe, 1960). Elbaum has stated that after the mid-60s affairs diminish because of increased security needs, fear of family disapproval and increased preoccupation with health concerns.

What Type of Marriage is Associated with EMI?

Cuber and Haroff (1963) related EMS to five different marital types. EMS is rare in the *total* marriage in which partners are intensely bound together by psychological, intellectual, and recreational compatibility. In a *vital* marriage, where there is a strong attachment, when EMS occurs it is usually related to a bohemian approach to life. EMS may provide an outlet for boredom in a *passive- congenial* marriage or be an attempt to recapture the lost romantic mood in a *devitalized* relationship. In a *conflict-habituated* marriage, EMS may provide either an escape or a reason for continued hostility. Whitehurst (1969) sampled upper-middle-class men, using Cuber typology, and found that extra- marital intercourse was associated with a negative Cuber type (*devitalized, pas- sive-congenial,* or *conflict-habituated*). There was a low incidence of extramari- tal intercourse among men in *vital* or *total* marriages; however, 70% of these men had engaged in "fooling around."

Teismann (1983) has described marital systems in which multiple affairs (de- fined as 5 or more) create a continuing series of crises. These affairs function to engage the marital pair in a recurrent pattern of anger, guilt, and reconcilia- tion. While the presenting problem is jealousy over an affair, the underlying issue is problems with intimacy and autonomy. In these conflict-habituated marriages, couples rarely divorce and the involved spouse seldom stops engag- ing in EMS. Family systems theorists believe that an affair is never an individual decision but is always a systemic problem (Elbaum, 1981; Teismann, 1983; Whi- taker et al., 1981). The extramarital partner often acts as an amateur therapist who activates either marital fights or marital intimacy. A wife who doesn't pro- test about her husband's late hours may be sanctioning his affair. According to a systems perspective, an affair does not create a new dyad but instead forms a triangle by adding a third leg to the marital dyad.

Hunt (1969) concluded from interview data that the level of involvement in an affair interacts with level of involvement in the marriage to produce either a positive or negative effect. The most durable affairs were of moderate involve- ment where the marriage was also semi-involved. He observed that marriages that benefit from an affair appear to be amiable rather than loving, tolerable rather than satisfying, and comfortable rather than close. There is no evidence that loving, close, satisfying marriages are helped by an affair. For those who once had a totally committed and involved marriage, the extramarital affair rarely remains casual or emotionally limited. It tends to be "a dynamic and dis- ruptive process that either grows by invading and claiming parts of the marriage, or is counter- attacked by it and driven off...must be resolved one way or the other" (p. 178).

Clinical Implications

It is apparent that EMI can occur in all types of marriages and may or may not be related to marital dissatisfaction. The implications of EMI differ accord- ing to the depth of involvement in the extramarital relationship, marital type, and length of stage or marriage. EMI can be a disruptive force leading to divorce, or it can stabilize a marriage when it supplements unmet needs, lowers expectations and decreases demands. Disruption but not stabilization is gener- ally seen in the clinical setting.

When EMI is associated with an unhappy marriage it may be the product of deficits in an already unhappy marriage; on the other hand, EMI may precipi- tate marital distress through its discovery or by creating an alternative emotional alliance. When a husband states that his EMI is merely a casual sexual encounter and has little to do with his marriage, he could very well be telling the truth. Mace assumes a traditional sex bias when he suggests that it is a sound policy to treat a sexual adventure quite lightly because after such an experience a *man* usually feels humiliated and wants to forget the whole thing. Mace (1965) advises that the wife can create more serious problems in the marriage than ever existed if she persists in dwelling on it. However, most women do perceive their husband's EMI as a personal rejection and proof of the wife's inadequacies, for women interpret extramarital relationships from the female perspective. Petersen (1983) found that 75% of the women versus 50% of the men surveyed believe that an affair indicates a problem in the marriage. One therapeutic strategy is to provide normative information about sex role differences in relationships in order to de-escalate some of the emotions and feelings of rejection generated by discovery of a husband's EMS.

Extramarital relationships that combine sexual intercourse with a strong emotional involvement are most often associated with an unhappy marriage. Therapists are well advised to note the more serious implications for the marriage and the therapeutic outcome when the involved spouse is both sexually and emotionally involved. Sexually involved women are more likely than sexually involved men to be very unhappy with their spouses and to be emotionally invested with their extramarital partners. They often feel hopeless about the marriage, and it may be difficult to engage them in marital therapy. In fact, when a wife (or husband) appears resistant to change, this may be a clue to the therapist that the resistant spouse may be already contemplating a more attractive alternative than working on the marital relationship. When the wife has experienced EMI, this is most often an indicator that the therapy will require an exploration of deficits in the marriage such as poor communication, lack of companionship and inadequate expressions of affection. Similar deficits in the marriage and guarded outcome can be expected when a husband is involved emotionally as well as sexually in an extramarital relationship.

When there is low need satisfaction in the marital relationship, the involved spouse can sometimes be the one who is "giving less" in the marriage rather than the one who is "receiving less." The therapist needs to guard against being triangulated and putting the burden of change on only one partner; it is important for both spouses to invest more in the marriage (if the basic patterns of interaction are to change) because both the overbenefitted and the underbenefitted partners are less happy than those in a more equitable relationship. It is frequently the belabored, devoted wife of a workaholic husband who is devastated by the revelation of his extramarital involvement with an employee, co-worker, or professional associate. Workaholics (who may also be women) are often only peripherally involved in their marriage and family life. As they gradually become emotionally involved with someone at work, they can become much more giving and invested in that relationship than they have ever been in their marriage. One of the parameters that they use to evaluate their ambivalence is that their feelings are so much more intense in the extramarital relationship; but they usually fail to recognize that degree of intensity is directly associated with degree of involvement. The therapeutic task is not only to discover what the involved spouse's partner needs to do to please him or her, but what the involved spouse needs to give in order to feel a greater sense of commitment to the marital partner. Their emotional link to their marital partners will be directly proportional to how much time they are willing to invest and how many considerate behaviors they share with their spouses. Furthermore, it has been our experience that the less committed partners who are not sure of their love will be moved as much or more through their own caring behaviors as by those of their spouses.

Case 1: Anne was exceptionally compassionate and understanding of Alan's ambivalence and pain regarding his "combined-type" extramarital involvement. During the marriage, Alan had invested most of his energy on his career while he could depend on Anne's total commitment to the marriage, children and the house. Conjoint sessions focused on Alan's terminating the EMI concretely and psychologically, and on his becoming more involved with Anne and the children. Individual sessions focused on Alan's resolving his ambivalence and Anne's getting support for her pain. Therapy was interrupted when Alan became seriously ill; for several months he was home from work and enjoyed peace of mind and his wife's unflagging devotion.
When he went back to work he encountered "the other woman" and became conflicted again about which woman he preferred. Anne was encouraged in individual sessions to take care of her own needs, to be *less* understanding, and to expect Alan to initiate and be responsible for "giving" as well as "taking." She wrote Alan a letter [extracted below] that changed the equity expectations in their relationship and resulted in Alan's making a strong and definite commitment to the marriage.

Dear Alan,

If you are on the fence and still trying to decide who you want to spend the rest of your life with, her or I, you are OFF the fence because I am shoving you off because I will not be in any race for your affection.
If you want to make it with me you better pick up the ball and start running because I am passing it to you. I am tired of carrying it...I look at our love as a nice comfortable burning ember after the blaze dies down. But you are blowing it out and there have been times you have stamped on it with both feet...if you want to keep the embers glowing you better pucker up and blow. You may be thinking she can't be serious but I am, Alan. I have never felt so strongly about anything like this in my life. This is a brand-new ball game. I want you to show me it's worth my time to stay in the game. I refuse to stay in unless there is an active participation from the other player...

I am tired of giving, you better start giving...Pretend I am your girl-friend, not your wife (who will always be there, because she won't be). Make an effort to impress me like a lover would...

Alan, I really want to go the whole nine yards with you. I'll be in the end zone waiting for you, but you are the quarterback now. The ball is in your hands and you are going to run for the touchdown (not me, I just passed it). I'll be waiting for you to win the game (I hope you do). If not I will have to start a new game without you.

I Love you,

Anne.

A systems perspective may reveal that an overbenefitted spouse who gets in-volved in an extramarital relationship may be a marginal member of the family constellation, and that the marital partner may be overly involved with the child-ren or with relatives. If the therapeutic intervention is to have any chance of per-manence, then a restructuring of the family system is necessary so that the strongest coalition is between husband and wife and that appropriate hierar-chies and boundaries with other family members are established.

INDIVIDUALISTIC REASONS FOR EMI: EMPIRICAL LITERATURE

Individualistic (vs. relational) reasons for EMI have been proposed by re-searchers and by clinicians. Researchers have focused on social-demographic characteristics and attitudinal variables, whereas clinicians have focused on in-dividual psychopathology and psychodynamic explanations for EMI. Most empirical studies have explored the influence of background variables but the results have yielded little explanatory or predictive value. Personal-readiness characteristics that involve justifications, attitudes, opportunities, and need states have been found to be more highly related to extramarital behavior. Re-search attempts to empirically validate clinical hypotheses and conclusions have been quite limited in scope and number.

Social Background/Demographic Variables

Most of the empirical studies of EMS have included background variables, such as age, liberal versus conservative values, education, ethnicity, gender, geo-graphic region, occupational status, political orientation, premarital sex, re-ligion, socioeconomic status, size of community, and wife's employment. Several studies have found modest correlations between these background variables and EMS (Athanasiou & Sarkin, 1974; Bell et al., 1975; Buunk, 1980; Edwards & Booth, 1976; Levin, 1975; Maykovich, 1976). Athanasiou and Sarkin found extensive premarital sexual activity to be related to extramarital sex, particularly where behavior and values are congruent. Bell et al. found that liberal sexuality and life-style explained variation in EMS more than did standard demographic variables. Thompson (1983), in a review of the EMS research literature, concluded that social background variables are of minimal importance in predicting and accounting for EMS.

Personal-Readiness Characteristics

Thompson (1983) presented two categories of individualistic reasons for EMS: extramarital sexual permissiveness attitudes and personal readiness characteristics. Thompson concluded that EMS permissiveness is related to premarital sexual permissiveness, but so far there is no clear demonstration that EMS permissiveness predicts EMS behavior. For example, Maykovich (1976) found discrepancies between EMS attitudes and EMS behavior in Japanese and American women; Japanese women were inclined to engage in EMS without approving of it and American women were more likely to approve without actual participation.

Personal-readiness characteristics include a cluster of variables that stress positive motives for EMS (need for intimacy, need for relational variety, sex role egalitarianism, and emotional independence), which Buunk (1980) found to be strongly correlated with actual EMI and with intentions to have an EMI. Atwater (1979) found that important steps for women becoming involved in their first EMS included knowing someone who had engaged in EMS, talking to that person, and thinking about EMS for an extended period of time after becoming aware of an opportunity for EMS.

Perceived opportunity for EMS has been linked to reported EMS behavior (Glass, 1981; Johnson, 1970b; Maykovich, 1976; Whitehurst, 1969). Men report more actual opportunities and are more likely than women to seek opportunities for EMS and to cite the lack of opportunity as the reason for noninvolvement (Glass, 1981; Johnson, 1970b). Glass suggested that happily married women may have a selective filter that inhibits their perception of opportunities for EMS.

Reasons/Justifications for EMI

Extramarital experience appears to be associated more with endorsing a specific rationale for EMI experience than with a general attitude of EMS permissiveness. Reasons and justifications for EMI have been proposed by a number of clinicians and researchers, based on clinical observations and survey responses of extramarital participants (see Table 13-1).

Sexual and marital reasons appear to predominate, but other reasons/justifications include companionate aspects, love, ego enhancement, psychodynamic formulations, and opportunity. Although revenge is a reason frequently cited by clinicians, only 6% of our nonclinical sample believe that "getting even with spouse" justified an EMI. Sexual excitement is a reason frequently cited by clinicians and researchers that was also endorsed by 75% of the men and 53% of the women in our sample who had engaged in extramarital intercourse. On the

Table 13.1.   Reasons and Justifications for Extramarital Involvement

	1	2	3	4	5	6	7	8	9	10	11
Sexual											
Novelty or variety		*	*h	*S		*	*		*		*
Curiosity			*h	*S	*					*	
Frustration or deprivation			*h	*	*	*	*	*		*	
Enjoyment				*S			*				
Excitement			*d	*S			*				
Unsatisfying marital sex				*		*	*	*		*	
Liberal sexual values	*					*	*			*	*
Marital											
Low marital satisfaction	*		*d	*		*	*				*
Boredom						*	*			*	*
Unattractive spouse								*			
Revenge, rebellion, or hostility	*		*d	*X	*		*	*	*		
Ego-bolstering			*d								
To enhance self-confidence or self-esteem		*		*E			*			*	
To get respect or recognition		*		*E	*		*			*	
To prove sexual attractiveness					*		*				*
To feel young				*			*				
Companionate											
Emotional satisfaction							*		*		*
Understanding				*E			*				
Companionship				*E			*				
Intellectual sharing	*			*E							
Fun				*							
Love			*h								
Falling in love				*L			*				
To get love and affection				*L			*				
For romantic experience				*			*				
Opportunity				*						*	
Physical separation	*							*	*	*	*
Propinquity						*					
To advance career				*X							

d = disturbed reason; h = healthy reason; S = Sexual factor; X = Extrinsic factor; E = Social-emotional factor; L = Love factor

1: Cuber & Hartoff (1983); 2: Elbaum (1981); 3: Ellis (1969); 4: Glass (1981); 5: Greene (1981); 6: Humphrey (1983b); 7: Hunt (1969); 8: Johnson (1970b); 9: Kinsey et al. (1953); 10: Mace (1965); 11: Weil (1975).

ATTITUDES ABOUT EXTRAMARITAL RELATIONSHIPS

Married persons frequently are involved in relationships with friends or acquaintances of the opposite sex. These relationships vary in degree of intimacy and may include emotional and/or sexual involvement.

Here is a list of reasons that people sometimes give to explain why they have been involved with someone of the opposite sex outside their marriage in a very close relationship.

To what extent would each of the following reasons justify either an emotional or sexual extramarital relationship for you?

I would feel _____ justified having an extramarital relationship for or to:

		I would feel completely justified	I would feel partially justified	I would feel not justified	I would feel completely unjustified
1.	For fun	1	2	3	4
2.	For intellectual sharing	1	2	3	4
3.	For a romantic experience.............	1	2	3	4
4.	To feel young.......................	1	2	3	4
5.	To relieve sexual deprivation or frustration	1	2	3	4
6.	For someone to understand problems and feelings	1	2	3	4
7.	To enjoy sexual relations	1	2	3	4
8.	For sexual experimentation or curiosity ..	1	2	3	4
9.	For companionship	1	2	3	4
10.	For sexual excitement	1	2	3	4
11.	To get love and affection	1	2	3	4
12.	To enhance self-confidence and self-esteem	1	2	3	4
13.	For novelty and change	1	2	3	4
14.	To be respected	1	2	3	4
15.	Falling in love with another person	1	2	3	4
16.	To get even with spouse	1	2	3	4
17.	To advance in my career	1	2	3	4
18.	Other _____	1	2	3	4

Figure 13.1 Justifications for Extramarital Involvement Questionnaire. (Copyright © 1986 by Shirley P. Glass).

other hand, 43% of the men and 77% of the women in the survey who had engaged in extramarital intercourse believed that "falling in love" justifies an extramarital involvement; however, love is infrequently cited as a reason for EMI by clinicians and researchers.

Glass (1981) reviewed the clinical and empirical literature for reasons and justifications (presented in Table 13-1) and then analyzed sex differences in justifications for sexual EMI and emotional EMI. She determined that seventeen justifications for EMI (see Figure 13-1) cluster into four factors for both

men and women: sexual, socio-emotional, love, and extrinsic. Sexual justifications are endorsed more by men, and love justifications are endorsed more by
women. People who have engaged in EMI are more likely to endorse specific
justifications for EMI than those who have never been sexually or emotionally
involved. The type of reason that people endorse as justification for an EMI
corresponds to the type of EMI that they are likely to have. For men and women,
sexual justifications (enjoyment, curiosity, excitement) are strongly associated
with EM sexual involvement. Love justifications are associated with men's
emotional EM involvement but with both sexual and emotional EM involvement
for women. These associations between justification attitudes and EM behavior
provide clear evidence for men's separating sex and love in extramarital relationships. For men, justification attitudes are more relevant for EMI than marital dissatisfaction. For women, the reverse is true; marital dissatisfaction is more
relevant to EMI than justification attitudes. Thus, women's EMI is related more
to deficits in the marriage, and men's EMI is related more to their beliefs and
value system. Glass and Wright (1985) have suggested that men take a more individualistic approach to EM involvement, whereas women take a more relational approach.

INDIVIDUALISTIC REASONS FOR EMI: CLINICAL LITERATURE

Clinical Diagnoses and EMI

Clinicians often view EMI as a sign of emotional disturbance (Greene, 1981;
Humphrey, 1983a; Mace, 1965), although it may be inappropriate to reach conclusions about nonclinical populations from observations of people who are
seen in therapy (Cuber & Haroff, 1963). Strean (1980) concluded from his psychoanalytic patients that "an occasional one night stand can be a fairly harmless regression, but a sustained extramarital affair is a form of neurotic compul-
sion in a person who is too immature to cope with the emotional and interpersonal tasks of marriage" (p. 19). Ellis (1969) differentiates between healthy and
disturbed reasons for EMI (see Table 13-1). "Healthy adultery," according to
Ellis, is noncompulsive and doesn't interfere with the marriage. Greene has associated EMS with several categories of psychopathology. He observed that "infidelity" is often an attempt by chronic alcoholics to overcome strong feelings
of insecurity and lowered self-esteem caused by premature ejaculation or impotence. In the affective disorders, infidelity can be an attempt to ward off a depressive reaction or can be a manifestation of increased motor activity in a hy-
pomanic phase. Greene noted that individuals with immature personalities or
character disorders may engage in EMS with no anxiety, remorse or guilt.

Additional psychodynamic explanations for EMS include feelings of inadequacy, denial of unconscious homosexuality, figurative penis envy (Greene,
1981) and difficulty with intimacy (Elbaum, 1981). Strean notes that EMS can

be an expression of profound bisexual conflict. A man who suffers from castration anxiety may enact a "Don Juan" promiscuous posture in order to "prove" his virility and to deny the passivity and feelings of vulnerability that he feels in the marital relationship. Similarly, a castrating woman may try to "prove" her femininity and sexual attractiveness through EMS.

There is little empirical evidence linking personality, psychopathology, and EMS. Neubeck and Schletzer (1962) concluded that low strength of conscience is associated with EMS. However, their small sample of 9 EMS subjects was not differentiated by sex, and the operational definition of strength of conscience (MMPI Pd Scale score > 60) is questionable. Whitehurst (1969) found that alienation and need for power are associated with EMS among middle-aged men.

Flight into Fantasy

"Extramarital liaisons, in particular, need to be discussed in relation to their escape or fantasy value" (Berman, Miller, Vines, & Lief, 1977, p. 204). "The affair with its island of bliss, excitement, and devilish abandon can offer more libidinal pleasure, but usually not without some conflict" (Strean, 1976, p. 103). Myers (1976) states, "The reality is that it is indeed quite possible for two mature, secure persons to meet in an escape world and be intimate in a sort of vacuum suspended in time, and after the allotted time, be it an hour, or a day, or a week, each return to the realities of job, marriage, or home" (p. 113).

Myers and Leggitt (1972) have noted that EMI often provides a temporary respite and diversion from the problems at home. We have observed that an extramarital involvement may be subsequent to some traumatic episode or loss — or associated with severe life stressors related to financial or occupational instability. The marital partner can be associated too much with the realities of the current life struggle or tragedy. When marital partners have different styles of handling stress and grief, they may drift apart and seek intimacy or diversion with an understanding third person. In some cases this interested third party is a therapist; in other cases it is an extramarital partner.

Splitting Sex and Affection

There is a tendency in some men and women to seek love gratification from one person and sexual satisfaction from another. Psychoanalytic interpretations, biological processes, sexual drives, and sex-role socialization theories have all been proposed to explain "splitting" sex and love.

Psychoanalytic explanations generally assume particular personality structures and projective phenomena in spousal perceptions and interactions. Weil (1975) states that when individuals relate to their mates as parental figures, incest taboos inhibit sexual gratification with their parentified spouse. Strean (1980) suggests that splitting occurs in some men whose strong oedipal attachment to the maternal introject causes them to maintain a platonic relationship with their "wife- mother" and a sexual relationship with their "whore- mistress."

Furthermore, an extramarital relationship may be a manifestation of a drive for autonomy and independence when the marital relationship is authoritarian, smothering, or symbiotic. The forbidden nature of EMS may make it exciting and romantic in a manner similar to the intensification of romantic feelings in dating relationships when there is significant parental interference (Driscoll et al., 1972).

Case 2: Bill and Belle's marital relationship paralleled Bill's relationship with his domineering, demanding mother. Bill procrastinated endlessly and Belle nagged him about household duties and lack of sexual interest. Belle separated from Bill after discovering Bill's sexual affair with a co-worker. Bill was very upset about the separation and agreed to marital therapy as a condition of reconciliation. During the course of therapy, Bill's anger at Belle for leaving him became apparent. Finally, Bill blurted out "*Mothers*—I mean *wives* aren't supposed to leave." The implications were clear: Belle should have been content to stay home with the light in the window while Bill was out having a good time. Belle should know Bill will always come home (to mother).

Case 3: Carl was 12 years older than Carla. He was a very traditional man who expected women to be content with their only roles in life as wife and mother. After a childhood as dutiful daughter and 15 years as devoted wife and supermother, Carla began to search for her own sense of identity and to resent Carl's paternal attitudes. During a domestic argument Carla became hysterical when Carl ordered her, "Go to your room!" Carla believed that there was no area of her life out of Carl's jurisdiction and she became involved in several casual EM sexual affairs as an exciting act of rebellion. When Carla subsequently became emotionally involved with an EM partner, Carl's desperate pleadings and intentions to change could not prevent Carla from leaving the marriage and terminating marital therapy after only three sessions.

Kinsey et al. (1953) cite a biological basis for increased sexual excitement with a new partner. "Among most species of mammals, sexual response is likely to become more vigorous when the animal encounters a new situation or meets a new sexual partner" (p. 411). In those over 40 years of age, physiological changes cause a change in sexual interactions. Some seek relief in the excitement of EMS, but it is only a temporary stimulant for problems of a less rigid penis, decreased vaginal lubrication, longer time for orgasmic experience, and longer male refractory period (Cleveland, 1976). Men, but not women, were found to engage in EMS because of an expressed need for exciting sex (Glass, 1981).

Balswick and Peek (1971) propose that men, in spite of a generalized inability to be emotionally expressive, may learn to be more expressive in the marriage by relating to their wives differentially than in their relating to women in general. If a husband remains emotionally expressive with his spouse but not with his extramarital sexual partner, marital stability can be maintained. There is some empirical evidence to support the concept that men may separate sex and affection. Rothstein (1960) found that authoritarian men (high F-Scale) tended to react sexually toward women whom they don't admire or respect and to inhibit sexual expression when respect and affection are felt. Glass & Wright (1985) found that men are much more likely than women to separate sex and love in their extramarital involvements.

Opportunity to Experience New Roles

An extramarital relationship may provide an individual with the opportunity to experience new roles that are different from the ones that they enact in the marriage. The dependent spouse can take on a more independent or equitable stance. The nurturant spouse can enjoy being cared for, and the taker can find great delight in giving. The sexually inhibited can be the initiator and experience new and freer sex. The insensitive spouse can assume the role of the empathic listener. Those who feel intellectually inferior in the marriage can feel that their ideas are valued and respected. In each of these cases, part of the appeal of the EM relationship is that the person has the opportunity to express different aspects of herself or himself in a new relationshp where the roles are not fixed. In trying out new roles in the EM relationship, the individual may discover a capacity for a wider range or depth of feelings and behaviors than they formerly believed possible.

> Case 4: Donna was supermother and superwife. She was a sensitive, responsible woman who was always there. Don was a hard-working, traditional male who was emotionally inexpressive. Donna protected and insulated him from family obligations. He became involved sexually first and then gradually developed an emotional involvement with a professional associate. He found that he was able to be sensitive and caring in a way that he and Donna had never realized. He valued this emotional renaissance and considered leaving the marriage to experience these feelings in the EM relationship, but he wanted to give his marriage a chance before making this choice.
>
> Donna came to marital therapy to save their marriage; Don's agenda was to decide which woman he wanted to be with. He was good friends with his wife but he was not "in love" with her. In conjoint marital therapy, Donna was encouraged to stop being Don's emotional interpreter and to allow Don to speak for himself. Don learned to express himself more openly with Donna, and he grew to feel more for Donna by giving more of himself to her. The key to therapy was that as Don expressed more caring and affection, and made more romantic overtures to Donna, he gradually discovered that he could experience a similar emotional renaissance with Donna. Once he discovered that he could experience the same feelings with Donna, his ambivalence was resolved.

Clinical Implications

The empirical literature suggests the importance of assessing attitudes toward EMI, opportunities for EMI, and the extent of premarital and extramarital sexual experience. Our Extramarital Justifications Questionnaire (see Figure 13-1) prepares the patient to report actual EMI by first asking them whether specific reasons for EMI are justified. Their endorsement of specific justifications for EMI permits us to evaluate their beliefs and values and alerts us to areas on which to focus in the marital therapy. What may be quite important clinically is the behavior-value congruence or discrepancy; for instance, an involved spouse who doesn't approve of EMI will experience guilt and be more motivated to work on the marriage, whereas it may be more difficult to stop extramarital behavior that is congruent with the person's value system. If husband and wife have different value systems regarding EMI, this will be a thorny clinical problem. Sprenkle and Weiss (1978) observed that if both spouses believe in the traditional"script" and one has "strayed," that is a much different therapeutic context than if one partner supports a traditional script and the other does not.

A key implication of individualistic aspects of the clinical literature is whether the treatment should be individual or conjoint. Our basic approach, regardless of our perception of individual dynamics and psychopathology, is to provide treatment primarily within the marital context. It is our belief that a therapist can establish an intimate relationship and supplant the extramarital partner, but that this does little to enhance the marital relationship and may, in fact, disrupt it. Connecting the present interpersonal problems with the patient's early history can be done with both spouses present; the marital partner is often an important source of information whose perceptions can facilitate the therapeutic process. Furthermore, parallel inquiries can be carried out with both spouses, so that they can develop more empathy for each other's experiential background.

If the EMI appears to have been a "flight into fantasy," one therapeutic strategy is to bring fun and romance back into the marriage. Couples who are stressed with parental and occupational responsibilities must be encouraged to structure "honeymoon hours" or "we-time" into their daily/weekly routines. The therapist's office can become a "dumping ground" in which they can safely confront and resolve problematic and painful issues. They should be directed to use their time together outside of therapy for relationship-enhancing experiences and to save the distress and pain for work within the therapy sessions.

If the involved spouse appears to be splitting sex and affection because the marital partner is perceived as an incestuous object, conjoint therapy can focus on restructuring their "parent-child" relationship. When the involved spouse is reacting against the marital partner's parental stance, it is important for the therapy to be conjoint in order to change the relationship to one where the power is more equitably distributed. "Parental" spouses must stop functioning as the partner's superego before they can become appealing sex objects. It is not uncommon for the parental spouse to nag partner routinely about duties and responsibilities that have been delayed, neglected, or not performed to the expected level. The concept of an equal partnership where responsibilities are owned jointly can help to change this pattern. The involved spouse may, on the other hand, be an authoritarian figure who feels sexually inhibited by a spouse who is seen as childlike and innocent. Sexual therapy is an important aspect of the marital therapy when the goal is exciting sex with the marital partner. Sharing sexual fantasies, working through sexual inhibitions, and psychoeducational approaches for sexual techniques can enhance the sexual aspects of the marriage and make an EMI less important. Unfortunately, it has been our experience that when the wife acts out against the husband's parental stance by engaging in EMS, the prognosis is the least favorable for the continuation of the marriage that we have yet encountered. Moreover, we have observed that when sexual excitement is enhanced by the forbidden nature of EMS, extramarital partners are likely to become less sexually attractive if they eventually become the marital partner.

When the involved spouse has used the extramarital relationship to experience new roles, the marital therapist can help the person use the new positive roles that were developed in the extramarital relationship to enhance the marital relationship. Focus on what the involved spouse experienced that was different and felt good in the EMI rather than on special characteristics of the extramarital partner. Frame questions about the extramarital experience to discover what can be brought back to the marital relationship, rather than question what deficits in the marriage and/or the spouse led to EMI. Help the non-involved spouse to accept these new roles as relationship enhancing, rather than as indictments of the self, the marriage, or the spouse. Help the couple to try out aspects of these new roles in their relationship. Help both partners change to accommodate these new roles.

SECRET EMI: DISCLOSURE, CONFIDENTIALITY, AND ALLIANCES

Disclosure, confidentiality, and secret coalitions are particularly troublesome issues for marital therapists when dealing with secret EMI. Even couples who do not present EMI as a source of marital distress may be experiencing the effects of secret EMI by one or both partners. Whether disclosure of an ongoing EMI is a necessary or appropriate condition for a successful therapeutic intervention is a widely debated issue.

Disclosure to Therapists: Should Initial Sessions be Conjoint or Individual?

Clinical opinions are divided about whether to begin marital therapy with individual or conjoint sessions. Secrecy about EMI is most likely to be maintained during conjoint sessions and disclosed during individual sessions. The structure and focus of the initial sessions of marital therapy reflect whether a therapist's primary focus is individualistic or relational. Therapists who are concerned about operating "in the dark" usually prefer to start marital therapy by seeing the spouses separately. Those who take a systems-oriented approach are more concerned about avoiding secret coalitions and usually prefer to begin marital therapy with both partners.

Therapists who begin their evaluation with individual history- taking sessions develop a separate, confidential alliance with each spouse, through which secrets can be revealed. Humphrey (1983a) emphatically states that the initial evaluation in marital therapy should always — without exception — include a minimum of one separate confidential interview with each spouse because of the large proportion of cases that involve EMS. Elbaum (1981) also places great importance on the therapist's being aware of ongoing extramarital relationships. The therapist who is deceived is not in control of the session, and treatment results are likely to be negative.

Jacobson and Margolin (1979) always begin marital therapy with a conjoint session in order to preserve a relationship focus. They are concerned that if secrets unfold during individual sessions, an alliance is formed that excludes the naive partner. On the other hand, they acknowledge that if the therapist is unaware of ongoing EMS, the treatment plan may be derived from inappropriate premises and therapy can be irrevocably harmed. They conclude that individual sessions, if utilized at all, should be used sparingly and only after careful consideration of the benefits and liabilities that may result. Ables (1982) believes that it is possible for the therapist to share a secret with one spouse and not have it interfere with marital therapy — unless the confiding spouse is attempting to manipulate the therapist into a unilateral alliance. He notes the difficulty of moving from individual to conjoint therapy, because of the original identification with one spouse, and concludes that it is better to begin marital therapy with conjoint sessions.

Should Conjoint Therapy Proceed if EMI Continues?

Once therapists become aware of secret EMI, they must decide how to use this information. Jacobson and Margolin (1979) make a strong case for the prevailing stance that conjoint marital therapy cannot proceed unless extramarital relationships are terminated or suspended (Elbaum, 1981; Liberman, et al., 1980). They state that marital therapy is an intensive experience requiring a full-time commitment from both partners. Because EMS creates an imbalance of power, spouses cannot proceed on an equal footing unless EMS is suspended. It is virtually impossible to devote the time and effort for marital therapy to be successful while maintaining a second "sexual" (they neglect the possibility of "emotional") relationship. Terminating EMS is the only way to give the marriage a fighting chance.

Both Humphrey (1983b) and Ables (1982) will proceed with conjoint and individual sessions if the EMI continues. Humphrey works with the involved spouse individually to resolve ambivalent feelings; he helps the other spouse to improve the marital relationship while preparing emotionally for a possible separation. Humphrey's individualistic approach is exemplified by his uncommon practice of offering the involved spouse's extramarital partner an opportunity for individual sessions. Therefore, he appears to treat several clients individually, rather than treating the marital relationship per se, despite the fact that he does see the marital couple in conjoint sessions.

Jacobson and Margolin warn of serious implications if a therapist refuses to treat a couple conjointly because of an ongoing EMI. This therapeutic stance may be viewed as a coercive ultimatum based on information attained under the guise of therapeutic confidentiality. The involved spouse who complies reluctantly may build up resentment toward the therapist. If the involved spouse refuses to suspend EMI, termination may seem abrupt and confusing to the naive partner; new agendas of mistrust and distress between the couple may then be generated by the process of disengaging from therapy. Thus, when therapist concern for preserving the relationship is rigidly applied, it can be a powerful force that leads to further deterioration of the marriage.

The intentions of the involved spouse can be an important factor in determining how to proceed. If the involved spouse is actively struggling with ambivalent feelings, conjoint sessions that enhance the marriage can tilt the balance in favor of the marital partner. On the other hand, a therapist can be compromised by holding conjoint sessions when the involved spouse's hidden agenda is to prove that the therapy won't help. It seems that any stance that is rigidly applied without recognizing the unique needs of each couple may be countertherapeutic.

Should the Spouse be Told about the EMI?

Should the therapist support or press for disclosure of extramarital involvement to the naive partner? Kinsey et al. (1953) reported that the most damaging effects of extramarital relationships were caused by their discovery rather than by their occurrence. Therapist opinions about spouse disclosure vary along a continuum from "must always tell" to "tell under certain circumstances" to "almost never tell." These diverse stances toward spouse disclosure are associated with therapist expectations regarding the probable consequences of disclosure on the marriage.

Scharff (1978) advocates complete disclosure of EMI as a precondition for beginning sex therapy, because he found through experience that lack of revelation increased the likelihood that the dysfunctional partner would remain stuck, commitment would be marginal, and therapeutic work would be "like pulling teeth." He now insists on full disclosure of secret affairs, one-night stands, or platonic unconsummated relationships. He does not urge revelation if the spouse is not committed to the marriage, and he respects patients' beliefs that their spouse could not stand the revelation, but he will not offer sex or marital therapy in either case. Scharff sees disclosure as a crisis, a major turning point, and a time of risk that needs to be guided in order to be a catalyst for growth instead of disintegration. The therapist must use clinical judgment to avoid raising anxiety above useful or tolerable levels, and risks such as potential suicide or incipient psychosis must be carefully assessed. Disclosure uncovers the dangerous state of the marriage and may give a "shot-in-the-arm" to the sexually dysfunctional partner. Disclosure may produce a "thawing of feelings so deeply frozen as to give no sign of being alive at all" (p. 49), and create a new, open, and firm foundation for the rebuilding and integration of a sexual and marital relationship.

Humphrey's (1983b) observations of the negative consequences of EMI disclosure have caused him to take a pessimistic outlook that is in direct contrast with that of Scharff. Humphrey predicts that upon disclosure, "all hell will break loose" in the marriage. Revelation of an unknown EMS activity is likely immediately to traumatize the marital partner, and to generate high levels of anger and mistrust. In Humphrey's experience, this virtually insures that a mammoth void — one that may never be bridged — will be formed between the marital partners.

Therapists need to determine individual motivations for and against EMI disclosure by the involved spouse. Ables (1982) no longer believes that complete honesty between spouses is necessary. First, it is important to understand the involved spouse's motivation to tell or not to tell. Motivations for telling may be to alleviate guilt, to punish the partner, or to elicit spouse retaliation in a way that will justify the infidelity. The motivation for not telling may be to avoid possible retaliation or because of a concern for the spouse's feelings.

The motivation of the naive spouse to know or not to know must also be considered. In some cases, the naive spouse is relieved to find out the truth because it validates the suspicious feelings that have been previously refuted and denied. Dicks (1967) states that the desire to know about spouse EMI ranges from "so long as I know nothing about what you do out there" to "the insult wasn't that he had that tart, but that he didn't trust me enough to tell me" (p. 165). The spouse who prefers not to know: (a) may be attempting to maintain an idealized image of spouse, (b) may have a strong need for security, or (c) may exhibit low sexual desire and appreciate the lowered demand for sex. The spouse who *must* know: (a) may need fuller dyadic communication, (b) may share vicariously in the EMI, or (c) may use the knowledge for moral blackmail.

The lack of therapist consensus about spouse disclosure reflects the diversity of spouse reactions and the range of effects on the marriage. Disclosure may serve no real purpose if the involved partner has ended EMI and is making a sincere effort on behalf of the marriage. Premature disclosure of EMI can have a catastrophic effect if the naive spouse reacts with rage and distrust before noteworthy positive changes in the marital relationship have been achieved. However, if secret EMI continues and the involved spouse is resistant to improving the marriage, the therapist could be colluding in the deception of the naive partner with no therapeutic gain possible. Scharff's firm position on disclosure appears to be utilized most effectively when sexual dysfunctions (or destructive interactions) are resistant to change. Disclosure creates a crisis, unbalances a "stuck" marital system, and allows significant changes to take place if the marriage survives the emotional upheaval that disclosure generally evokes.

A Proposal for Dealing with Secret EMI

The issue of secrets and alliances emerges as a source of concern not only for the marriage but also in the therapeutic relationship. We have developed an approach that maintains a system perspective while allowing us to obtain information about EMI. We use confidential precounseling questionnaires that include a section on EMI in order to become informed, while maintaining a conjoint approach for the initial sessions.

If the confidential questionnaire reveals that a secret EMI is ongoing, we plan to see the spouses separately for 15 to 20 minutes at some point during the initial session. We explain to the couple at the beginning of the session that it is a part of our routine (in cases of secret EMI), in order to give each spouse an opportunity to meet with one of us individually. They are advised that confidentiality will be maintained between marital partners but not between the cotherapists.

The involved spouse is offered three options:

1. S/he can terminate the EMI or discontinue the EMI for a specific initial period of commitment to conjoint marital therapy (6 to 12 sessions).
2. If s/he is ambivalent or does not wish to terminate the EMI, s/he can disclose the EMI to the marital partner, with help from the therapist, and give the spouse the choice whether to continue in the marriage and/or the marital therapy.
3. If s/he does not want either to stop the EMI *or* disclose to the marital partner, s/he can make an excuse for choosing not to engage our services when, toward the end of the first session, we present a contract for conjoint marital therapy.

This structure allows us to delineate where the boundaries of confidentiality and alliances are. We believe it is inappropriate to conduct conjoint marital therapy when there is a secret alliance between one spouse and an extramarital partner that is being supported by another secret alliance between the involved spouse and the therapist. If the EMI is terminated and the involved spouse makes a sincere effort to work on the marriage, the therapist is acting equally on behalf of both marital partners. If the EMI continues but the noninvolved spouse wants to fight for the marriage with full knowledge of the EMI, the therapist can again act on behalf of the marriage. If the involved spouse refuses therapy, the therapist can usually avoid creating suspicions or new agendas and act therapeutically to delineate appropriate boundaries.

Treatment Model After EMI Disclosure or Discovery

It is frequently the case that disclosure of an EMI is the precipitating event that propels a couple into marital therapy. Disclosure may have taken place through inadvertent discovery, confession, or suspicious tracking of the involved spouse. Dealing with the effects of EMI disclosure requires specific approaches in marital therapy, regardless of whether spouses were found out as part of on-going therapy or if such disclosure was the reason for beginning therapy.

We have developed an approach to cases of marital therapy that are precip-itated by disclosure or discovery of an extramarital involvement, an approach that successfully uses this crisis as a means to motivate change in both spouses.

We begin with a broad assessment of the marital and extramarital relation-ships and negotiate a therapeutic contract for a specified period, during which the EMI must be suspended. We discreetly use confidential information about the extramarital relationship in structuring the marital therapy. We focus on strengthening the marriage by increasing caring behaviors and improving com-munication skills. We are ready to deal specifically with the extramarital involve-ment after carefully developing a degree of stability and satisfaction in the mari-tal relationship. The extent to which we delve into the details of the extramari-tal involvement is derived for each couple as a unique set of conditions rather than as a generalized policy. The primary goal in therapy is to improve the marriage (Jacobson, 1981; Taibbi, 1983); insight about the EMI is important only as it pertains to this primary goal.

Assessment

We begin the assessment process at intake on the telephone by inquiring about the presenting problems and the level of distress. Then we either mail our assessment package to each spouse under separate cover or have them come in to take the tests before the first session begins. Our intake procedure and our assessment package of paper-pencil tests allows us to do some preliminary loose structuring even before the first session. We establish the confidentiality of the responses to our questionnaires, but we also make it clear that we will utilize the responses to develop therapeutic goals.

Utilizing diagnostic tests enables the therapist to intervene with the marital relationship as the principal focus. The therapist cannot purge the occurrence of an extramarital involvement from the history of a marriage, but efforts can be directed at what can be learned from the extramarital involvement about the marriage and each of the marital partners. Assessing characteristics of the EMI can implicitly direct therapeutic interventions so the involved spouse can begin to experience the positive aspects of the EMI in the marriage.

We evaluate marital satisfaction (16 Aspects of Marital Satisfaction, Glass; see Figure 13-2), commitment (Dyadic Adjustment Scale, Spanier, 1976), caring agendas (Stuart, 1982), sexual adjustment (Sexual Adjustment Inventory, Stu-art et al., 1975), relational efficacy (Marital Agendas Protocol, Notarius & Van-zetti, 1983), marital adjustment (Marital Adjustment Scale, Locke & Wallace, 1958), areas of desired change (Areas of Change Questionnaire, Weiss & Bir-chler, 1975), relationship equity (Who Does More? Glass & Wright, 1985; see Figure 13-3), extramarital attitudes (Justifications for EMI, Glass; see Figure

SATISFACTION AND IMPORTANCE OF SIXTEEN ASPECTS OF MARRIAGE

Directions: For each of the 16 aspects of marriage listed below, circle the rating that answers...

How satisfied are you with each of these aspects of your marriage?

How important to your marriage is each of these?

Satisfaction scale: 1 = Enthusiastic—it could not be any better; 2 = Quite satisfied; 3 = It's all right, I guess—can't complain; 4 = A little disappointed—it could be better; 5 = Really disappointed

Importance scale: 1 = not what I expected; 2 = Absolutely essential; 3 = Extremely important; 4 = Very important; 5 = Moderately important; 6 = Slightly important / Not at all important

Aspect	Satisfaction					Importance					
1. Opportunity to raise children	1	2	3	4	5	1	2	3	4	5	6
2. Enjoying sexual relations with spouse	1	2	3	4	5	1	2	3	4	5	6
3. Understanding by spouse of your problems and feelings	1	2	3	4	5	1	2	3	4	5	6
4. Standard of living—kind of house, car, etc.	1	2	3	4	5	1	2	3	4	5	6
5. Finding sex with your spouse to be exciting	1	2	3	4	5	1	2	3	4	5	6
6. Expression of love and affection by spouse	1	2	3	4	5	1	2	3	4	5	6
7. Household tasks which are done by spouse	1	2	3	4	5	1	2	3	4	5	6
8. Having sexual relations as often as desired	1	2	3	4	5	1	2	3	4	5	6
9. Companionship in doing things with spouse	1	2	3	4	5	1	2	3	4	5	6
10. Having sexual relations bound up with love and affection	1	2	3	4	5	1	2	3	4	5	6
11. Having fun with spouse	1	2	3	4	5	1	2	3	4	5	6
12. Romantic experiences with spouse	1	2	3	4	5	1	2	3	4	5	6
13. Being respected by spouse	1	2	3	4	5	1	2	3	4	5	6
14. Having similar intellectual interests with spouse	1	2	3	4	5	1	2	3	4	5	6
15. Being in love with spouse	1	2	3	4	5	1	2	3	4	5	6
16. Self-confidence or self-esteem enhanced by spouse	1	2	3	4	5	1	2	3	4	5	6

Figure 13.2 16 Aspects of Marital Satisfaction Questionnaire. (Copyright © 1986 by Shirley P. Glass).

13-1) and extramarital behaviors (Glass, 1981, pp. 118-121) We are able to contrast specific aspects of marital satisfaction and specific justifications for EMI such as understanding, companionship, expression of love and affection, respect, and sexual enjoyment and excitement. Sexual EMI is generally less significant than EMI that is both emotional and sexual. We are also able to contrast perceived roles and equity both in the marriage and in the extramarital relationship. Assessing behaviors that would be pleasing or that would indicate caring provides concrete behavioral goals for directed therapeutic change and specific caring agendas. Specific problem areas—such as alcohol/drug abuse, religion, friends, children, relatives, and jealousy—can be quickly surveyed in the questionnaires and outlined in the first session. Marital commitment and love for the spouse are more important prognostic indicators of the course of therapy than are number or range of problems. Initial assessments provide a baseline for change markers, if periodic reassessments are done.*

During the initial session, we outline the major problems and form a judgment of the severity of marital distress and the motivation for treatment. We try to obtain a brief historical perspective of their marital relationship in order to understand "why now?"; that is, "why now" was there an EMI, and "why now" are they choosing to come for marital therapy. We determine whether the problems are longstanding ones, whether they appear to be of recent origin, or whether they are related to developmental changes in the spouses or in the marriage. We tell them that we don't want to go back to what they had before the EMI. We prefer to move forward to something better—the best that their relationship can be. We emphasize that this crisis can be an opportunity to put the pieces back together in a new and better way.

Contract

At the end of the first session, we recommend that the couple verbally contract for a specific number of conjoint sessions. Contracting for a specific period of time adds a degree of stability and commitment that alleviates some of the tension, because it insures that both partners will give the marriage a chance for that given period of time. We prefer to get a commitment for 12 sessions of conjoint therapy; however, when there is marked ambivalence and fragile com-

---

* Degree of extramarital sexual involvement is assessed on a 6-point continuum parallel to measurement of premarital sexual behavior by Ehrmann (1959): What is the greatest extent that you have been sexually involved with someone other than your spouse while still married? (1) No sexual or physical involvement. (2) Kissing. (3) Hugging and caressing. (4) Petting. (5) Sexually intimate without intercourse. (6) Sexual intercourse.

   Degree of extramarital emotional involvement is assessed on a 5-point continuum: What is the greatest extent that you have been emotionally involved with someone other than your spouse while you have been married? (1) No emotional involvement. (2) Slight emotional involvement. (3) Moderate emotional involvement. (4) Strong emotional involvement. (5) Extremely deep emotional involvement.

   An item characterizing EM relationships as more emotional or more sexual was derived from Bowers and Furstenberg (1967): Some extramarital involvements are mainly emotional with little or no sexual involvement and others are just the opposite. How would you describe your extramarital relationship(s)? (0) Never involved sexually or emotionally. (1) Entirely sexual. (2) Mainly sexual. (3)More sexual than emotional. (4) More emotional than sexual. (5)Mainly emotional. (6) Entirely emotional.

SATISFACTION AND IMPORTANCE OF SIXTEEN ASPECTS OF MARRIAGE

Directions: For each of the 16 aspects of marriage listed below, circle the rating that answers...

I. WHO DOES MORE

In your marriage, which spouse does more of the following:

	I always do more	I often do more	We do it equally as often	My spouse often does more	I always do more
1. Who enhances the other's self-confidence more	1	2	3	4	5
2. Who tells more about how the day went	1	2	3	4	5
3. Who does more romantic things	1	2	3	4	5
4. Who understands the other's problems and feelings more	1	2	3	4	5
5. Who respects the other more	1	2	3	4	5
6. Who expresses more love and affection	1	2	3	4	5
7. Who wants to have sexual relations more ...	1	2	3	4	5
8. Who enjoys sexual relations more	1	2	3	4	5

II. WHO DOES MORE

In your most intimate or most recent extramarital relationship(s), who has done more of the following:

(If not applicable, check here _____.)

	I always do more	I often do more	We do it equally as often	My friend often does more	My friend always does more	
1. Who enhances the other's self-confidence more	1	2	3	4	5	NA*
2. Who tells more about how the day went	1	2	3	4	5	NA
3. Who does more romantic things	1	2	3	4	5	NA
4. Who understands the other's problems and feelings more	1	2	3	4	5	NA
5. Who respects the other more	1	2	3	4	5	NA
6. Who expresses more love and affection	1	2	3	4	5	NA
7. Who wants to have sexual relations more ...	1	2	3	4	5	NA
8. Who enjoys sexual relations more	1	2	3	4	5	NA

*NA = Not Applicable in this relationship

Figure 13.3 Relationship Equity Questionnaires: I. Who Does More in the Marriage? II. Who Does More in the EMI? (Copyright © 1986 by Thomas L. Wright and Shirley P. Glass).

mitment, it may be more prudent to suggest a 6-week initial phase. We state that at the end of the given period the four of us will evaluate whether it seems worthwhile to continue marital therapy. The initial stage of marital therapy is a trial period during which the goal is to maximize the marital relationship so *both* partners can make a decision about whether to remain married, based on the *best* that they can aspire to rather than based on the worst that they have experienced. It is clear that commitment to the marital therapy is a metaphor for commitment to the marriage. We see couples weekly or every other week until they are able to get along better, to work out more of their problems on their own, and are relatively satisfied with the marriage. We provide monthly "booster" sessions until the couple is ready to "graduate" from therapy.

The involved spouse is asked to agree to discontinue the EMI during the contracted period. The therapist has to know that the EMI is stopped or on hold during marital therapy, so that the marriage can have its best chance to succeed. Because this will also aid the noninvolved (NI) spouse, it is useful to get this commitment to suspend the EMI from the involved spouse in the first conjoint session.

Developing Caring: Strengthening the Marriage

When EMI is the presenting problem it is usually best to delay exploration of the extramarital involvement until there has been time to develop some "caring behaviors" (Stuart, 1980) in the marital relationship. Couples are advised that it is necessary to build up some credits in their marital account (via "caring" agendas) before discussing the painful issues that have depleted their marital account; premature discussion of negatively charged topics could bankrupt their marriage. If the initial impression is that of a relatively satisfying marital relationship disrupted by a casual sexual extramarital contact, then the focus will be on validating the love and commitment to the marriage and establishing trust. Where the extramarital relationship included an emotional involvement, it is quite likely that deficits in the marital relationship contributed to the development of an extramarital involvement. Only when the marital relationship shows potential for offering comfort, companionship, and caring is it appropriate to conduct an inquiry into the ramifications of the extramarital relationship.

The initial phase of therapy focuses on positive exchanges (particularly at home) as suggested by Stuart. Couples are encouraged to use the therapist's office as a safe, neutral place to "dump" their anger and hurt and are discouraged from holding "heavy" or "hot" discussions at home. Grappling with the heavy issues of the EMI in conjoint sessions is postponed for a later stage in marital therapy when the marital relationship is stronger. The NI spouse, who appears unable to contain anger about the EMI during the initial phases of therapy when EMI discussion is discouraged, can be invited to dump angry feelings at an individual session. Couples will accomplish more by concentrating at home on giving each other the best that each has to offer. Sometimes it is useful to suggest that they pretend (Madanes, 1981) that their relationship has already become what they hope it will be at the conclusion of therapy. Stuart (1982) advises couples to treat each other as nicely as they would treat a stranger. This is an interesting metaphor that is especially useful in treating couples with EMI because the directive allows them to utilize the resources and roles that may have been rewarding in their EMI. It is essential to find an intervention technique that allows the spouses to reestablish caring attitudes and behaviors so their negative feelings of disillusionment and hopelessness will not become a self-fulfilling prophecy. The first assignments consist of desired instrumental behaviors such as calling each other during the day, picking up after oneself, making a nice meal, coming home on time, and kissing hello and good-bye.

The first few sessions of therapy begin by asking about what kinds of caring each spouse *received* during the preceding week. This provides feedback about which caring behaviors and messages got through. Then each spouse is asked what caring behaviors they *sent* that were not acknowledged. This highlights the fact that caring involves both sending and receiving; there can be a breakdown in either end. Most couples expect to begin each session with their complaint list; the report on caring agendas encourages them to perceive positive sides of their relationship and not to overgeneralize the negatives. Although time is allotted in each session to discuss negatives, it is best to begin and end each session with positives.

As the initial caring behaviors become established, additional caring agendas are generated. The EMI assessment is used by the therapist to guide the caring agendas covertly, so that the marital relationship can be broadened and developed to become more like the desired aspects of the EM relationship. The rationale for these changes is best left covert so the NI spouse won't resist outright and so the involved spouse can "discover" that the marital relationship can be as satisfying as the EM relationship.

One evidence of resistance in either spouse is their attributing positive changes and caring behaviors solely to the therapists' assignments. "You only did this because they said to," thus discounting any changes. Spouses who are reluctant to perceive positive motives in their marital partner may be maintaining a negative image of their spouse so that they won't have to change or so they can leave without guilt.

The noninvolved spouse may resist doing the assigned caring behaviors because of anger or numbness. The NI hostile spouse may be unwilling to do anything nice for their partner because they feel "wronged"; they may be inclined to sit back and wait for their partner to "jump through hoops" in order to avenge the infidelity. The therapist can easily become triangulated by buying into a construction of the therapy as the unfaithful spouse "proving" his love. The NI spouse may resist doing caring behaviors because they may presently feel indifferent, cold, or numb. We encourage spouses to do caring behaviors for each other even if they are angry or don't feel caring, because behavior can not only precede feelings but can elicit feelings. If they act in caring ways, they are more likely to recognize emotional arousals that indicate feelings that they still care.

The involved spouse can resist the assigned caring behaviors because of ambivalence or hidden agendas. The involved spouse, who is ambivalent about the marital versus extramarital partners, may be reluctant to display caring behaviors or any spontaneous feelings of warmth toward the marital partner for fear that any loving gestures may be misinterpreted as evidence of a decision or commitment to stay. We reassure them that their caring behaviors will only be taken as evidence of their efforts to give the marriage its best chance for survival, while emphasizing to both spouses that we are still in a trial period with no long-term commitment. Ables (1982) has stated that ambivalent spouses, who claim not to know which partner is preferred, are usually not being honest; in reality they want both but are being forced to choose because of the marital partner's protest.

When involved spouses appear resistant to changes in caring behaviors, it may be an indication that they came into marital therapy with a hidden agenda to prove that the marriage is not salvageable, so they can leave without guilt — because "We tried everything, even counseling, but it just didn't work." If the involved spouse continues to show resistance, we raise the question of a hidden agenda and/or continued involvement with the EMI partner in an individual session.

Improving Communication Skills

Although a deficit in communication skills may or may not be related to the occurrence of EMI, it is important that couples demonstrate constructive communication patterns before a discussion of EMI becomes the appropriate agenda for therapy. Destructive patterns such as cross-complaining, digging up the past, overgeneralization, and "district attorney" questioning can turn conflict over trivial issues into major flare-ups. It is clear that couples who cannot talk to each other constructively about common problem areas can be even more destructive when discussing an explosive, painful topic like an EMI.

Whenever possible or appropriate, we encourage spouses to talk to each other rather than to us so we can observe their communication patterns across a broad range of topics and emotions. The spouse who complains about an inexpressive partner often contributes to the problem by speaking for that partner, by interrupting, interpreting, mind reading, and interrogating. We encourage them to shift to a communication process that resembles ping-pong — that is, one in which the conversation bounces back and forth with each one taking a short turn. We stop monologues and raise awareness of the contribution that each partner makes to the couple's maladaptive conversational style. It is important to control and confront dominant communicators, and to offer gentle encouragement and invitations to reluctant communicators to express their opinions. We model the desired interactional pattern with each other and with the clients.

Spouses who complain that they are not listened to or understood by their partners usually mean that their point of view is not validated or acknowledged. Nondistressed couples acknowledge each other's point of view, whereas distressed couples do not (Gottman, Notarius, Gonzo, & Markman, 1976). Couples are instructed to paraphrase each other's position and to demonstrate that they understand even if they do not agree. This is a particularly helpful strategy when a couple appears to be deadlocked on opposing sides of an issue, because it softens their stance to perceive that they have been heard and understood.

Couples who are volatile and explosive tend to use the past as a weapon, stray from the original topic to everything under the sun, make lots of "You" statements, and answer complaints with their own complaints. These couples are able to use rules, structure, and metaphor to contain their explosive patterns. They are instructed to make "I" statements instead of "You" statements and to stay in the present instead of going to the past. Moreover, they may be given a list of "hot" or "forbidden" topics that they are not allowed to bring up at home. If one of them becomes verbally abusive, the other one is to call for "time out"; during time out, one of them goes off to a neutral place until things have cooled down. An authoritarian approach, delivered with a calm, gentle voice has been an effective therapeutic technique for many verbally abusive spouses.

Issues about EMI Disclosure

It is appropriate to discuss the EMI *after* caring behaviors have been established, commitment to the marriage is definite, and communication patterns are constructive. Couples who enter marital therapy because of an EMI disclosure have painfully discussed the EMI before entering therapy. The therapeutic questions become what more do the therapist and the noninvolved spouse need to know about the EMI, how to find it out, and how to use it in marital therapy.

One of the most important things to know about the EMI is whether it is over. We think that it is important to have learned privately, early in marital therapy, several important aspects about the EMI: (1) Is the type of EMS sexual, emotional, or both? (2) What are the spouses' attitudes and beliefs about EMI? (3) What needs were being met by the extramarital relationship that appear to be compensating for perceived inadequacies in the marriage? (4) What role did the involved spouse take in the extramarital relationship that makes him or her feel good about himself or herself? (5) What growth or insights, developed through this new relationship, can be shared or integrated back into the marital relationship? The therapist maintains the involved spouse's confidentiality but needs the freedom to use clinical judgment in recommending the extent, manner, and timing of the involved spouse's EMI disclosure to the other spouse in order to facilitate alliances inside the marriage rather than outside.

We have found that being part of a male-female cotherapy team allows for greater flexibility in approaching the complex issues of disclosure and alliances. During individual and conjoint sessions, each spouse can identify with a particular therapist, usually of the same sex. Confidentiality regarding the other spouse is assured for individual sessions, but we make it clear that there will be no secrets between the therapists. Any detailed inquiry during conjoint sessions is usually done by the cotherapist who does not see that spouse individually, in order to avoid collusions or in order to ask for information that has already been revealed. Furthermore, one therapist can ask questions *for* the NI spouse, with attention to the details that the NI spouse desires but without the emotional intensity and "district attorney" inquisitions that the spouse could display. The other therapist's position is to protect and support the concerns of the involved spouse during the exploration of the EMI.

Extent of EMI Disclosure

Until both spouses have committed themselves to the therapy and to the continuation of the marriage, it could be extremely destructive to conduct an inquiry of the "sordid" details of the EMI. The NI spouse is asked what use they will make of the information that is disclosed. If the therapist believes that the information will be used as a weapon or that it will be a source of obsessive thoughts, then the therapist may need to align on the side of suppression. It may also be apparent that the details may be used by the NI to confirm the deceitfulness of the involved spouse by pointing out inconsistencies in "stories" that were told during the EMI in order to cover up or avoid discovery. These apparent inconsistencies could be seen as "lies" and as evidence of further proof for continuing distrust. The therapist can reframe these confabulations as the involved spouse's determination to protect the marriage by avoiding discovery. It can be evidence of a continued commitment to preserving the marital relationship even during the time of the EMI.

Greene (1981) has observed that a familiar reaction to disclosure is that a spouse develops a "district attorney syndrome" and asks incessant questions about the details of the affair. In some cases, obsession with the partner's EMI may be used to deprecate the partner, or it can heighten the partner's effect as a sexual object. While some will forgive, others will find this sufficient grounds for divorce. Scharff (1978), on the other hand, supports the betrayed spouse's need to know everything. He reports that couples commonly experience a honeymoon during the crisis of revelation. Feeling closer than they have for years, they share sorrow, grief, anger, love, panic, and sexual feelings. The new alliance is a painful process that may require 2 or 3 years of painstaking therapeutic work.

Where the marital relationship has been happy and sexually satisfying until discovery of a primarily sexual extramarital relationship, the focus can be on the details of the extramarital sexual encounter and the value systems of the spouses. If the participating spouse is regretful and demonstrates love and sexual interest in the marital partner, it can be therapeutically helpful to discuss what led up to the EMS experience and what that experience was like. Although it is painful to discuss such an incident, the therapist can inquire about the event in the role of a benign investigator in place of the "betrayed" spouse carrying on their own courtroomlike inquisition. The following is abstracted from a conjoint session that took place after therapeutic work on caring, commitment, and communication. Here the therapist asked questions on behalf of Edie, the betrayed spouse, who "needed to know all the details" of her spouse Ed's one-night stand, which she inadvertently discovered by calling his hotel room one morning while he was away on a business trip.

Case 5: *Therapist: Let's hear the facts about the incident.*

Ed: I probably got caught at a weak moment. I wasn't the aggressor. It wasn't planned. I had known her for 1-1/2 months. She called and said she would be at the convention. When I went into the hotel bar lounge, I accidentally ran into her. I wasn't drunk. She talked about lots of problems with her kids, and about how lonely she's been since her divorce. She's by no means as attractive as Edie.

What did she do to turn you on, then?

She flattered me. She said appealing things about my looks. She was lonely and troubled. She wasn't looking for a long-term thing, just something casual with no strings.

Did she invite you to her room?

No. There was a sixth sense. There was a dialogue just before, an emotional plea. She was lonely and what would it hurt.

How did you walk out of the bar?

Not touching.

How did you feel? Excited?

Intrigued, not aroused. When I got in the elevator a tape was playing in my head—God forbid I ever get caught [laughing].

What happened when you got to your room?

I went into the bathroom for 5 to 6 minutes. When I came out, she was in bed.

Were you surprised?

Yeah, I thought, "Holy mackerel, this is really going to happen." She said, "Please join me."

Who undressed you?

Myself.

When you got into bed, did you have a hard-on?

Yes.

Excited?

Yes; she approached me.

How?

She tried to kiss me on the mouth. I gave her my cheek. I was mad. Physically excited, but mentally mad at myself.

Not at her?

No, it went very fast.

She kissed you and you stuck it in.

Not right then. Some foreplay.

Did you kiss her breast?

I had to speed up. I would have lost it. If I didn't do it quickly, I would lose it. It was over quickly.

How many thrusts?

[shrugs his shoulders]

Did you talk to her at all?

From the bathroom — just general bullshit. Once I walked out, nothing.

No dialogue, during or after?

I just pulled out and turned over.

How was it. Good or bad?

After 10 minutes it was awful. I couldn't wait to get out of the room. I regretted it very badly and wanted to get out.

Did you satisfy her in any way?

Not very satisfied.

Did you play with her genitals?

No foreplay, no oral sex, once it was over, it was over. I rolled over. I had to get some sleep. I got up at 5:30, showered and dressed in the bathroom. At 6:30 I left and told her to have a good trip home.

Could it have happened if things were different between you and Edie?

I'm not sexually starved. My marriage is good. There have been lots of opportunities before, but I never wandered.

Sounds like she tugged at your penis through your heartstrings, through your senses.

Yes, but it's a betrayal of trust. I lost my own self- respect. I responded to her emotional weakness.

Edie: You said you could talk to her. That hurt as much as the physical thing. She didn't pressure me like you do to communicate.

Edie: Is it abnormal for me to want to know the details of it? If I had never called, would you have told me?

I would not have told you…too guilty. If I'm quiet, things go away. I would not have pursued her.

Therapist: Have you spoken to her since the incident?

No.

What are your chances of running into her?

I don't want any.

What will it be like when you do eventually see her?

Strange. Not bitter. My own fault. It still hurts. My guilt is so great. I couldn't do it again. I'll never do it again. I felt like a real piece of dirt.

Discussing the incident openly enables the NI spouse to feel that the basic loyalty is within the marriage rather than with the EMI.

The Issue of Alliances and Loyalties

The issue of alliances and loyalties is basic in the treatment of extramarital relationships. If the involved spouse protects the identity of the extramarital partner and the nature of the extramarital relationship, then the noninvolved marital partner will feel like the outside person in a triangle. One of the most devastating effects of EMI for the naive spouse is the secrecy and intimacy that exists between the involved spouse and the EM partner. Feelings of being excluded are frequently more destructive than knowledge of actual sexual intimacies. Trust and intimacy can be reestablished more readily if the participating spouse is willing to discuss the extramarital relationship, because the question of loyalties and secrecy is inherent to the resolution of the crisis generated by a betrayal of trust. Therapeutic discussion of EMI details opens the window on the EMI and allows the marital partners to use this negative experience, and the feelings generated, as something they can share together with the EM partner finally on the outside.

> Case 6: Frank and Fran began therapy after Frank's EMI disclosure to Fran. Initially, the purpose of marital therapy was to help Frank resolve his ambivalence about whether to continue in the marriage or leave for "the other woman." Frank agreed to suspend EMI for a contracted period of 12 weeks in order to work on the marital relationship. Fran worked hard to be empathic and a fun-loving companion while suppressing most of her own feelings of hurt and anger in order to give the marriage a fighting chance. The marital relationship improved steadily and became a vastly closer relationship than Frank and Fran had experienced at any previous time. Frank permanently severed ties with his EM partner and was very happy and relieved about his decision. Fran, however, began to obsess over the identity of the EM partner, who she knew was a professional associate of Frank's. Frank's firm refusal to disclose this identity symbolized to Fran that his loyalty was still not to her, and she threatened to end the marriage. When Frank, under much duress, reluctantly made the revelation because he did not want to lose his wife, Fran was greatly relieved and was able to invest in the marriage without further reservations because the boundaries and loyalties were now clear.

A therapeutic purpose can be accomplished when the dredging up of details helps to rebuild cohesion through obvious honesty and undisputed desire to accomplish a reliance with the spouse. The NI spouse frequently feels like an outsider because a "secret life" has been experienced outside the marriage with the "other" person. Sharing intimacies about the extramarital involvement can extinguish unfounded fantasies and reestablish boundaries within the marital dyad.

> Case 7: At George's retirement party, Georgia learned that he had been taking a prolonged coffee break every morning for 5 years with a 32-year-old female employee. Georgia's rage was directed at the secrecy of the liaisons and the feeling that she had been deceived for so many years. Her belief system was based on the assumption that she and George were completely open and shared everything in their lives. Georgia was shattered by this apparent betrayal of faith. Although she believed George's protestations that he did not love the other woman and had not been sexually involved with her, Georgia was prepared to end a 41-year marriage that had been satisfying, close, and sexually exciting. Therapy focused on detailing the nature and extent of the "coffee breaks," with attention to sexual innuendoes, shared intimacies, and physical contact, using the female cotherapist as the investigator. Georgia was encouraged to write pressing questions or signs of deceit on index cards as the inquiry proceeded in order for the therapist to cover all of her concerns. This allowed Georgia to remain calm and protected George from Georgia's previous punishing barrages.

ISSUES OF TRUST, JEALOUSY, AND FORGIVING

Trust

The issue of rebuilding trust is paramount when extramarital relationships are discovered or revealed. Trust cannot be earned by oaths of fidelity, but belief in a partner's love and devotion through mutual companionship, affection, communication, and understanding can gradually reduce suspicion and rebuild trust. The secrecy, deception, and alibis that accompany a secret extramarital involvement can be more destructive to the reconstruction of the marriage than the actual act of extramarital sex. Jacobson & Margolin (1979) note that mistrust is normal and will have to be tolerated while the trust and jealousy issues remain to be resolved.

The accused spouses who believe that trust can never be regained are frequently tempted to get involved again, since their partner doesn't trust them anyway. The point needs to be made that the choice and responsibility for future behavior lies with the individual rather than with the distrusting spouse. The errant spouse can attempt to build trust by focusing on what can be done in the present to demonstrate commitment to the marriage.

Jealousy

Jealousy can be a reaction to problems in the marital relationship or may be a manifestation of individual pathology. There is more to jealousy than fear of losing a beloved partner. The intensity of a jealous response is not necessarily related to the degree of love felt, but rather to the degree of dependency on the partner for positive self-regard. The feelings of rejection and deprivation triggered by a partner's extramarital involvement are associated with loss of self-esteem and self-worth (Jacobson & Margolin, 1979). The client is dealing not only with the emotional loss of the spouse, but loss of image, dream, and the marriage.

Jealousy reactions will be determined by previous losses, unresolved mourning from the past, and level of adaptive mechanisms (Taibbi, 1983). Elbaum (1981) asserts that the more comfortable the "injured" spouse is as an individual, the easier it is to work through the anger, jealousy, hurt, and injured self-esteem. Ables (1982) states that early disturbances in basic trust can predispose a spouse to have continuous doubts.

> Case 8: Harriett's rage over Harry's indiscretion was intense and prolonged, and appeared to be an extreme overreaction on her part. She recognized that his EMI was sexually exciting because of the provocative discussions and physical intimacies, and accepted his explanation that there had been no sexual intercourse or strong emotional attachment. Furthermore, she accepted that Harry had terminated all contact with the EM partner and knew that the marriage ties were based on love and companionship. However, Harriett became physically violent on several occasions and threatened to end the marriage. Inquiry into her family history revealed that she still harbored tremendous bitterness over her father's desertion of her mother for a younger woman 30 years earlier. Her basic distrust of men and love-hate feelings toward her father were unleashed by revelation of Harry's extramarital encounter.

Greene (1981) has observed in his clinical practice that in 4% of the cases, a partner was unjustly accused of infidelity by a spouse suffering from a paranoid condition. Dougherty and Ellis (1976) reported that several men with an obsessive delusional form of pathological jealousy had seen their mothers engage in sexual infidelity when they were young adolescents. Unwillingness to forget the past, even after the extramarital involvement has ceased, is often rooted in disappointments and anger from earlier developmental stages, which must be worked through before the present situation can be improved. In any case, however, treatment must include a relationship perspective that can enhance the mutual development of trust *and* autonomy.

The cognitions that mediate jealousy can be the main target for therapy through cognitive restructuring (Jacobson & Margolin, 1979). If a spouse believes that they are no longer loved because their partner has been involved with someone else, their emotional reactions and behavioral responses will be markedly different than if an extramarital involvement is viewed as just a harmless sexual diversion by the spouse.

Buunk (1982) studied jealousy-coping styles among 100 Dutch spouses. Avoiding the involved spouse was the major coping strategy by those with low marital satisfaction and/or those with high neuroticism scores. Women and men with high marital satisfaction attempted to have open and frank discussions with their spouse. Buunk concluded that jealous responses were prevalent and usual, even among the sexually liberal who professed accepting attitudes regarding spouse EMI.

Forgiving

When the injured spouse seems unable to forgive, it may be necessary to explore the need to hold onto the anger. Forgiving may be seen as condoning the behavior. Not forgiving may be a signal that serves as a constant reminder not to let such a thing happen ever again. Not forgiving may also be a means of making the involved spouse suffer—to pay back for the pain that was inflicted. "We have at times asked how much longer the spouse is going to punish the other" (Ables, 1982, p. 230). Teisman (1983) suggests establishing a strategic intervention whereby atonement can be accomplished through specific acts.

SUMMARY AND CONCLUSIONS

Empirical researchers and clinicians can benefit by integrating both their literatures. Research suggests that men and women may experience and approach EMI along lines that fit traditional sex roles (i.e., male extramarital involvements are more sexual, and female extramarital involvements are more emotional). EMI can occur in all types of marriages and may or may not be related to marital dissatisfaction (providing it is not discovered). Therapists and researchers should be sure to assess the depth of extramarital emotional involvement. Extramarital relationships that combine sexual intercourse with a deep emotional attachment are associated with the least happy marriages and pose the greatest threat to marital stability. When there is low need satisfaction in the marriage, the involved spouse may be the one who is "giving less" and "receiving more." Such spouses who aren't sure of their love may be moved as much or more by an increase in their own caring behaviors as they are through increased caring by their marital partners.

Therapists with an individualistic perspective may stress psychodynamic explanations of EMI. However, there is no evidence in the empirical literature that EMI participants have any particular personality disorder that differentiates them from EMI non-participants. Although there is no specific individual pathology associated with EMI, individuals do differ in their attitudes toward EMI and in the personal readiness characteristics that lead to EMI. Even when the EM behavior is associated with individual pathology, the best context for change is within the marital relationship. The existing patterns in the marriage can either maintain acting-out behaviors or inhibit the individual's ability to change. Conjoint therapy can reveal destructive interpersonal patterns in the marriage and can provide a context for promoting individual and mutual change. Occasional individual sessions (within the larger context of conjoint therapy) are useful for support, disclosure, resolving ambivalence, and expressing destructive hostility. A destructive triangle can be created by a therapist who develops a more intimate relationship with the individual spouses than is promoted between the spouses.

Issues about confidentiality, disclosure, and secret coalitions are particularly troublesome for marital therapists dealing with EMI. Some clinicians begin marital therapy by seeing the spouses separately in order to uncover secrets such as EMI whereas other clinicians begin with conjoint sessions because they are concerned about avoiding secret coalitions. We prefer to begin with conjoint sessions and a paper-and-pencil assessment that is confidential from the spouse. There is a general consensus by therapists that the involved spouse should terminate or suspend an ongoing EMI as a condition for participating in conjoint therapy. If the EMI is unknown to the spouse, this request must be made in an individual session. Therapists are divided on whether EMI should be disclosed to the spouse. Disclosure can create a crisis that may end in divorce, or it may act as a cataylst for positive change in a "stuck" marital system. We believe that it is important to consider the unique characteristics of each couple in order to take a stance on spousal disclosure that will allow the marital relationship to improve and endure.

Disclosure or discovery of EMI is frequently the precipating event that propels a couple into marital therapy. Our treatment model includes an extensive assessment of the marital and extramarital relationships, a contracted period of therapy during which the EMI must be suspended, the development of caring behaviors to strengthen the marriage, training in communication skills, and teaching couples how to recognize and change destructive interactional patterns. We use information about the EMI covertly to determine which aspects of the marriage can benefit by restructuring. After caring behaviors have been established, commitment to the marriage is definite, and communication patterns are constructive, the therapeutic question becomes how much more does the noninvolved spouse need to know about the EMI.

REFERENCES

Ables, B.S., (with Brandsma, J.). (1982). *Therapy for couples.* San Francisco: Jossey-Bass.

Athanasiou, R., & Sarkin, R. (1974). Premarital sexual behavior and postmarital adjustment. *Archives of Sexual Behavior, 3,*(3), 207-225.

Athanasiou, R., Shaver, P., & Tavris, C. (1970, July). Sex (a report to *Psychology Today* readers). *Psychology Today, 4,* 39-52.

Atwater, L. (1979). Getting involved: Women's transition to first extramarital sex. *Alternative Lifestyles, 1*(2), 33-68.

Balswick, J., & Peek, C.W. (1971). The inexpressive male: A tragedy of American society. *Family Coordinator, 20,* 363-368.

Bell, R.R., Turner, S., & Rosen, L. (1975). A multivariate analysis of female extramarital coitus. *Journal of Marriage and the Family, 37*(2), 375-383.

Berger, E.M. (1972). *Triangle: The betrayed wife.* Chicago: Nelson-Hall.

Berman, E.M., Miller, W.R., Vines, N., & Lief, H.I. (1977). The age 30 crisis and the 7-year itch. *Journal of Sex and Marital Therapy, 3*(3), 197-204.

Bernard, J. (1974). Infidelity: Some moral and social issues. In J.R. Smith & L.G. Smith (Eds.), *Beyond monogamy.* Baltimore: Johns Hopkins University Press.

Block, J. (1978). *The other man, the other woman.* New York: Grosset & Dunlap.

Blood, R.O., & Wolfe, D.M. (1960). *Husbands and wives: The dynamics of married living.* Glencoe, IL: Free Press.

Blumstein, P., & Schwartz, P. (1983). *American couples: Money, work, sex.* New York: Morrow.

Bowers, W.J., & Furstenberg, F. (1967). *Attitudes and opinions on marital fidelity.* Russell B. Stearns Study, Northeastern University, Boston.

Boylan, B.R. (1971). *Infidelity.* Englewood Cliffs, NJ: Prentice-Hall.

Buunk, B. (1980). Extramarital sex in the Netherlands: Motivation in social and marital context. *Alternative Lifestyles, 3,* 11-39.

Buunk, B. (1982). Strategies of jealousy: Styles of coping with extramarital involvement of the spouse. *Family Relations, 31,* 13-18.

Cleveland, M. (1976). Sex in marriage: At 40 and beyond. *Family Coordinator, 25*(3), 431-440.

Cuber, J.F., & Haroff, P.B. (1963). *The significant Americans.* New York: Appleton-Century-Crofts.

DeBurgher, J.E. (1972). Sex in troubled marriages. *Sexual Behavior, 2*(5), 23-26.

Dicks, H.V. (1967). *Marital tensions.* New York: Basic Books.

Dougherty, J.P., & Ellis, J. (1976). A new concept and finding in morbid jealousy. *American Journal of Psychiatry, 133*(6), 679-683.

Driscoll, R., Davis, K.E., & Lipetz, M.E. (1972). Parental interference and romantic love: The Romeo and Juliet effect. *Journal of Personality and Social Psychology, 24*(1), 1-10.

Edwards, J.N., & Booth, A. (1976). Sexual behavior in and out of marriage: An assessment of correlates. *Journal of Marriage and the Family, 38*(1), 73-81.

Ehrmann, W.W. (1959). *Premarital dating behavior.* New York: Holt.

Elbaum, P.L. (1981). The dynamics, implications, and treatment of extramarital sexual relationships for the family therapist. *Journal of Marital and Family Therapy, 7,* 489-495.

Ellis, A. (1969). *The civilized couples' guide to extramarital adventure.* New York: Peter H. Wyden.

Francis, J.L. (1977). Toward the management of heterosexual jealousy. *Journal of Marriage and Family Counseling, 3,* 61-69.

Glass, S.P. (1981). Sex differences in the relationship between satisfaction with various aspects of marriage and types of extramarital involvements. Doctoral dissertation, Catholic University, 1980. *Dissertation Abstracts International, 41*(10), 3889B.

Glass, S.P., & Wright, T.L. (1977). The relationship of extramarital sex, length of marriage, and sex differences on marital satisfaction and romanticism: Athanasiou's data reanalyzed. *Journal of Marriage and the Family, 398*(4), 691-703.

Glass, S.P., & Wright, T.L. (1985). Sex differences in type of extramarital involvement and marital dissatisfaction. *Sex Roles, 12*(9/10), 1101-1119.

Gottman, J., Notarius, C., Gonzo, J., & Markman, H. (1976). *A couple's guide to communication.* Champaign, IL: Research Press.

Greene, B.L. (1981). *A clinical approach to marital problems.* Springfield, IL: Charles C. Thomas.

Gross, A.E. (1978). The male role and heterosexual behavior. *Journal of Social Issues, 34*(1), 87-107.

Gurgul, D., Bowers, W., & Furstenberg, F. (1969). *Marital infidelity.* Unpublished manuscript, Northeastern University, Boston.

Humphrey, F.G. (1983a). *Extramarital relationships: Therapy issues for marriage and family therapists.* Paper presented at meeting of American Association for Marriage and Family Therapy, Washington, DC.

Humphrey, F.G. (1983b). *Marital therapy.* Englewood Cliffs, NJ: Prentice-Hall.

Humphrey, F.G., & Strong, L. (1976). *Treatment of extramarital sexual relationships as reported by clinical members of the American Association of Marriage and Family Counselors.* Paper presented at meeting of AAMFC, Hartford, CT.

Hunt, M. (1969). *The affair.* New York: World Publishing Company.

Hunt, M. (1974). *Sexual behavior in the 1970's.* Chicago: Playboy Press.

Jacobson, N.S. (1981). Behavioral marital therapy. In A.S. Gurman & D.P. Kniskern (Eds.), *Handbook of family therapy.* New York: Brunner/Mazel.

Jacobson, N.S., & Margolin, G. (1979). *Marital therapy: Strategies based on social learning and behavior exchange principles.* New York: Brunner/Mazel.

Johnson, R.E. (1970a). Extramarital sexual intercourse: A methodological note. *Journal of Marriage and the Family, 40*(2), 249-255.

Johnson, R.E. (1970b). Some correlates of extramarital coitus. *Journal of Marriage and the Family, 32*(3), 449-456.

Johnson, R.E. (1972). Attitudes toward extramarital relationships. *Medical Aspects of Human Sexuality, 6*(4),168-191.

Kanin, E.J., & Davidson, K.R. (1972). Some evidence bearing on the aim-inhibition hypothesis of love. *Sociological Quarterly, 13*(spring), 210-217.

Kinsey, A., Pomeroy, W., & Martin, C. (1953). *Sexual behavior in the human female.* Philadelphia: Saunders.

Knapp, J. (1975). Some non-monogamous marriage styles and related attitudes and practices of marriage counselors. *The Family Coordinator, 24,* 505-514.

Leigh, W. (1985). *The infidelity report: An investigation of extramarital affairs.* New York: Morrow.

Levin, R.J. (1975, October). The Redbook report on premarital and extramarital sex. *Redbook,* 38, ff.

Levinger, G. (1964). Task and social behavior in marriage. *Sociometry, 27,* 433-448.

Liberman, R.P., Wheeler, E.G., de Visser, L., Kuehnel, J., & Kuehnel, T. (1980). *Handbook of marital therapy.* New York: Plenum.

Locke, H.J., & Wallace, K.M. (1958). Short marital adjustment and prediction tests: Their reliability and validity. *Marriage and Family Living, 21*(3), 251-255.

Mace, D. (1965). Problems of marital infidelity. In R.J. Klemer (Ed.), *Counseling in marital and sexual problems: A physicians' handbook.* Baltimore: Williams & Wilkins.

Madanes, C. (1981). *Strategic family therapy.* San Francisco: Jossey-Bass.

Maykovich, N.K. (1976). Attitudes versus behavior in extramarital sexual relations. *Journal of Marriage and the Family, 38*(4), 693-699.

McGinnis, T.C. (1981). *More than just a friend: The joys and disappointments of extramarital affairs.* Englewood Cliffs, NJ: Prentice-Hall.

Myers, L. (1976). Extramarital sex: Is the neglect of its positive aspects justified? In W.W. Oaks & G. Melchiode (Eds.), *Sex and the life cycle.* New York: Grune & Stratton.

Myers, L., & Leggitt, H. (1972). A new kind of adultery. *Sexual Behavior, 2*(2), 52-62.

Neubeck, G. (1969). *Extramarital relations.* Englewood Cliffs, NJ: Prentice-Hall.

Neubeck, G., & Schletzer, V.M. (1962). A study of extramarital relationships. *Marriage and Family Living, 24*(3), 279-281.

Notarius, C., & Vanzetti, N. (1983). The marital agendas protocol. In L. Filsinger (Ed.), *A sourcebook of marital and family assessment.* Beverly Hills, CA: Sage.

Petersen, J.R. (1983). The Playboy readers' sex survey, part II. *Playboy, 30*(3),90-92, 178-184.

Reiss, I.L. (1960). *Premarital sexual standards in America.* Glencoe, IL: Free Press.

Reiss, I.L. (1967). *The social context of premarital sexual permissiveness.* New York: Holt, Rinehart, & Winston.

Reiss, I.L., Anderson, R.E., & Sponaugle, G.C. (1980). A multivariate model of the determinants of extramarital sexual permissiveness. *Journal of Marriage and the Family, 42*(2), 395-411.

Roebuck, J., & Spray, S.L. (1967). The cocktail lounge: A study of heterosexual relations in a public organization. *American Journal of Sociology, 72,* 388-395.

Rothstein, R. (1960). Authoritariansim and men's reactions to sexuality and affection in women. *Journal of Abnormal and Social Psychology, 61*(3), 329-334.

Salzman, L. (1974). Viewpoints: What is the chief cause of marital infidelity? *Medical Aspects of Human Sexuality, 8*(1), 103.

Scharff, D.E. (1978). Truth and consequences in sex and marital therapy: The revelation of secrets in the therapeutic setting *Journal of Sex and Marital Therapy, 4*(1), 37-51.

Simon, W., & Gagnon, J.H. (1970). *Psychosexual development in the sexual scene.* New Brunswick, NJ: Transaction.

Singh, B.K., Walton, B.L., & Williams, J.S. (1976). Extramarital sexual permissiveness: Conditions and contingencies. *Journal of Marriage and the Family, 38*(4), 701-712.

Smith, J.R., & Smith, L.G. (1974). *Beyond monogamy.* Baltimore: Johns Hopkins University Press.

Spanier, G.B. (1976). Measuring dyadic adjustment: New scales for assessing the quality of marriage and similar dyads. *Journal of Marriage and the Family, 38,* 15-28.

Spanier, G.B., & Margolis, R.L. (1983). Marital separation and extramarital sexual behavior. *Journal of Sex Research, 19*(1), 23-48.

Sprenkle, D.J., & Weiss, D.L. (1978). Extramarital sexuality: Implications for marital therapists. *Journal of Sex and Marital Therapy, 4*(4), 279-291.

Sprey, J. (1972). Extramarital relationships. *Sexual Behavior, 2*(8), 34-40.

Strean, H.S. (1976). The extramarital affair: A psychoanalytic view. *Psychoanalytic Review, 63*(1), 101-113.

Strean, H.S. (1980). *The extramarital affair.* New York: Free Press.

Stuart, F., Stuart, R.B., Maurice, W.L., & Szasz, G. (1975). *Sexual Adjustment Inventory.* Champaign, IL: Research Press.

Stuart, R.B. (1980). *Helping couples change.* New York: Guilford.

Stuart, R.B. (1982). *Short term treatment of marital distress.* National Association of Social Workers Workshop Presentation, Washington, DC.

Taibbi, R. (1983). Handling extramarital affairs in clinical treatment. *Social Casework, 64,* 200-204.

Teismann, M.W. (1983). *Extramarital relationships: Therapy issues for marriage and family therapists.* Paper presented at meeting of American Association for Marriage and Family Therapy, Washington, DC.

Thompson, A.P. (1983). Extramarital sex: A review of research literature. *Journal of Sex Research, 19*(1), 1-22.

Thompson, A.P. (1984). Emotional and sexual components of extramarital relations. *Journal of Marriage and the Family 46*(1), 35-42.

Weil, M.W. (1975). Extramarital relationships: A reappraisal. *Journal of Clinical Psychology, 3*(4), 723-725.

Weiss, R.L., & Birchler, G.R. (1975). *Areas of change questionnaire (ACQ).* Eugene, OR: Oregon Marital Studies Program. University of Oregon.

Whitaker, C.A., Greenberg, A., & Greenberg, M.L. (1981). Existential marital therapy: A synthesis. In G.P. Sholevar (Ed.), *The handbook of marriage and marital therapy.* Jamaica, NY: Spectrum.

Whitehurst, R.N. (1969). Extramarital sex: Alienation or extension of normal behavior. In G. Neubeck (Ed.), *Extramarital relations.* Englewood Cliffs, NJ: Prentice-Hall.

Wolfe, L. (1976). *Playing around.* New York: New American Library.

Zetterberg, H. (1966). The secret ranking. *Journal of Marriage and the Family, 28,* 134-143.

Chapter 14

Erotosexual Orientations: Understanding and Treating Homosexuals

Gregory K. Lehne

INTRODUCTION

The human species forms pairbonded relationships based on sexual and affectional compatibilities. This pairbonding is selective, with compatibility on a number of individual differences in the characteristics of the partners necessary for successful bonding to occur. An individual's erotosexual orientation basically defines the parameters of the characteristics that a partner should possess for successful affectional and/or sexual unions to occur, including the specification of attributes, situations, objects or activities associated with genital-sexual arousal. An erotosexual orientation is the lovemap of an individual (Money, 1986).

It is popular to describe sexual orientations (or sexual preferences) based simply on the gender-identity/role of *both* of the individuals in a potentially pairbonded relationship. Thus a homosexual orientation generally refers to a person who can fall in love with and have satisfying sexual relations with another person of the same gender-identity/role (prefix homo-, derived from Greek *homos* = same). A bisexual is capable of pairbonding with individuals of both sexes, whereas heterosexuals pairbond with individuals of the other sex (hetero = other). Clinicians are more likely to classify individuals according to the Kinsey continuum, from exclusively heterosexual (0) through bisexual (2-4) to exclusively homosexual (6), based on an analysis of erotosexual fantasies and behavior throughout the life history.

These tripart or continuum concepts of sexual orientation are simplistic, and are thus misleading for contemporary clinicians to use in conceptualizing their patients. However, they do represent the cognitive categories that many patients will struggle with in trying to develop viable erotosexually labeled social identities. The gender of the partners in a sexual love affair is important by social standards, and thus individuals will be labeled by others and will label themselves using this criterion. But defining an individual as heterosexual does not mean that he/she is potentially capable of being erotosexually attracted to every member of the other sex, nor are homosexuals capable of sexual arousal or pairbonding with respect to every willing member of their own gender.

An individual's erotosexual orientation (lovemap) describes more specifically the field of characteristics that a partner must possess for the maximum or minimum amount of bonding (and associated genital-sexual arousal) to occur. For most but not all individuals, the gender-identity/role of the partner is only one important specific component of the erotosexual orientation. Note that the gender-identity/role incorporates both a self concept and social concept of erotosexual status, as well as the status of being male or female. Thus there are some self-defined heterosexual women who fall in love with and copulate with men who consider themselves homosexual, just as there are homosexual men who fall in love only with heterosexual men, and so forth.

In addition, an erotosexual orientation commonly specifies an age range of attractiveness for the potential partner, which may remain the same or may change over the life history. Many other characteristics may be specified or not, including physical-appearance parameters, personality or life-style dimensions, as well as racial, ethnic or religious characteristics. Any characteristic on which people may differ, as well as any erotosexual activity that may be engaged in, can be included (or excluded) as an obligatory feature of an erotosexual orientation. An erotosexual orientation may also incorporate attributes, situations, objects, or activities that in the extreme case may preclude the specification of a partner. Individuals also vary in the total specificity of their erotosexual orientation. Some people are potentially capable of sexual arousal or pairbonding with only a relatively small and specific group of individuals, whereas others have generalized erotosexual orientations that encompass a diversity of available partners. In some cases, such as in some of the paraphilias, the erotosexual orientation may be so specific and non-partner-oriented that pairbonding may not occur.

The remaining sections of this chapter use the concept of erotosexual orientations as the basis for understanding the typical courses of development of an adult status as a homosexual. Gay male and lesbian issues are not discussed separately, because this would require a more specific and hence much lengthier presentation, although most of the basic developmental issues are similar.

In the next section, clinical issues in diagnosis related to the use of the term *homosexual* are discussed. Then specific issues of erotosexual orientation and homosexual statuses from individual, clinical, and social perspectives are raised. The professional literature on developing a homosexual status (identity) is briefly reviewed or cited. The next four sections present typical stages in the development of a homosexual status: Sensitization; Exploration; Acceptance;

Stabilization. In each section, problematic strategies that have implications for clinical services are discussed.

The remaining sections discuss some special cases and treatment issues, including the role of the therapist in providing clinical services for individuals in the course of developing a homosexual-identity/role.

CLINICAL ISSUES IN DIAGNOSIS

The labeling terms *homosexual, bisexual,* and *heterosexual* specify erotosexual orientation based only on the conjunction of the genders of the two potentially pairbonded partners. Note that homosexuality, bisexuality or heterosexuality are not diagnoses or disorders in themselves, but are merely components of differential diagnosis when the problem is thought to be psychosexual. For the clinician, the use of these three discrete categories as diagnostic terms, except as an occasional shorthand reference, creates insoluble problems in dealing with some of the psychosexual disorders (see DeCecco, 1984a, 1984b; DeCecco & Shively, 1983/1984; Klein & Wolf, 1985).

For example in cases of difficult differential diagnosis, what criterion of gender for both individuals is going to be used (see Money, 1982)? Would one use the chromosomes—so that a 46, XX individual with the adrenogenital syndrome who has a complete, functional penis and a male gender-identity/role would be considered homosexual if married to a female, and would the partner likewise be considered homosexual or bisexual (Money & Dalery, 1976)? Would one use the genitalia—so that a preoperative 46, XY transsexual with male genitalia would be considered homosexual if pairbonded to a 46, XY male with male genitalia? Do the transsexual (and partner) then become heterosexual after surgical reassignment of the genitalia? Would one use the self-defined gender, regardless of chromosomes or genitalia, so that the self-defined preoperative transsexual could be considered heterosexual (and what would the erotosexual status of the partner be)?

These examples may seem extreme, but they are only a few of the many examples that occur with significant frequency in the caseloads of clinicians who specialize in sexual medicine and sexual therapy. The problem of categorization is also one that plagues the patient and others as well as the clinicians. Transsexuals and, less frequently, transvestites, for example, are commonly misdiagnosed as homosexuals (or bisexuals with a penchant for cross-dressing), based on overly simplistic conceptualizations of erotosexual orientation. Likewise, transsexuals themselves may share this confusion and refer to their sexual orientation as changing from homosexual to heterosexual following surgery. Within the homosexual subculture, where some transsexuals play an active role, there is also considerable dispute over the sexual orientation of transsexuals: "male" transsexuals who present as female, for example, may define themselves as gay when they seek male partners in the company of gay-identified males, while they identify themselves (as gay females) with lesbians in other political/social gatherings. Yet most gay males and lesbians do not consider transsexuals to be gay, regardless of whom they socialize with, although they do have a social category for "gay drag queens," which probably includes some individuals who are undergoing sex-reassignment procedures.

The paraphilias provide other examples where the homosexual/bisexual/heterosexual system of categorization of erotosexual status is inadequate. In pedophilia, for example, a man's erotosexual orientation may include as sexual partners prepubescent boys, girls, or both, and may or may not also include men, women, or both. Thus, a man with adult "heterosexual attractions" may have powerful "homosexual attractions" to young boys, which technically ought to make him "bisexual" — attracted to both women and boys. Some of these men identify themselves with the gay community, although the gay community generally does not accept them as gay unless they have an erotosexual interest in adults of their own gender. Many clinicians would consider this person to be a homosexual pedophile as well as a heterosexual male, which sounds like a contradiction in terms, especially since a "homosexual pedophile" with no adult interests would then have to be similarly considered an "asexual male." The imprecision of this limited system of categorization is also apparent in all of the paraphilias in which there is not necessarily any adult pairbonded partner. For example, in some of the fetishes or other paraphilias where the entire range of genital activity may involve a repetitive autoerotic or masturbatory ritual without a partner, the individual is certainly not asexual but may not be able to be classified as homosexual, bisexual, or heterosexual.

The reconceptualization and specification of erotosexual orientation eliminates many of the problems of the definition and classification of homosexuality, which has plagued the clinical, historical and research literature (see, for example, DeCecco, 1981, 1984b; DeCecco & Shively, 1983/1984; MacDonald, 1981, 1983; Paul & Weinrich, 1982; Shively & DeCecco, 1977). An erotosexual orientation is that component of the gender-identity/role that *specifies* the parameters expressed in fantasy and behavior in an individual's life history (with reference to the characteristics of others, objects or situations, and corresponding erotosexual activities) that are the basis of erotosexual behavior (measured by genital arousal) and pairbonding (or its absence). It is specifically individualistic and multidimensional, rather than categorically based on gender, although it probably has a phyletic basis as well as an origin associated with experience (Money, 1981a, 1981b, 1986).

An example can most readily illustrate the advantage for clinicians of this reconceptualization of erotosexual orientation. Consider a 40-year-old man, with an incidental teenaged history of limited sexual exploratory activity with male and female peers, whose sexual experiences have otherwise been exclusively limited to intercourse with his wife. Although his erotosexual fantasies are not essential for sexual/genital arousal, his fantasies are exclusively of fellatio with men of a certain physical type, and at times these fantasies are obligatory for him to function genitally with his wife. Would he be considered heterosexual, bisexual, or homosexual? He has come to the clinician for help in resolving this confusion, since for a variety of reasons his marriage is not functioning well. His wife has had several affairs with other men; he has not ever been tempted by the possibility of sexual activity with other men or women. He considers himself to be heterosexual, leading a typical heterosexual life-style, and in fact is somewhat antigay in his attitudes.

There would be considerable disagreement among clinicians on how to classify the man, in this relatively simple and common situation, using the heterosexual-bisexual-homosexual continuum (see Klein & Wolf, 1985). Consequently he may receive a very different treatment, depending on the implicit diagnosis of the clinician who treats him. The result may be a disservice to him, and an embarrassment to the profession if he goes "doctor shopping." But all of the clinicians (and the patient) could readily agree on a description of the content of the erotosexual orientation of this individual, as summarized in the paragraph above. In this case, the description of erotosexual orientation would be based primarily on self-report of fantasies, attitudes, and behavioral history—although visual and verbal stimuli could also be used, and sexual arousal measured for the behaviorally inclined and technologically sophisticated. Clinicians could then agree and discuss fruitfully the psychological effects of the discrepancies between components of the gender-identity/role. The clinical issues include erotosexual orientation; individual identity and social status as homosexual, bisexual or heterosexual; and associated behaviors. The focus would be to examine the effects of discrepancies on the adaptive functioning of the individual. But the simplistic pseudopsychological question of whether this man is "really" a homosexual, bisexual or heterosexual cannot be resolved with a high level of agreement among clinicians, for it is a matter of definition.

The conceptualization of the clinician, especially one with expertise in sexology, is not necessarily shared by the patient. Patients (like sociologists, anthropologists, and historians), will press for a social classification of sexual orientation. Homosexuality, bisexuality, or heterosexuality (and other variations, across the life history or different social/cultural/historical settings) are properly considered *statuses,* which individuals may use to identify themselves and which others may use to label an individual. A status necessarily obscures the complexity of an erotosexual orientation by simplifying the description of an individual into a socially-defined category that may or may not correspond particularly well to an individual's reality. The status of being homosexual or bisexual is a relatively recent phenomenon, as is the corresponding development of individuals with a homosexual or gay identity (identity refers to the internal cognitive representation of a socially defined category or status). Certainly across cultures and throughout history there were many individuals with erotosexual orientations very similar to those commonly found among contemporary Americans. But the social status and its internalized representation has varied with the culture and historical time (see, for example, Bullough, 1976; Boswell, 1980; Carrier, 1980; Sprague, 1984; Weeks, 1977).

ISSUES OF EROTOSEXUAL ORIENTATIONS AND HOMOSEXUAL STATUSES

It is beyond the scope of this paper to discuss the hypotheses concerning the *why* and the *how* in the development of different erotosexual orientations (see, for example, Money, 1980, 1981a, 1986; Money & Ehrhardt, 1972; Money & Wiedeking, 1980). Suffice it to say that erotosexual orientation is largely developed, in conjunction with the other aspects of gender-identity/role, in the period from conception to puberty. The process of development is sequential, with certain critical periods being of determining importance as a result of the interactions of biological processes and cognitive and social events. Individuals differ in their thresholds or vulnerabilities to the different components of the interactions, so that the course of atypical development is usually difficult to identify or predict, with no single outcome being 100% assured. Childhood gender incongruity, for example, is predictive of adult homosexual status (Money & Russo, 1979, 1981), although the majority of sissy boys and tomboy girls do not become homosexuals — nor were the majority of homosexuals once sissy boys or tomboy girls (Bell, Weinberg, Hammersmith, 1981). However, once components are established as part of the gender-identity/role, they influence further development.

The resulting erotosexual orientations are generally extremely difficult to change, if they are even amenable to change with present techniques and technologies. The earlier that components are incorporated into development, the more intractable to change they seem to be later in development. Most of the basic components of erotosexual orientation, such as the sex of the preferred partner, are believed to be incorporated early in development, although the specifics are embellished later. The tentative result of erotosexual development becomes most accessible to the individual's own self-reflection at puberty and later (Lehne, 1978).

A useful metaphor for describing erotosexual orientation is that of a lovemap (Money, 1986). The outlines of the significant features are indelibly drawn in childhood, but the process of exploration and discovery occurs throughout adulthood. The map determines where one explores, and different individuals map their territories out in differing amounts of detail. Individuals can vary quite dramatically in the size and scope of their individual travels and maps, but no amount of adult experience will create a new territory that was not already outlined on an individual's map.

The metaphor of the map is a useful heuristic that can be elaborated extensively. Different societies provide different tools and vehicles for exploration.

Exploration of some areas may be prohibited, or trespassing may be severely punished. There are a lot of fellow explorers helping each other out in some areas, while exploration is a lonely business in others. There are different social values associated with different areas and neighborhoods. Some people get stuck on some limited route, in a circumscribed neighborhood, or in the repetition of a short train ride from which they can never get off; others may never find an area where they are comfortable.

The role of the clinician in this process is to be a guide. The therapist needs to explore with the client the available territory in hopes of finding a viable neighborhood to explore or in which to settle down. The therapist may try to help the client stay away from forbidden territory, but should not maintain the delusion that a territory can be talked out of existence or that new land can be created where none existed before.

The primary issues of erotosexual orientations are sex, love and social adaptation: how to find a self-satisfying way to conduct a sex life that in most cases will include the possibility of pairbonding with another individual while existing as a functional member of society. Each society sets up its road maps for guidance for the majority of individuals who are expected to follow a typical course in exploring and hopefully resolving the issues of sex, love and social adaptation. In contemporary American society, the route markers predominantly guide the way to monogamous heterosexual marriage, with the nuclear family being the basic unit of childrearing and economic support and stability. For people who cannot follow this route, the alternative paths for exploration are less clearly marked, and the possibility of getting lost are hence greater.

Contemporary American society does offer an alternative and less well-marked territory for individuals to explore in order to determine whether the social status and/or individual identity of being a homosexual leads the way to a neighborhood where a person can live and resolve the issues of sex, love and social adaptation. Because the route is less well marked, less socially sanctioned, individuals on this course may get lost occasionally and seek the professional guidance of a clinician. The next section of this paper describes some of the paths most commonly taken by men and women in developing the identity and social status of a homosexual.

DEVELOPING A HOMOSEXUAL STATUS: FROM ADOLESCENCE TO AIDS

Infants and children do not have the status or identity/role of being homosexual, bisexual or heterosexual. These terms are only applied to adolescents and adults. The process of developing a homosexual status, although it builds on the erotosexual orientation that has been outlined in childhood, properly begins in adolescence. The making of an adult homosexual, as Plummer (1975) has skillfully pointed out, is a developmental process separate from the etiology of homosexuality as a component of an individual erotosexual orientation. The process is that of reconciling cognitions with socially derived information and experiences, and thus cannot be considered independently of the social context of homosexuality.

The clinician whose assistance may be sought at problematic or difficult times in the adolescent and adult developmental process is one important source of information about the social context of homosexuality. Insofar as the clinician is knowledgeable and truthful about the developmental process and the social status of homosexuality, the client can benefit from seeking professional guidance. When the clinician is judgmental or moralistic, however covertly, the client will not derive useful guidance, but instead may be led down false paths. In many cases, the result of this is an enduring hostility, resentment, suspiciousness and degradation of the helping professions, based on the experience that, rather than providing guidance, the misguided professional has instead assumed the role of a moral or legal authority.

It is clear that with reference to the development of a homosexual status in contemporary American society, the prevalent social, moral and legal norms are that heterosexuality for everyone, not homosexuality for some, are the appropriate adult outcomes, although there is also the recognition that some individuals will nevertheless have a homosexual status. Although a homosexual status is certainly a viable identity/role in Western societies, it is considered to be socially less desirable than heterosexuality for a large number of reasons, some valid and others fallacious (see Lehne, 1976). Homosexuality is still a stigmatized status, and this is not likely to change in the 20th century. It is this situation that makes it difficult for individuals to develop a homosexual status (Fein & Nuehring, 1981; Nungesser, 1983; Plummer, 1975). This usually detours all but the most committed from following this path.

Homosexuality is the path of most resistance, not of least resistance, in the process of developing an adult identity/role status based on the information available to individuals from their own erotosexual-orientation cognitive maps. It is true that homosexuality and homosexuals themselves have become more socially accepted and visible in American society during the last 20 years, but the increasing fears of the public about the AIDS epidemic, which is affecting homosexual males, only too poignantly points out how very tenuous the social tolerance of homosexuality actually is. Whereas before the path of homosexuality was thought to end in unhappiness, loneliness, and possibly blackmail and suicide, now the endpoint of that route is increasingly believed to be death by the 20th-century plague disease of AIDS. These drastic outcomes are, of course, greatly exaggerated in the public minds, but the point is that no type of deterrence, especially the well-meaning deterrence of a clinician, will stop the explorations of travelers following the dictates of their own erotosexual maps.

The process of developing a homosexual status is best viewed as an adolescent and adult development process, which occurs in a society where a homosexual identity is a stigmatized status. Four empirical studies have examined this process in terms of milestone events as retrospectively reported by large numbers of respondents: Kooden et al. (1979; N = 138); Dank (1971; N = 180); Troiden (1979; N = 150); McDonald (1982; N = 199). Although there was considerable variation among the ages for specific events reported by respondents, there was general agreement among the studies on the mean ages at which the milestone events occurred (from McDonald, 1982):

Milestone Event	Mean Age Reported
Awareness of same-sex attractions	12-13
Same-sex acts and experiences	13-15
Understood what word "homosexual" meant	15-17
Questioned socially-prescribed heterosexual identity (Troiden only).	17
Feelings labeled homosexual, but not self (Troiden only)	19
Self-designation as homosexual	19-21
First homosexual relationship	21-23
Disclosure to significant nongay others	23-28
See self as having positive gay identity	22-28

Not each study asked about all the above-listed events. One study (Troiden & Goode, 1980) also reported variability in the sequence of milestones for different groups of respondents.

Other researchers have not focused on empirically determining an age-graded progression in the development of a homosexual identity, and have instead used smaller numbers of respondents to develop a theoretical model of "coming out" (Cass, 1979, 1984; Coleman, 1982; Hart & Richardson, 1981; Lee, 1977; Minton & McDonald, 1984; Moses & Hawkins, 1982; Plummer, 1975; Troiden, 1979; Warren, 1974, 1980; Weinberg, 1983). Large-scale survey research studies of the gay community also provide information on aspects of homosexual identity formation, such as those conducted by the Kinsey Institute (Bell & Weinberg, 1978; Bell, Weinberg & Hammersmith, 1982; Weinberg & Williams, 1974; Weinberg, 1978) or by researchers within the gay community (Jay & Young, 1979), although their sociological approach is not specifically directed at explaining the psychological process of developing individual gay identities. More of a micro analysis of specific populations, issues, or the dynamics described in case histories, can be found in other publications (Babuscio, 1976; DeMonteflores & Schultz, 1978; Goode, 1981; Hencken &

O'Dowd, 1977; Humphreys & Miller, 1980; Kimmel, 1978; Larson, 1981; Ponse, 1980; Seabrook, 1976; Silverstein, 1981). In addition, there are a variety of fictionalized and autobiographical accounts of the process of developing a gay identity (for example, Brown, 1976; Kantrowitz, 1977; Kopay & Young, 1977; Reid, 1973).

In the discussion of the development of a homosexual status that follows, the organizing framework is based upon Plummer's (1975) interactionist account, and Cass's (1979, 1984) interpersonal congruency theoretical perspective, which also provided a substantial amount of the supporting detail. Readers should consult these sources for a more extensive discussion and interpretation of the theoretical and empirical rationale of these models, which reflect the dominant sociological and social-psychological perspectives for analyzing the development of social statuses, social roles and individual identities.

Plummer analyzes the developmental process into four stages: Sensitization; Signification and Disorientation; Coming Out; Stabilizing Homosexuality. Cass's analysis is somewhat parallel to that of Plummer, positing six stages: Identity Confusion; Identity Comparison; Identity Tolerance; Identity Acceptance; Identity Pride; Identity Synthesis. Although neither Plummer nor Cass are sex-specific in their models, Plummer's research is based more upon the experiences of male homosexuals, while Cass's theory was initially derived more from her own work with lesbians, and then empirically tested (N = 166) with male and female homosexuals. My own analysis, which melds together Plummer's and Cass's perspectives, is presented in four stages, each discussed with an emphasis on the issues they present to the individual and clinician: Homosexual-Identity/Role (H-I/R) Sensitization; H-I/R Exploration; H-I/R Acceptance; H-I/R Stabilization. The underlying themes of the analysis of the development of homosexual status (H-I/R) is that this process is an interactive one of finding a match between cognitively identified inner realities and the social world as it is explored and understood by the individual.

HOMOSEXUAL-IDENTITY/ROLE SENSITIZATION

The first step in the development of a homosexual-identity/role is based in uncertainty and confusion. As a result of the influence of the hormones of puberty, the individual begins to review private cognitions (such as fantasies, see Lehne, 1978), recollections of prior experiences, and new experiences as they occur, in order to begin exploring the types of partners that will be sought for sexual and affectional relationships. The peer culture of teenagers provides the markers for the most commonly followed and the most socially desirable paths. The heterosexual norm, with social standards for the most desirable types of partners of the other sex, is also presented by family and the media, as well as by peers, sometimes with minor discrepancies in content.

Some individuals realize that their fantasies do not correspond clearly to the presumed normative fantasies of their peers: same-sex affection, however vague; and, in many cases, recognizable associations with genital arousal or sexual situations. There may be recalled the experiences of crushes and even sexual involvement with same-sex partners. The result is a sensitization (Plummer, 1975) to the status of homosexuality, without necessarily any realization that this may apply to the self.

Identity Confusion

Case (1979, 1984) labels this stage Identity Confusion, and describes many of the following characteristics of it. For some of these youths, the sensitization leads to seeking information to answer the question, "Am I homosexual?" Labeling of the self by others as homosexual may also be a factor, as is the availability of information about homosexuality that is viewed as being relevant to the self. The result of the sensitization for some may be the early "realization" that the homosexual status correctly applies. If the realization has the force of a strong conviction and the individual has not been overly traumatized by homophobia, then the homosexual status may also be acceptable. The next developmental task is then to figure out what it means in terms of social behavior.

For other youths, the sensitization poses questions that are not so readily resolved. They may recognize the correctness of the possibility that the homosexual status may apply to themselves, but if they also share the social disdain of homosexuality, they may reject this self-labeling as undesirable. They may then attempt to inhibit any homosexual fantasies or behaviors. Their denial may develop into attempts at conformity with the dating and mating standards of their peers, or there may be a more complete denial of sexuality into asexuality, and a corresponding high level of involvement with studies, work, or hobbies and activities without a sexual content. They may limit their access to any information about homosexuality. This may include making antihomosexual comments to others, which has the effect of limiting their opportunities to learn accurate information about homosexuality from the casual conversations wherein the subject may arise. This approach to dealing with identity confusion can lead to a negative or self-hating identity. This may be specific to the status of sexuality and homosexuality, or it may generalize into sarcastic, hostile and negative personality styles. The individual may increase the use of obsessive or compulsive defense mechanisms, which has the effect of limiting interactions with potentially threatening information or situations. This type of resolution of the identity confusion/sensitization is initially unstable, and may not be long lived. If it endures, however, it can cause serious dislocations of future development, as well as set the stage for homosexual panic reactions later, which can have violent repercussions for the self (e.g., suicide) or others. Depression is also a possible outcome. Clinical assistance would be valuable for youths who are trapped in this dilemma, but it is rarely sought except in cases of attempted suicide or serious depression.

A third reaction to the identity confusion arising out of sensitization to homosexual cognitions is to reject a homosexual status as being inapplicable to the self, as well as being socially undesirable. Cognitive restructuring can be used to redefine the unacceptable cognitions. For example, sex and emotion may be separated. For males, homosexual attraction and behavior may be viewed as "just fooling around" or "a phase," while affection toward other males is denied. For females, the affection may be recognized while genital involvement is denied. For both sexes, the context of any sexual behavior will be redefined, for example, as "an accident," "I was taken advantage of," "it was an experiment," "an easy way to earn money," "I was drunk" or "drugged," "everyone does it in my neighborhood," "it was just a sex act (I didn't think of my partner as being of the same sex, but rather what it would feel like if it was with a person of the other sex)," or "I was horny, but afraid" of pregnancy, disease, and so forth. This type of resolution, even if perpetuated for many, many years, can be stable and without associated problems. In some situations, however, it can lead to marriages at great risk of divorce, and other problems related to the separation of sexuality and affection—such as lack of sexual desire, impotence, and anorgasmia. It most frequently presents to clinicians at these later stages rather than during adolescence, under the guise of relationship problems, sexual dysfunctions, or lack of sexual desire.

Identity Comparison

The next step in the process of sensitization arises only for those individuals who consider the question that they may be homosexual, and are exploring what this means for their social relations. Cass (1979, 1984) calls this the stage of Identity Comparison, and has described its major characteristics as follows. The central concern is with social alienation, with the likely resulting conclusion that "I'm different" from the norm, and therefore much of the life plan that has been socially taught to me is irrelevant. The task is therefore to compare the self with others in order to reach some sense of identity knowledge.

Some people feel that they have always been different. They later label themselves homosexual when they encounter a group of homosexuals with whom to affiliate. Others may adopt a general stance of nonconformity, rejecting heterosexual roles in a process of self-legitimization, which may not necessarily culminate in adopting homosexual roles as a guide for either identification or behavior. Others find being different to be special or exciting.

Homosexuals are not the only group of people in society who may consider themselves different, or who decide that the conventional standards and norms do not fit them. There are subcultures in which individuals with a wide variety of differences mingle. In some locales there are homosexual subcultures accessible to the novice, in other locales these may be lacking or too invisible to detect. In the adolescent world, subcultures proliferate to include a range of "different" or "deviant" groups, including most prominently those organized around religion, drug use, music/cultural styles, political action, and the intellectual or artistic "elites," not to mention groups of people involved in delinquency. People struggling with the difference of homosexuality may find themselves aligned against social norms in many areas if they follow this path. In the extreme, for example, they may develop problems with drugs or law-breaking behavior, in an attempt to deal with their sense of being different through subcultures in the nonsexual arena.

Likewise, other individuals in such groups may experiment with homosexuality as an aspect of their own difference, although this rarely has much influence on their own development of their sexual status, which ultimately depends on whatever their erotosexual orientation dictates. Some of these subcultures are also characteristically antihomosexual. So, for the person trying to resolve the issues of Identity Comparison through involvement with different subcultures, the path to resolution may be difficult and problematic. For the clinician, the problem of differential diagnosis is very difficult when dealing with adolescents who present with problems associated with a subculture. In general, the issues of the development of a sexual status should not be overlooked, even when the presenting problem may be as apparently far removed as drugs or antisocial behavior.

In the stage of Identity Comparison, the evaluation of others is always a critical concern. When individuals are concerned with determining how they compare to others, they are also equally concerned with how others compare or evaluate them. Several strategies are commonly relied upon to deal with the reflexive evaluation process.

If the comparison process suggests that the individual indeed is like others who are homosexuals, the strategy will depend upon the evaluation of other homosexuals. When there are positive homosexual role models and social beliefs, the identity-comparison stage can be easily negotiated, with a resulting general improvement in the well-being of the individual. When homosexuality in the comparison process is devalued, for example, as being sex-role nonconforming or "sick," there may be a splitting into good and bad (homosexual) selves. Or there may instead be a move in the direction of the comparison persons or stereotypes. The individual, for example, may attempt to act in a less sex-role conformist manner, even though this had previously been evaluated as undesirable and inconsistent with the self-concept. This alternative may also be accompanied by general devaluation of the importance and beliefs of others, expressed either through strategies of withdrawal, or acting out and taunting others (flaunting it).

The clinician needs to be aware of different components of the negative social evaluation and stereotypes of homosexuality, their prevalence as social beliefs, their social functions and personal effects, and how they correspond to the actual experiences of most homosexuals. Those attitudes are collectively called *homophobia.* There is a literature that should be consulted for additional information (see, for example, DeCecco, 1984c; Lehne, 1976; Morin & Garfinkle, 1978).

Another method of resolving identity-comparison issues may be overcompensation through identification with the socially desirable norms. This is the "best little boy" or "best little girl" strategy. The presentation of conventional social values and achievement through the attainment of status becomes paramount for the individual. Emotionality is denied and replaced by conventionality. The individuals seek to be all things to all people, or to become so accomplished in achievement that their erotosexual status cannot be questioned. This strategy may be carried out through marriage and high-level professional achievement, until the pressures of being the model person or model couple become too much to manage in the face of anger and rage related to repression and self-denial of erotosexual satisfaction. Upward social mobility, which tends to set apart the individuals from their families and social origins, is often associated with the use of this strategy.

Another strategy for managing identity comparison is called *passing.* It occurs when individuals conclude that they are similar to other homosexuals, while at the same time avoiding the stigmatization of accepting the status of homosexual in a society where homosexuality is devalued.

Many older homosexuals have a long history of passing themselves off as heterosexuals because of the negative antihomosexual social attitudes (homophobia) that were evident during their youth. This strategy is most successful prior to the socially typical age of marriage, and less successful after that unless the homosexual marries for social cover. This is not to deny that they may also appreciate and marry for other values of this social institution, such as companionship, economic stability, or to have children.

Common passing techniques include avoiding situations that potentially raise heterosexual issues. Dating may be avoided, for example, by pleading lack of time, money, car, or energy due to involvement in work, study, or hobbies. Passing individuals will also be cautious in controlling the personal information available to others about the self, from adopting very conventional characteristics to restricting friendships and conversations on personal topics. They may develop the role of a good listener, but only a theoretical or intellectual speaker. The cultural image of heterosexuality or asexuality may be deliberately developed or dissimulated. A person may have nonsexual dates of convenience, a putative lover who lives in another geographical locale, or have sincere or affected religious beliefs about premarital chastity, restrictions on dating, or celibacy (including the option of joining religious orders). Work in all-male institutions (such as the military services or as merchant seamen) may also provide a cover of presumed heterosexuality, while also minimizing situations in which an individual is compelled to provide verifiable evidence of typical heterosexual sexual activities.

Passing also usually involves distancing oneself from homosexual situations, to avoid guilt by association. As Plummer (1975) points out, this is one of the main pitfalls of passing during the stage of sensitization. Because contact with homosexuals is so limited by strategies of passing, these persons are also deprived of firsthand experiences that could potentially help them learn about the homosexual status in society. For the individual who successfully passes, information available about homosexuality tends to come more often from less-informed, presumably heterosexual sources, rather than from people whose own experience has directly taught them about the varieties of the homosexual experience.

The person who passes as a strategy for dealing with the issues of identity comparison is always vulnerable to social labeling or exposure, and the realization that they have been unduly constrained in living their lives as a sham or a lie, with generally demoralizing consequences. Others who continue to pass as a social management strategy, while maintaining social contact with homosexual friends, are much better insulated from the potential trauma of exposure, probably without being at any greater risk of exposure.

Clients will also pass, often successfully, with clinicians whom they may see for assistance. In the initial clinical interviews, the clinician must always be alert to asking questions in a form so as not to encourage passing. In diagnosis and treatment, passing as a way of avoiding the development of a homosexual status needs to be differentiated from the highly similar forms of passing that are used for social management of a stigmatized identity. Nonsexist, nonjudgmental interview styles are most useful here, where open-ended questions are followed up by questions that more specifically probe a variety of topics related to sexuality.

There are other strategies used to avoid adopting a homosexual status in the stage of identity comparison. They include cognitive conceptualizations of homosexuality only in relationship to one particular person (the "special case"). Alternatively, persons may consider themselves bisexual or ambisexual, with the associated belief that most people are bisexual. This belief may be maintained even in the absence of any heterosexual experience, for the heterosexuality may be considered potential and not realized because of the lack of an appropriate partner — a rationalization that is often more clear to the clinician than the client. Even an extensive amount of heterosexual experience, of course, does not preclude a homosexual status. Most self-identified homosexuals have had significant amounts of heterosexual experience, but the self-defined quality of these experiences was different and less positively valued than were homosexual experiences. Other individuals adopt a homosexual status prior to any interpersonal sexual experiences. One may also avoid the commitment to a homosexual-identity/role by maintaining that the homosexual status is only a temporary identity, with the possibility that one could in the future choose to be heterosexual.

Particularly where there is self-hate or a negatively valued identity, the individual may accept the homosexual role but give a non-self-blaming attribution for the homosexual identity. The use of etiological pseudo-explanations is one strategy to avoid guilt and self-blame. For example, they may claim, "I was born this way," "I can't help it," or blame it on their parents or some childhood experience. The excessive concern with etiology, which presumes that they have realized that the label of homosexual applies to themselves, is actually a strategy to avoid accepting the negative valuation of a homosexual status as part of their identity. That it is a strategy of the identity-comparison stage is evident partly because these individuals have usually sought out a great deal of information about homosexuality to determine (or overdetermine) whether they do merit the homosexual-status label.

Individuals at the social-comparison stage may also use a variety of strategies to avoid homosexual behavior. Even though homosexual behavior is not a necessary component of this stage, for these individuals the ability to engage in the behavior is threatening because it makes them unable to avoid the comparison with other homosexuals who presumably engage in homosexual behavior. These individuals may present to the clinician with the problems of asexualism, lack of sexual desire or impotence, being unable to express their underlying concern that if they were capable of engaging in sexual behavior, it might be homosexual. When there are very negative views regarding homosexuality and a desire to be heterosexual, all homosexual behavior may be inhibited; homosexuality is then excessively devalued while heterosexuality is positively portrayed as the cure-all for every ailment. This negative self-identity puts the individual at great risk of depression and suicide should the strategy for sexual realignment fail (as it usually does).

Finally, for some people, it is difficult to resolve the concern with social approval, and yet the individuals believe that the identity/role of homosexuality corresponds to their self-assessment. In this situation the person may change reference group by, for example, changing friends, social or professional circles, or religious associations. In many cases this is accomplished by a geographic move, away from family and childhood friends, to an (urban) area where the individual is not known by history. In this new context, which may be going away to college or perhaps only a shorter vacation or business trip out of town, the individual can explore the identity/role of homosexuality while avoiding the problems of social comparison. This strategy is a particularly common resolution of the difficulties of the identity comparison stage.

HOMOSEXUAL-IDENTITY/ROLE EXPLORATION

The sensitization stage in the development of a homosexual-identity/role is predominantly worked through alone, but the exploration stage involves seeking contact with other homosexuals. Cass (1979) refers to this as the stage of identity tolerance. The individual's possible homosexual status is generally kept secret from others. The process is that of trying out the social and sexual roles of homosexuals to determine their applicability to the person's own situation. Although a homosexual status may be professed to one's homosexual contacts, it has not necessarily been accepted as a personal identity/role during the stage of exploration.

The social context of the exploration process is crucial. Because of the conceptualized need for secrecy about sexual behavior (reinforced by the frequently illegal status of the behavior), the more general social context is presumed to be negative toward homosexuality. This conception of socialized homophobia may approach the proportions of paranoia. In extreme cases, the paranoia may have clinical characteristics, in that homophobia is conceived of as being everywhere, and this leads to serious distortions of behavior. Suspiciousness may abound, accompanied by the use of a fictionalized name and identity. Although the individual may have had no experiences to support the paranoid ideation, the paranoia does not recede with accumulated positively valued experiences and is not influenced by the denials and countersuggestions and interpretations of the homosexual reference group or by those of the clinician. Most typically, the paranoia is short-lived, never achieving independence totally unrelated to the individual's own experiences of fearfully making initial contact with homosexuals. In some cases, however, the paranoia may become characterological.

The underlying issue is that increased social alienation results in the individual's seeking out other homosexuals or a homosexual subculture where the exploration of a homosexual-identity/role can be explored in ways in which it cannot be with nonhomosexuals. The novice may have great difficulty in detecting ways of meeting other homosexuals. Early encounters may be by chance, or as a result of the information-seeking of the previous stage.

Although the emotional quality of the early contacts is important, it is the availability of role models who are perceived as similar to the explorer that is crucial. These models may be difficult to find, which can result in a period of withdrawal to previous stages. The novices' lack of information about the homosexual subculture may not lead them to situations where they can find the types of models who exemplify the type of life-style they can envision themselves leading.

The novice also begins the journey with the need to learn the somewhat different social skills of the homosexual subculture. A process of resocialization must often be undergone before the novices are able to make personal contacts with individuals whom they perceive as appropriate or desirable. This resocialization may be hampered by poor social skills in general, as a consequence of strategies used in the previous stages of development. Low self-esteem is also a frequent factor, although the personal characteristics that are devalued in the novice's previous nonhomosexual experiences may not be similarly devalued within some of the possible homosexual subcultures. A concern about the fear of exposure, police, and the general fear of the unknown do not help to make the early process of exploration comfortable. These fears and anxieties may also interfere with successful and enjoyable sexual functioning.

Surprisingly enough, considering all these possible and realistic difficulties, most novices negotiate the activities of exploration with a remarkable degree of success. Part of the reason for this is that the experience of fearful exploration is a normative experience within the homosexual subcultures, so that others will readily acknowledge and sympathize with the novice, often by sharing their own experience.

A series of unrewarding contacts may lead to the devaluation of the homosexual subculture, a reevaluation or negative evaluation of homosexual experiences, and a more difficult journey in the process of developing a sexual status. The result may be periods of depression. If professional assistance is sought, the clinician must be extremely cautious about supporting the depression by devaluing the homosexual subculture in the belief that this will encourage the development of a heterosexual status. Instead the clinician can interpret the clients' experiences in light of their presentation of self and knowledge of the homosexual subculture. A lack of success in exploring the homosexual subculture is often predictive of a lack of success in exploring the heterosexual culture, so the issues of concern are best pursued from that perspective (i.e., socialization skills, along with an absence of blaming or transference of responsibility onto the subculture).

A series of rewarding contacts may lead to one of several paths of further exploration. Some males go through a phase of "tricking" (having sexual relations) with a large number of partners. This may help them develop their self-esteem and sexual confidence, while also exposing them to a wide variety of homosexuals from whom they can learn about the many varieties of homosexual experiences and life-styles. There is certainly risk involved in this course – either of physical danger, conflict with the law, and, of course, of sexually transmitted diseases such as AIDS. Given the increasing prevalence of AIDS among male homosexuals the pattern of a large number of different sexual partners has already changed, if not because of the novices' fears, then because of the increasing unwillingness of individuals in the gay male community to engage in sexual activities with a large number of different partners.

The tricking strategy has other pitfalls, if it becomes a habit that consumes the time available for other types of socializing. This is especially so if it continues to the point where novices are longing to develop a friendship circle or a relationship and become frustrated and devalue themselves as people who are only desired for their bodies.

Another pattern is to go through a series of love affairs, constantly falling in love, and then falling out of love or being rejected by a partner. This may lead to persistent beliefs that all homosexuals are interested only in sex, and that nobody ever develops a stable relationship. This pattern is most prevalent in those individuals who have more of an affectional than a sexual priority in their developing homosexual-identity/role. Consequently, it may lead to disillusionment and depression.

Still others may find a lover and settle down, very early in the exploration stage. In some cases these relationships may be quite successful and long lasting. In other cases, they may be constricting because the partner of the novice, after an initial period of teaching, may restrict the future development and learning of the partner out of an inability to cope with the consequent changes which this would entail for the relationship. This is more common in relationships where the novice is young, and the partner is considerably older with a well-established life-style.

Homosexual/gay consciousness-raising or rap groups, as well as group therapy, may be useful adjuncts for some individuals in the process of negotiating the exploration stage. The utility of these groups derives from the sharing of experiences and conceptions of social reality of the participants. Although most individuals are able to gain this knowledge in the course of their own explorations, some are not, for a variety of reasons. Individual psychotherapy can be useful if there are personality problems or a lack of social interaction skills, although most therapists are not familiar enough with the many by ways of the homosexual subcultures to function single handedly as effective guides, unless they can also skillfully refer their client to appropriate resources within the homosexual community for additional information and viewpoints.

The stage of exploration ends when the novice is skilled and comfortable in the ways of the homosexual community, and, consequent upon finding a satisfactory niche for the present, no longer merely dissembles a homosexual status, but incorporates it as a homosexual-identity/role.

HOMOSEXUAL-IDENTITY/ROLE ACCEPTANCE

The stage of homosexual-identity/role acceptance is the least problematical from the point of view of the individual. Relatively few people seek professional assistance during this period. However, the resolution of the issues of this stage have a predisposing effect on life satisfaction for the remainder of many individuals' adult lives. This is the time when an individual moves from being "homosexual" to accepting the label of "a homosexual." The content that label implies will have a great effect on future patterns of love, sex, socialization, and social adaptation.

In the course of the exploration of the previous period, the individual develops increased contacts with other homosexuals. In situations where the individual is positively evaluated, there is a tendency to become a member of a subculture with a close reference-group of gay friends. The attitudes of this group are gradually adopted by the individual, which provides a basis for the validation and normalization of homosexuality as an identity and life-style. The individual may gradually reform his own life-style, restructuring it based on the model of the reference group.

There is a tremendous diversity among different homosexual life-styles in the United States. Some groups, for example, are extremely secretive about their homosexuality. Thus passing may be incorporated as a relatively permanent component of a life-style, with its implications for compartmentalized activities and social contacts. Other subcultures may be much more open in "flaunting" their homosexuality, perhaps with political commitment and involvement. Some individuals lead life-styles that totally revolve around the gay liberation movement, the feminist movement or gay organizations dedicated to political and social change.

Still other subcultures are organized around a specific interest — a certain religion, an interest in music, opera, dance, theater or other arts. Some subcultures revolve around certain gay activities, be it the commerical gay scene of the bars or discos, or the circuit of summer and winter resorts. Other subcultures convene around specific ways to satisfy sexual urges, from street cruisers or "tea room" (public toilet) aficionados to those whose interests, for example, may be exclusively limited to partners of another race or social background. Additionally, there are subcultures composed exclusively of couples who revolve on a cycle of private entertaining. These brief descriptions barely begin to scratch the surface of the variety of homosexual subcultures to which individuals may be drawn and may gradually reconstruct themselves — according to the attitudes and values of the subculture. Acceptance of an identity/role often implies that the individual accepts the standards of a subculture as one's own.

Homosexual-identity/role acceptance becomes the basis of disclosure of that identity/role to others, to the extent that disclosure is practiced within the subculture. This disclosure may be predominantly to other homosexuals within the subculture, to selected homosexuals in other subcultures, or perhaps even disclosure to a limited number of heterosexuals, most typically family.

Coming Out. The process of self-disclosure to others is called coming out. The advice and support of a clinician can be useful, both for the individual and also for the targets of disclosure. As a result of the sometimes difficult path to self-acceptance, there may be anger at others who are viewed as contributing to the difficulty of the journey. This anger may be symbolically directed, as at all individuals who hold conventional values or are authority figures. Or the anger may be specific, and related to difficulties resulting from the negative attitudes or treatment of others. In either case, self-disclosure can be used as a weapon to hurt others, rather than as a process of very personal sharing that can lead to greater intimacy and better communication.

In other cases, the price of self-acceptance of what is seen as a socially devalued identity is paid at the cost of generally devaluing heterosexuality and conventionality. Homosexuality is overvalued, and viewed as directly confrontational to heterosexual statuses.

The advantages of coming out to others are many. Most importantly, it makes it possible to live life with less deception. Individuals are more able to share their highs and lows with others, their successes and their defeats. Coming out can eliminate the fear of detection or exposure, which preoccupies some individuals. It can improve communication with others who are important parts of the life of an individual. It provides an opportunity to live a more integrated life, with the full range of support systems available.

There are also risks in coming out. When personal information is shared, it becomes public property and can never be taken back; it may be used for better or worse. Some parents still reject their children when they learn about their homosexuality. People still get fired from jobs, or are not hired, because they are gay. Individuals can be subject to public abuse and harassment, should their erotosexual status become known. Full disclosure may immunize an individual from the risks of blackmail, but partial disclosure, which is more common, may provide the evidence to be used against a person. This is particularly true in certain occupations (including religious and the military professions), where homosexuality may preclude ordination or security clearances, or licensing where the behavior is considered to be immoral or illegal. As a result of public concern about homosexual transmission or affliction with AIDS, discrimination against homosexuals appears to be increasing.

In coming out to others, it is difficult to predict their response. Generally liberal social beliefs may correlate with the general acceptance of homosexuality. But the reaction to a specific individual is not necessarily the same as the more generalized social acceptance or rejection of homosexuality. All people have certain beliefs, expectations, fantasies about others who are important in their lives. Almost all parents, for example, have fantasies based on the assumption that their children are heterosexual, will marry and produce grandchildren, and be a credit to the family in conventional social terms. They are also concerned that their children will be happy. These expectations and fantasies are abruptly confronted when a son or daughter "comes out" to their parents.

Thus, while coming out may be an ultimate act for the individual in the process of accepting self-labeling as a homosexual, for the parent or person who is told, it is only the first step in the process of accepting homosexuality. As it took the individual many years to accept his or her homosexuality, it should likewise be expected that it will take others some time before they reach the stage of acceptance. It is important, therefore, that the process of coming out (if done) be carefully managed to avoid damaging future relationships with important non-homosexual others.

The clinician can offer some simple suggestions that may maximize the value and likelihood of a reasonable response to coming out. The individual, however, not the clinician, must take full responsibility for the decision to come out. Following are some general considerations that can be discussed by clinicians when a patient raises the issue of coming out. First, an individual must choose an appropriate occasion for coming out to important others, such as family. Family-oriented holidays and occasions (such as weddings) should be avoided. The emotionalism of these situations, and the contrast between the conventional heterosexual imagery they provoke and the message of revealing homosexuality and asking for acceptance, is too great a discrepancy for others to bridge at the time of telling. Likewise, times of stress or distress should be avoided, because parents are likely initially to regard their child's revelation of homosexuality as another piece of bad news, because of its own content and by association with the distressing situation. In these situations, the initial response of parents is not likely to be as loving and accepting as it might be under other circumstances.

A neutral time is the best time to share a revelation of homosexuality. Forewarning others generally tends to create suspense, as well as the expectation that good news is not the purpose of the requested meeting. The context of coming out to parents or others should most properly be a sharing of intimacy with a view to improving the closeness of the relationship between the involved individuals. The revelation does not mean that the now-labeled homosexual is a different person from before, but only that there is more shared understanding and communication possible among the participants.

When telling parents, the issue of blame is certain to arise, and should be avoided at the outset. Blame is associated with bad outcomes, not positive results. Although the homosexual turned out differently than the family would have expected, if there is genuine acceptance of a homosexual status that is the basis of a happy and satisfying life-style, there is no need for blame. When relevant people (such as both parents) are told at the same time, the blame issue can be defused additionally.

Homosexuality is most positively understood by others when related to falling in love, rather than related to either the real or imagined details of sexual encounters. The issue of coming out is most likely to arise when one can share the excitement and pleasure of being in love. This is an aspect of life that people in American society do endeavor to share with others, or may feel pain and pressure when they cannot proclaim their love publicly. People do not typically share or proclaim intimate details of their sexual functioning.

Coming out or telling parents and important others about a personal homosexual status is only the first part of the process of mutual acceptance. It is important to follow up initial revelations with continued communication and education.

Other than with parents and close friends, who may have a long history with an individual wherein it was assumed that the individual was conventionally heterosexual, it is not generally advisable to sit other people down and come out to them. Coming out in work and other social situations can more appropriately be handled by avoiding the creation of the presumption that the individual is heterosexual. Individuals may want to proclaim their homosexuality to the world, as part of their own acceptance and perhaps sense of "Identity

Pride" (Cass, 1979, 1984). But this type of proclamation goes beyond the conventionally accepted values and standards of American customs, and thus should be avoided unless the individual has certain political rather than personal purposes in mind. Coming out as a political act designed to influence and change social concepts of homosexuality is only for those who are prepared to deal with the consequences of politicizing their otherwise essentially personal erotosexual life-styles.

In some situations, the clinician will become involved as a follow-up resource for homosexual clients who have come out to their parents and significant others. When the client is already in family therapy, the initial revelation may be made in a family session. Otherwise, the initial revelation should be made privately by the client—it is not the function of the clinician to initially share information about the client's erotosexual orientation with others, even at the client's request. To do so places too much responsibility upon the clinician, who is then vulnerable to repercussions for violating confidentiality (even with signed consent), and may be seen as labeling or inappropriately "pushing" a client into an inappropriate identity or revelation. Also, the clinician's pronouncement carries a weight of finality that cannot be justified or substantiated. In follow-up consultation with parents, if requested, the clinicians can explain in terms of probabilities and generalities what homosexual erotosexual status involves, and it can then be left to the client to fill in the relevant personal details. In this way, also, the client maintains personal responsibility for the decision to come out and for the sharing of any personal information.

Since homosexuality is not a DSM III-diagnosible condition, it is not necessarily a relevant aspect of an individual's life to report or discuss with others in the context of a general authorization to release information. The process of coming out is an individual decision that some clients will make in the process of accepting the status of a homosexual/identity-role. The decision to label an individual as a homosexual should never be made independently by a treating clinician. When a client authorizes the release of information about psychological status or treatment, the therapist should specifically determine with the client whether the released information should include references to erotosexual status. In some legal situations, such partial disclosure may not be possible.

The result of the process of identity acceptance is that the individual becomes comfortable with applying the social-category label of "a homosexual" to the self, and has developed a strategy for the social management of this status. The individual then moves into the final stage of the process, that of homosexual-identity/role stabilization.

HOMOSEXUAL-IDENTITY/ROLE STABILIZATION

Stabilization is a process of developing an identity/role synthesis that becomes the basis for a normalized life-style. Synthesis involves achieving a rapprochement with society, which will tolerate many types of homosexual life-styles, while not actually encouraging, condoning or openly accepting the viability of such a life-style. By social convention, but not necessarily by individual choice, the individual lives spanning two very different worlds: the presumptively heterosexual world of society in general and the more accepting personal/social world of other homosexuals and accepting heterosexuals. A flawless, seamless merger of these two aspects of existence is rarely achieved.

Retreat into a basically homosexual environment, such as can be found in parts of San Francisco, New York or other areas where an individual can work, live, and socialize in a totally homosexual environment, is achieved by some. This retreat is usually more of a transitional stabilization, because relatively few individuals can encompass the majority of their interests within such socially and geographically restricted environs, and have a productive, fulfilling work life at the same time. Such styles of ghetto living, by necessity or choice, however, have a long history of success for a variety of social minorities or outcasts. Thus one viable form of stabilization for some gay people can be found in gay urban neighborhoods.

For most others, stabilization involves achieving success in a workplace where the individual's homosexual status (even if not known) does not interfere with being secure and productive. Socialization usually includes a range of different groups, from those which are presumptively heterosexual, to socially mixed groupings, and to exclusively homosexual associations. Socializing with work companions may become less of a priority for many homosexual individuals when events are more couple oriented, and hence exclude loved companions of one's own gender. Other forms of socialization with married couples, who are often in the process of raising their own families, may decrease in interest and frequency as life situations become more divergent.

Developing a living situation, with or without a lover, where the individual can be comfortable in living a homosexual (or mixed) life-style, is definitely a priority in the process of stabilization. Otherwise, conventional social pressures will decrease the pleasure in comfortable and casual socialization at home, which can lead to isolation. The increase in neighborhoods and apartment developments not characterized by families with children has contributed to the viability of alternative life-styles, including those which can be comfortable for homosexuals.

A primary factor in stabilization is developing a satisfactory way of conducting a sexual and love life. For most gay people this includes developing a stable relationship, and eventually a network of other gay couples with whom to participate in social activities. For others, there may be stabilization through a close-knit friendship circle, with sexual liaisons and affairs being conducted outside this support group and tending to be more ephemeral.

The problems of gay couples are similar to those of heterosexual couples, differing mainly in the intensity of the forces that can contribute to the establishment or break-up of a relationship. (See Blumstein & Schwartz, 1983;

McWhirter & Mattison, 1984; Silverstein, 1981). The lack of social recognition and sanctions, such as marriage, increases the ease with which individuals can get into and out of such relationships.

A mutual interest in sexual activities is one of the chief factors that brings potential partners in a gay relationship together. Some meetings may occur through the gay commercial scene, such as bars and bathhouses for men, and to a somewhat lesser extent for women. Meeting others through private parties and friendship networks is also prevalent, especially among lesbians. Relationships, of course, can also develop through work situations, neighborhood contacts, and in the course of recreational activities. The frequency with which individuals share a sexual orientation and mutual attraction is lower in nongay subcultural events, although the likelihood that the two people who meet share common interests that may provide the basis for a stable relationship is higher.

The gay subculture is not as stratified on social variables as is the equivalent heterosexual culture. There may be more mixing of age groups, of educational, occupational, and social class backgrounds, in addition to cultural, racial and religious dimensions. The result is that there may be more divergence in backgrounds among individuals developing a potential relationship than is typical among heterosexual dating customs. These difference factors pose more obstacles that must be negotiated as the basis of developing a stable relationship. A homosexual status is in many senses a great equalizer for different types of people. It is also relatively easy to get involved in a relationship based on initial sexual attraction and compatibility, although the prospects for the relationship stabilizing may not be excellent because of other differences between the partners.

The ground rules of each relationship must be negotiated separately. There is no set of norms for the division of responsibility and social roles in gay relationships, because these relationships are not socially sanctioned or socially modeled. Thus a newly in-love couple will have more issues to resolve at the outset, and their success in resolving these issues is one of the most important determinants for the stability of their relationship.

The relationship issue of monogamy versus nonmonogamy is critical. Most gay relationships are not, in the long term, monogamous, although they may be at the outset. Nonmonogamy is found more often than monogamy in longstanding gay relationships, yet paradoxically it is often this issue that leads to the most disruptive disputes and contributes to the early break-up of many gay relationships. The gay subculture offers many opportunities for sexual liaisons, creating the impression that it is often easier to abandon a relationship that needs work, where sexual passions are waning, than to increase the individual commitments to the ongoing relationship. In many cases, by the time a gay couple makes a decision to seek couple counseling for their relationship, one member of the relationship will have already decided that nonmonogamy is more important than the current relationship, which the other member is trying to preserve with untenable demands for monogamy.

Some gay individuals seeking stabilization through a relationship will come for professional assistance extremely discouraged by the difficulty in meeting potential lovers. They may maintain that gay people are only interested in sex, not in relationships. Usually there are two factors operating. First, the individuals are often pursuing routes for meeting partners that are not compatible with their personal styles. For example, if years of trying to meet a partner through gay bars has not been successful in the past, the likelihood is that it will not be successful in the future. New approaches to socialization need to be explored. Second, most likely these individuals, through their past patterns of socialization, have not been exposed to the role models of successful gay relationships. Established gay couples do not tend to socialize in the same types of settings as those single individuals seeking a sexual partner or potential relationship. The lack of couple role models is a significant factor in the inability of many gay individuals to develop the expectations and skills for successful long-term relationships.

Stabilization is always a goal, but never a finalized reality. Individuals keep changing during the course of their lives. Also, the social situation of homosexuality is constantly changing. Homosexual life-styles that were stabilized in the 1960s or 1970s may be in states of flux in the 1980s. The 1970s and 1980s were times of rapid expansion in the public acceptance of homosexuality, the development of gay liberation organizations, and expansion of the political, social, and commercial gay subculture. Sexual liberation was increasingly expressed through the opportunities for increased numbers of different sexual partners, and openness in the expression of homosexuality.

Social change in the 1980s is also likely to have an impact on the stabilization of gay life-styles. Three factors are particularly notable: increasing social conventionalism; the increase in the mean age of the gay population; and the influence of the fatal contagious disease of AIDS.

Social values and norms are becoming more conventional, meaning more traditional or conservative. Alternative life-styles are being replaced with "making it" attitudes in a time of economic and political retrenchment. "Dress-for-success" thinking is replacing individualistic display. There has always been an attitude of conventionality and conservativism within many gay people, which is again coming to the forefront. From flaunting homosexuality as a desirable form of difference, current attitudes are more in tune with the idea that gay people are just like everyone else, except that they fall in love with people of the same sex. This trend has the advantage of encouraging social synthesis, but possibly at the disadvantage of ultimately decreasing the public acceptance of homosexuality. Gay people, for example, are increasingly turning back to religion, at a time when some religious denominations are becoming more supportive in their tolerance of homosexuality, while other, fundamentalist religions are more vocal in their denigration of homosexuality. Thus, the visibility of positive aspects of gay life-styles may become less accessible to the novice, while antihomosexual attitudes may become more apparent.

Now that the baby boom has topped out, the general population and the gay population is getting older. The gay subculture has been typified in the past as being preoccupied with youth. Normative gay life-styles, however, are changing—with increasing emphasis on somewhat older models. The perceived social acceptance and associated life-styles of more middle-aged gay people can be expected to improve in tandem with the aging of the population.

AIDS has posed a serious threat to the sexual behavior patterns, well-being and social acceptance of the gay community. In the past, casual sexual relationships were the focal point of some gay subcultures, and an important part of the process through which individuals came to accept their own homosexual status. This pattern has already changed dramatically with a deemphasis and decline in the frequency of casual sexual coupling, and an increase in the support for gay friendships and relationships. At the same time, the crisis of AIDS has had a unifying, supportive impact on the gay community to an extent that had never been previously obtained through either gay political organizations or the social networks of the gay community. On the negative side, fear of AIDS is leading to increased social intolerance and discrimination against homosexuals.

Thus, the process of homosexual-identity/role stabilization is affected by changes in the social climate. Insofar as individuals have achieved a normalized homosexual life-style, the problems presented to the clinicians are similar to those of heterosexuals: problems with relationships, problems in living, and with work. All of these problems are characterized by the nature of the interrelationship between an individual who has accepted a homosexual status and others, who may be homosexual (as friends and lovers) or not (as in the social and work environment).

OTHER CLINICAL PROBLEMS

This paper has described fairly typical processes in the development of homosexual status, with detours of clinical importance. In this section, additional clinical problems of some homosexuals are discussed.

Sexual Disorders (among males). Sexual disorders are prevalent among homosexual males, as well as among heterosexual males, although there are probably some differences in the incidence of different dysfunctions. Homosexual male impotence, for example, although not frequently a presenting problem for treatment, has causes similar to those commonly seen among all men. These causes include impotence due to organic factors including the abuse of alcohol or substances, or reflective of a lack of sexual arousal associated with a loved partner, or due to performance fears. In other cases, impotence may not be a problem in casual sexual contacts, but occurs in potential or actual relationship situations. This often is reflective of fears of emotional and sexual intimacy, or of the idea that sex is too degrading to do with someone who is loved (the playboy/provider or madonna/whore syndrome).

Atypical sexual imagery, including concurrent paraphilias, may be present in male homosexual as well as in heterosexual life-styles. Attraction to partners of different ages (as in pedophilia, but also in individuals attracted to adolescents) may result in a series of sexual contacts that do not last. Cross-dressing (usually not transvestism, which is typically heterosexual), and sexual sadism and masochism may also be present in gay men. These factors can interfere with pair-bonding, and may also be expressed through compulsive behavior that makes an individual a prisoner of sex rather than responsibly in control of his own sex life. The clinician must differentiate between atypical, fantasy imagery, which is acted upon in a spirit of playfulness without any injurious effects upon the individual's life-style, and the clinical presentation of a paraphilia.

Because a wide variety of sexual imagery and exploration is tolerated and even encouraged within the gay male social subcultures, it is important that the clinician be comfortable and nonjudgmental when clients describe their sexual interests. If there is a clinical paraphilia concurrent with a homosexual status, treatment of the paraphilia independently of the homosexual status may be indicated. The success of treatment for the paraphilias with, for example, combined group therapy and Depo-Provera, is similar regardless of whether the individuals are homosexual or heterosexual. The possible exception here is that the paraphilia may be more ego-syntonic in some homosexual men, and supported by a subculture that is accepting and encouraging of the paraphilic activity. Pairbonding with an individual who shares a complementary paraphilia is also more frequently found among homosexual men than in heterosexual couples. In these cases, individuals may not seek psychotherapy unless the behaviors are destructive or compulsively preoccupying.

Two hyperphilias are seen with significant frequency among gay males: compulsive cruising and multiphilia. Both of these may have their roots in earlier adaptations to a homosexual status. In compulsive cruising, the individual's life-styles revolve around opportunities for sexual encounters, where the agenda is usually an anonymous sexual contact without an interest in developing intimate relationships. In multiphilia, the pattern is a series of love affairs, without settling down in a relationship for longer than a few weeks or months: when the initial limerence or intense love (Tennov, 1979) dies down, the person is off in search of a new partner. Gay men are increasingly seeking therapy or participating in sexual addiction groups to change these patterns due to fears of AIDS. However, both of these patterns are difficult to change, although the ideal resolution in each case is the same: an enduring, reciprocal love affair.

Sexual dysfunctions among lesbians are infrequently reported. Their prevalence, therefore, is unknown. Lesbians may complain of inhibited sexual desire or difficulty in achieving orgasm. Genuine paraphilias or sexual addictions are rare.

Psychopathology. Serious psychopathology can coexist with a homosexual status as well as with a heterosexual status. It may be more prevalent among homosexuals who have both a vulnerability toward psychopathology and less ability to tolerate the increased pressures of trying to come to terms with a homosexual status in a society that is not sympathetic toward or supportive of such a status.

The diagnosis of psychopathology must be made independently of homosexual status: the erotosexual status of an individual is not a definitional criterion or indicative of any type of psychopathology. Treatment approaches for psychopathology, although they are similar to those used in the general population may have to be tailored to the special issues stemming from the erotosexual status of the client.

Depression (*dysthymic disorder*) is the most prevalent type of psychopathology in clients presenting for treatment. The clinician must differentiate depression which is related to life-styles issues (isolation, loneliness) from that which is a result of other factors (e.g., manic-depressive or bipolar disorders; reactive depression; and more characterological forms of depression). The approach to treatment, including possible referral for medication, is closely related to the diagnosis.

Depression that is related to life-style issues, where there is evidence that the client is engaging in inappropriate or ineffective behavior, can frequently be handled with behavioral tasks. Developing new approaches and arenas for socialization can be handled by giving the client tasks to carry out that result in increased client knowledge and contact with different activities and subcultures within the gay community. Group psychotherapy, in groups composed exclusively of gay individuals, can also be very beneficial.

Both individual and group psychotherapy are beneficial for dealing with characterological depression involving adjustment to a homosexual-identity/role. Cognitive restructuring is a necessary part of the resolution of depressive thought patterns that center on a negative view of homosexuality and its implications for future life-styles. Providing information about gay life-styles is an important component of this type of therapy, although the information that comes firsthand from other individuals within the gay community is likely to have more impact than information provided through books or by the therapist. The therapist can incorporate into therapy parables or stories based on the actual experiences of individuals similar to the client, including the ways in which they resolved their situations.

In *borderline* personality disorders there is often a confusion over gender-identity/role or erotosexual status issues, combined with an inability or difficulty in pairbonding. Some individuals struggling to adopt a homosexual-identity/role may appear to present as a case of borderline personality disorder. Differential diagnosis is crucial, since the approach to treatment of borderline personality disorders (with the essential use of transference and the assumption of ego functioning, following the establishment of trust with the therapist) differs from the more direct guidance that the therapist may offer a floundering traveler who is attempting to test out a homosexual-identity/role. In general, when the patient presents the problem as being related to atypical sexual interests, the clinician should be particularly cautious about using borderline personality disorder as the diagnostic basis for the therapeutic plan, unless the full criteria for the diagnosis are rigorously met.

Narcissistic personality disorders also present a problem of differential diagnosis when dealing with individuals struggling with issues of erotosexual status. Some ways of dealing with these issues may interfere with pairbonding. One common early-life strategy for coping with a budding awareness of being "different" is to become the "best little boy" or "best little girl" in the world. When this strategy is maintained inappropriately long into adulthood, the results may resemble a narcissistic personality disorder. The difference is often that in these homosexual-identity/role cases the amount of anger concealed by the superior-appearing facade is considerable. An acceptance of or adjustment to a homosexual-identity/role may precipitate a period of overreaction into socially questionable behavior. There may also be key issues of guilt. Treatment of this maladaptive coping strategy progresses more rapidly than does that for narcissistic personality disorders, and the prognosis is very good.

Dependent, avoidant, and *compulsive* personality disorders can often be found in conjunction with a history of difficulty in accepting the legitimacy of a homosexual- identity/role. Paranoidlike ideation may also be present. Dealing with the underlying issues related to homosexuality is not sufficient to provide relief from the effects of these personality disorders. Therapy must also directly address the general personality disorder, as well as the concurrent anxiety. The anxiety must be defused with reference both to homosexual and heterosexual situations.

Gay and Married. Being gay and married is one of the more common— and also one of the more difficult and problematic—situations that are brought to therapists. The issue is complicated by the many different patterns of marriage that couples adopt or can tolerate, and becomes further complicated when there are children involved (Klein & Wolf, 1985; Ross, 1983).

Individuals with sexual interests that cannot be satisfied within a marriage are more likely to seek satisfaction outside of the marriage than are those individuals with conventional interests. Thus, for example, a man who fantasizes about other men is more likely to seek homosexual contact outside of the marriage than is a man who fantasizes about other women likely to seek heterosexual contact outside the marriage.

The erotosexual status of married individuals is more typically some variation of bisexuality than exclusive homosexuality. Nevertheless, the individuals will often strive to put themselves into one of two categories: heterosexual or homosexual. Thus, the presenting problem of gay and married individuals is twofold – a problem of identity as well as a problem of role as it relates to the marriage. It is often useful to explain to clients the implications of the continuum model of human erotosexual interests from 100% homosexual to 100% heterosexual, with most individuals falling somewhere in between. Most self-defined gay people are less than 100% homosexual on the continuum. This is a categorization of *general* erotosexual interests. But people are more interested in relationships with *one* other person than general interests. For persons who characterize their erotosexual status as 80% homosexual, for example, one would predict that they may have a better likelihood of falling in love with other individuals of the same sex. However, if they meet and fall in love with one person of the other sex, then they can have a pairbonded relationship with the potential for lasting. What counts is the *one* individual with whom they fall in love, not the odds of whether in a general sense that individual is more likely to be male or female.

Thus, many predominantly homosexually oriented people fall in love and marry for love. Others may marry for different reasons. The problems come in when the relationship stabilizes, the initial limerence diminishes, and the love becomes routinized or in some cases diminishes – as it does in the nearly 50% of all married couples who eventually get divorced. It is important for couples to realize, when one member is grappling with issues of homosexual-identity/role, that the current state of the marriage does not mean that from the start the marriage was a sham or a deception. Without this realization, the couple is unlikely to be able to work together either to continue the marriage in whatever way they are capable, or to separate amicably.

In many locales there are groups for individuals who are gay and married, and their memberships show a wide range of resolutions to this marital problem. Some couples divorce, either amicably or very acrimonously. Others allow for sexual liaisons or love affairs outside the marriage. Some relationships evolve into ménages a trois, or more communal living situations. When both the husband and the wife have an opportunity to explore these options by firsthand contact with other gay and married persons, they are more likely to come to a mutually satisfying resolution of their marital difficulties.

The problems, and resolutions, for gay and married couples are so diverse that the therapist can only provide information about the range of factors to be considered. There is no standard advice that can be offered, other than the fact that a homosexual or bisexual erotosexual status is a chronic condition that does not change over time (although behavior and life-styles may change). The therapist must be cautious never to discourage the continuation of a marital relationship, for this is solely the decision of both of the spouses.

In working with a couple, issues of confidentiality are paramount. Limits of confidentiality need to be established immediately when beginning the treatment. While honesty and open communication may in general be a healthy policy for married couples, this rule does not necessarily apply when dealing with the presenting problem of an individual who is gay and married. Thus there are situations in which a therapist may be drawn into apparent collusion with a married client when it would be inappropriate to divulge any information about the client's erotosexual status or activities to the spouse. The use of cotherapists for the husband and the wife is one method to avoid being compromised by collusion. In other situations, only one member of a couple may be seen, rather than seeing both in conjoint couple counseling.

Ego-dystonic homosexuality is a *DSM III* diagnosis applied to individuals who desire to increase heterosexual interests where the predominant and unwanted erotosexual interests are homosexual. This desire, however, while in many cases resulting from the internalized negative social evaluation of homosexuality, cannot simply reflect conflict between a homosexual and society. There are many individuals who, for a variety of reasons, desire to eliminate homosexual interests and replace them with heterosexual interests. In practice, however, there are many unresolved difficulties inherent in the diagnosis of ego-dystonic homosexuality as a mental disorder (see Suppe, 1984). Thus the diagnosis of ego-dystonic homosexuality cannot be made with any high degree of confidence.

Nevertheless, the presenting problem may be a desire to change an erotosexual status (typically from homosexual to heterosexual; rarely the reverse except in some unusual cases of paraphilia). In this situation, the therapist bears the responsibility of discussing reasonable goals of therapy with the client. It is much more feasible to change ego-dystonic into ego-syntonic than it is to change homosexuality into heterosexuality. But the bipolar categorization of homosexuality/heterosexuality is misleading, especially when the dimensions of identity and role/behavior are considered. A bisexual erotosexual orientation has the potential for being expressed in behavior through both homosexual and heterosexual relationships. Most of the cases of "change" of homosexuality reported in the literature are merely changes in the behavioral expression of bisexuality. In some cases "heterosexual behavior" may be possible in the presence of "homosexual fantasies," although usually with an impairment in the pairbondedness of the relationship. The therapist should also be sensitive to issues of the long-term stability of reported changes of erotosexual status.

The initial discussion of feasible goals of therapy is crucial in cases where the presenting problem is self-described as a desire to "change" erotosexual orientation. The client needs to understand that sexual behavior patterns are difficult to change, and that the object with whom one falls in love (which is the other component of erotosexual orientation) is most difficult to change. It is also important to provide the new client with an explanation of the continuum concept of erotosexual orientation (as described with reference to gay and married individuals). With this type of discussion as the basis for developing goals for therapy, most apparent cases of "ego-dystonic homosexuality" can be reconceptualized in a more therapeutically useful manner. In some cases, however, the clients may seek another therapist, to embark on the path of proving paradoxically that their erotosexual status cannot be changed (a means of avoiding self-responsibility for a stigmatized erotosexual status). But it is a discredit to the profession to take on a client who has goals for therapy that cannot be realized in the form in which the client understands them as the basis of the therapeutic relationship/contract.

Some therapists have been impressed with the effectiveness of Depo-Provera in treating the paraphilias, which they may see as an example of "changing" erotosexual orientation. Depo-Provera does not change typical adult homosexuality, in either its sexual or affectional manifestation. It does lower the sex drive, for both heterosexual and homosexual interests, making it more possible to control behavior. Thus it is useful to assist in the control of compulsive sexual behavior. Some types of compulsive homosexual behaviors reflect a paraphilia, and may respond to treatment incorporating Depo-Provera. This treatment does not, however, "change" erotosexual status, particularly when that status determines love rather than more simply sexual behavior.

Other clients may present to the clinician as heterosexual, when all the evidence indicates a predominant homosexual erotosexual orientation. In these cases, as well as in cases initially presenting as ego-dystonic homosexuality, the clinician is best advised to encourage heterosexual involvement at the onset. To encourage homosexual involvement would most likely result in panic and in the client's changing therapists. When the client is more sensitive to the difficulties (if any) of the heterosexual involvement, the possibility of learning more about homosexuality can be raised. Both of these types of problems are likely to be present in individuals at the first stage in the process of developing a homosexual-identity/role. Assuming that the eventual outcome is a homosexual-identity/role, the developmental process, augmented and supported by therapy, is along the routes described in the earlier sections of this paper.

SELECTED TREATMENT ISSUES

The preceding sections of this paper have focused on the development of a homosexual-identity/role from the point of view of normative development and the clinical characteristics of the client. In this last section, selected issues in treatment related to the therapist are discussed.

Knowledge of the subculture. It should not be the task of the client to educate the therapist about the homosexual subculture. An effective therapist for homosexual individuals should be knowledgeable about the multitude of lifestyles and resources within the local gay community, and the range of subculturally accepted standards of behavior. Without such familiarity, the therapist is at a loss to differentiate reported problems of the client as being due to personal difficulties or to a mismatch between the individual and the social settings for homosexual behavior. Similarly, suggestions for resolution of real-world problems cannot be made effectively by a therapist who is unfamiliar with local resources. It is not as useful to point out that a behavior pattern is self-defeating as it is to provide suggestions for modified patterns and different social milieus. Many of the problems homosexuals face are the result of the social stigmatization of homosexuality. Because the therapist is not in a situation to change social attitudes readily, and has little hope of changing individuals' erotosexual orientations, the compromise solution is to develop better techniques for social adaptation. Knowledge of the subculture is essential in this endeavor.

Behavioral tasks are often important in assisting a client to begin the process of changing ineffective or self-defeating behavioral patterns. Tasks can also be used to increase the client's knowledge of the subculture, which places more responsibility on the client, and less upon the therapist, as a provider of information. Behavioral tasks may include reading literature on homosexuality, as well as tasks of going to different groups or places, or trying different activities with partners.

Therapist's erotosexual orientation. Many therapists do not discuss their erotosexual orientation because it complicates transference and countertransference issues. However, the presumption is that most therapists are heterosexual, although some people presume that knowledgeable therapists who frequently see homosexual clients are homosexual. The homosexual therapist is often known and sought out by homosexual clients, because a higher level of knowledge about the homosexual subculture and a greater acceptance of homosexual life-styles is assumed. This assumption is not necessarily valid in practice. The converse belief, that a homosexual therapist is less likely to be supportive of a bisexual person who is attempting to live a conventional heterosexual life-style, is also not particularly valid.

The primary concerns of the client who seeks a therapist when issues of homosexuality are involved are those of knowledge, acceptance and nonjudgmentalism. These characteristics can be found in most therapists, independent of the therapists' sexual orientation. Some homosexual therapists, for example, are not comfortable with their own erotosexual status – and as a result may not be as comfortable in dealing with homosexual clients as are other, heterosexual therapists, who are secure and comfortable with their own sexuality. Some heterosexual therapists, likewise, are not comfortable or knowledgeable in dealing with homosexual clients. In these cases it is most appropriate to refer the client to a therapist who is known to be knowledgeable and comfortable in seeing homosexual clients.

When a potential client asks about the therapist's erotosexual status, the best policy is usually to answer the underlying question first: that the therapist is knowledgeable and nonjudgmental about human sexuality, including homosexuality. Once this question is answered, therapists may want to state that their standard policy is not to discuss their own personal lives with clients.

It is appropriate to add that the therapist, with the possible exception of a professional sexual surrogate therapist, does not become sexually involved with clients. Since the norms of the homosexual subculture may be more accepting of casual sexual liaisons than is typical of the heterosexual community, it is usually best in the beginning to define clearly the parameters of the therapeutic relationship.

For the homosexual therapist who sees many homosexual clients, it is often impossible not to encounter clients in social situations. Because the homosexual subculture is smaller and more focused than the heterosexual culture, it is not usually feasible to avoid all client contacts in social settings. Clients therefore need to be forewarned that if the therapist is encountered in a social situation, a social greeting is appropriate, with the understanding that the therapist will not divulge the presence or absence of a therapeutic relationship. In addition, the therapist has the responsibility to keep disengaged from the client's social/sexual life, which requires special consideration with reference to client confidentiality. It is not unusual for a therapist to have several clients who are socially and sexually involved with each other, where the clients do not realize that their friends may also be seeing the same therapist. Managing these types of professional relationships requires considerable skill on the part of the therapist.

Transference and Countertransference are present in perhaps a majority of all therapeutic relationships. It is essential that therapists be secure and comfortable in their own sexuality in order to handle these issues properly with homosexual clients. Transference is often a turning point in a therapeutic relationship, which if handled poorly can have a disastrous effect on the effectiveness of therapy. The techniques for handling transference and countertransference are the same regardless of the sexual orientation of the client or therapist. Two responses that are not appropriate are to be threatened by erotic transference because it is inconsistent with the therapist's own erotosexual status, or to deflect transference (rather than process it) by reference to an erotosexual status that is different from that of the client. Tranference is often a result of the intimacy created by the therapeutic relationship, rather than a product of the personal attractiveness of the therapist. Involvement in the personal life of the therapist is not a solution to the presenting problems of the client. For homosexual clients and therapists, as noted above, total separation of professional and social interactions may not be possible — but it is always possible to avoid any appearance or reality of sexual intimacy with patients.

Confidentiality and Nonjudgmentalism are the norm for all clinical relationships,and are especially important when dealing with homosexual clients. Even if the client signs a release of information, details about a client's erotosexual status should only be divulged by the client, because it does not properly constitute a diagnosis. Since erotosexual statuses are generally chronic characteristics of individuals, once such information is divulged it cannot be taken back. Homosexuality does not go "into remission" like other conditions, although an individual may or may not be living a homosexual life-style at any given time. Therefore, confidentiality should not be breached on this issue, without the specific consent and knowledge of the client (who is also informed of the long-term consequences).

Nonjudgmentalism is again standard practice. There is no quicker way to lose a client than to be moral or judgmental about erotosexual practices. But the issue here is also tied into confidentiality. Some homosexual clients may be behaving in ways that are strongly counter to the therapist's moral beliefs, and which may also be contrary to the law. Homosexual behavior itself is illegal in many jurisdictions. In addition, homosexuals may be engaging in other types of illegal behavior — most commonly, public or semipublic solicitation, but also in some situations, sexual relationships with minors, or physically dangerous sexual practices. Some clients are charged with illegal behavior during the process of therapy; for others, legal charges may be a precipitating event that brings a patient into therapy. In some cases, the therapist may feel an obligation to report illegal behavior to criminal justice authorities. The therapist may also have a moral responsibility (and a legal responsibility in some cases) to protect the well-being of others. Every sexual problem involving atypical sexual imagery or behavior may be a potential forensic case. Therapists who are not skilled in handling forensic cases, or who fear that they may feel compelled to breach patient confidentiality with reference to potentially illegal behavior, have an obligation to inform potential patients of their legal and ethical positions before becoming compromised. Errors of judgment in this area (including violation of patient confidentiality by inappropriate reporting of illegal behavior) may lead to malpractice suits.

CONCLUSIONS

Homosexuality has changed from a sin, to a sickness, to a social status over the past two hundred years. As a social status, it is still evaluated negatively, with few positive role models and social examples to help guide the individual on the paths of self-discovery and exploration. Understanding the social context in which individuals learn in adulthood to label themselves as "homosexual" is critical in understanding the process of developing a homosexual-identity/role.

The trend for the future will be away from categorizing homosexuality as distinct from bisexuality and heterosexuality, although these are the social-status labels that individuals still struggle to apply to themselves. The Kinsey continuum concept of sexuality, from exclusive heterosexuality to exclusive homosexuality in imagery and behavior, will most likely be replaced increasingly by the concept of erotosexual status, which incorporates both love/pairbonding and sexual/genital activity in a multidimensional, phenomenological format. Erotosexual status, including in some cases a homosexual-identity/role, is an integral component of gender-identity/role.

The process of developing a homosexual-identity/role is strongly influenced by the content of a homosexual status (or even the absence of that social status) in a society. It is a process of self-identification, labeling, and learning social roles for the expression of behavior. This adult developmental process can be conceptualized in four phases: Sensitization; Exploration; Acceptance; Stabilization. Various detours, some of which are maladjustive and may require clinical assistance to negotiate successfully, may occur in each phase.

In general, the progression starts with sensitization to evidence suggesting that an individual's erotosexual interests are atypical insofar as they include or are focused upon partners of the same sex. There are various ways in which this can be incorporated into the identity, and there are, as well, strategies for avoiding incorporation and for modification. Exploration provides opportunities to compare the self with others, to determine the adequacy of the self-labeling process. Acceptance develops when individuals are able to merge their own developing identity with a recognizable social setting and role. Stabilization is never complete, but represents a rapprochement between an individual's homosexual-identity/role and a normalized pattern of social relationships.

Although homosexuality itself is not a psychopathological condition, a homosexual individual can suffer from any type of psychopathology. These run the full gamut, from sexual disorders to personality disorders. In some cases, diagnosis of homosexual individuals is difficult, while in other cases there are special considerations for therapy with homosexuals. In general, however, the process for treating psychopathology in homosexuals is similar to that for all erotosexual orientations.

Treating homosexuals also raises some special therapeutic issues for the professional, ranging from knowledge of the homosexual subcultures to special concerns about transference, confidentiality, and professional nonjudgmentalism.

Issues of more serious psychopathology aside, the general role for the clinician in working with individuals who are struggling with issues of erotosexual status is that of a guide. The client is exploring both inner and outer space, in an attempt to find a fulfilling place to live a life. The better the therapist knows the territory, the more effective the therapist can be in this process.

REFERENCES

Babuscio, J. (1976). *We speak for ourselves: Experiences in homosexual counseling.* London: SPCK.

Bell, A.P., & Weinberg, M.S. (1978). *Homosexualities: A study of diversity among men and women.* New York: Simon & Schuster.

Bell, A.P., Weinberg, M.S., & Hammersmith, S.K. (1981). *Sexual preference: Its development in men and women.* Bloomington: Indiana University Press.

Brown, H.C. (1976). *Familiar faces, hidden lives: The story of homosexual men in America today.* New York: Harcourt Brace Jovanovich.

Blumstein, P., & Schwartz, P. (1983). *American couples: Money, work, sex.* New York: Morrow.

Bullough, V.L. (1976). *Sexual variance in society and history.* New York: Wiley.

Boswell, J. (1980). *Christianity, social tolerance, and homosexuality.* Chicago: University of Chicago Press.

Carrier, J.M. (1980). Homosexual behavior in cross-cultural perspective. In J. Mormon (Ed.), *Homosexual behavior: A modern reappraisal.* New York: Basic Books.

Cass, V.C. (1979). Homosexual identity formation: A theoretical model. *Journal of Homosexuality, 4*(3), 219-235.

Cass, V.C. (1984). Homosexual identity formation: Testing a theoretical model. *Journal of Sex Research. 20*(2), 143-167.

Coleman, E. (1982). Developmental stages of the coming-out process. In W. Paul, J.D. Weinreich, J.D. Gonsiorek, & M.E. Hotvedt (Eds.), *Homosexuality: Social, psychological, and biological issues.* Beverly Hills: Sage.

Dank, B.M. (1971). Coming out in the gay world. *Psychiatry, 34,* 180-197.

DeCecco, J.P. (1981). Definition and meaning of sexual orientation. *Journal of Homosexuality, 6*(4), 51-67.

DeCecco, J.P.(Ed.). (1984a). *Bisexual and homosexual identities: Critical clinical issues.* New York: Haworth Press. (Also published as *Journal of Homosexuality, 9*[4]).

DeCecco, J.P. (Ed.). (1984b). *Controversy over the bisexual and homosexual identities; Commentaries and reactions. Journal of Homosexuality, 10*[3/4]).

DeCecco, J.P. (Ed.). (1984c). *Homophobia: An overview.* New York: Haworth Press. (Also published as *Journal of Homosexuality, 10*[1/2]).

DeCecco, J.P., & Shively, M.G. (Eds.). (1983/1984). *Bisexual and homosexual identities: Critical theoretical issues.* New York: Haworth Press. (Also published as *Journal of Homosexuality,9*[2/3]).

DeMonteflores, C., & Schultz, S.J. (1978). Coming out: Similarities and differences for lesbians and gay men. *Journal of Social Issues, 34*(3), 59-72.

Fein, S.B., & Nuhring, E.M. (1981). Intrapsychic effects of stigma: A process of breakdown and reconstruction of social reality. *Journal of Homosexuality, 7*(1), 3-13.

Goode, E. (1981). Comments on the homosexual role. *Journal of Sex Research, 17,* 54-65.

Hart, J., & Richardson, D. (1981). *The theory and practice of homosexuality.* London: Routledge & Kegan Paul.

Hencken, J.D., & O'Dowd, W.T. (1977). Coming out as an aspect of identity formation. *Gay Academic Union Journal: Gai Saber, 1*(1), 18-26.

Humphreys, L., & Miller, B. (1980). Identities in the emerging gay culture. In J. Mormon (Ed.), *Homosexual behavior.* New York: Basic Books.

Jay, K., & Young, A.(1979). *The gay report: Lesbians and gay men speak out about sexual experiences & lifestyles.* New York: Summit Books.

Kantrowitz, A. (1977). *Under the rainbow: Growing up gay.* New York: Morrow.

Kimmel, D.C. (1978). Adult development and aging: A gay perspective.*Journal of Social Isues, 34*(3), 113-130.

Klein, F., & Wolf, T.J. (Eds.). (1985). *Bisexualities: Theory and research.* New York: Haworth Press. (Also published as *Journal of Homosexuality, 11*[1/2]).

Kooden, H.D., Morin, S.F., Riddle, D.I., Rogers, M., Sang, B.E., & Strassburger, F. (1979). *Removing the stigma: Final report of the Board of Social and Ethical Responsibility for Psychology's Task Force on the Status of Lesbian and Gay Male Psychologists.* Washington, DC: American Psychological Association.

Kopay, D., & Young, P.D. (1977). *The David Kopay story.* New York: Arbor House.

Larson, P.C. (1981). Sexual identity and self-concept. *Journal of Homosexuality, 7*(1), 15-32.

Lee, J.A. (1977). Going public: A study in the sociology of homosexual liberation. *Journal of Homosexuality, 3*(1), 49- 78.

Lehne, G.K. (1976). Homophobia among men. In D. David & R. Brannon (Eds.), *The forty-nine percent majority: The male sex role.* Reading, MA: Addison-Wesley.

Lehne, G.K. (1978). Gay male fantasies and realities. *Journal of Social Issues, 34*(3), 28-37.

MacDonald, A.P., Jr. (1981). Bisexuality: Some comments on research and theory. *Journal of Homosexuality,6*(3), 21-35.

MacDonald, A.P., Jr. (1983). A little bit of lavender goes a long way: A critique of research on sexual orientation. *Journal of Sex Research, 19*(1), 94-100.

McDonald, G.J. (1982). Individual differences in the coming out process for gay men: Implications for theoretical models. *Journal of Homosexuality, 8*(1), 47-60.

McWhirter, D., & Mattison, A. (1984). *The male couple: How relationships develop.* Englewood Cliffs, NJ: Prentice-Hall.

Minton, H.L., & McDonald, G.J. (1984). Homosexual identity formation as a developmental process. *Journal of Homosexuality, 9*(2/3), 91-104.

Money, J. (1980). *Love & lovesickness: The science of sex, gender difference, and pair-bonding.* Baltimore: Johns Hopkins University Press.

Money, J. (1981a). The development of sexuality and eroticism in humankind. *Quarterly Review of Biology, 56*(4), 379-404.

Money, J. (1981b). Paraphilias: Phyletic origins of erotosexual dysfunction. *International Journal of Mental Health, 10*(2/3), 75-109.

Money, J. (1982). Lesbian lizards. *Psychoneuroendocrinology, 7*(4), 257-258.

Money, J. (1986). *Lovemaps.* New York: Irvington.

Money, J., & Daléry, J. (1976). Iatrogenic homosexuality: Gender identity in seven 46, XX chromosomal females with hyperadrenocortical hermaphroditism born with a penis, three reared as boys, four reared as girls. *Journal of Homosexuality, 1*(4), 357-371.

Money, J., & Ehrhardt, A.A. (1972). *Man and woman, boy and girl: The differentiation and dimorphism of gender identity from conception to maturity.* Baltimore: Johns Hopkins University Press.

Money, J., & Russo, A. (1979). Homosexual outcome of discordant gender-identity/role in childhood: Longitudinal follow-up. *Journal of Pediatric Psychology,4*(1), 29-41.

Money, J., & Russo, A. (1981). Homosexual vs. transvestite or transsexual gender-identity/role: Outcome study in boys. *International Journal of Psychiatry, 2,* 139-145.

Money, J., & Wiedeking, C. (1980). Gender identity role: Normal differentiation and its transpositions. In B.B. Wolman & J. Money (Eds.), *Handbook of Human Sexuality.* Englewood Cliffs, NJ: Prentice-Hall.

Morin, S., & Garfinkle, E. (1978). Male homophobia. *Journal of Social Issues, 34,* 29-47.

Moses, A.E., & Hawkins, R.O., Jr. (1982).*Counseling lesbian women and gay men: A life-issues approach.* St. Louis, MO: Mosby.

Nungesser, L.G. (1983). *Homosexual acts, actors, and identities.* New York: Praeger.

Paul, W., & Weinreich, J.D. (1982). Whom and what we study: Definition and scope of sexual orientation. In W. Paul, J.D. Weinreich, J.D.. Gonsiorek, & M.E. Hotvedt, *Homosexuality: Social, psychological, and biological issues.* Beverly Hills: Sage.

Paul, W., Weinreich, J.D., Gonsiorek, J.D., & Hotvedt, M.E. (1982). *Homosexuality: Social, psychological, and biological issues. Beverly Hills: Sage.*

Plummer, K. (1975). *Sexual stigma: An interactionist account.* London: Routledge & Kegan Paul.

Ponse, B. (1980). Lesbians and their worlds. In J. Marmor (Ed.), *Homosexual behavior.* New York: Basic Books.

Reid, J. (1973). *The best little boy in the world.* New York: Putnam.

Ross, M.W. (1983). *The married homosexual man.* London: Routledge & Kegan Paul.

Seabrook, J. (1976). *A lasting relationship: Homosexuals and society.* London: Allen Lane.

Shively, M., & DeCecco, J.P. (1977). Components of sexual identity. *Journal of Homosexuality, 3*(1),41-48.

Silverstein, C. (1977). *A family matter: A parents' guide to homosexuality.* New York: McGraw-Hall.

Silverstein, C. (1981). *Man to man: Gay couples in America.* New York: Morrow.

Sprague, G.A. (1984). Male homosexuality in Western culture: The dilemma of identity and subculture in historical research. *Journal of Homosexuality, 10*(3/4), 29-43.

Suppe, F. (1984). Classifying sexual disorders: *The diagnostic and statistical manual* of the American Psychiatric Association. *Journal of Homosexuality, 9*(4), 9-28.

Tennov, D. (1979). *Love and limerence: The experience of being in love.* New York: Stein & Day.

Troiden, R.R. (1979). Becoming homosexual: A model of gay identity acquisition. *Psychiatry, 42,* 362-373.

Troiden, R.R., & Goode, E. (1980). Variables related to the acquisition of a gay identity. *Journal of Homosexuality, 5*(4), 383-392.

Warren, C. (1974). *Identity and community in the gay world.* New York: Wiley.

Warren, C. (1980). Homosexuality and stigma. In J. Marmor (Ed.), *Homosexual behavior: A modern reappraisal.* New York: Basic Books.

Weeks, J. (1977). *Coming out: Homosexual politics in Britain from the nineteenth century to the present.* London: Quartet Books.

Weinberg, M.S., & Williams, C.J. (1974). *Male homosexuals: Their problems and adaptations.* New York: Harper & Row.

Weinberg, T.S. (1983). *Gay men, gay selves: The social construction of homosexual identities.* New York: Irvington.

Weinberg, T.S. (1978). On "doing" and "being" gay: Sexual behavior and homosexual male self-identity. *Journal of Homosexuality, 4*(2), 143-156.

Chapter 15

Ethical and Professional Issues in Sex Therapy

Robert A. Brown and Robert Sollod

The field of sex therapy is so new and its practitioners so diverse that professional and ethical standards for sex therapy have not been clearly elaborated (Gorovitz, 1980). Many organizations have formulated guidelines for practice (American Association for Marriage and Family Therapy (AAMFT), 1985; American Association of Sex Educators, Counselors, and Therapists (AASECT), 1980; Society for the Scientific Study of Sex (SSSS), 1985), but no single organization has captured the field to the point of turning its guidelines into mandatory rules. Although the field has avoided the disadvantages of premature codification, it is clearly of great importance to review ethical issues and practices and to note those principles around which a consensus exists or is beginning to emerge. In this chapter, a variety of those ethical and practice issues that challenge sex therapists will be presented. General areas of agreement and of controversy will be indicated. In addition, wherever possible, implications for clinical practice will be explored.

There are a variety of explanations for the observation that every society prescribes rules for "right" professional conduct. Some see rules and standards as growing out of the public's lack of knowledge about which procedures are useful and which are common practice. Clients may not be able to discern professional impropriety (AASECT, 1980). Without guidelines, anything goes, and consumers are not protected from financial or even sexual exploitation (Lief, 1982). Another view is that ethical rules may grow out of the homeostatic needs of a society to maintain the status quo (Marmor, 1980). They may even represent a power move by individuals or organizations to capture a field (Pomeroy, cited in Lief, 1982). Mudd (1977) suggests that ethical standards protect both the public and the profession. If there were no standards, professional practice could deteriorate to the point at which clients would suffer, and the profession would be discredited.

Whatever the source, many writers agree on the advantages and disadvantages of ethical guidelines and standards (e.g., Lief, 1982; Masters, Johnson, & Kolodny, 1977; Masters, Johnson, Kolodny, & Weems, 1980). Clear rules and principles are helpful in guarding privacy and rights to informed consent to treatment, in ensuring access to a competent professional, and generally in protecting the public from harm and exploitation. On the negative side, even if care is taken to protect the legitimate interests of clients, ethical rules may suppress questioning and stifle innovation. Guidelines, which in the short run appear to protect the public, may in the long run perpetuate ignorance and incompetence.

Many ethical or professional problems that arise in sex therapy also occur in any form of psychotherapy, such as the necessity to ensure confidentiality and informed consent. Some of these issues may be even more important in sex therapy. For example, others' simply knowing that a person is in sex therapy may be humiliating to some clients. Other problems may be peculiar to sex therapy, for example, the use of sexual surrogates or the possible observation of sexual activity by the therapist. Here, the focus will be on those issues that appear to be more important in, or specific to, sex therapy. More general psychotherapy questions will only be included through discussion of specific implications for sex therapy. The chapter will begin with a general discussion of values in sex therapy and will then explore a number of areas where guidelines for conduct are useful. The list of areas, partially taken from Stoltz and Associates (1978), includes setting goals, identifying the client, defining the problem, selecting and implementing an intervention, evaluating the quality of the intervenor and of the intervention, as well as insuring informed consent, confidentiality and the client's right to terminate treatment.

VALUES IN SEX THERAPY

A number of writers have suggested values that specifically impact on sexual therapy (e.g., Margolin, 1982; Redlich, 1977). These values include beliefs about the importance of sexual pleasure in relationships, sex as a natural function, sex roles, homosexuality, extramarital relationships, masturbation, orgasm, sexual fantasy, fantasy of other-than-the-partner during intercourse, oral-genital contact, vibrators, and the role of nudity or touching in treatment. There is a general consensus by sex therapists in some areas. LoPiccolo (1978), for example, notes that sex therapists share many values and beliefs. Many therapists suggest that individuals or couples are mutually responsible for maintenance and change of sexual dysfunction. They further agree on the importance of information and education as a necessary but not sufficient condition of therapy and on the importance of changing client attitudes toward sex roles, the double standard, or the acceptability of sexual activity. Most sex therapists also share values about the importance of reducing demands for superior sexual performance by focusing on pleasure and not outcome, open and direct communication, egalitarian sex roles, and directed, structured treatment. It is probably safe to add to this list that most therapists also agree on the importance of confidentiality and on the avoidance of sexual activity with clients. In spite of this general consensus, there are some conflicting views on each of these items. Moreover, there may be passionate controversy over specific issues pertaining to sexual pathology or treatment procedures, such as the use of masturbation as a treatment technique (Bailey, 1978). Also, it is important to recognize that the general consensus portrayed above is one of professional beliefs that are informed more by social values and practical experience than by empirical research.

There no longer seems to be much controversy over whether therapists' personal and professional values influence the course of psychotherapy. Most therapists now agree that those aspects of themselves or of the world that they find desirable (e.g., independence, freedom) or obligatory (e.g., individual responsibility) are at least partially involved in the selection of therapeutic goals and do influence therapist behaviors. For example, if one assumes, following Masters and Johnson (Redlich, 1977), that sex is a natural function and that sex therapy should consist of removing learned obstacles to sexual pleasure, then one has clearly adopted a value stance only partly based on factual knowledge. Additional value implications of this stance include views that sexual pleasure is a desirable property of human functioning and that obstacles to pleasure should be removed. Sex therapists may then further "medicalize" that moral judgment by defining a lack of sexual pleasure as pathological, and then develop typologies of sexual dysfunction. Then, given a diagnosis of pathology, the helping professional is obligated to "treat" or "cure" it (Englehardt, 1980, Szasz, 1980). Even the diagnosis of sexual dysfunction, which appears at first to be objective and factual, is based in part on a complex chain of values and beliefs.

One danger of this rather paternalistic view of sexual problems is that professionals may adhere to their beliefs about what constitutes pathology even though the definition of sexual normality and psychopathology may change from culture to culture or from time to time (Money, 1977). Szasz (1980, p. xiv) notes that at one time in history our belief was that women should have as many children and as few orgasms as possible, while many people currently hold the opposite view! Moreover, our society has shifted in a few decades from believing that masturbation causes insanity to many viewing it as natural and even necessary to healthy sexual development. In fact, the development of the practice of sex therapy over the past 20 years is probably due as much to change in societal values regarding sexuality as to an increase in information. Even social changes over brief periods of time may affect professional beliefs and practices. The 60s and 70s represented a period of rebellion against social and sexual restrictiveness, and sexual therapy offered one of many routes to individual freedom and self-expression. There was little emphasis within the field on the importance of the values that were being challenged—such as marital fidelity, the importance of sexual activity occurring within a committed and caring relationship, or the possibility of celibacy as a healthy life-style. However, a number of writers referenced in this chapter have attempted, in the last ten years, to integrate treatment of sexual difficulties with traditional values concerning individual responsibility and freedom and relationships. A historical and cross-cultural perspective thus suggests that it would be naive to assume that society's and the various helping professions' current beliefs about ideal sexual functioning and sexual pathology represent the final truth.

A number of writers (e.g., Hiltner, 1977) have discussed the relationship between religious beliefs and the diagnosis and treatment of sexual problems. Sex therapists' or clients' views of the relationship between sexual problems and moral/religious beliefs will impact heavily on the therapy process. For some, moral and religious beliefs about sexuality are seen as based on natural law of right and wrong. For clients or therapists with such convictions, no amount of change in social attitudes or advances in knowledge about human sexuality would significantly change their beliefs about sexual behavior. Many mental health professionals believe that such inflexibility is associated with archaic and even destructive views (e.g., the Vatican stand that masturbation is a seriously disordered act). Some professionals even believe that moral and religious values are not basic givens but represent psychopathology or serve a defensive function. Strong values or moral objections may ward off decompensation for some people. In this view, religious and other values are viewed as learned and may be dealt with as any other kind of psychopathology. The danger here is that if one does not agree with a belief, it may be labeled as pathological even though there is no empirical data to indicate that one belief is inherently any more "true" or healthy than another. More moderate theologians and mental health professionals attempt to resolve differences without devaluing each others' views. But each sex therapist must decide, in any particular case, the degree to which a contradiction between sexuality and religious beliefs should be either sidestepped or resolved in favor of one or the other.

Perhaps the major lesson to be learned from a careful examination of the literature on religion, values, and sex therapy is to be humble. In a pluralistic society such as ours, at one point in time, one cannot count on cornering the market on ultimate truth. A number of writers have given similar cautions. The SSSS (1985) statement warns therapists to respect the right of the client to hold different values, and Jonsen (1980) has suggested further that sex therapists need to understand the client's values and work within them. Jonsen and the AASECT code (1980) both suggest that professionals request a change in values from their clients only where it is necessary to eliminate the dysfunction, while Lief (1982) notes that we should not recommend such practices as masturbation or oral-genital contact without first finding out the client's views. The AASECT code (1980) goes so far as to admonish sex therapists to disapprove only those sex acts that are coercive or involve deceit. Indeed, for many individuals, holding to their religious or other moral values about divorce or sexual activity may be far more important to them than sexual performance or pleasure.

Humility and caution concerning the imposition of sexual values also seems well advised on other grounds. There appears to be a general movement in the mental health professions away from a paternalistic view of the practitioner as the absolute authority (Wasserstrom, 1980) toward a view that portrays the client as an autonomous entity encouraged to enter into a collaborative relationship with a knowledgeable professional. Responsibility for change is shared. The advantages of this stance include enhancement of the client's autonomy and sense of competence, reducing defensiveness by not demanding that the client relinquish control, and joint responsibility for failure (a not inconsiderable advantage in this litigious society). Actually, even such a collaborative stance still puts therapists in a position of power by virtue of their professional position. Any therapist statement or request may be seen as containing an element of coercion due to the socially sanctioned role of expert, even if neither the client nor the therapist is aware of it (Lief, Sarrel, & Sarrel, 1980).

There do not seem to be data on deterioration effects in sexual therapy, but findings from other treatment modalities would also seem to favor a collaborative approach. For example, Lieberman, Yalom, and Miles (1973), studying deterioration effects in encounter groups, found that the groups most likely to produce casualties were those led by strong, charismatic leaders. Whether the same finding would hold for sex therapy is an empirical question, as yet unanswered. But there may be considerable potential harm in a highly authoritarian therapist who challenges a client's long-held beliefs and values in the complex and sensitive area of sexuality, even though such confrontation could sometimes be helpful.

One markedly value-laden area of intervention involves sex roles. Sex therapists generally take a stance of sexual egalitarianism (Lassen, 1976, LoPiccolo, 1978). LoPiccolo suggests that such a position is a necessary aspect of all sex therapy, and Margolin (1982) states expicitly that marital therapists should attempt to change destructive sex-role behaviors. In general, it would appear advisable for therapists to be sensitive to and deal with those sex-role issues that interfere with sexual functioning, while at the same time to be careful in addressing those issues they personally believe to be destructive but which do not necessarily affect the sexual dysfunction. In addressing the latter issues, it could be useful to state the therapist's belief that these issues are important but maybe not crucial for the sexual relationship, and allow the couple the option of pursuing them or not. Edelwich and Brodsky (1982) have a useful discussion of this point.

One important feminist concern, particularly directed toward systems theory, is that an extreme egalitarian view may dismiss the concept of "responsibility" or "victim" altogether (Taggert, 1985). At the extreme, for example, a woman married to a man who has a history of psychogenic impotence with a variety of partners could be seen both as contributing equally to the etiology and maintenance of his problem and as sharing the responsiblity of improvement. Practically, many sex therapists deal with this by avoiding the concepts of responsibility and blame for problem development, and by recognizing that one partner may be more vulnerable to sexual dysfunction than the other. But even if the sexual dysfunction is not due *to* the relationship, it is likely to be a problem *for* the relationship. Indeed, current literature suggests that the involvement of both parties in *treatment* is the most efficient approach to remediation and the one that has the most likely long-term benefit to the couple's sexual satisfaction.

Finally, even though there seems to be agreement on the importance of the therapist's values, there has been little discussion on how much and in what manner to reveal one's values to the client. No one, apparently, suggests that therapists should reveal values unrelated to the current problem and its treatment. But what about the case where the therapist's beliefs may clash with those of the client? For example, a client may feel that masturbation is wrong and should not be a part of any sexual treatment plan. It may not be helpful for the therapist to state that masturbation is a natural phenomenon and is often useful in overcoming sexual dysfunctions. Such a statement simply pits the client's moral value system against the values and sanctioned expertise of the therapist. It would probably be more helpful to the client if therapists revealed the *source* of their views. For example, some views are based on empirical data, others on a general consensus of professionals, others on general societal norms, and still others on personal experience. It would be of great value to clients and would probably enhance therapists' creditability and authoritativeness if they could say, for example, "There are experiments to support the effectiveness of two different approaches to rapid ejaculation; in my experience the stop/start technique is easier and more acceptable to my clients." Or in the situation portrayed above, the therapist may say, "We have considerable evidence that masturbation is helpful in learning to reach orgasm. However, in cases such as yours, where you have a strong moral objection to it, we don't have good evidence on whether it is helpful or not. I personally believe, however..." The therapist could go on to express the opinion that masturbation either would not be necessary or that it would be helpful. However, with the admonitions of the experienced therapists above to respect the client's values, it is useful to ask whether any specific intervention is so critical that it cannot be by-passed. The answer to that probably lies as much in the therapist's ingenuity as in the available treatment literature.

ISSUES RELATING TO THERAPEUTIC GOALS

The very process of formulating the goals of psychosexual therapy involves a variety of ethical and professional judgments. Stoltz & Associates (1978) has indicated that therapeutic goals should be realistic, explicitly presented and serve the best interests of the client. These admirable intentions are not always readily achieved within the context of psychosexual therapy.

Currently, many clients seeking sex therapy present with major individual psychopathology or with marital problems such as lack of trust or commitment, so success rates will probably not be as high or as predictable as in the original work of Masters and Johnson (Kaplan, 1977; Masters & Johnson, 1970; Sollod & Kaplan, 1976). At times, problems interfering with reaching seemingly realistic goals may not emerge until well into the course of therapy. For example, it may take considerable time for some clients to admit to an ongoing affair, to reveal the presence of a longstanding paraphilia, or to remember an early sexual trauma. In other cases, the presence of individual or dyadic pathology may be apparent, but it may not be possible to predict the extent to which such problems will impede progress in sexual functioning. Probably all therapists have had experiences in which couples with seemingly serious psychopathology profited quickly from treatment, while other couples, not as obviously disturbed, were highly resistant to change.

It is not always clear what goal/s would be in the best interests and would increase the overall happiness and well-being of a particular client. For example, many couples present sexual dysfunction/s as well as significant marital distress. The therapist could indicate that, for the majority of couples, a fulfilling long-term sexual relationship is usually possible only within a satisfactory interpersonal context. The therapist could add that sometimes, but not always, remediation of a dysfunction may greatly improve the relationship. As a result of ensuing discussions, a couple may decide either to focus on marital goals prior to continuing with sex therapy, to continue with sex therapy and then to focus on relational issues, or to continue with either sex therapy or marital therapy alone.

Another issue in regard to goal setting is that the clients' stated goals may mask a hidden agenda. In a treatment program structured to provide progressive emotional and physical intimacy, such a hidden agenda may come to the fore in the form of resistance. The therapist may, as a result, find the original goals to be based on invalid premises and therefore not realistic. For example, a male in his late 20s sought treatment for premature ejaculation. His wife was openly supportive of the treatment goal of ejaculatory control. As therapy progressed, however, she participated with increasing reluctance and often sabotaged the stop/start exercise. She stated that she felt isolated, unsatisfied and exploited during these encounters. Attempts to restructure the exercise by having the male pleasure her to orgasm afterward were not successful. Exploration of the relationship indicated that the husband was unsatisfied in the relationship. However, as a result of his history of premature ejaculation, he felt that he could not cope adequately with the singles scene. His hidden agenda was to attain ejaculatory control, separate from his wife, and have new sexual partners. Her difficulty in cooperating with the treatment process was apparently because at a prereflective level, she was aware that her effective assistance in the stop/start exercises would have facilitated her own abandonment.

Another therapist dilemma with respect to goal setting relates to discussing goals with the client. On one hand, therapists want to be as honest as possible in evaluating and presenting the feasibility of goals. On the other hand, they should be sufficiently optimistic so as not to discourage clients who could be helped potentially. One way of dealing with the dilemma is to present in a general way those intrapsychic or other issues that may impede progress toward the specified goal. These factors may then need to be addressed only if therapy does not progress satisfactorily.

IDENTIFICATION OF THE CLIENT

There is debate in the marital and sexual therapy literature as to whether the client is the individual or the couple (Katz, 1977, Margolin, 1982). Katz cites the medical dictum, *primum non nocere:* first (do) no harm. But who does one avoid harming? An individual? A couple? Society? All of these parties may have different goals and vested interests, so a helpful change in one may not always be in the best interests of another (cf. Strupp & Hadley, 1977). Without a clear identification of the client, it is difficult to specify goals.

A case example may help clarify this dilemma. An unmarried cohabiting college couple presented with his complaint about the frequency (nonexistent) of intercourse. He had insisted they come for treatment, and she had reluctantly agreed. When asked about her satisfaction with the sexual relationship, she said that she also desired more frequent intercourse but somehow "we never get around to it." After several sessions, it seemed clear that she was neither comfortable with sexual relations nor able to speak directly of her discomfort. She "gave ground" in their sexual bargaining to the point of having intercourse once or twice. Even though this frequency of intercourse was nowhere near what he wanted, it did reduce his anger to a point at which he felt unjustified and guilty for complaining. Her agenda was to avoid intercourse as well as therapy, his was to have both, and the couple's agenda seemed to be to maintain the relationship at any cost. Was it ethical to urge the continuation of therapy when she indicated indirectly that she was there against her will (e.g., she often suggested they could work this out on their own)? Should one assume that the couple should terminate at the point where the relationship was stabilized by their negotiations around balancing sex, anger, guilt, and anxiety? In supervision, the therapists were urged to continue to attempt to clarify and understand the basis for her hidden agenda and to encourage the open expression of his continued frustration. This strategy eventually had the effect of helping her begin to deal with her sexual anxieties. She also began to confront him with her concerns about his sexual technique. However, the fact remains that the early stages of treatment involved subtle coercion on the part of the therapists in the service of what *they* judged to be the best long-term interests of the couple. And it is clear that each constituent (the individuals and the couple) had conflicting goals.

DEFINITION OF THE PROBLEM

John Money (1977) says that there are no exhibitionists in a nudist colony. In other words, defining a sexual behavior as pathological or problematic reflects cultural, professional, and personal values. Because most therapists hold definite views about sexuality, it is important to follow professional consensus in diagnosing problems rather than relying on one's idiosyncratic beliefs. Using consensual definitions, as reflected in standard nomenclature and the sex therapy literature, reduces the possibility that therapists will influence clients to adopt values or patterns of behavior that could bring them into conflict with society's, their partner's, or their own values. For example, many people find oral and anal sex enjoyable. Regardless of the therapist's personal preferences, the literature does not suggest that dislike of these practices necessarily represents pathological inhibition. A therapist who diagnoses dislike of such practices as necessarily pathological and encourages clients to engage in them could generate more problems than solutions.

Some therapists may think that holding to a professional party line could stifle their originality and creativity. This conflicts with a principle of professional autonomy and the responsibility to challenge the profession and society when they may be wrong. It is better, however, to issue such challenges in the literature and at professional meetings rather than through clinical practice.

Probably the best problem definition — the one that would best address the concerns indicated above — would be based on agreement by all involved parties, that is, the couple, therapist, profession, and society. For example, one would seem to be on safe ground when dealing with a joint complaint of anorgasmia by a husband and wife. This process of problem definition becomes more difficult, however, when there is disagreement between the clients. For example, two lovers may express divergent preferences regarding frequency, with one wanting intercourse four times weekly and the other being content with once a week. Or a wife may be concerned that her husband seems not to enjoy sexual relations, but he is not particularly concerned about it. One reasonable approach in such cases is to discuss the spouses' differing views of the problem, to inform them about the usual range of sexual preferences, and then to negotiate a problem definition with them.

Another area to consider in the assessment of a sexual disorder is the advisability of routine and automatic referrals for physical examinations. Determining whether the sexual difficulty has a biogenic origin or component has critical implications for treatment. Because the therapist has an ethical responsibility to provide appropriate treatment, taking necessary steps to ensure an accurate diagnosis is mandatory. Many sex therapists strongly advise automatic referral for a physical examination for all clients.

Practically, however, the nature of the problem dictates the relative urgency of the need for immediate referral for physical examination. For example, secondary impotence in a married man without apparent marital distress should be referred immediately—even in the face of occasionally adequate erections. The same would hold true for any case of dyspareunia. However, automatic referral does not appear indicated for a man with premature ejaculation who can maintain his erection for long periods of time during masturbation. Nor would it likely be helpful for the insecure man who regularly masturbates to orgasm with full erections but who has had several erectile failures with new partners. In such cases it would seem reasonable at least to begin treatment without an immediate physician referral. However, if the problem does not begin to yield to treatment, a referral may well be in order.

One important guideline that has been inadequately emphasized is that the therapist has the responsibility to make the best possible referral; it is not sufficient simply to refer for a physical examination. It is strongly recommended that therapists dealing with sexual dysfunctions establish a working consultative relationship with at least three sensitive, reliable physicians—a gynecologist, a urologist and an internist with expertise in endocrinology. These specialists should be comfortable and knowledgeable in dealing with clients with sexual dysfunctions. In this way, the therapist can be more certain that the client will receive an adequate physical examination, a medical diagnosis in line with current knowledge, and an interview that will facilitate the therapy.

PROFESSIONAL AND ETHICAL ISSUES INVOLVED IN PSYCHOSEXUAL INTERVENTIONS

All major codes of ethics say that psychotherapists should stay within their area of competence in diagnostic and treatment activities (e.g., American Association for Marriage and Family Therapy, 1985; American Psychological Association, 1981). This guideline relates partially to formal training standards (to be discussed subsequently), but it relates as well to the therapist's judgment as to the appropriateness of usual treatment methods. If the therapist is trying a new approach or is significantly modifying familiar procedures, it is often advisable to discuss the case or receive supervision from someone with additional expertise.

Stoltz & Associates (1978) suggests that the therapist should choose the least intrusive, coercive and restrictive treatment available. Annon's (1977) PLISSIT model, discussed by Sprei and Courtois (Chapter 12 in this volume), provides one useful way of thinking about this guideline in psychosexual therapy. If a client has a specific sexual complaint and limited information is sufficient for the problem to be resolved to the client's satisfaction, this model suggests that it would be unjustified for the therapist to impose a more intensive or extensive course of therapy. If the therapist believes that there are additional intrapsychic or interpersonal problems that might be useful to address, however, the most responsible approach would be to discuss this with the client in a manner that would leave to the client the choice of proceeding or not.

The ethical codes of all the organizations surveyed for this chapter state that sexual activities or intimacies with clients are unethical. These statements were usually added to the codes in the last decade, probably as a result of growing appreciation of feminist concerns as well as empirical evidence of substantial numbers of psychotherapists and other professionals having had sexual relations with clients. Even after the establishment of these guidelines, a large number of malpractice claims continue to allege sexual activities between psychotherapists and their clients. No sound survey results are currently available to indicate whether sexual therapists are more or less likely to be sexually involved with their clients than other therapists.

In recent years, few writers have attempted to justify therapist-client sexual relations. Those who have addressed the issue have reasoned that the therapist holds a highly influential position of trust and parent-like authority with clients. Overt sexual activity with the client violates this trust and misuses the authority. Lief (1982) has stated that clients are in a helpless and vulnerable position and are often seeking love and attempting to avoid loneliness. Sexual seduction by a therapist exploits the client's vulnerability. Lowry and Lowry (1975) suggest that therapist-client sexual intimacies violate incest taboos and that the loss of the therapist as a caretaker is "serious, since good lovers are easier to find than good caretakers" (p. 233).

Both Lief and Lowry and Lowry also question therapists' ability to understand their own motivations for sexual activity with clients. Therapists' needs for power, control, self-esteem, love, avoidance of loneliness, and reassurance as to their own attractiveness and sexual prowess can motivate the sexual behaviors, which the therapist justifies as therapeutic. Lowry and Lowry say that one way for therapists to be sure of their own motives for sexual contact with clients is to "make sure he provides such services to the elderly, ugly, to the crippled, to the incontinent, to the same sex, and to all races, creeds and religions" (p.233). In addition, the American Psychological Association (1981), whose code of ethics specifically prohibits therapist-client sexual relations, also demands that psychologists abstain from "dual relationships," such as treating relatives or involving themselves in business dealings with clients. Sexual relations with clients clearly falls under this prohibition.

For most writers, the injunction against sexual activities between therapists and clients extends to a prohibition against observing a client's sexual activity alone or with a partner (Lief, 1982). As in the case of direct sexual involvement, it would be difficult for therapists to be fully aware of their motives. The opportunities for exploitation are quite evident. None of the leading researchers or sex therapists seem to use direct observation of sexual behavior as an assessment or therapeutic technique. They appear to stay within the guideline that one should be only as intrusive as is absolutely necessary to accomplish therapeutic goals. There is no empirical evidence that the degree of intrusiveness involved in direct observation of sexual behavior is necessary or helpful. However, the AASECT Code (1980) is tolerant regarding the advisability of this practice. The code notes that direct observation of client's sexual activity goes beyond the boundaries of established practice. It further indicates, however, that it "may be used...when there is good evidence that it is in the best interests of the client" (p. 7). The code does not define what would constitute "good evidence" or "best interests."

There are no clear guidelines for professionals concerning participation in, or touching sexual organs during, physical and sexual examinations. The literature portrays a variety of levels of physical exposure and involvement — from a standard pelvic examination, to examination of the sexual organs with the spouse present, through sexual self-stimulation or masturbation within the context of a physical examination. To the extent that physicians go beyond the traditional examination, with the spouse present or not, they would appear to be treading on somewhat shaky ethical and possibly legal ground. For example, in the case of a therapist's observing masturbatory behavior, there could be considerable difficulty in separating power and voyeuristic motives from professional concerns. Moreover, only physicians are sanctioned by society to conduct physical examinations of sexual organs. At most, nonphysicians could possibly have a place in the examining room as an adjunct to the physician. But even such a role appears unwarranted. The nonphysician simply is best advised to avoid physical examination of genitalia.

Most psychosexual therapists prefer to involve a cooperative spouse or partner in the treatment program. For example, it is extremely difficult if not impossible to work successfully with clients who evidence premature ejaculation, erectile dysfunction, or vaginismus if there is no regular sexual partner with whom they might develop improved patterns of sexual behavior.

In cases in which the client has no regular sexual partner, many therapists have concluded that the simplest and best solution is to urge the individual to find a cooperative partner. There are real dangers, however, that in doing so the client's moral standards regarding premarital, extramarital or casual sexual relations may be violated. Many therapists would be wary of separating sexual behavior from genuine intimacy or commitment. Furthermore, there is the potential danger that clients might select partners who are not as caring, accepting or helpful as they may initially appear. Moreover, if, at the therapist's urging, the client selects a partner who transmits herpes or AIDS, the therapist could be in a very vulnerable legal position. Probably the most ethical and professional course of action would be to explain the advantages and drawbacks of this course of action. If individual clients choose not to involve themselves with a partner for the sake of psychosexual therapy, they can return for treatment at some point in the future when a relationship does develop. Or, if indicated, the therapist may help the client develop the interpersonal and social skills necessary to develop such an intimate relationship.

Some clients present a Catch-22 situation where they feel unable to enter into any relationship unless they believe they can engage adequately in sexual intimacy. One helpful course of action is to work with such clients to develop more self-esteem and openness, as well as to initiate dating patterns that do not involve attempting heroic sexual performances at the onset.

An additional option considered by some psychosexual therapists for a client without a cooperative partner is to use a sexual *surrogate,* a hired stand-in, for a partner. Masters and Johnson developed a program involving surrogates, even though they later terminated it, and there is currently an international association for surrogates. Most professional organizations have not taken a strong, well-articulated stand on the use of surrogates, though the AASECT (1980) indicates that the practice is controversial but ethically permissible. The AASECT also provides guidelines for using surrogates. However, Bersoff (1982), in an opinion to the American Psychological Association, noted that the use of surrogates would be illegal in most jurisdictions. It would violate one or more statutes pertaining to prostitution, adultery, or deviate sex practices. Leroy (1972) further cautions that involvement of surrogates could violate the Mann Act if either party crossed state lines. Hall and Hare-Mustin (1983) note that a spouse could file an ethics complaint against the therapist on the basis of the surrogate's infringing upon the spouse's civil or legal rights. On the other hand, Leroy (1972) argues that it could be seen as discrimination for the therapist not to treat single clients without partners, and that it is probably unlikely that a sex therapist or clinician would be found guilty of violating the above statutes due to the therapist's goal of rehabilitation and treatment.

The legal issues in this area are murky and untested, and the associated practical issues also do not give rise to comfort in employing surrogates. Leroy felt, for example, that practical difficulties were severe even in a clinic in a large medical school with a training program for surrogates. Referring to the Masters and Johnson program, he said that there were breaches of confidentiality and that some surrogates became overly emotionally involved with their clients. Masters, Johnson, and Kolodny (1977) indicated that the surrogates began considering themselves to be therapists. The implication seemed to be that they began to operate somewhat independently of the therapy team, even though they were not trained as counselors. Lief (1982) raises the additional practical question of whether the client can transfer skills from the surrogate to other partners. And, as noted above, some therapists may be reluctant to encourage sexual relations in nonintimate, uncommitted relationships.

Perhaps in the future, the use of surrogates, as trained teachers of sexual skills, will be commonplace and acceptable. At the present time, however, due to legal and ethical considerations as well as practical problems, the use of surrogates cannot be recommended. Such a practice is particularly inadvisable for therapists in individual or small group practices.

ASSURING THE QUALITY OF THE INTERVENTION

Ideally, specific standards for psychosexual therapy could be established such that the therapist's major ethical responsibility would be to learn the procedures and how to apply them. As Gorovitz (1980) has noted, however, the standards for sex therapy are simply not clear; sexual complaints are dealt with by diverse professionals in a wide variety of ways.

This section will be brief, because many of the preceding and following sections address issues relating to the quality of the intervention, such as setting realistic and well-articulated goals, ensuring informed consent, or making appropriate referrals for physical examinations. And the next section is addressed to the issue of assuring the quality of the *intervenor;* even if the precise treatment of choice cannot be specified, the extent to which the therapist has the breadth and depth of training, knowledge, and skill to deal with sexual problems can be evaluated.

One ethical paradox in treatment will be useful to address. It has long been known that one source of ineffective pharmacologic therapy is the tendency to give doses too low to be useful. McCarthy, in Chapter 10 of this volume, points out the analogous situation in psychosexual therapy. Therapists may be sidetracked by the temporary failure of an exercise and may not be sufficiently persistent for the behavioral prescriptions to be effective. On the other hand, various codes of ethics (e.g., American Psychological Association, 1981) state that it is the ethical responsibility of the therapist to terminate a client if treatment is not helping. How much is not enough and how much is too much? Probably the best aids to clinical judgment here are the therapist's experience and willingness to seek consultation. Even if therapists cannot say exactly how long a treatment will take, they should have a good idea of the client behaviors or other changes which would indicate at least micromovement toward accomplishing the goals. If these signs of change are not occurring, it behooves the therapist to seek a second opinion in the form of peer or other supervision. In Chapter 9 in this volume, Sollod discusses the advantages of an eclectic strategy to deal with therapeutic impasse.

The treatment format and nature of the professional setting affect the ability of therapists to evaluate the effectiveness of their interventions. Clinics and hospital settings often offer case conferences, interdisciplinary seminars, and consultation opportunities, which greatly facilitate evaluation. Cotherapy also opens up, to some extent, the private relationship between one therapist and the client/s. Individual practitioners ideally should work with other psychosexual therapists and training facilities to obtain necessary consultation, support and professional development resources. In an area as private as sexuality, where an individual's beliefs, values and feelings about sex and the therapy process can be highly idiosyncratic, the involvement of other professionals can offer important corrective feedback.

ASSURING THE QUALITY OF THE INTERVENORS

The AASECT guidelines (1980) address training of sex therapists in considerable detail. They indicate that the therapist should have basic understanding of sexual and reproductive anatomy and physiology, sexual development, interpersonal relationships, marital/family dynamics, sociocultural factors in sexual values and behavior, and ethical and medical issues affecting sexuality and sex therapy. In addition, therapists should have knowledge, clinical skills and supervised clinical training in the diagnosis of psychopathology and sexual disorders, and in the techniques of sex therapy and psychotherapy. These guidelines point out clearly that training in a mental health profession does not automatically assure adequate training in sex therapy.

Katz (1977) discusses the important issues of the degree to which the state and/or profession should take responsibility to assure the quality of the intervention and the competence of the intervenor. How much power should the profession and the state have in controlling the relationship between the client and therapist? Should the professions declare unethical any therapist who does not precisely meet training or experience guidelines? Should the state regulate (i.e., license or certify) sex therapists so that only certain professionals can legally attempt to remediate sexual dysfunctions? All of the questions concerning the justification for professional standards discussed in the introduction apply here also. Requiring a license or certification may be a move to protect the public, promote the status quo, capture the field for a certain "elite," allow the state to control a profession, or all of these. And although state regulation may indeed serve the public or the professional interest or both, in so doing it may stifle innovation and artificially limit professional practice. There is clearly no right or wrong here; one's value stance on the issue of state and professional regulation is probably complexly determined for each individual. As a practical matter, most states do not currently have legislation that controls the practice of sex therapy specifically, over and above regulations associated with other professional licenses. At present, professionals in these states must assess their own credentials in order to judge which services they are qualified by education and training to offer.

A final point here has to do with the personal qualities of the therapist. Again, a universal ethical principle (e.g., American Psychological Association, 1981) involves refusing to undertake an activity if personal problems may lead to the provision of inadequate services. In addition to the types of psychopathology that may interfere with any psychotherapy with culturally deviant (e.g., paraphilias) sexual practices or with sexual dysfunctions, therapists should be exceedingly cautious in offering sexual psychotherapy. It is certainly not impossible for someone with a sexual problem to aid others, but the possibilities of overinvolvement or underinvolvement with the client, or of destructive countertransference reactions, pose real dangers. Supervised experience and ongoing peer consultation should help clarify those dangers. Training programs are well advised to offer programs that enhance awareness of the would-be therapist's own sexual preferences and behaviors and how they may impact on professional effectiveness.

CLIENT RIGHTS

Informed Consent

A variety of laws and regulations demand that a client give informed consent to a proposed course of treatment. There are three conditions that must be met in order to ensure that the client has given truly informed consent (cf., Corey, Corey & Callahan, 1979). These are:

1. The consent must be voluntary.
2. The client must have sufficient knowledge to choose.
3. The client must be competent to understand and judge the information.

The essential element in voluntary consent is freedom from coercion. As discussed above, subtle coercion by a therapist or by one member of a couple is difficult to avoid. In the sexual arena, there are additional problems of coercion due to the social sensitivities, taboos and laws associated with sexual behavior. Can individuals with a paraphilia or who are homosexual voluntarily decide to change, or are they coerced by a social milieu that condemns their behavior (Lief, 1982)? Can individuals who see a therapist under court order ever be considered to make a fully voluntary choice for treatment, even if they indicate that they want to change (Lehne, personal communication, 1985)? Is it possible to differentiate in such circumstances between those who freely *consent* and those who *capitulate* (Bailey, 1978)? In truth, human motivations are so complex and multidetermined that such distinctions may be impossible to make in some situations. If there are rigid demands for absolute assurance of voluntary choice, this could lead to the paradoxical situation in which the state (through laws or regulation) or organizations (through codes of ethics or standards) may actually deny individuals' rights to treatment in order to protect them from being unduly pressured by professionals or society. Perhaps the only way out of this dilemma at the present time is for the client and therapist to proceed in therapy only after having examined in depth whether the best interests of the client are served by attempts to change and to what extent motivation for treatment is based on social or legal pressures.

The complicated issue of voluntary consent is brought into even sharper focus by a situation that commonly occurs in sexual therapy. A client forces a dysfunctional mate into treatment by threatening to leave if the dysfunction is not remedied, and the dysfunctional partner agrees to treatment in order to keep the spouse. People can be coerced to volunteer, but can they also volunteer to be coerced? There is clearly no neat solution to this paradox. It is helpful, however, to explore questions such as whether the demanded change is feasible, whether the relationship is worth the effort, and whether anger generated by the coercion will defeat attempts to change.

The second requirement for informed consent is that the client have sufficient knowledge to make choices. Margolin (1982) indicates that requisite knowledge includes the client's understanding of the therapist's qualifications and role; proposed treatment procedures and their purposes, benefits, and risks; treatment alternatives; and rights to ask questions and to withdraw from treatment. Corey, Corey & Callanan (1979) add that clients should know which statements are empirically based and which are the therapist's opinion. Clients also should be informed of the nature and extent of their expected participation inside and outside the therapy sessions and the locus of responsiblity for change.

There is a real question, however, as to how far to pursue discussion of treatment risks and alternatives. Jonsen (1980) notes that part of the efficacy of treatment has to do with the client's trust in the therapist and confidence in the procedures. If too much detail regarding risks and discomforts is given, do therapists run the risk of sabotaging their efforts by reducing hope? Do they build in expectations of failure or of negative side effects? In the authors' experience, explanation of treatment procedures, risks and alternatives actually enhances client confidence and comfort. It heightens the credibility of the therapist and the treatment plan by demonstrating expertise and by clearly indicating that the proposed treatment regime was chosen specifically for this client to deal with this particular problem. Moreover, it portrays the model of therapy as collaborative, in which both parties have and make choices and where the responsibility for change is shared.

A final comment here has to do with treatment techniques, such as paradoxical interventions, which do not allow the client to be fully informed of the purpose of the procedure (e.g., Weeks & L'Abate, 1982). An example should clarify the nature of this concern. An involuntarily childless couple complains that the man cannot get an erection at midcycle, when fertilization is most likely. The therapist diagnoses the problem as performance anxiety. He recommends to the couple that they begin adoption proceedings. The reasoning is that since the erectile failure is due to performance anxiety, the focus on adoption should reduce the man's immediate pressure to perform and enhance the probability of erections. If this does not work, however, the therapist has launched (coerced?) the couple on the road to adoption, which they may or may not have decided on in other circumstances. Therapists using such interventions should be fully aware of the implications of such techniques. At the very least, therapists should make only those paradoxical recommendations that, if they are actually followed, would not be harmful.

Confidentiality

All professional codes of ethics reviewed in this chapter address confidentiality in detail. A number of writers have suggested that confidentiality in sexual therapy is even more critical than in other forms of psychotherapy. Wasserstrom (1980) says that sexuality and privacy are highly related; people do not want to be held accountable for their sexual thoughts and feelings and want to maintain control over access to them. Similarly, Lief (1982) says that we could be humiliated by the revelation of our private sexual impulses or behaviors. Lief further notes that sexual adequacy, pride, and self-esteem are closely linked, so that disclosure, even disclosure of the client's presence in sex therapy, could be embarrassing and represent an insult to self-esteem.

Although all therapists strongly favor holding in confidence material revealed in therapy, few will or can take the absolute stand that Gebhard followed in his sex research. He said that if he were studying a tribe of headhunters, he would neither warn the neighboring tribes of the danger nor tell the headhunters that they were committing murder; he would simply "count the heads as they came in" (Gebhard, 1977, p. 12). Because of multiple clients (e.g., couples) and current regulations regarding child abuse reports and duty to warn, clinicians do not have the luxury of that straightforward standard of absolute confidentiality.

As in any form of psychotherapy, the sex therapist should tell the client what records are being kept, who has access to them (Stoltz & Associates, 1978), and should clearly establish the limits of confidentiality (Margolin, 1982) — that is, who can waive privilege, and under what circumstances the therapist will unilaterally reveal information. All therapists, of course, have an obligation to be familiar with state laws that govern their practice in this regard.

Sex therapists need to have and to communicate to their clients their policy on confidentiality of telephone calls or individual interviews with one member of a couple. If therapists make ad hoc decisions about what to disclose to the partner under such circumstances, it puts them in a position of considerable discretionary power and of great responsibility to predict the consequences of the revelation accurately (Margolin, 1982). Rigid rules of complete disclosure or complete nondisclosure can also be problematic. If all information gained in individual interviews or through telephone calls is disclosed to a partner, clients may withhold important information due to fears of embarrassment or of their partner's reaction. Complete nondisclosure, on the other hand, can lead to manipulation or co-opting of the therapist. There are, however, a number of intermediate stances that enhance information flow but reduce the chance of manipulation. For example, the therapist may tell the client that the occurrence—but not the content—of any phone calls or individual sessions will be revealed. The clients may be urged to disclose appropriate content themselves. They also may be told that the therapist will disclose a confidence in life-threatening circumstances or in situations of irreversible harm, with a clear indication to the clients as to the purpose and details of any such disclosure. Glass and Wright (Chapter 13 of this volume) deal directly with the issue of confidentiality and extramarital relationships.

Complete disclosure of all information to each partner does not always seem to be necessary or even desirable. In many situations, it does not appear to be crucial for the couple to exchange their deepest sexual fantasies and impulses in order to remediate the dysfunction. Revelations of such fantasies, or disclosure of sexual liaisons terminated before marriage or years before, may simply not be helpful. The gains in intimacy and knowledge of one another can be more than offset by increased anxiety, distrust or anger.

The AASECT Code (1980) takes an interesting stand with respect to individual confidentiality. It states that if a client does not request confidentiality, but it appears to the therapist that a revelation could be damaging, the therapist is obligated to point out the possible danger and get permission to disclose.

There does not appear to be a comprehensive review of the implications of duty-to-warn statutes and court decisions as they pertain to confidentiality in sex therapy. However, in cases of ongoing incest or child molestation, or repeated rapes, the therapist could well be on shaky ground in treating the individual without taking steps to warn or protect the victims (Wasserstrom, 1980). Lehne (personal communication, 1985) raises the interesting question of statutory rape in the treatment of homosexuals; if an adult is having sexual relations with an apparently cooperative teenager below the legal age of consent, does the therapist have the responsibility to reveal this to authorities or to the "victim's" parents? The same dilemma could occur, of course, with a heterosexual child or adult.

In cases where more than one person is seen, neither ethical rules nor most state laws spell out clearly the exact nature of the client's confidentiality privilege. For example, one partner may demand that a sexual therapist testify in a divorce case and the other may refuse to waive privilege. It would appear that the most sensible thing to do would be to attempt to limit testimony to material pertaining only to the former, but a neat division of information into *his* and *hers* may not be feasible. Moreover, it is not clear if the courts would even agree with this tack, or whether they would say that once information is revealed in the presence of both the partner and a sexual therapist it is no longer privileged.

There are other situations that point out the complexity of maintaining confidentiality. Many therapists run groups for individuals with sexual dysfunctions. Although group members are almost certainly urged not to reveal confidences gained in the group, information revealed may not be legally safeguarded by privilege statutes. Another problem may arise with therapists working with adolescents who may reveal homosexuality or paraphilias. Should the family be told? If a 15-year-old is beginning to test his sexuality through multiple sexual relations, is the risk of venereal disease or AIDS sufficient ground for disclosure? Most therapists would take the responsibility on themselves to apprise adolescents of danger and to inform the parents of the limits of confidentiality, but they should know that there are still less than perfect guides for therapists in such cases.

CONCLUDING REMARKS

It is important for therapists to be cognizant of and sensitive to the general issues of values, coercion, confidentiality, victimization and the like, and then to use their best clinical judgment and common sense to map specific therapeutic strategy. As a practical matter, it does not seem feasible or even desirable to develop minutely detailed standards of therapist conduct. A legalistic approach to ethical and professional practices in sex therapy would impair the therapist's ability to develop new approaches and to modify old ones in line with new scientific findings.

The sex therapy literature does not include extensive casebooks that explore the clinical implications of general ethical principles, but there are a number of helpful resources available. The ethical codes referenced in this chapter are readily obtainable. There are many new books and articles on ethical and legal principles for mental health professionals, and much of this material is directly applicable to sex therapy. Professional organizations, such as the American Psychological Association, sponsor symposia on ethics and professional practices in a variety of areas. A collaborative treatment model engages the client in the therapy process, making it more likely that client needs, rights and sensitivities will surface. And it is essential to have knowledgeable and trusted colleagues comment on whether therapy plans seem to be in the best interests of all concerned.

Complex clinical, ethical, and value considerations underlie many current assumptions and practices in sexual therapy. A greater appreciation of such issues should lead therapists to deeper understanding of and greater sensitivity to client needs and the intricacies of the sexual therapy process.

REFERENCES

American Association for Marriage and Family Therapy. (1985). *Code of professional ethics.* Washington, DC: Author.

American Association of Sex Educators, Counselors, and Therapists. (1980). *AASECT code of ethics.* Washington, DC: Author.

American Psychological Association. (1981). *Ethical principles of psychologists.* Washington, DC: Author.

Annon, J.S. (1977). THE PLISSIT model: A proposed conceptual scheme for the behavioral treatment of sexual problems. In J. Fischer and H.L. Gochros (Eds.), *Handbook of behavior therapy with sexual problems* (Vol. 1). New York: Pergamon.

Bailey, K.G. (1978). Psychotherapy or massage parlor technology? Comments on the Zeiss, Rosen and Zeiss treatment procedure. *Journal of Consulting and Clinical Psychology, 46*(6), 1502-1506.

Bersoff, D.N. (1982). *Criminal liability of sexual surrogates.* Unpublished memorandum. Washington, DC: American Psychological Association.

Corey, G., Corey, M., & Callanan, P. (1979). *Professional and ethical issues in counseling and psychotherapy.* Monterey, CA: Brooks/Cole.

Edelwich, J., with Brodsky, A. (1982). *Sexual dilemmas for the helping professional.* New York: Brunner/Mazel.

Engelhardt, H.T., Jr. (1980). Value imperialism and exploitation in sex therapy. In W.H. Masters, V.E. Johnson, R.C. Kolodny, & S.M. Weems, *Ethical issues in sex therapy and research* (Vol. 2, pp. 109-137). Boston: Little, Brown.

Gebhard, P.H. (1977). Designated discussion. In W.H. Masters, V.E. Johnson, & R.C. Kolodny, *Ethical issues in sex therapy and research* (Vol. 1, pp. 11-15). Boston: Little, Brown.

Gorowitz, S. (1980). Remarks. In W.H. Masters, V.E. Johnson, R.C. Kolodny, & S.M. Weems, *Ethical issues in sex therapy and research* (Vol. 2, pp. 201-205). Boston: Little, Brown.

Hall, J.E., & Hare-Mustin, R.T. (1983). Sanctions and diversity of complaints against psychologists. *American Psychologist, 38*(6), 714-729.

Hiltner, S. (1977). Theological perspectives on the ethics of scientific investigation and treatment of human sexuality. In W.H. Masters, V.E. Johnson, & R.C. Kolodny, *Ethical issues in sex therapy and research* (Vol. 1, pp. 20-32). Boston: Little, Brown.

Jonsen, A.R. (1980). Informed consent. In W.H. Masters, V.E. Johnson, R.C. Kolodny, & S.M. Weems. *Ethical issues in sex therapy and research* (Vol. 2, pp. 206-207). Boston: Little, Brown.

Kaplan, H.S. (1977). Training of sex therapists. In W.H. Masters, V.E. Johnson, & R.C. Kolodny. *Ethical issues in sex therapy and research* (Vol. 1, pp. 182-189). Boston: Little, Brown.

Katz, J. (1977). Designated discussion. In W.H. Masters, V.E. Johnson, & R.C. Kolodny, *Ethical issues in sex therapy and research* (Vol. 1, pp. 161-165). Boston: Little, Brown.

Lassen, C.L. (1976). Issues and dilemmas in sexual treatment. *Journal of Sex and Marital Therapy, 2,* 32-39.

Leroy, D.H. (1972). The potential criminal liability of human sex clinics and their patients. *St. Louis University Law Journal, 16,* 586-603.

Lieberman, M.A., Yalom, I.D., & Miles, M.B. (1973). *Encounter groups: First facts.* New York: Basic Books.

Lief, H.I. (1982). Ethical problems in sex therapy. In M. Rosenbaum (Ed.), *Ethics and values in psychotherapy: A guidebook* (pp. 269-296). New York: Free Press.

Lief, H.I., Sarrel, L.J., & Sarrel, P.M. (1980). Accreditation and training in sex therapy. In W.H. Masters, V.E. Johnson, R.C. Kolodny, & S.M. Weems, *Ethical issues in sex therapy and research* (Vol. 2, pp. 138-162). Boston: Little, Brown.

LoPiccolo, J. (1978). Direct treatment of sexual dysfunction. In J. LoPiccolo & L. LoPiccolo (Eds.), *Handbook of sex therapy* (pp. 1-17). New York: Plenum.

Lowry, T.S., & Lowry, T.P. (1975). Ethical considerations in sex therapy. *Journal of Marriage and Family Counseling, 1*(3), 229-236.

Margolin, G. (1982). Ethical and legal considerations in marital and family therapy. *American Psychologist, 37*(7), 788-801.

Marmor, J. (1980). Remarks. In W.H. Masters, V.E. Johnson, R.C. Kolodny, & S.M. Weems. *Ethical Issues in sex therapy and research* (Vol. 2, pp. 274-276). Boston: Little, Brown.

Masters, W.H., & Johnson, V.E. (1970). *Human sexual inadequacy.* Boston, Little, Brown.

Masters, W.H., Johnson, V.E., & Kolodny, R.C. (1977). *Ethical issues in sex therapy and research.* (Vol. 1). Boston: Little, Brown.

Masters, W.H., Johnson, V.E., Kolodny,R.C., & Weems, S.M. (1980). *Ethical issues in sex therapy and research.* (Vol. 2). Boston: Little, Brown.

Money, J. (1977). Issues and attitudes in research and treatment of variant forms of human sexual behavior. In W.H. Masters, V.E. Johnson, & R.C. Kolodny. *Ethical issues in sex therapy and research* (Vol. 1, pp. 119-132). Boston: Little, Brown.

Mudd, E.H. (1977). The historical background of ethical considerations in sex research and sex therapy. In W.H. Masters, V.E. Johnson, & R.C. Kolodny. *Ethical issues in sex therapy and research,* (Vol. 1, pp. 1-10). Boston: Little, Brown.

Pomeroy, W.B. Cited in Lief, H.I. (1982).

Redlich, F. (1977). The ethics of sex therapy. In W.H. Masters, V.E. Johnson, & R.C. Kolodny, *Ethical issues in sex therapy and research* (Vol. 1, pp. 142-157). Boston: Little, Brown.

Society for the Scientific Study of Sex. (1985). *Statement of ethical principles.* Philadelphia: Author.

Sollod, R., & Kaplan, H. (1976). The new sex therapy: An integration of behavioral, psychodynamic, and interpersonal approaches. In J. Clayborn (Ed.), *Successful psychotherapy* (pp. 140-152). New York: Brunner/Mazel.

Stoltz, J.B., & Associates. (1978). *Ethical issues in behavior modification.* San Francisco: Jossey-Bass.

Strupp, H.H., & Hadley, S.W. (1977). A tripartite model of mental health and therapeutic outcomes: With special reference to negative effects in psychotherapy. *American Psychologist, 32,* 187-196.

Szasz, T. (1980). *Sex by prescription.* New York: Anchor Press/Doubleday.

Taggert, M. (1985). The feminist critique in epistemological perspective: Questions of context in family therapy. *Journal of Marital and Family Therapy, 11,* 113-126.

Wasserstrom, R. (1980). Issues of privacy and confidentiality in sex therapy and sex research. In W.H. Masters, V.E. Johnson, R.C. Kolodny, & S.M. Weems, *Ethical issues in sex therapy and research* (Vol. 2, pp. 42-60). Boston: Little, Brown.

Weeks, G.R., & L'Abate, L. (1982). *Paradoxical psychotherapy: Theory and practice with individuals, couples, and families.* New York: Brunner/Mazel.

Index